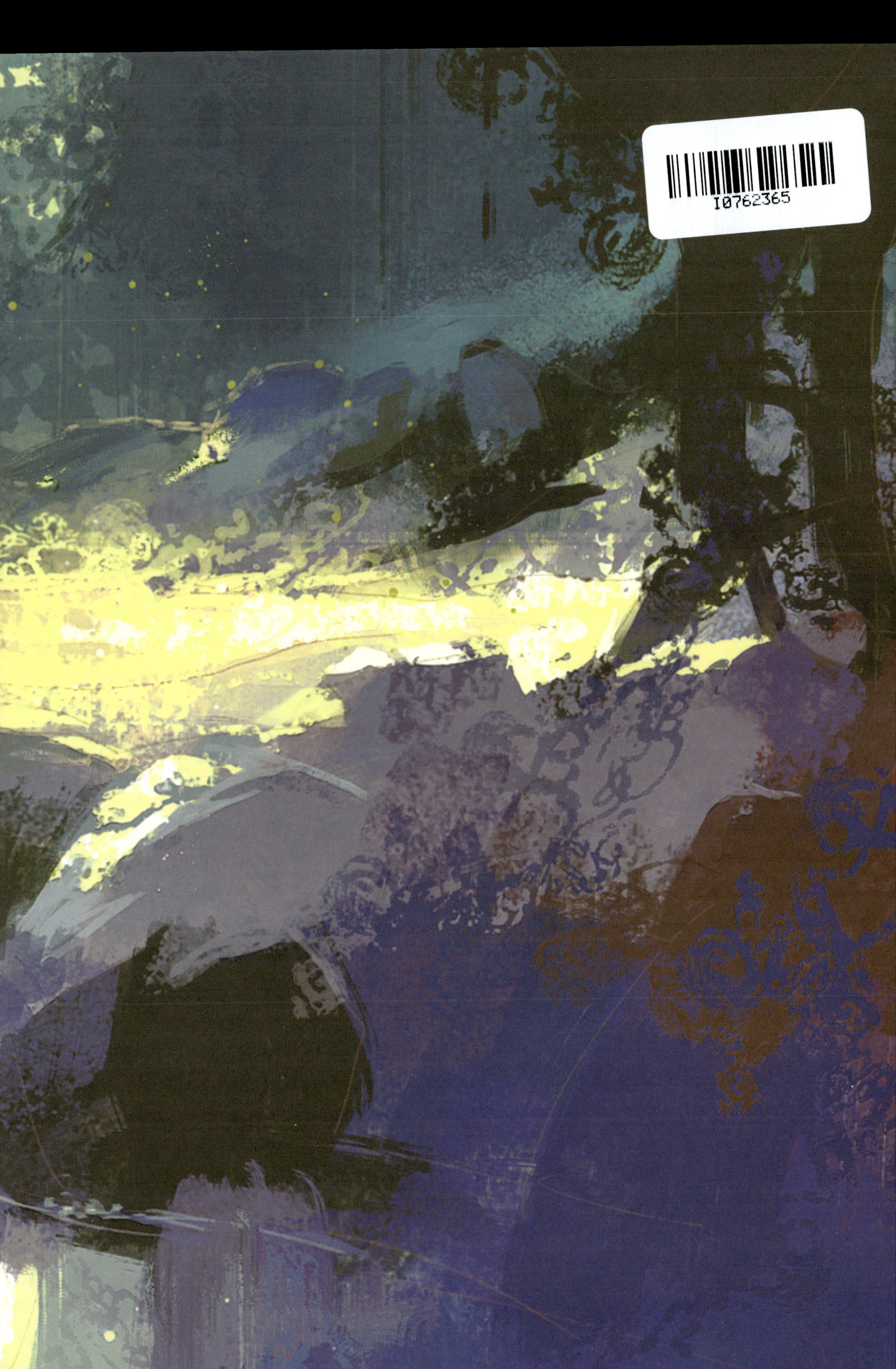
I0762365

ARTISTS' MASTER SERIES

PERSPECTIVE & DEPTH

3dtotalPublishing

3dtotalPublishing

Correspondence: publishing@3dtotal.com
Website: store.3dtotal.com

First published in the United Kingdom, 2024, by 3dtotal Publishing.

Address: 3dtotal.com Ltd,
6 Sansome Street, Worcester,
WR1 1UH, United Kingdom.

Reprinted in 2025 by 3dtotal Publishing

Hard cover ISBN: 978-1-912843-83-1
Printed and bound in China by
C&C Offset Printing Co., Ltd
www.candcprinting.com

Visit store.3dtotal.com for a complete list of available book titles.

Editor: Philippa Barker
Designer: Matthew Lewis
Lead Editor: Samantha Rigby
Lead Designer: Joseph Cartwright
Studio Manager: Simon Morse
Managing Director: Tom Greenway

Front cover image © Mike Hernandez
Back cover image © Guweiz
End papers images © Nathan Fowkes

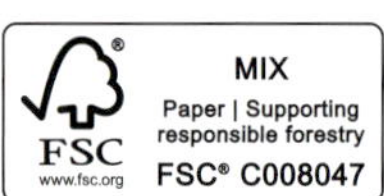

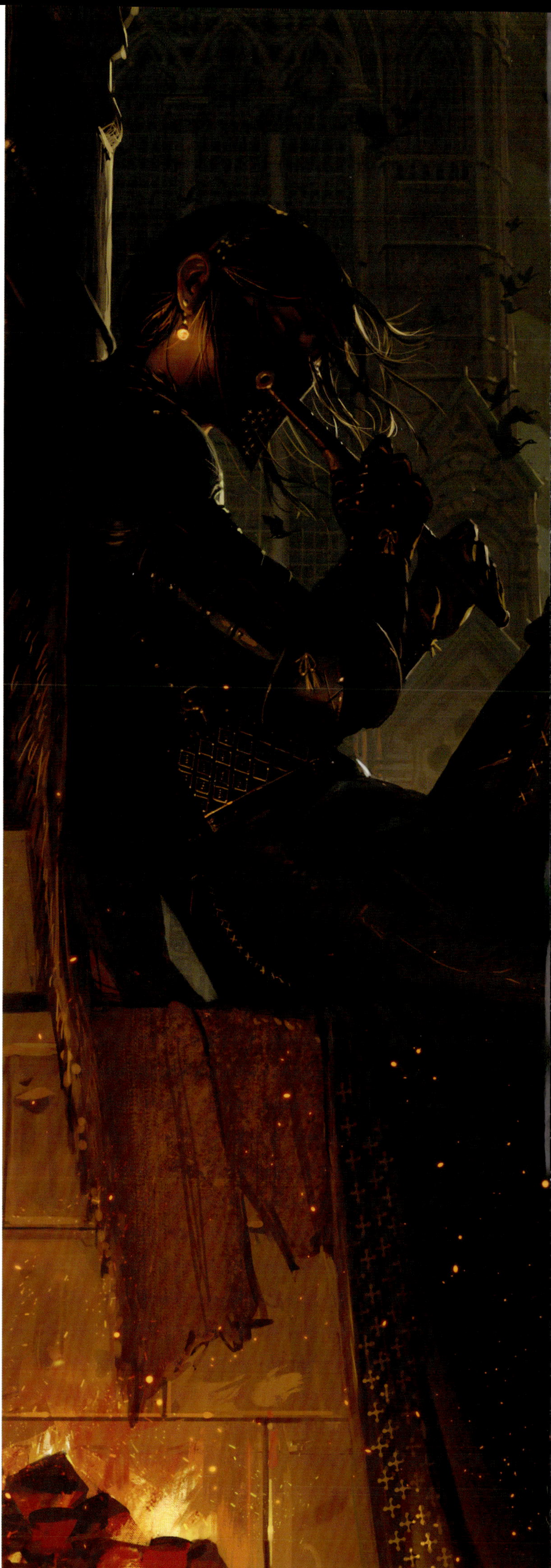

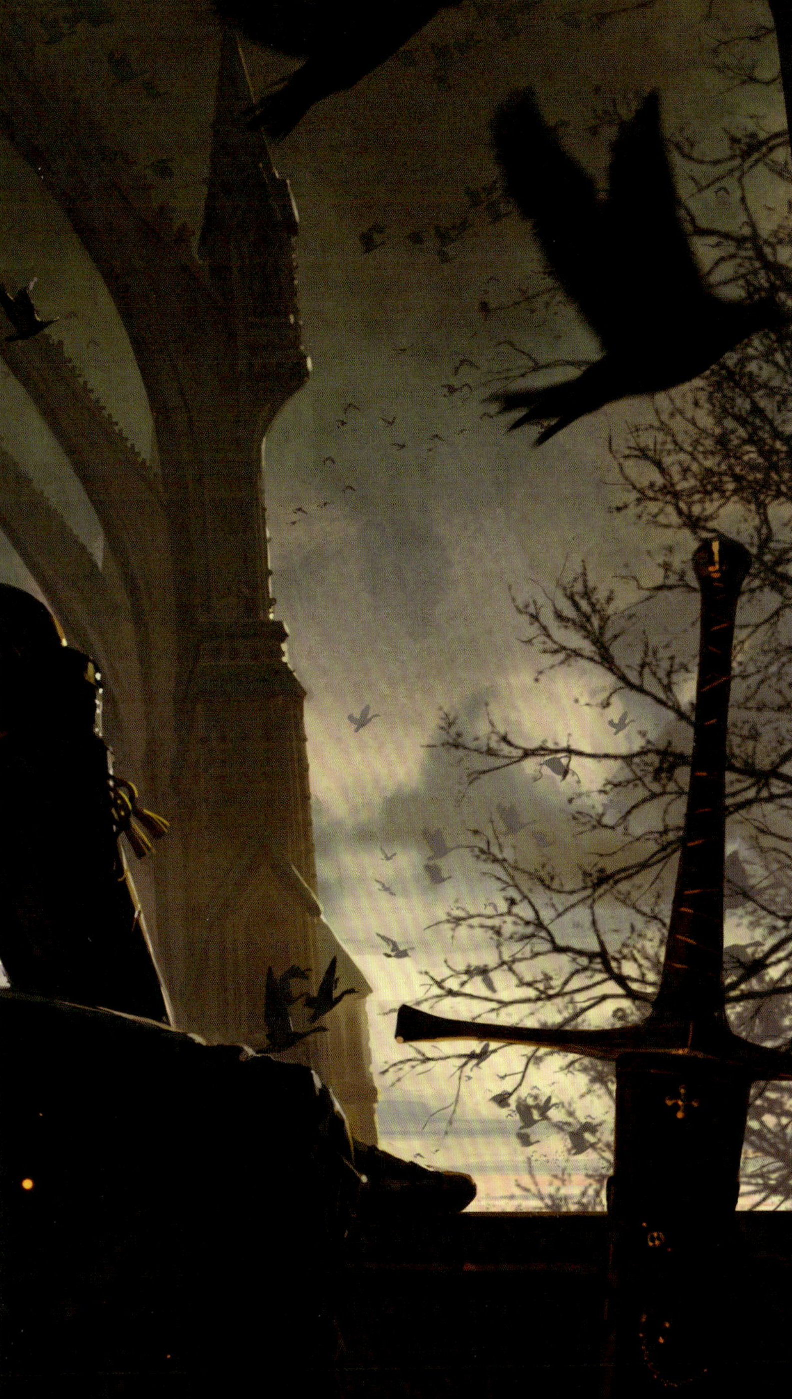

50%

of net profits donated

TO CHARITY

In 2022, 3dtotal Publishing became successful enough to make a pledge to donate **50% of its net profits to charity**. This continues to be possible due to the incredible support from all our customers, employees, and partners. At the time of printing, we have donated over $1.62 million (USD) to charity.

We focus our giving on three charitable areas: **environmental, humanitarian, and animal welfare**. We use organizations such as Effective Altruism and Founders Pledge to guide who we help within these causes. Some ways of doing good are over 100 times more effective than others, so donating this way hugely increases the impact of our contributions.

See 3dtotal.com/charity for full details.

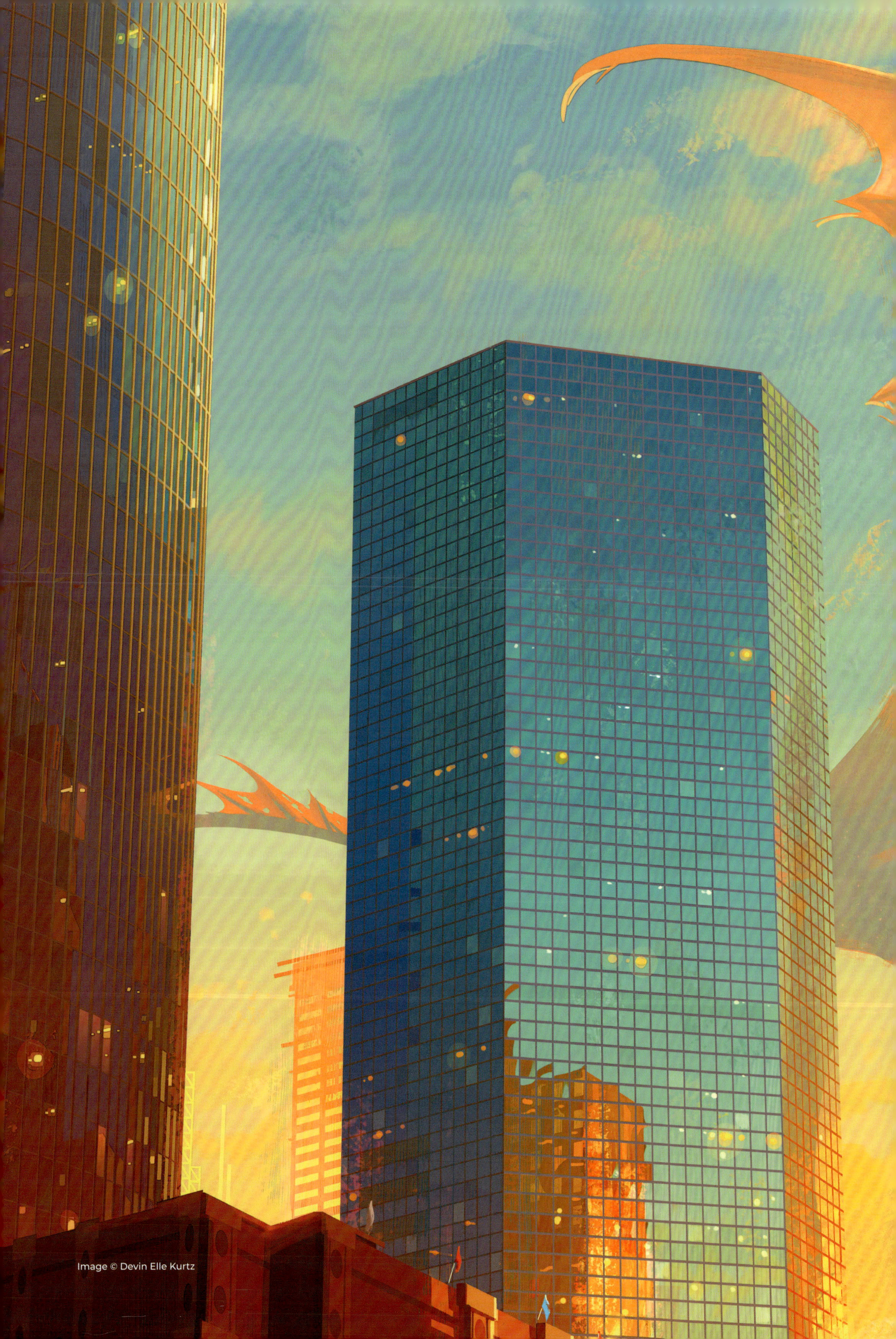

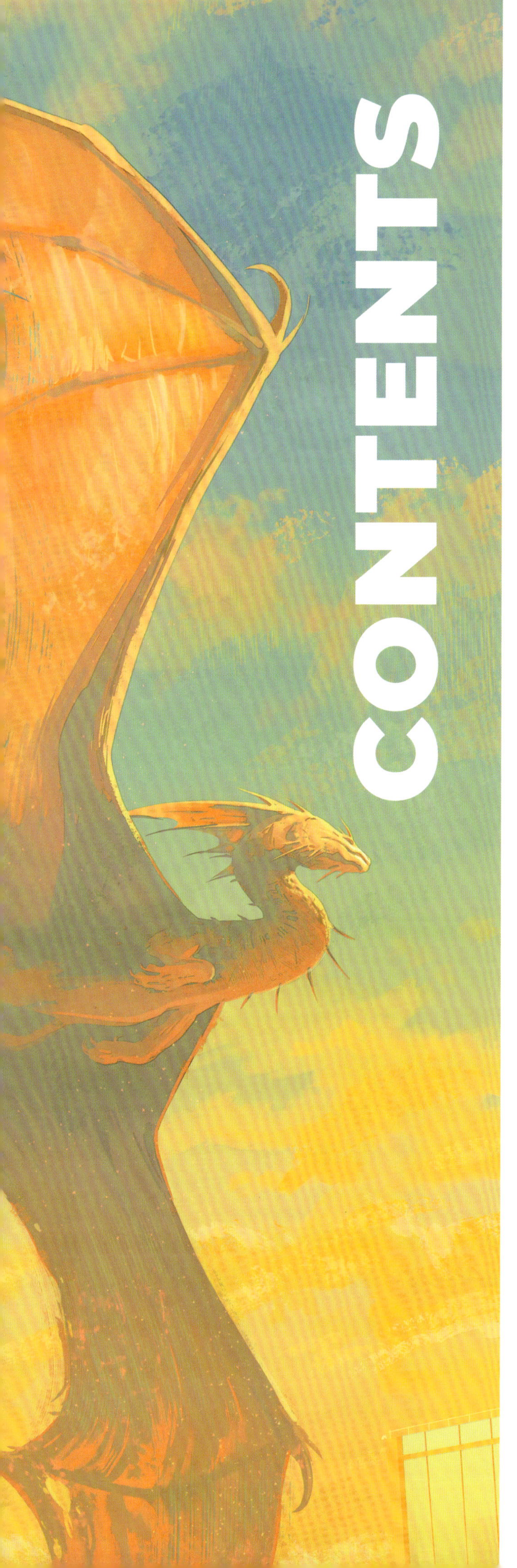

CONTENTS

HOW TO USE THIS BOOK

Welcome to *Artists' Master Series: Perspective & Depth*. This book contains three main sections: the theory chapters, the tutorials, and the gallery.

We recommend that you begin by reading through Mike Hernandez's introductory chapters on **Perspective & Depth** (page 8 to page 81) to expand your knowledge and understanding of these fundamental topics. **Perspective & Depth Throughout History** (page 10) explores how they have been used in artwork through the ages. **Types of Perspective** (page 16) discusses the various different types of perspective that can be used to create the illusion of depth and realism, covering one-point perspective all the way up to four-point and above, in addition to schematic view, worm's-eye view, and bird's-eye view. **Foreshortening & Depth of Field** (page 34) explores alternative methods that can be used to create a sense of distance without the need for measurements and vanishing points, including looking at the placement of focus in the foreground, middle ground, or background for storytelling purposes. Next, **Atmospheric Perspective & Depth Perception** (page 44) examines the role that wavelengths, colour, contrast, value, light reflection, and the Fresnel effect play in achieving the illusion of depth. Unpacking how shadows can be used to create a believable object in space, **Shadows** (page 56) unpacks artificial and natural lighting, form and cast shadows, linear and radial lighting, measuring shadows in perspective, parallel perspective, and viewing shadows in the abstract. **Shapes** (page 66) explores how perspective can be used to change the appearance of shapes in a scene, with sections discussing depth cues, primitives, and the use of grids. To finish, **Breaking the Rules** (page 74) suggests how the established rules and principles can be intentionally broken to produce certain artistic effects or to challenge conventional representations of space, with sections on distorting perspective, including multiple or no vanishing points, and flat, isometric, and curvilinear perspective.

The four **Tutorials** that follow, by Devin Elle Kurtz (page 84), Nathan Fowkes (page 134), Orenjikun (page 168), and Guweiz (page 202), can be treated as standalone projects, but you will benefit from reading the knowledge and terminology shared in the introductory chapters before starting them. Each tutorial artist has their own unique style, creative background, and skilled approach to creating perspective and depth in their artwork. Follow each tutorial in turn to observe how they apply their knowledge of these core topics in practice.

Finally, the **Gallery** (page 256) showcases the portfolios of the four tutorial artists, plus six additional professionals, each of whom shares valuable insights into their expert use of perspective and depth in their artwork.

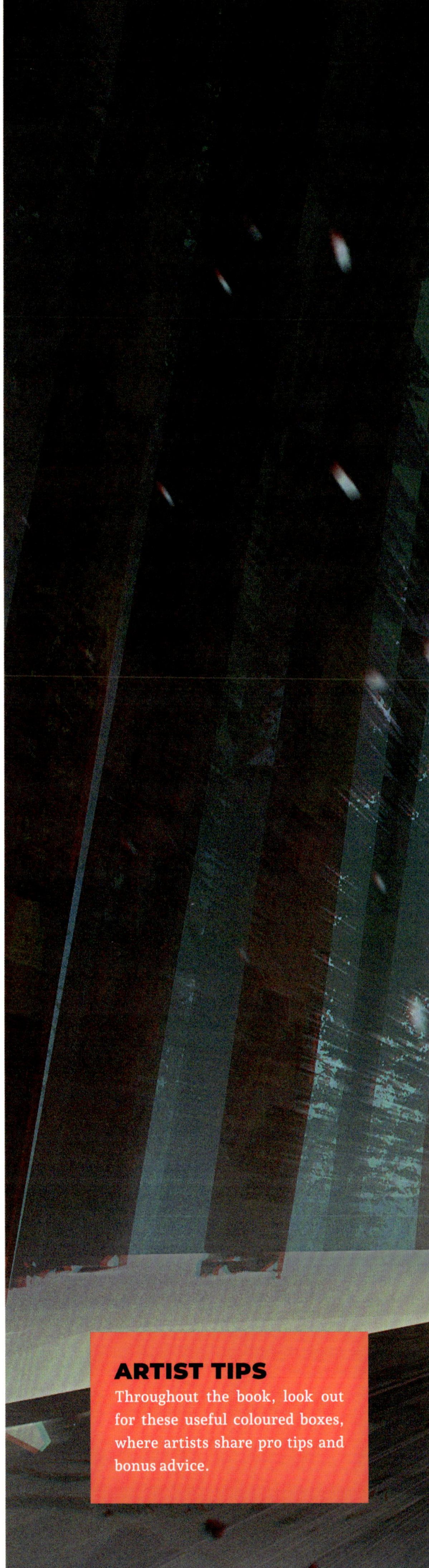

ARTIST TIPS

Throughout the book, look out for these useful coloured boxes, where artists share pro tips and bonus advice.

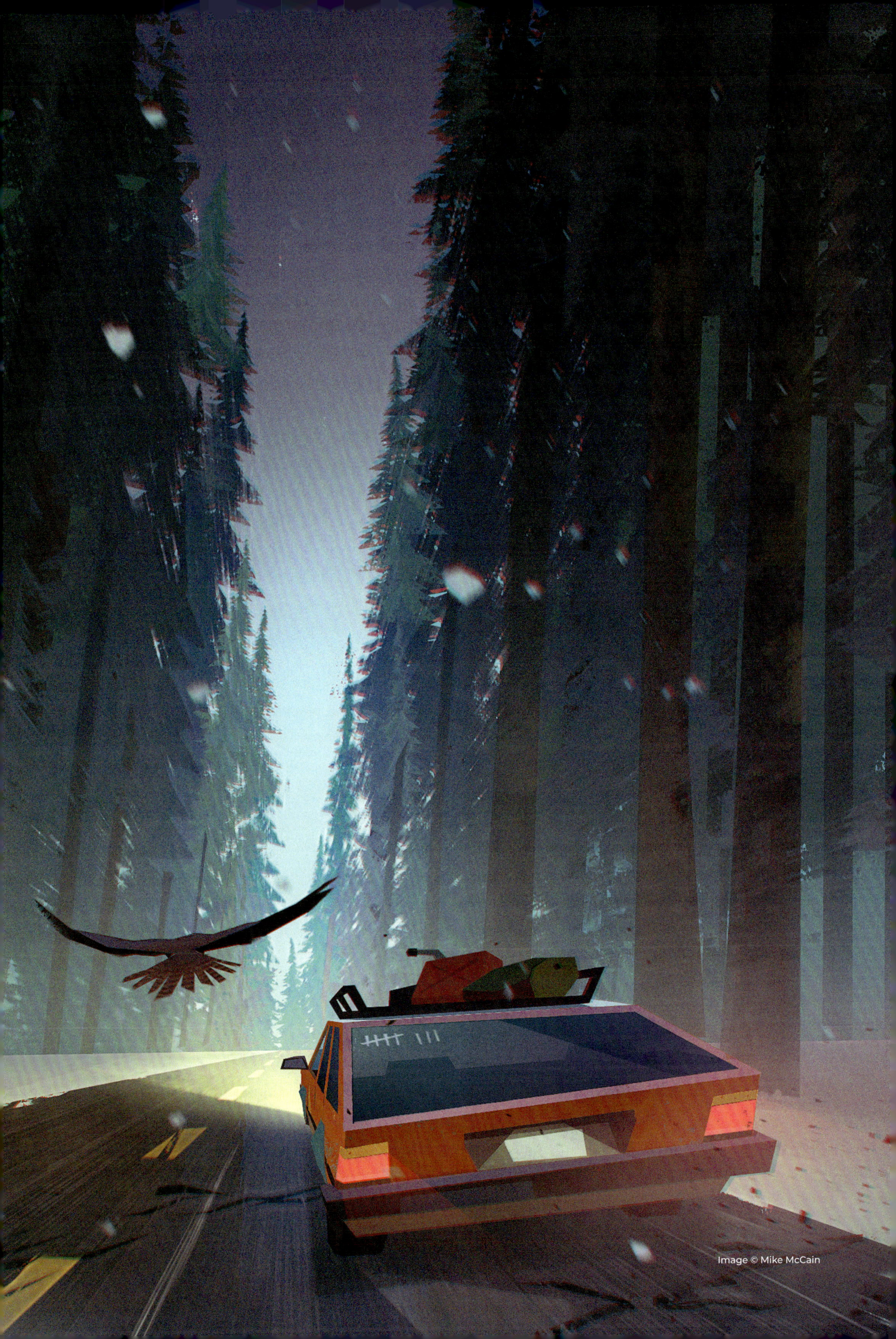

Image © Mike Hernandez

PERSPECTIVE & DEPTH

MIKE HERNANDEZ

Perspective in art is the fundamental technique that allows artists to represent three-dimensional space onto a two-dimensional surface. It depicts the way that objects appear in relation to one another, creating a sense of depth, distance, and realism. Whether using linear perspective to establish vanishing points and convergence, applying isometric perspective for a more stylized approach, or experimenting with unconventional methods, a comprehensive yet simple understanding of perspective is essential for artists seeking to convey a convincing and dynamic sense of space in their art.

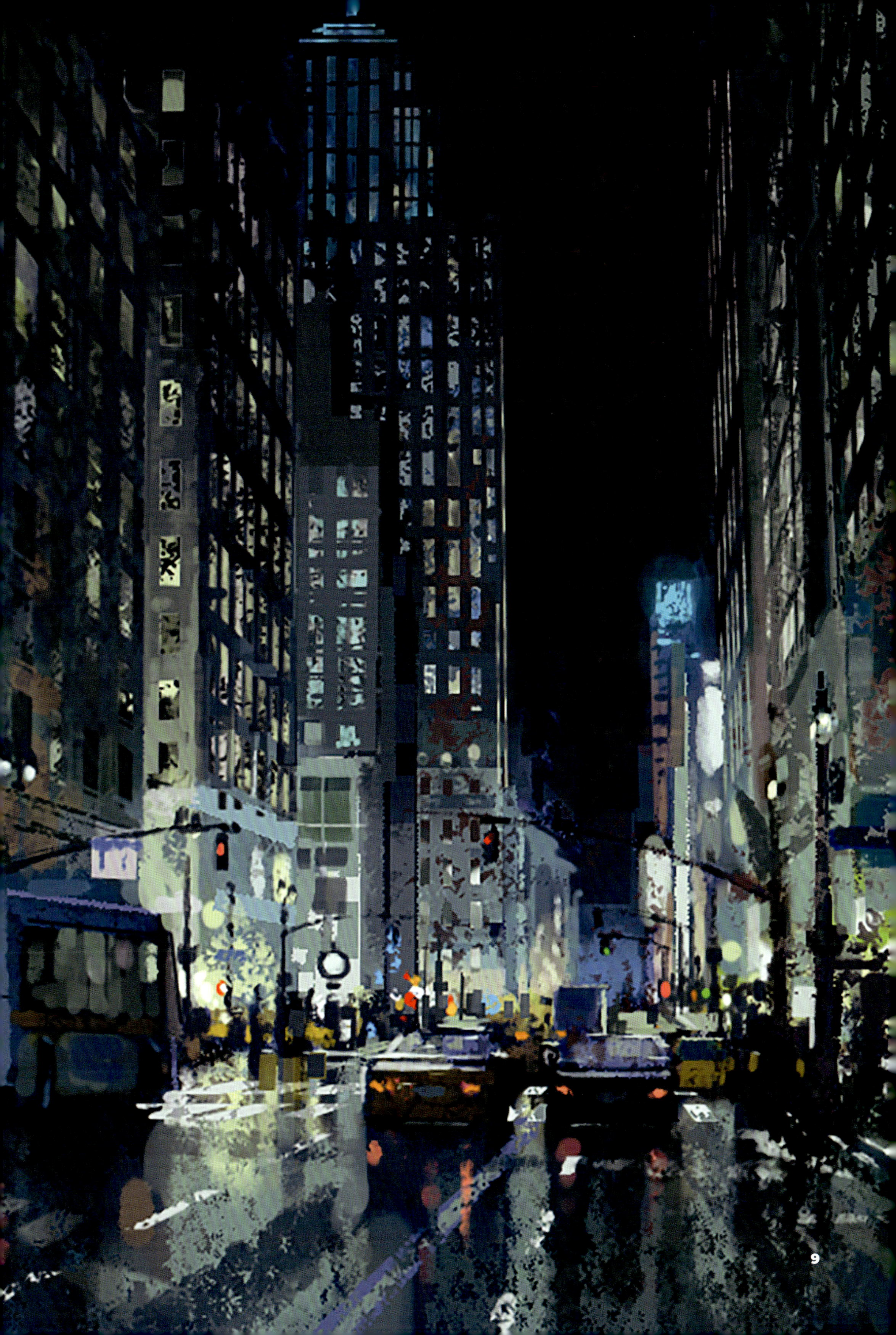

PERSPECTIVE & DEPTH THROUGHOUT HISTORY

Perspective in art has evolved through time from simple applications to sophisticated techniques. It has played a pivotal role in transforming two-dimensional paintings into immersive, realistic, and imaginative visual experiences. This chapter will take a look at how perspective and depth have been used in art, from Egyptian hieroglyphs to contemporary digital artwork.

THE EVOLUTION OF PERSPECTIVE & DEPTH IN VISUAL ART

In visual art, perspective refers to the technique used to create the illusion of depth and three-dimensionality on a two-dimensional surface, such as a canvas or a piece of paper. It is an aspect of Western art that has evolved over centuries and various historical periods, and its roots can be traced back to ancient civilizations.

The earliest known forms of perspective were used in ancient Egyptian and Mesopotamian art, such as flat graphic hieroglyphs and symbols **(01)**. These cultures depicted objects in a way that emphasized their importance, rather than striving for realism.

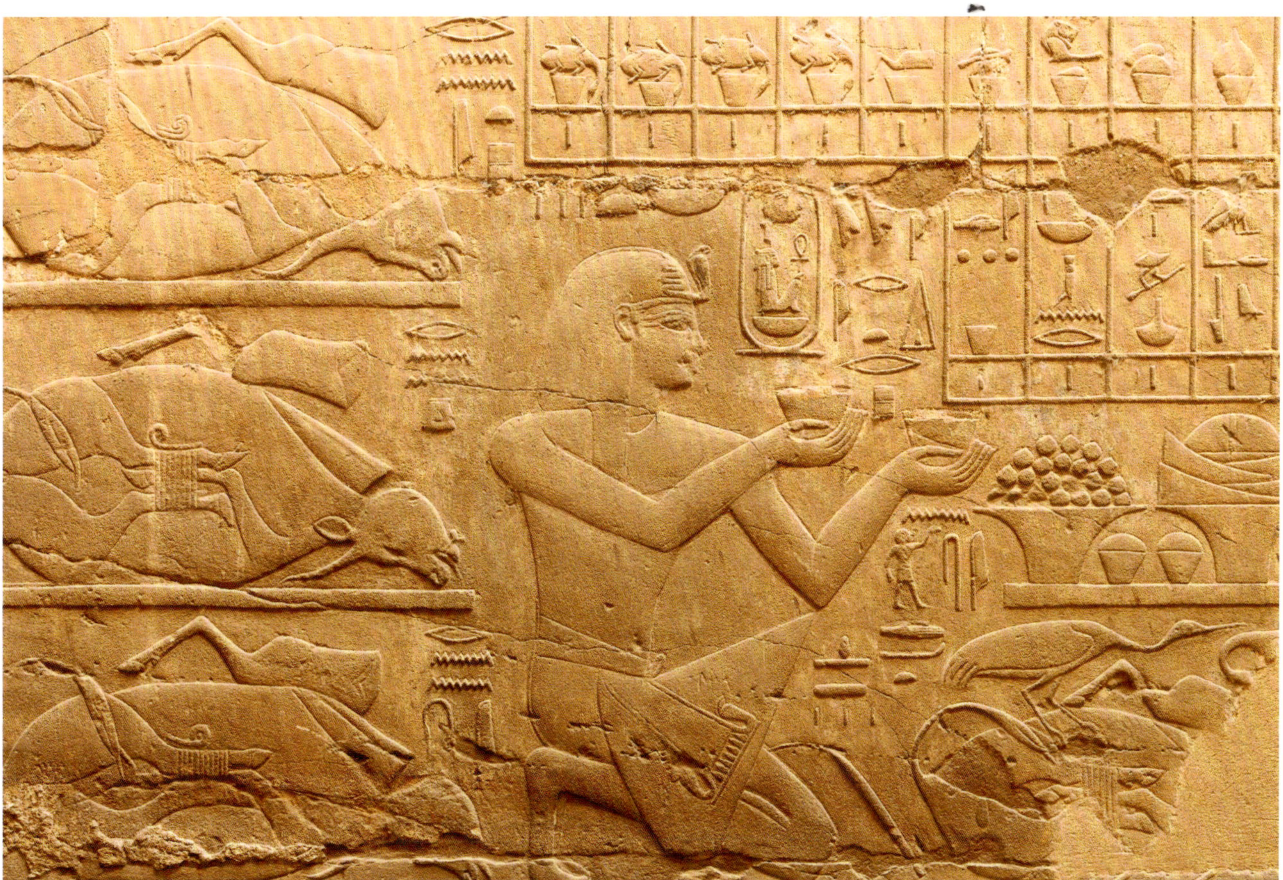

01 This image of an Egyptian hieroglyph carving shows an example of early perspective and depth through the use of foreshortening. Notice how the right arm is placed over the left arm, suggesting the subtleties of depth and volume.

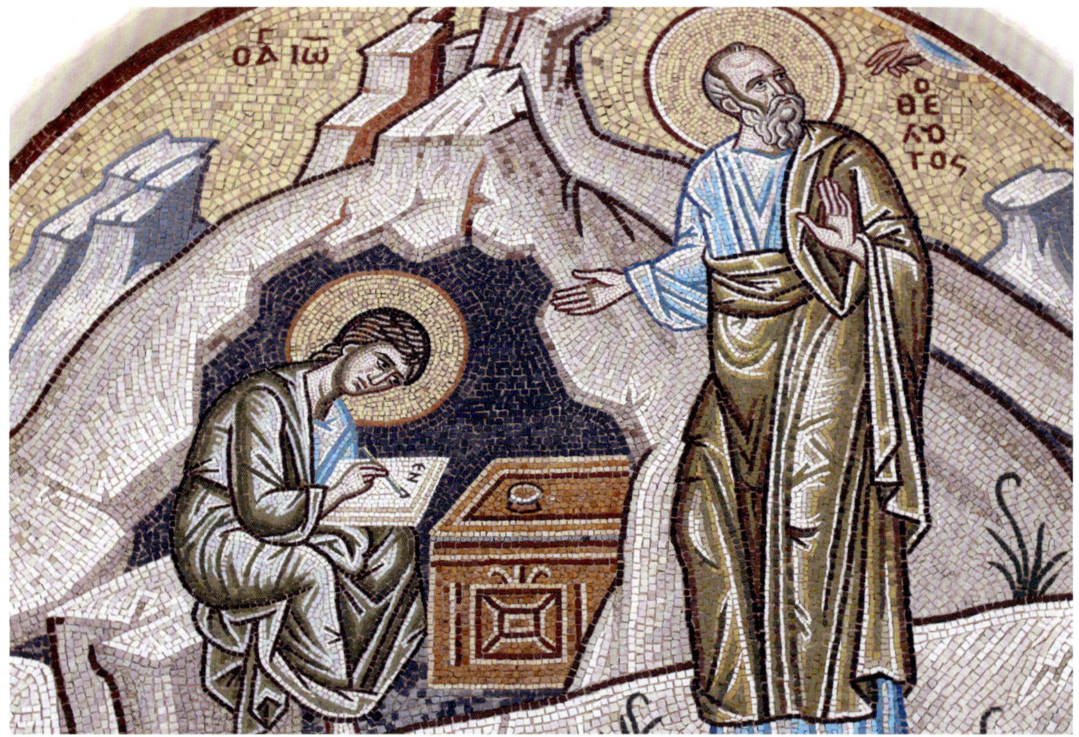

02 This image of Byzantine artwork provides an example of perspective cues. Notice the volume of the table, as well as the hierarchy of scale and size implied by the figure in the foreground.

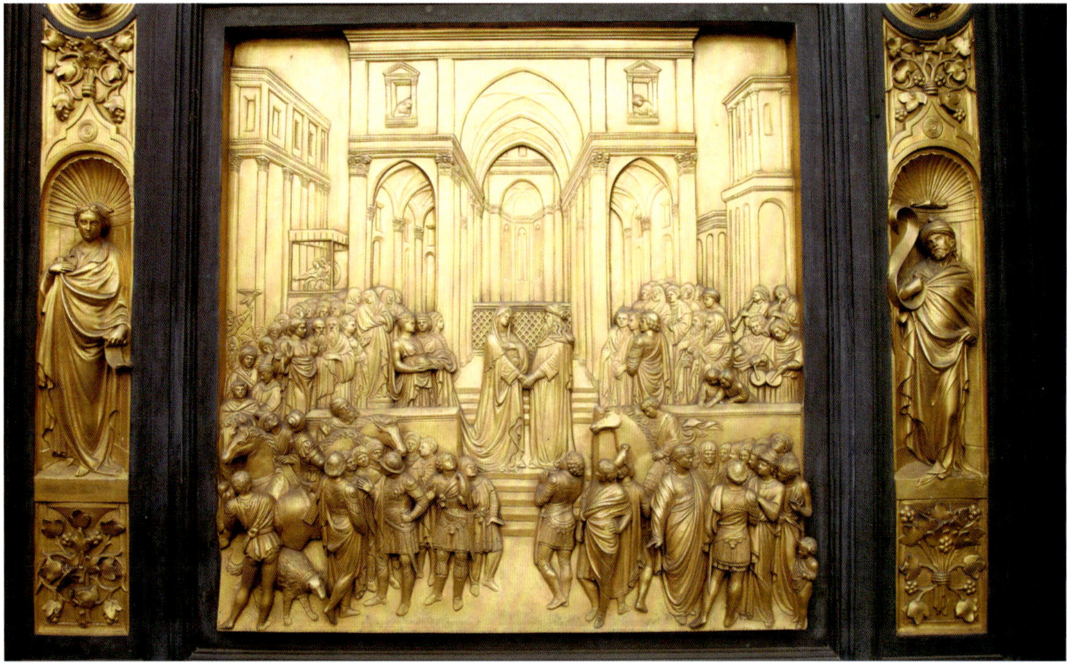

03 This image, taken from the *Gates of Paradise* (1401–1422) by Lorenzo Ghiberti in Florence, Italy, is an example of early linear perspective in the Renaissance era.

Early Christian and Byzantine art were primarily focused on religious subjects and spirituality **(02)**, rather than the concept of perspective itself. Figures were often shown in hierarchy, with people of higher importance presented as larger in scale than those of lesser value. In the Renaissance era, artists such as Lorenzo Ghiberti and Leon Battista Alberti created the concept of linear perspective, where the illusion of depth was created by the use of converging lines to a single vanishing point on the horizon **(03)**. Artists such as Leonardo da Vinci further refined the use of perspective in their art, which helped to create the feel of accurate spatial representation **(04, 05)**. These refinements also spread to Northern Europe during this period.

Image 02, iStock.com/Socha
Image 03, iStock.com/Massimo Merlini

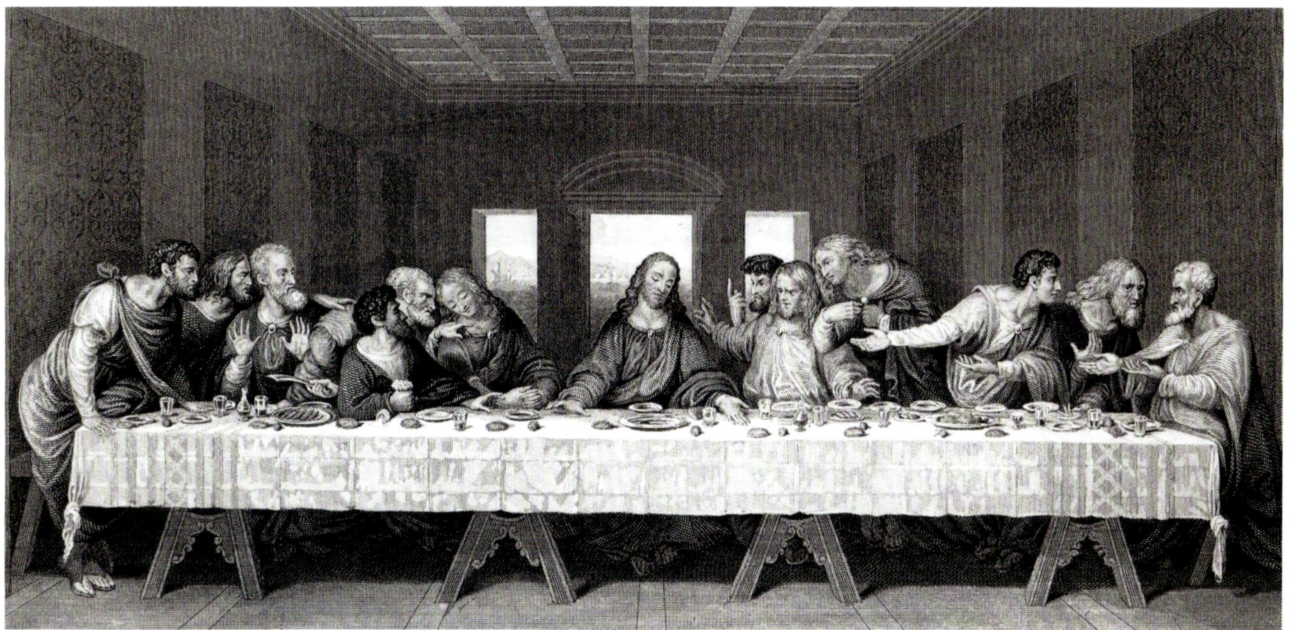

04 This etching of *The Last Supper* by Renaissance artist Leonardo da Vinci shows a clear example of his use of linear perspective.

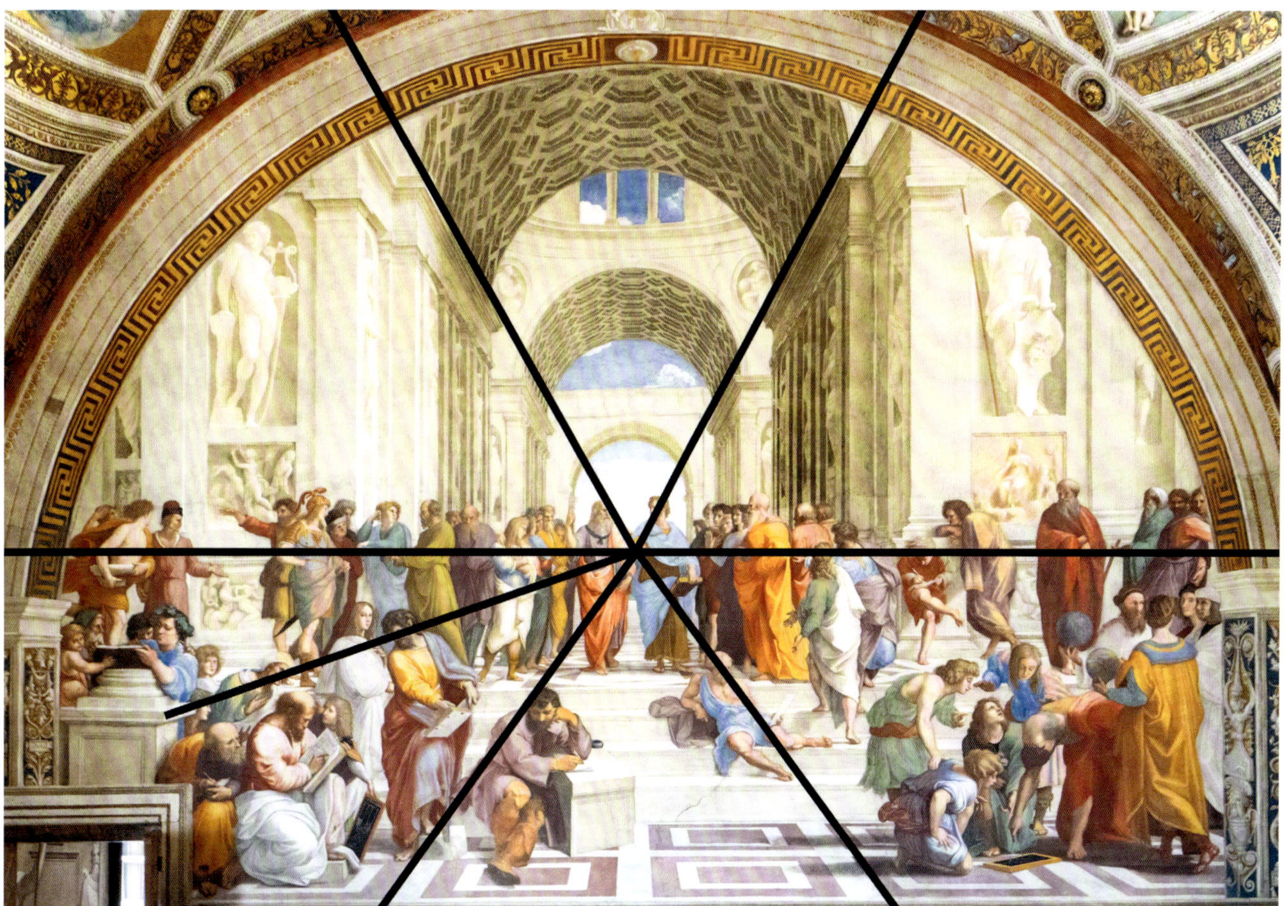

05 *School of Athens* by Raphael is one of the most famous frescos of the Italian Renaissance for its accurate mathematical depiction of one-point perspective.

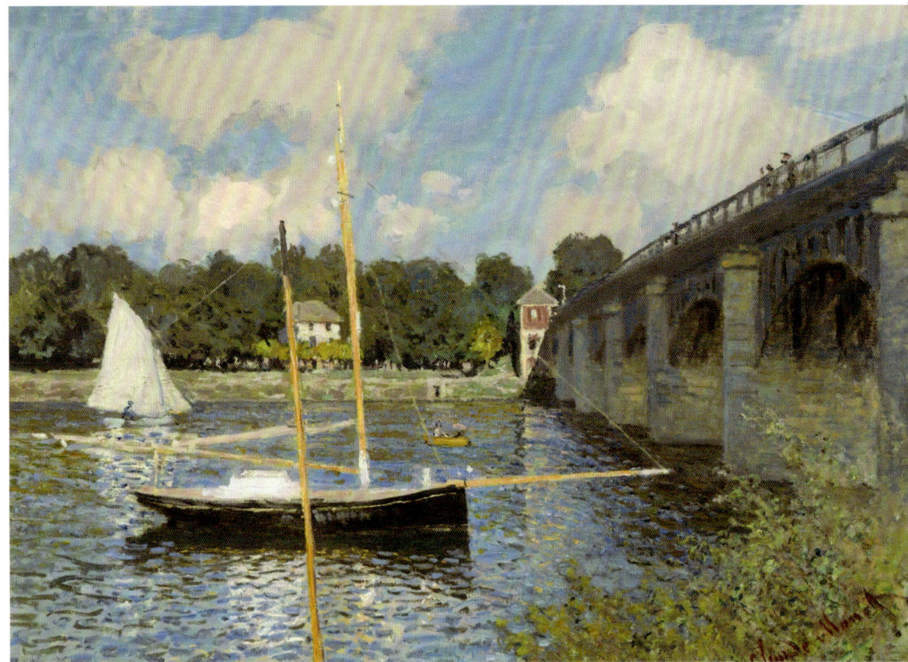

06 *The Bridge at Argenteuil* (1874) by Claude Monet is a great example of how perspective evolved well into the nineteenth century, giving way to beautiful images filled with light, atmosphere, and depth.

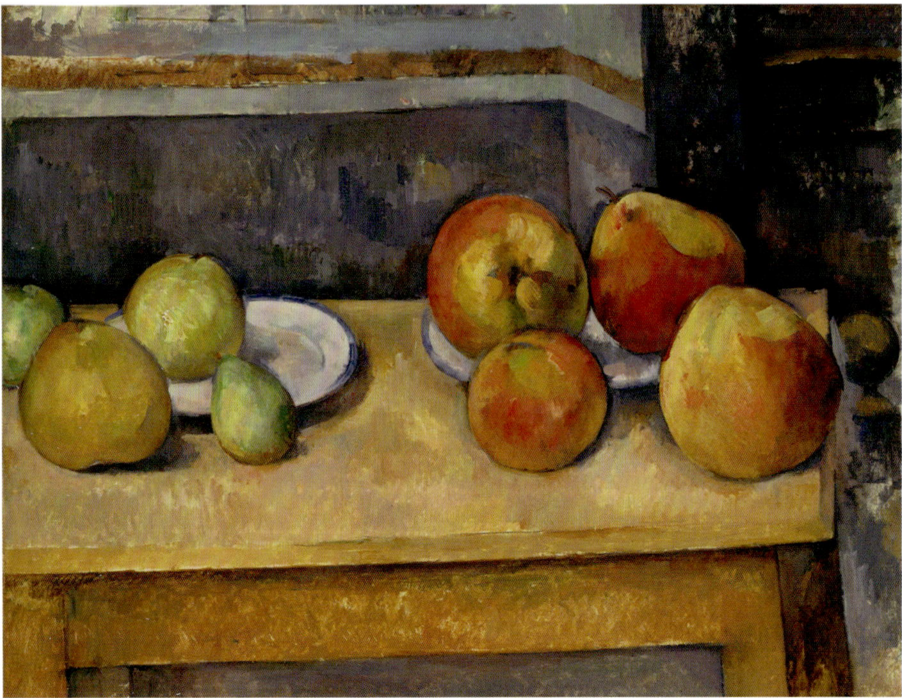

07 *Still Life with Apples and Pears* by Cubist painter Paul Cézanne was a great departure from the traditional rules and standards of perspective in that era. Notice the statements being made by the forced awkwardness of the vanishing points suggested by the foreground table and background wall.

In the nineteenth century, artists such as Edgar Degas and Claude Monet challenged traditional perspective and focused more on capturing the essence of lighting and atmosphere **(06)**. Movements like Cubism and Surrealism pushed the boundaries of perspective even further, sometimes abandoning it altogether in order to achieve a better sense of abstraction **(07)**.

In the early 1900s, the Modernist era of art rejected realistic depictions of reality and were more concerned with experimentation and innovation. Their thinking created new rules for how some artists would go on to use design to first establish their artistic statement beyond reality, then reinforce this idea with implied perspective. Such an idea can be seen in the works of both Richard Diebenkorn and Eyvind Earle.

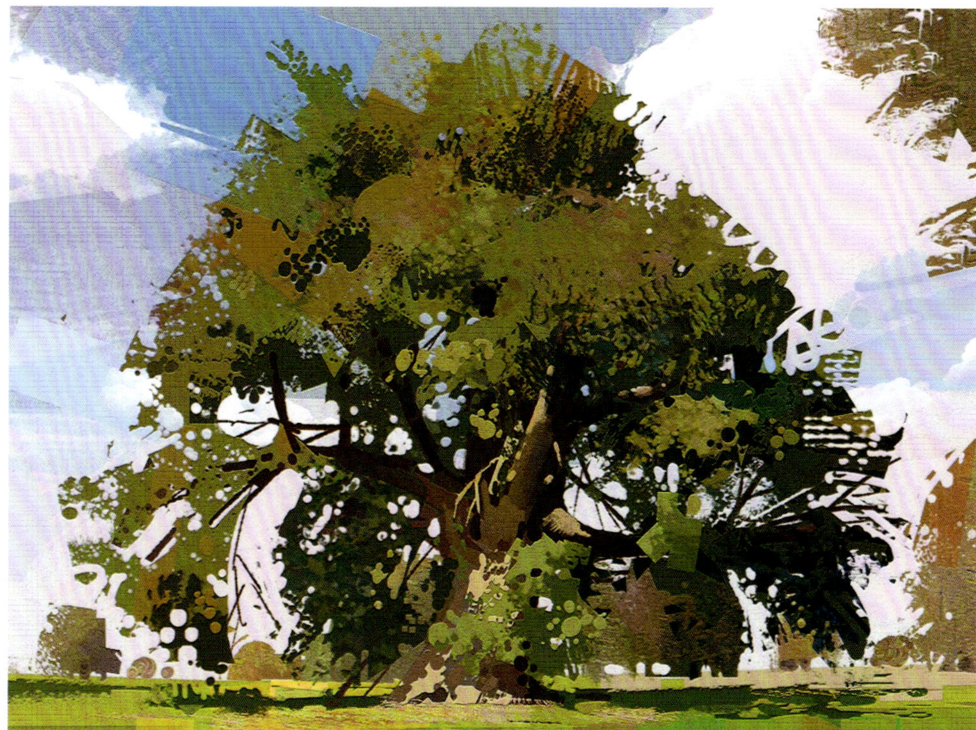

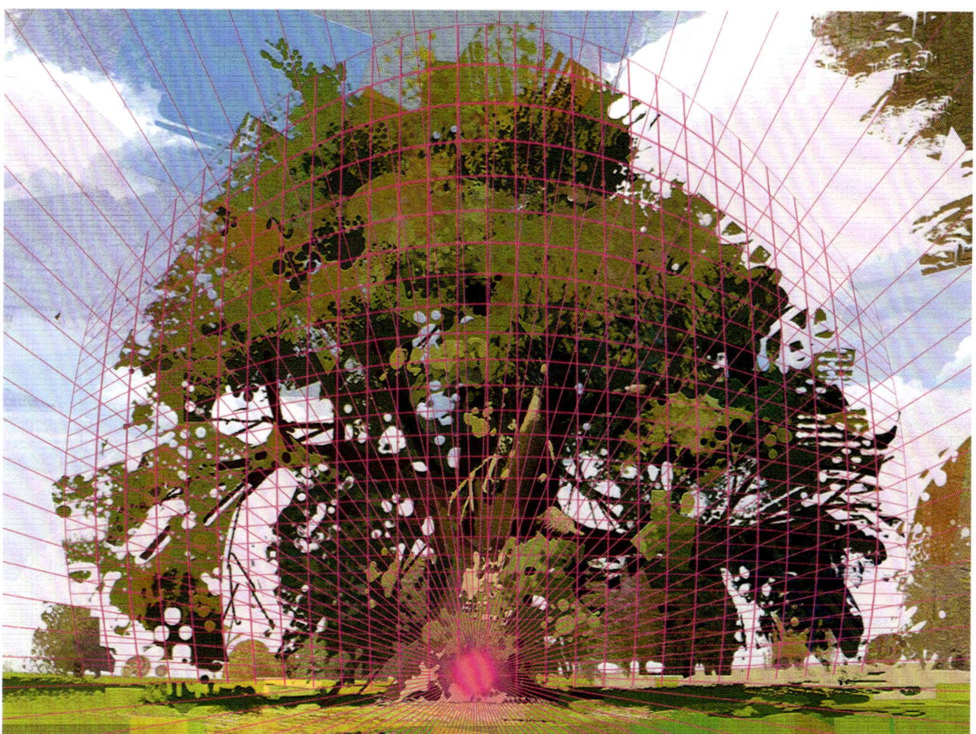

08 This digital painting is an example of how traditional thinking and digital skill sets can come together to bring a more abstract experience, while maintaining realistic depth and volume in perspective.

In contemporary art, perspective continues to evolve. Artists in both the entertainment and fine-art industries explore new techniques and concepts. Digital art, virtual reality, and social media have expanded the possibilities for creating a more dimensional and immersive experience. While traditional linear perspective techniques have been used for centuries to create realistic depth and volume, many contemporary artists now push the boundaries of perspective in order to challenge and explore abstract concepts **(08)**.

TYPES OF PERSPECTIVE

There are several types of perspective, each offering a unique approach to achieving the illusion of depth and realism. The different types provide artists and designers with a range of tools and techniques to convey depth, space, and realism in their work. Depending on the artistic intention and visual effect required, artists can choose the most suitable perspective method to achieve their goals.

THE HORIZON LINE & PICTURE PLANE

When studying depth and perspective, there are many aspects of maths and theory that may at first seem daunting and intimidating to the average layperson, leading them to avoid the subject matter altogether. A good way to make the subject more approachable is to break depth into four simple dimensions: one-, two-, three-, and four-point (also known as multi-point) perspective.

For the purposes of our discussion and understanding of perspective, you should always begin with a known horizon line **(01)**. The horizon line, or eye level, refers to a physical, visual boundary where the sky separates from land or water. This is the actual height of the viewer's eyes when looking at an object, interior scene, or exterior scene. Knowing where the horizon line is at all times gives the artist a measuring point for perspective and depth in order to feel grounded in the artwork.

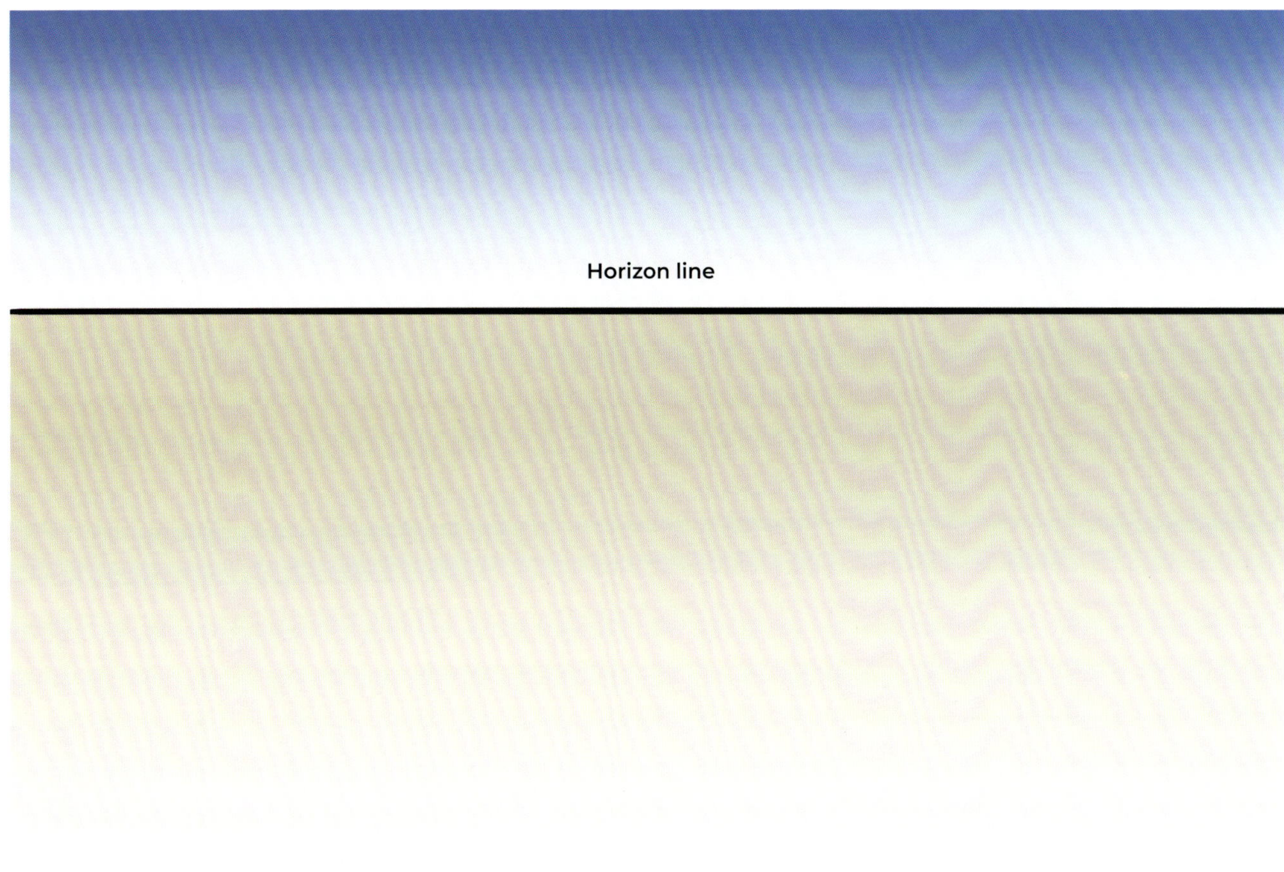

01 The horizon line is the starting point in establishing perspective in a scene. It's where the sky meets the ground plane, or water, and is also referred to as the viewer's eye level.

It's also important to consider that paintings or drawings are working within a picture plane **(02)**, which is like a glass window through which the viewer sees the subject. The scene beyond the picture plane is where the volume and depth originates **(03)**.

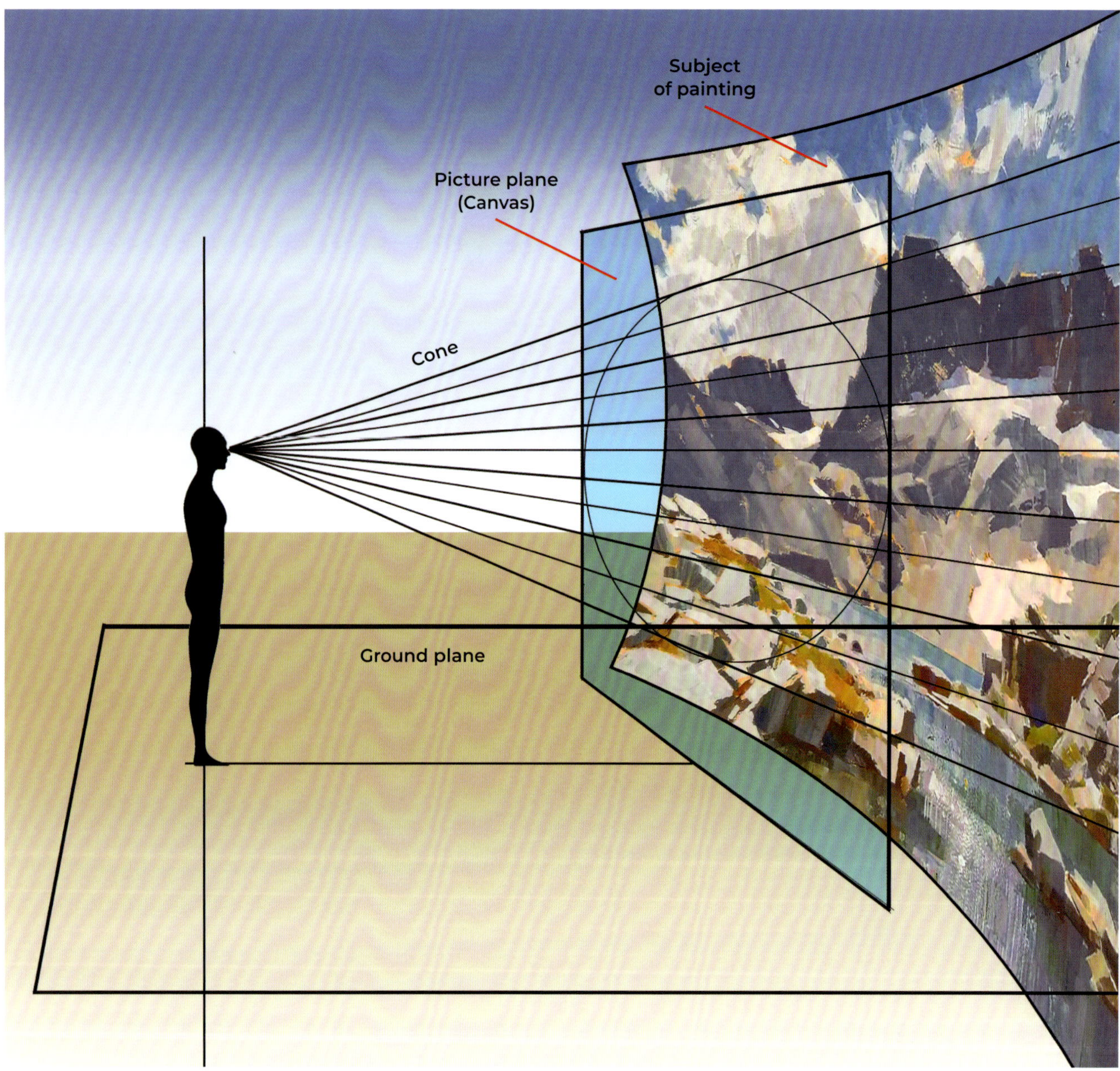

02 Here you can see the horizon level as it pertains to the viewer standing eye level to the picture plane. The world beyond the picture plane is the painting and where you measure perspective.

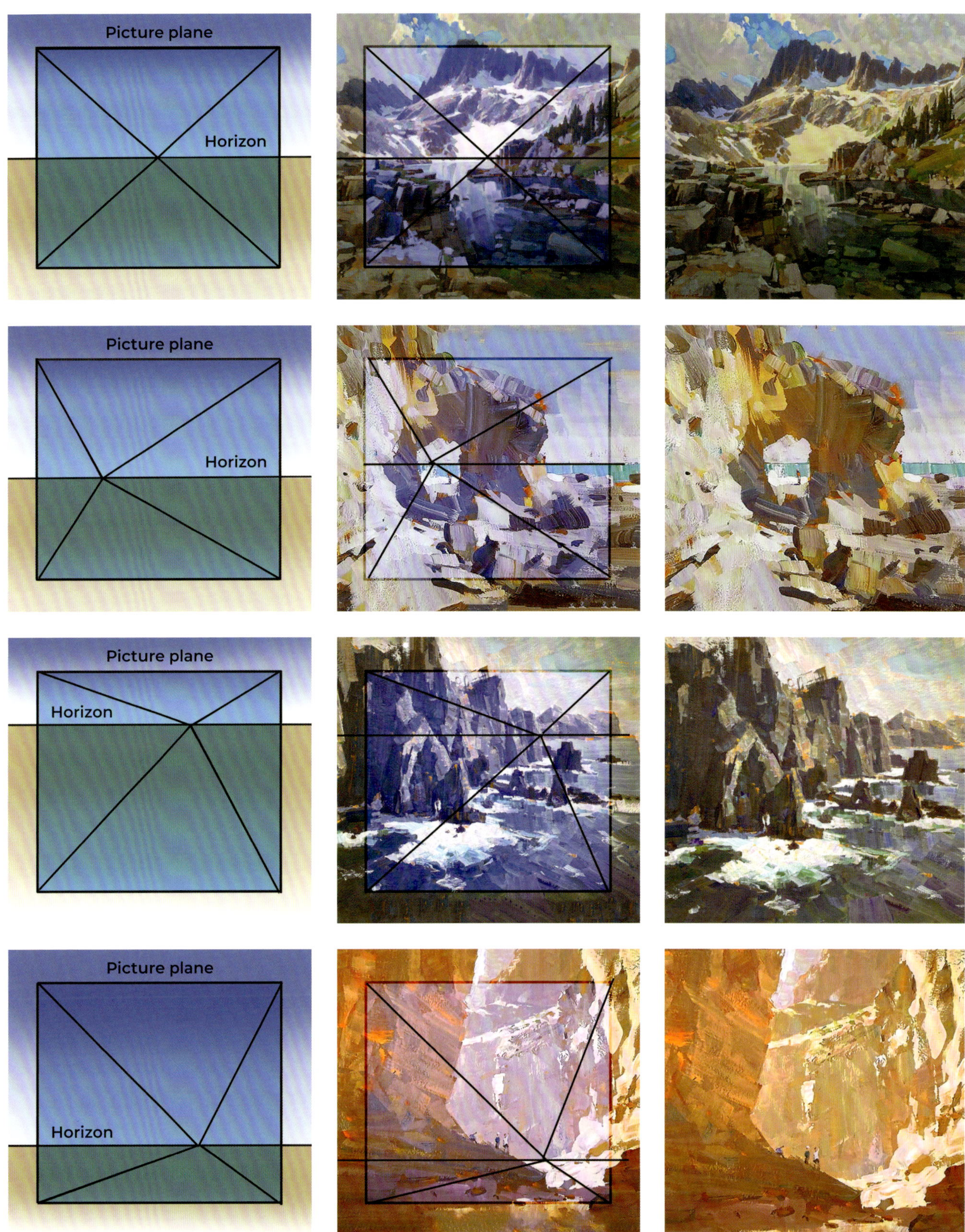

03 Four examples of how volume and depth are perceived beyond the picture plane, dependent on the placement of the horizon and vanishing points.

SCHEMATIC VIEW

Let's start with a cube in what is called the 'schematic view'. This offers the face of only one side of an object at any given view. It represents a 90-degree angle from the viewer's eye. In order to see more views of the object simultaneously, you would need to apply several points of perspective. However, from this schematic view, you only see one square face of the cube **(04)**.

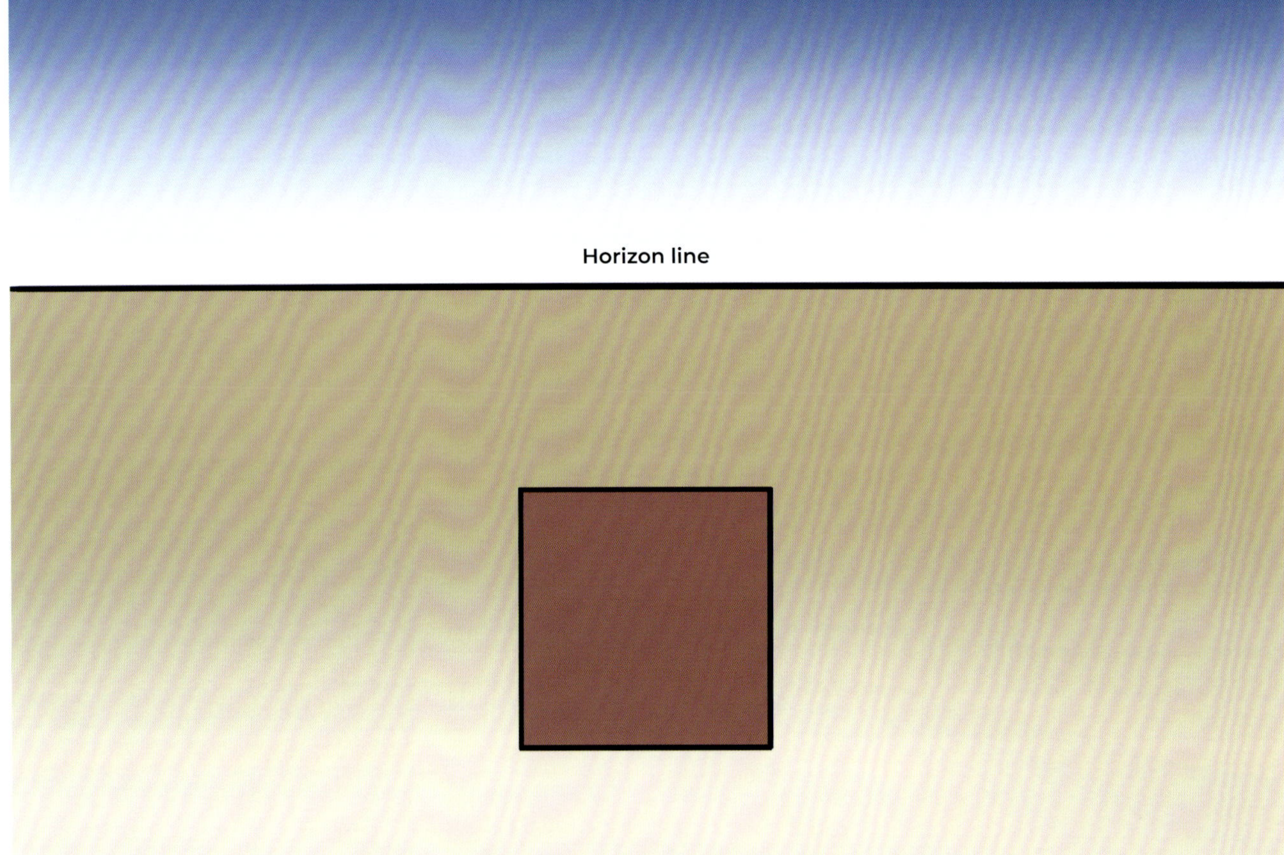

04 Schematic view of a cube placed in our view, below the horizon line, without an established vanishing point. As there is no perspective, this is considered frontal plane view.

ONE-POINT PERSPECTIVE

When introducing a single vanishing point somewhere on the horizon line, this creates a measuring point that allows you to see another side as well as the top of the square, creating a cube **(05)**. This is one-point perspective.

With one-point perspective, only one side converges to the horizon, while the face remains schematic, or square. By following the lines connected to the corner of the square, you will observe the cube become increasingly smaller as the lines stretch into the distance and finally meet at the vanishing point on the horizon line.

One-point perspective has its benefits. For example, you might want to show an undistorted view of the face of a building, while also showing its depth **(06)**. This is important if the focus of your artwork is the object or building in the foreground needing to be facing the viewer, in order to convey proper proportion and storytelling. It's also a good option for artists who have little to no understanding of complex perspective.

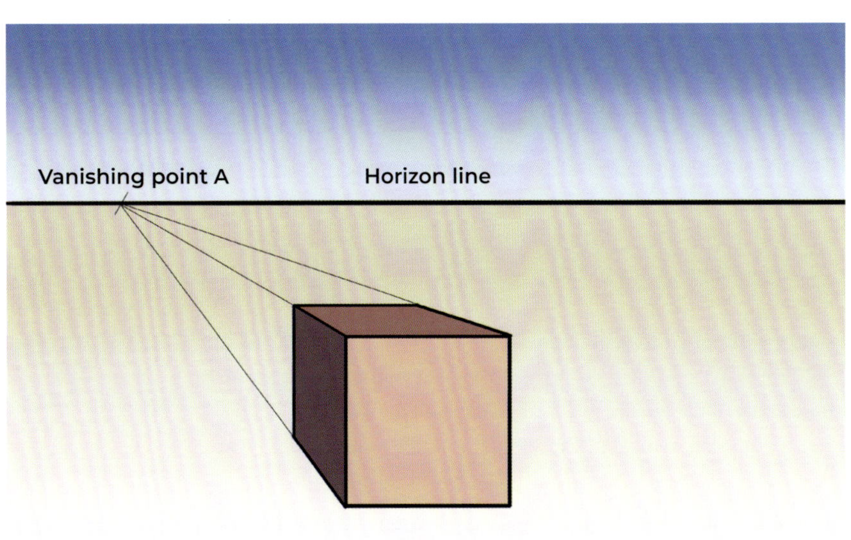

05 The first vanishing point on the horizon reveals two other sides of the square, creating a cube in one-point perspective and an image with depth.

Sometimes a little perspective can go a long way in conveying depth. Another advantage of one-point perspective is the inherent subtlety of distortion due to the limited number of vanishing points of objects in a scene.

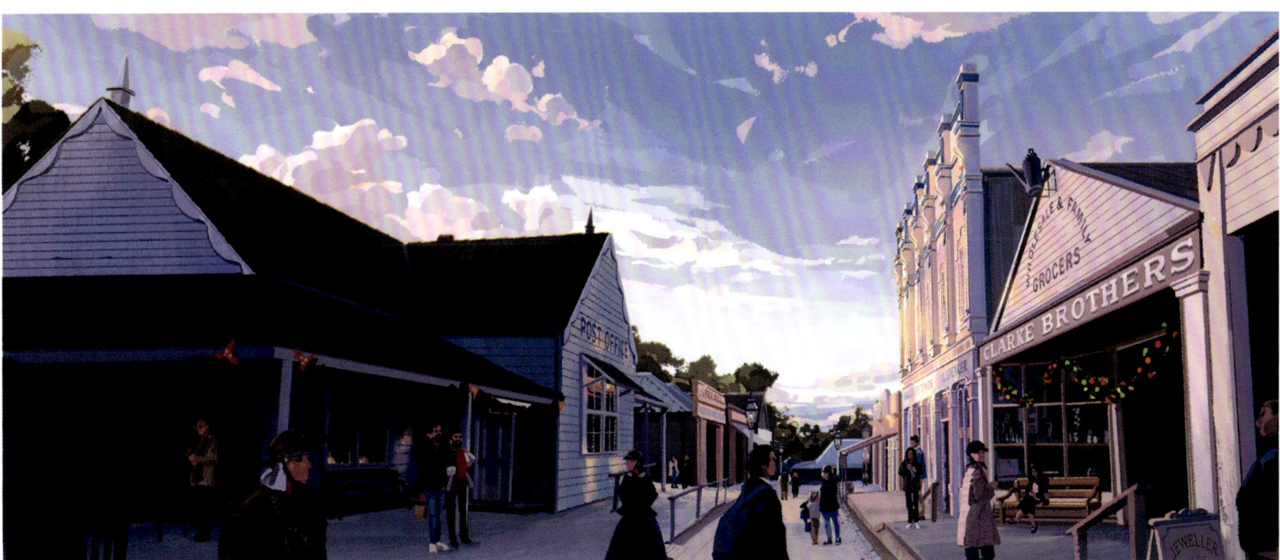

06 This painting by Orenjikun is a great example of how to use one-point perspective in a scene. Notice the convergence of lines that vanish to a single point on the horizon in the centre of the painting, while the left and right horizontal lines remain parallel.

TWO-POINT PERSPECTIVE

If you introduce another vanishing point on the horizon line, across from the first point, this provides the second measurement needed to create two-point perspective. Now the cube takes on a different dimension where you no longer see the square faces of the box, but rather distorted sides that create volume and depth **(07)**.

Two-point perspective presents an object from the side with two vanishing points. It provides a realistic view of the object, as it shows the item edge-on, as you would typically view it. Two-point perspective is often used to produce realistic drawings of an object. With its more neutral sense of distortion, it's often favoured by contemporary outdoor painters who want to capture a simple and neutral composition in landscape **(08)**.

From a human point of view, we tend to paint within the confines of our comfortable range of vision, which doesn't usually cause much distortion. This range is what is known as the 'cone of vision', which will be discussed on page 80. When you paint within your cone of vision, you minimize distortion and reduce the risk of having to introduce too many dimensions and vanishing points. This is where two-point perspective usually makes sense. It's not a hard rule, but rather an average that can help you to instil a composition with a simple, calm appearance.

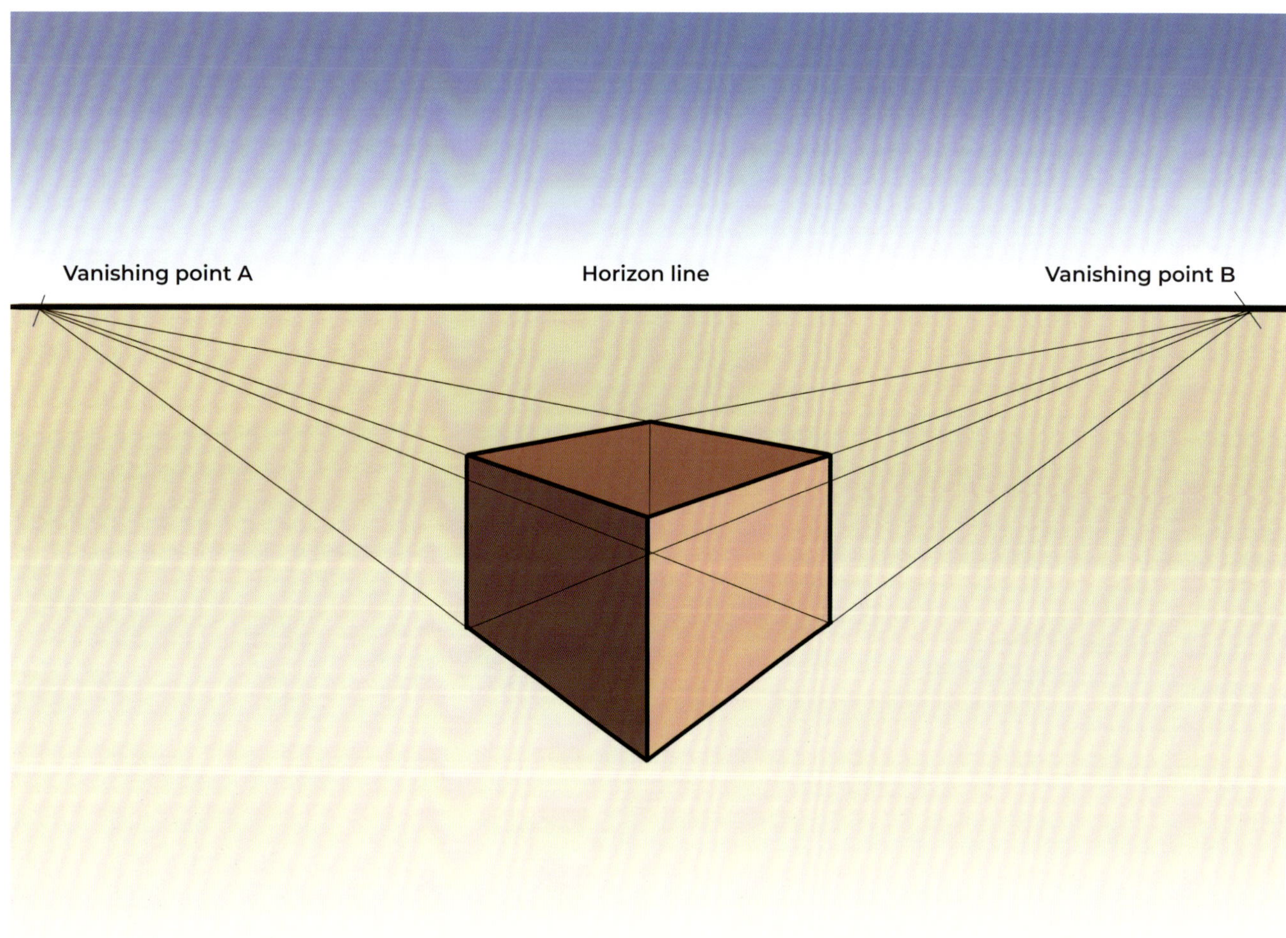

07 The addition of a second vanishing point on the opposite side creates two-point perspective. Here you can see three sides of the cube. Notice how the vertical sides of the cube lines are parallel to one another.

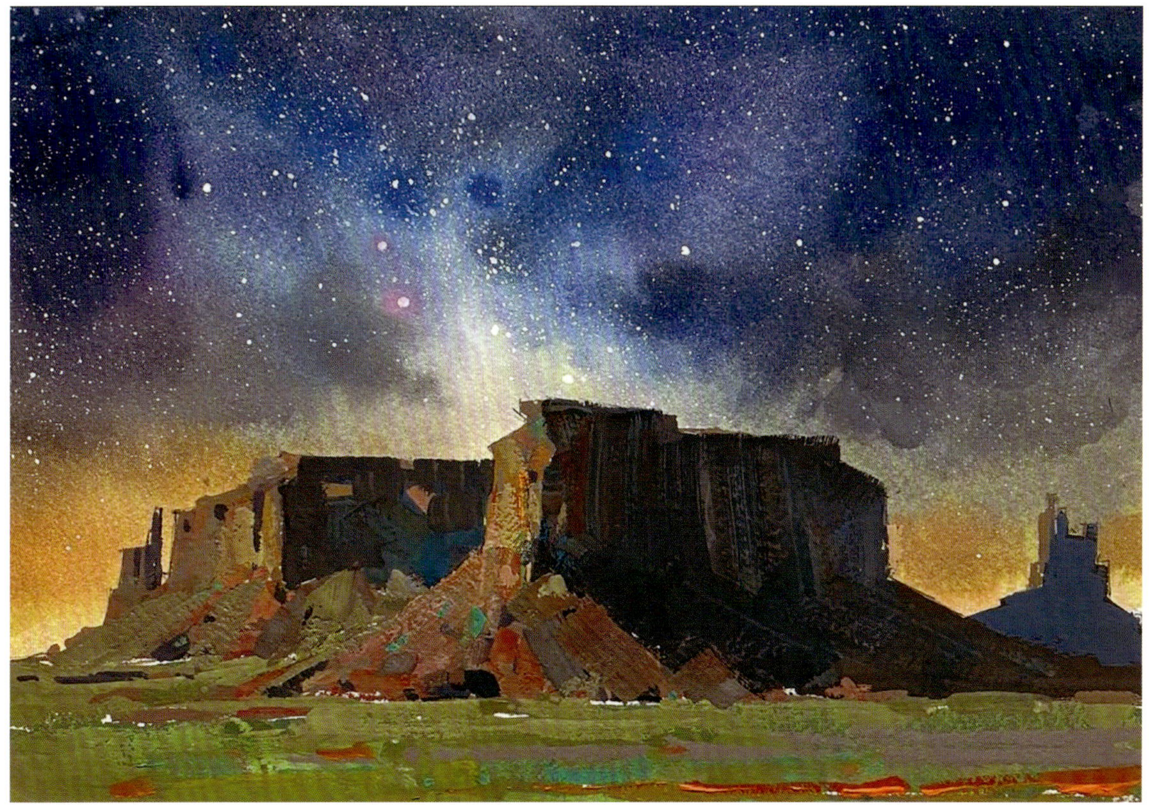

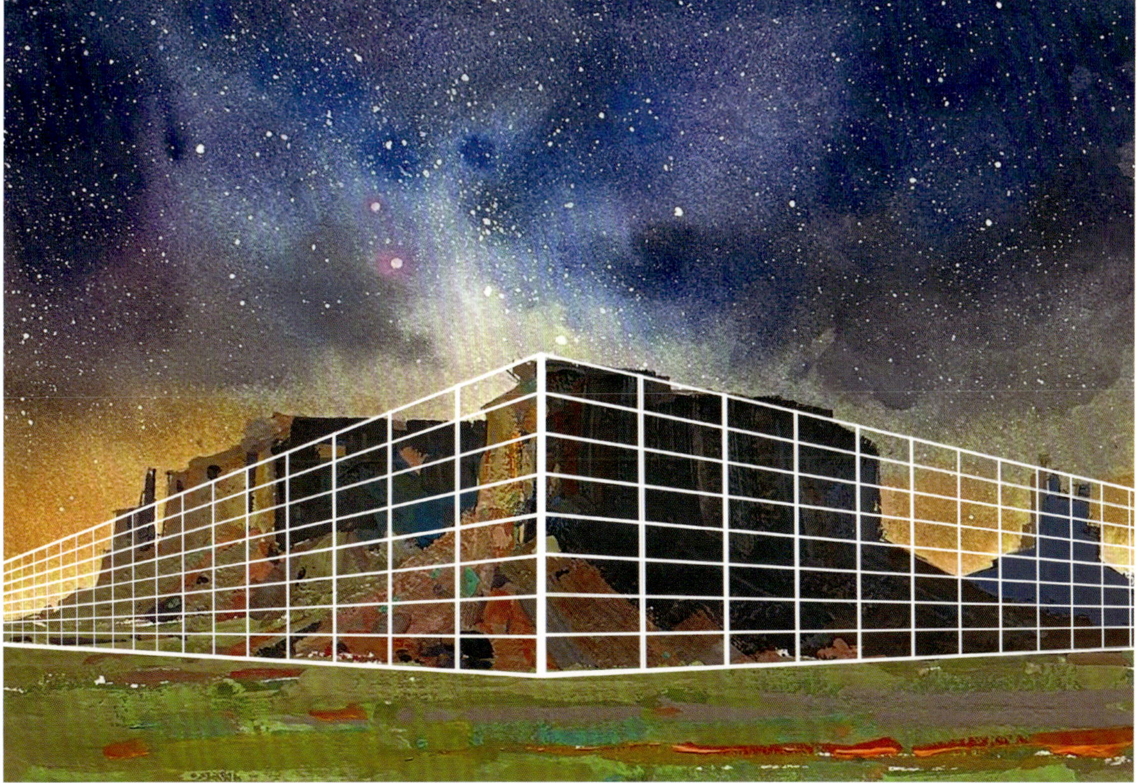

08 This gouache nocturne painting is a good example of two-point perspective.

Notice how both sides of the mesas vanish to different points on the horizon.

THREE-POINT PERSPECTIVE

Adding an additional vanishing point forty-five degrees vertically to the horizon line provides another measurement and creates three-point perspective **(09)**. Boasting yet more benefits, three-point perspective provides the most realistic feeling of depth and dimension for an object in a lifelike scenario. Humans tend to see the world from a wide-angle view. Three-point perspective conveys that view most accurately, without overly distorting the composition **(10)**.

Another advantage is its ability to convey a low-to-high eye level. For example, if you were standing at the base of a building, looking up slightly, three-point perspective would create the illusion of that distortion in volume **(11)**.

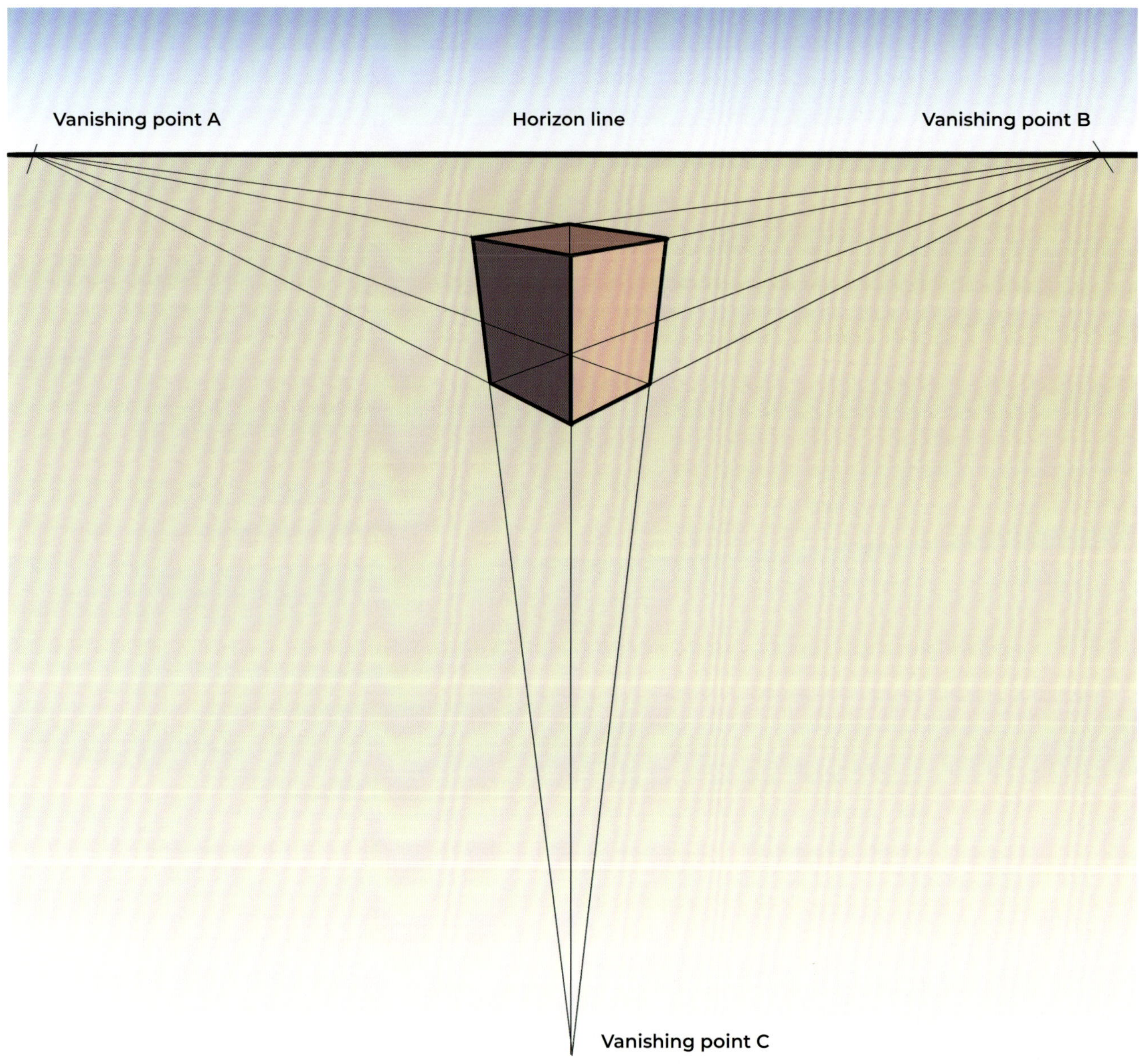

09 Adding a third vanishing point 45 degrees vertically to the horizon produces three-point perspective. Notice the distortion where the side lines are no longer parallel.

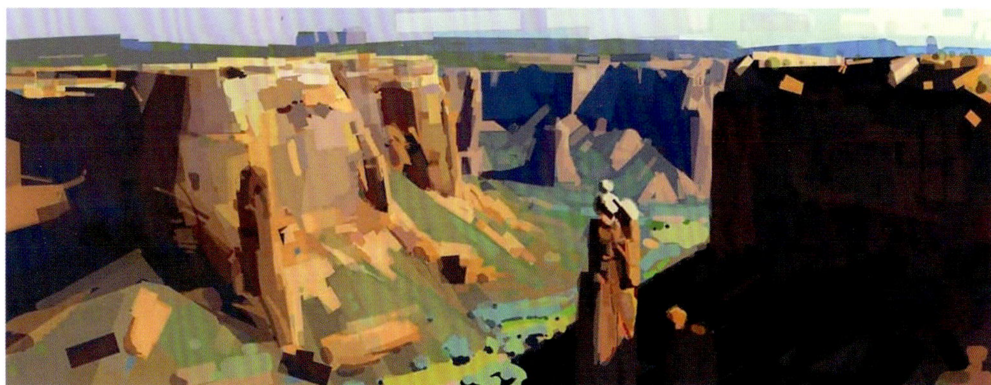

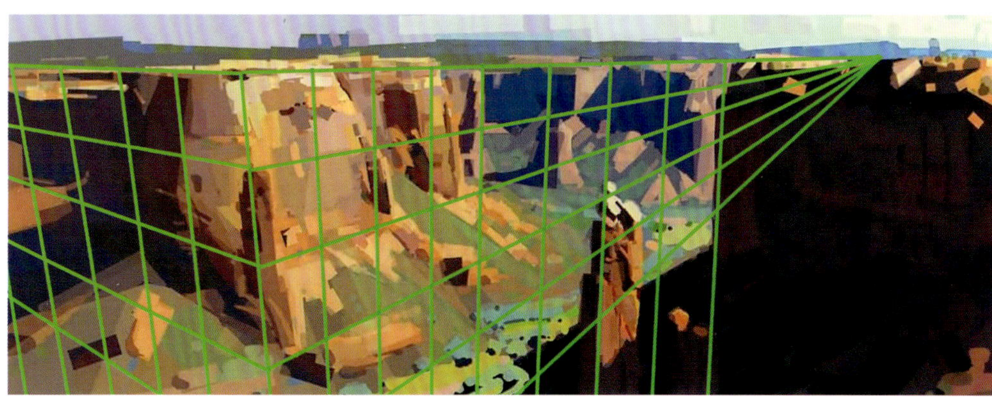

10 This digital painting of Canyon de Chelly illustrates three-point perspective as viewed from a higher point of view. Notice how the vertical lines converge to a lower vanishing point beyond the picture plane.

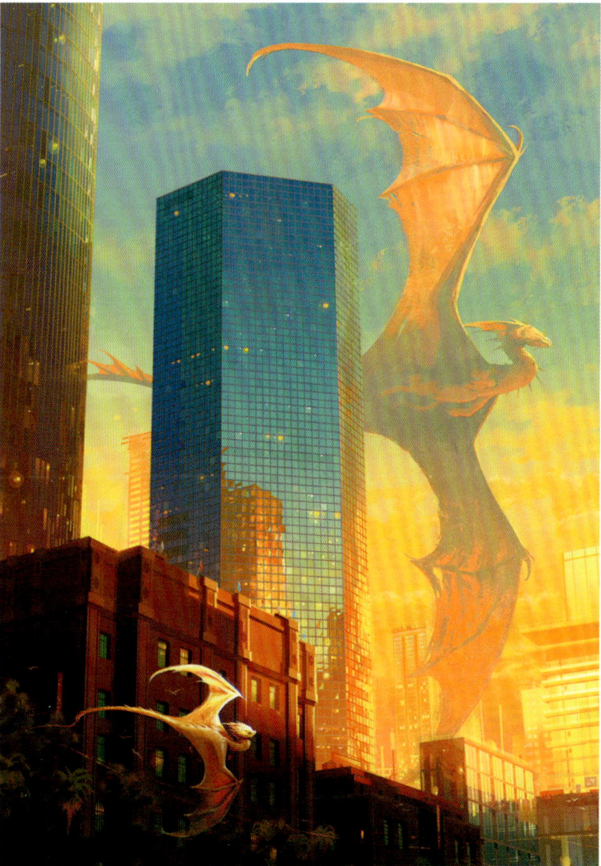

11 This digital painting by Devin Elle Kurtz is another example of how to use three-point perspective in a scene. Notice the convergence of left and right horizontal lines from the buildings, as well as the convergence to a single vertical vanishing point on top. Find the tutorial on page 84.

FOUR-POINT PERSPECTIVE & ABOVE

Most art and design work stays within the confines of one-, two-, or three-point perspective, as moving beyond this causes further distortion and what is called 'fish-eye view'. Sometimes the inclusion of distortions created by four-point perspective (or higher) is justified, such as in production work with the use of multiple camera styles for film and entertainment. The purpose of these shots in film would be to cram as much information into the scene as possible **(12)**.

The same effect is evident when looking through the peephole of a door. To produce this type of measurement, you would use four-point or multi-point perspective by adding in another vanishing point 45 degrees above the horizon line **(13)**. Perspectives using four or more points are by far the most complex to master, as they require additional mathematical calculations and measurements **(14)**.

As for my personal history with perspective, as both an art director for animated films and a plein-air painter in contemporary fine art, I've rarely ever felt the need to venture beyond three-point perspective. One-, two-, and three-point have typically proved all I've needed.

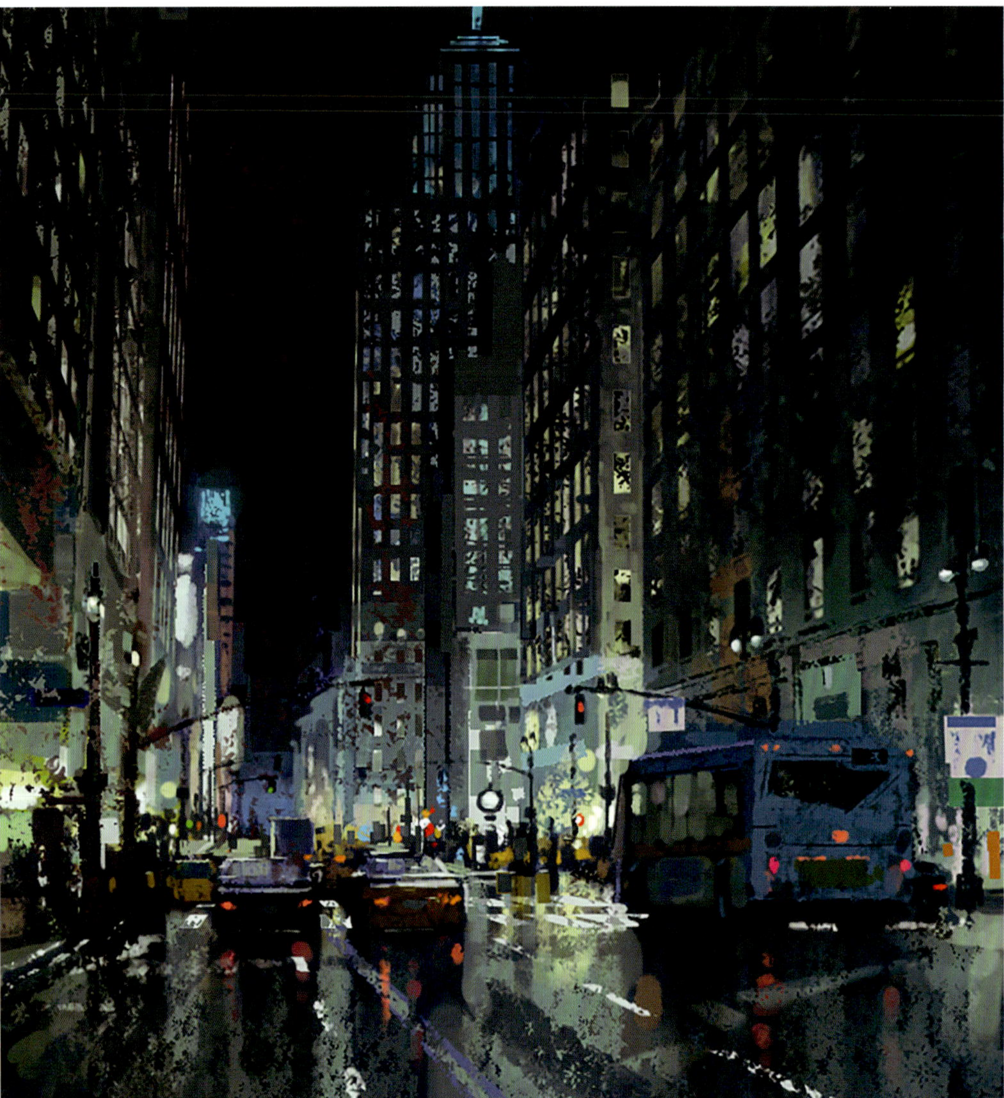

12 This digital painting of a downtown city scene demonstrates the use four-point perspective in a more naturalistic way. Notice the subtle vertical distortion due to the view outside of the cone of vision.

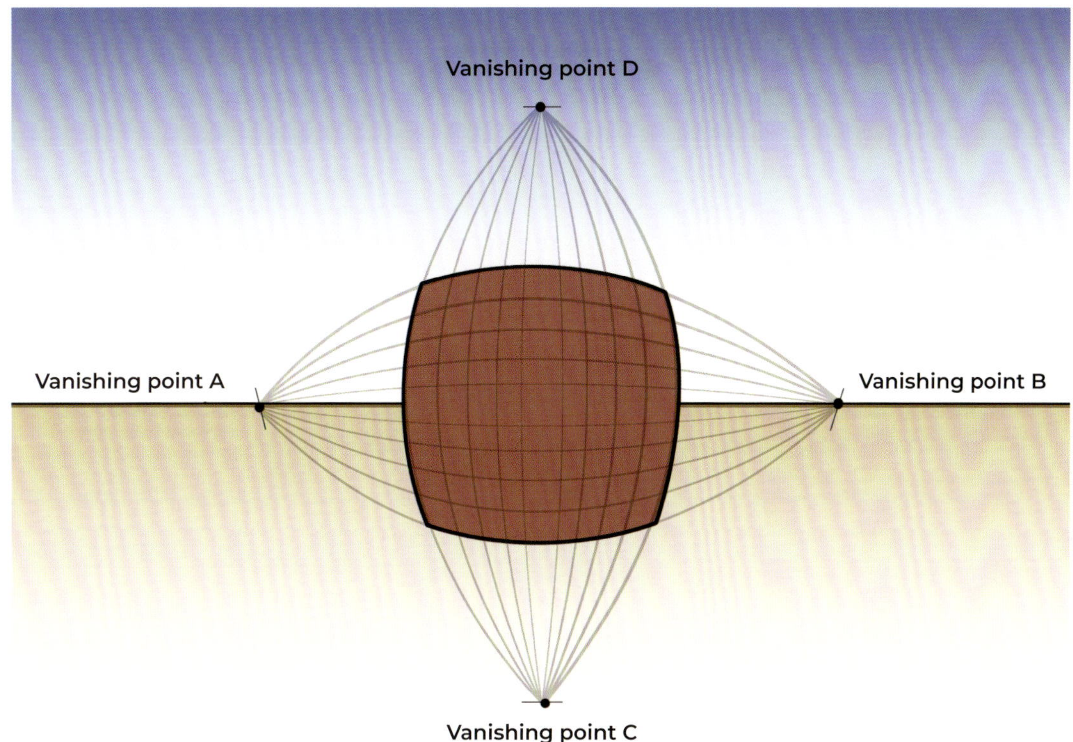

13 Adding the fourth vanishing point 45 degrees vertically above the horizon creates four-point perspective. Notice the rounded effect of the cube on all four sides.

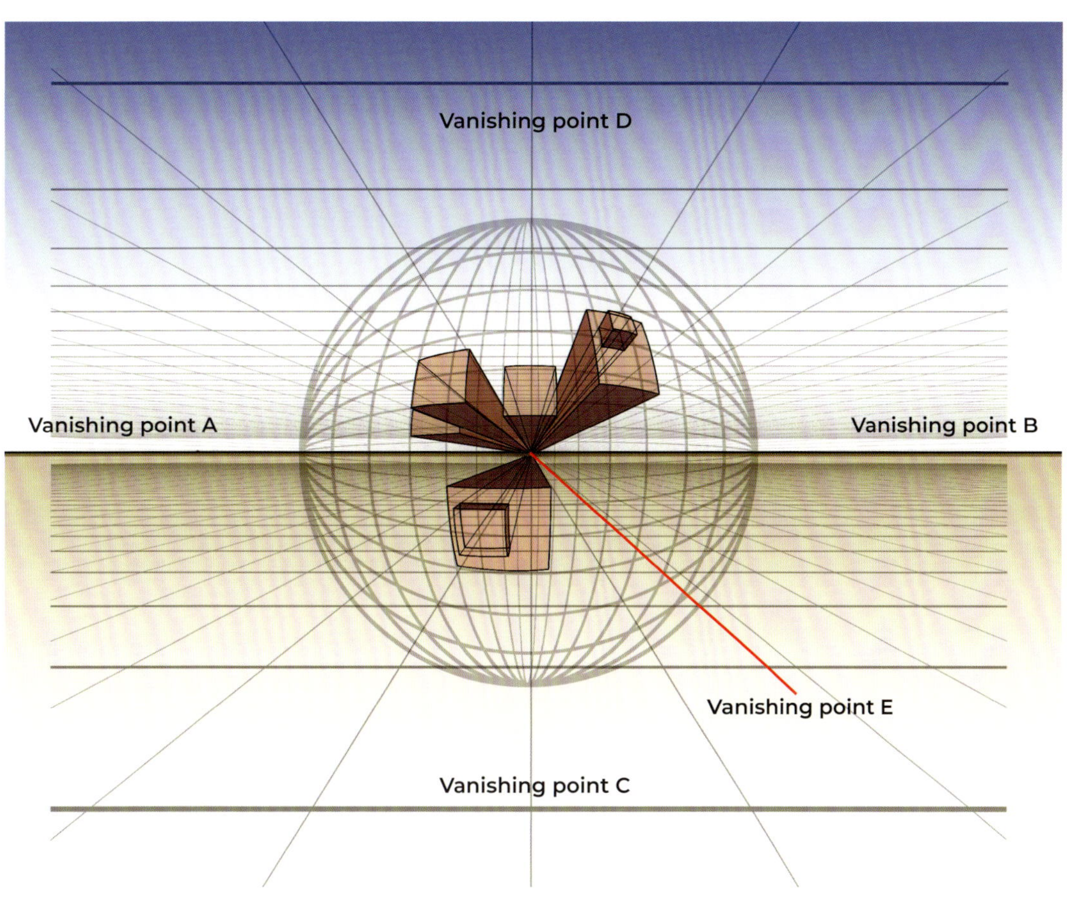

14 Adding another vanishing point in the middle, radiating out in a star-like formation, produces five-point perspective. This is known as the 'fish-eye view'.

WORM'S-EYE VIEW

If you were to force the three points of three-point perspective closer together, while placing the viewer's eye level on the floor, this would create what is called 'worm's-eye view' **(15)**. This view yields much heavier distortions. Very rarely would you see this type of view in a landscape painter's artwork, as it requires you to lie on the floor with your eye to the ground, looking up. You could, however, use this method to create a more stylized feel in a scene **(16)**, such as in a movie where a character is experiencing vertigo from staring up at the city skyscrapers towering above them. Worm's-eye view would help to capture that sense of dizziness and overwhelm.

Another example of how to use worm's-eye view would be to capture the hero motif. The term 'hero' does more than describe an important character. It also conveys a sense of hierarchy in staging a scene. Whether the painting is of a building, tree, or person, forced three-point perspective in worm's-eye view can been used to achieve a more heroic shape.

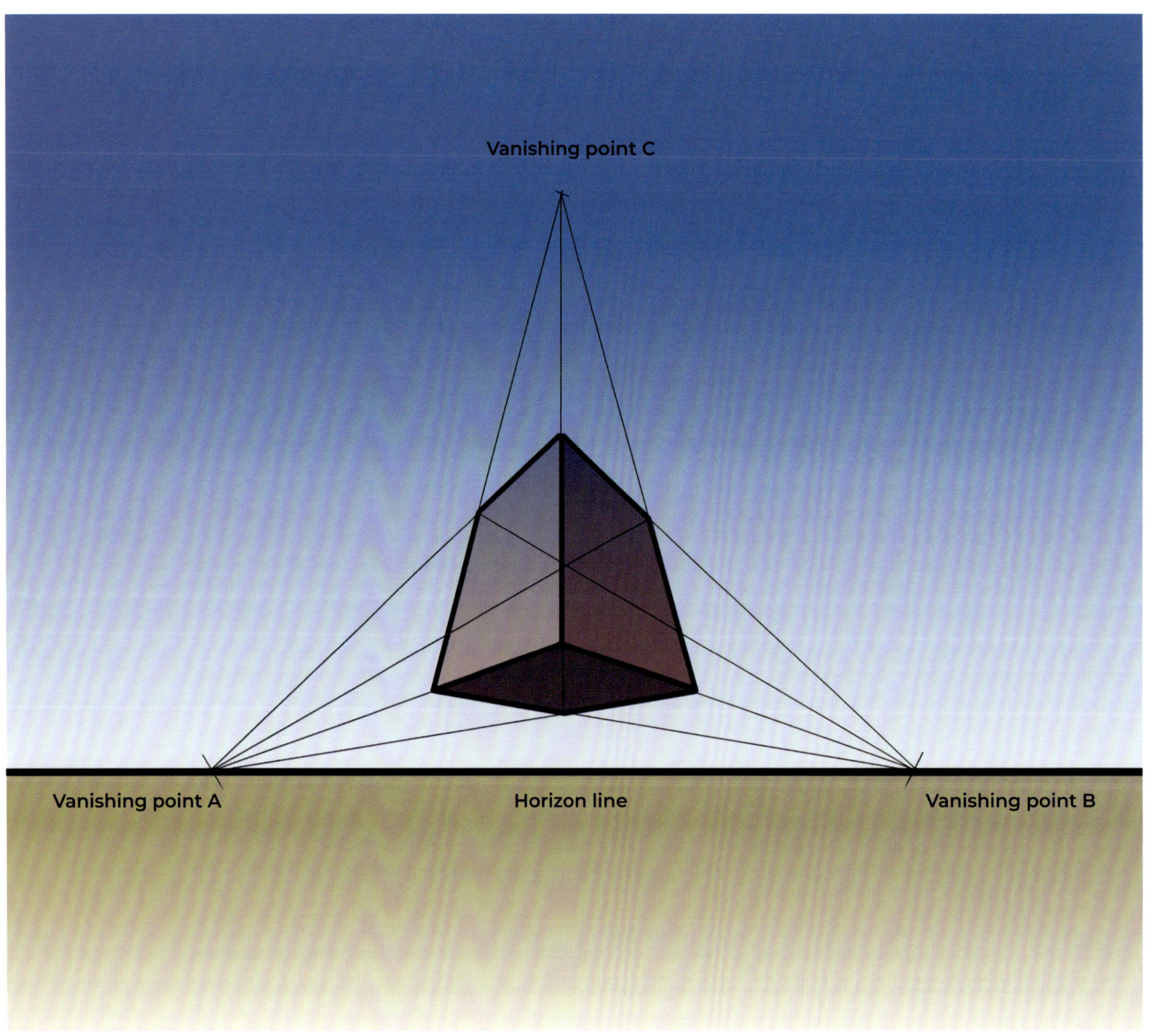

15 Worm's-eye view is a forced perspective created from a point of view looking up from below.

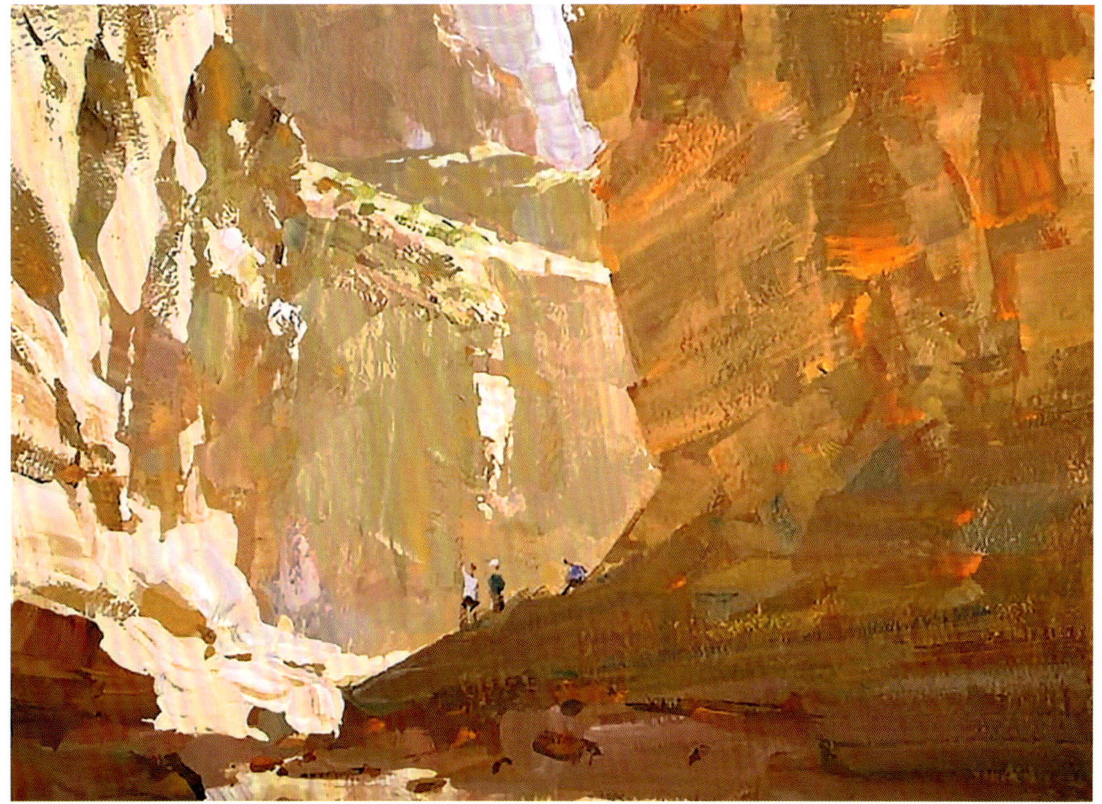

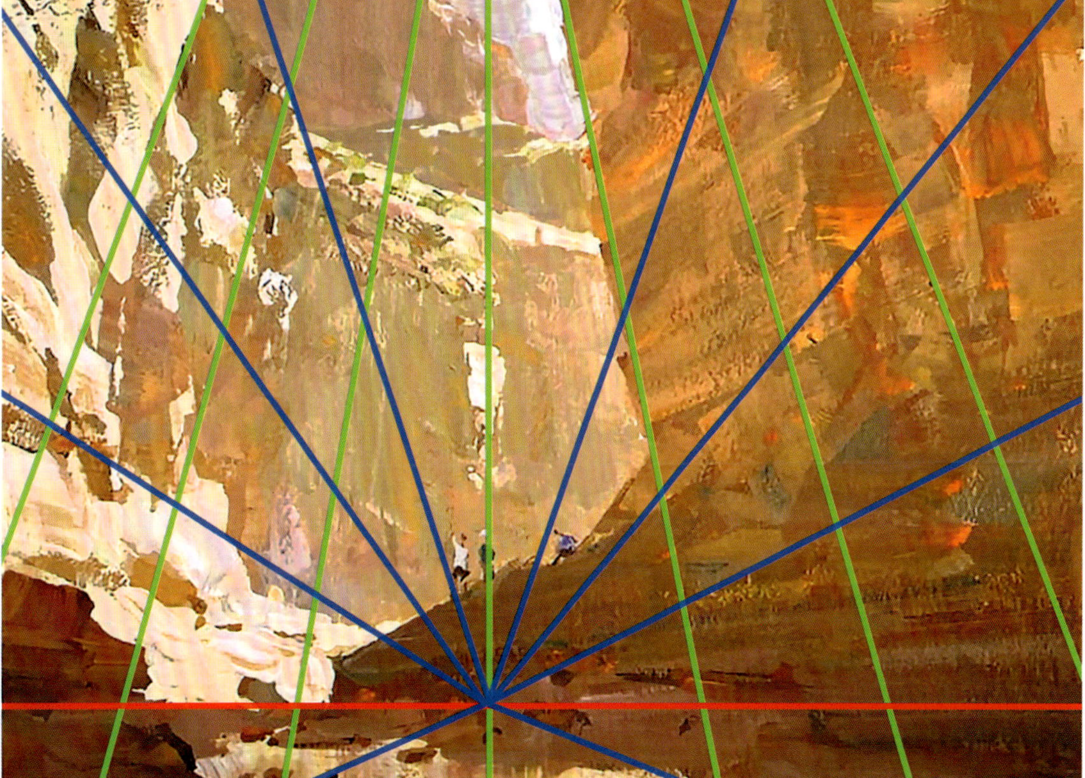

16 This gouache painting from the Grand Canyon is a good example of worm's-eye view, thanks to the extremely low point of view looking up at the towering rock walls.

BIRD'S-EYE VIEW

The opposite can be achieved when looking down on an object from an elevated viewpoint, described as 'bird's-eye view' **(17)**. This angle is useful when artists wish to establish a greater scope and scale of an environment. Examples of this could be figures looking down over a cliff top **(18)**, or a person overlooking the city from their high balcony.

An example of bird's-eye view used in film would be a dynamic view looking straight down into a city street from the top of a skyscraper, as is often seen in superhero movies such as *Spider-Man*. This type of bird's-eye view can also be achieved in four-point through to six-point perspective, where the scene takes on that circular fish-eye lens look.

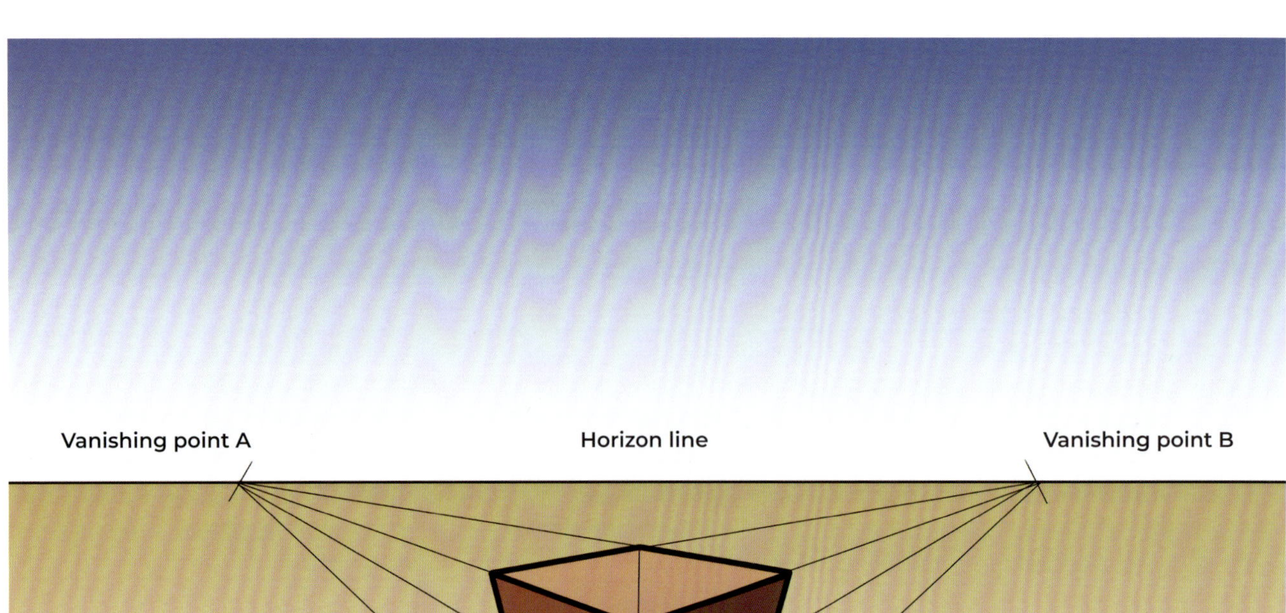

17 Pulling the vanishing points closer together creates a forced perspective that is also referred to as bird's-eye view.

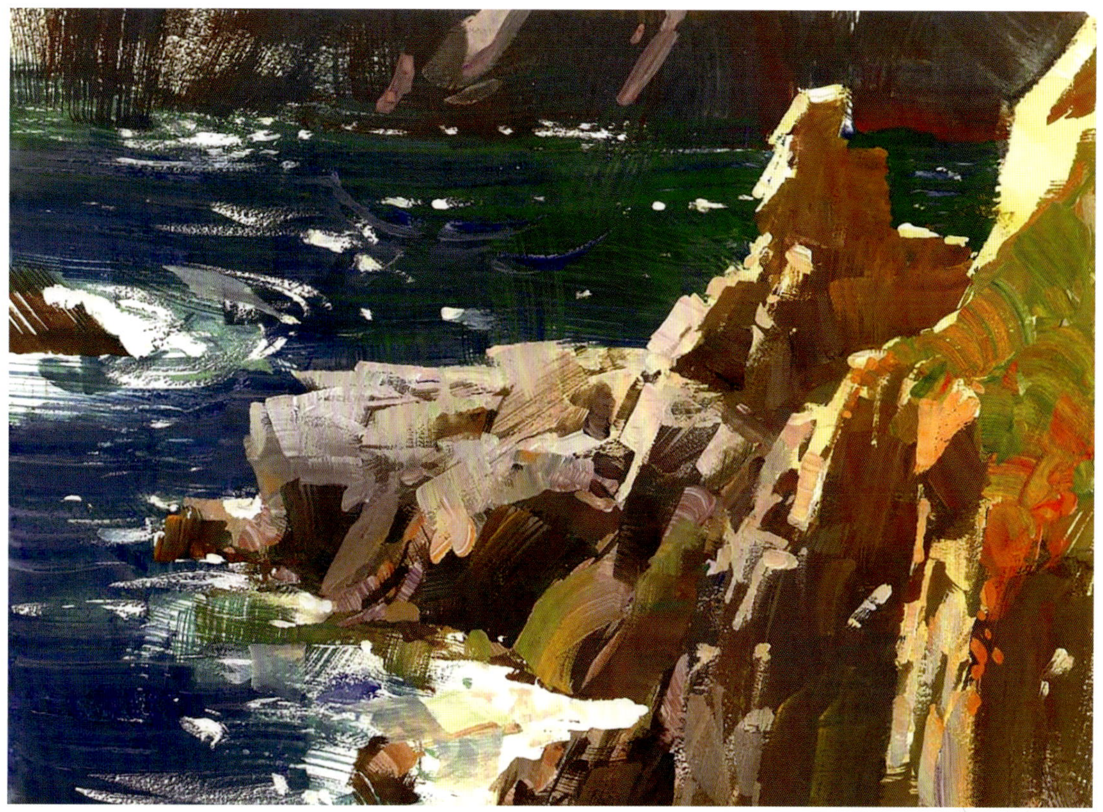

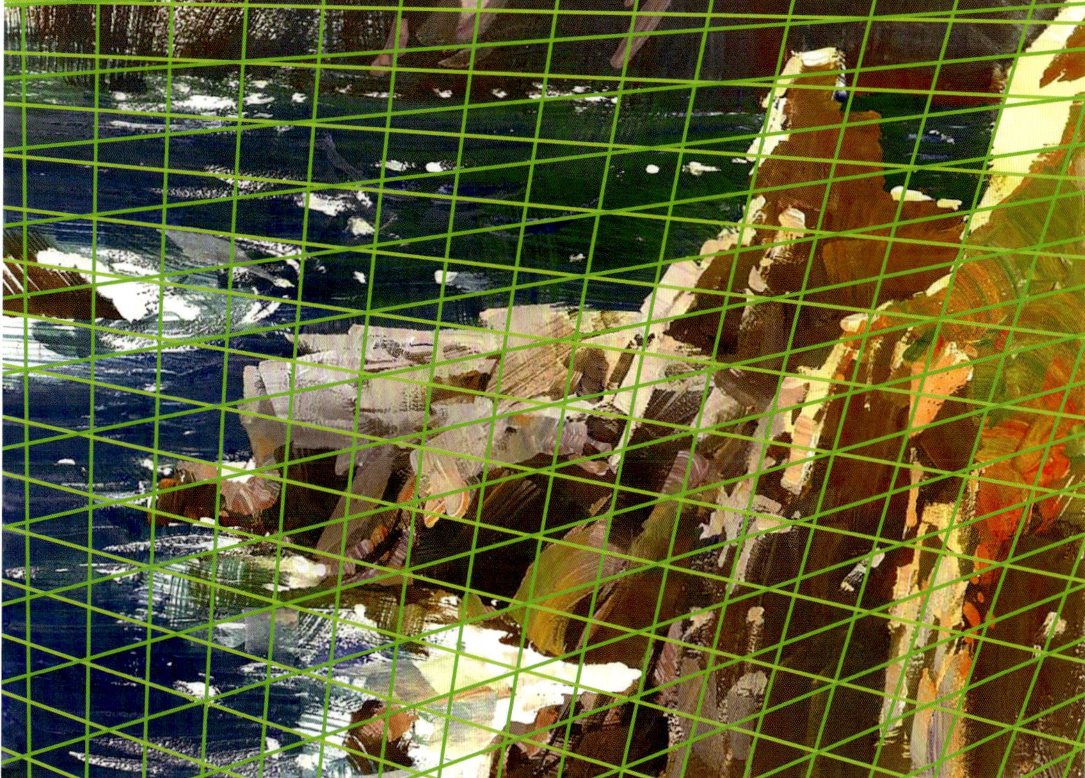

18 This gouache painting of Garrapata Beach, California, is a good example of bird's-eye view due to the higher vantage point looking down on the rocks.

Four-point through to six-point perspective is best used when you want achieve a truly dynamic sense of depth and distortion in a scene, which is why it's rarely used in contemporary outdoor painting. It's the least realistic way in which we view the world through our eyes due to the limitations of our cone of vision. Interestingly, bird's-eye view can also be achieved in two-point perspective where the view has a limited sense of distortion **(19, 20)**. These types of perspectives in bird's-eye are typical in long-lens shots, which will be discussed on page 214.

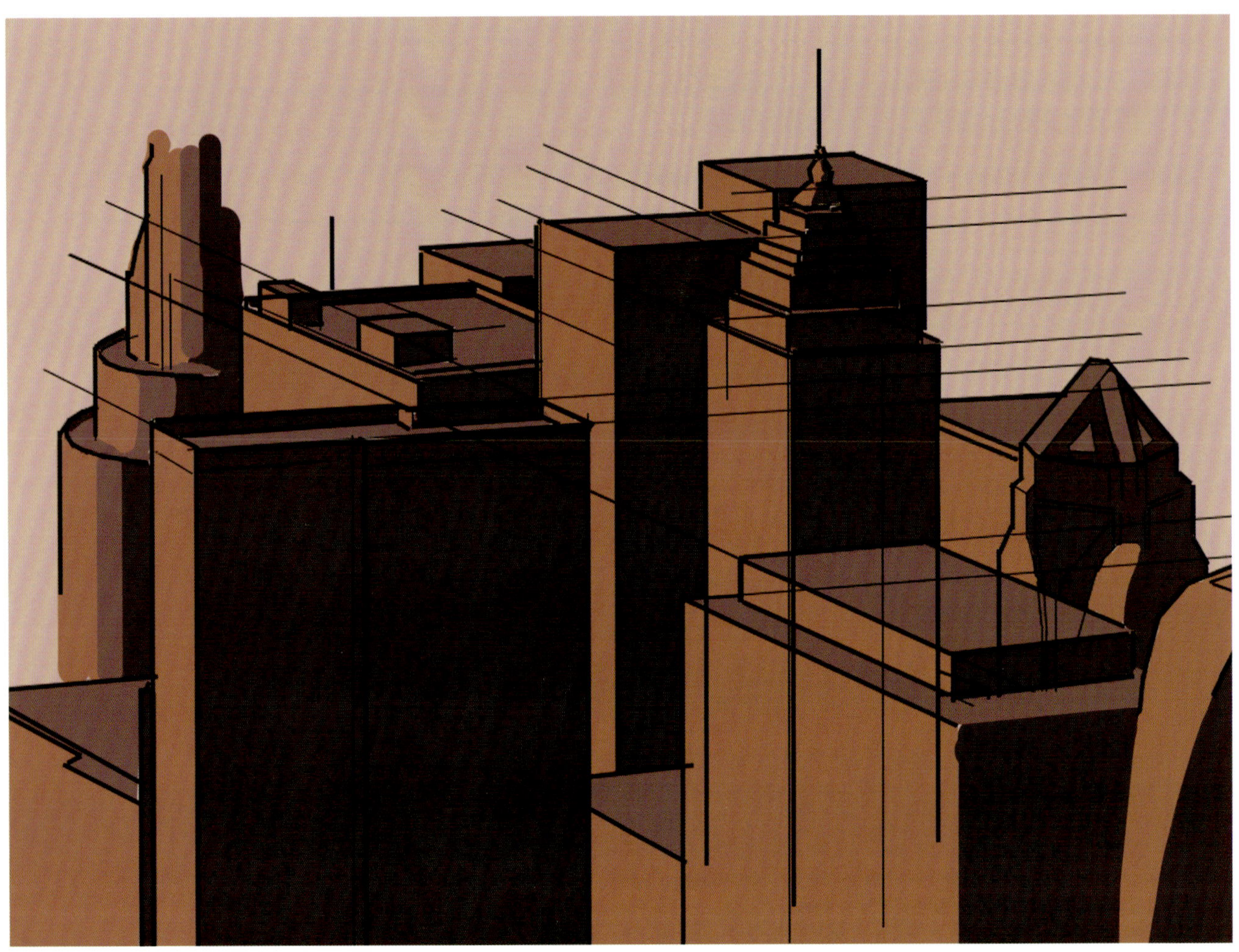

19 The illustration above is an example of bird's-eye view using two-point perspective. Notice the parallel vertical lines.

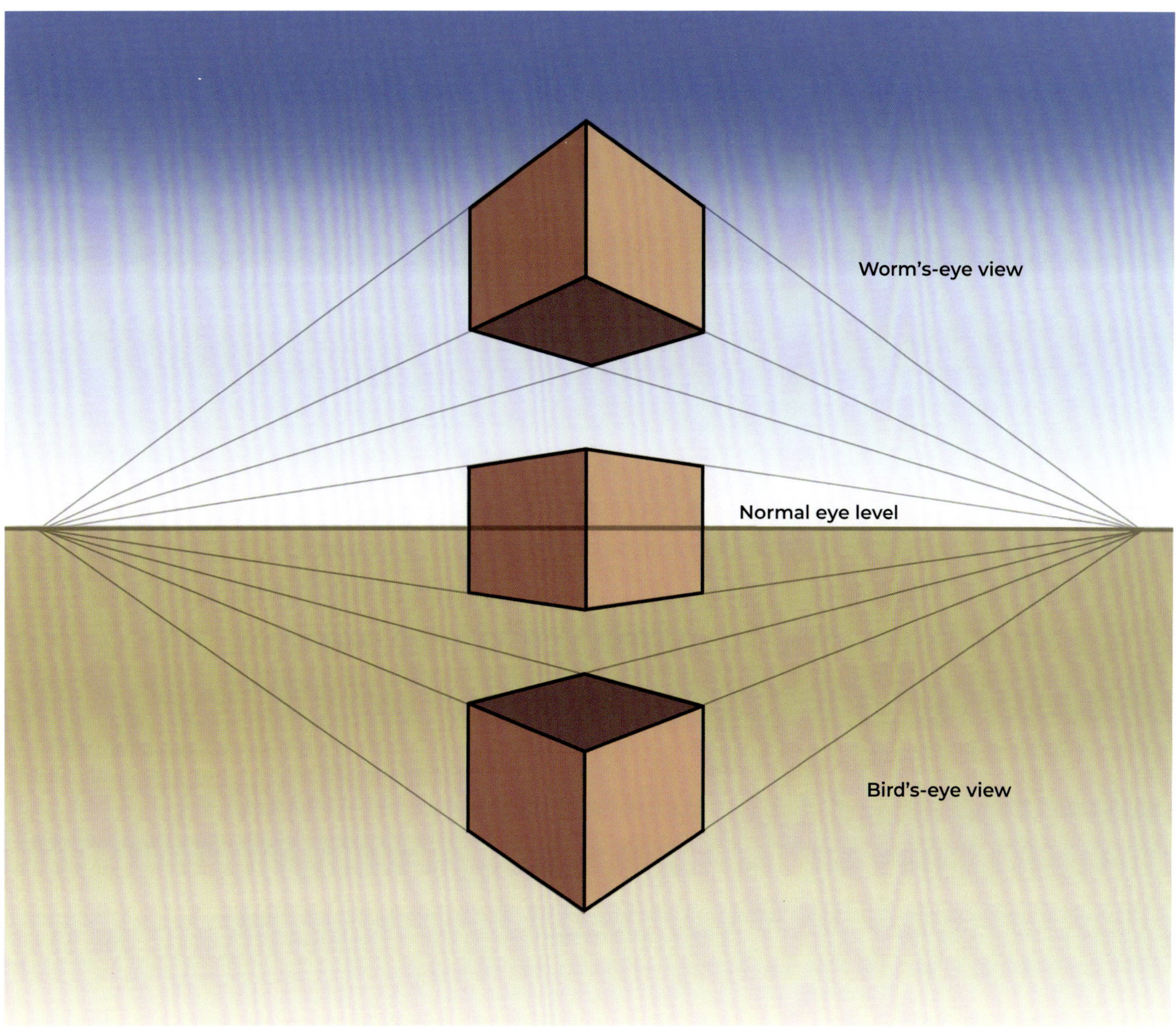

20 An example of the three basic levels, illustrated in two-point perspective.

CHOOSE WISELY

Choosing which type of perspective to use for a painting is an important decision, as it plays a crucial role in how an artwork is perceived and how it communicates its message or story. The type of perspective can influence the composition, depth, and emotional impact of the artwork. It needs to work well with the intended concept of the image. Artists should consider what they want to communicate and choose the perspective that best serves that statement.

FORESHORTENING & DEPTH OF FIELD

While foreshortening and depth of field are sometimes thought of as the easier and less impactful options, because they don't involve mathematics or measuring vanishing points, this is simply not true. Both take practice to achieve and can be used to create impressive artwork.

FORESHORTENING

Foreshortening can be described as the simplest form of depth in art. It creates the illusion of depth and perspective by shortening an object through the use of overlapping forms and lines **(01)**. Objects or figures are depicted at an angle that appears to shorten their length in the picture plane, creating a three-dimensional look. Put simply, foreshortening is how an object appears much shorter when viewed from a sharper angle.

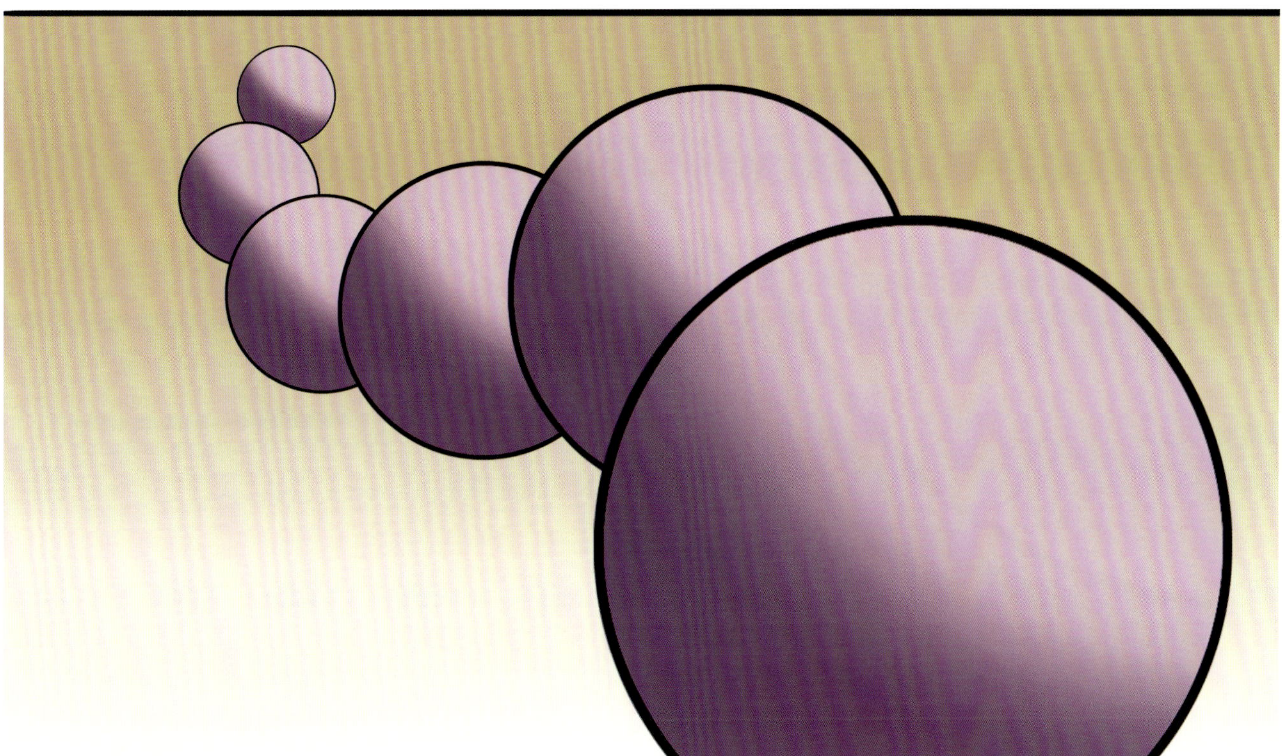

01 This illustration is a good example of how objects layered in space create a sense of depth and perspective.

Raise your arm so it's pointing straight out in front of you. By looking down the length of your arm, starting from your shoulder, you will notice how the various muscles and anatomical parts overlap each other and compress, making your hand appear far away. Most of what you see in everyday life is viewed with this foreshortening, as everything in front of you typically overlaps the other objects beyond. For example, when walking down a street you will notice buildings, signs, and storefront shapes overlapping each other. Similarly in nature, you may observe hills or cliffs overlapping one another as they recede into the distance **(02)**. Each object appears smaller as it is overlapped by a larger object in front, creating the illusion of depth **(03)**.

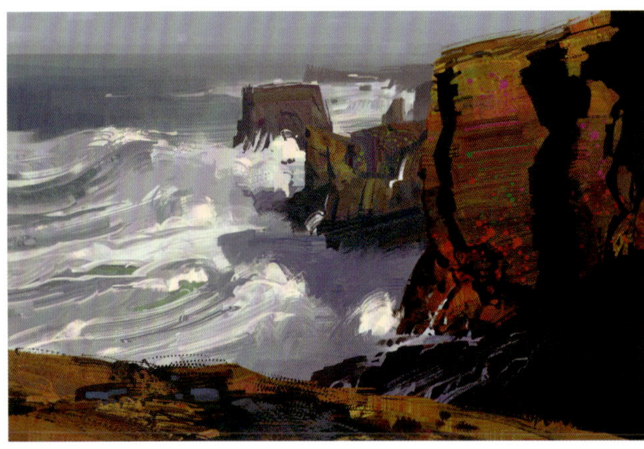

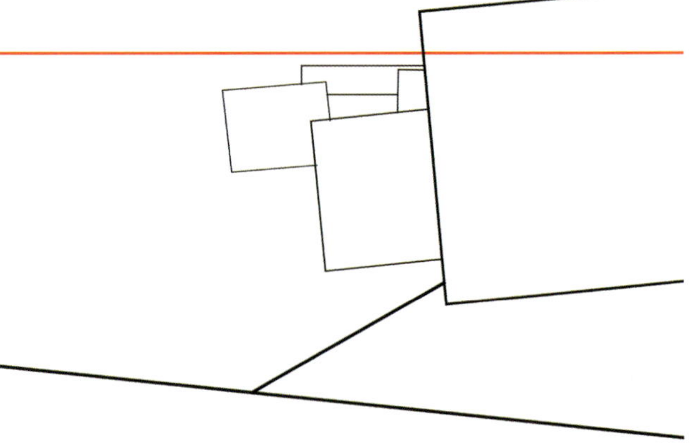

02 This digital painting of sea cliffs in Scotland (above left) shows how simple and effective foreshortening can be, with the layering of larger cliff shapes in the foreground to smaller ones in the distance. This is a very simple and effective way of achieving perspective and depth. If we break down the scene into primitive shapes (above right), the effect is more apparent.

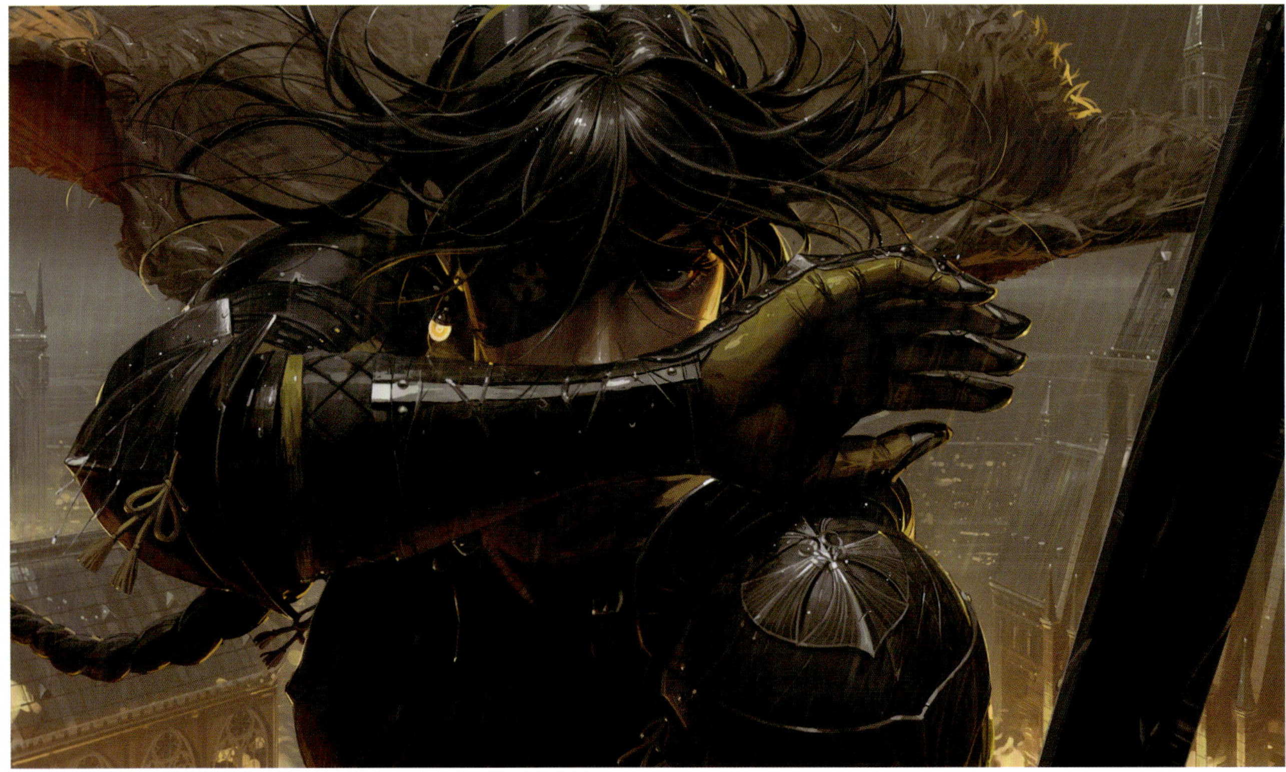

03 This painting by Guweiz is a great example of how to use foreshortening in order to achieve volume in the foreground character. Notice how the overlapping of anatomical forms and the layering of hair strands creates the illusion of depth. Find the tutorial on page 202.

EXAGGERATE PROPORTIONS

With foreshortening, objects or body parts closer to the viewer can appear larger than they would in reality. Don't be afraid to exaggerate proportions to emphasize this effect. Exaggerating proportions in perspective can add depth, drama, and personality to your artwork.

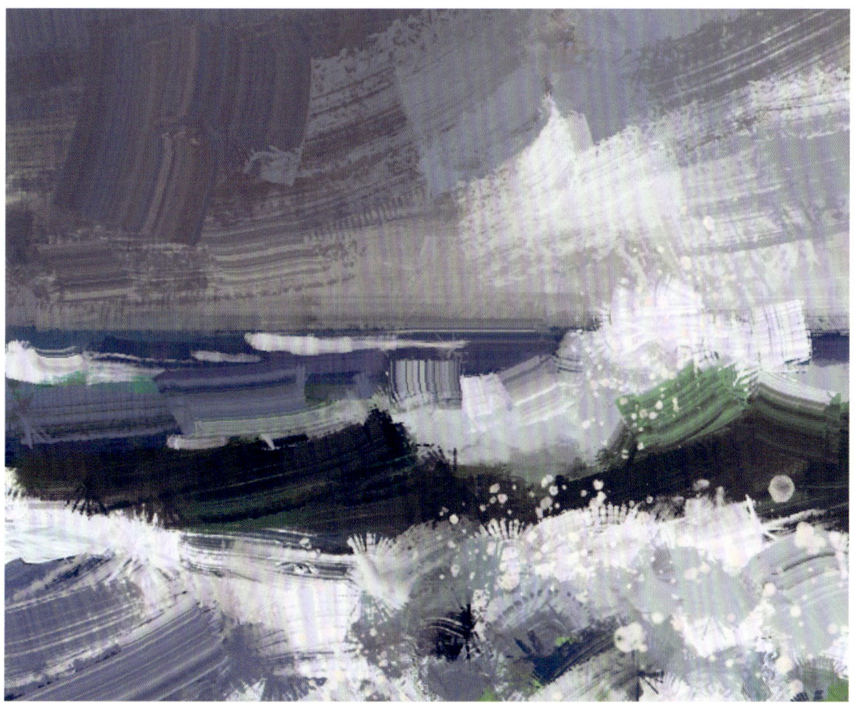

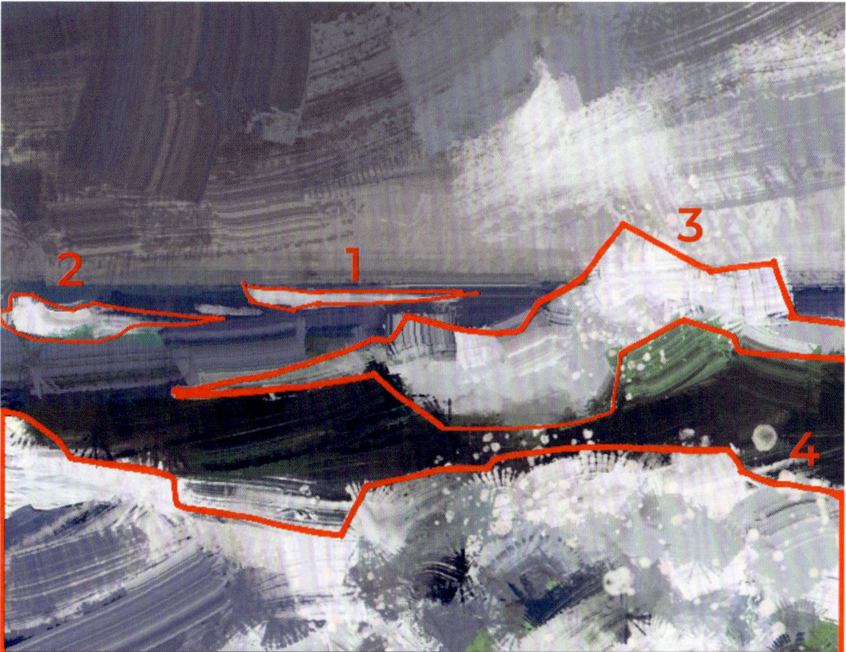

There are, however, exceptions. For example, you might be looking at a smaller building in front of a larger one. While you may think that this situation would defy the rules of foreshortening, it does not. Since the object closest to you is still overlapping the one further away, you will always perceive this as order and hierarchy, which will then create depth and perspective. It is just greatly enhanced when the objects beyond are smaller in comparison. Eventually, all objects of equal size will appear smaller than one another as they overlap and recede into the distance, creating a compressed distortion.

COMPRESSION

Compression provides another form of depth, distorting how distances change in proportion as they recede. When viewing a desert scene at eye level, for example, the shadows from clouds cast onto the foreground plane appear larger compared to the compressed shadow shapes in the distant middle and background planes. One might assume that because each shadow shape is thinner as it recedes, that they are smaller shadows, when in fact they are the same size. This is the illusion of compressed space. A scene showing waves on the ocean can also show compression in action **(04)**.

04 This digital painting illustrates the principles of foreshortening through compression of size and space. Notice how the size and spacing of waves progress from small to large as they move forward from the vanishing point. The largest wave in the front has also been greatly exaggerated to imply forced perspective. This gives the scene a deeper dynamic.

DEPTH OF FIELD

Depth of field is another important factor in how we perceive distance. Objects appear to us as in-focus or sharper in the foreground, and distant and out of focus in the background. The human eye can generally only focus on one detail at a time, therefore we only articulate details through hierarchy. Photographers also rely on these principles through the technology of the camera. A zoom lens and various camera settings will allow the photographer to focus on objects near or far away. This allows the photographer the ability to gain a sense of depth and staging of the subject. The eye has the ability to do the same, but at a more accurate and faster speed.

One way to test this theory out for yourself is to place your finger in front of your face and with both eyes open, focus on your finger. Once your finger is in focus, look past your finger and focus on objects beyond it. Now try focusing on your finger in front and anything beyond it simultaneously. You will find this is impossible because of the rules of hierarchy **(05)**.

As artists we can use this tool to understand depth of field as a way of enhancing our subject matter in a painting. For example, you could paint the subject in the foreground with more articulation and sharpness, while painting the background loosely, to suggest depth and focus. Watercolour or gouache artists can use a wet-on-wet technique to make the edges of objects bleed in the distance, while maintaining harder edges in the foreground. The wet bleed makes the softer effect of objects appear out of focus.

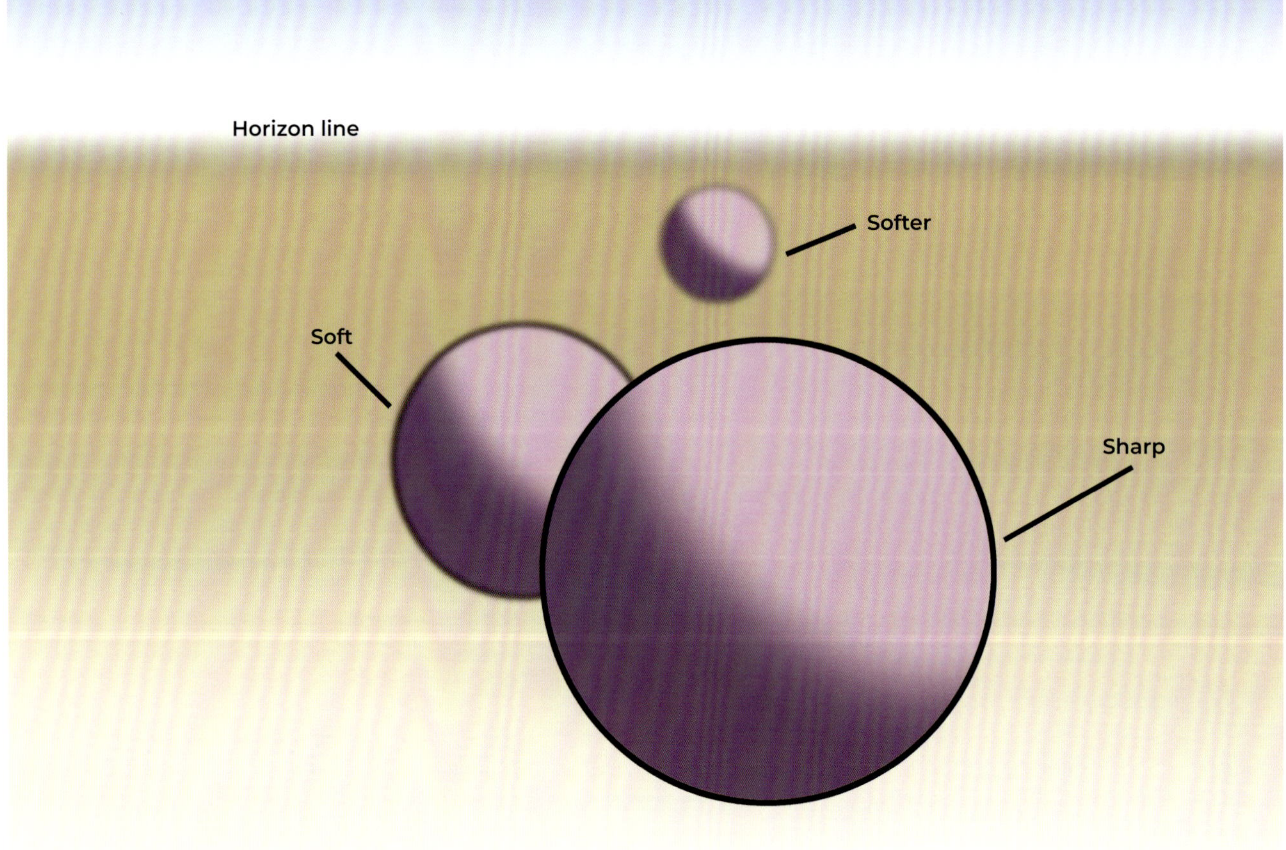

05 This illustration demonstrates how objects in the foreground can appear sharper and more in focus, while objects further away blur out of focus as they recede towards the horizon.

THREE FIELDS

In general, depth of field can be broken up into three fields: foreground, middle ground, and background. The foreground is typically sharp, the middle ground soft, and the background softer still **(06)**. This is not a hard-and-fast rule, however. In cinematography, photography, and any style of art or storytelling, you can place your focus anywhere within these three fields.

One intimate form of storytelling typically used in cinema is to make the foreground and background out of focus, giving hierarchy to the subject in the middle ground. This effect is also known in photography as 'tilt-shift', where the foreground and background perspective are greatly altered **(07, 08, 09)**. This method places the viewer in the foreground scene, peering into the middle ground while keeping the distant details out of focus.

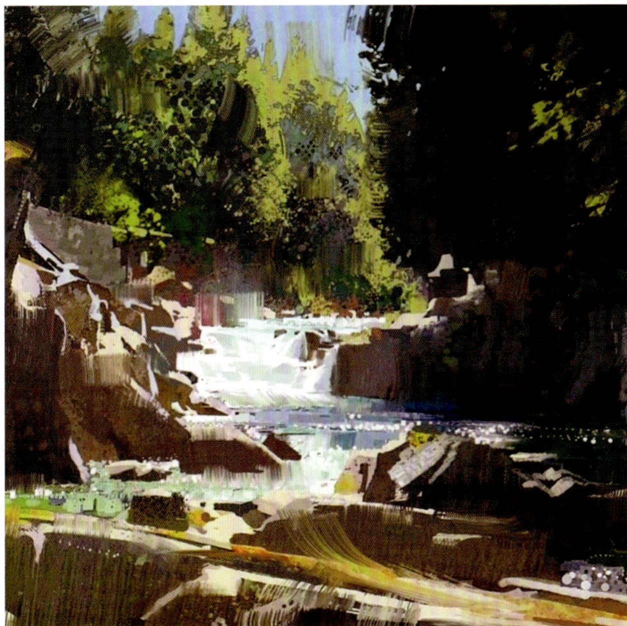

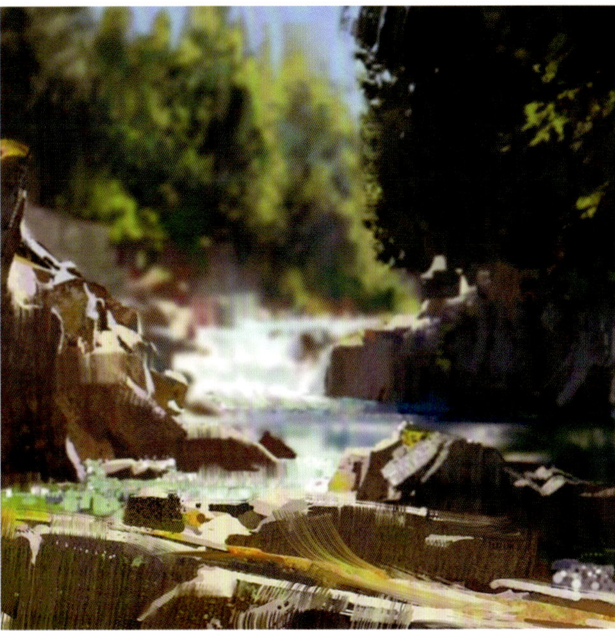

06 This image comparison demonstrates how depth of field can enhance a stronger sense of depth in a scene. The image on the right has been cut into three simple fields, with the foreground being the sharpest in focus, the middle ground a little softer, and the background out of focus.

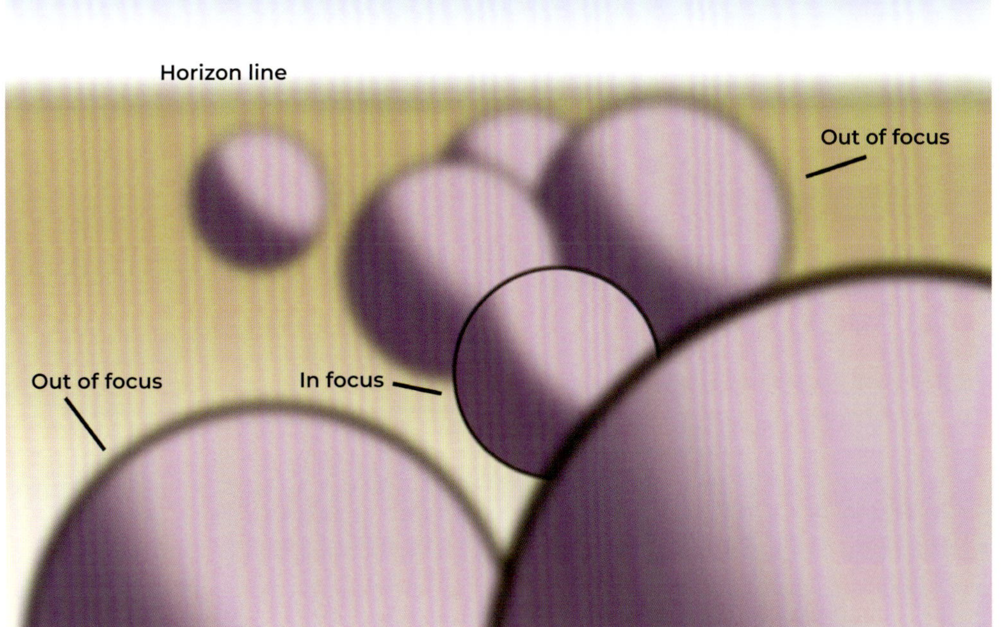

07 Here you can see the tilt–shift effect where the middle ground is in focus while the foreground and background remain way out of focus. This effect gives the subject a more intimate, miniature feel.

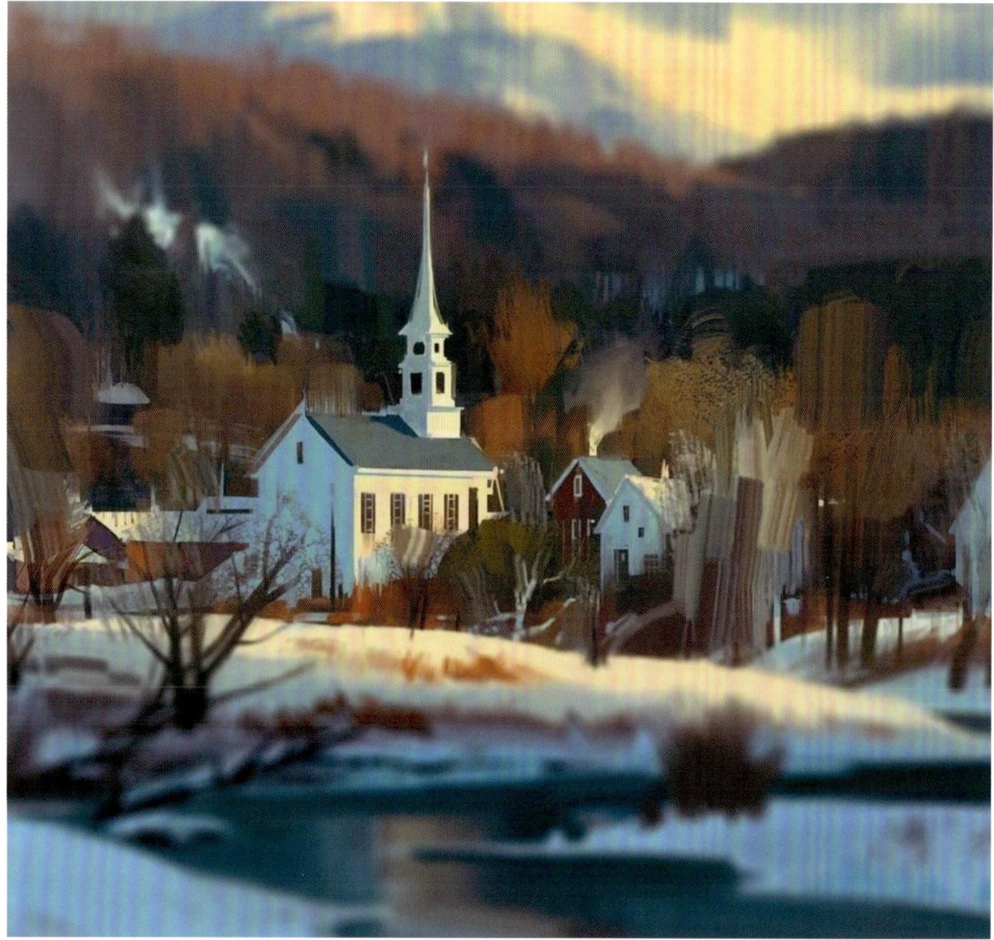

08 This image demonstrates the tilt–shift method. The foreground and background are out of focus, which gives the subject in the middle ground more focus and attention. Tilt–shift can sometimes give the scene a miniature-like quality, depending on how far the blur has been pushed.

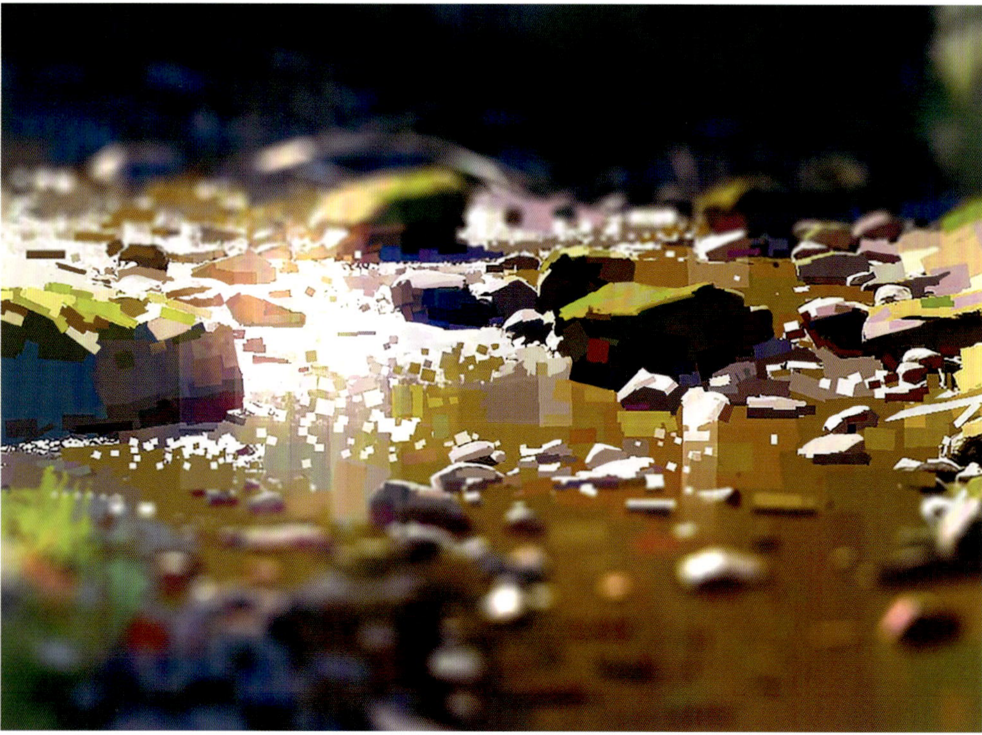

09 Here is another digital painting that illustrates the tilt–shift effect, but with an added bokeh effect. The bokeh adds more of a blown-out colour and light effect to the highlights in the blurred regions of the image.

Image 08, *Stowe in Snow* © Mike Hernandez
Image 09, *Umpqua River* © Mike Hernandez

A great tool in Adobe Photoshop is the Iris filter, found in the Filter menu under the Blur gallery. This filter will focus on any part of the painting you choose, blurring out from the centre of interest to create a shallow depth of field. A similar yet slightly different method can be found in macro photography, where the subject in the foreground is sharp and in focus, set against a very out-of-focus background **(10, 11)**. Both examples can be seen in cinema through a technique called 'rack focus'. This is where the camera moves from focusing on a subject in the foreground to focusing on the background instead, or vice versa.

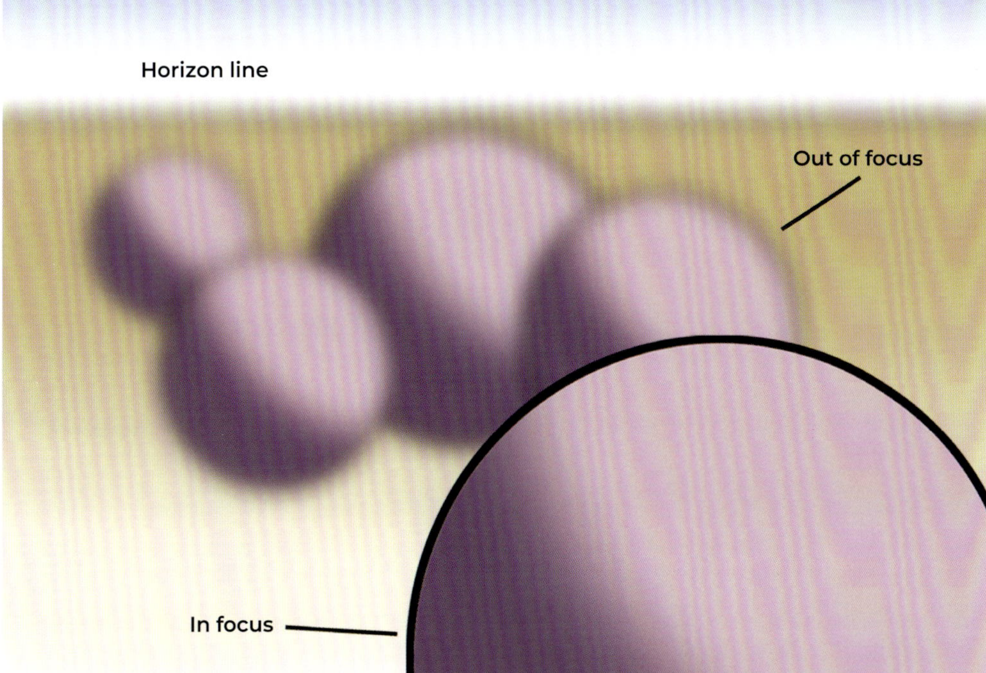

10 This illustration demonstrates what is known as the macro effect, where objects in the extreme foreground have a sharp focus, while the middle ground and background are completely out of focus. This effect can give images a photographic or cinematic look.

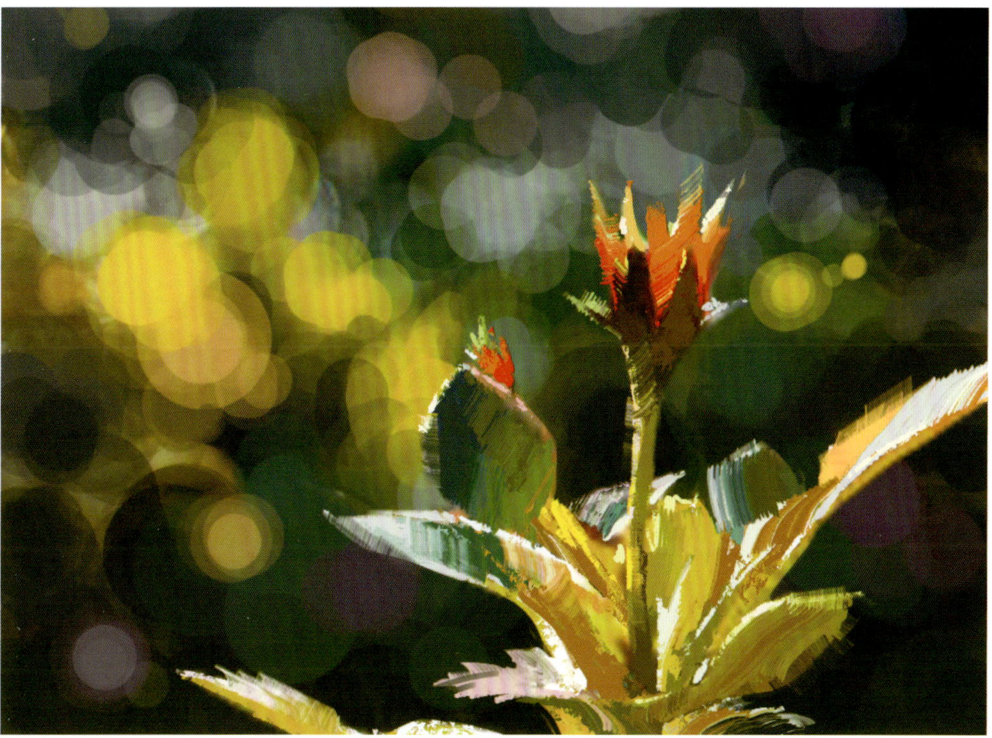

11 This digital painting is a perfect example of the macro effect. The object in the foreground is in crisp focus, while the background is blurred and completely out of focus. This yields a more intimate look to the subject matter. (See page 46 for a further explanation of the bokeh effect.)

As an artist working in the worlds of both production art and fine art, I tend to use these methods unilaterally. For example, it would be difficult to justify the use of a macro effect in an outdoor landscape painting, as it's unlikely that I'd be painting something so close-up. When landscape painting outdoors, I tend to stage my focus on subjects with more articulation and harder edging, while using broken or softer edges to create that sense of push-and-pull depth in a scene **(12)**.

In cinematography for animation, however, I rely heavily on the use of depth extremes by pushing and pulling fields even further apart than is seen in contemporary outdoor painting to get the viewers' attention faster **(13)**. In cinema, you only have split seconds to make the audience look where you want them to, whereas with contemporary outdoor painting, the viewer has more time to appreciate the first, second, and third read. This is where subtlety can play a part in outdoor painting.

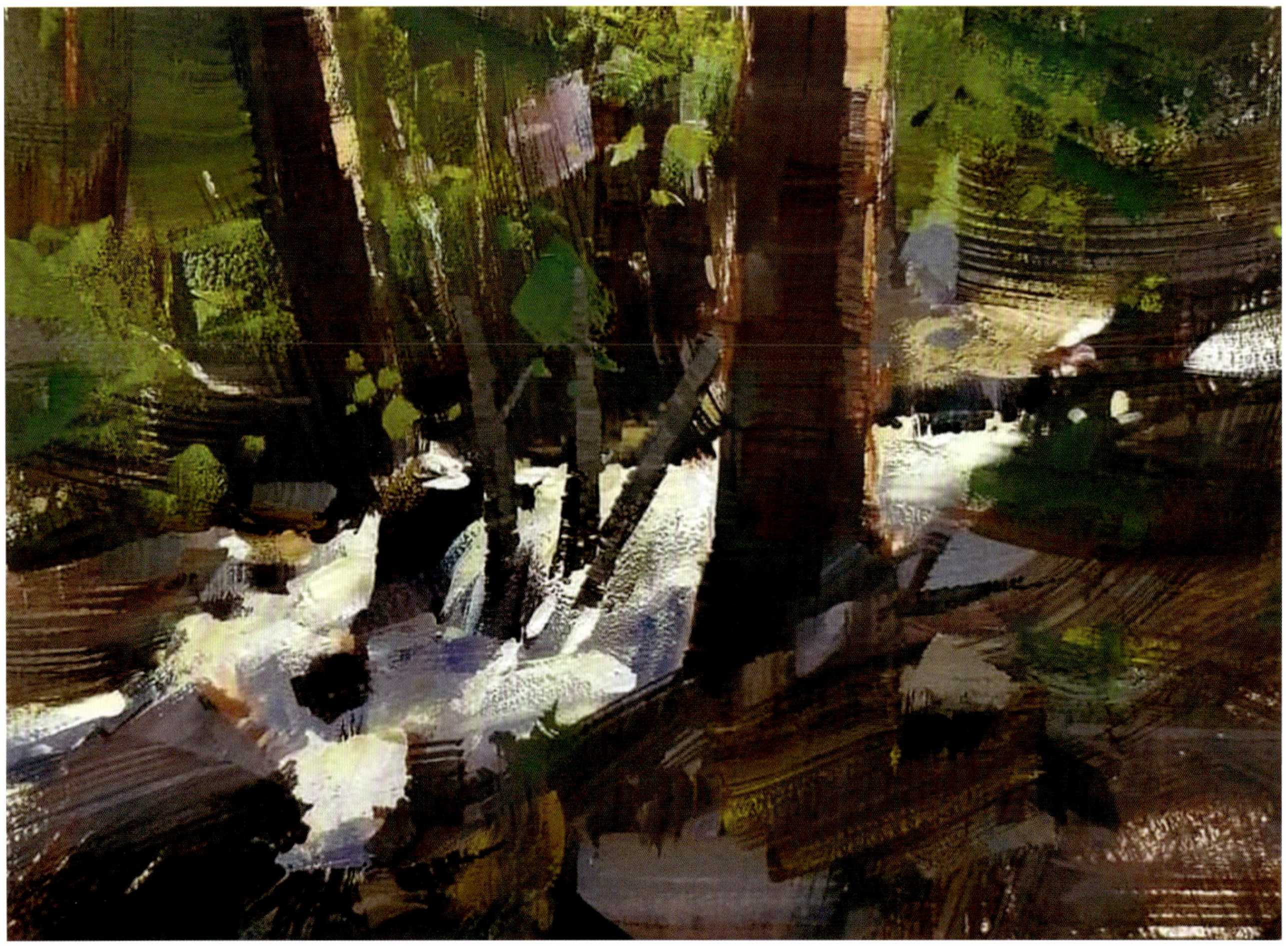

12 This image is a good example of how a traditional painter can use depth of field in plein-air painting. I painted this gouache image outdoors in the High Sierra within a creek setting. The scene was very busy with lots of scattered trees, textures, and lighting, but I wanted to keep the middle-ground creek in focus while maintaining the scope of the forest. I achieved this by loosening up my strokes and losing details in the foreground and background, giving the scene a tilt-shift-like quality.

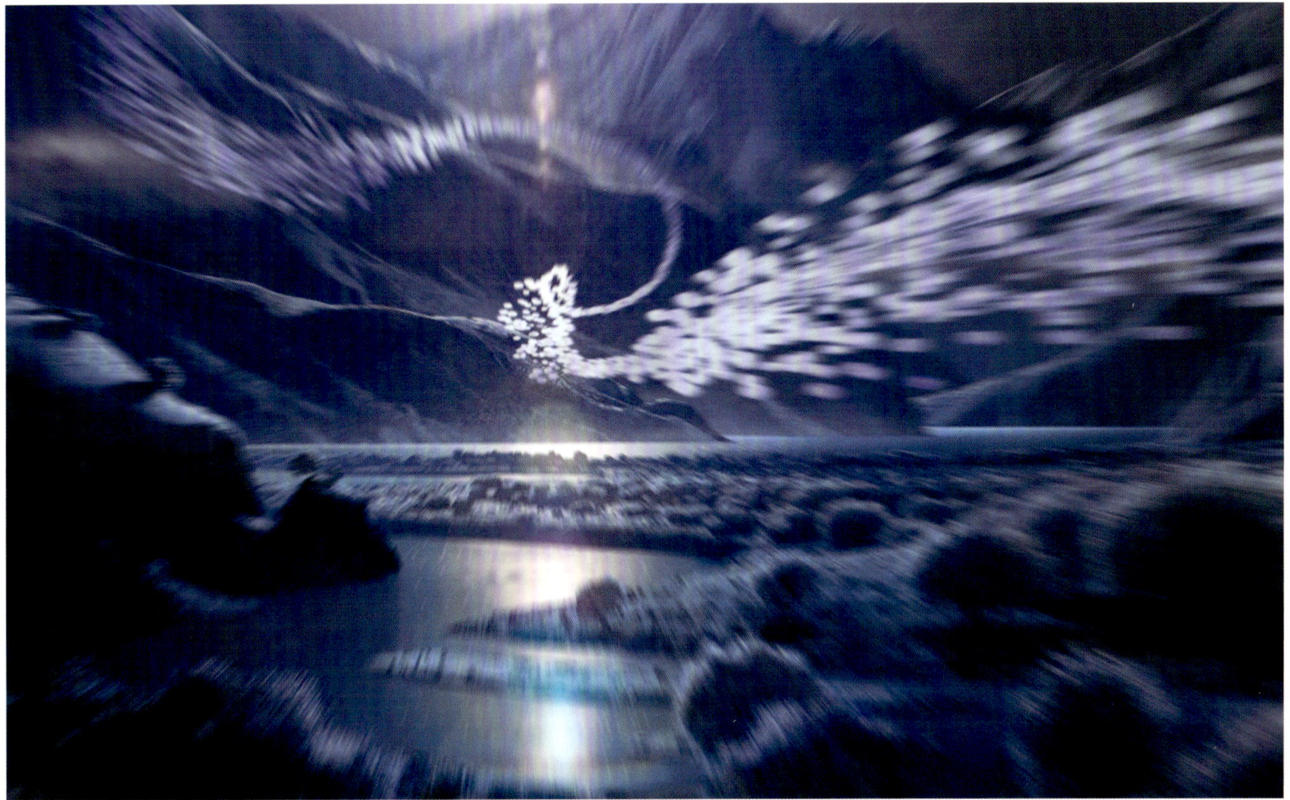

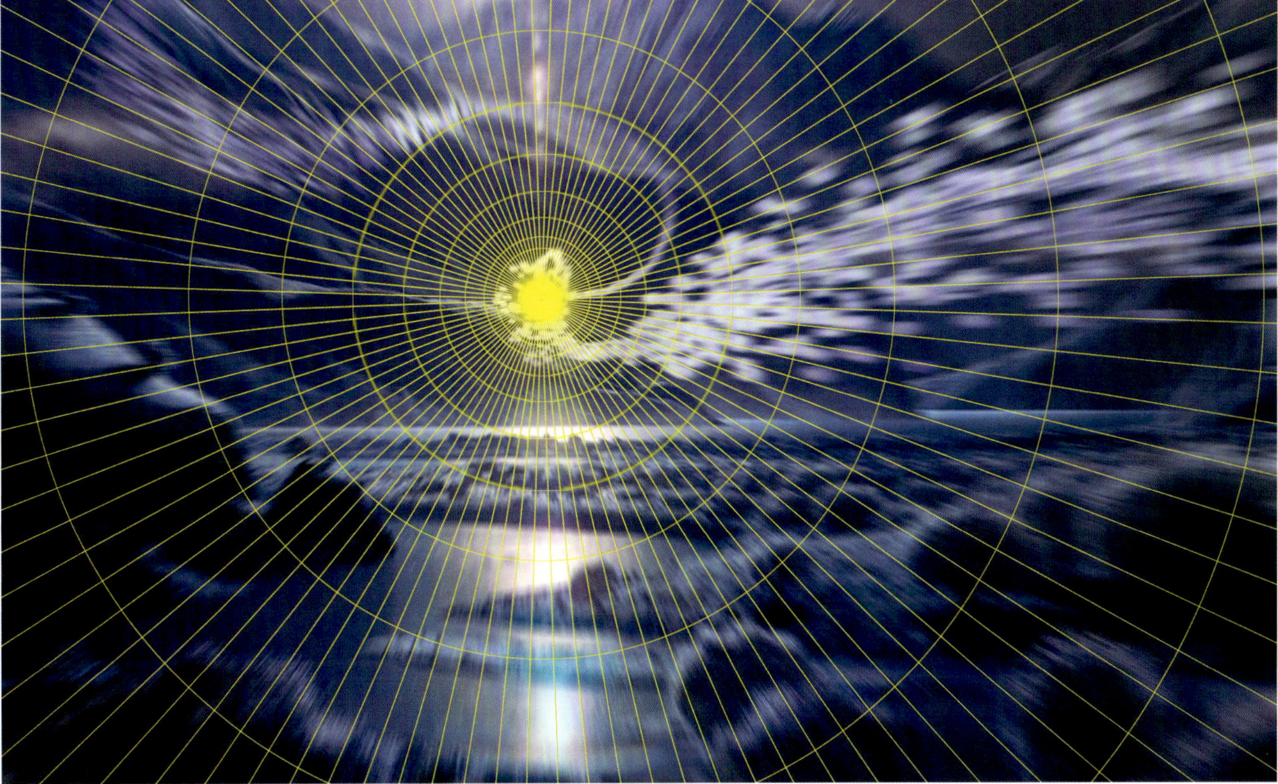

13 This digital painting is an example of how I push volume and dimensional extremes in my industry work by applying a radial zoom to the perspective in order to achieve a more focused effect.

ATMOSPHERIC PERSPECTIVE & DEPTH PERCEPTION

This chapter will discuss the theories and practicalities of atmospheric perspective as it pertains to depth perception through colour, contrast, value, details, simplification, and grouping. As humans, we depend on these attributes in order to perceive depth and distance beyond the perspective of shapes. Atmosphere creates a sense of hierarchies that inform us of the depth in front of us. Ever since the day we were born, we've been calibrating our distances and awareness in space based on these principles.

ATMOSPHERIC PERSPECTIVE & THE ILLUSION OF DEPTH

Atmospheric perspective, also known as aerial perspective, creates the illusion of depth by the definition of objects appearing less clear and less saturated the further they recede from the viewer. The method goes back as far as the Pompeiian-style frescos (01), dating as early as 30 BCE, and Leonardo da Vinci's lessons on painting (02) where he stated: 'Colours become weaker in proportion to their distance from the person who is looking at them.' Polymaths such as Leon Battista Alberti also wrote explanations of the effects of atmospheric perspective. One of the strongest contributors to atmospheric perspective is the many particles in the air. These particles can range anywhere from the microscopic to the granular, including elements such as moisture, fog, dust, smog, and chemicals.

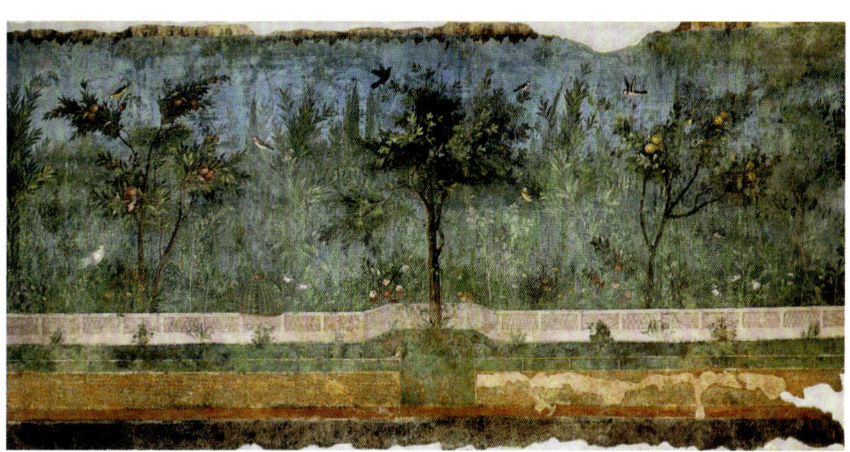

01 *Villa de Livia, jardin (v. 30 av JC).* Fresque, Museo Nazionale Romano, Rome. This fresco from Pompeiian art demonstrates an early understanding of atmospheric perspective through contrast and colour.

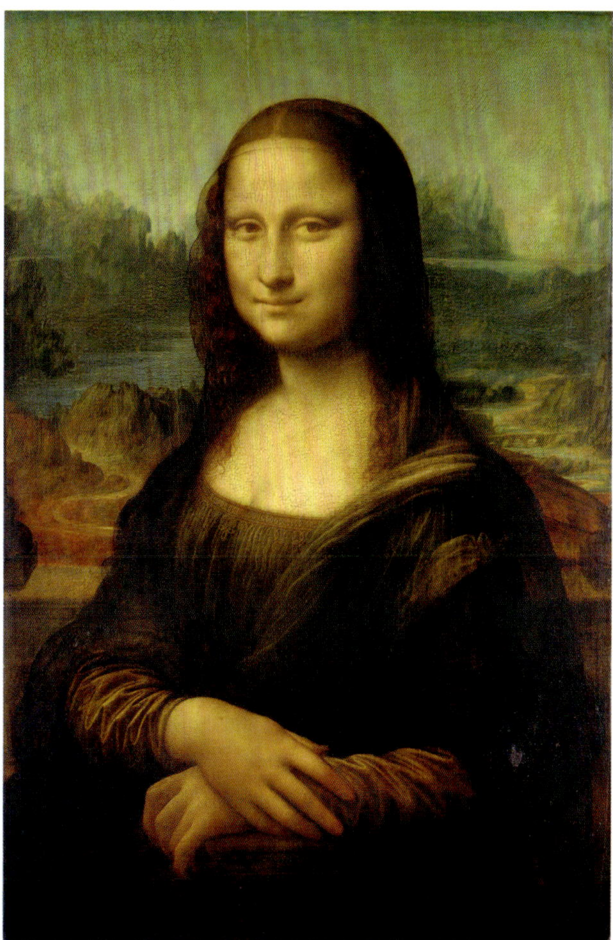

02 *Mona Lisa* (circa 1503–1519) by Leonardo da Vinci. This is a perfect example of how Leonardo used atmospheric perspective to convey a sense of depth and vastness in this scene. Notice the warmer colours in the foreground compared to the cooler grey colours in the background.

As light rays pass through these particles, they have a scattered effect that tends to create a more opaque quality in the atmosphere. The degree of scattering will depend on the amount of particles in the air. Think of a foggy day where you're driving down a road and can only see objects within thirty feet in front of you. This effect becomes exaggerated when you increase the brightness of light by turning on your full-beam headlights; as a result, the light becomes more scattered and opaque. Artists, photographers, and filmmakers can enhance this effect by using an optical effect called bokeh. Bokeh is an aesthetically pleasing blurry effect found in out-of-focus areas in a photograph **(03)**.

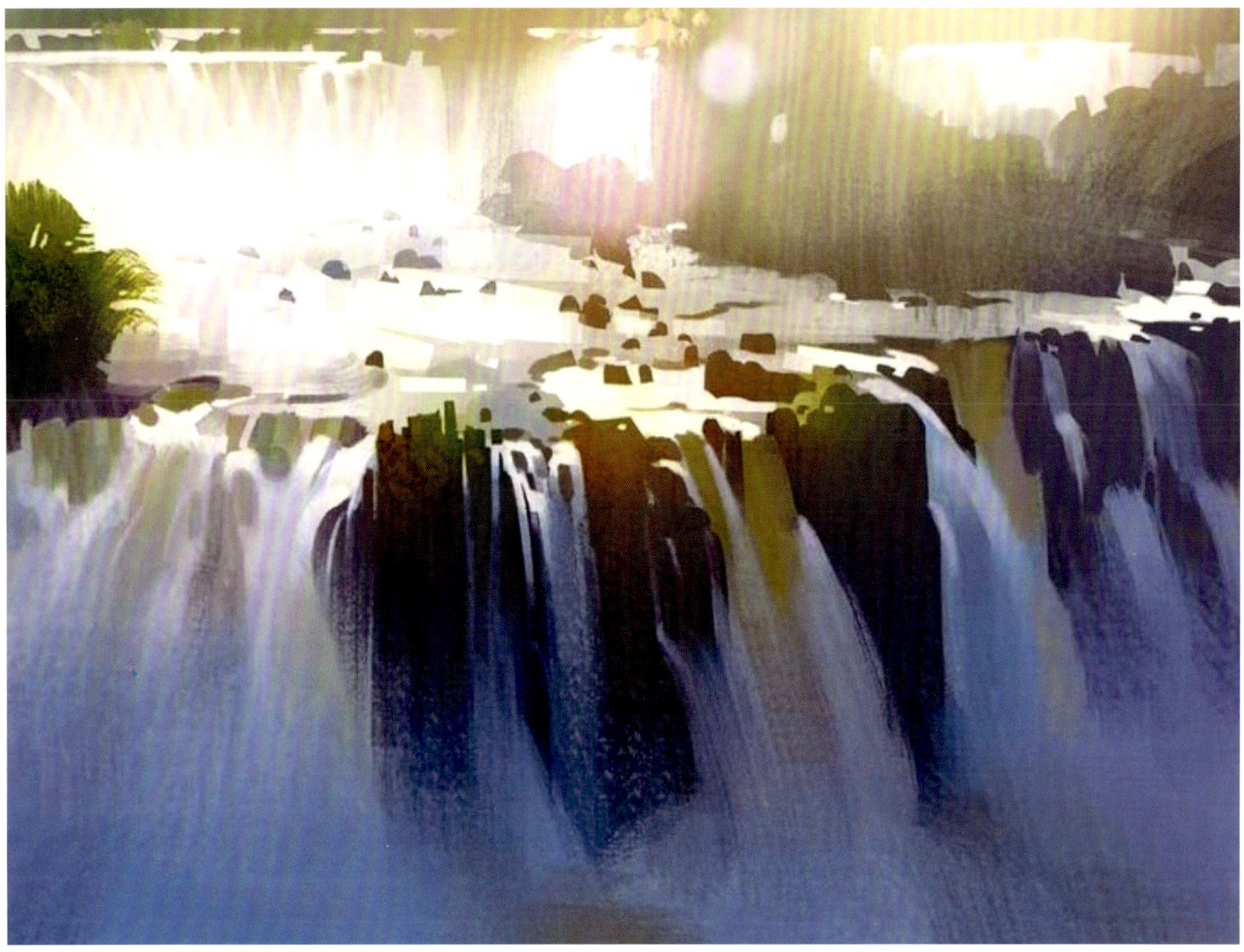

03 This painting captures how moisture particles exaggerate the effect of light scatter in atmosphere, creating a light bokeh effect.

Image 03, *Misty Falls* © Mike Hernandez

THE SCIENCE OF WAVELENGTHS

Another aspect of atmospheric depth is the science of wavelengths. The sky is made up of many coloured wavelengths. Among those colours are blue and red light photons **(04)**. Blue light has much shorter waves, with wavelengths between around 450 and 495 nanometres. Red light has longer wavelengths of around 620 to 750 nanometres. Between these two wavelengths, blue light has a higher frequency, and therefore it carries more energy than red light. When light passes through these wavelengths, different effects are created based on the corresponding colour of light. As blue light has the higher frequency, it will also have the greater degree of light scatter. This is why the furthest and darkest objects tend to have a bluish cast on them, whereas longer red wavelengths of light scatter the least and show up on lighter distant objects. The reason for this is the blue cast is lost in the light values in the distance, revealing the weaker red left behind in the highlights **(05)**.

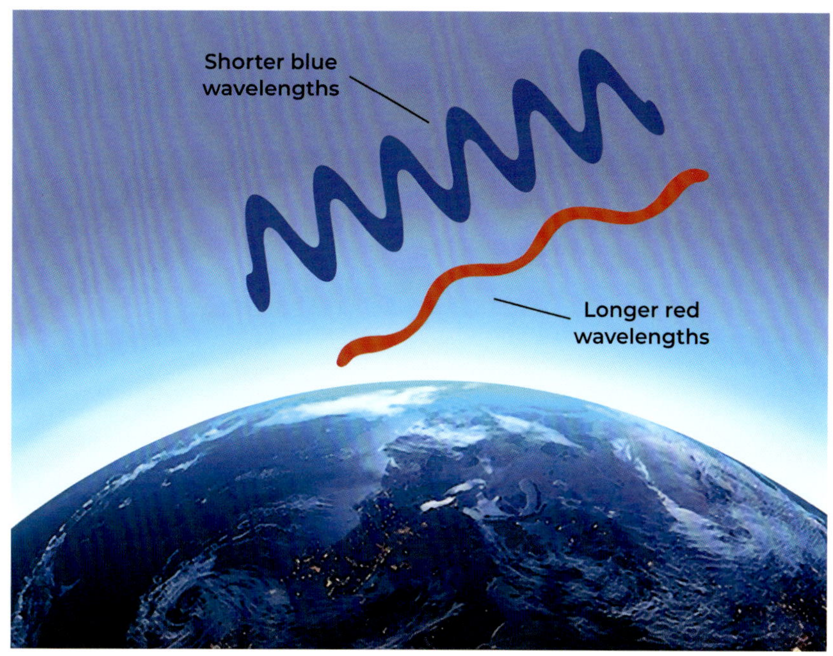

04 This image illustrates the wavelengths of both blue and red photons. Shorter wavelengths, like blue, are diffused by the atmosphere more than longer red wavelengths, causing the sky to have a blue cast. The longer red wavelengths travel further through the atmosphere without much scattering.

The sun, as we know it, burns reddish-yellow, but it emits all spectrums of colour through a process called RGB light (red, green, and blue), which is additive light. When you add all three of these colours together in light, it creates white, and therefore sunlight is white. The reason we perceive it as warm light is due to the weaker and shorter wavelengths of yellow, orange, and red trying to pass through the blue scatter in the sky. The longer wavelengths of yellow and orange that pass through our atmosphere without much scattering or absorption are what are left over. When the sun is at its brightest and directly above us, the light scatters through the shorter blue photons, creating a blue hue to the sky. When the sun's brightness is at its weakest and the angle of light passing through the atmosphere is longest at sunset, you can see the additive effects of the weaker wavelengths of yellow, orange, and red scattered throughout the atmosphere.

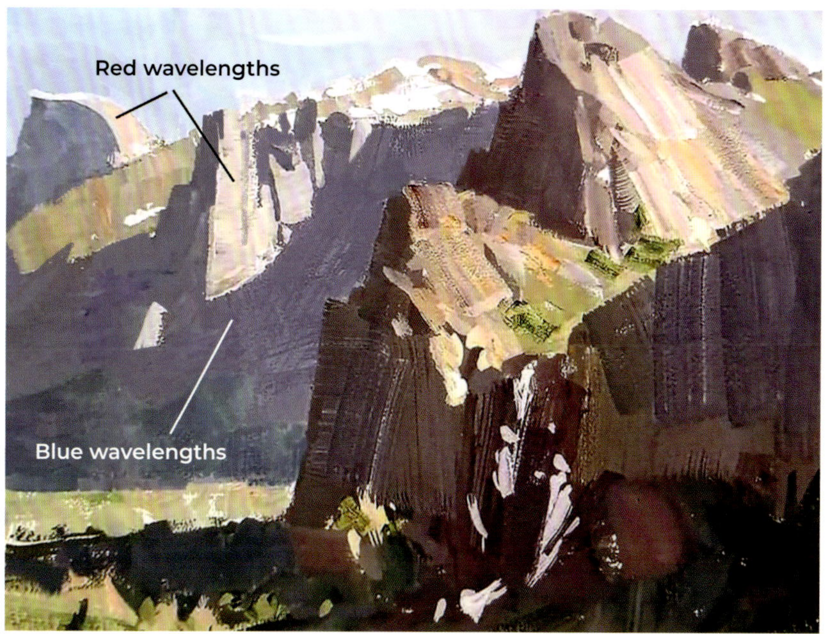

05 This painting of Yosemite National Park is a good example of how blue and red wavelengths affect landscape. Notice the warmer light as it appears on the distant rock in higher value, as opposed to the cooler light in lower value shadow.

COLOUR, CONTRAST, & VALUE

Through colour perspective, warmer colours appear closer to the viewer's eyes due to the absence of atmospheric particles scattered by blue light. Among the weakest of these warm colours is yellow, since its colour saturation point is around eighty to ninety per cent value range, so it tends to fall off first in the foreground **(06)**. This is why colours like greens and oranges hold their fullest saturation in the foreground, then recede into greyer and weaker versions in the distant blue scatter **(07)**.

Most foreground colours will eventually recede into a blue, grey, or violet shade in the distant landscape, producing a beautiful hierarchy of depth through colour **(08)**. Colours of higher importance have more saturation and typically grab your attention most. This is how we use nature's hierarchies of colour to discern the objects that are closest to us and of more immediate importance. Even cooler objects will have more colour and attention in the foreground than in the background. All colours, warm or cool, will eventually lose their saturation as they recede into the distant landscape **(09)**.

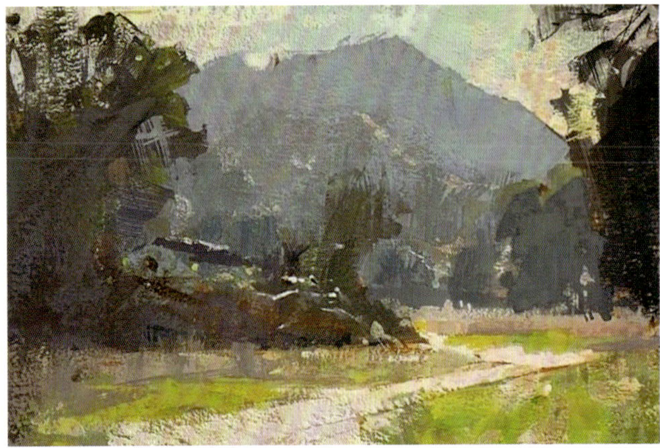

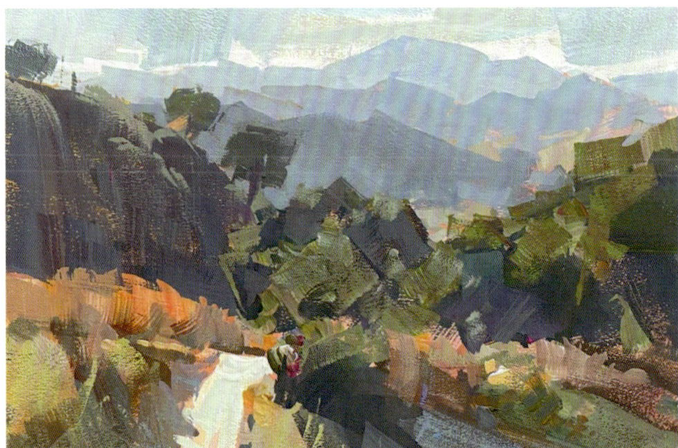

06 These two gouache paintings convey how particles create a sense of haze and fall-off from foreground to background. Notice the lack of contrast and colour in the distant mountains.

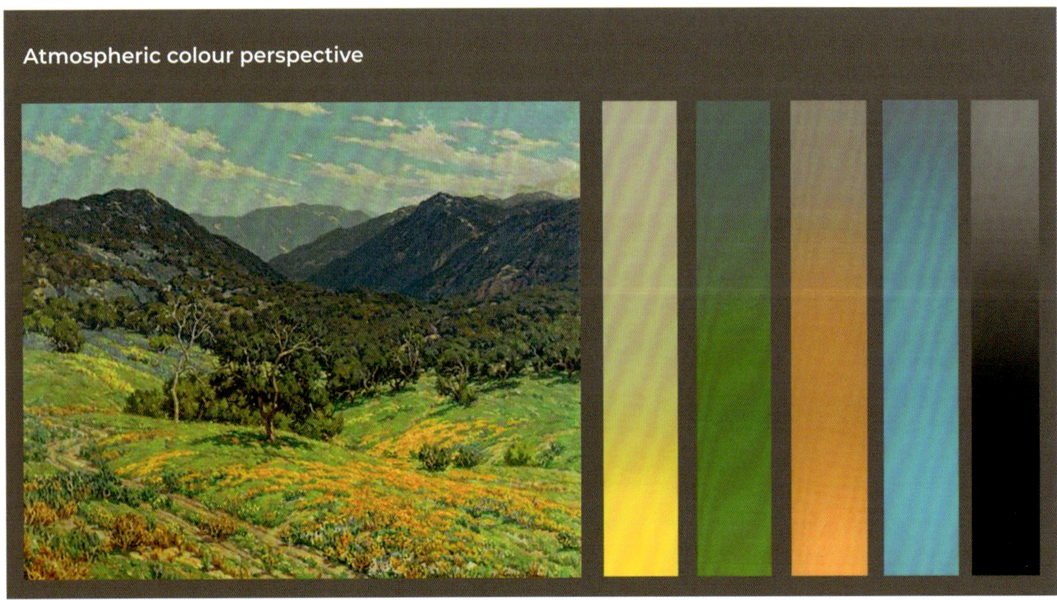

07 *Spring in Southern California* (1931) by Granville Redmond demonstrates the levels of loss as certain colours recede into the distant atmosphere. Notice how yellow and green recede faster, while blues hold their colour further out.

Image 06a, *The Healing Trail* © Mike Hernandez
Image 06b, *Just One More Mike* © Mike Hernandez

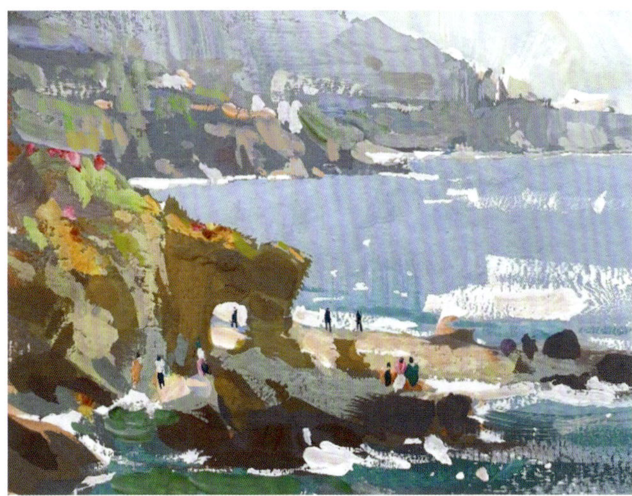

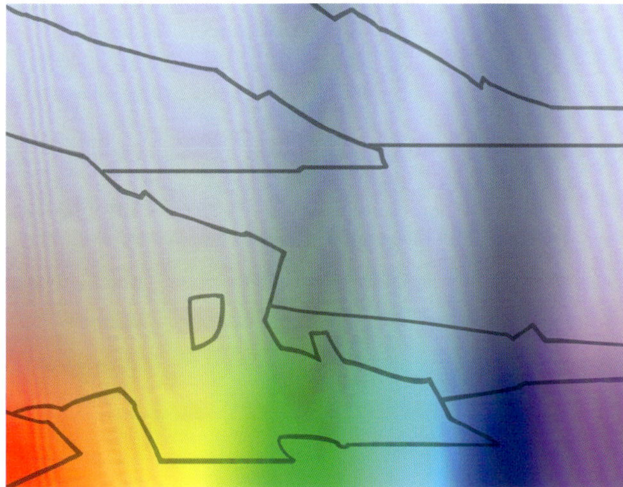

08 This painting of Keyhole Arch, Laguna Beach, illustrates how all colour loses its saturation and contrast as it recedes into the distance. Notice how all of the colours eventually turn towards a violet-grey-blue hue.

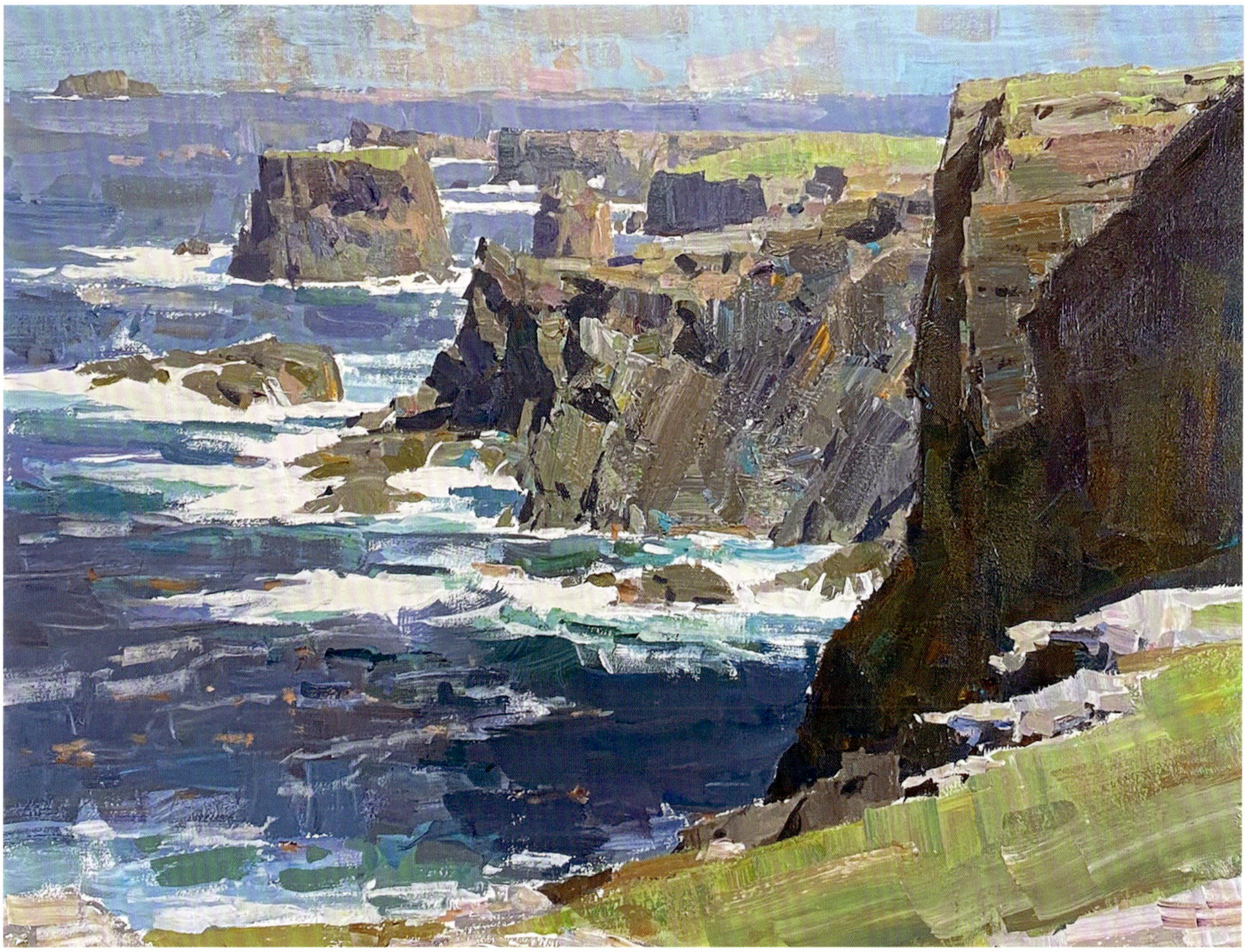

09 This painting of the Eshaness Cliffs in Scotland shows how warm colours in the foreground recede to cooler colours in the background. Notice the warmer shadow colour in the foreground rock. This represents the local colour of the rock without the blue wavelength photons and atmospheric particles. The small hints of pink in the distant horizon represent hints of red photons on clouds.

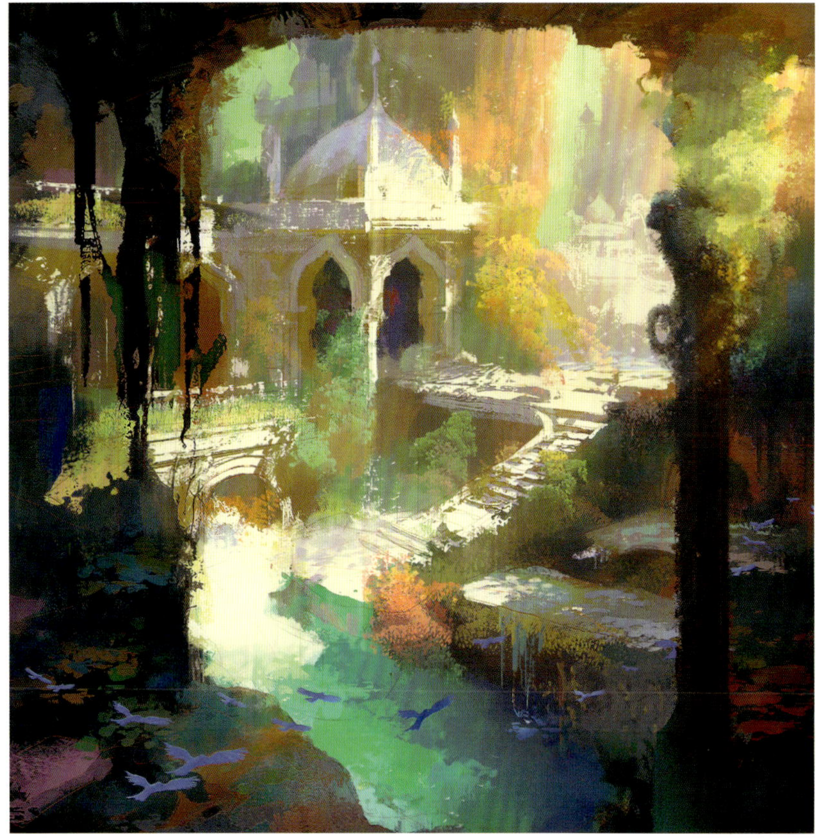

10 This digital painting by Nathan Fowkes is a great example of how to use atmospheric perspective in a scene. Notice the use of higher contrast value and colour in the foreground versus the higher key of colour and contrast in the background. This establishes depth and perspective through the use of hierarchy.

Contrast and value also play a part in establishing hierarchies in perspective and depth. Because of scattered particles and wavelengths of light and colour, lighting from the sun affects the atmosphere through contrast. There are fewer particles of light scattered between our eyes and objects that appear closer to us. Therefore these foreground objects have fewer of the strong blue wavelengths that would normally show up in darker values such as shadows, making the object appear closer due to having more contrast between light and dark. As objects recede into the distance, there are more particles scattered between the viewer's eyes and the object, making the shadows appear lighter and bluer **(10, 11)**. This will also make objects appear further away from the viewer's eyes.

In art, we can reinforce the concept of depth through distant contrast by forcing shadows and highlights much closer to one another than they would actually appear. One artist who was known for doing this was Albert Bierstadt. In some of his sunset paintings where he pushed atmosphere and distant scale, he would use a method known as 'simultaneous colour contrast' where the values of the shadows were the same as the highlights. What set them apart as sunlight and shadow was the use of warm and cool temperature.

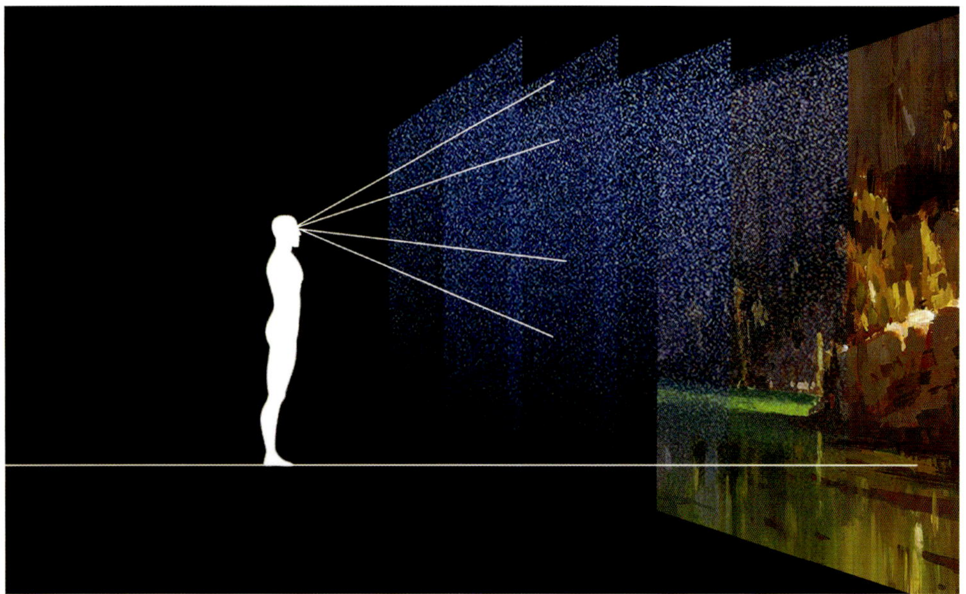

11 This image illustrates how we perceive atmosphere and haze through a layered process of particles. The more particles between the viewer and the subject in the scene, the more atmosphere there is.

Image 10, *Jungle Ruins* © Nathan Fowkes

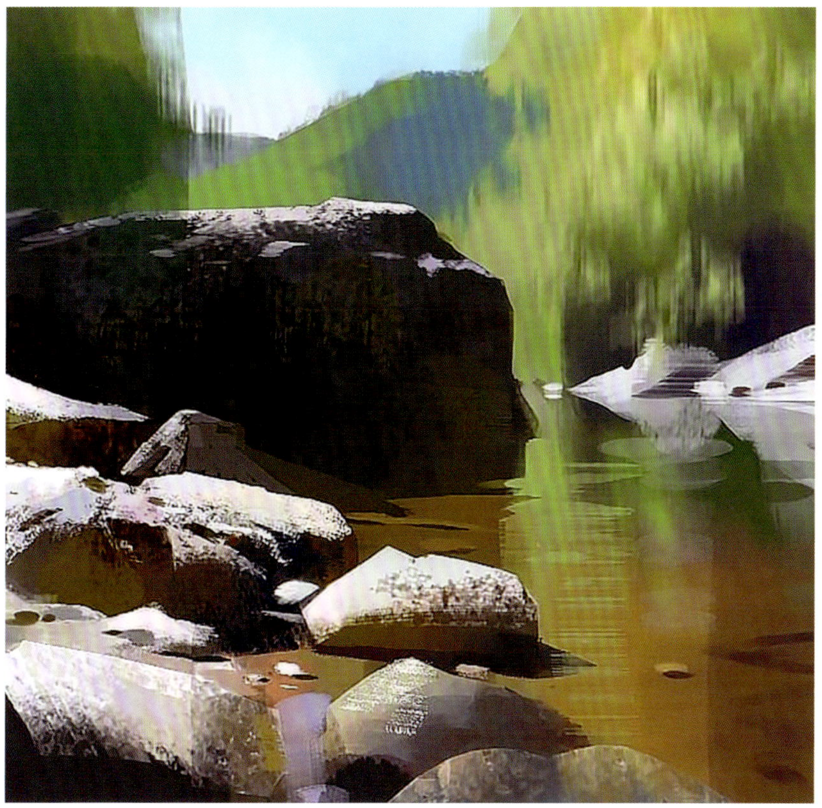

12 This digital illustration shows how depth can be achieved by loosening details and textures as the landscape recedes towards the horizon.

Details will also be lost in the distant atmosphere due to the scattering of particles. You will typically see more clarity in foreground objects; they will tend to separate and become more complex in the foreground, while bodies of objects will appear to group together and simplify in the distance **(12)**. This phenomenon is also due to the limitations of our mind when handling too many details at once. The human brain is designed to function on levels of hierarchy and importance, not multiple tasks of the same importance all at the same time. Our minds are constantly reading the world and the landscape in front of us, but we can't take it all in at once. It would be like having lots of books open and trying to read them all simultaneously. You need to focus your attention on one book at a time in order to read the words and appreciate it fully. Thankfully nature has found a way to help us by establishing these hierarchies through atmospheric perspective **(13)**.

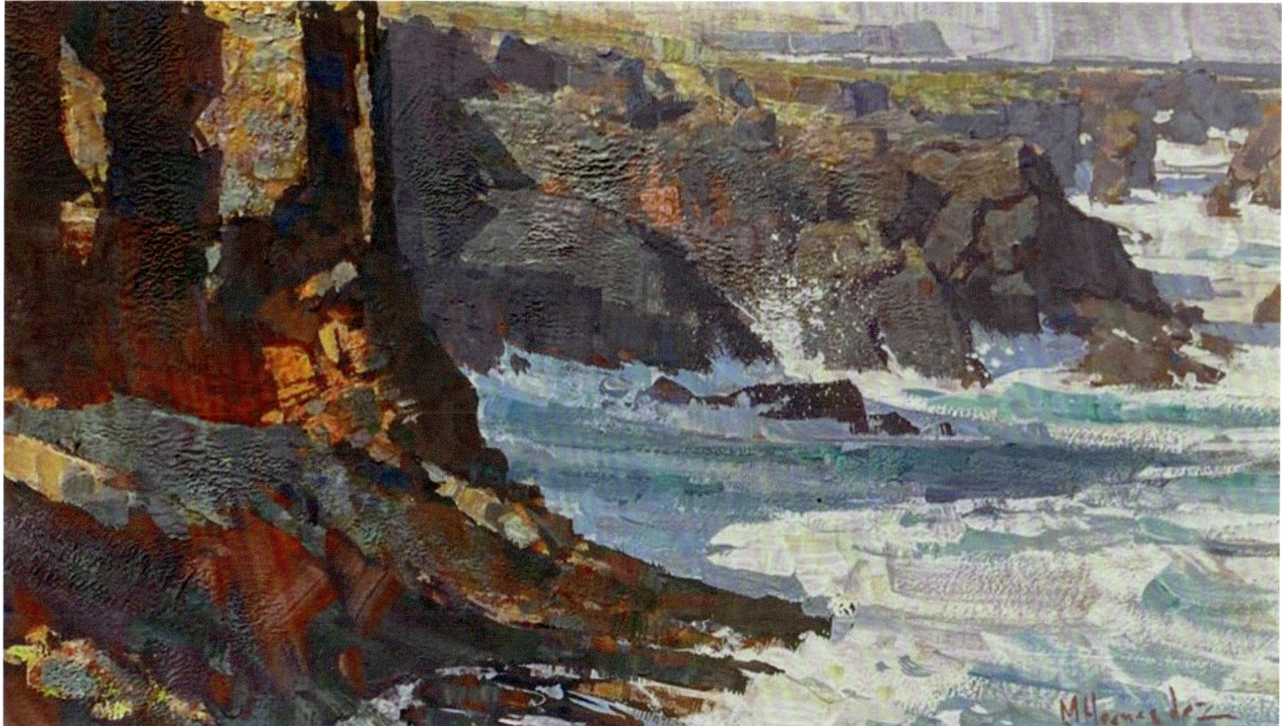

13 This gouache painting is a good example of how to use simultaneous value and colour contrast to achieve depth in a landscape. Notice how the distant highlights and shadows get closer together in value, while the temperatures of warm and cool set them apart.

Image 12, *Sawtooth Creek* © Mike Hernandez
Image 13, *Eshaness Gray* © Mike Hernandez

This phenomenon can also be observed in the sky **(17)**. When looking at the distant horizon, the light gathers to create an opaque quality of light. When you look straight up at the sky, with the sun at an angle, you will see a darker, bluer sky, suggesting less gathering of light or photon particles. In other words, we almost glimpse the darkness of outer space, but the blue scattering of photons from the sunlight prevents that, instead presenting as a dark blue. This gradient effect creates a strong sense of depth towards the lighter horizon.

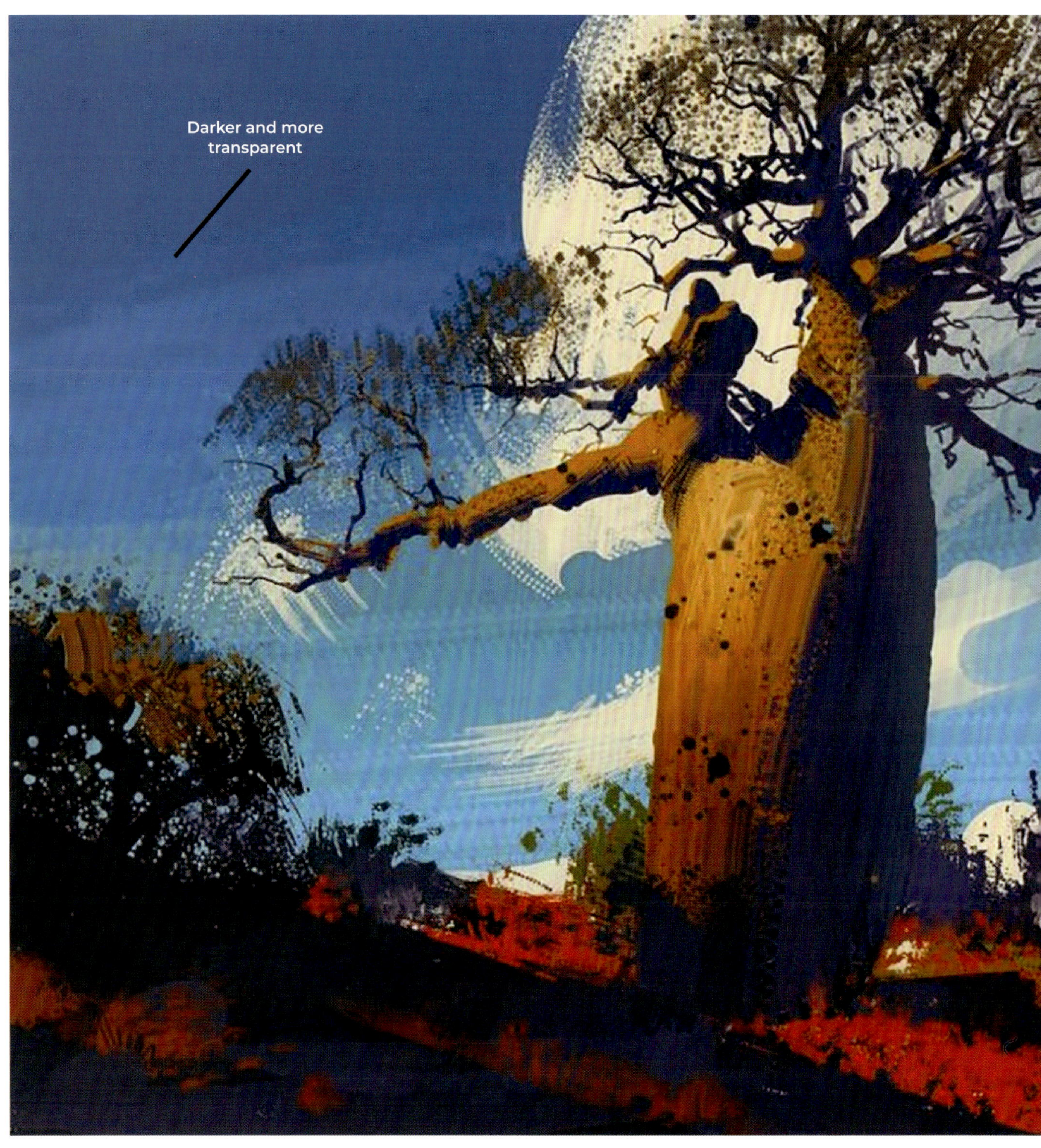

Image 17, *Baobab* © Mike Hernandez

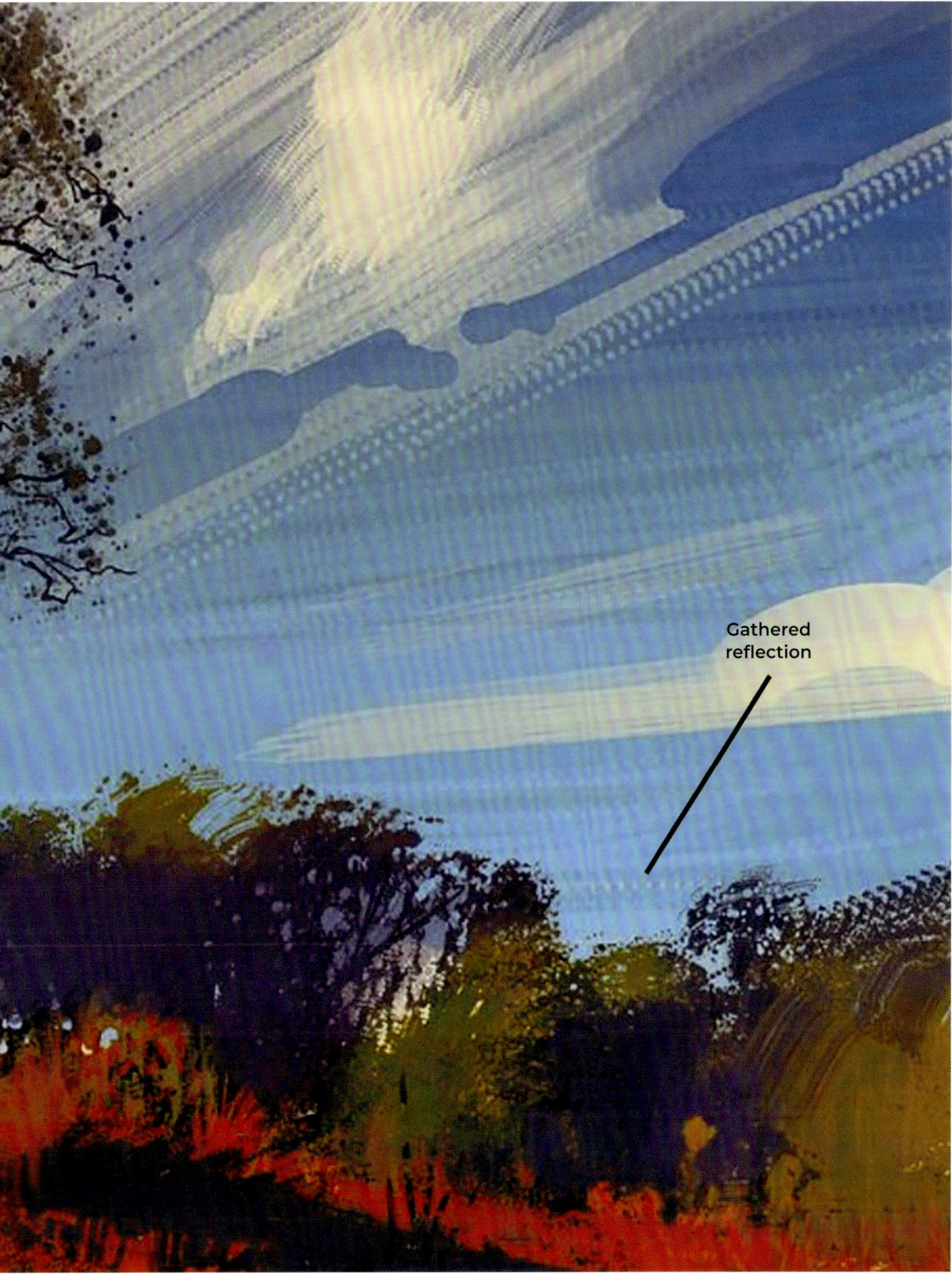

17 This digital image painted in three-point worm's-eye view is a good example of the Fresnel effect as it relates to the sky. Notice the lighter opaque colour on the horizon and its gradation towards the upper dark-blue sky dome.

SHADOWS

As an artist or photographer, when striving for volume, form, and depth, we rely on the use of shadows to create a believable object in space. Lighting has multiple effects on how we perceive shadows, depending on the type. This chapter will look at the only two types of lighting that need to be discussed in relation to perspective and depth: natural and artificial lighting.

FORM & CAST SHADOWS

Natural lighting is the sun or sunlight (01). Artificial lighting is any light form created by humans, or any light that is not produced by the sun (02). Artificial light sources include candles, torches, lamps, home decor lighting, street lamps, car headlights, phones, and TV screens. There are two types of shadows created by these two kinds of lighting: form shadows and cast shadows.

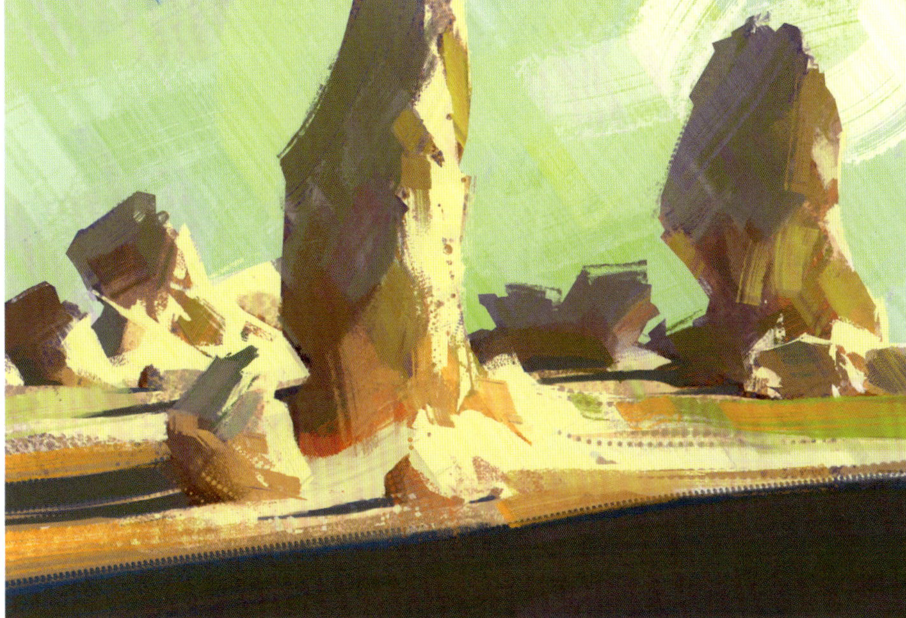

01 This digital painting of rocks is a good example of natural lighting from the sun. Notice the parallel effect of the shadow shapes cast across the ground plane.

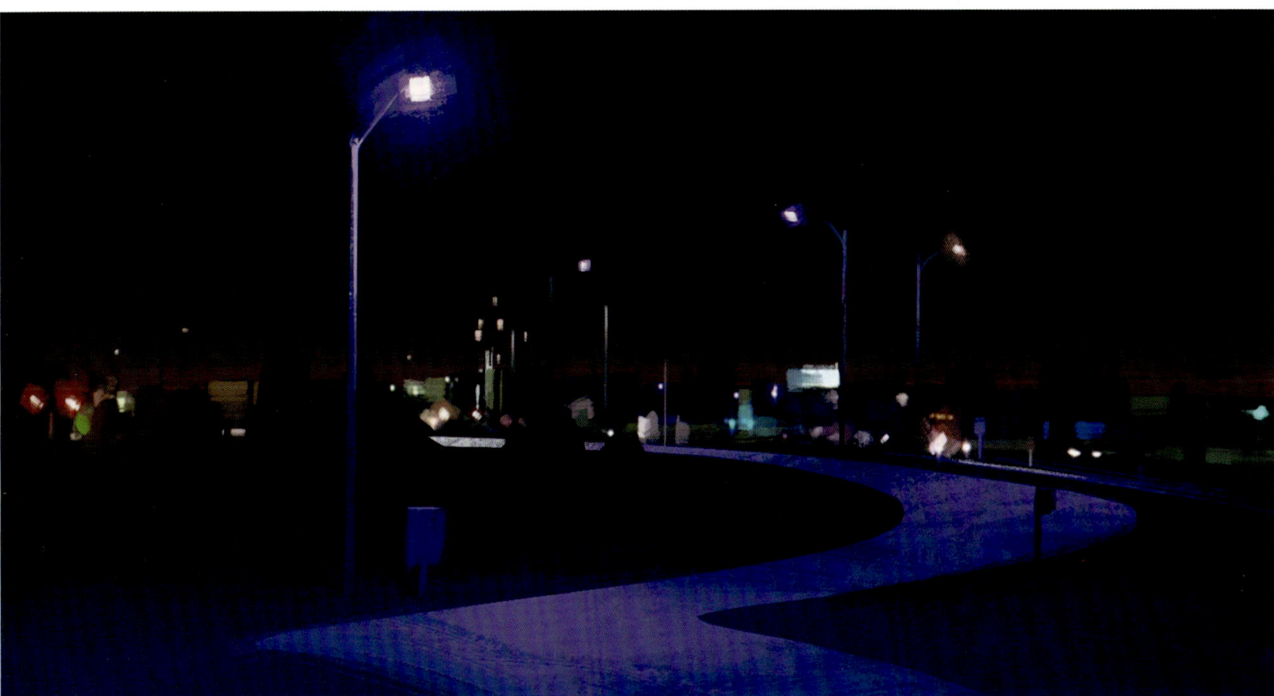

02 This digital illustration of a city street scene depicts artificial lighting used in a night-time setting. The only hint of natural light can be seen on the distant horizon due to the scattering of red wavelengths from the setting sun.

Form shadows fall within an object, on its surface, while cast shadows fall outside of an object. On a form shadow, there is a core or terminator point where the light and shadow are divided **(03)**. This is what creates that solid architectural structure of light and shadow in landscapes. The terminator is also where the light can no longer reflect onto the object, therefore moving past it until the light hits another object, such as the floor. You can then observe the silhouette of the terminator cast onto the floor or object adjacent to the lighting direction, which creates the cast shadow. Think of a cast shadow as a 'mimic' of the object it is casting from.

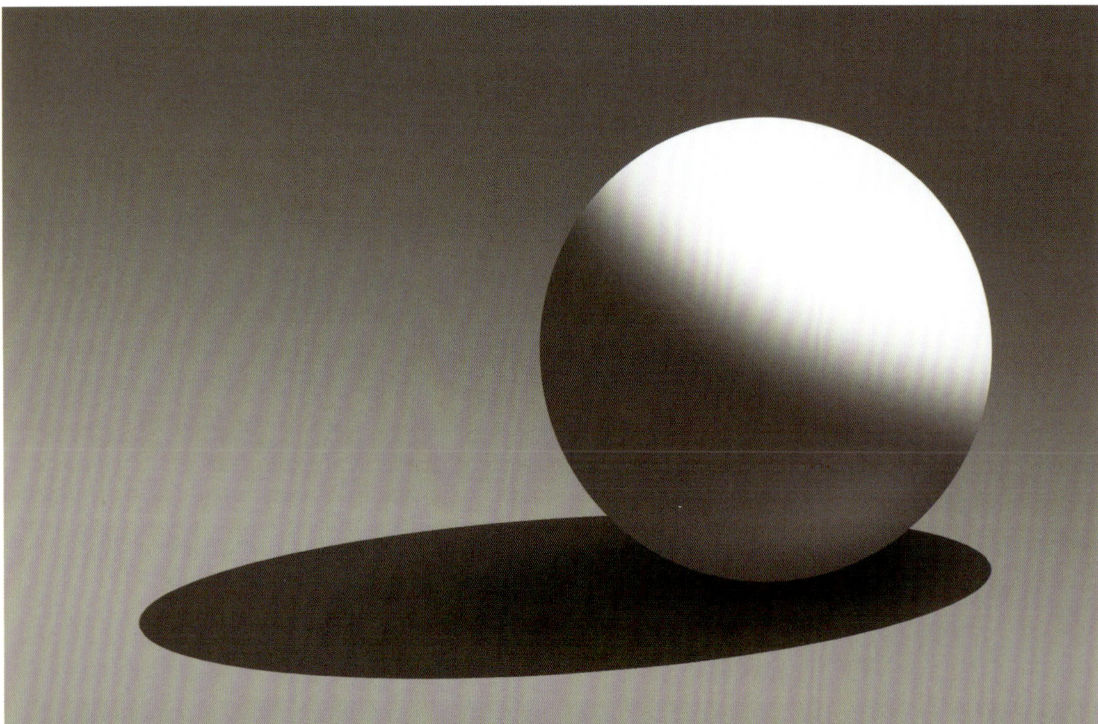

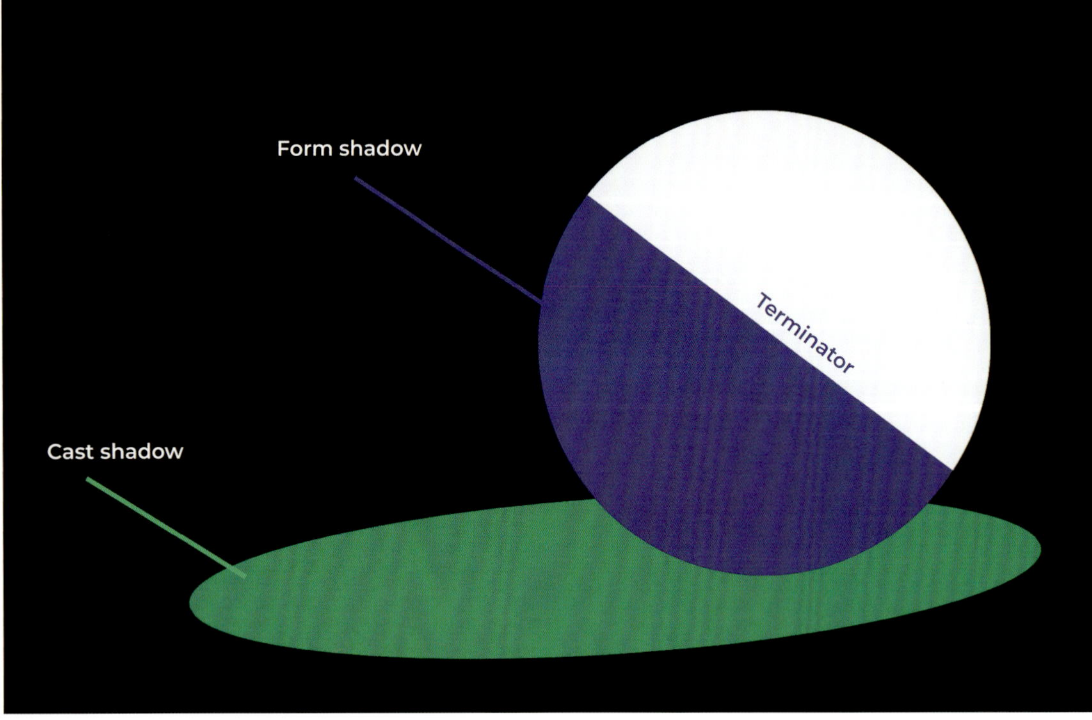

03 The image of the sphere, lit by a single light source from the upper right, reveals the light and shadow play between form and cast shadows. Notice the split between light and shadow on the sphere that creates the dividing terminator line.

SOFT & HARD EDGES

Shadows can have soft or hard edges, depending on the light source and the surface. Soft shadows are often seen in diffused lighting, such as a lamp light with limited reach, whereas hard shadows typically occur with a concentrated, powerful light source, such as the sun. Hard and soft shadows also play a role in drama. Hard shadows typically create a dynamic look, while softer shadows lend themselves more towards romance.

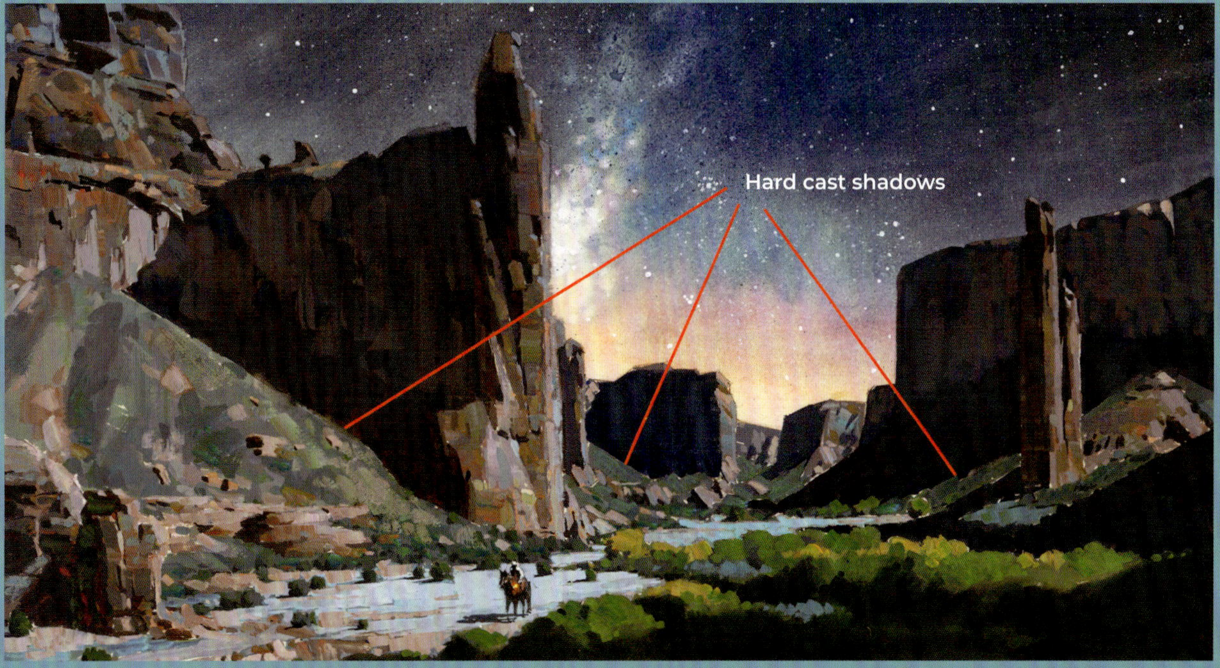

A. This gouache painting shows how natural light, such as sunlight or, as seen here, bright reflected moonlight, creates hard and sharp cast shadows in the landscape.

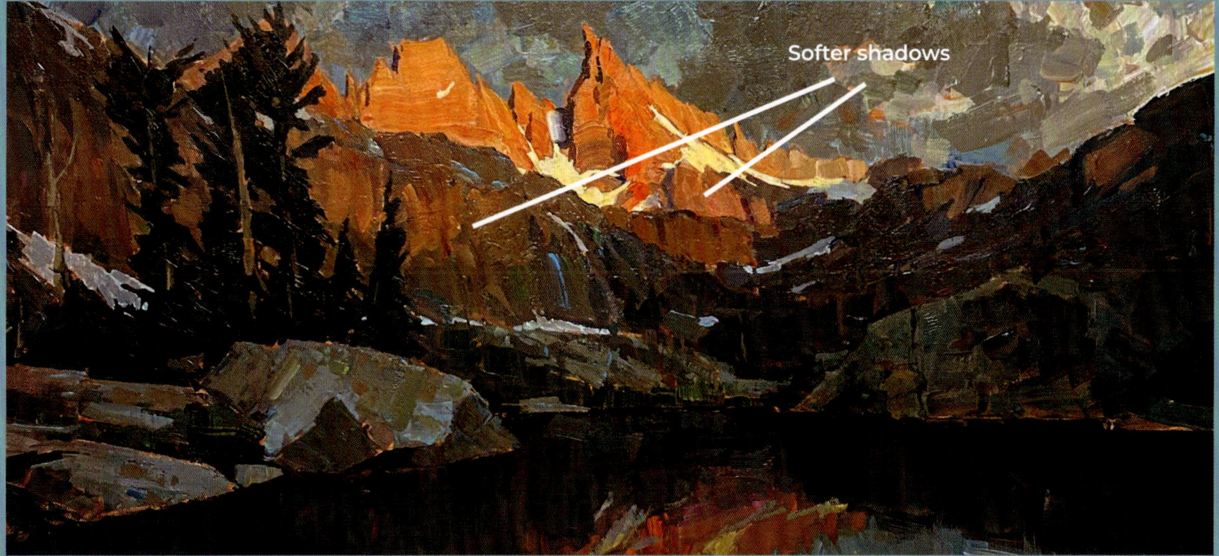

B. This acrylic painting illustrates how sunlight is diffused through clouds, creating softer shadows on the mountainscape, while balancing harder shadows in other areas that are not obscured or diffused by cloud coverage.

Image A, *Knight Ryder* © Mike Hernandez
Image B, *Fire Light* © Mike Hernandez

LINEAR & RADIAL LIGHTING

Now that you're familiar with the basic differences between the light sources and shadow types, you can move on to how to measure them in perspective. To do this you must first understand that there are only two types of lighting in perspective. One is radial lighting and the other is linear or parallel lighting **(04)**.

All lighting is radial to begin with, which is to say that light radiates in all directions, like a star. The sun is a star that radiates lines of light from all sides. However, when you take one very small section of those light rays directed towards our planet, you only receive a limited range of lines. We perceive this small range of light rays as parallel or linear light, seeming to shine in only one direction **(05, 06)**. This is due to the larger size of the sun in comparison to our very small planet and the vast distance between them. Artificial light, such as from a light bulb, is radiant like the sun, and we see it as radiant rather than linear due to its smaller size and close proximity.

Linear and radial light usually only apply to the light rays from the source light and the directions or distortions of the cast shadow from the object. When using linear lighting in perspective, the cast shadow lines will be parallel to one another. In radial lighting, the cast shadows will distort in a fan-like direction away from the object. The closer the light source is to the object, the greater the distortion. This is why the sun's lighting appears parallel, due to its immense distance from anything on our planet. The best vantage point to see this example is from a bird's-eye view of people walking on the street in a sunset environment. Take note of how parallel all of the shadows are in a crowd. The best way to demonstrate radial lighting would be to place multiple objects around an artificial light source. Notice the distortions of each individual shadow, as well as the star-like directions of all the shadows as they radiate away from the centre of the light source **(07)**.

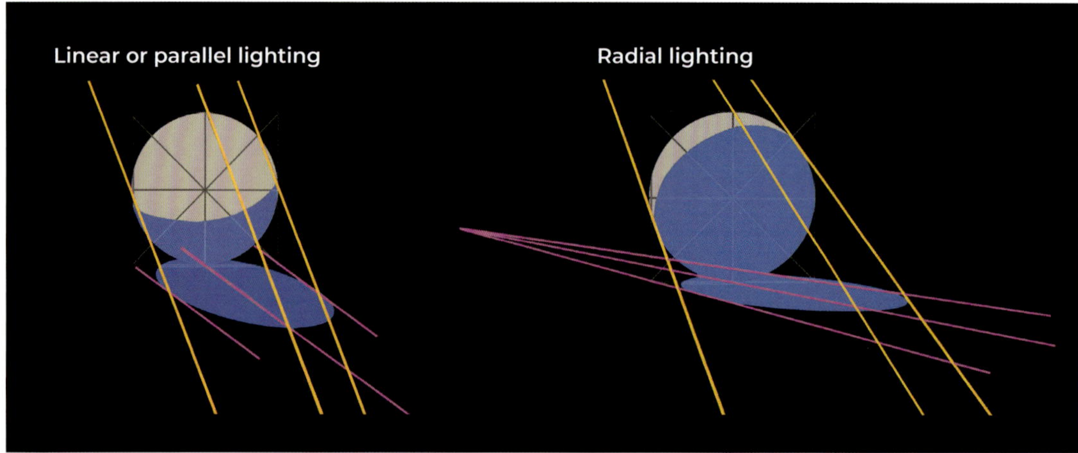

04 These diagrams use a sphere to illustrate the differences between linear and radial perspective in lighting. The yellow lines represent the key light direction and the magenta lines represent cast shadow direction.

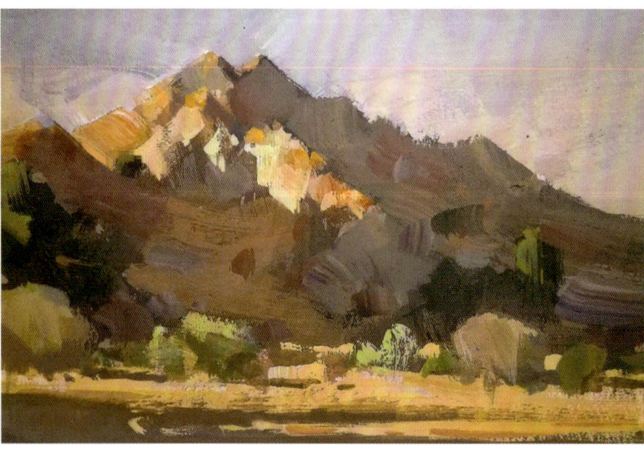

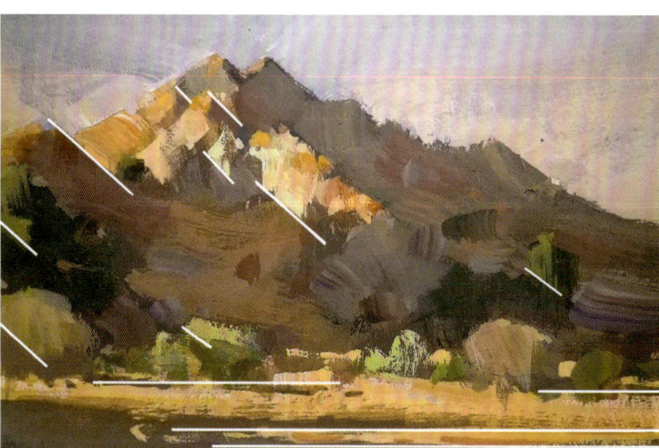

05 This gouache painting captures how sunlight creates parallel shadows in landscapes. Notice all of the small, medium, and large cast shadows on the mountainside, as well as the long shadows on the ground plane.

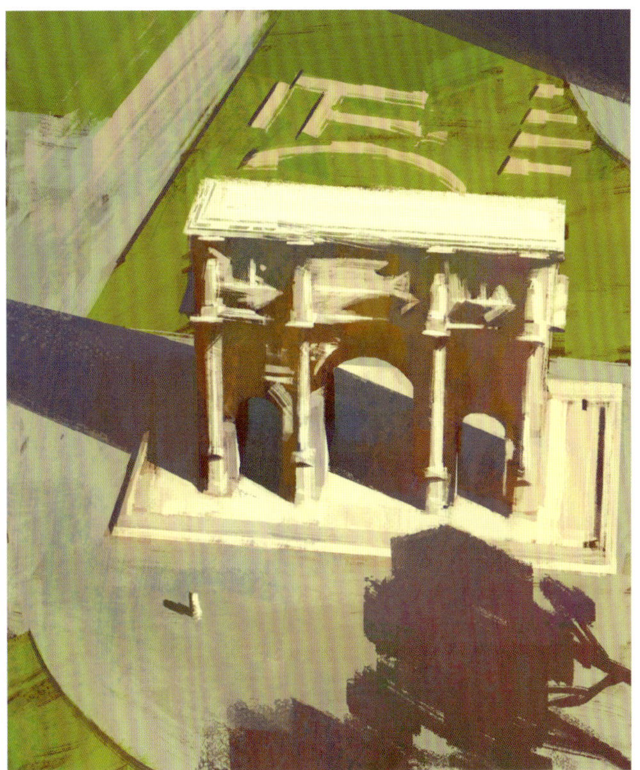

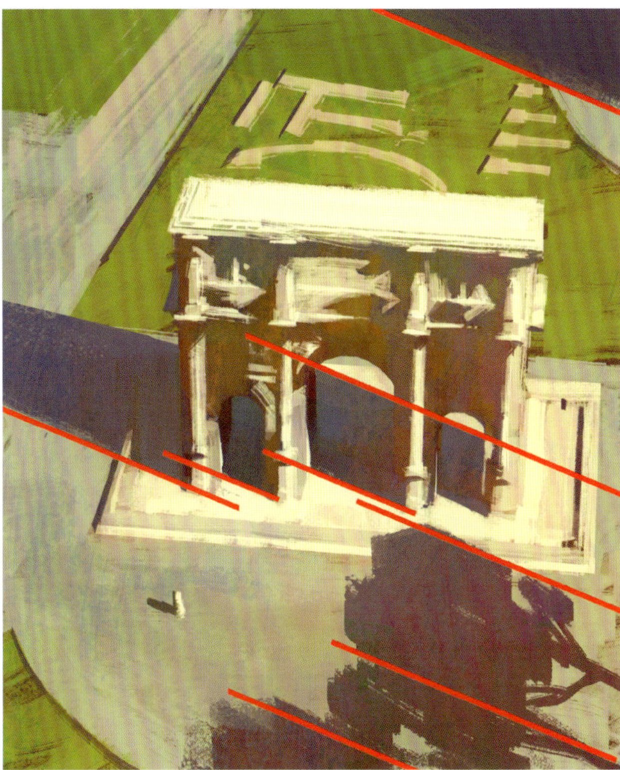

06 This digital painting of Roman architecture is another good example of natural sunlight creating parallel shadow shapes.

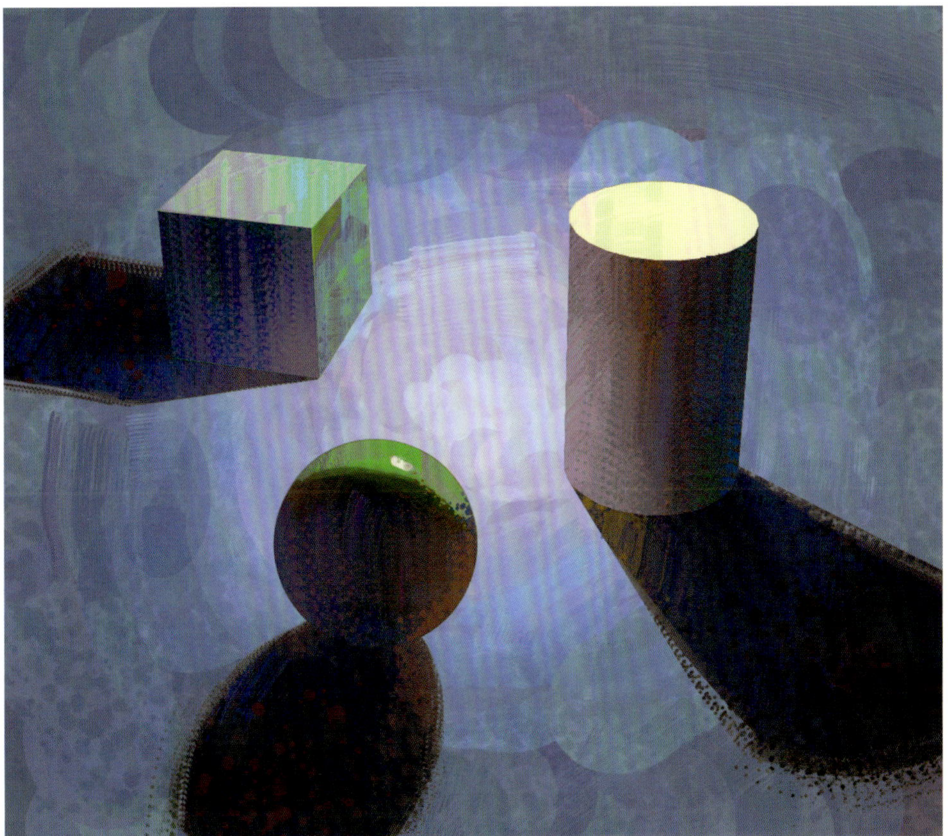

07 Here objects are placed around an artificial light source to demonstrate radiant light, which radiates in all directions and casts individual shadows.

MEASURING SHADOWS IN PERSPECTIVE

To measure any kind of shadow in perspective, you should always start with a ground plane, as this will allow you to create vanishing points from which to measure objects and lighting. In the case of sunlight, you would start with a point above the ground plane to create the primary light source (the sun). This will act as the measuring point for your light direction. From there you will draw a vertical line down to the ground plane. This will be the measuring point for your cast shadow. Once you have both of these points, you can connect them to their corresponding points on an object and see how it will cast a shadow **(08, 09)**.

For a three-dimensional example that isn't too complex, let's look at a cube **(10)**. From the light source (sun) point, you can draw a line that touches all of the outside top points of the cube, then from those points continue onto the ground plane. You can then draw lines from the cast shadow measuring point on the ground plane to the outside bottom points of the cube, and then past those points until they meet with the light source lines. Once you connect these intersections, it creates the map for the form and cast shadow.

When measuring for fixed or artificial light, such as a street lamps or indoor light, you can follow exactly the same methods as above, except you don't need to measure cast shadow lines from the ground plane. You would find this measuring point by drawing a line vertically from the light source, then plotting a point somewhere on the ground plane behind the object. This would indicate that the light is somewhere within close proximity of the object being cast, as opposed to a place on the horizon that indicates the distant sunlight.

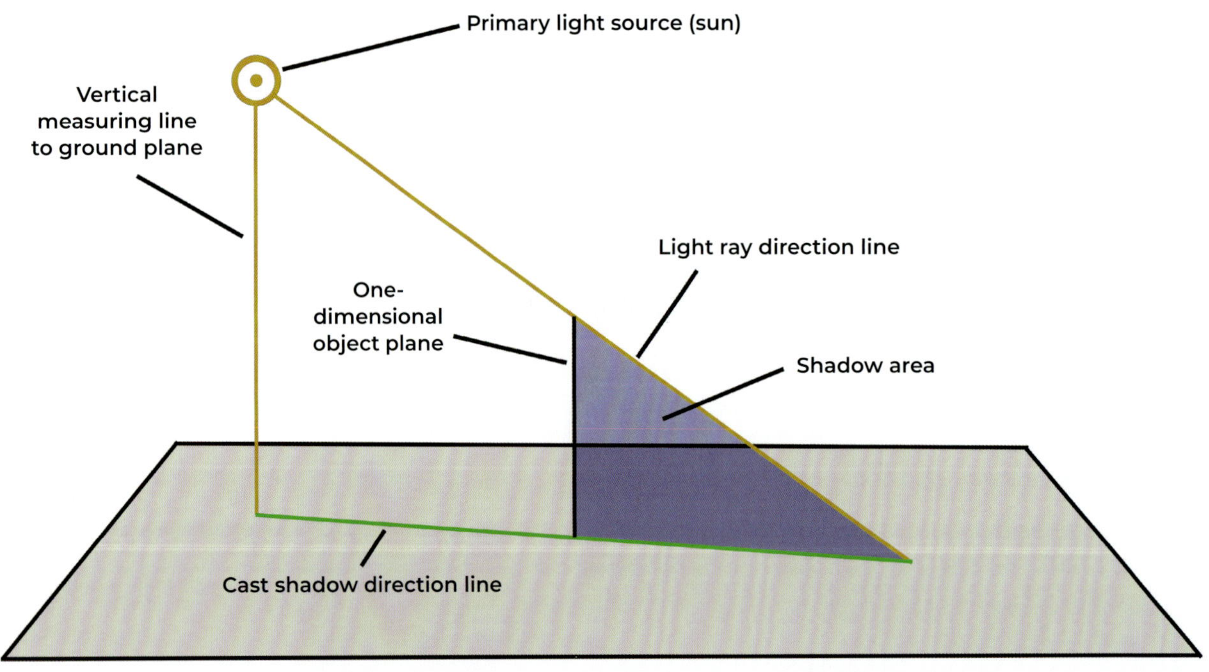

08 This diagram shows the use of a primary light source (the sun) in one-point perspective on a one-dimensional object in space to create a shadow area. The shadow is created by connecting the light to the top and bottom points of the plane.

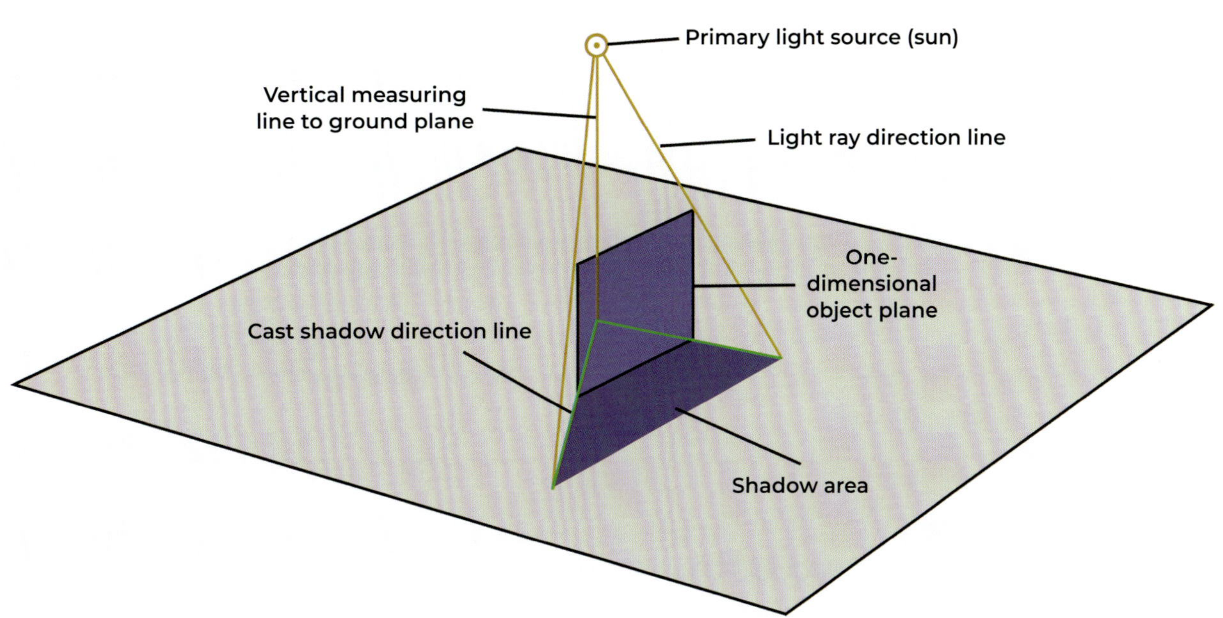

09 This image represents lighting a one-dimensional object in two-point perspective by measuring the top and bottom-most outer points of the plane.

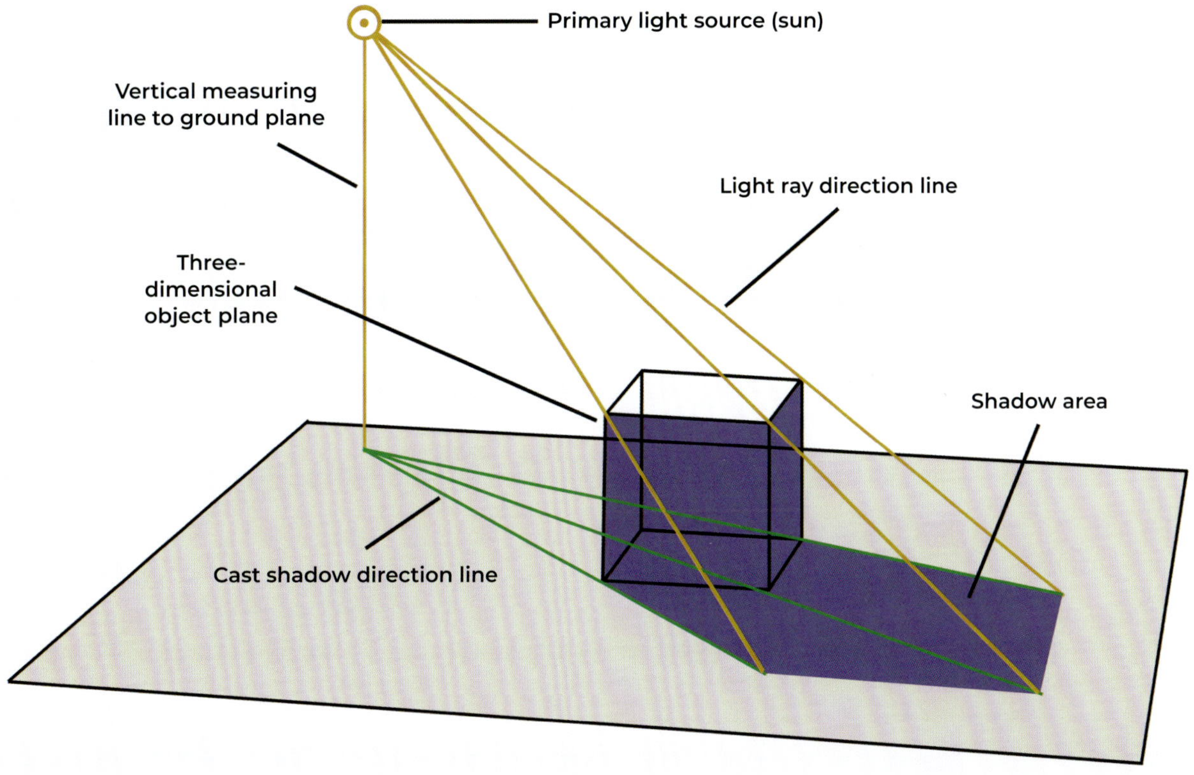

10 The image above illustrates how lighting a three-dimensional cube using three-point perspective can create more volume and form.

PARALLEL PERSPECTIVE

A simpler method of drawing shadows cast by sunlight is to use parallel perspective. This method doesn't require you to find the vertical measuring points like before, rather you are only using parallel directional lines for sunlight direction and parallel directional lines for cast shadow direction. The only similarity here is that you will be connecting these points to the top and bottom outer points of the cube to get the dimensions. Where these lines meet will determine the form and cast shadow shapes **(11)**.

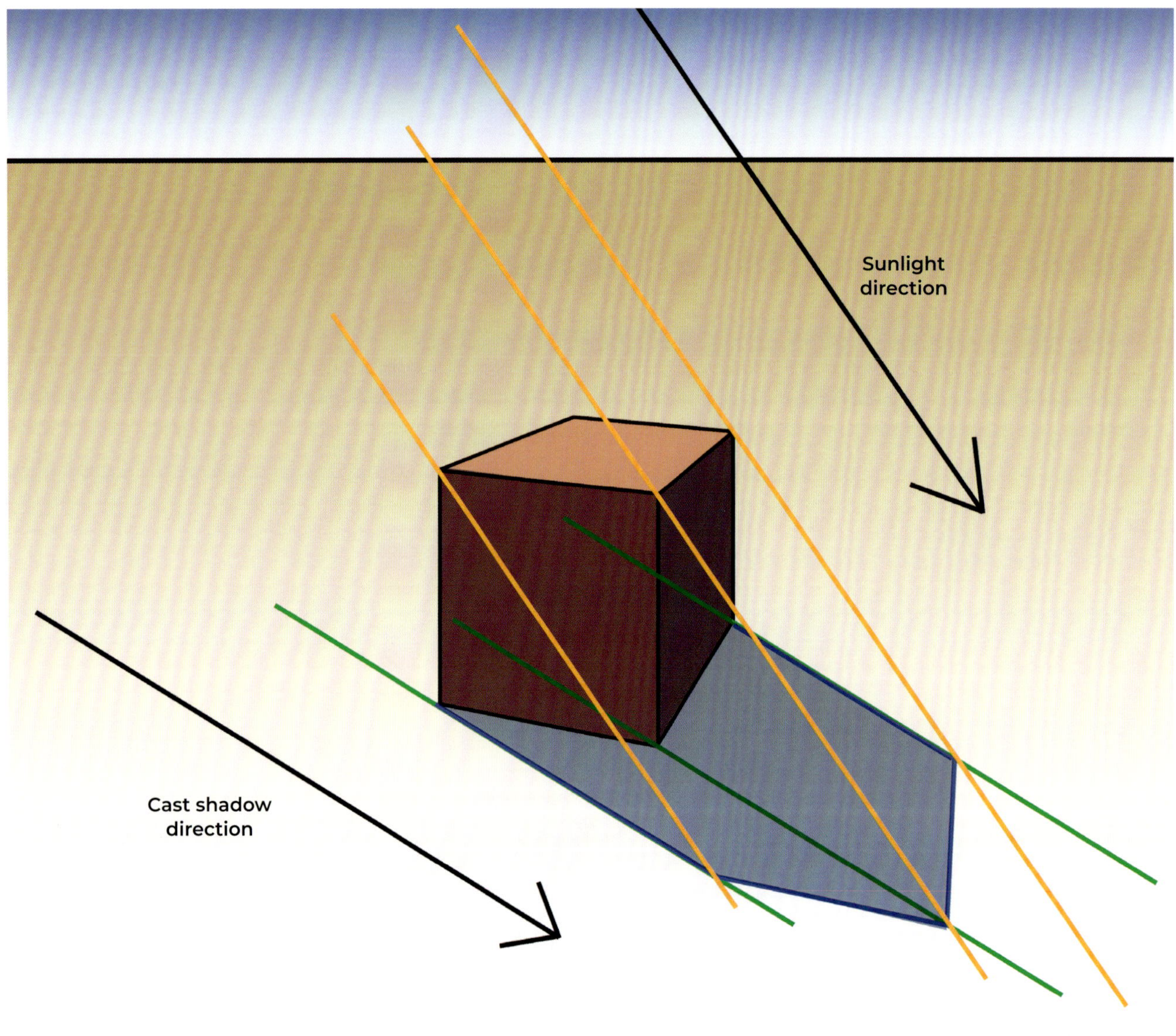

11 This image illustrates a simpler method of using parallel perspective in sunlight, without having to find measuring vanishing points for the sun's rays and shadow direction.

VIEWING SHADOWS IN THE ABSTRACT

Understanding the science of light and shadow in perspective is essential for an artist to learn, but in order to comprehend a better sense of design aesthetic, beauty, and style, this is only the beginning. It's important to look at light and shadow as a way to make literal sense of our environment, but it's also essential to view shadows in the abstract. Most people who will view your artwork are more interested in the aesthetic and appealing aspects of the image, rather than the literal sense. True, art *is* in the eye of the beholder, but you as the artist need to know that you can break or enhance the rules in order to make your artistic statement.

As a designer in the animation industry, I found it very useful to be able to create art and environments that communicated the story with more accuracy and tone, but then when I would paint from life, I would sometimes feel limited by what was in front of me. I began to take the lessons I had learned as a storyteller in animation and apply them to the real world; which is to say that I always tried to create a narrative or be intentional with my outdoor painting.

Looking at shadow shapes in the abstract helped me to take advantage of tools I could use in storytelling or to direct the eye. Cast shadow shapes, for example, could point in a particular direction or frame a subject matter. Cast shadow lines could also be used as mood stabilizers to convey excitement or calm, depending on whether the edge was busy or uninterrupted. Shadows can be used to create more form and depth by layering them over other objects. I would often cheat this effect by having an unjustified shadow just cast across a large middle-ground or foreground object, giving it more depth and dimension. The viewer's eye would never think to question it if it felt balanced in the scene or in the context of the lighting. If the object casting the shadow was off screen, we could assume that it could do that.

It is also important to consider the ratio of light to shadow when mapping out shapes in a scene. A good rule to follow is the golden mean or golden ratio. There is some maths required to create the golden ratio, but in simple terms it is best described as a seventy-to-thirty ratio. These ratios can be pushed and pulled in order to achieve various visual dynamics. For example, a ratio of twenty per cent light to eighty per cent shadow will have a very dramatic look, giving the scene a different mood **(12)**.

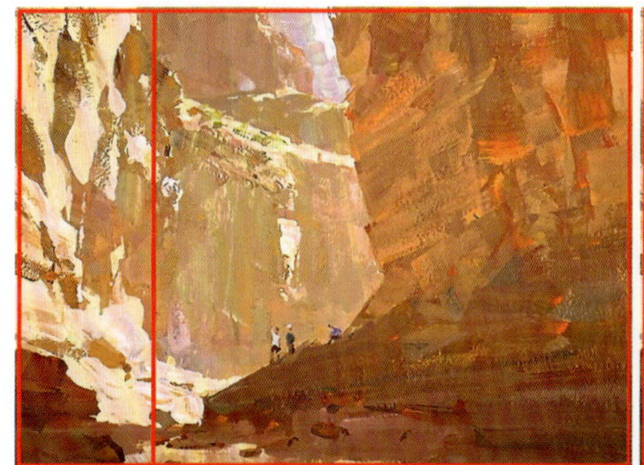

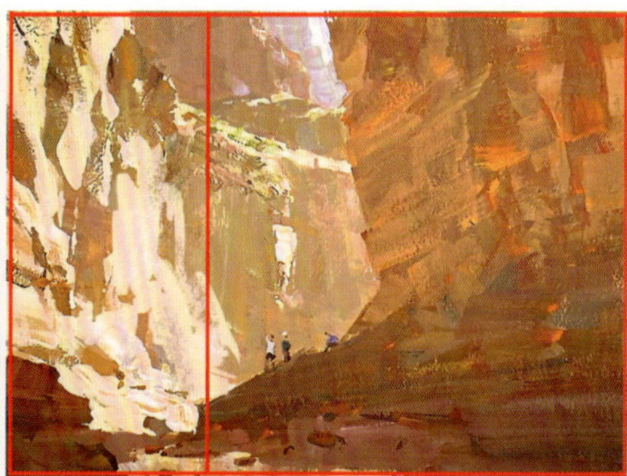

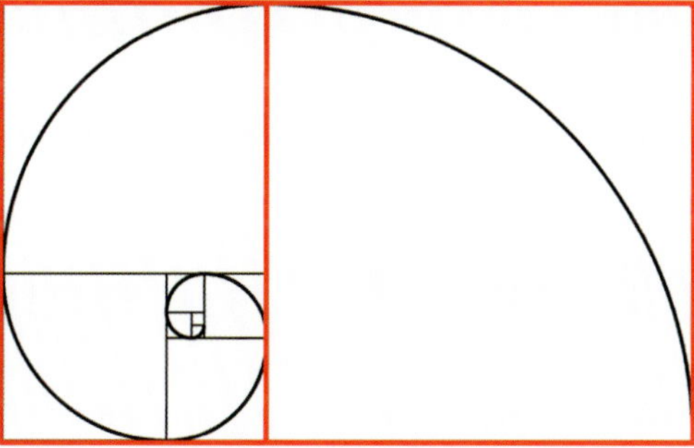

12 This gouache painting depicts the proportions of the golden ratio. The painting on the left depicts a relatively close 80/20 proportion of sunlight to shadow, while the painting on the right and diagram below illustrate a ratio of 70/30 proportion. These types of proportions yield a stronger dynamic of dramatic lighting.

SHAPES

This chapter will discuss how shapes can be used to inform the viewer of the perspective and depth present in a scene. We view and understand the world as various different shapes, from big to small, complex to simple, geometric to organic. When a shape is placed in a scene, perspective can change its appearance and may even create a more distorted feature that informs us less about the subject itself and more about the depth of the scene and where our eyes are drawn into space.

DEPTH CUES

If we were to dissect the various different shapes that make up a landscape and think of them more as flattened puzzle pieces, rather than volumetric shapes, we can explore how the abstract shapes inform us about the direction and movement the viewer's eye can take into and through the composition. These are known as depth cues (01, 02). In landscape or city scenes, the eye is drawn away from complex textures and instead drawn to simple paths first, such as trails, pavements, streets, buildings, and groups of shapes moving in one direction (03, 04). This tells us that the eye is drawn to the path of least resistance, which we can use to our advantage in a composition.

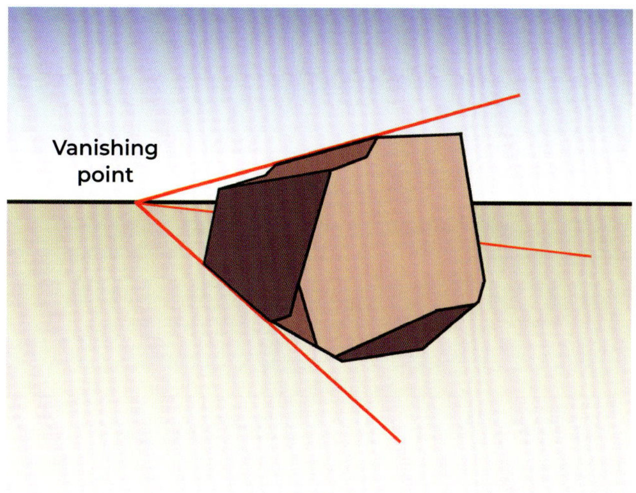

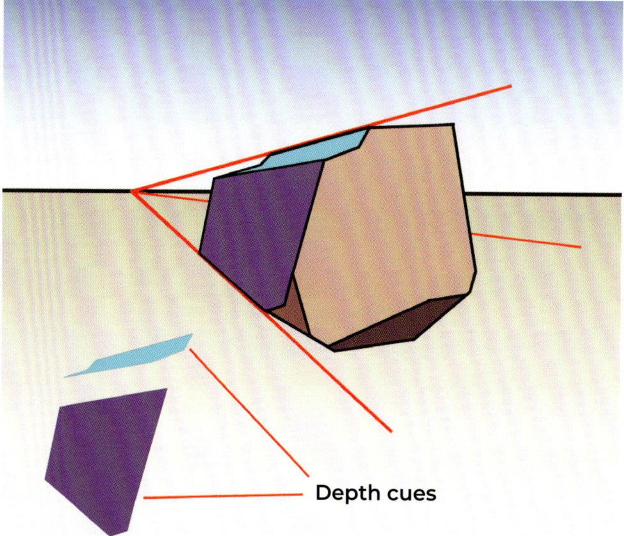

01 This illustration of a rock in one-point perspective is a good example of how shape cues inform us of depth. The front-facing plane has a square-like shape, while the side creates distorted shapes that point towards the horizon. Simple shape changes like this are a great way to imply perspective and depth.

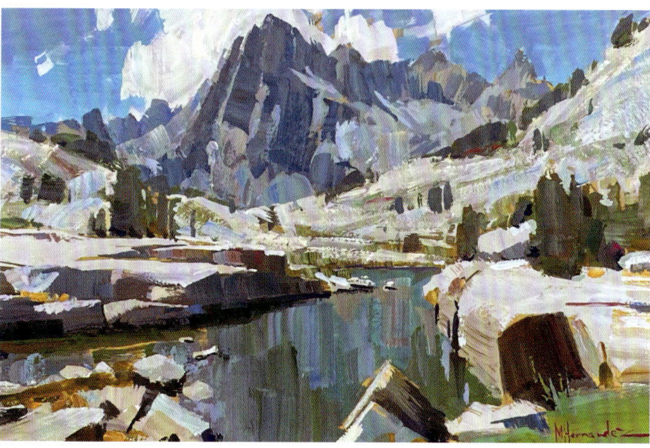

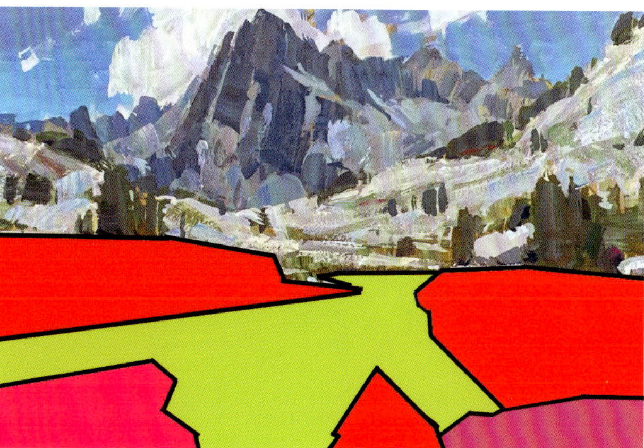

02 The foreground in this gouache painting has been broken down into several puzzle-like pieces to reveal the shape cues that inform perspective and depth.

PRIMITIVES

A useful exercise to train your eye to notice these cues in organic shapes is to break them down into primitives, such as squares, triangles, and rectangles **(06)**. This reinforces a better sense of architecture and structure in an organic scene, helping to inform perspective **(07)**. Clouds are a perfect example of an ambiguous subject matter for structure, as they often lack straight lines and easy-to-read shapes. This is because we see the world in its literal sense, rather than applied design. By applying design to cloud shapes, we can reveal a simple structure of form that we can then place into perspective, creating more depth and volume **(08)**. Learning to apply this method to all of the natural and ambiguous shapes in nature will always yield a stronger sense of design, depth, and perspective. Another bonus to simplifying shapes is that it creates a kind of visual grammar – a set of rules or guides to help you break down and interpret what you see. A further simplified look can help to communicate a form of stylization in one's own artwork.

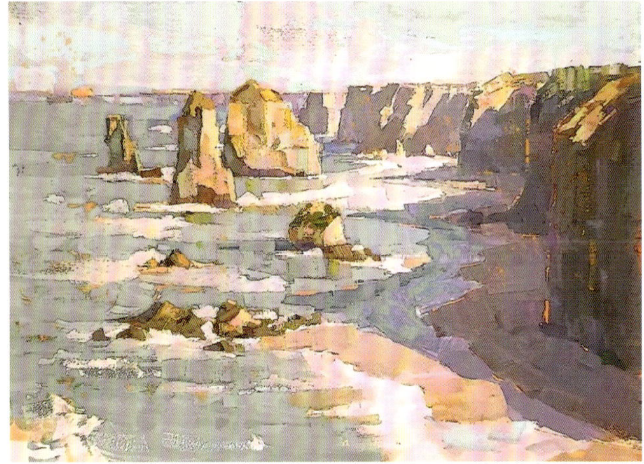

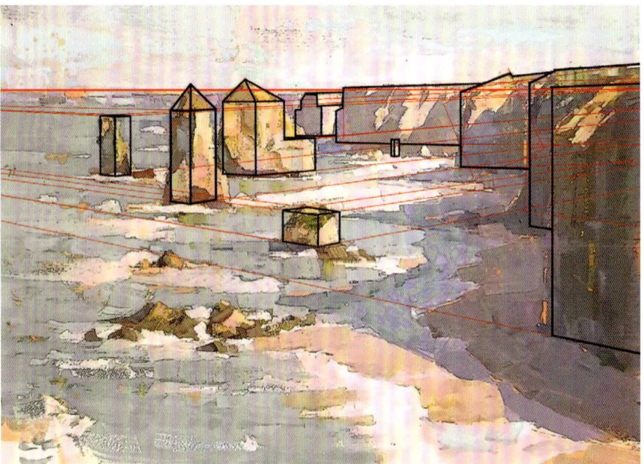

06 This gouache painting is a good example of how to break down forms into simple primitives, such as squares, rectangles, triangles, and cones, to help create a better sense of dimension in a scene.

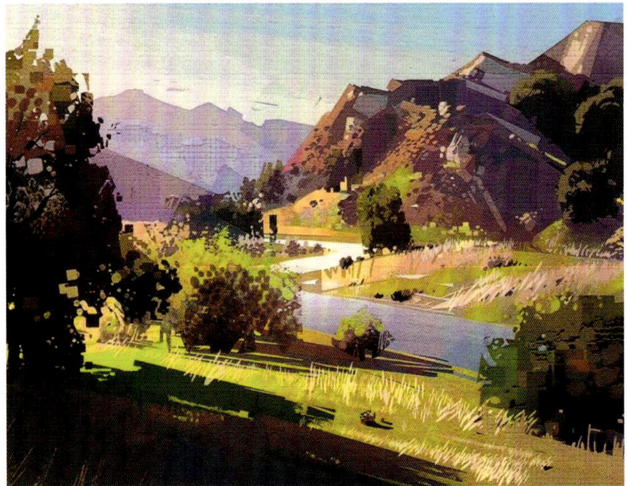

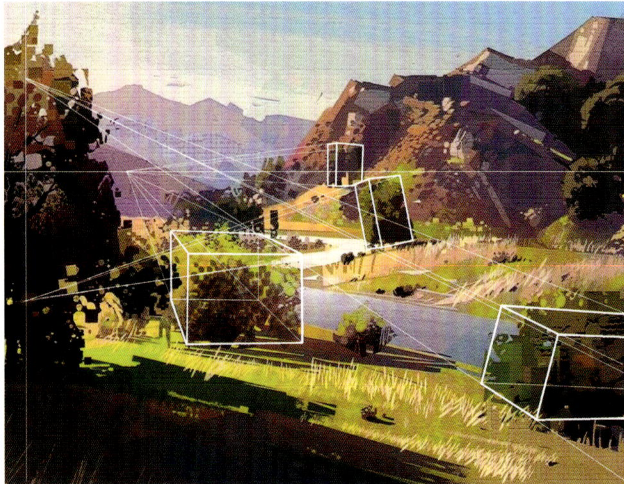

07 This digital painting also shows how to break down complex and organic shapes into primitive building blocks, then apply them to perspective in order to achieve depth. When I simplify shapes into geometric forms, it helps to establish a stylized look to my paintings.

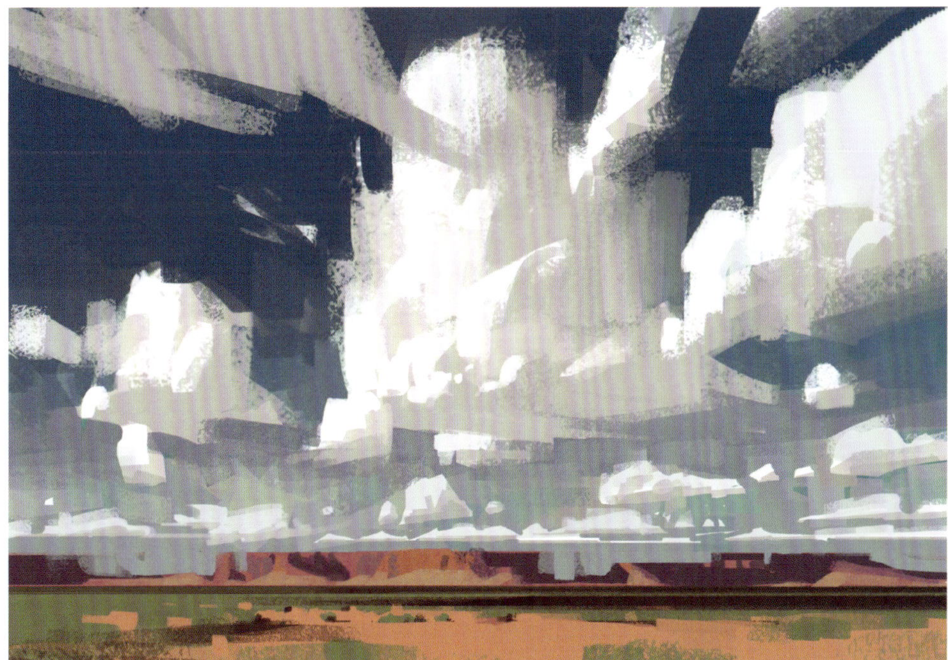

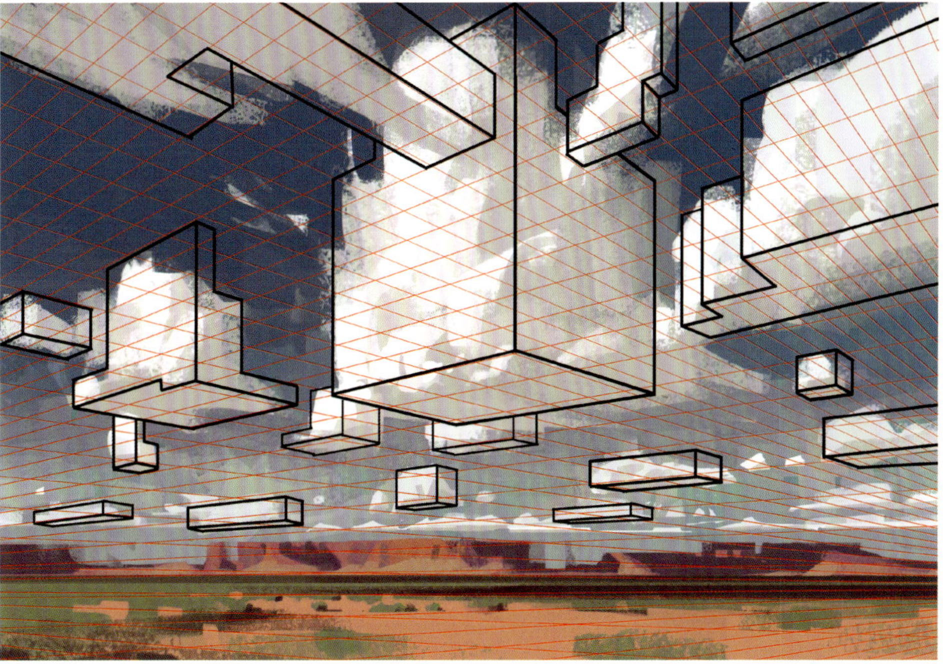

08 This digital painting of clouds is a good example of how I use primitive blocks in perspective to enhance a better sense of structure, form, volume, and depth.

START WITH SIMPLE SHAPES

Begin by practising with basic geometric shapes, such as cubes, spheres, cylinders, and pyramids. These forms are known as primitives and are excellent for mastering the fundamentals of perspective. Add the details gradually after first establishing the basic shapes. As always, observe real objects and how their shapes change when viewed from different angles and perspectives.

GRIDS

Grids are another very useful tool for creating and understanding depth and perspective in a landscape, while also enhancing form and volume in shape. They are also helpful in understanding how to measure the foreshortening of objects and the eyeballing of ratios in space. By placing simple grids in a scene and dissecting them into planes, they reveal a lot of information about how the form changes direction and movement. A grid reveals the volume and simplicity of forms, plus how they relate to one another in scale. A great example of how a grid can be useful in a complex scene is to use one on a mountain terrain with trees **(09, 10)**. By placing grids that are smaller in the distance and larger in the foreground, you can use the squares in the grids as measurements of how the trees relate to them by ratio. This ratio can be applied to all objects, such as bushes, rocks, and people.

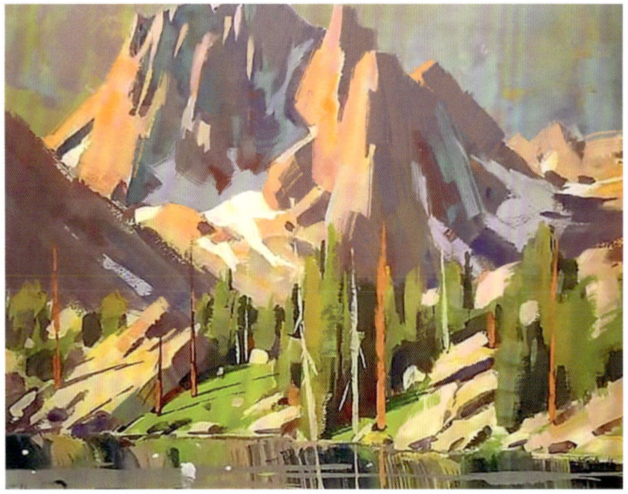

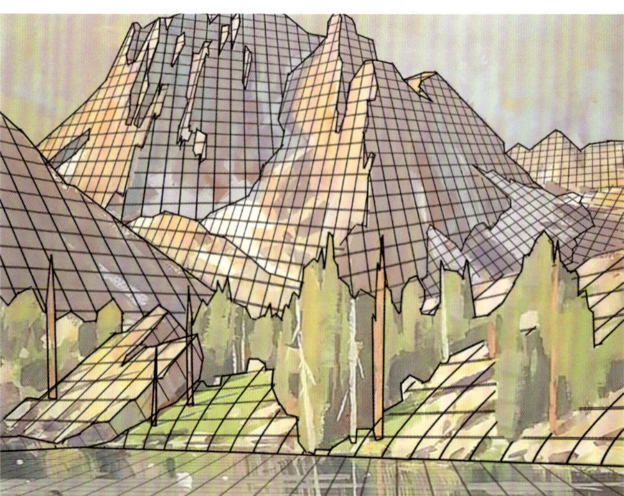

09 Here I've taken a gouache painting and applied grids to illustrate form, depth, and dimension. Notice the progression from smaller grids in the background, to larger ones in the foreground. This creates a better sense of foreshortening.

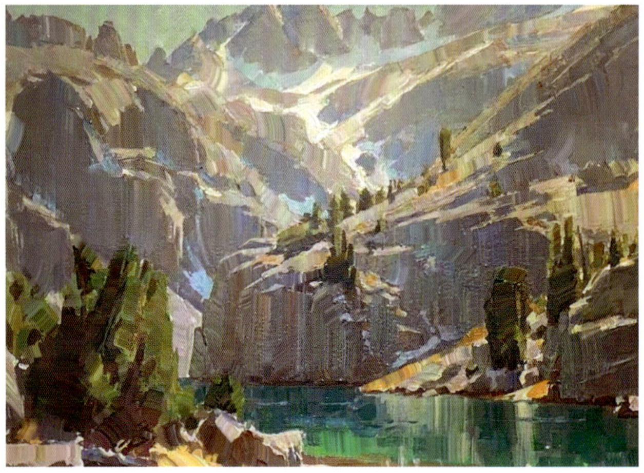

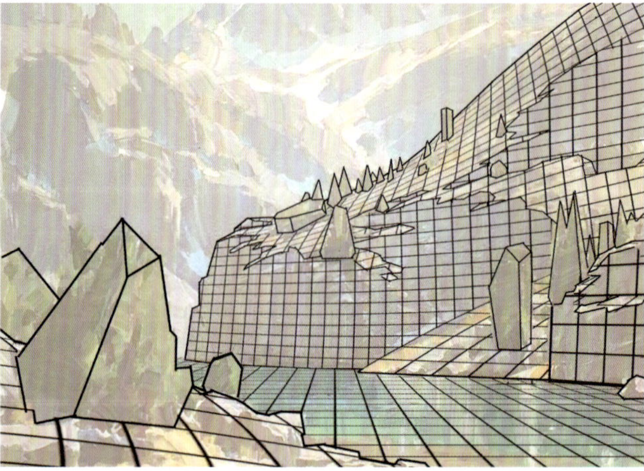

10 Here is another of my gouache paintings where I've applied grids to the middle ground and foreground to illustrate depth by ratio and proportion. Notice how the size of the trees and bushes correspond in size and shape with the grids as they recede into the landscape.

Grids can also be useful in enhancing movement and direction in perspective **(11)**. Large land masses, such as mountains and hills, can sometimes seem ambiguous, but with the help of grids they can act as pathways for the viewer's eye in a scene. By taking simple grids and applying them to the forms in an image, they will follow perspective, which creates leading lines for the viewer's eye to follow. Leading lines can be used in art and cinema to help guide the viewer, or the subject, in storytelling.

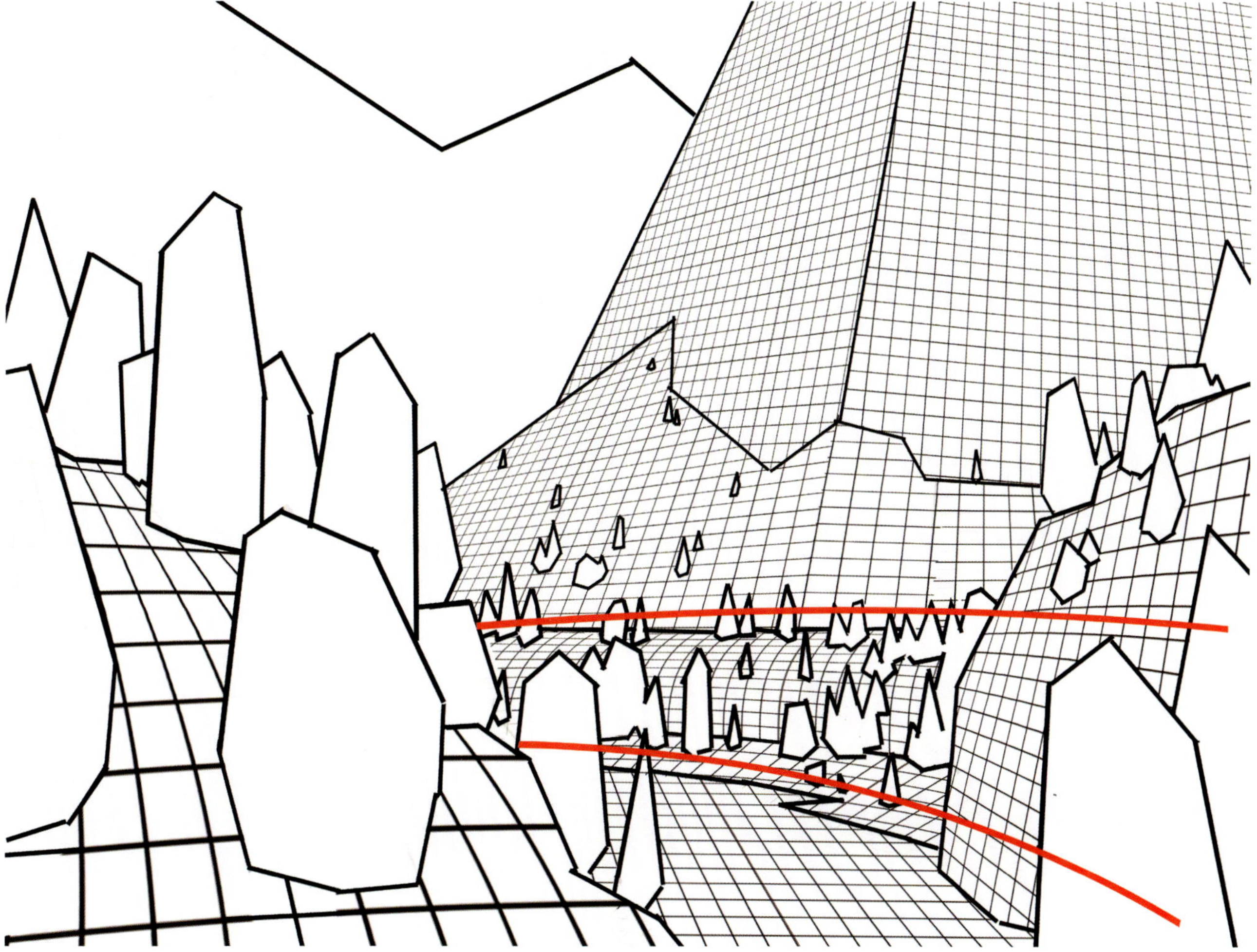

11 This illustration is another good example of how grids reinforce depth and movement in a scene. Notice the leading lines that create direction and depth.

BREAKING THE RULES

In traditional linear perspective, there are established rules and principles that artists use to create the illusion of depth and three-dimensionality on a two-dimensional surface. However, artists sometimes intentionally break these rules to achieve certain artistic effects or to challenge conventional representations of space. There were many times in my career as a concept artist that I found myself departing from the established principles and techniques of perspective in order to achieve an artistic statement or stylization. This chapter will explore a few ways artists can break the rules in linear perspective.

DISTORTING THE PERSPECTIVE

Artists sometimes choose to break the traditional rules of linear perspective as a form of artistic experimentation. They may distort or manipulate the perspective to create a unique and visually compelling composition. This can lead to interesting and visually striking artwork. Artists may also deliberately distort perspective to create a sense of unease, or to emphasize specific elements in their composition. This type of distortion can be seen in the works of artists such as Salvador Dalí, who used a technique called 'crazy perspective' to create dreamlike and surreal scenes **(01)**.

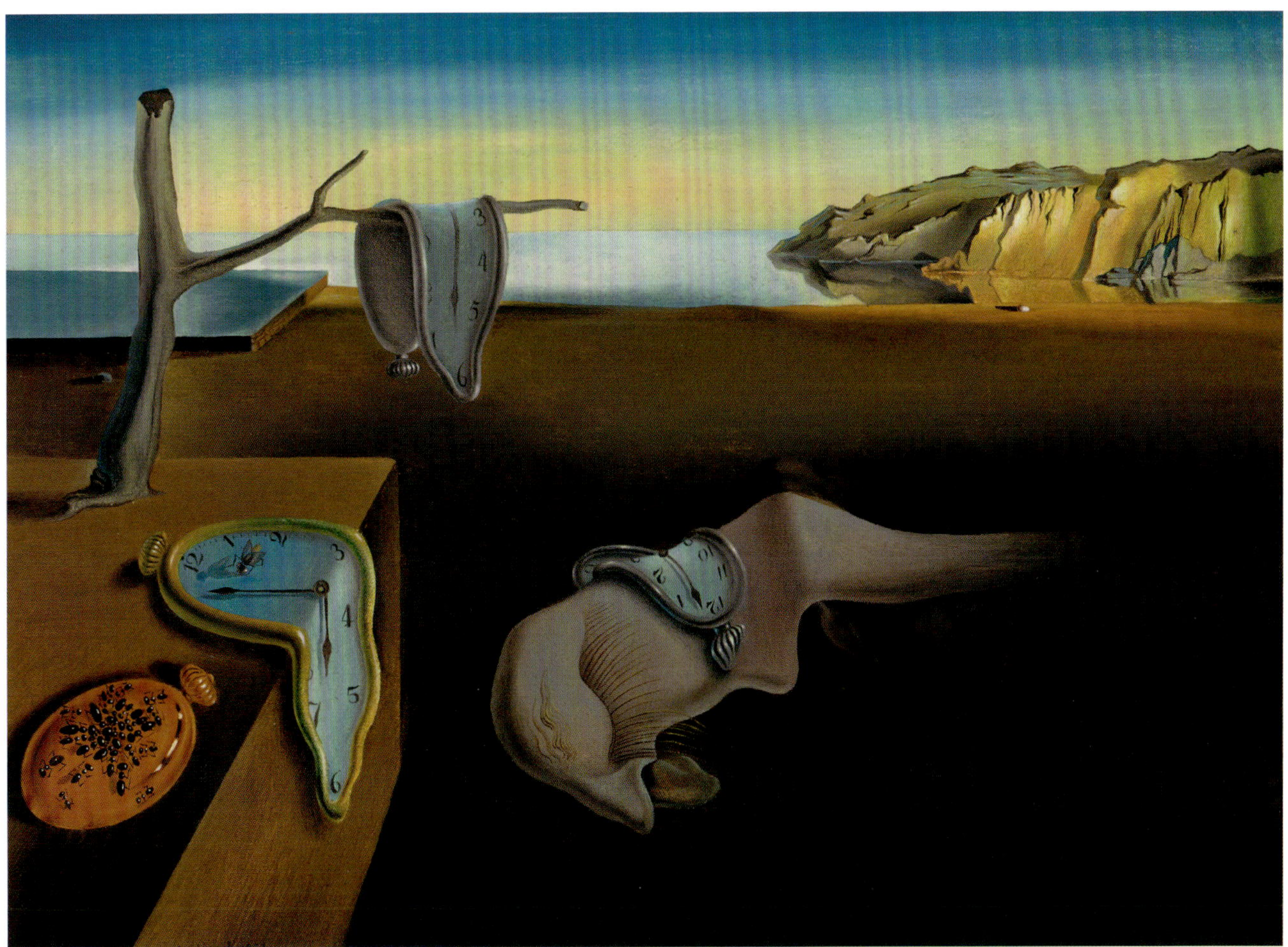

01 *The Persistence of Memory* (1931) by Salvador Dalí demonstrates how compelling and innovative an image can be by manipulating and distorting the rules of traditional perspective. Notice the dreamlike quality that this image evokes.

MULTIPLE OR NO VANISHING POINTS

Artists might also use multiple vanishing points, or even create scenes with no clear vanishing points at all. This technique creates a simultaneous sense of disorder and rhythm and can feel otherworldly and unique **(02)**.

Another useful technique I was taught when I first started work as a concept artist at DreamWorks was how to split a single vanishing point into two different points. This allows the artist to open up a scene, such as a city that appears too narrow or too deep **(03)**. By moving the points apart, the artist has room to stage action in the foreground, such as a character moment where the background needs to function as a backdrop rather than the focus.

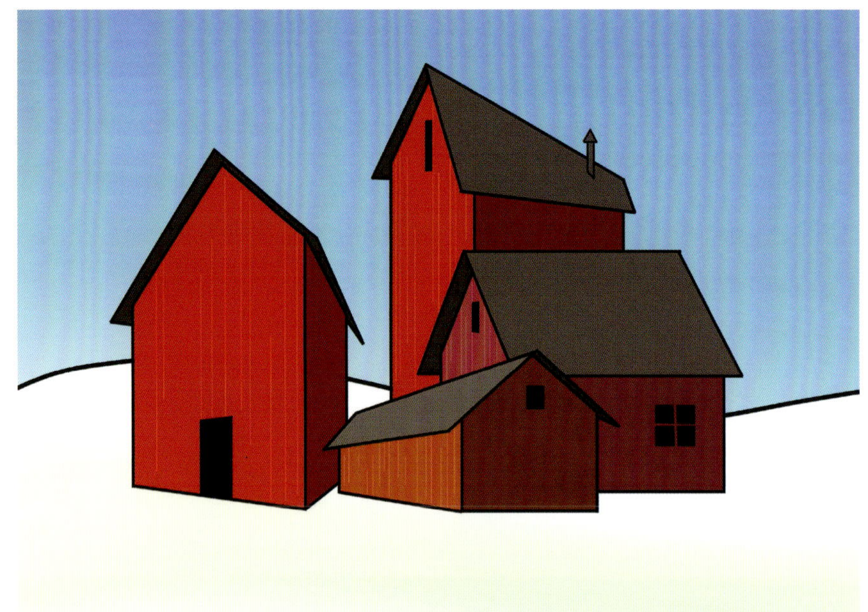

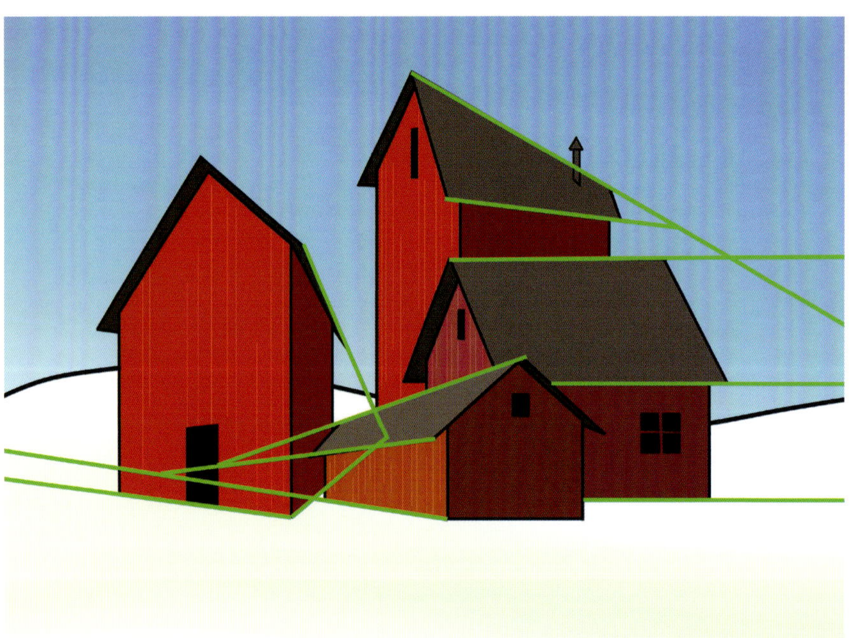

02 This illustration is a good example of how artists can manipulate the rules by the use of chaos to create rhythm and movement. By creating broken multiple vanishing points, the buildings take on an abstract stylization.

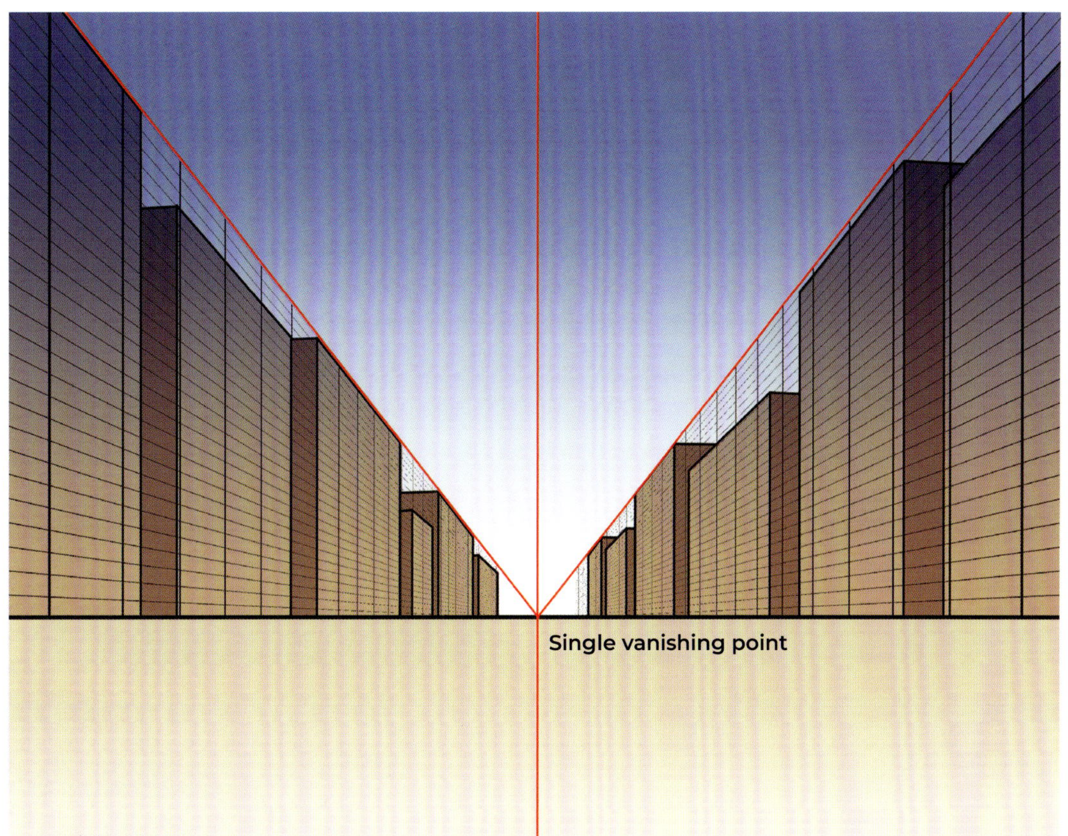

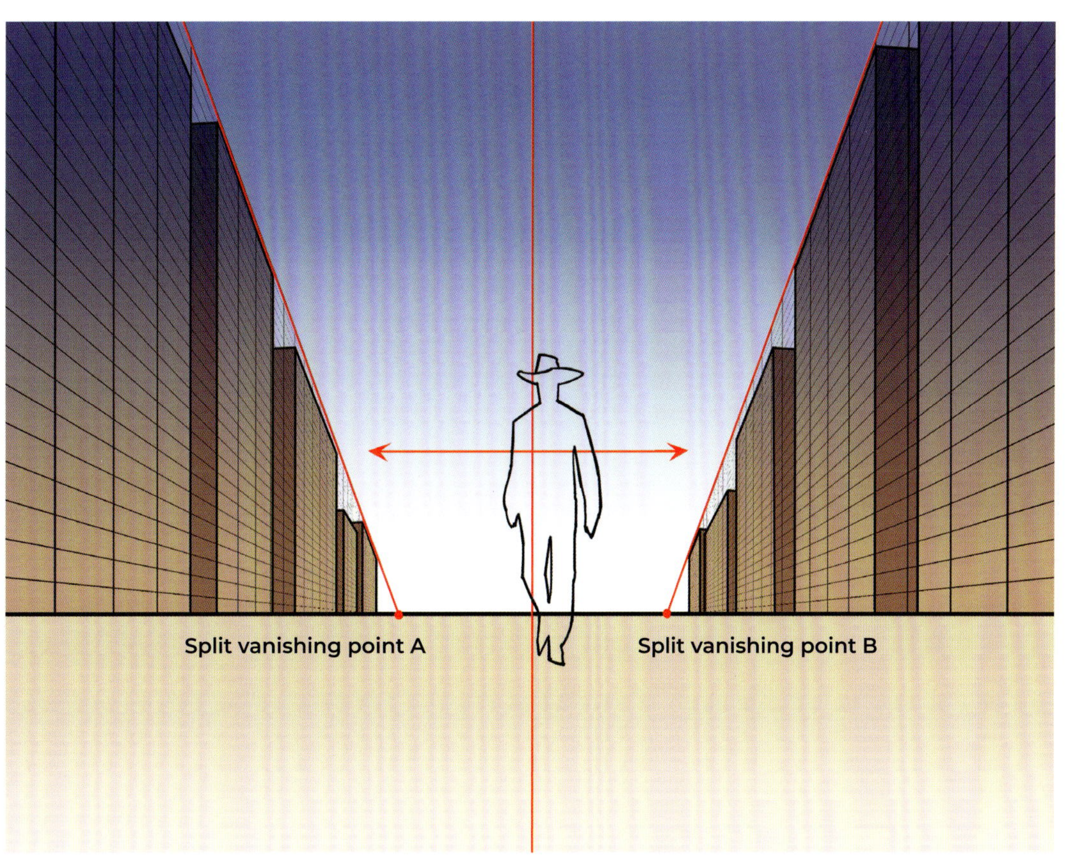

03 This illustration illustrates how a single vanishing point can be split into two separate points in order to open up a scene. The character now has a more breathable staging area to perform in isolation.

FLAT, ISOMETRIC, & CURVILINEAR PERSPECTIVE

Another method used in stylized art is flat perspective, which refers to a simplified or flattened version of traditional linear perspective. In this case, artists may choose to use some elements of perspective, but simplify them to create a more stylized or less realistic representation of space **(04)**. Artists may choose to use flattened perspective for symbolic or expressive purposes. The absence of depth can convey a sense of focus and attention on other aspects of the artwork, such as colour or composition **(05)**.

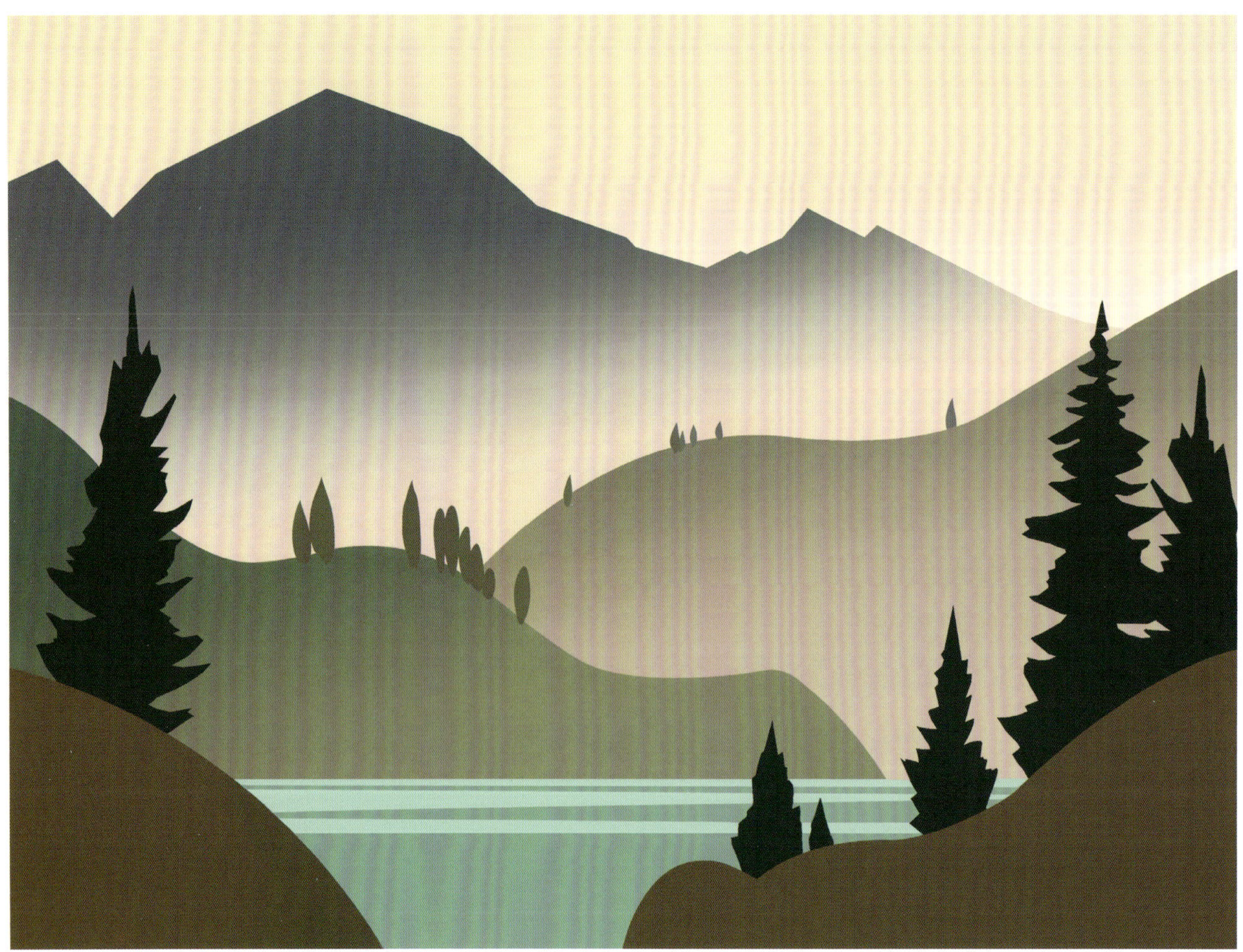

04 This is a simple example of how flattened perspective can be used to convey a quick stylistic read without volume. The only perspective cues used here are overlapping objects that create that subtle foreshortened look.

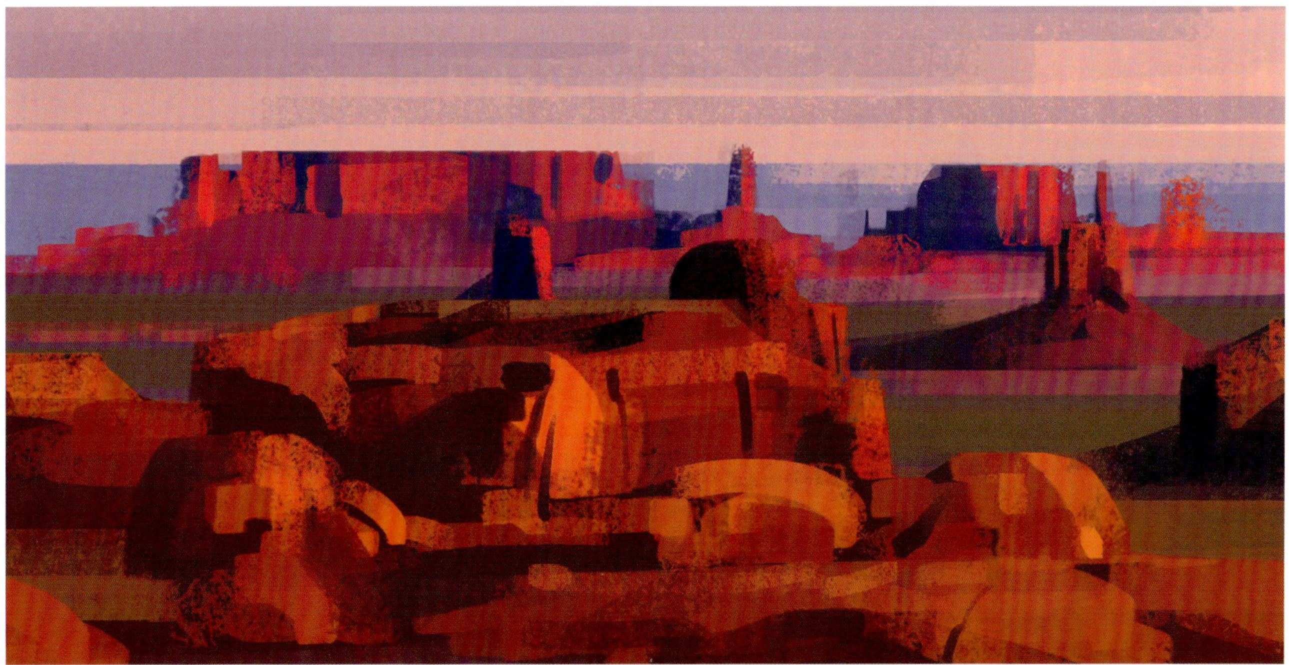

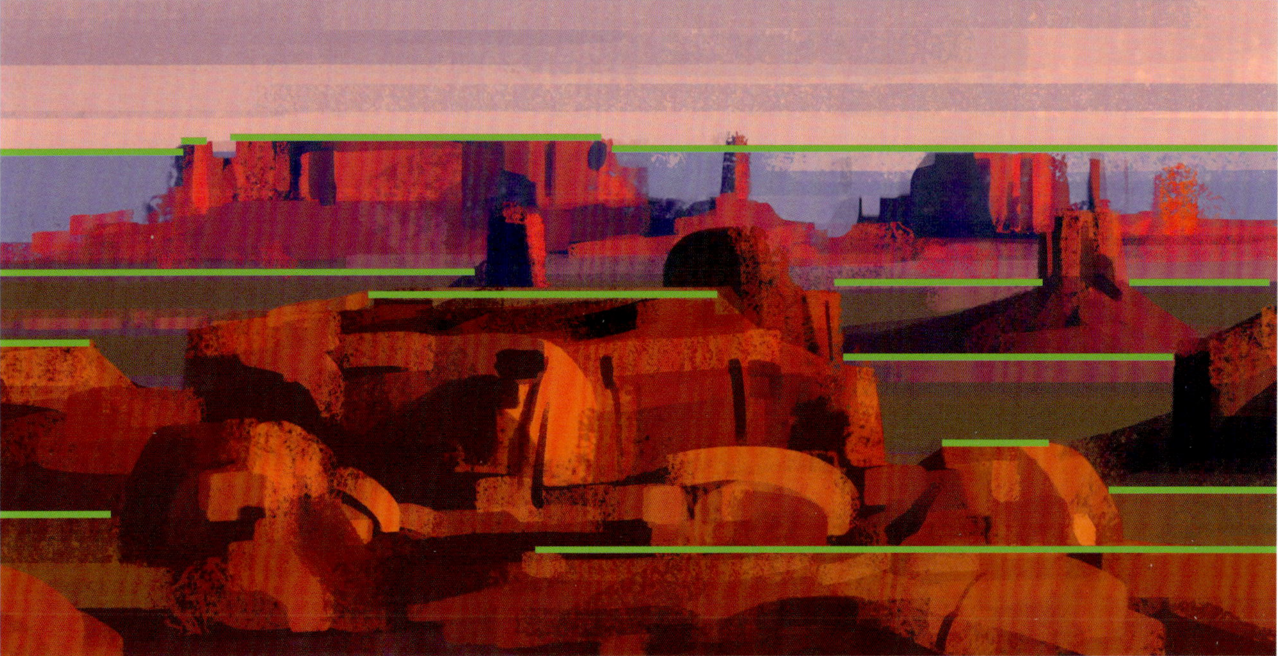

05 This illustration also captures how flattened perspective can be utilized to create an artistic statement. Notice how all of the perfect parallel lines convey a stylized look.

Isometric perspective is a form of perspective used primarily in technical drawing. Unlike traditional linear perspective, which uses vanishing points to convey the illusion of depth, isometric perspective maintains consistent angles and dimensions for all three axes of length, width, and height **(06)**. Although isometric perspective isn't commonly used in traditional art, because it is primarily associated with architectural drawings, there are instances where it has been incorporated into concept art. When this happens, it is typically used to create an abstract or stylized effect in artistic expression.

An additional way to enhance volume and depth is through the use of curvilinear perspective. One of the key aspects of curvilinear perspective is the use of the 'cone of vision'. This cone represents the area in front of you that you can see clearly, while objects outside of this cone appear more distorted and curved **(07)**. It's important to understand and work within this cone to maintain the illusion of depth and space in the artwork. Another fascinating aspect of curvilinear perspective is that it can create a sense of movement and dynamism in compositions **(08)**. The curved lines and arcs suggest a dynamic flow in a scene, which can add energy and interest.

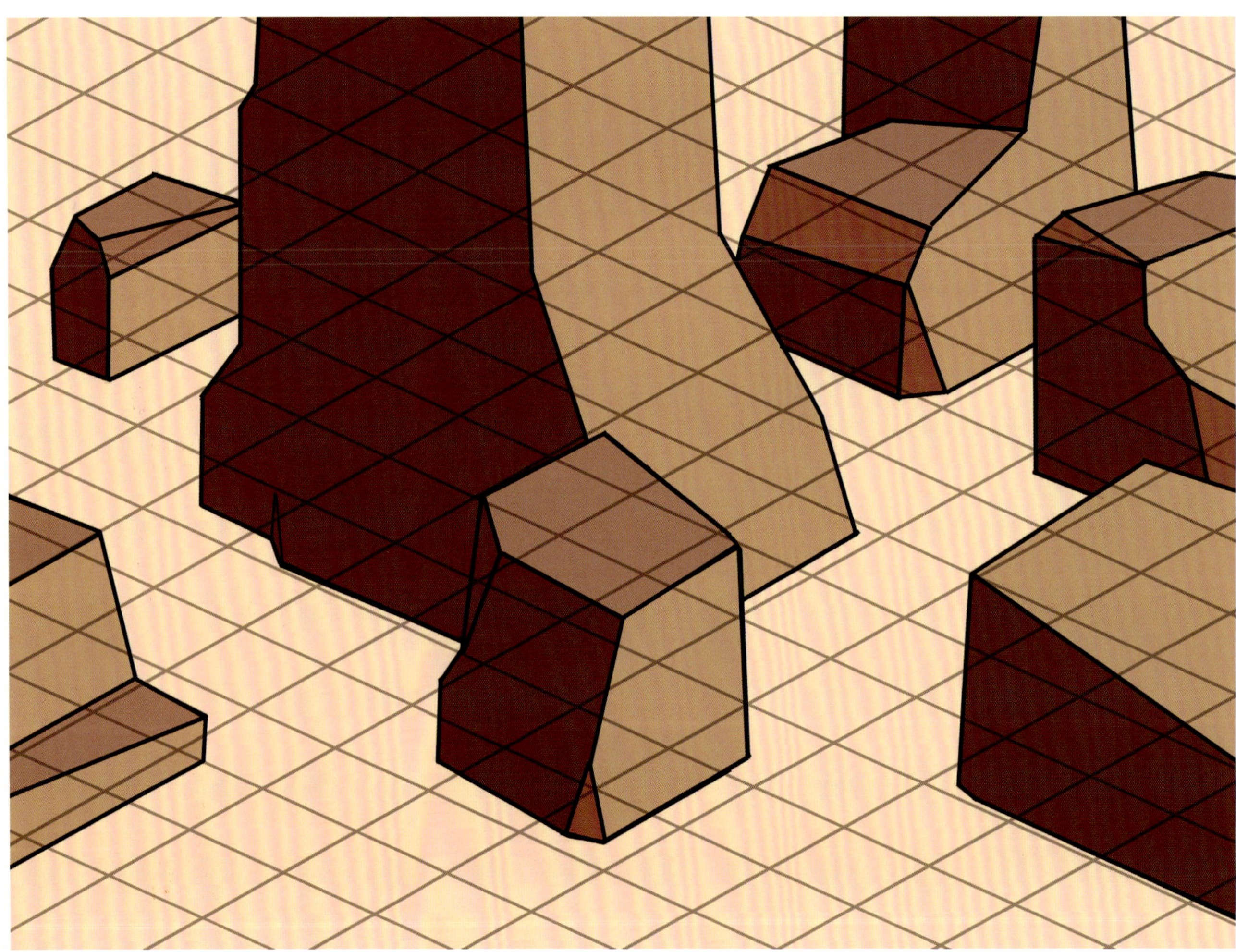

06 This demonstrates the use of isometric perspective in order to achieve a plan-like view of the landscape. This type of perspective has been widely used in simple video-game platforms.

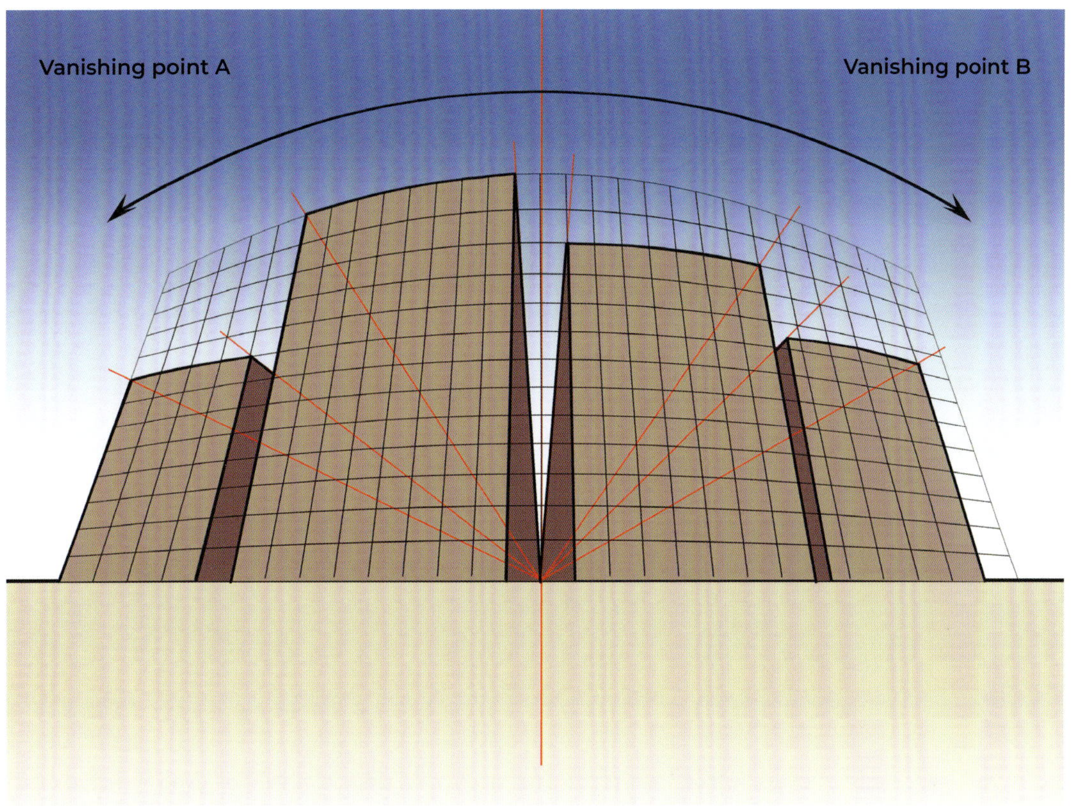

07 Here you can observe the use of curvilinear perspective in order to accommodate the distortion viewed through a wide cone of vision.

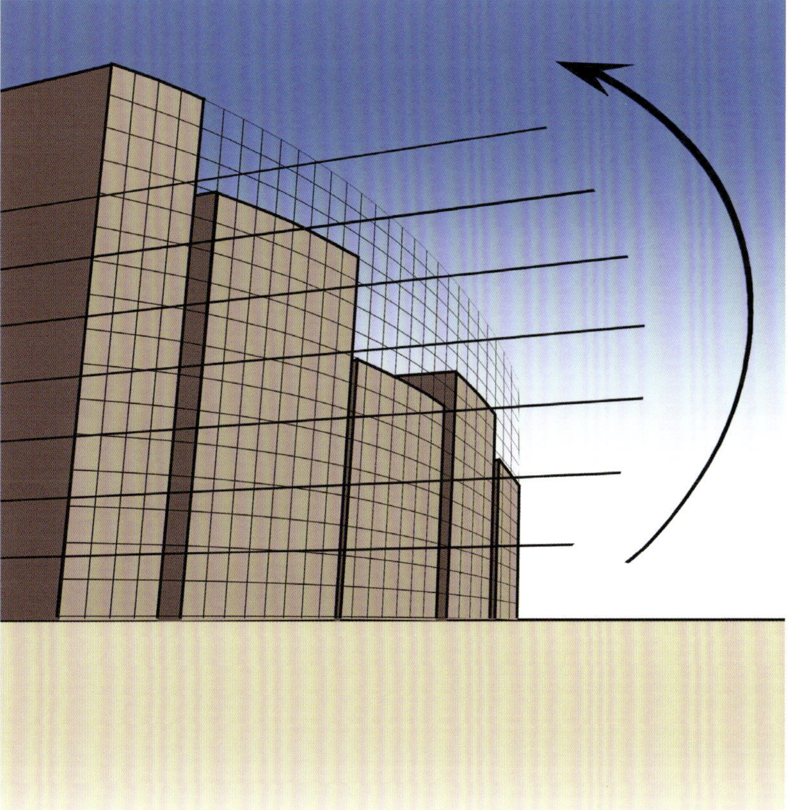

08 Here curvilinear perspective is used to create direction and dynamic movement in a scene.

EXAGGERATING PROPORTIONS

Making certain objects or figures larger or smaller than they should be in reality can convey a sense of drama or emotion. By playing with scale, objects can appear disproportionately larger or smaller within the scene to evoke a sense of wonder or distortion. Embrace distortion techniques like elongation, compression, or exaggeration to achieve creative effects.

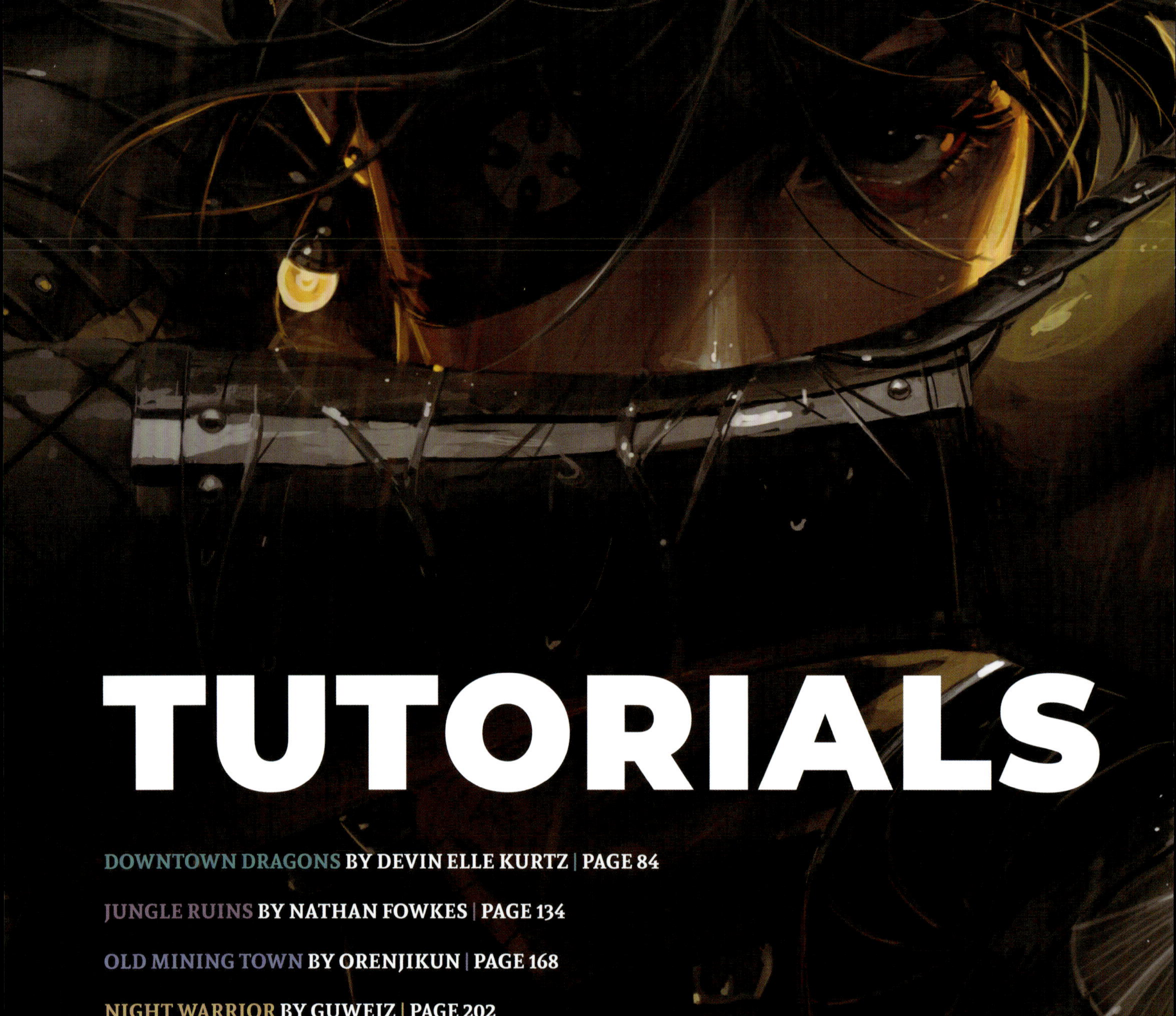

TUTORIALS

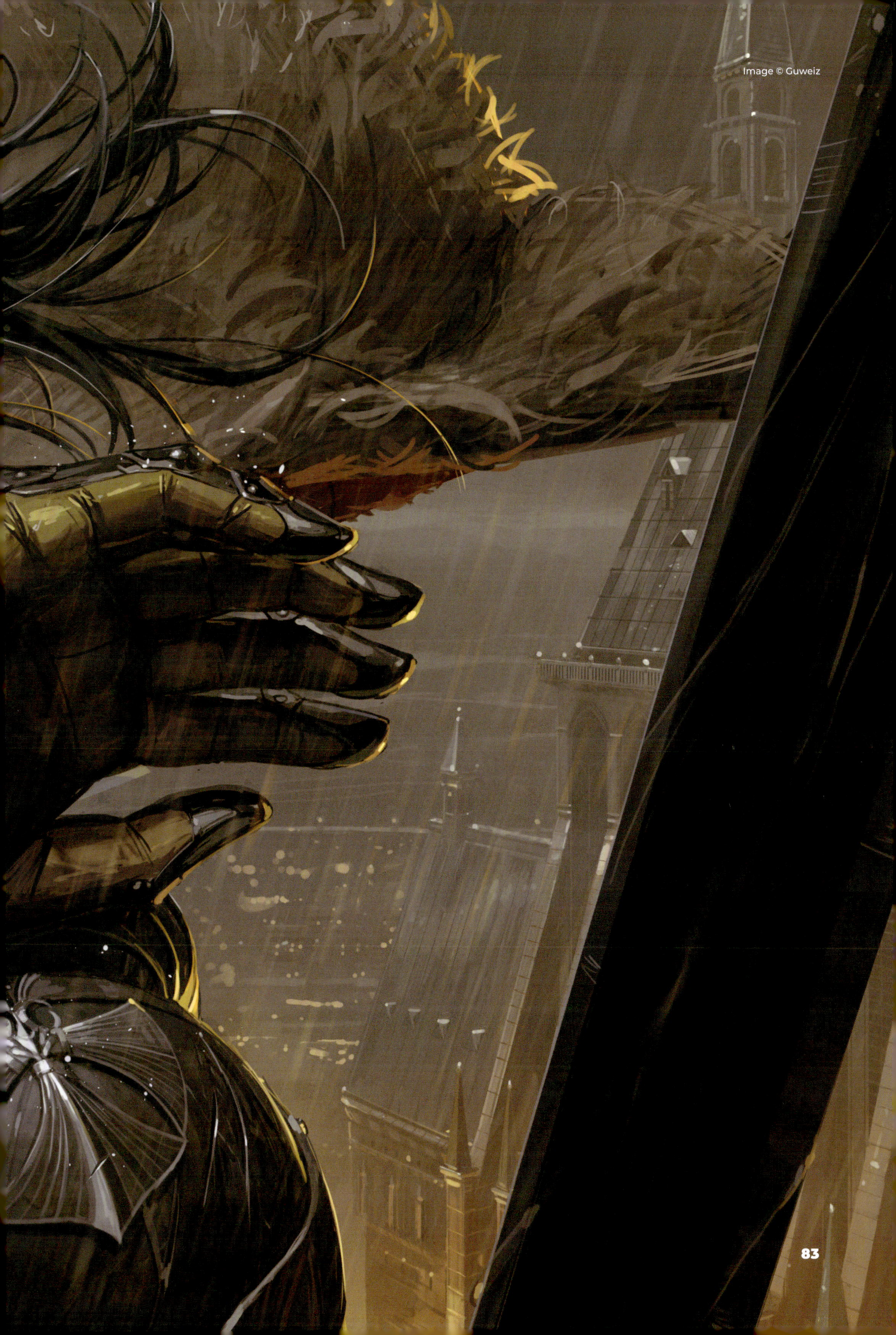

DOWNTOWN DRAGONS

DEVIN ELLE KURTZ

I always aim to create illustrations that feel visceral and alive, with an immersive quality that pulls viewers into the image and holds their attention. Lifelike perspective and depth are key tools for achieving this. In order for my illustrations to feel like real and believable spaces, they must contain convincing perspective and a true sense of depth.

Throughout my years as a production artist painting environments for both animation and games, I've developed a number of speed and efficiency tools for the purpose of achieving the maximum artistic impact, while working at the (sometimes frantic) pace that many productions require. This tutorial aims to take you through a number of these digital efficiency techniques, and to hopefully make painting complex city scenery feel less daunting and more easily achievable. Buildings are largely just a collection of boxes and rectangles – the most basic of three-dimensional forms and the easiest to put into perspective. With the right tools and knowledge, anybody can learn to construct an appealing city scene out of these simple shapes and forms. I will be using Clip Studio Paint for the initial construction drawing, followed by Adobe Photoshop for the remainder of the painting process, but you can follow along with your program or medium of choice.

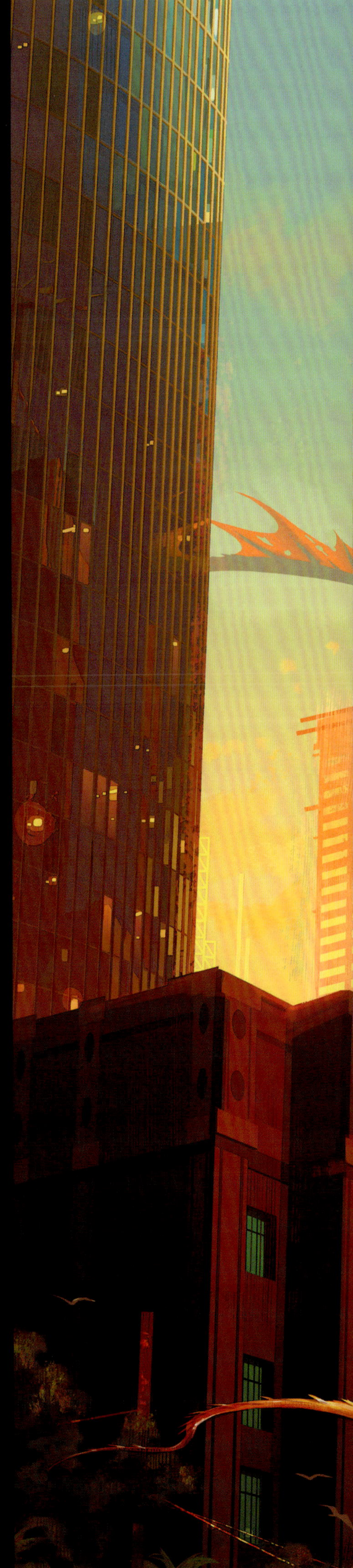

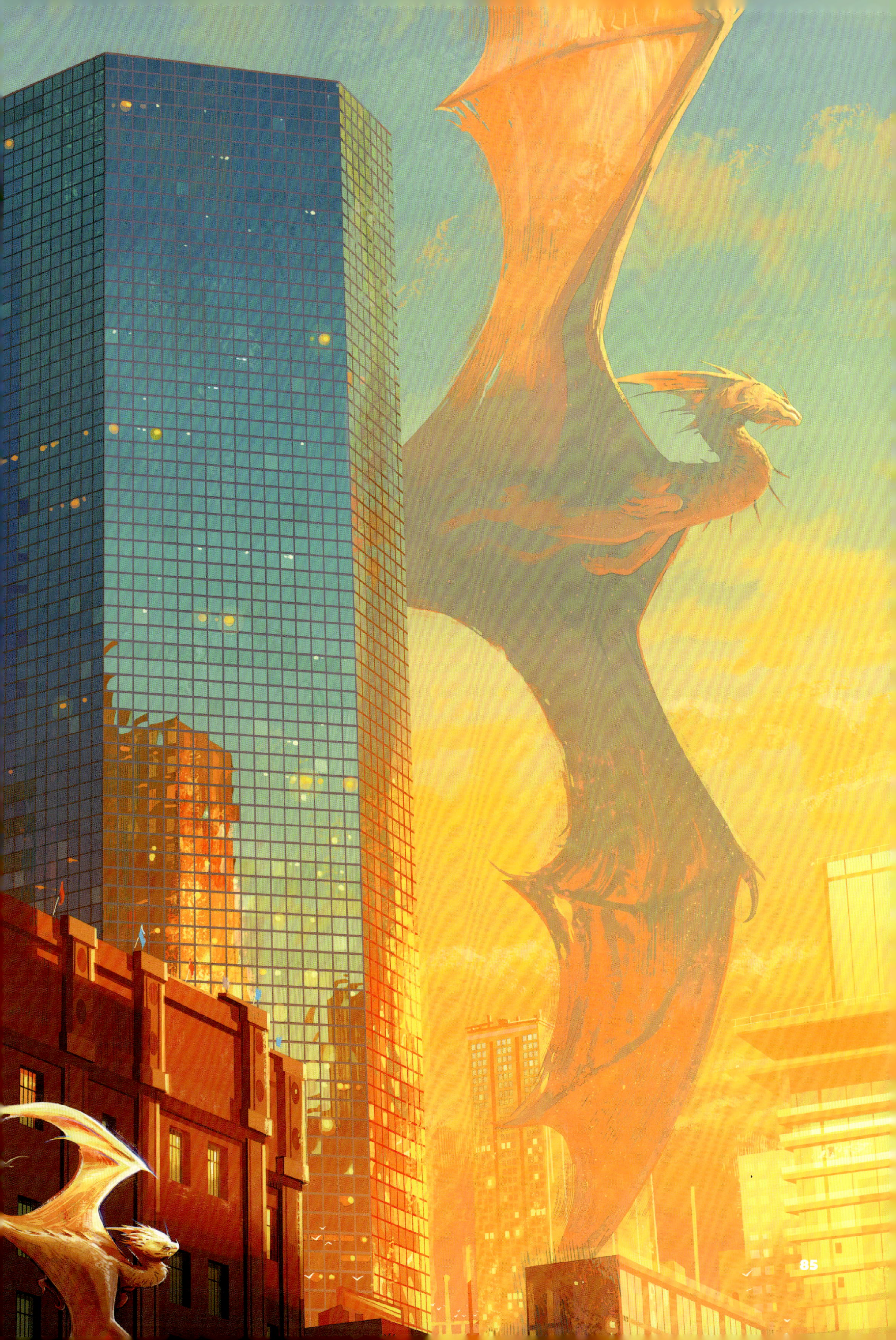

01 GATHERING REFERENCES

On the Saturday night of San Diego Comic-Con this summer, I walked through downtown San Diego with a group of friends. One of them commented that the golden hour scenery looked a lot like a 'Devin Elle Kurtz painting' – and he was right! Nestled in the hazy mist of the sea, downtown San Diego is one of my favourite locations to explore for inspiration. Towering skyscrapers reflect different pieces of the sunset sky on every face, horizontal shafts of light beam through alleyways, and the whole city glints with gold and blue.

When I set out to gather references for this project, I looked for a few things in particular: I wanted to capture buildings reflecting in the windows of other buildings, structures casting shadows onto one another, and window towers reflecting glimpses of skies out of frame **(01a–d)**. These are all city characteristics that leave me feeling awestruck and inspired by the scale and dynamism of the world around me. When you gather references for your projects, wherever you choose to go, try to walk through the streets like a director. What draws you into the depth and scale of the environment around you? What aspects of the space you're photographing leave you feeling full of awe?

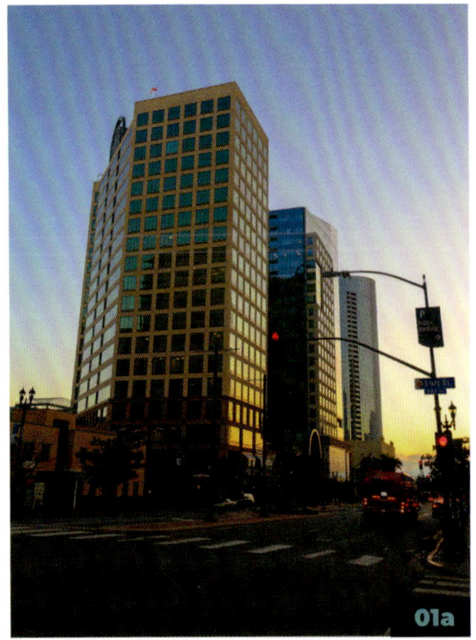

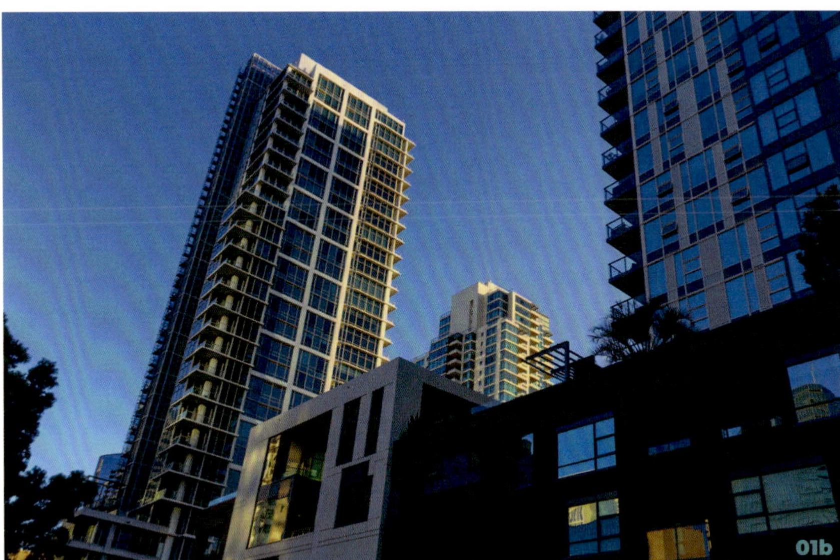

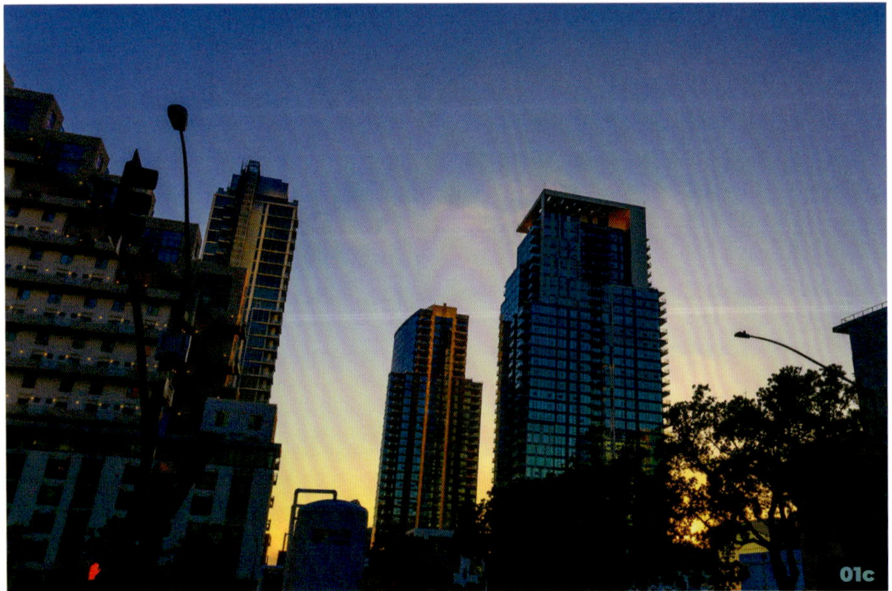

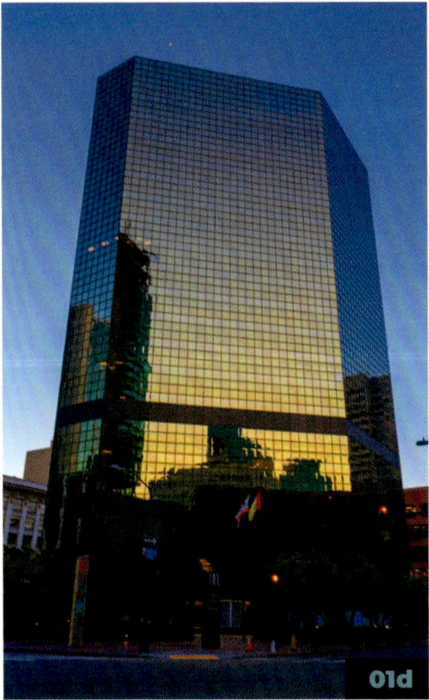

01a – 01d A few of the photos I took as reference for this illustration, shot on my trusty old Canon 6D with a wide lens, then edited in Adobe Lightroom.

EXPLORE ROOFTOPS FOR UNIQUE REFERENCE PHOTOS

If you have the chance to visit a large city, try to find a skyscraper rooftop that you can publicly access. This fresh perspective of the cityscape will lend itself to exciting reference material, so bring a camera (or your phone!).

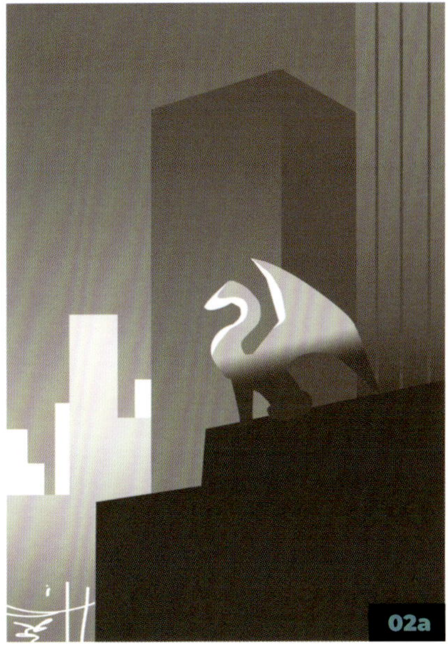

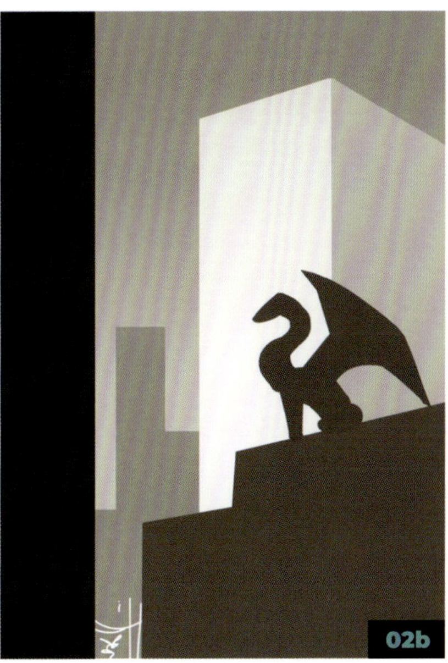

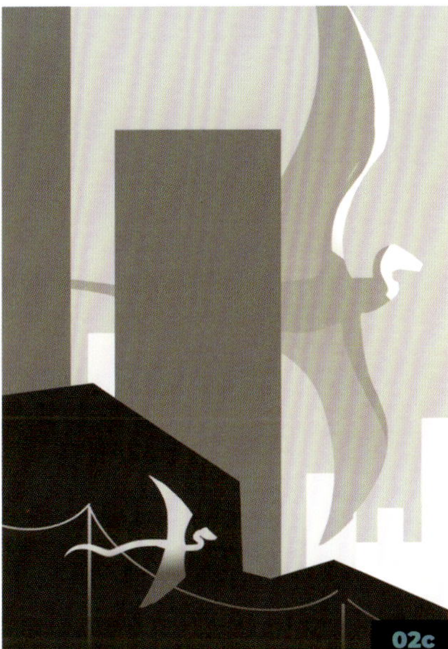

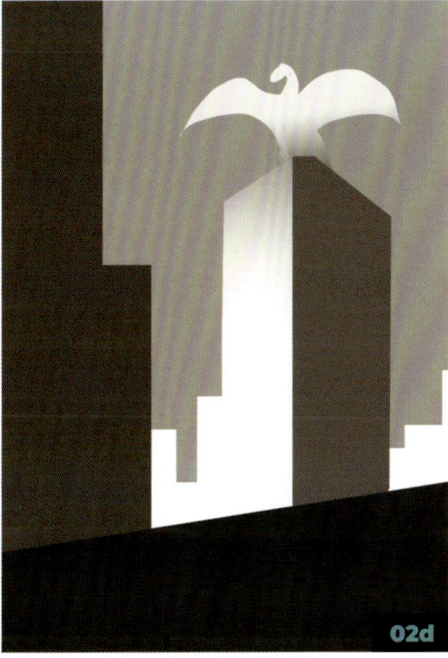

02a – 02d Various greyscale thumbnail explorations, composed with shape and value instead of line.

02 ROUGH VALUE THUMBNAILS

Rather than using just one photo as a direct reference, I want to design a brand-new composition – something inspired by bits and pieces of the photos I've taken, but stitched together into an entirely new arrangement. I'm working with the Rectangular Marquee tool, the Gradient tool, and a hard round brush. I lay down shape and value with no consideration for careful mark-making or line quality. At this stage I'm searching purely for an appealing composition in its most basic form **(02a–d)**.

If you typically sketch with line, challenge yourself to try composing in value when working with city imagery. Because cities are composed of such simple shapes, you can achieve a fairly accurate glimpse of what the finished composition might look like, even at this early thumbnail stage.

I don't concern myself with accurate perspective here, so long as the composition reflects an arrangement of shapes that could roughly exist in reality. I slowly find the story of the image as I work. From the start I know that I want to paint a piece for my city dragon series. As I sketch, I'm inspired by the concept of a mother and baby dragon, flying in and out of the long afternoon shadows cast by the skyscrapers. It presents an enticing challenge: establishing a smaller subject in the foreground, while a much larger version of the same creature must sit back in the background. This is a reversal of one of the most important depth cues – objects and subjects typically reduce in size as they move back in space.

03 SETTING UP A PERSPECTIVE GRID

Having selected the mother and baby dragon concept **(02c)**, I take it into Clip Studio Paint for a drawing pass. You can create a perspective ruler in Clip Studio Paint by selecting Layer > Ruler > Create Perspective Ruler. For this piece, I use a three-point perspective grid. A collection of lines will appear on the screen. The horizontal line is the horizon line. Start by dragging that line to wherever your horizon should be. In this case, it's down below the bottom of the canvas. Next, you can adjust the two points that sit along the horizon: the vanishing points (VP1 and VP2). These are the perspective points present in a two-point perspective grid and they always sit along the horizon line. If you're unclear about where the horizon should be in your drawing, you can place these two vanishing points first using lines in your thumbnail, and then connect them to locate the horizon. Drag the lines radiating out from the VPs to roughly match up to your thumbnail. Finally, drag the third perspective point into position. Here the third VP is placed a great distance off the canvas in the sky – this will create drama, but not too severe of an up-shot **(03a, 03b)**!

PERSPECTIVE RULERS IN CLIP STUDIO PAINT

Although I paint in Photoshop, this year I started using Clip Studio Paint's intuitive perspective rulers to build the majority of my perspective grids. It's easy to switch the ruler on and off with the visibility of the layer it occupies, which is useful. I don't always match the perspective perfectly with every line, particularly when drawing older and quirkier architecture. Sometimes imperfections are needed to create character and a feeling of history.

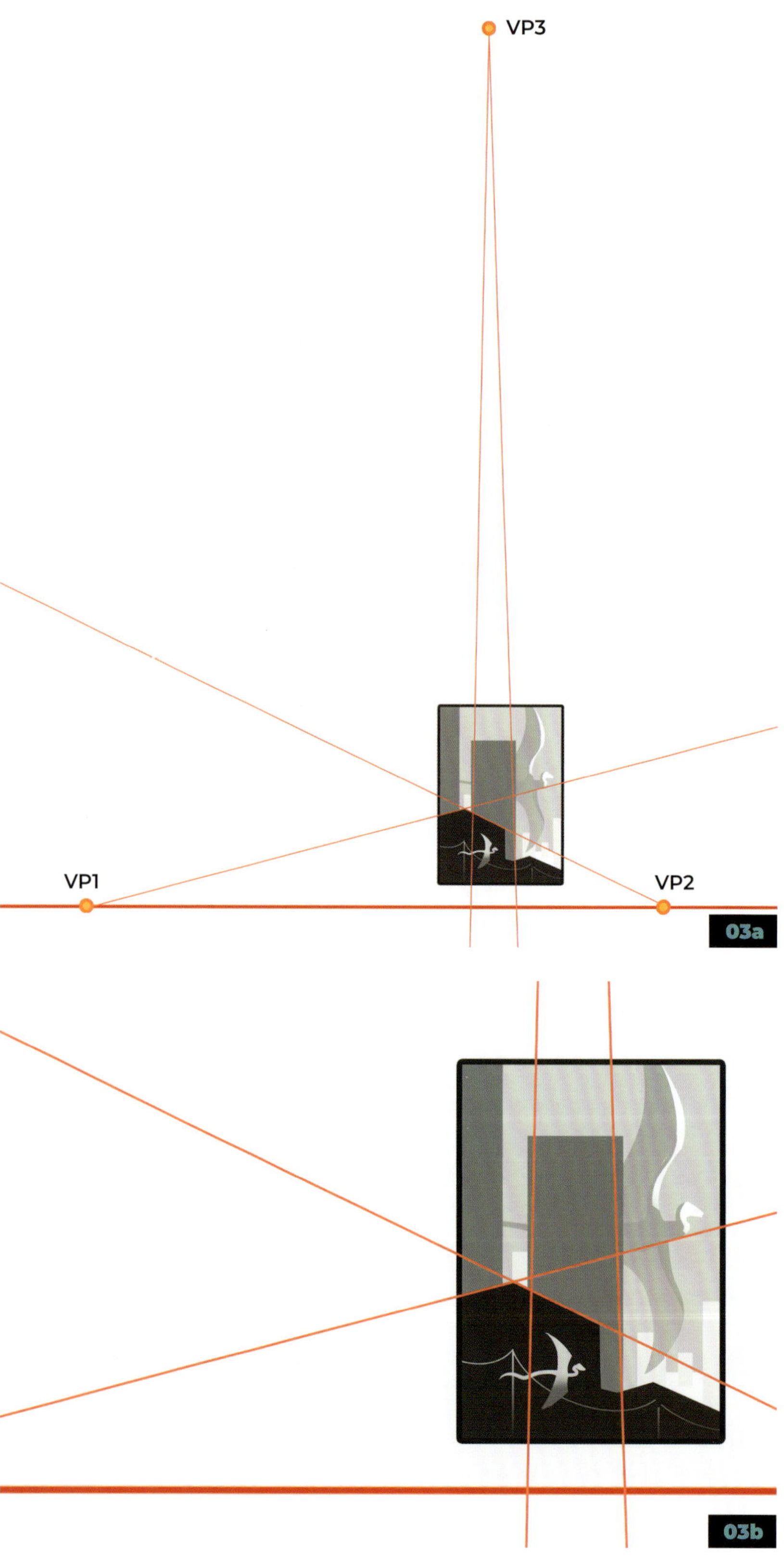

03a & 03b A recreation of the perspective grid, coloured for additional clarity. Try to match the perspective lines roughly to the thumbnail.

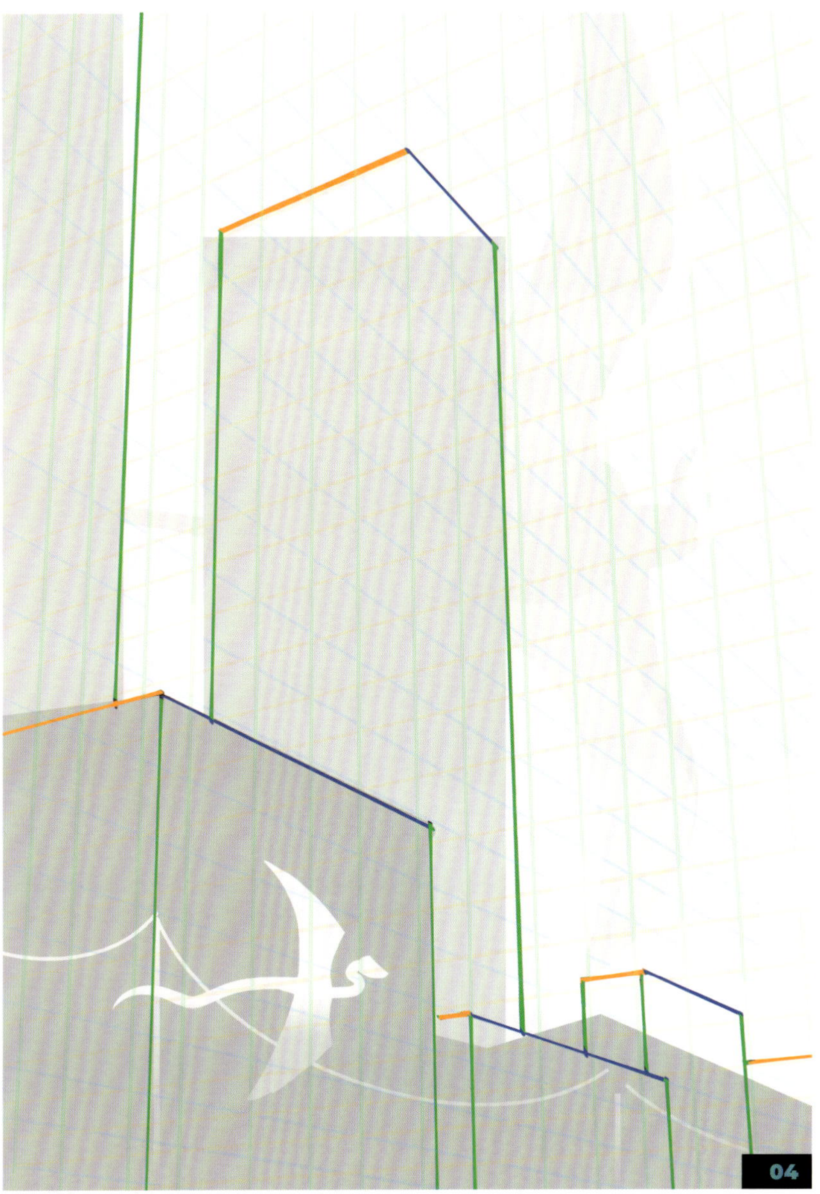

04 An early block-in sketch of the cuboid buildings, colour-coded for clarity.

04 SKETCHING THE BASIC BUILDING BLOCKS

If the perspective in your thumbnail is too nonsensical to match easily, you may need to experiment. Place the vanishing points (VPs) somewhere in the general vicinity, try it out, and see how the sketch looks. You can always move the VPs and try again if the resulting perspective is too flat or too severe. Over time, you will gain an intuition for how the position of each VP will impact the perspective in your drawing.

Once you're satisfied with how the perspective looks, it's time to turn down the opacity on the thumbnail and create a block-in pass. Each cuboid building in three-point perspective will have a set of lines that converge to VP1, a set of lines that converge to VP2, and a set of lines that converge to VP3. If you find yourself getting confused, it may be useful for you to use a different colour to sketch each set of converging lines to encourage your brain to start separating the sets from one another. The goal is to eventually be able to easily distinguish which VP any line in your drawing converges to, even when drawing in one solid colour.

LEARN TO SEE PERSPECTIVE BY DRAWING OVER PHOTOS

If you struggle to see and understand perspective, try tracing directly on top of city photos and following the perspective lines until they converge. Find the VP1 and VP2 by tracing the horizontal lines of the buildings, and then connect them to find the horizon line. Next, trace the vertical lines to see whether they converge above or below the horizon line. This exercise will help your brain start to make connections between what you see visually and the underlying perspective.

05 CUTTING CORNERS

Composing with box forms is an easy way to quickly lay in a city. Boxes are the easiest form to put into perspective. If you want to spice up your boxy skyline and introduce more interesting building shapes, you can carve out sections of some boxes to create new planes and more unique silhouettes.

Draw two parallel lines in perspective from front to back, top to bottom, or side to side on two adjacent planes **(A)**. Then, connect the end points of those lines **(B)** to create a new plane cutting through your box form at a diagonal angle **(C).** This technique can be used to efficiently craft all sorts of interesting buildings, without needing to

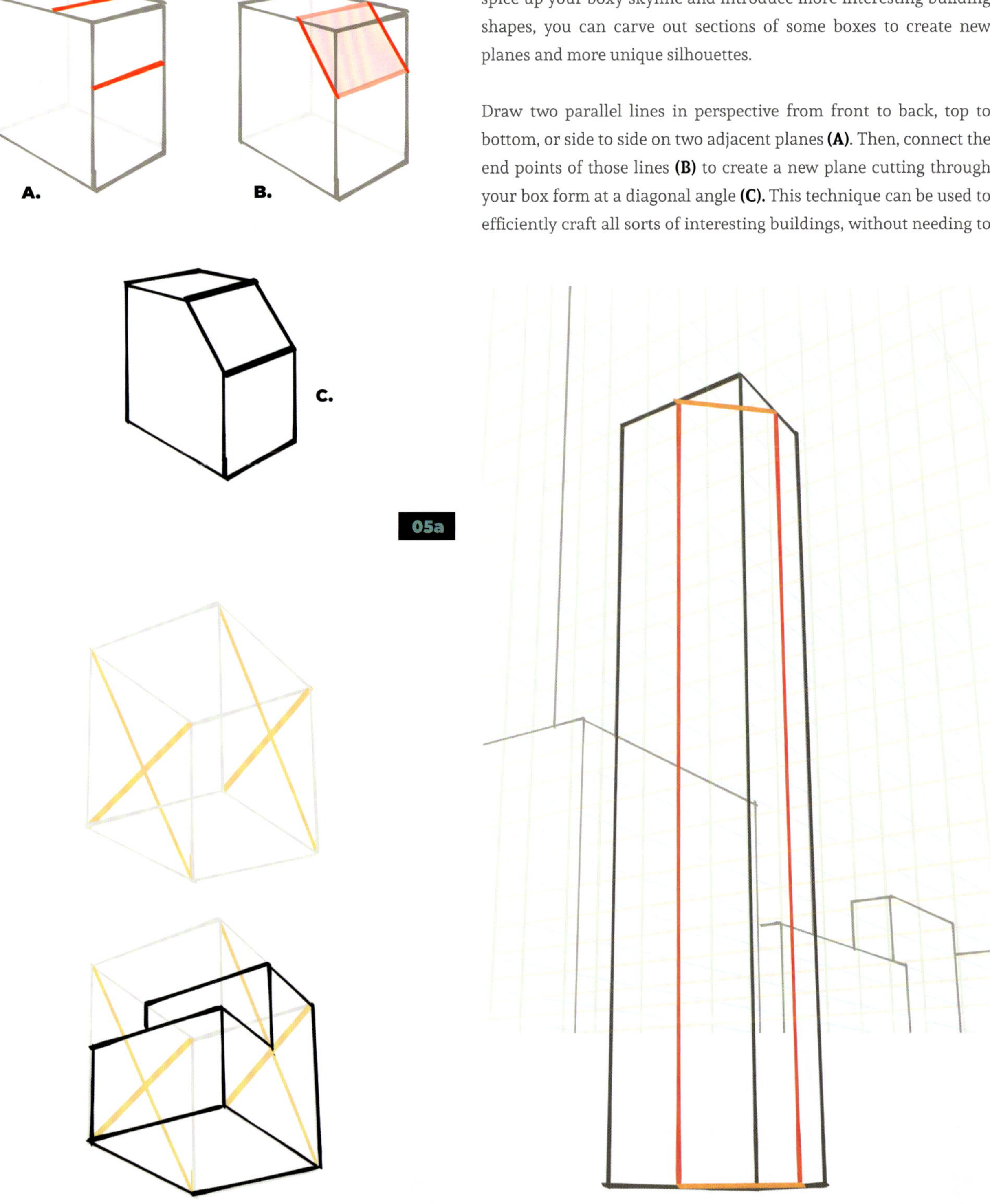

05a – 05c I use the corner-cutting technique to carve out a fifth face on the main building in my drawing.

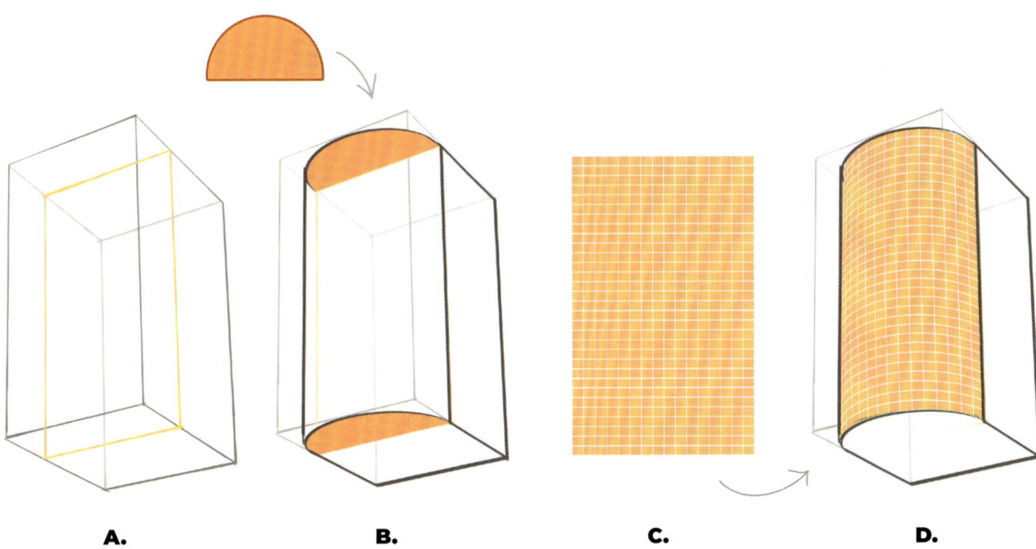

06a An example of adding a curved face to a box.

use reference points on the horizon line. Use this technique to add diagonal slants or make a building with five (or more) sides **(05a)**.

You can quite easily find the midpoint of any plane in perspective by drawing an X from corner to corner **(05b)**. This technique can be used to carve out planes or sections in a proportional way, or to divide buildings into even sections **(05c)**.

06 DRAWING A CURVED BUILDING

It's possible to add a curved front face to a box too **(06a)**, which can be translated onto a curved building **(06b)**. First, cut a vertical plane out of somewhere in the front-middle section of the box by following the perspective **(A)**. To create a subtle curve, cut out a shallow section. For a deep, round curve, cut a plane further into the middle of the box. Second, drag a circle out using the Shape tool in your chosen software, then use the Rectangular Marquee to cut the circle in half and delete the bottom half. Select Transform > Distort if using Photoshop or Procreate, or Transform > Free Transform if using Clip Studio Paint, and a bound box will appear around your half circle. Match the corners of the bound box to the four top corners of the section you cut out of your box. Repeat with the base, draw around the perimeter, and you will have an easy, efficiently drawn, curved building **(B)**. To add windows that match the curve, you can draw the window facade flat **(C)** and then use Transform > Warp to curve it around the building, using the top and bottom curves as guides **(D)**.

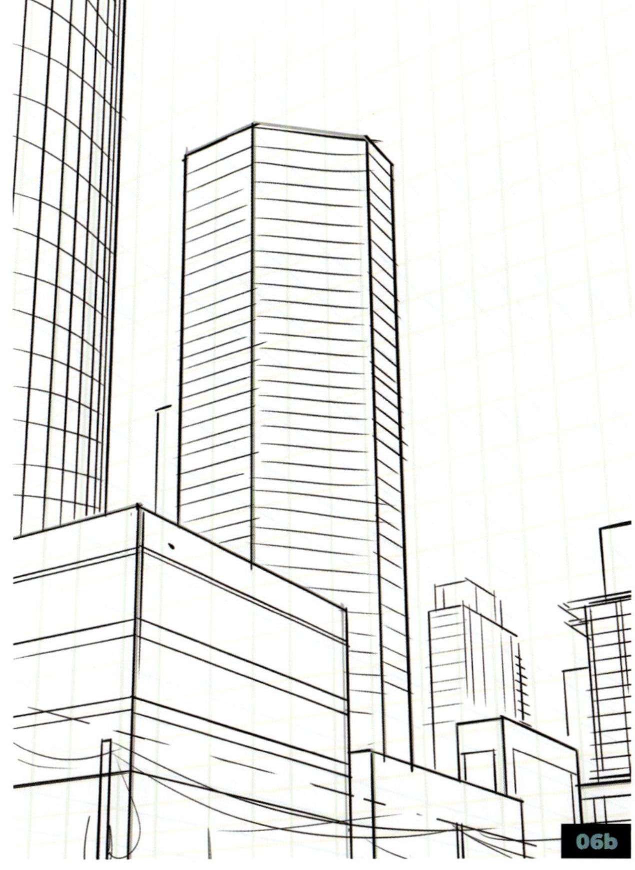

06b I eyeball a curved building on the left of my drawing. I'll figure out the curves more precisely at the painting stage.

07 SKETCHING THE DRAGONS

As I sketch the dragons, I envision them in the real, three-dimensional space they occupy. I want the mother dragon to cut through the buildings, forcing viewers to recognize the depth in the scene. Overlap is a key tool for depicting depth. I make sure that she's nestled amidst the buildings: in front of distant buildings and behind foreground structures. Overlaps in busy city scenes can be challenging to achieve without causing tangents (places where two lines awkwardly touch and make the spatial positioning unclear). Whenever possible, try not to create overlap at the very edge of a form. The more breathing space you can give each overlap, the better visual clarity there will be. Generally, try to avoid overlapping right in the middle of a form. A 30:70 or 20:80 distribution will, in most cases, feel more organic and appealing. Finally, avoid placing objects too close to one another without overlap. The tension can become distracting and produces a flattening effect.

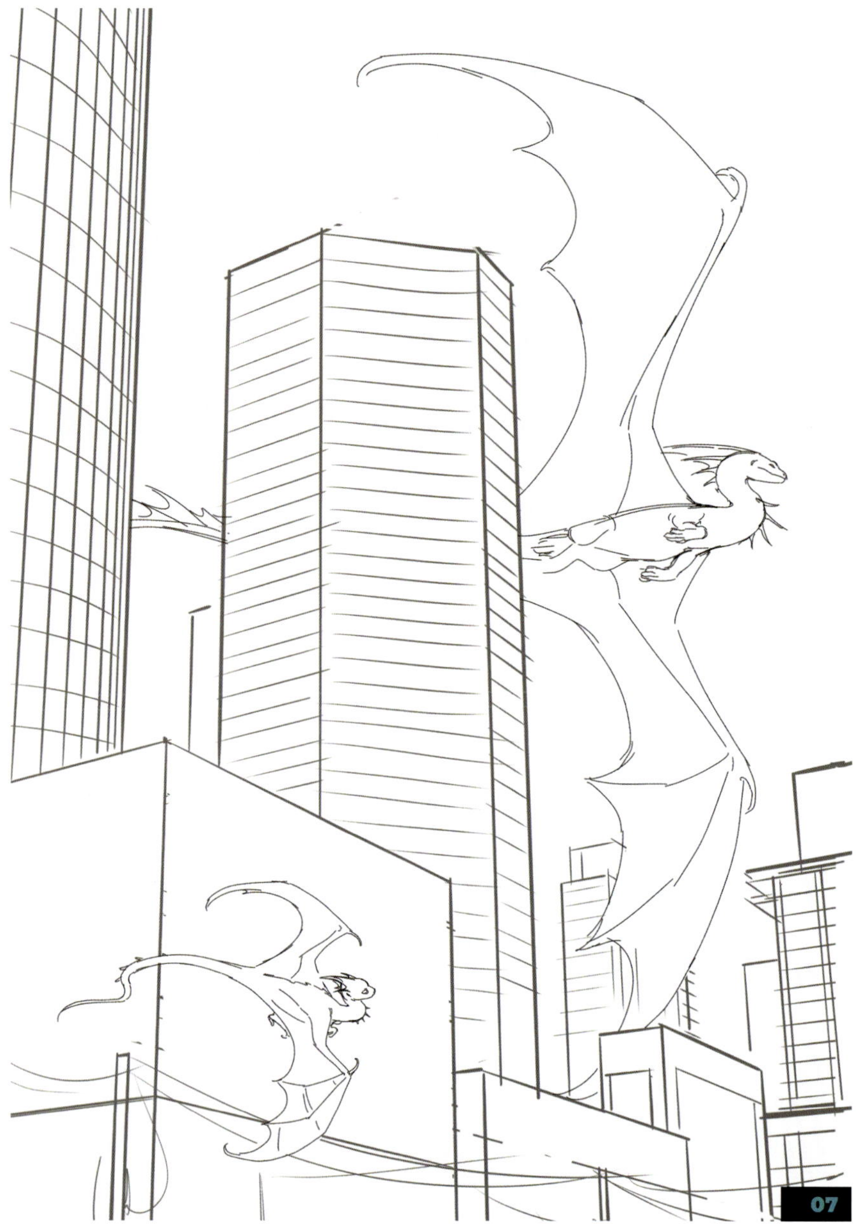

07 The finished sketch, depicting the dragons flying through the city.

08 PAINTING A VALUE KEY

I use Photoshop to expand my initial thumbnail into a full value key. The general formula I follow is to decrease the contrast and narrow the range of value as objects recede into the distance. In the world around us, the space between objects is full of fog, debris, and other particles. The further you are from an object, the more particles will be in the air between your eyes and the object. These particles cause distant objects to present with lower contrast, fewer details, and fuzzier edges within shadows.

The baby dragon is closest in space, followed by the foreground building it silhouettes against. I give this lower left section of the painting the widest range of values, from very dark darks to very light lights. I methodically decrease the contrast and narrow the value range of each subsequent spatial plane of the environment, with the most distant buildings simplifying into a very narrow value range.

I use shadow and light to create a sense of depth and distance between the foreground, middle-ground, and background buildings. Sunlight cuts through a gap and illuminates the distant buildings, while the foreground and middle-ground buildings remain mostly in shadow. This separates the foreground, middle ground, and background from one another.

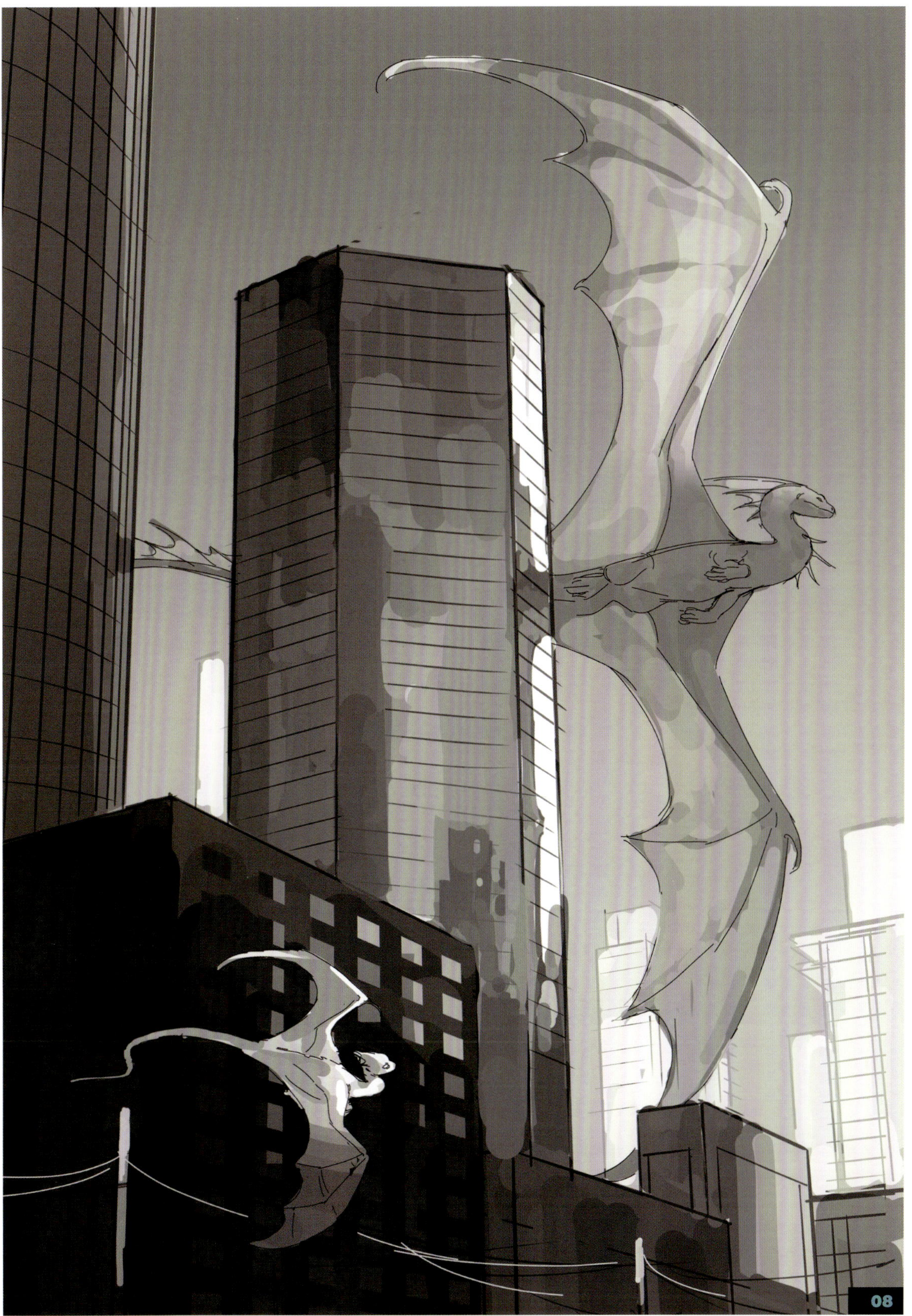

08 The final value key for my painting; the foreground contains a wide value range, while the background has a narrower value range.

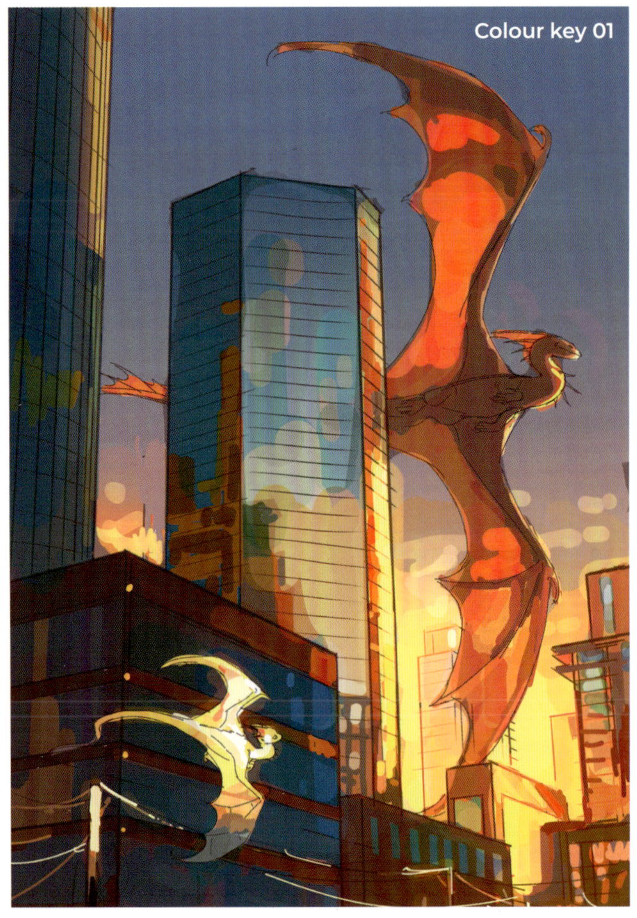

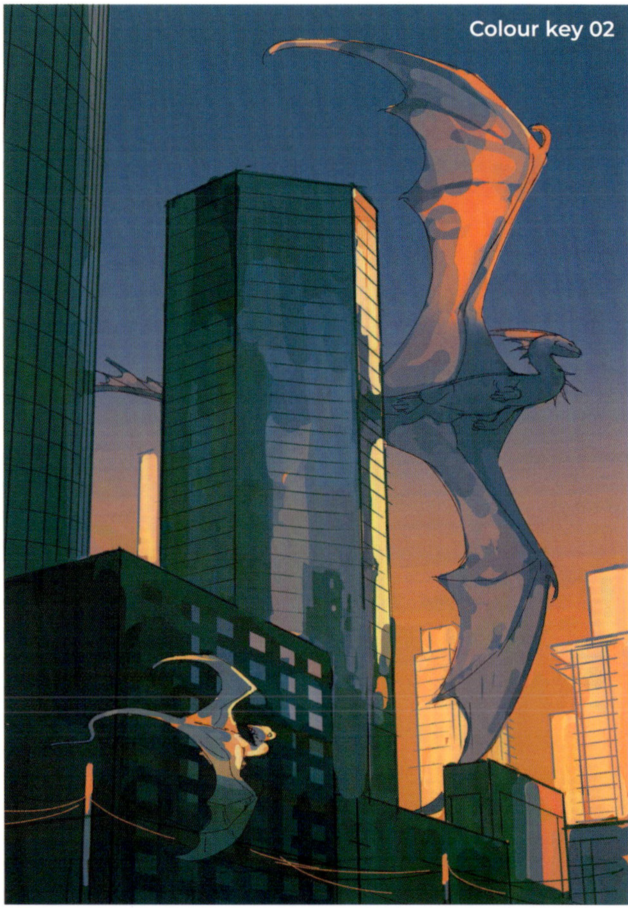

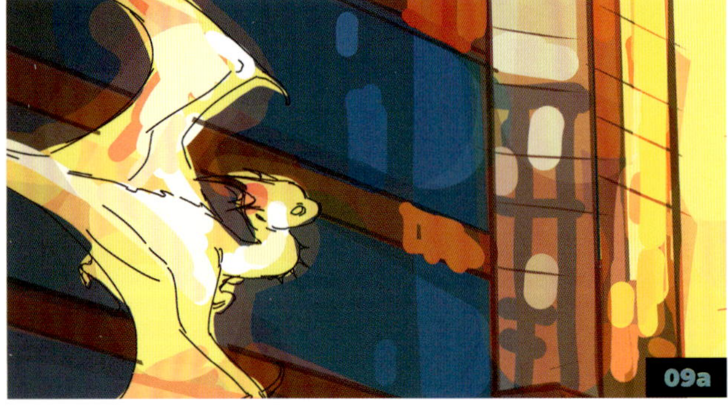

09a Colour key 01: painted directly from the line art.

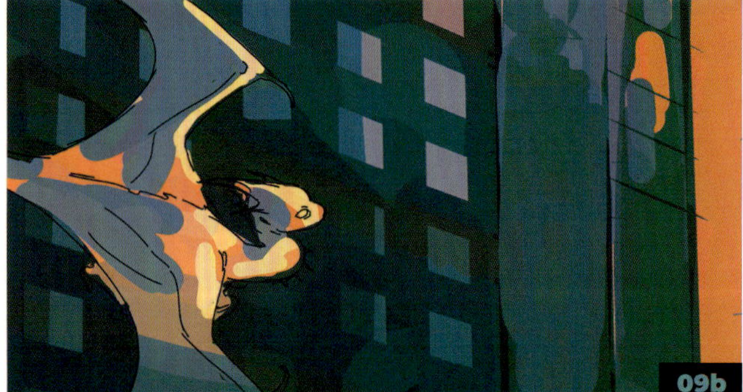

09b Colour key 02: created using a gradient map with little to no paint on top.

09 PAINTING COLOUR KEYS

I use a variety of Photoshop techniques to explore colour and light in my colour keys. In some, I start fresh from the line art alone **(09a, 09d)**, and rather than trying to make use of the value key, I use it only as reference and experiment directly with painted colour. In others, I start by using a gradient map on top of my value key to experiment with colour and mood **(09b)**, and then paint on top until I achieve a pleasing result **(09c)**.

If you want to try exploring colour using a gradient map, you can do so in Photoshop, Procreate, Clip Studio Paint, or other digital painting software. Gradient maps work by mapping colours you select to each value zone of an image. In order to retain your value structure, you will need to pick colours that generally align in value to each value range you assign them to.

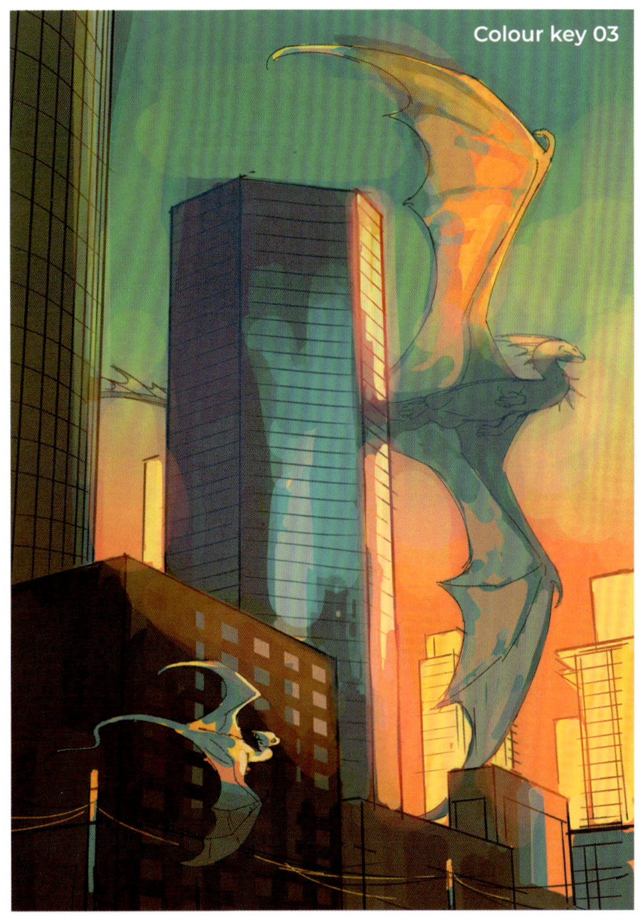

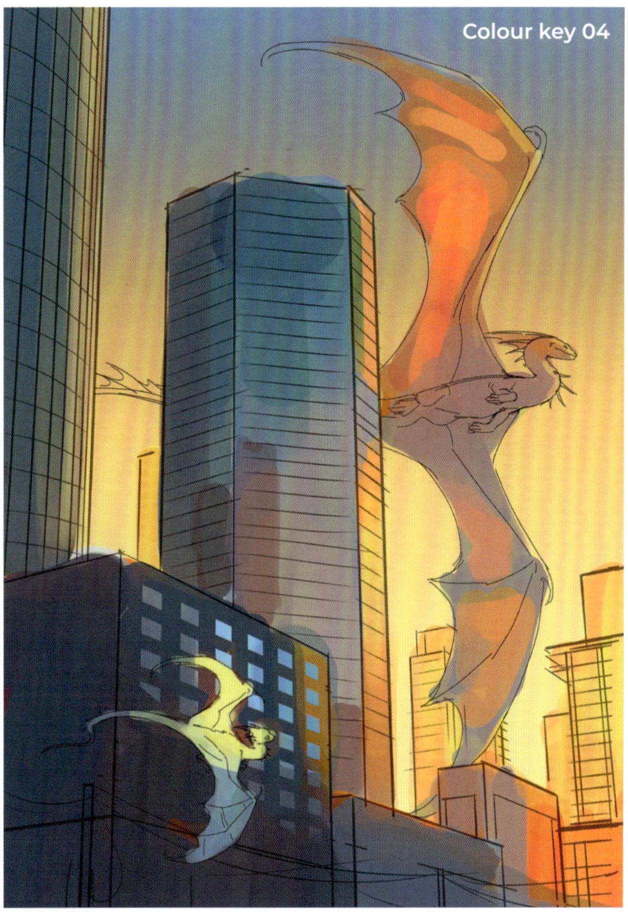

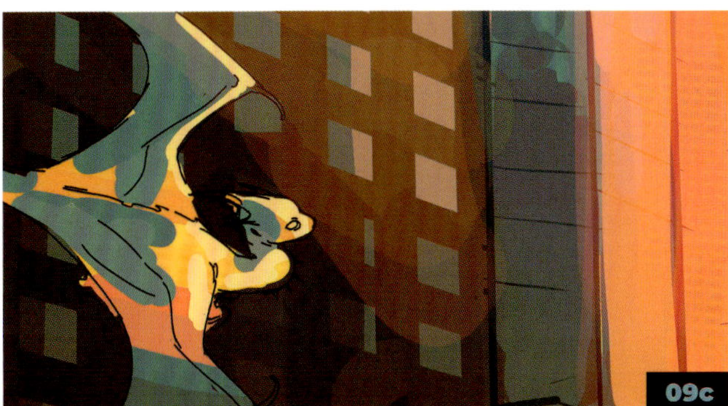

09c Colour key 03: I used a gradient map initially, before finishing by painting directly on top.

09d Colour key 04: painted directly from the line art.

After experimenting, I'm happiest with **09c**, and decide to move forward with it, while remaining open to changing it as I paint. I'll talk more about how the colours I chose interact with depth in the coming steps.

USING BOXES TO CONSTRUCT MORE CITY FORMS

This tip will show you how to use basic boxes as guidelines to sketch all kinds of unique forms in perspective. All you need is a little geometric knowledge and the Transform tool. These skills can be used to add set-dressing and personality to your cityscapes.

Starting from a fairly even box **(A)**, use the Shape tool to drag out a perfect circle, and then transform that circle so that the four corners of the bound box match up perfectly with the four corners of the top and bottom planes of your box **(B)**. Now, if you connect the top and bottom circles **(C)**, you have a cylinder in perspective. You can construct all sorts of city details out of a cylinder: round buildings, poles, and silos to name a few. Using the 'X' technique to find the midpoint (see page 90), you can create a cone-shaped roof **(D)** and turn it into a water tower **(E)**.

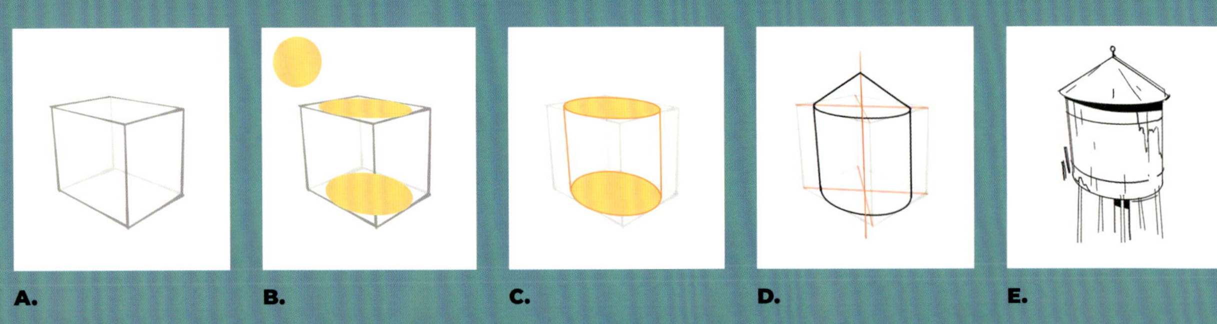

A. **B.** **C.** **D.** **E.**

If you carve a slanting triangular section out of the top of a long box **(F)**, you can construct a rubbish bin **(G)**.

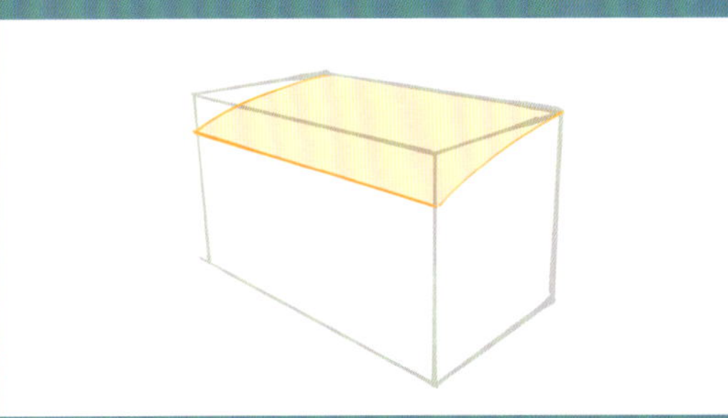

F.

G.

Using the 'X' technique to find the centreline of a tall, narrow box **(H, I)** will allow you to construct a welcome sign **(J)**.

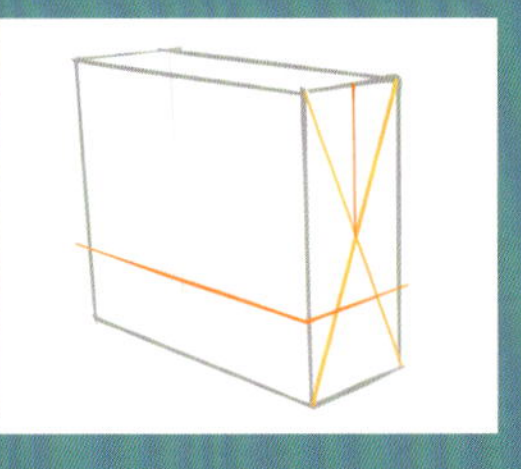

H.

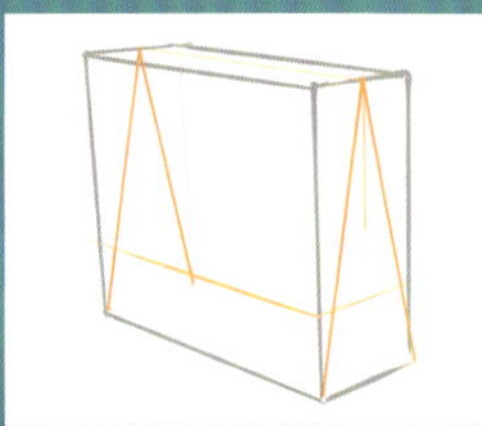

I.

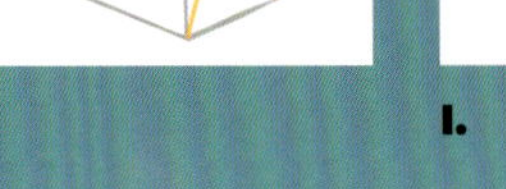

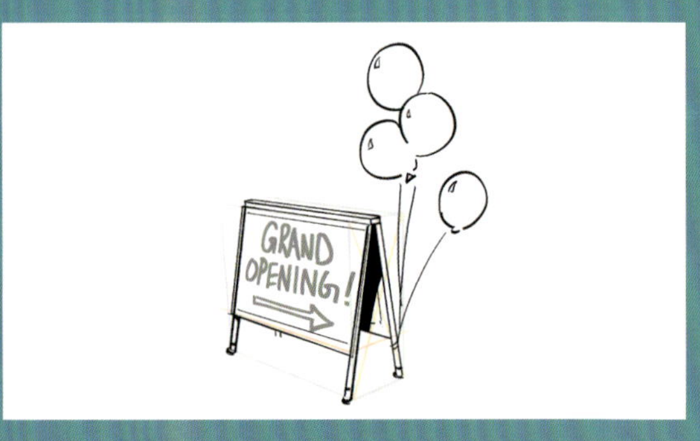

J.

You can easily place complex forms in perspective by transforming the flat version of the complex face onto both the back and front of the box it occupies **(K)**, then connecting each corner following the perspective grid. Here I construct a letter from a giant sign that could sit atop a skyscraper, generously covered in bird droppings **(L)**.

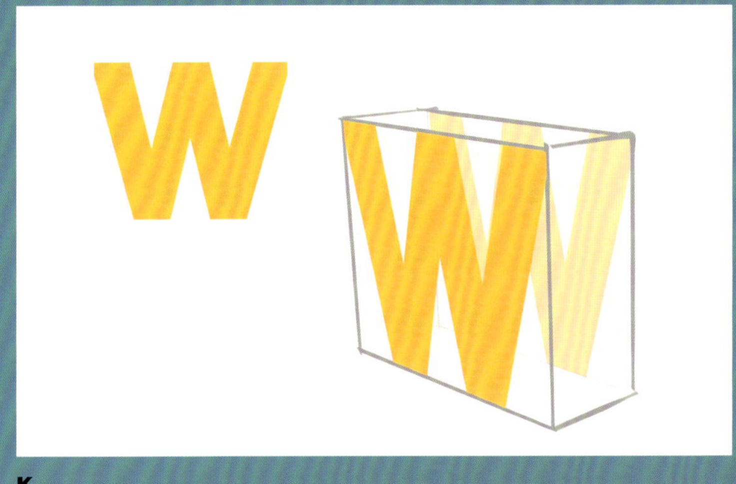

K.

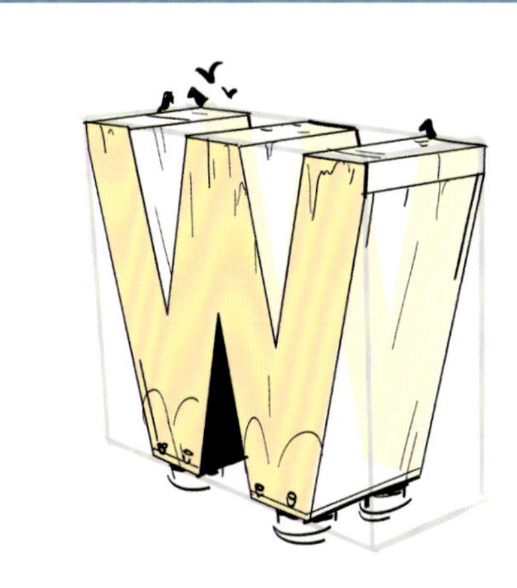

L.

If you struggle with conceptualizing the way forms can be 'carved' out of a 3D box, try playing around in the free web version of SketchUp. You can use the Rectangle tool to draw out a rectangle on the ground plane, then use the Push/Pull tool to pull it up into a building. Next, use the Curve or Line tool to make a cutaway shape on a plane of your choosing. Here I use the Curve tool to create a curve on the top plane **(M)**. I use the Push/Pull tool to carve it out of the box form **(N)**, and watch as the new carved-out form appears right in front of my eyes **(O)**!

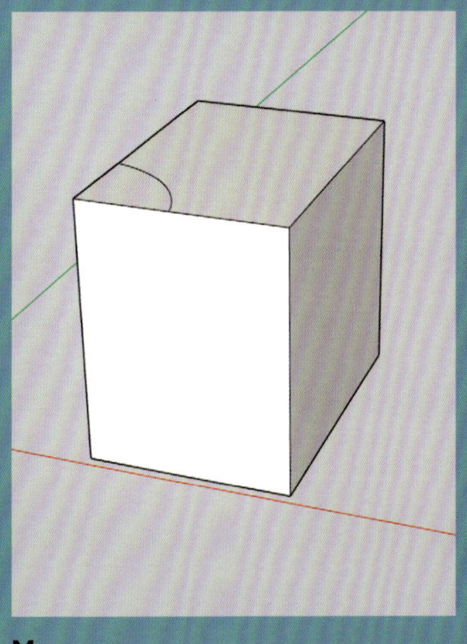

M.

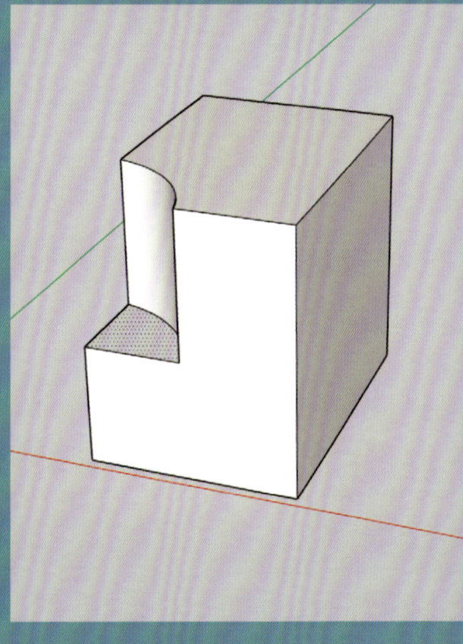

N.

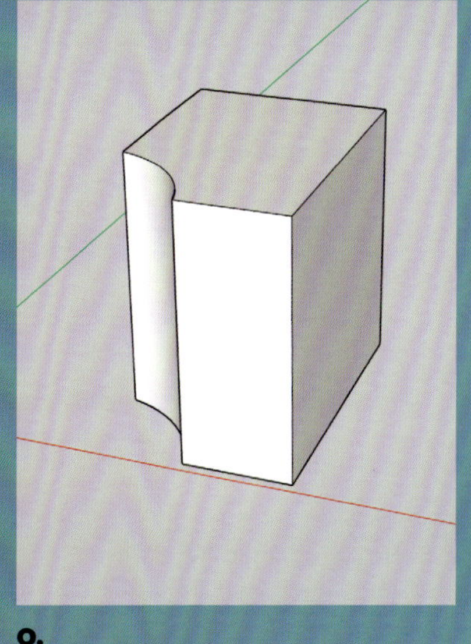

O.

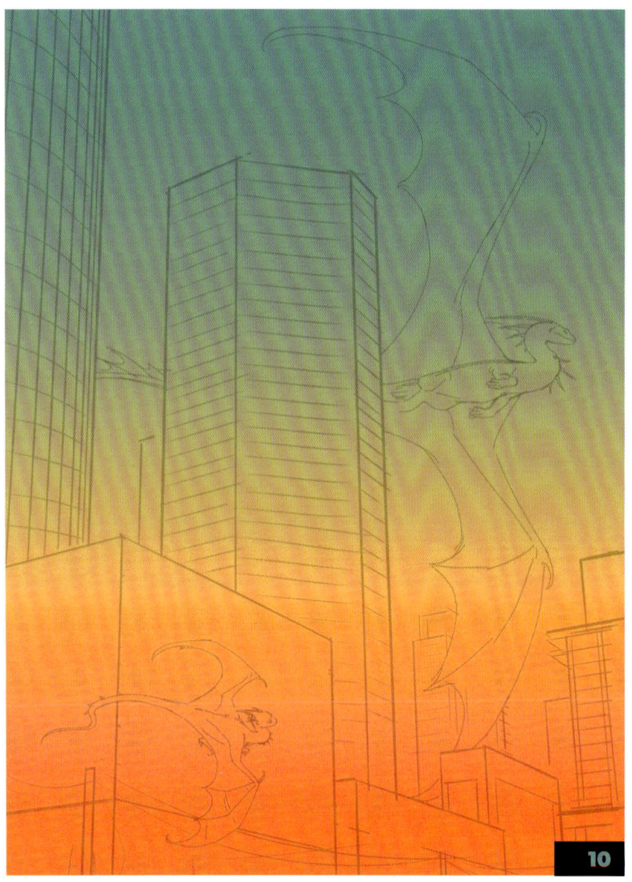

10 The sky gradient is established using the Gradient tool.

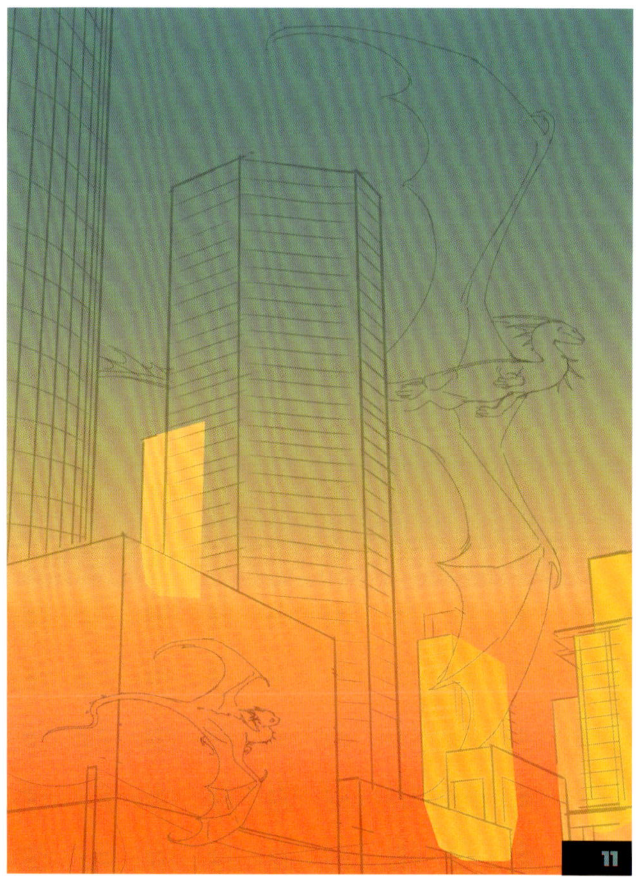

11 The distant buildings are blocked in using the Lasso tool.

10 SETTING UP MY LAYERS

With a finished sketch, value key, and colour key ready to use, it's time to paint. I lower the opacity on my sketch layer and begin work, starting by setting up folders: one for each general plane of the image. At the bottom of my layers is the sky folder, then the distant buildings, then the mama dragon, followed by the middle-ground buildings, the foreground buildings, and finally the baby dragon at the top of my layer structure. When organizing my layers, I generally put the 'closest' object at the top of my Layer menu, while putting the object 'furthest away', which is often the sky, at the bottom of the Layer menu.

Keeping the different spatial planes layered and grouped like this is immensely helpful when painting an image with a lot of depth. It allows you to easily add global light and atmosphere to each spatial layer, plus to always retain the overall silhouettes of each section.

With my layers and groups established, I scroll down to my sky folder and use the Gradient tool to establish the colours of the sky. A layer of thick atmosphere is catching warm light towards the horizon, and I use a saturated salmon pink to indicate that layer of fog.

11 BLOCKING WITH THE LASSO TOOL

I love using the Polygonal Lasso tool to block in buildings, as it's exceptionally speedy. I click on each corner of the building, complete the lasso shape, and then fill the building in with the appropriate colour. Keyboard or button shortcuts also help to speed up this process, allowing me to instinctually move between tools. In Clip Studio Paint, the rectangular selection tool is capable of automatically following your perspective rulers. This can speed up the process of blocking in buildings in perspective.

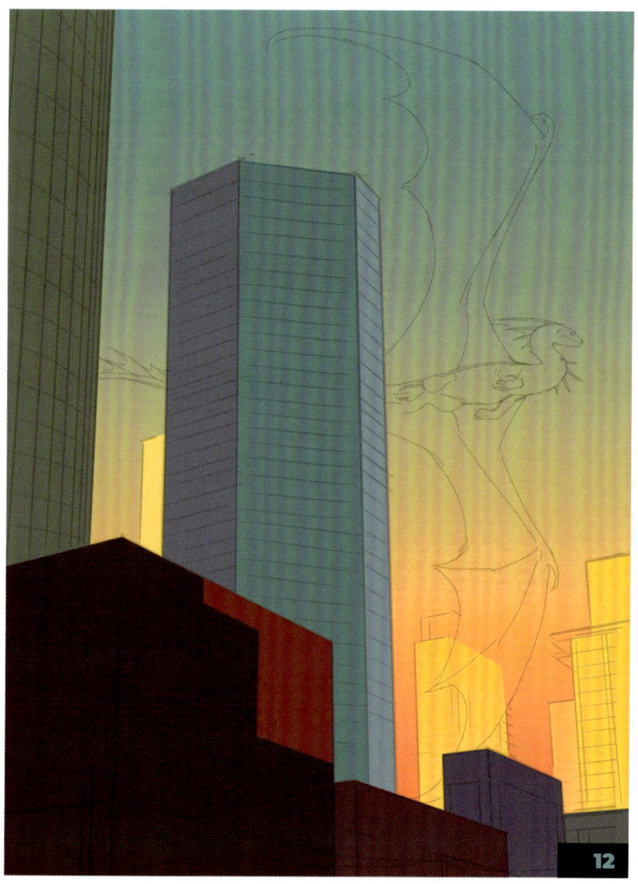

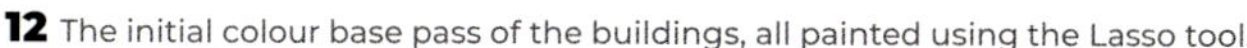

12 The initial colour base pass of the buildings, all painted using the Lasso tool.

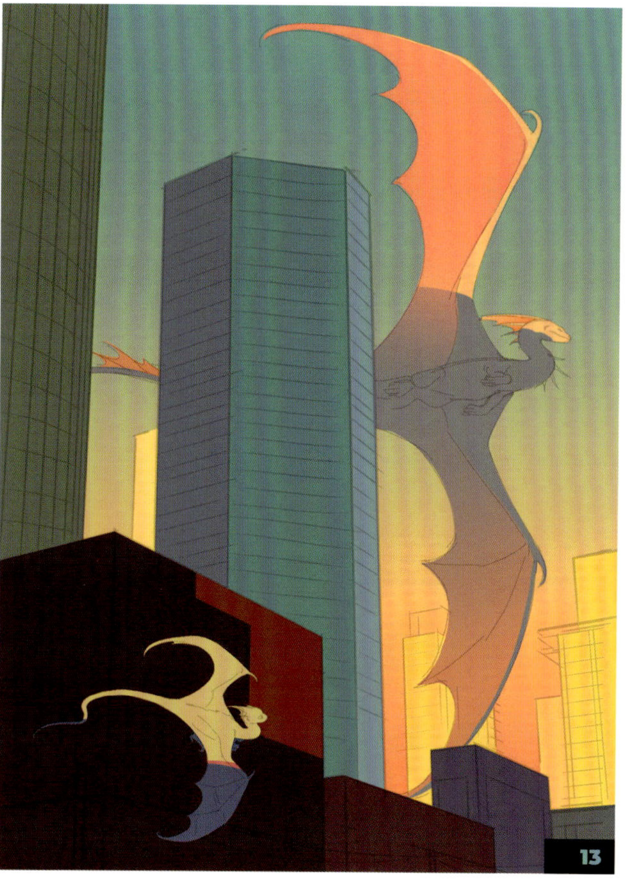

13 The initial colour base of the dragons, blocked in with the Lasso tool.

12 SETTING UP DEPTH WITH HUE

Hue can be used to indicate depth and create a feeling of distance, in addition to the value structure. Grouping the spatial planes of the environment into general hue families, distinct from one another, helps to visually separate each layer. Even in this very simple block-in stage, there is already a sense of the depth. The most distant zone of the image groups into light warms. The middle zone groups into midtone cools. The foreground graduates into rich, deep warms. These hue cues aid the value and size cues in establishing a clear read of the distance and depth.

13 BLOCKING IN THE DRAGONS

I pull colours that are already found within the composition to establish the dragons, but lean the lightest yellow towards a whiter cream to give them a unique pop against the backdrop. Pulling from comfortably within the existing palette for the main subjects creates harmony within the image, but means you must be strategic about placement, value, and silhouette in order to achieve a clean and instantaneous read of the scene.

For example, with the mama dragon, I place the shadow across the body very purposefully. It allows the bottom two-thirds of the dragon to silhouette neutral-cool against the warm yellow sky. In the top third of her body, the warm creams and pinks silhouette lightly and warmly against the cool, darker sky. This creates contrast and separation all the way around the dragon, even as the backdrop graduates colour drastically from top to bottom. I make sure that the colour of the mama dragon is more muted and dull than the buildings she passes behind, to stay in line with my value and hue formula for depth.

The baby dragon is easy to silhouette lightly against the dark foreground building, but I have to be careful not to lose the cool shadowed wing. The cool versus warm contrast against the building allows the silhouette to remain readable, even with the shadow transition across the lower wing.

MAKING WINDOW BRUSHES IN PHOTOSHOP

In this section, I'll be explaining how to create window brushes in Photoshop. The process is very similar in both Clip Studio Paint and Procreate. Window brushes can be used to save time when drawing out the flat tower windows for cities. I have a set of free city window brushes for all three programs available on my Gumroad store if you want to experiment with pre-made brushes. You can find my City Brushset here: tamberella.gumroad.com

Start by using the Rectangle tool to create a single window **(A)**. This window should be pure black against a pure white background. Next, select the window and hold Option+Command+Shift and drag to the side to copy that window repeatedly, until you have a horizontal line of windows **(B)**. This will be one row in your window tower, and the base for your brush. Now, select the whole line using the Marquee tool and select Edit > Define Brush Preset. A Brush Name dialogue box will pop up. Name the brush and select OK to save your window stamp. Next, you can edit the stamp in the Brush menu to turn it into a usable brush. Go to Window > Brush Settings to open the Brush panel.

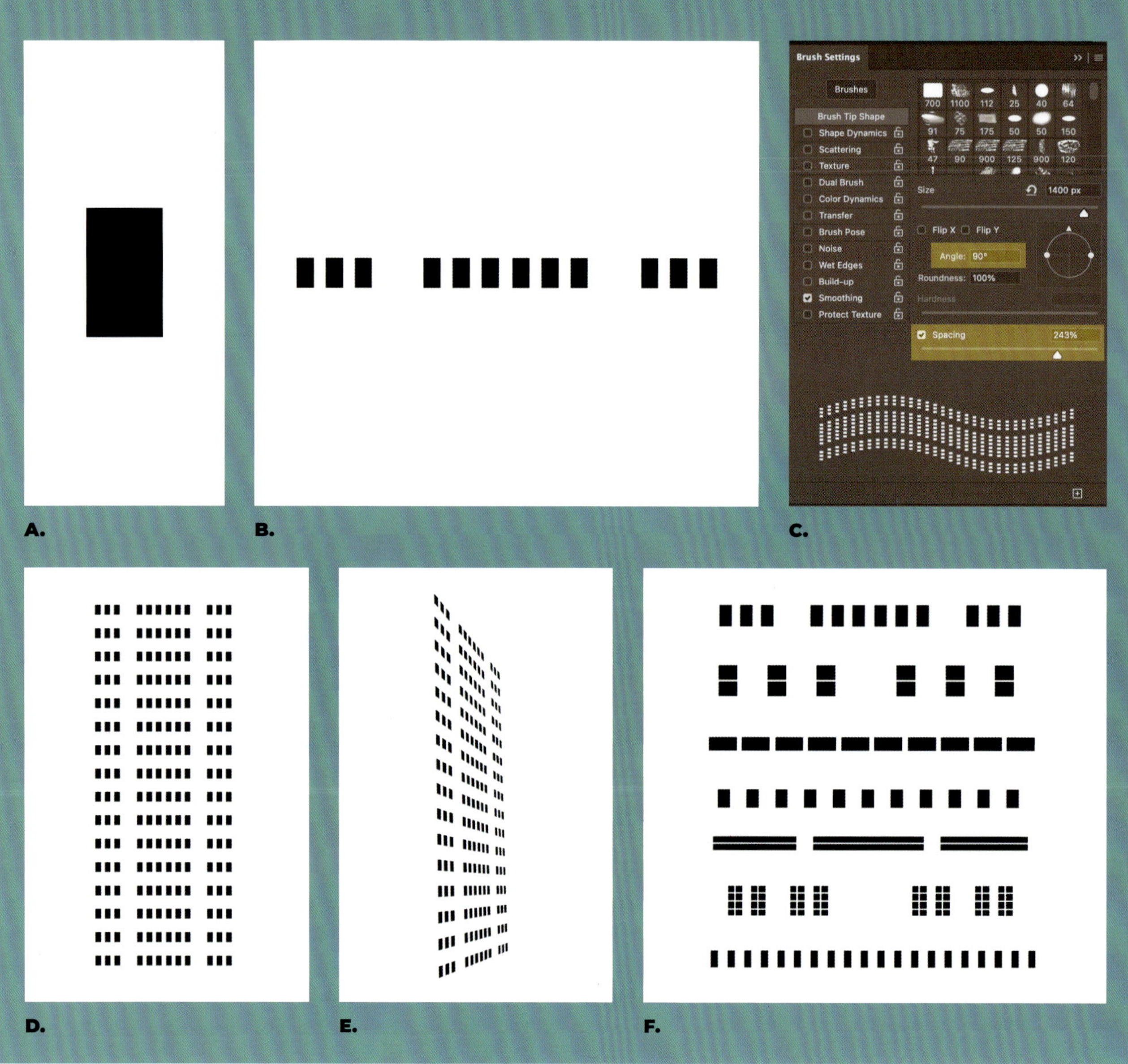

A. B. C.

D. E. F.

Select Brush Tip Shape to get to this page of the menu **(C)**. Temporarily set the angle to 90 degrees. You will change the angle back to 0 later, but you need to adjust it now in order to see the spacing of the brush in the brush panel. Next, drag the bar under Spacing until the rows of windows separate from one another. You can create a wide gap or a narrow gap. Once you're satisfied with the spacing between your window rows, reset the angle to 0 degrees. Click the + at the bottom right of the window to open the dialogue box to save and name your brush.

Now, you can hold Shift and draw in a vertical line to easily create a window tower **(D)**. Finally, use Transform > Distort to put it into perspective in your painting **(E)**!

Repeat these same steps with a variety of window shapes and configurations to build your own unique library of window brushes. Vary the size, shape, and spacing of each window row to create endless variations **(F)**. Once you have a stockpile of window brushes, blocking in a skyline is quick and easy! Lock the window layer to add reflections or illuminate lit windows at night **(G)**.

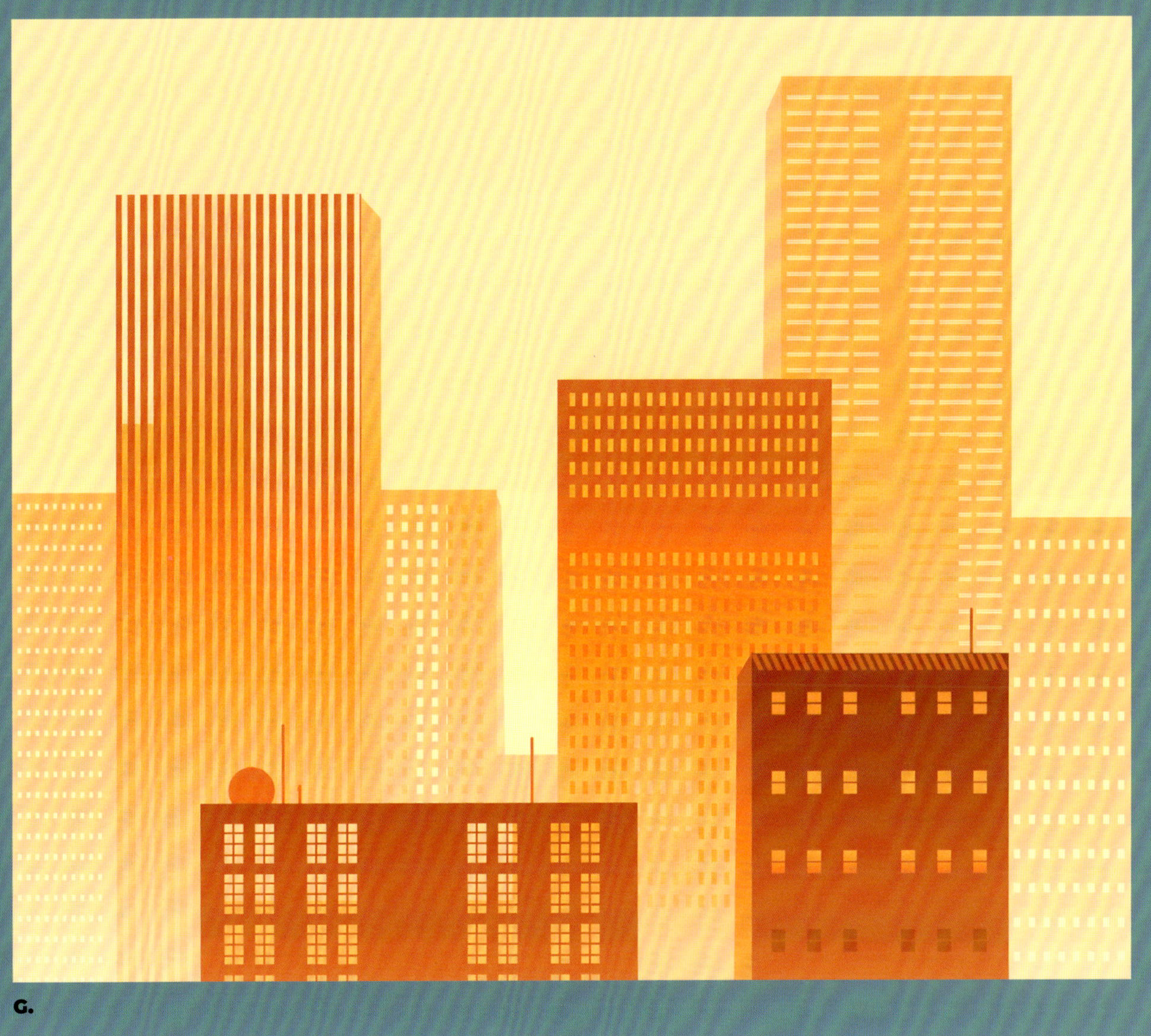

G.

17 MAINTAINING THE LAYER STRUCTURE

I repeat the Transform > Distort process on the left and right faces of the tower. I keep each of these transformed window columns on their own layer, clipped to the base. It's key to keep things like windows layered out, so that they can be locked and painted within at various stages of the process. I try not to merge anything until I'm fully satisfied with my composition and am only making final touches. This may be a challenge if your computer or tablet struggles with large files. If you need to merge layers to keep your software running smoothly, try saving out selections or silhouettes instead.

18 REFLECTIONS IN WINDOWS

I use the same Transform > Distort process to add a unique pattern of windows to the building in the lower right of the composition. Next, I block in reflections. Windows are not perfect mirrors, so the scenery that they reflect is distorted and discoloured compared to the source material. They reflect a warped version of reality, which allows you to be creative and use their reflections to the benefit of the composition. They can reflect colours entirely out of the frame of the canvas, allowing you to add fresh, contrasting colours if the composition needs them **(18a)**.

Because each window is its own surface, there is typically some variation between what is reflected in one window compared to its neighbour **(18b–e)**. Replicating this uneven, disjointed quality by selecting a handful of windows and moving or recolouring them can very quickly add realism to your painting.

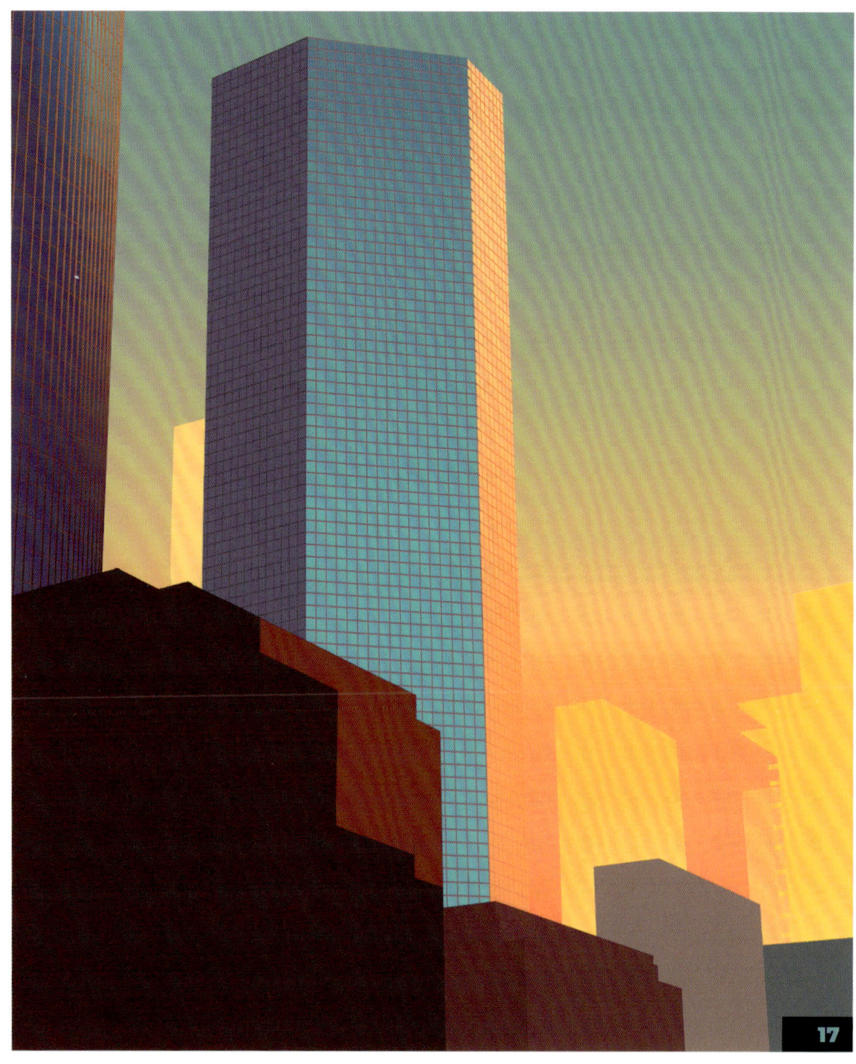

17 The tower is now fully covered with windows.

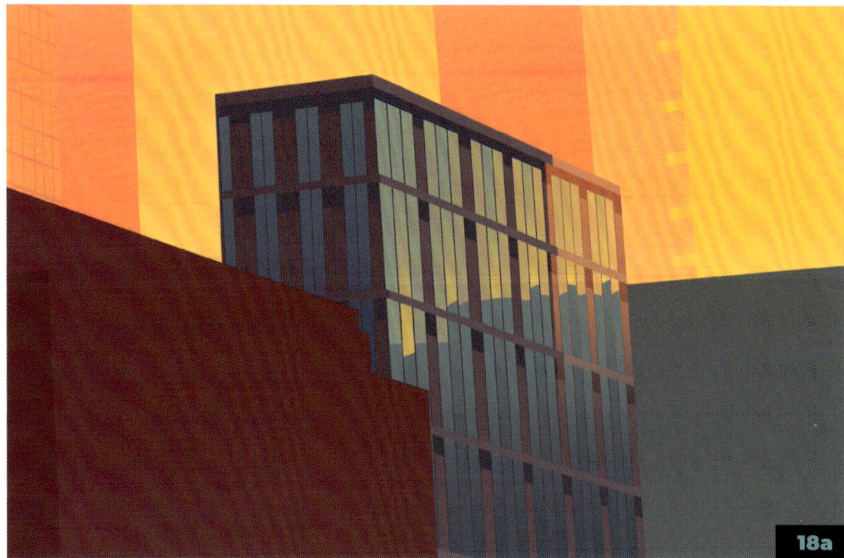

18a The lower right-hand building with disjointed, wavy reflections on the window surface.

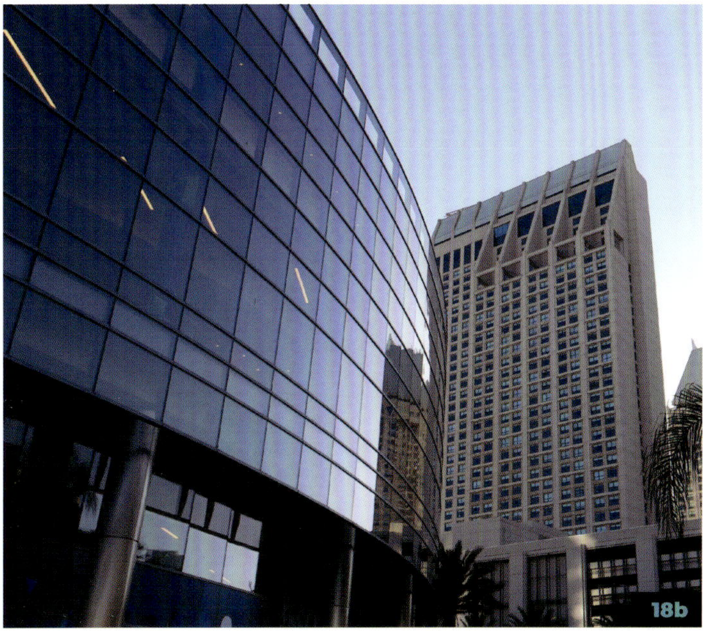

18b Photo reference: Note the condensed, highly warped appearance of reflections in curved buildings. Observe how the reflected hues are warmer and darker than the source material.

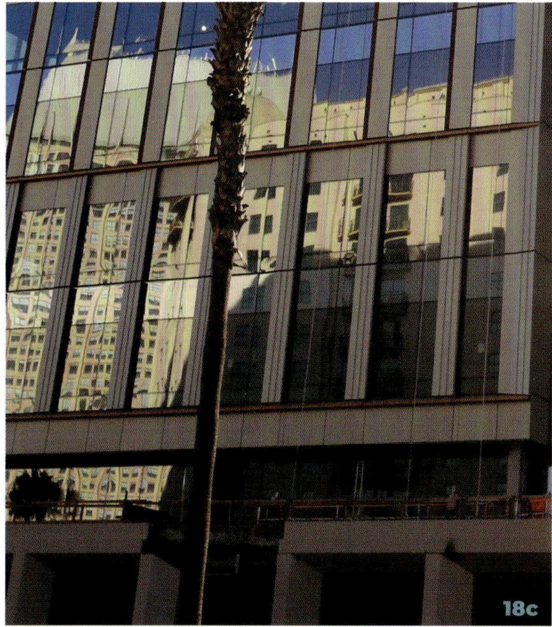

18c Photo reference: Windows that are even slightly concave or convex will create greatly distorted reflections that stretch oddly around each edge.

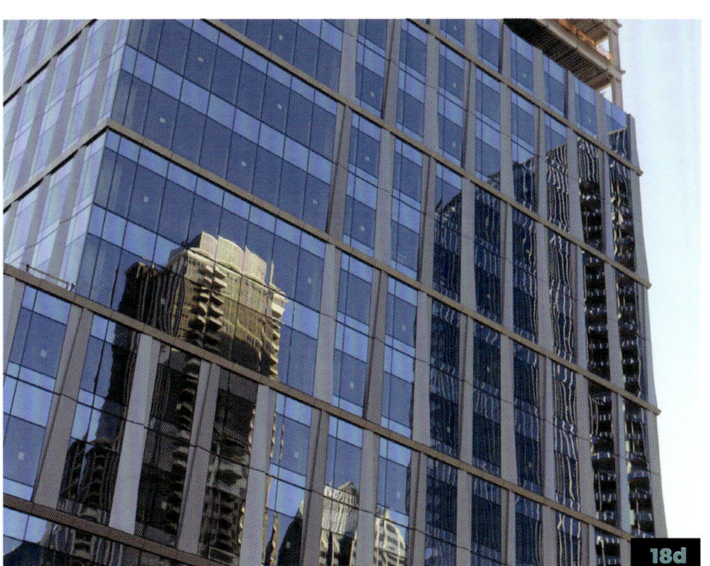

18d Photo reference: This building has narrow sections of glass that cover walls, plus wider sections that open transparently into the offices. Note how the reflections vary between the two sections.

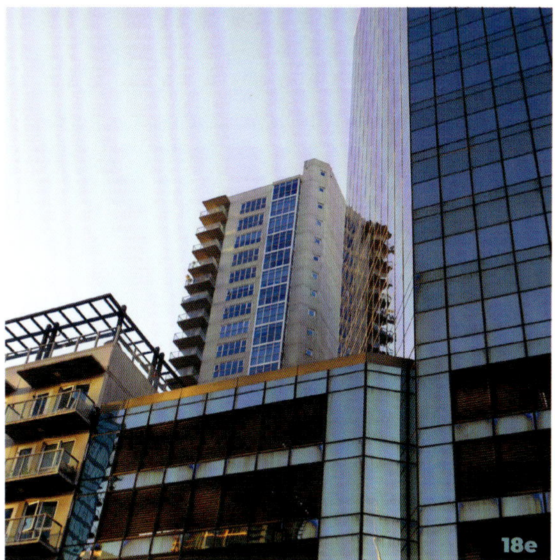

18e Photo reference: The window leading and reflections vary in the lit areas versus the shadow areas. The leading is darker than the windows on the shadow face, and lighter than some of the reflections on the lit face.

19 PAINTING A FLAT FACADE

This tutorial has already covered flat tower windows that are distorted into perspective (page 102). You can also use this technique with entire building facades. It's much easier to proportionally design a flat building facade than to try to draw all the details individually in perspective. When working flat, you can use the Symmetry tool to mark out distances. Hold Option+Command+Shift to easily copy out parallel elements on the same layer. It's easier to focus on design and creativity when working in flat perspective.

Here I paint a facade for the building on the lower left. I keep the windows on their own layer, as well as the columns and cross elements that will need to separate from the main surface to read with accurate depth. Now I can group the entire painted facade into one layer group, and then transform that layer group into perspective while retaining the layer structure.

20 TRANSFORMING THE FACADE INTO PERSPECTIVE

I use the Transform > Distort technique to move my facade into perspective. You'll notice that it looks very flat and unrealistic at the moment, like a facade painted onto a building, rather than a real one with depth. At this stage, take note of which elements of your facade need to nudge in or out in order to create a feeling of depth. Here the windows should nudge left and down to sit deeper into the wall, whereas the columns should nudge right and up to come forward from the wall.

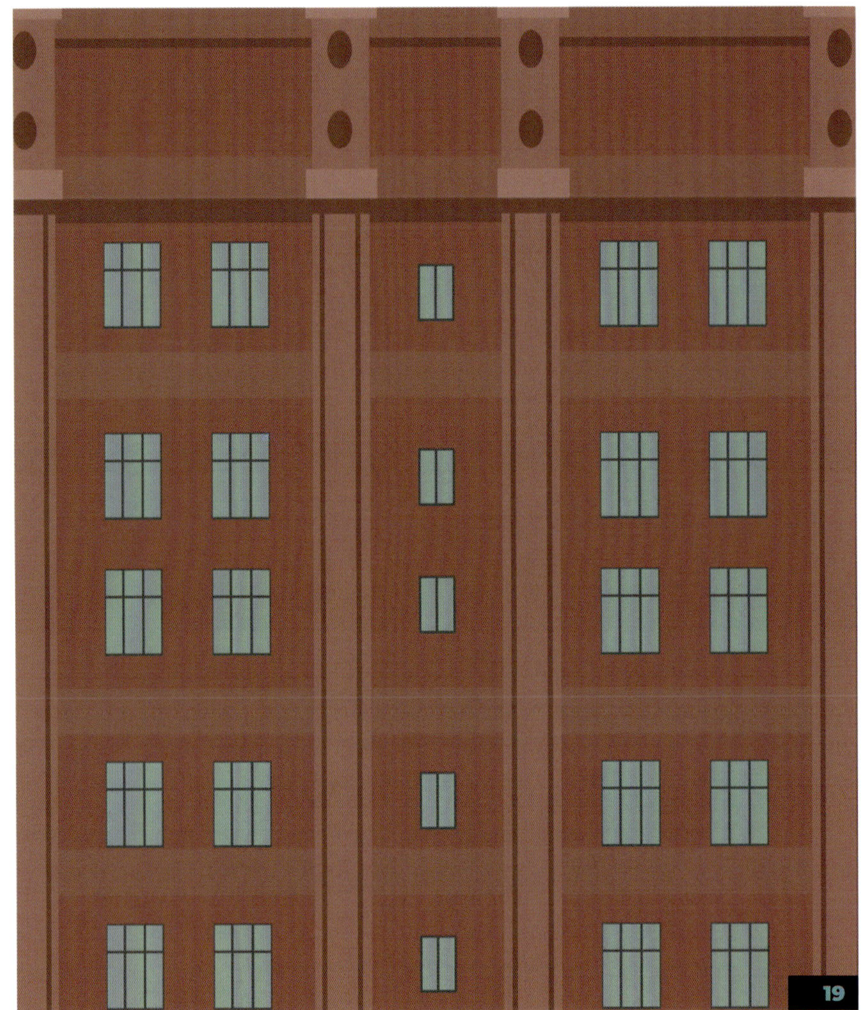

19 The flat facade is blocked in.

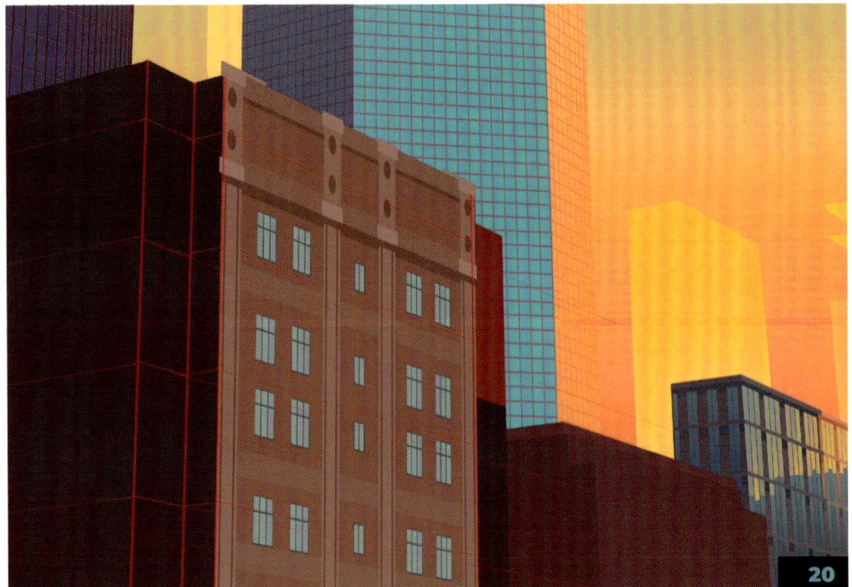

20 The flat facade is transformed into perspective.

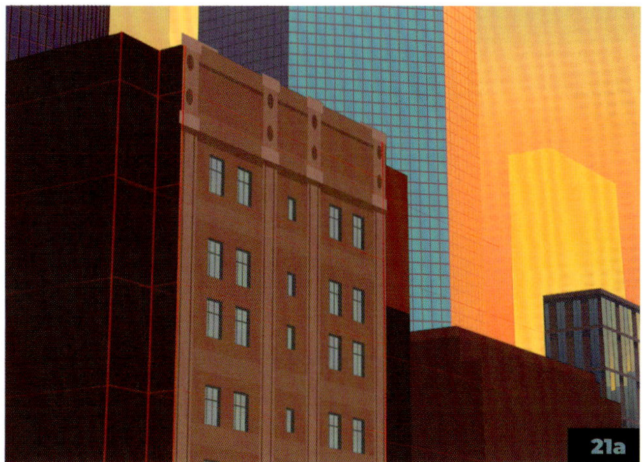

21a The facade with depth added to the windows.

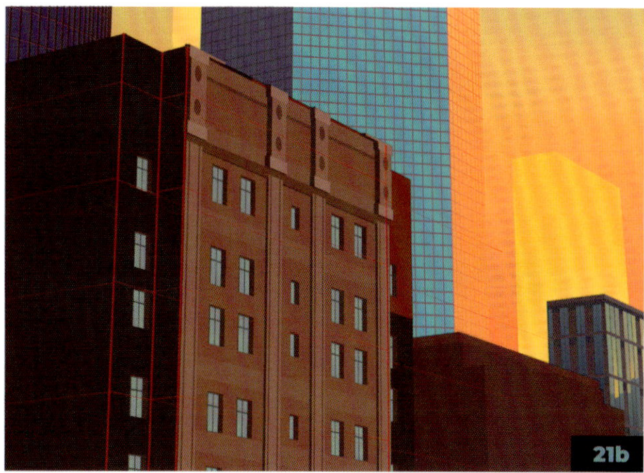

21b The facade with depth added to the columns.

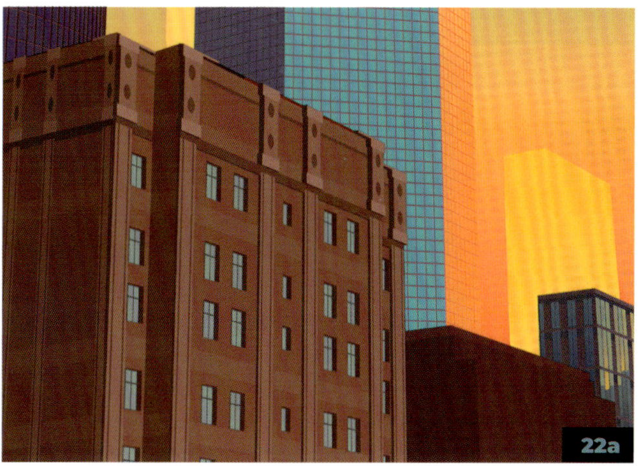

22a The building before shading.

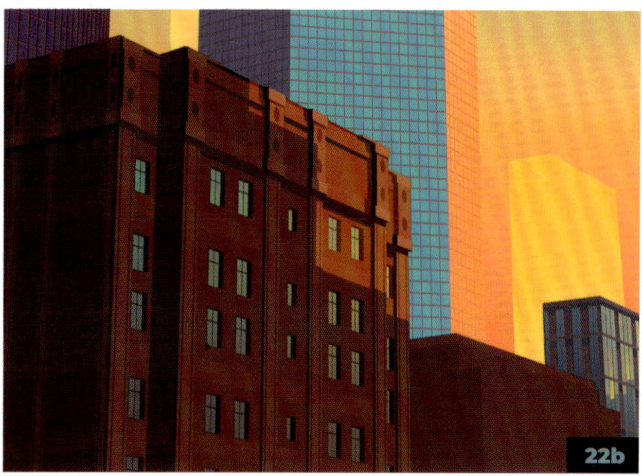

22b The building with shading, creating depth and a sense of realism.

21 GIVING THE FACADE DEPTH

Giving the windows depth is a multi-step process. First, I duplicate the window layer. I select the copy on top and clip it to the original window layer with a clipping mask. Next, I fill the base window layer with a darker colour. Finally, I select back onto the lighter window layer on top, and with the arrow keys I nudge that layer down and to the left to situate it deeper into the building. Because the lighter windows are locked to the original base, this creates a feeling of real depth **(21a)**.

Second, I repeat this process with the columns, but nudge them in the other direction in order to lift them away from the building **(21b)**. I also copy windows onto the two side sections. You can repeat these steps with any number of elements in order to create depth and volume.

22 SHADING THE BUILDING

I follow the perspective grid to fill out the rest of the building **(22a)**, then begin my shadow and light pass. Alongside reflections, cast shadows are a way you can indicate scenery outside the bounds of the canvas. Indications of a world outside the frame make the space feel more real and add to the sense of depth by reminding viewers that there is a world behind the 'camera'.

I add a cast shadow zigzagging across the front plane of the building using a cool purple-grey colour set to Multiply, then add a warm light in the space outside of the shadow using an Overlay layer. When adding cast shadows across building facades, make sure that you adjust the shadows based on the depth of each element of the facade. The columns in my painting come forward, so the shadow across them sits higher than the shadow line across the building beneath them **(22b)**. These small variations in the shadow line do a lot of heavy lifting when it comes to imparting volume and dimension.

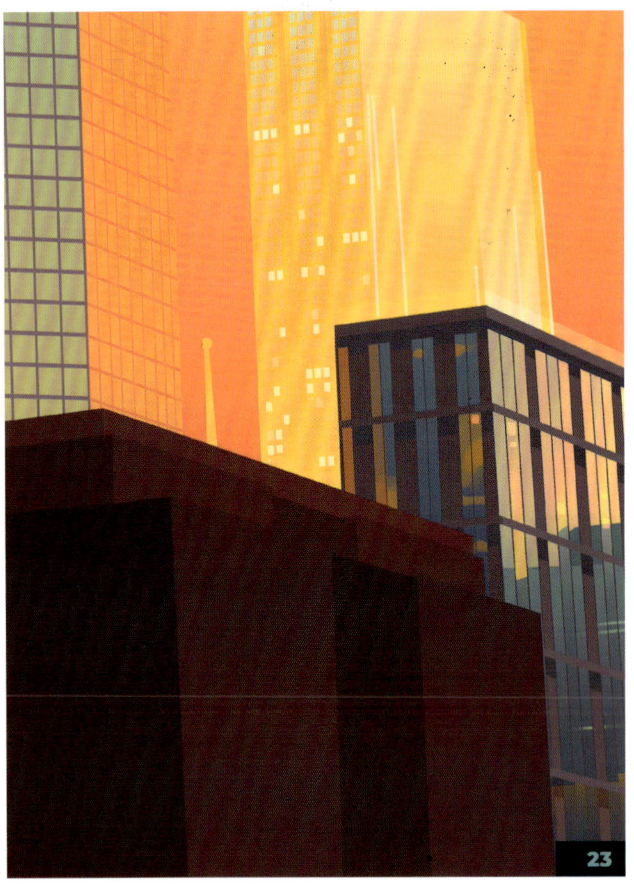

23 A close-up of the rendered buildings in the distance, with added roof elements.

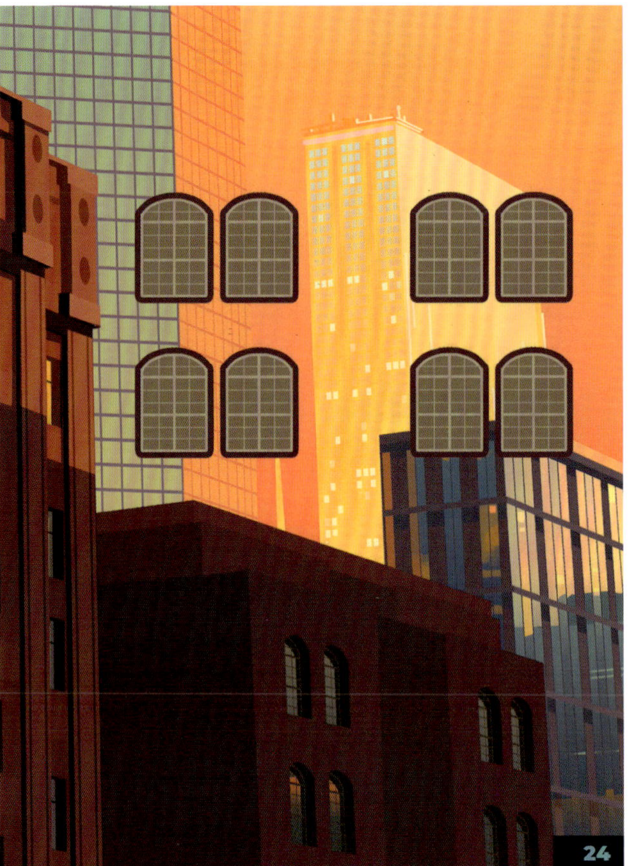

24 A close-up of the building with arched windows, which have been transformed into perspective. The flat version of the windows are shown above.

23 RENDERING THE DISTANT BUILDINGS

Next, I render out the most distant buildings. I keep them relatively simple, including only enough detail to make them feel real and populated. The heavy atmosphere and bright blooming sun will simplify these buildings considerably by the end. I add some roof structures across various buildings too. Little noisy details on a roof can add a lot of realism to a city skyline. I maintain the very narrow value range in the distant buildings, as I want them to sit back solidly into the distance. Consider a 'less is more' approach when rendering your distant buildings. Too much contrast and detail will break the illusion of depth, pulling too much attention from your middle ground and foreground.

24 VARYING THE DETAILS

I use a similar process with these arched windows as I did with the windows in step 21, first clipping them to a darker base and then nudging them over using the arrow keys. As these windows are larger, I include a dark reflection of the overhang by erasing out the sky reflection along the outer right rim. Because the grey window leading sits on top of the reflections without being impacted by their colour variation, it makes the windows feel more real and solid.

Throughout your cityscapes, try to vary both the macro and micro shape language. This will help your cities to appear more lifelike and interesting. I try to give each building a unique silhouette, window shape, and proportion. The smaller buildings in a city are typically the oldest, with the architectural aesthetics of a bygone era. These older buildings tend to have more ornate design elements and more unique window shapes, designed in a time before sleek minimalism took hold.

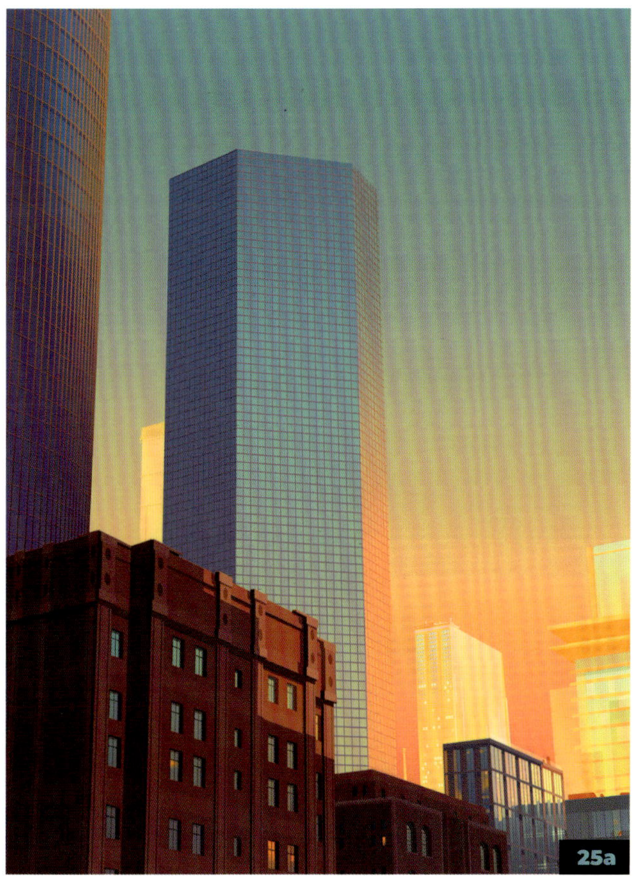

25a My current painting progress in colour.

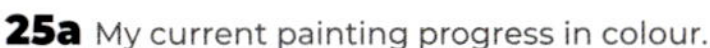

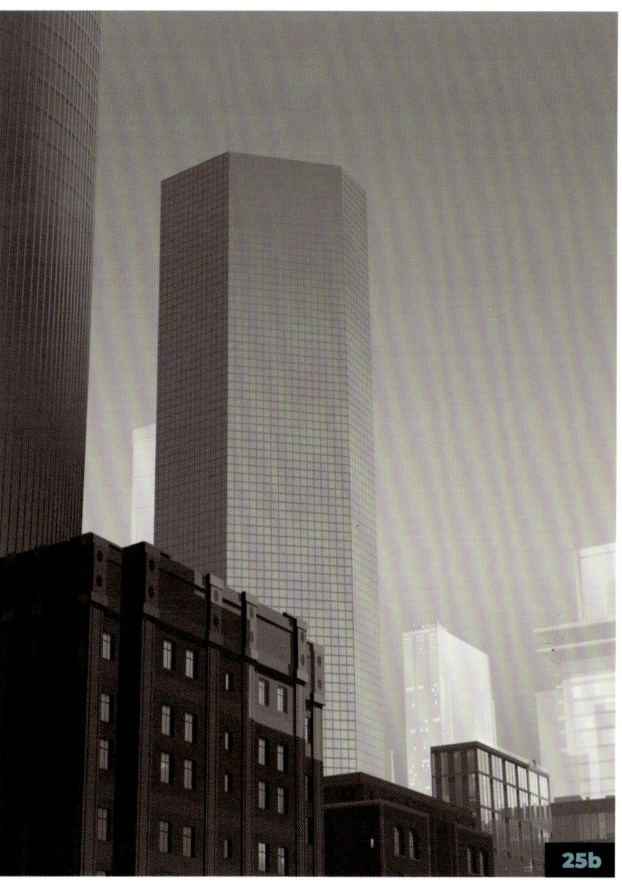

25b The painting in greyscale, which is useful for checking the values.

25 CHECKING THE VALUE STATEMENT

Pause to check your values from time to time to ensure you're staying on track with your value goals for the painting **(25a)**. It can be easy to get lost and 'lose the plot', especially when working on an environment as complex as a cityscape. I keep a layer filled with pure black set to the Colour blending mode at the top of my layer structure. This allows me to easily check my values at any time during the painting process. I find this digital greyscale conversion process to be a lot more accurate than using the Desaturate feature or the Saturation slider.

When looking at my current progress in greyscale, it feels in line with my goals for the image **(25b)**. The distant buildings illuminate against the sky, the middle buildings group into a wider (but still fairly neutral) midtone value range, and the foreground buildings contain the highest contrast and widest value range. This is a green light to continue without needing to make any major adjustments. If you find your values no longer align with your plan, take some time to make adjustments before progressing further with the rendering stage.

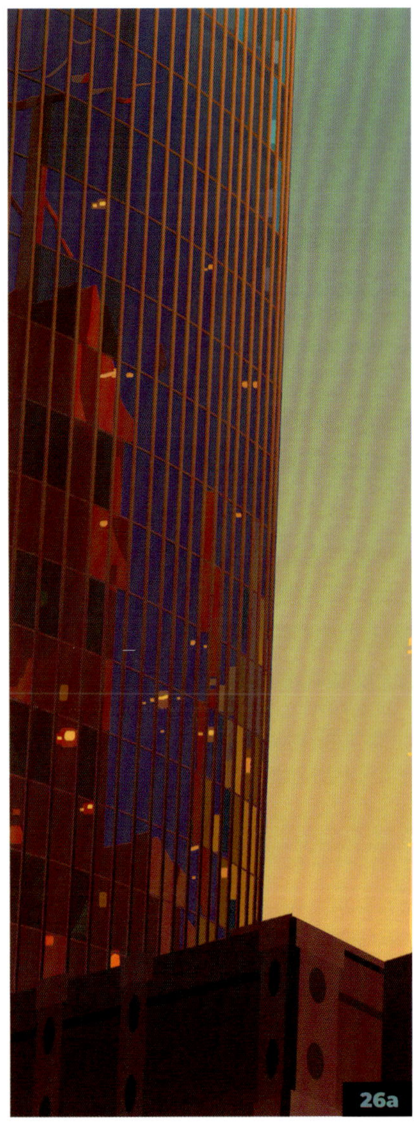

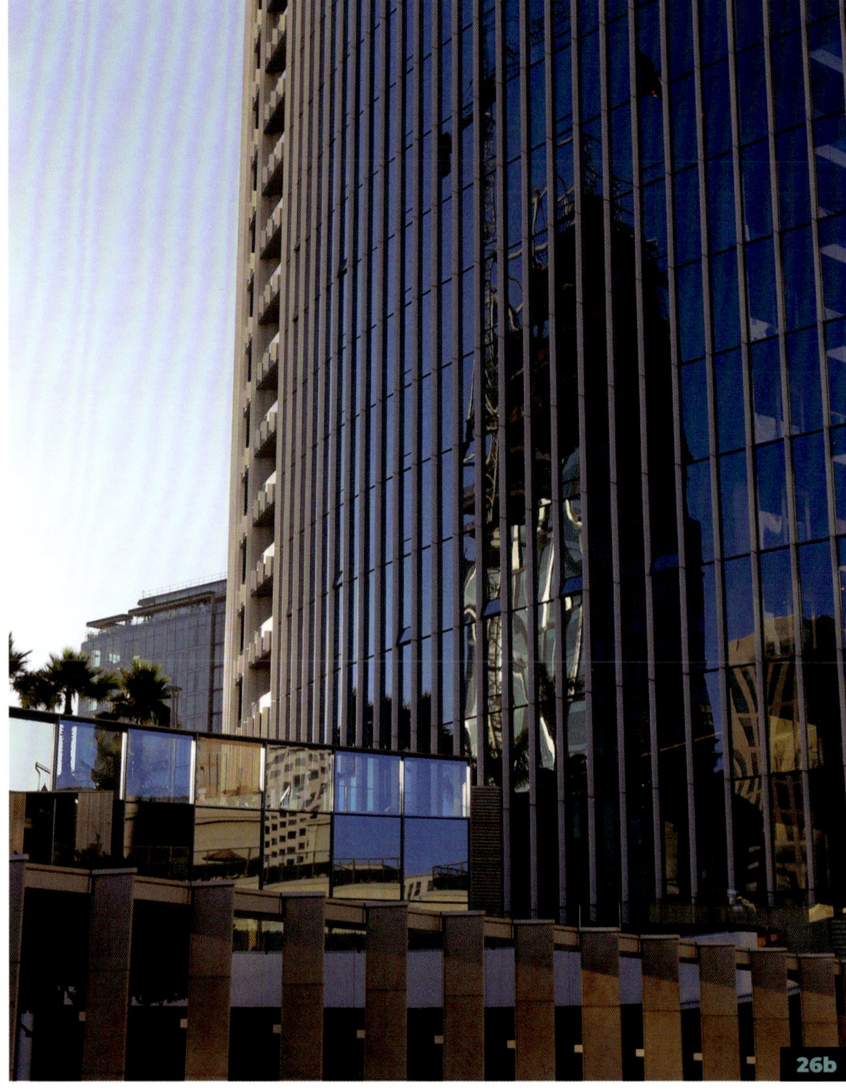

26a A detail pass across the curved office tower.

26b A close-up of a reference photo I took of a curved building in downtown San Diego.

26 DETAILING THE CURVED BUILDING

Using reference photos of curved buildings from my walk through San Diego, I add a reflected building and some other reflected details to the curved tower on the left **(26a)**. I look closely at my reference and notice that various bits of the reflection curve diagonally across warped windows **(26b)**. I do my best to mimic this effect, selecting individual windows and drawing in swooping motions within them. I also add lights within offices inside the building. These tiny specular lights are to remind viewers of the scale.

27 DETAILING THE MAIN WINDOW TOWER

Next, I detail the main tower. I add building reflections in the middle face, using reference photos as a general guide for how these reflections might ripple and warp across the many individual windows. I also include subtle indications of windows on the reflected building. Little details like this will generally go unnoticed, but will add to the overall immersion and reality of the painting.

I select windows here and there to lighten and darken, maintaining the overall gradient but breaking it up with imperfections and noise. I also pick some sections of window panels to darken, a feature I see in various reference photos. I add some subtle drips from those panels, perhaps fluid from AC or ventilation.

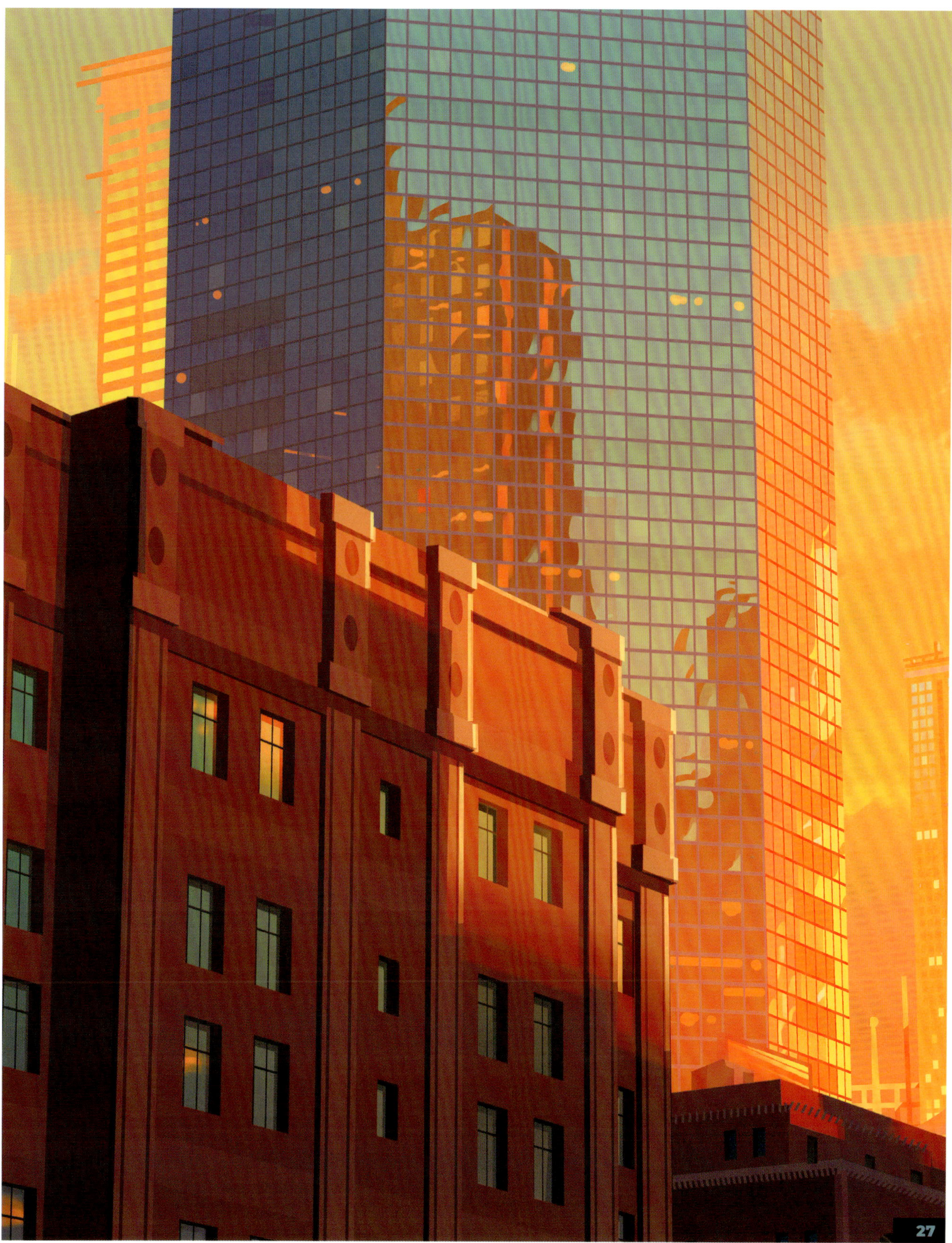

27 A close-up of the main tower, with added reflections and window rendering.

USING LIGHTEN LAYERS FOR ATMOSPHERIC PERSPECTIVE

If you find that you're struggling to separate the spatial planes of your environment, try using the Lighten blending mode. This blending mode comes closest to portraying how fog and atmosphere truly interact with real-life distant objects. The technique will allow you to first paint your scenery using a full value range, then add atmosphere on top to suggest depth.

In diagram **A**, the buildings are all painted with a similar value range, which flattens the composition. In diagram **B**, I use Lighten layers to create a feeling of depth in the image. Note how the highlights mostly remain intact. This is fairly true to how fog and atmosphere interact in the real world.

If you want to try this technique, first use the Rectangle tool and window brushes to block in a rough city skyline. Make sure to keep each building on its own layer, with the furthest building at the bottom of your Layer menu and the nearest building at the top of your Layer menu. Next, clip a layer set to the Lighten blending mode to each of your building layers. Finally, fill the Lighten layers with a neutral colour that resembles the general sky and atmosphere, working from back to front. Use a light version of your neutral colour to lighten the most distant buildings, then slowly darken the colour as you approach the foreground **(C)**. Experiment with various hues to try out different effects!

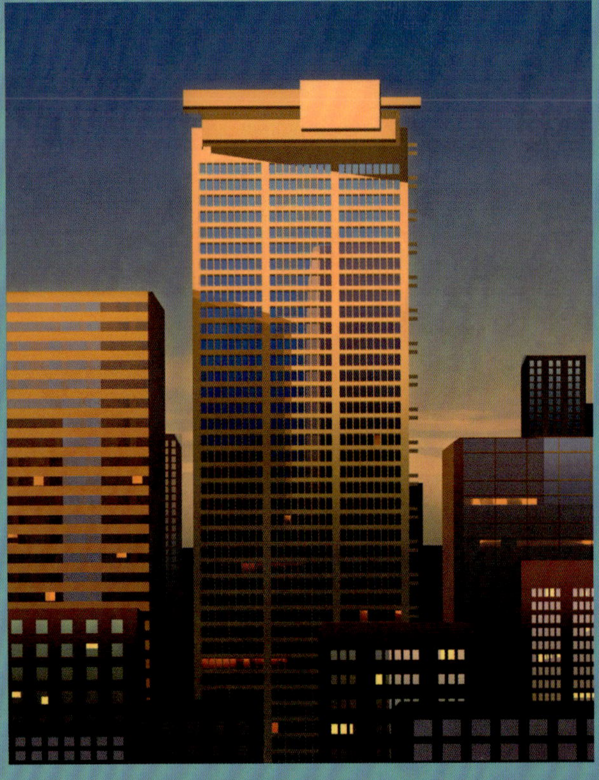

A.

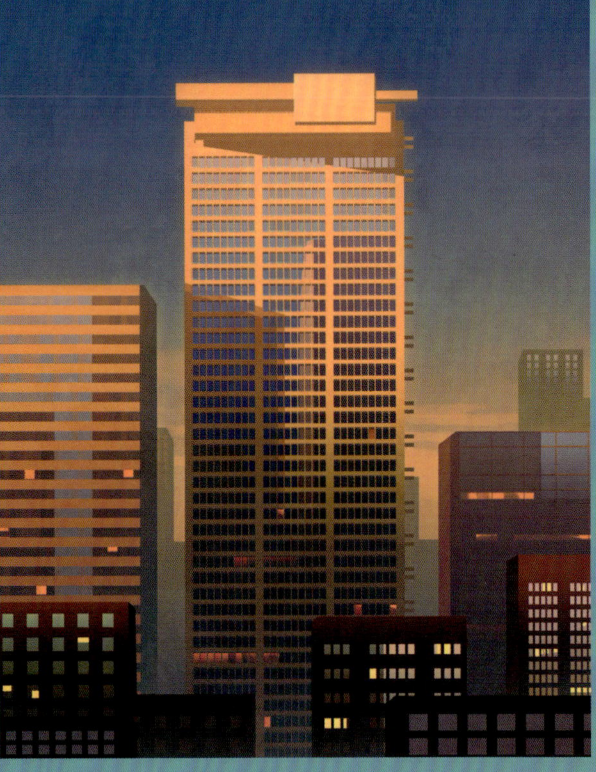

B.

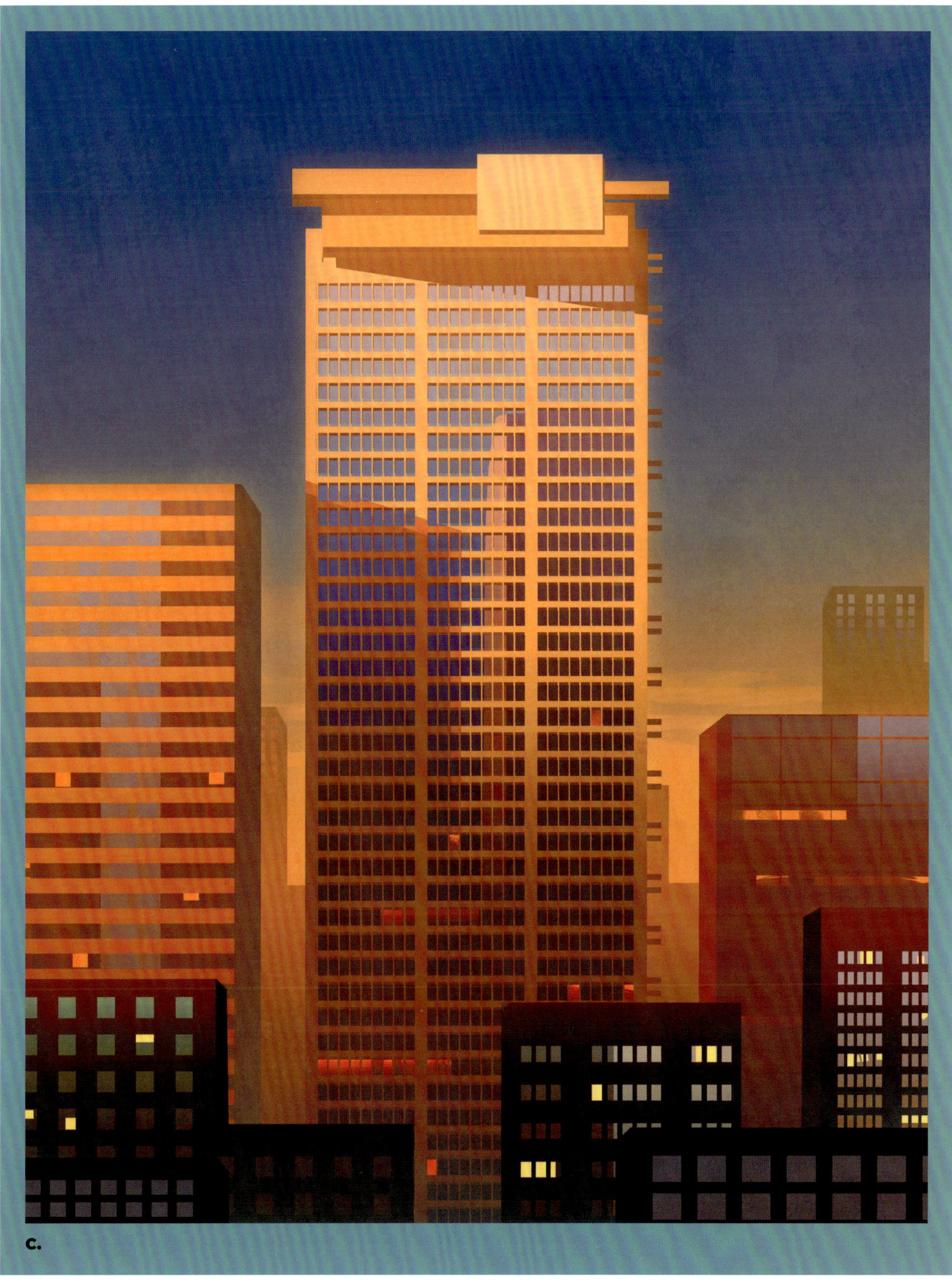

C.

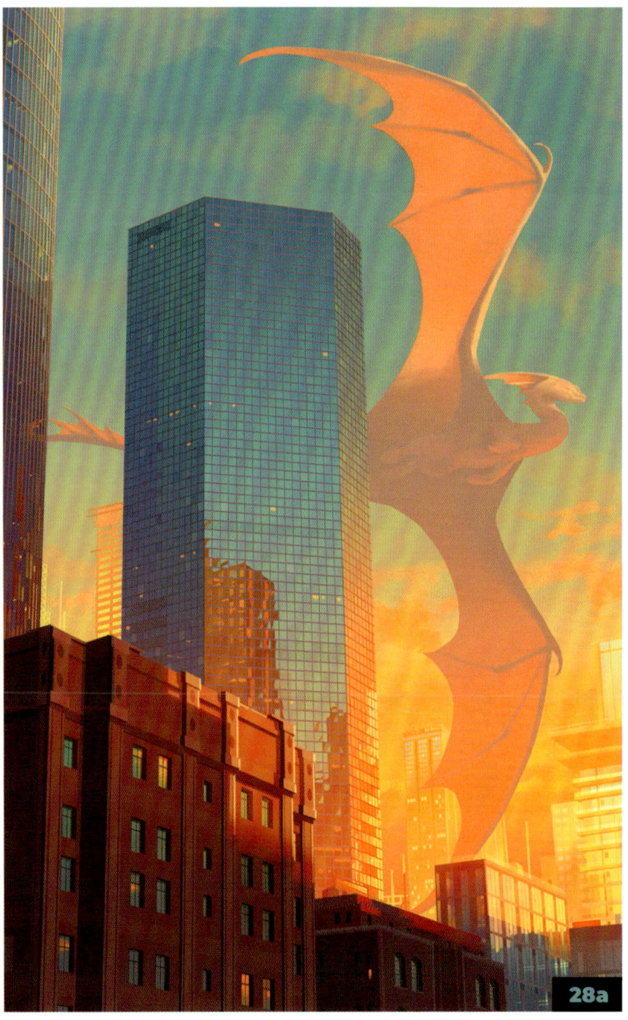

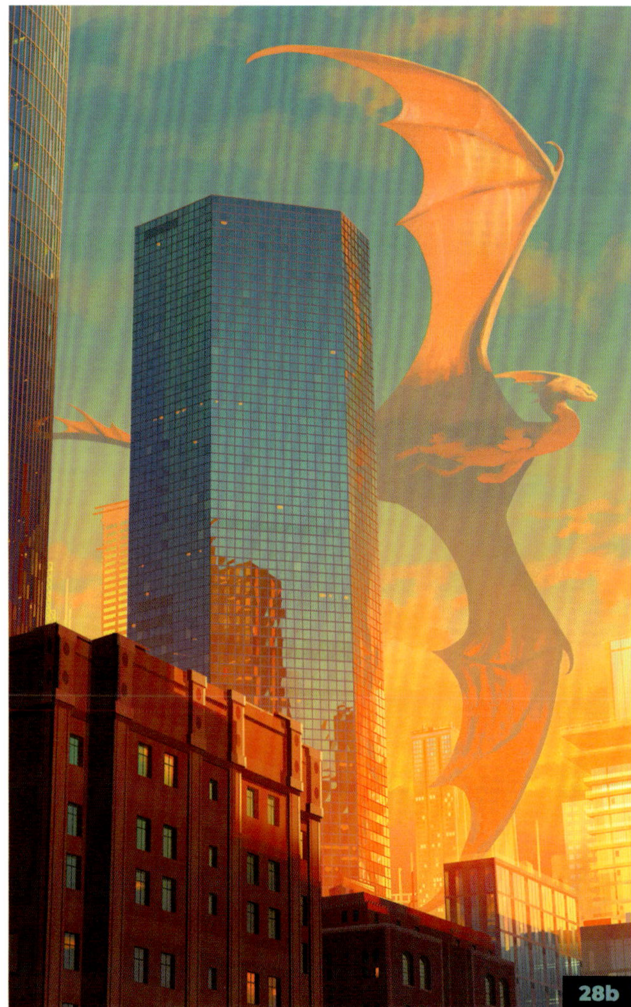

28a & 28b The first **(28a)** and second **(28b)** paint pass across the mama dragon.

28 PAINTING THE MAMA DRAGON

To render the mama dragon, I begin by taking the colours already present in my block-in pass and use them in a detail pass across the dragon **(28a)**. Next, I follow with a pass intensifying the cool shadows and warm light **(28b)**. I want the dragon to appear as a colossal figure within the image. A creature at this impossibly large scale needs to be handled differently than a creature of typical scale. An organic form this large will inevitably contain a great deal of texture and detail. Due to the distance, and therefore the atmospheric perspective, this detail must only be hinted at in my painting, particularly in the shadow masses. Fully rendering the dragon's body with scale and skin details would ruin the immersion and depth.

The terminator line (the division between light and shadow) is a choice location to display hints of detail in a huge and distant form. I concentrate texture, noise, and detail right at this transition between light and shadow, hinting at tiny scales, skin folds, and other surface variations. I use bounced light from the glowing city below to illuminate anatomical detail across the dragon's chest and body. The lower wing is detailed through subsurface scattering alone. Subsurface scattering describes the warm, saturated glow that appears within semi-translucent materials as light penetrates the surface and is scattered wildly inside. This phenomenon is present in the translucent membrane of the dragon's wings, neck fins, and tail fins. You can observe this in your own body by holding a lit torch up against your fingers.

I keep the interior shadow and bounce light zones mostly absent of detail, signalling to the viewer that a great deal of atmospheric interference is present. This atmospheric interference is interpreted as distance. Shadows group into one midtone mass, with crevice shadows and details disappearing into the larger shadow form. Only the face and upper wing, illuminated by sunlight, are allowed more detail and rendering.

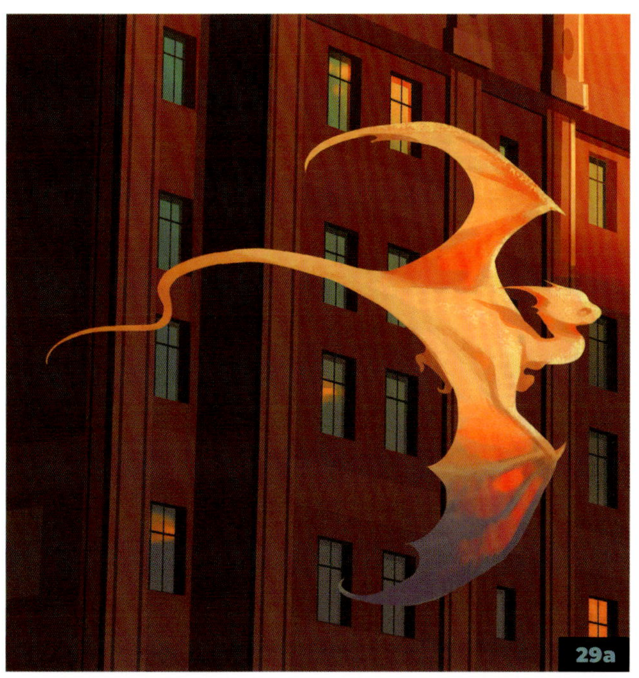

29 RENDERING A CLOSE-UP SUBJECT

Rendering the baby dragon in the foreground requires largely the opposite of what I've done for the mama dragon in the distance. Where the mama dragon's shadows group onto one flat mass, the baby dragon's must expand into subtle value transitions and rendered crevices **(29a)**. I include lots of tiny spikes, scales, and specular highlights. I render the skin folds of wings, the shine in the eye, and whisker-like lines on the nose and chin. Subsurface scattering illuminates the thin membranes of the lower wing in shadow. During this rendering process I also elongate the baby dragon's tail, encouraging a sleek and aerodynamic appearance **(29b)**. I render each body part with a wide range of colour and value. This pulls the dragon close to the camera, as it displays very little atmospheric interference. This value and colour range will widen even further as the painting develops.

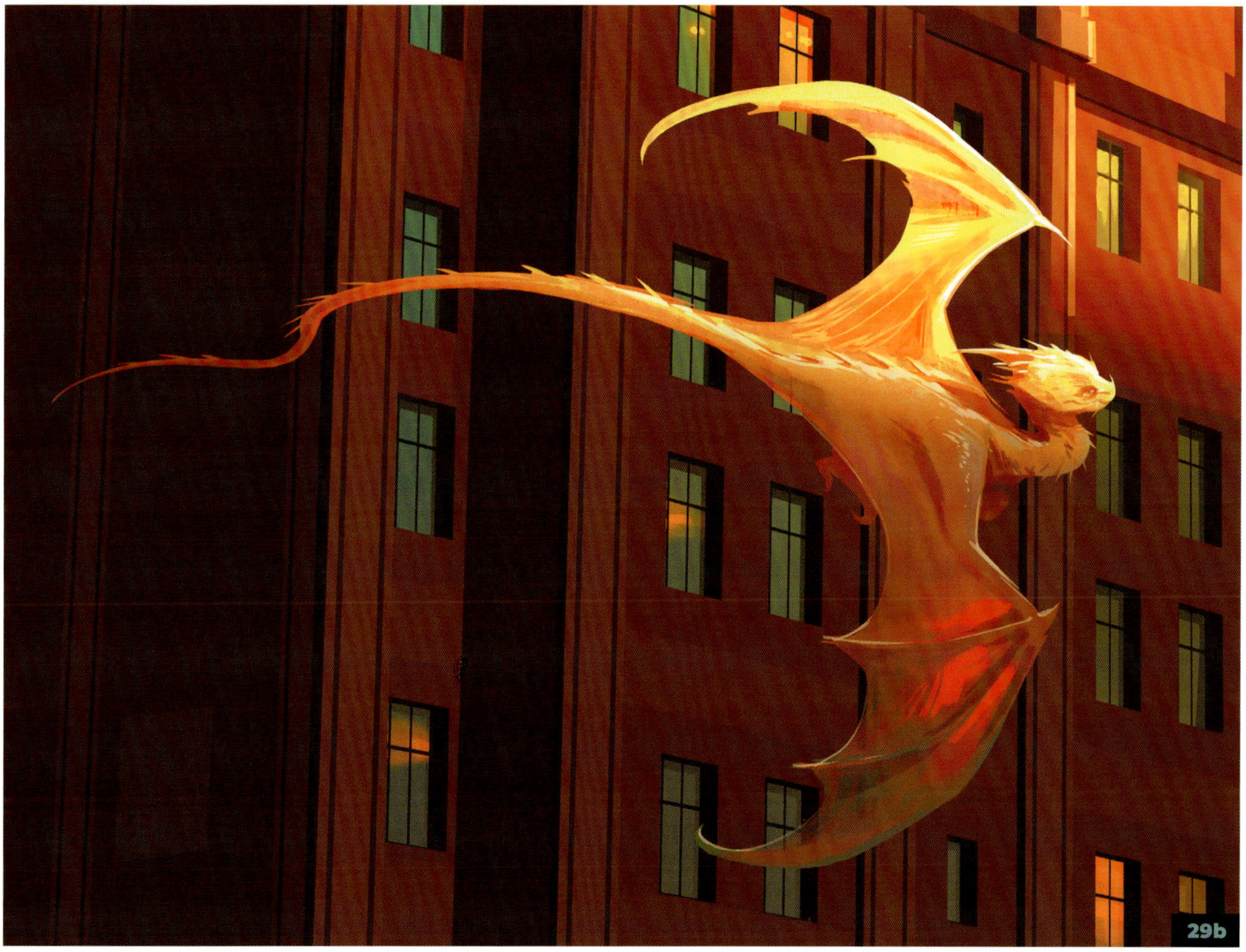

29b

29a & 29b The first **(29a)** and second **(29b)** paint pass across the baby dragon.

30 DETAILING A MASSIVE DISTANT SUBJECT

Painting a subject that is both very large and very distant presents some unique challenges. If your silhouette and form appear too simple, the scale of the subject will not read correctly, so a degree of silhouette complexity and overall noise must be present. However, if that noisy detail is given too much value contrast, the illusion of distance will be broken and your subject will not settle back into the atmosphere. Therefore, you must be careful to include noisy silhouette changes and details, but they must be placed and coloured very strategically in order to achieve a proper impression of distance and scale.

I've already mentioned the efficacy of detailing along the terminator line, and you can note the various details I've placed along the divisions between light and shadow forms. The overall silhouette of the subject is another handy location to add indications of small details. I break up the dragon's silhouette with a variety of silhouette details **(30a)** – particularly details that hint at the dragon's age, such as wear and tear on the thinner membrane of the wings **(30b)**. The value diagram **(30c)** shows how the values are handled differently between the mama and baby dragon.

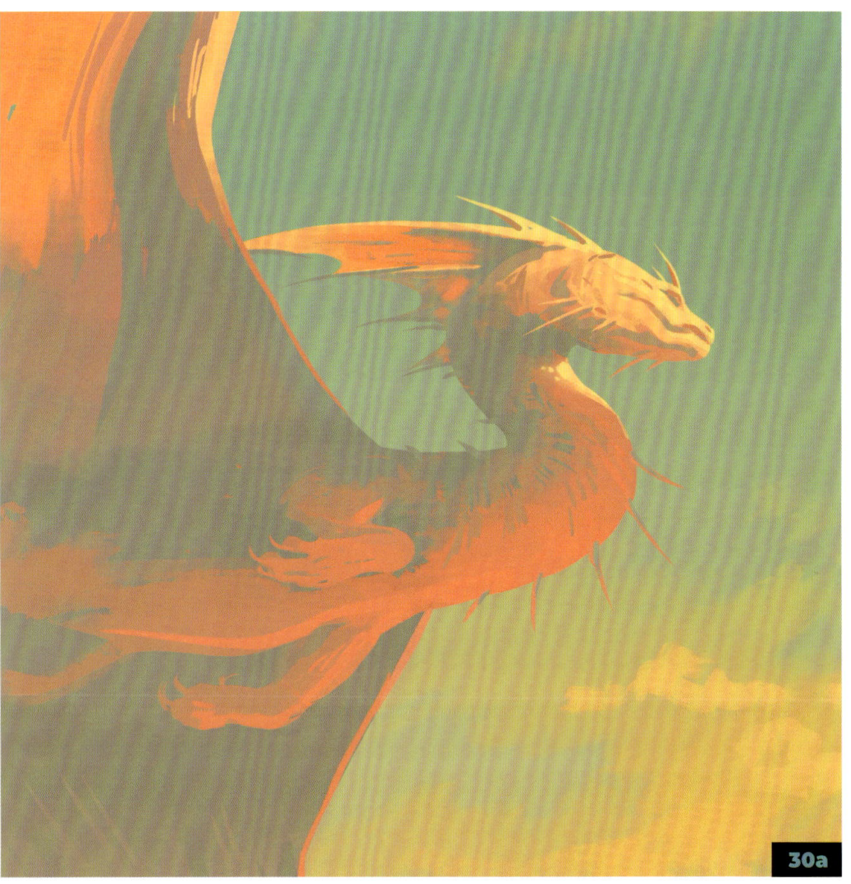

30a A close-up of the detail in the mama dragon's silhouette and form.

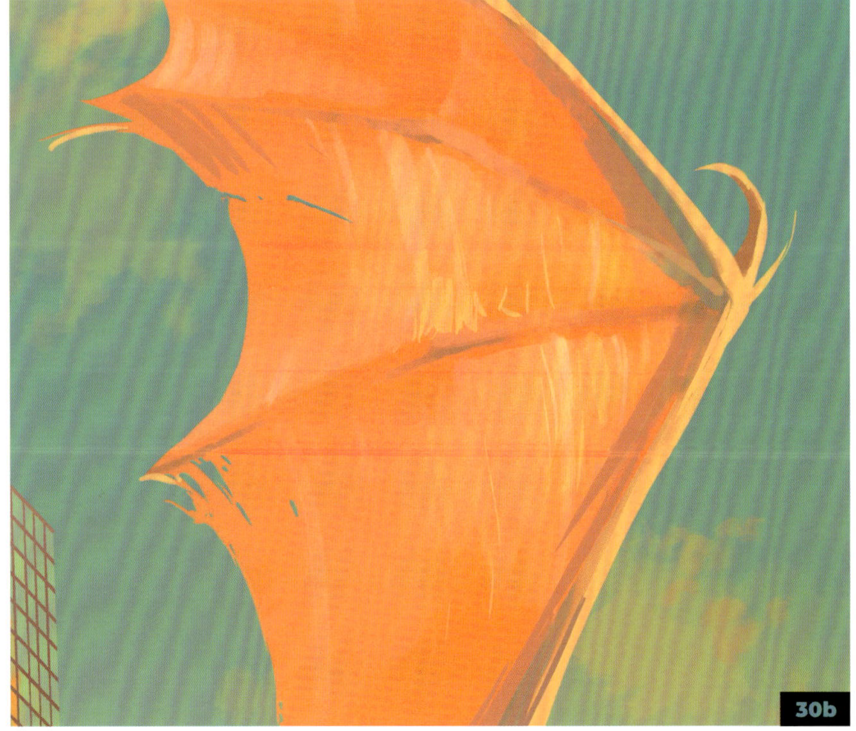

30b Details such as tears in the wing hint at the dragon's age.

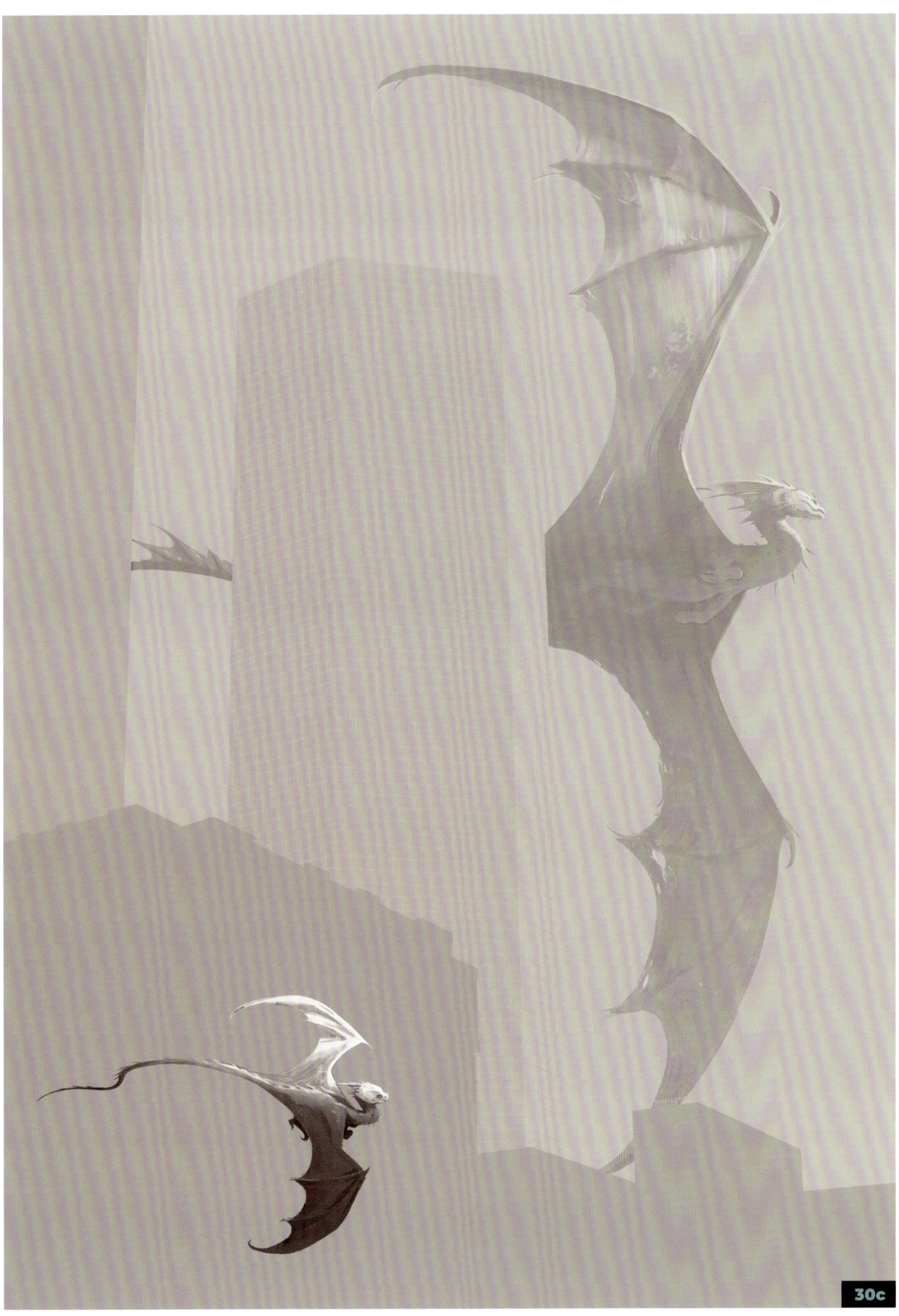

30c A diagram depicting the difference in value range between the mama and baby dragon.

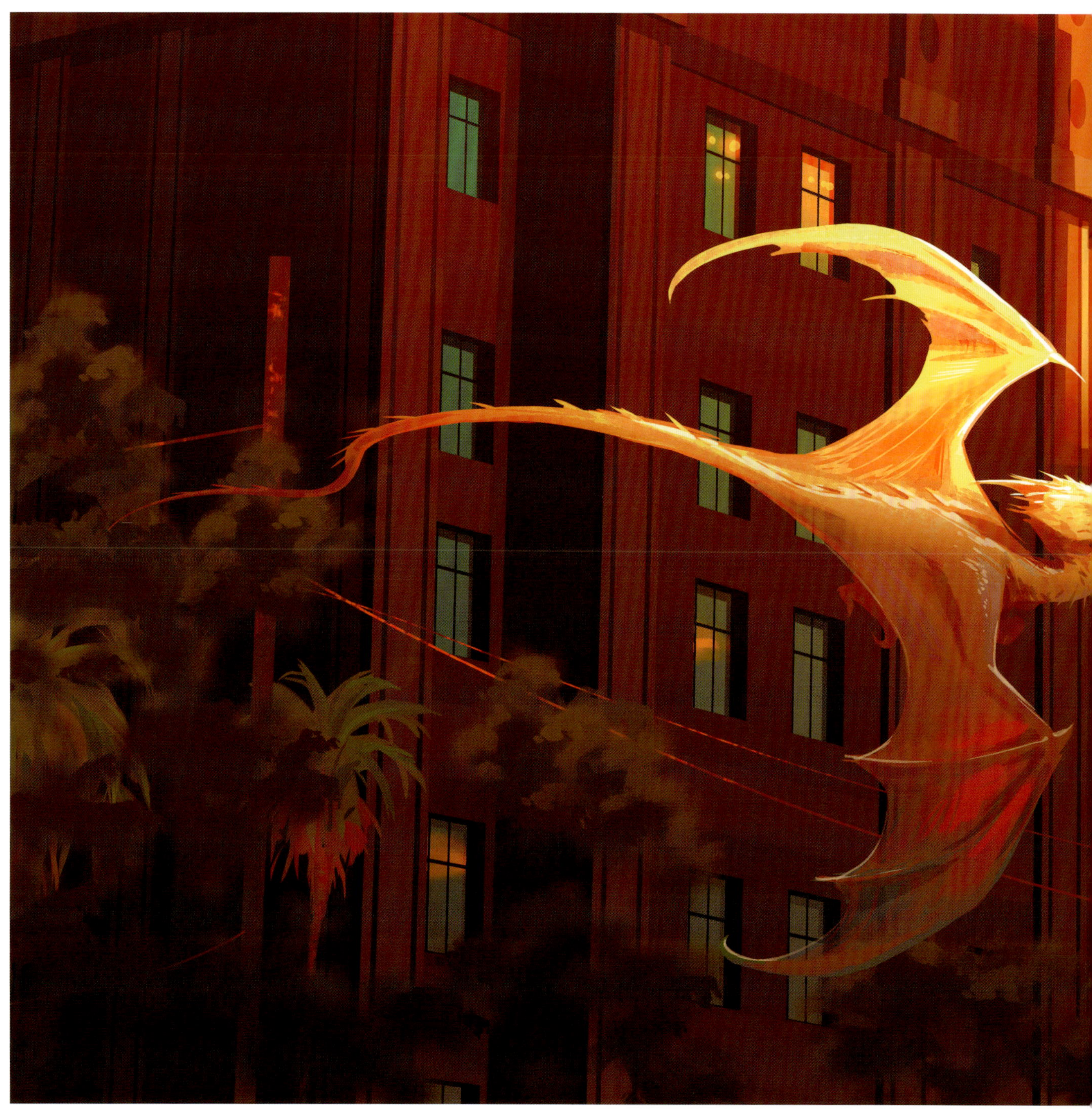

31 A close-up of the trees and telephone wires at the bottom of the painting.

31 ADDING SCALE CUES

I introduce additional details to the bottom section of my painting to further the depth and distance read. Including multiples of the same object, such as trees or telephone poles, at various distances throughout your painting is an effective way to show the viewer exactly how much distance elapses between each repetition of the object. If it's an object that is easily recognizable, such as a bird or a street sign, viewers will immediately be able to cue into the scale of the object, and will therefore have a reference point for the scale of your overall image. You can scale objects or subjects into your environment by following the lines of your perspective grid.

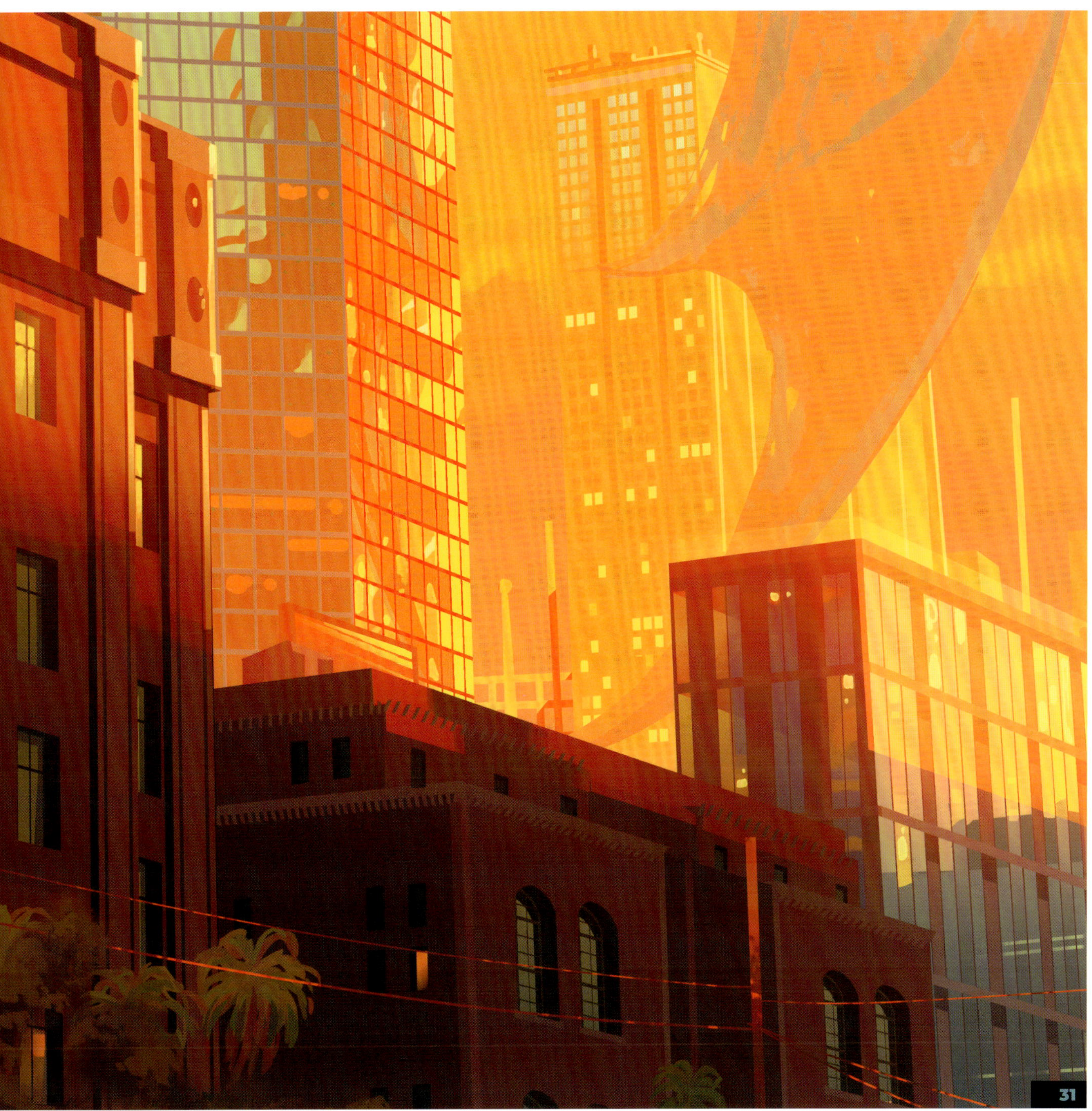

Placing the little dragon in front of these recognizable scale cues helps us to recognize just how much smaller it is compared to its mother. Dragons sure must eat a lot to grow that much over the course of their lifetime!

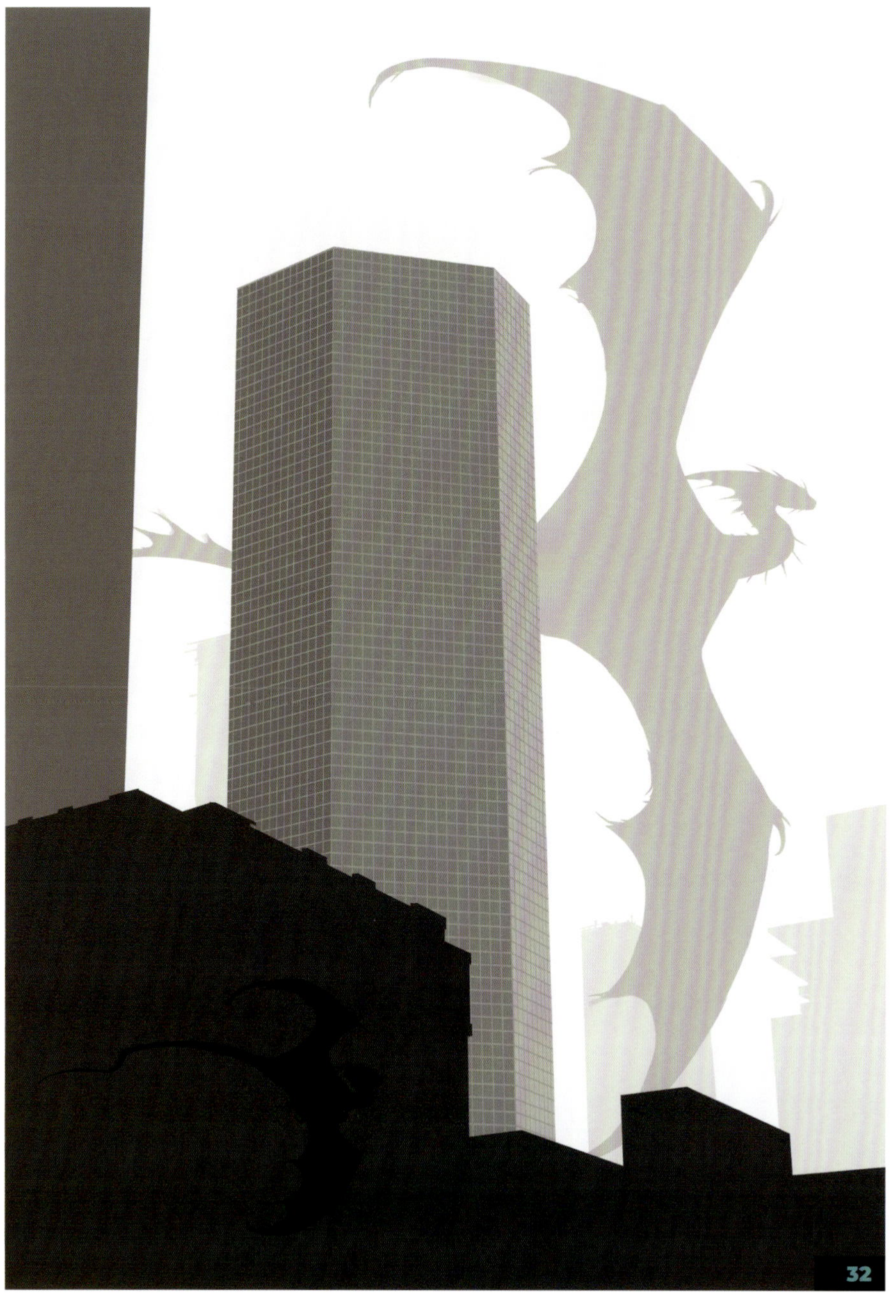

32 An example of the various silhouettes I save as alpha channels in this illustration.

32 SAVING SELECTIONS OF SILHOUETTES

As you draw closer to the finish line of your illustration, it may be beneficial for you to save out selections of your major silhouettes. You can use these silhouettes to easily make final adjustments to the image. I will detail how to do this in Photoshop.

Determine which silhouettes you want to save out. I generally save out each of the major buildings, each of the major subjects, and then general selections for the foreground, middle-ground, and background planes. If, for instance, your background plane consists of five or six different buildings, it may prove tiresome to scroll through the Layer panel and select each one individually in order to perform a value adjustment to the entire background plane. Compiling all of those silhouettes together into one saved selection will speed up the process of doing final adjustments.

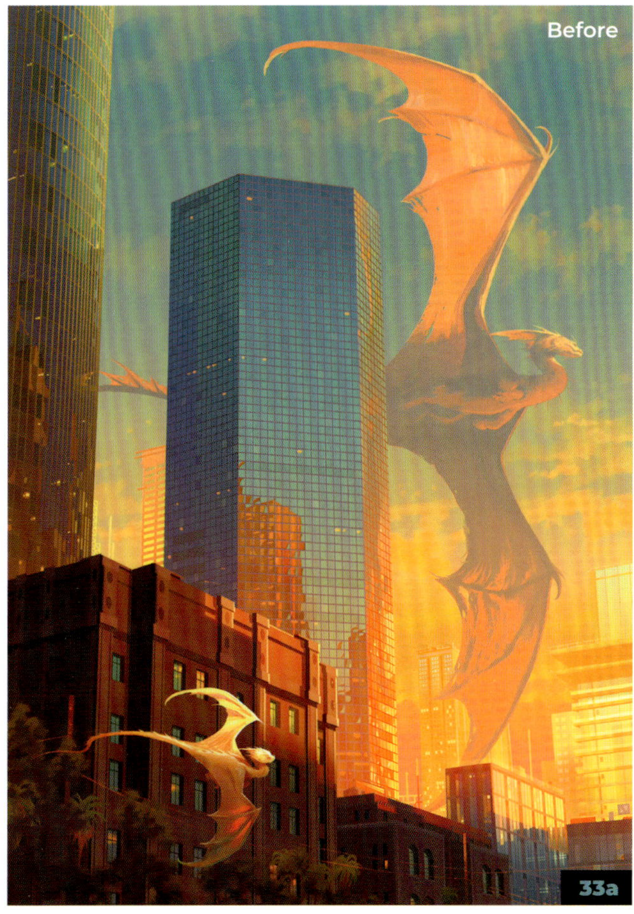

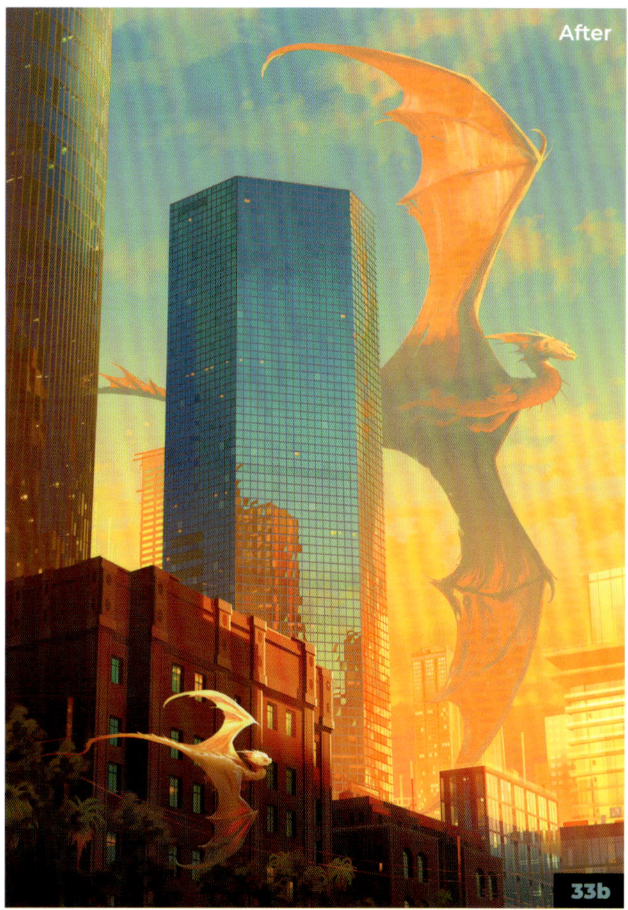

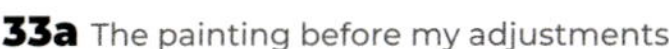
33a The painting before my adjustments.

33b The painting after my adjustments.

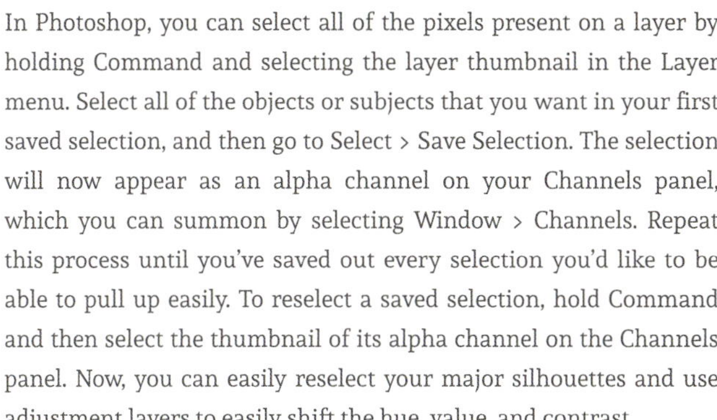
In Photoshop, you can select all of the pixels present on a layer by holding Command and selecting the layer thumbnail in the Layer menu. Select all of the objects or subjects that you want in your first saved selection, and then go to Select > Save Selection. The selection will now appear as an alpha channel on your Channels panel, which you can summon by selecting Window > Channels. Repeat this process until you've saved out every selection you'd like to be able to pull up easily. To reselect a saved selection, hold Command and then select the thumbnail of its alpha channel on the Channels panel. Now, you can easily reselect your major silhouettes and use adjustment layers to easily shift the hue, value, and contrast.

If using a different digital painting program that doesn't allow you to save selections, you can select your desired silhouettes and then fill them in with a solid colour, each on a new layer. Keep the visibility of these layers off, but leave them in a group at the top of your Layer menu so that you can easily select from them as needed.

33 MAKING COLOUR ADJUSTMENTS WITH SAVED SELECTIONS

I use my saved selections to make hue and value changes to large areas of my painting using adjustment layers **(33a, 33b)**. You can read more about these techniques on page 124.

My primary goal is to bring more clarity to the silhouettes. The painting is currently too neutral in value, so I will be aiming to create separation and visual impact through my adjustments. The sky feels too dark, so I use a Levels adjustment to brighten it. I also use selective colour to lean the hues away from peach and towards gold, to create more separation between the mama dragon and the sky behind. Next, I push the cyans and blacks of the main window tower using a Selective Colour adjustment. This gives it more impact and pulls it forward in front of the mama dragon. I warm up the foreground using a Selective Colour layer as well, then create a subtle gradation in the blacks to ensure they're lighter towards the top of the foreground buildings and darker towards the base. I add more contrast to the baby dragon and lean the mama dragon's shadow forms towards cyan, rather than magenta.

LOSING EDGES WITH TEXTURE

Softening or blurring out-of-focus edges is an incredibly useful tool for crafting depth. But if a standard Gaussian blur or airbrush doesn't suit your style, you can soften edges by going over them with a rake brush, grainy brush, or any other kind of textured brush. Any brush that breaks up the solid silhouette will allow you to soften or 'lose' edges.

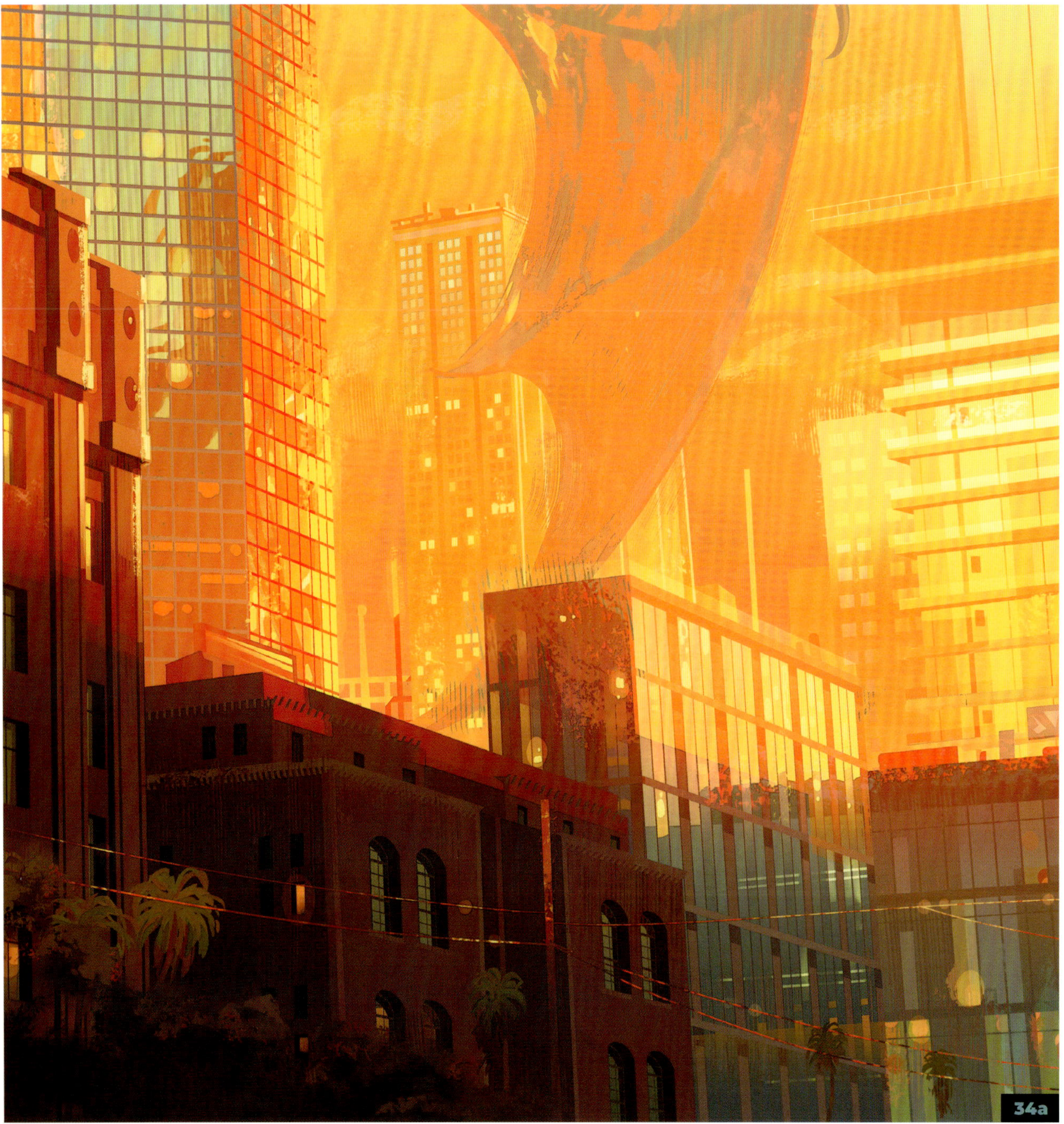

34a – 34c Close-ups of the noisy details and lost edges across the painting.

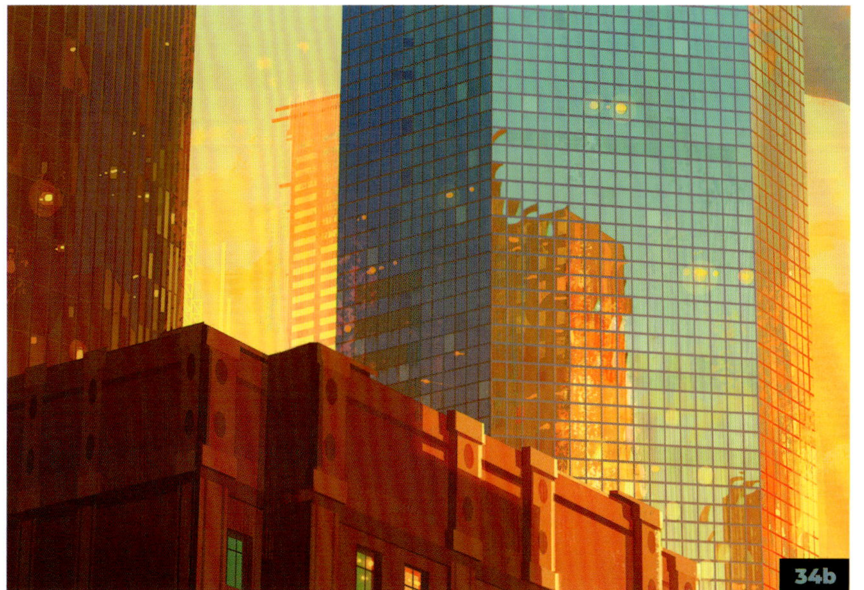
34b

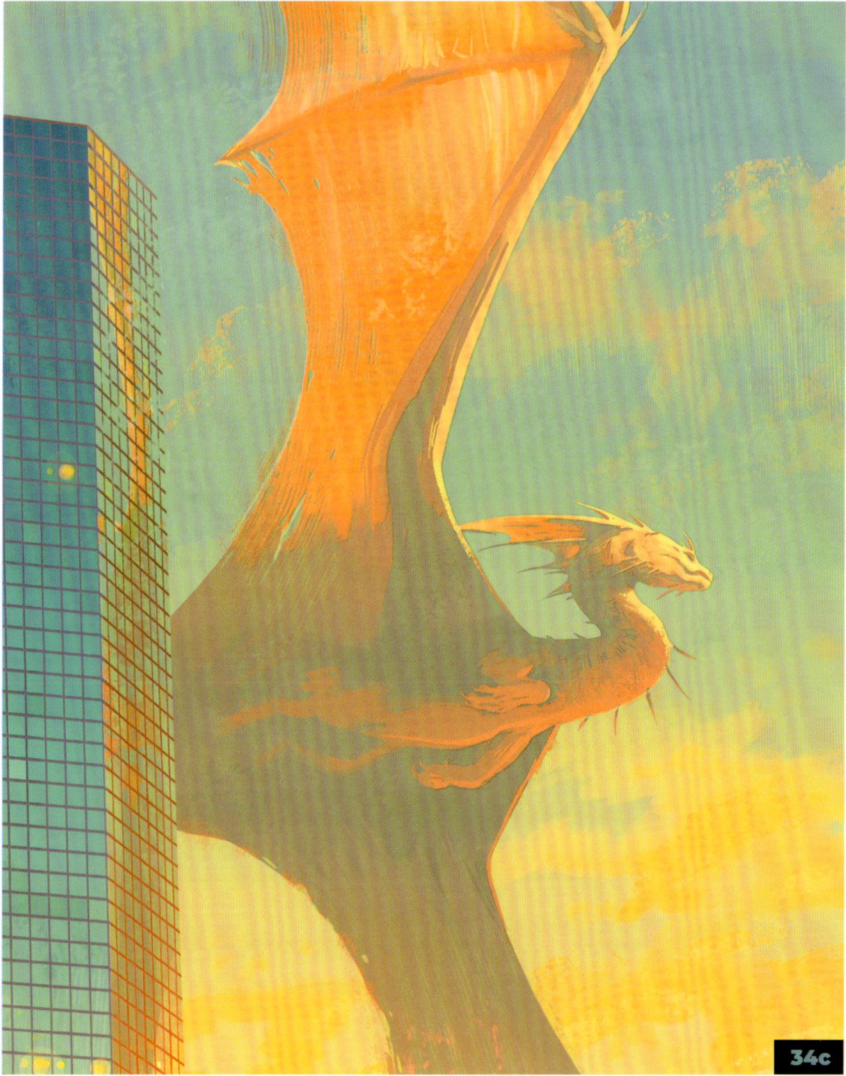
34c

34 ATMOSPHERE, LIGHT, EDGES, & NOISE

Satisfied with my overall image, I zoom in to do a final detail and paint pass across the environment. I begin by softening edges within the brightly lit areas of the city **(34a)**. The gleaming light bloom from the setting sun will make these areas look fuzzy and blinding. Losing edges within the light bloom will appear to make the light intensify. Note the highly saturated, reddish border between the lit areas and shadow areas. This light bloom transitions the light and shadow masses gently, encouraging a brighter appearance in the process.

I also include hints of texture across the rest of the painting **(34b, 34c)** to unify the overall texture and give the rest of the buildings a level of noise that suggests their large size and years of weathering.

ADJUSTMENT LAYER TECHNIQUES

The last ten to twenty per cent of my painting process nearly always involves making hue, saturation, and value changes to saved silhouettes using Photoshop's adjustment layers. In Step 32, I detailed how I save out selections that I use to reselect the major subjects and objects in my paintings easily. In this section, I'll explain how you can use adjustment layers to balance and finalize your paintings.

Adjustment layers are one of Photoshop's greatest features. They allow you to make non-destructive changes to your colour and value. The changes you make will be tied to a layer in your Layer menu. You can switch this adjustment layer off and on, decrease the opacity, change the blending mode, or mask areas out with a clipping mask. You can create an adjustment layer by clicking on the half-light, half-dark circle at the bottom of the layer panel.

My favourite type of Photoshop adjustment layer is the Selective Colour tool **(A)**. It allows you to select a hue family (reds, yellows, greens, cyans, blues, magentas, whites, neutrals, or blacks) and then manipulate the CMYK values of just that hue family. Select a colour from the Colour menu, and then drag the bars left and right to make your adjustments. You can set your changes to Relative or Absolute. Typically I select Absolute.

Let's experiment by making some adjustments to this dragon painting **(B)**. First, I try a global adjustment. By

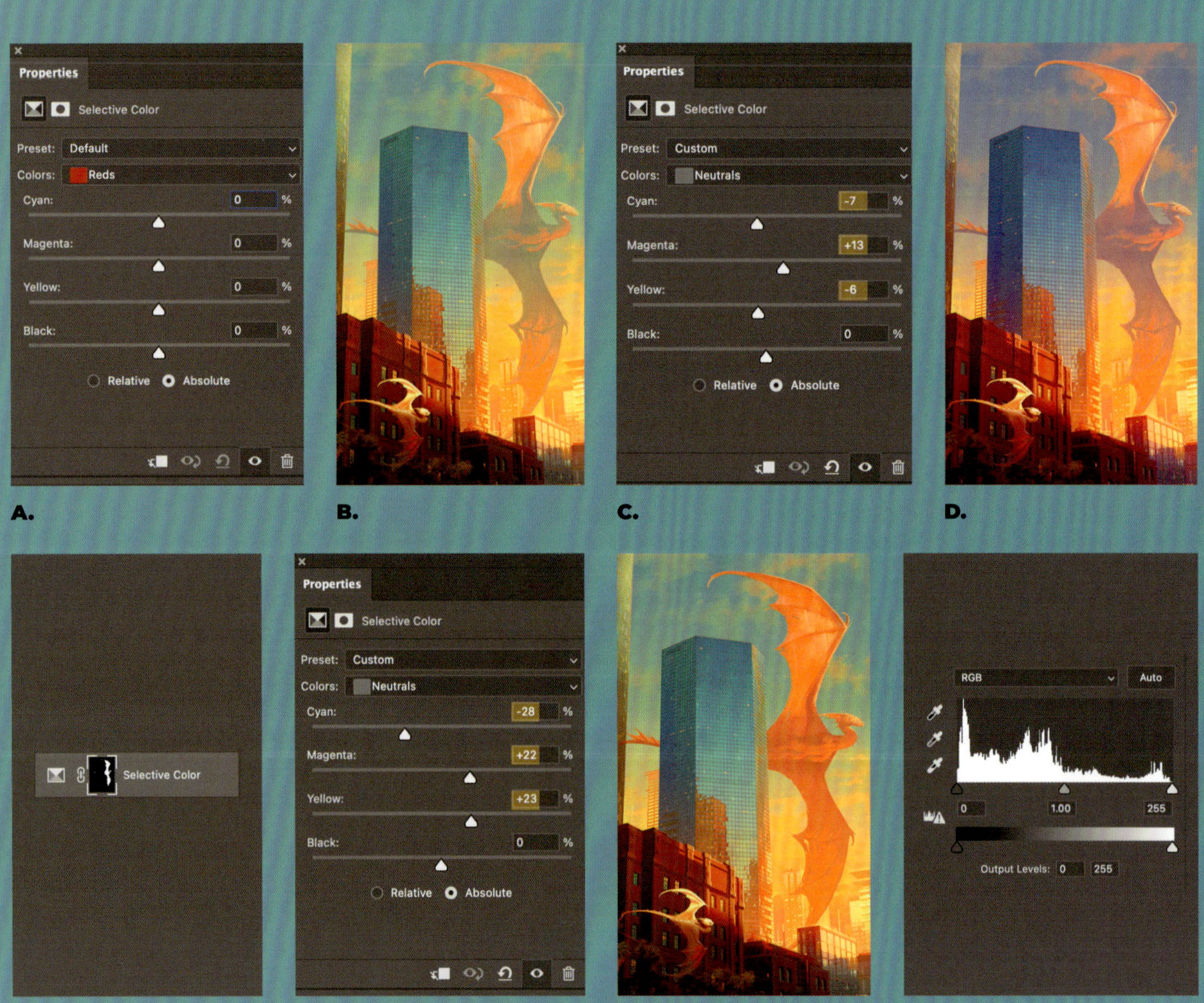

A. B. C. D. E. F. G. H.

selecting the neutrals and decreasing the cyan, increasing the magenta, and decreasing the yellow **(C)**, we end up with a lovely, purple-tinted scene **(D)**. I quite like this version of the image and nearly continue in this direction with my final painting. Sometimes, playing around with this tool leads me to discover new colour options for my paintings that I hadn't previously considered.

Second, I try using one of the selections to adjust one area of the painting. Here I select just the silhouette of the mama dragon. When you select an area first, and then create the adjustment layer, it will automatically apply a layer mask so that the adjustment layer only touches the selected pixels **(E)**. I decide to create a more graphic, solidly warm silhouette for the mama dragon, something similar to my piece *Dragon Migration*, which you can view in the gallery section of this book (page 259). This would be a more graphic depiction of distance and scale than the direction I choose for my final painting. Here I select the neutrals, decrease the cyan, increase the magenta, and increase the yellow **(F, G)**.

Now let's try an adjustment more specific to depth and perspective. Perhaps you have a foreground subject that feels too light in value to sit solidly in the foreground. Using a Multiply layer to darken it may feel flat. Instead, try using a levels adjustment **(H)**. Look at the three triangles on the top bar first. The leftmost triangle on the top bar allows you to push the dark tones darker. The middle triangle allows you to lighten or darken your midtones. The triangle on the right allows you to lighten your light tones. The bar along the bottom allows you to push all values lighter or darker, with the left triangle pushing values lighter and the right triangle pushing values darker. This sounds complex, but is quite intuitive when you experiment with it yourself.

For example, if I want to darken just the buildings in the foreground, I can select them with my alpha channel, deselect the baby dragon, and then create a levels adjustment clipped to the shape of the buildings **(I)**. In my Levels panel, I drag the midtones to the right to darken them. I also pull the overall values darker using the bottom bar **(J)**. This results in darker, richer foreground buildings **(K)**.

You can use these adjustment layers to fix all sorts of depth issues in your painting. If distant structures or objects aren't sitting back into the atmosphere properly, you can desaturate them, lighten them, and narrow their value range in just a couple of minutes. If your focal point needs an extra pop of contrast, you can lean the hue towards a complementary colour of the surroundings, or increase the value contrast with Levels. I recommend you experiment with other types of adjustment layers too, such as Curves, Colour Balance, and Brightness/Contrast.

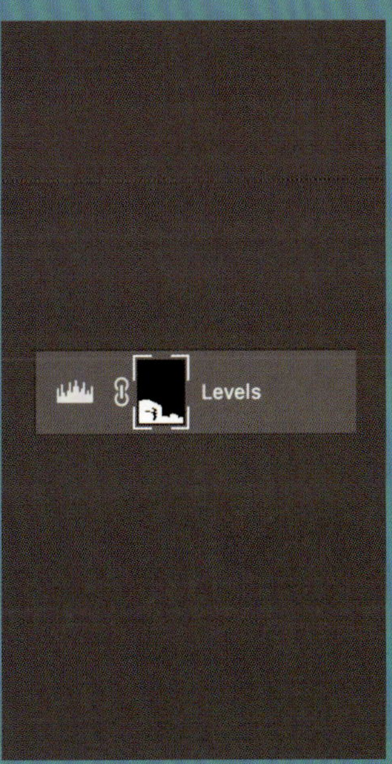

I.

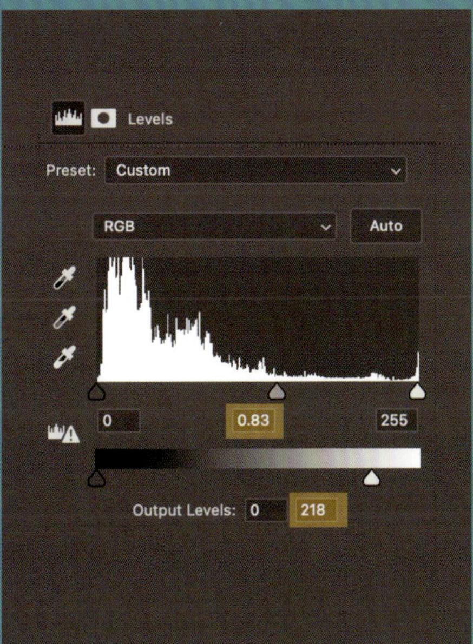

J.

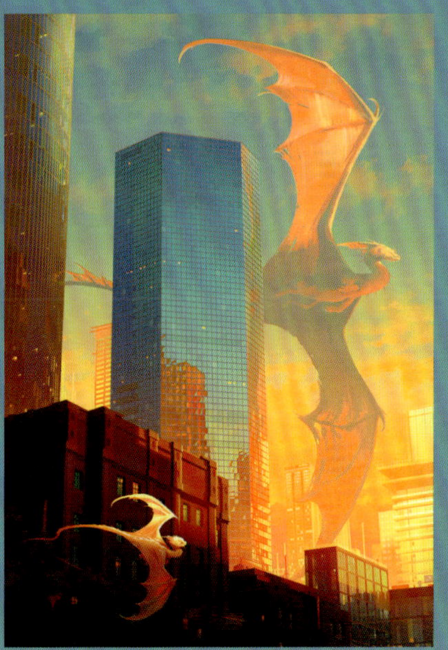

K.

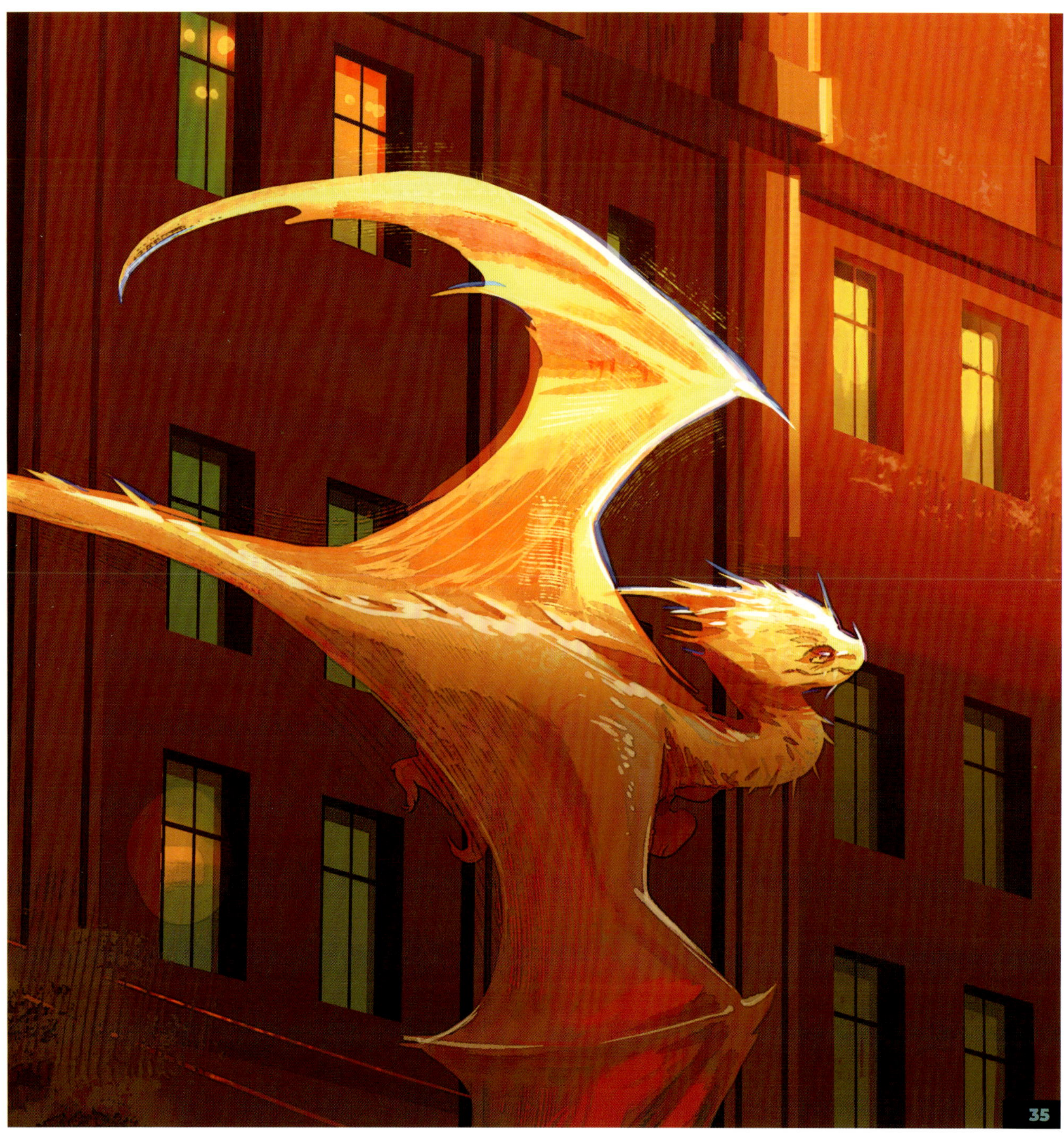

35 A close-up of the baby dragon with the added blue highlight.

35 ADDING A HIGH-CONTRAST GLOW

One fun method to make a bright, white highlight appear even brighter is to give it a neon glow in a hue opposite to the local colour of the subject. The baby dragon is warm, so I use a very saturated blue to encourage the white highlights to glisten. This is a technique I picked up from looking at blown-out photos. When highlights blow out in photography, our phones and cameras compensate by creating a neon border to the highlight. These neon lights tend to also replicate the way looking at a bright highlight feels in life. This additional contrast on the baby dragon also pulls it closer to the camera. You can try this technique using either a Hard Light blending mode, or a Normal blending mode.

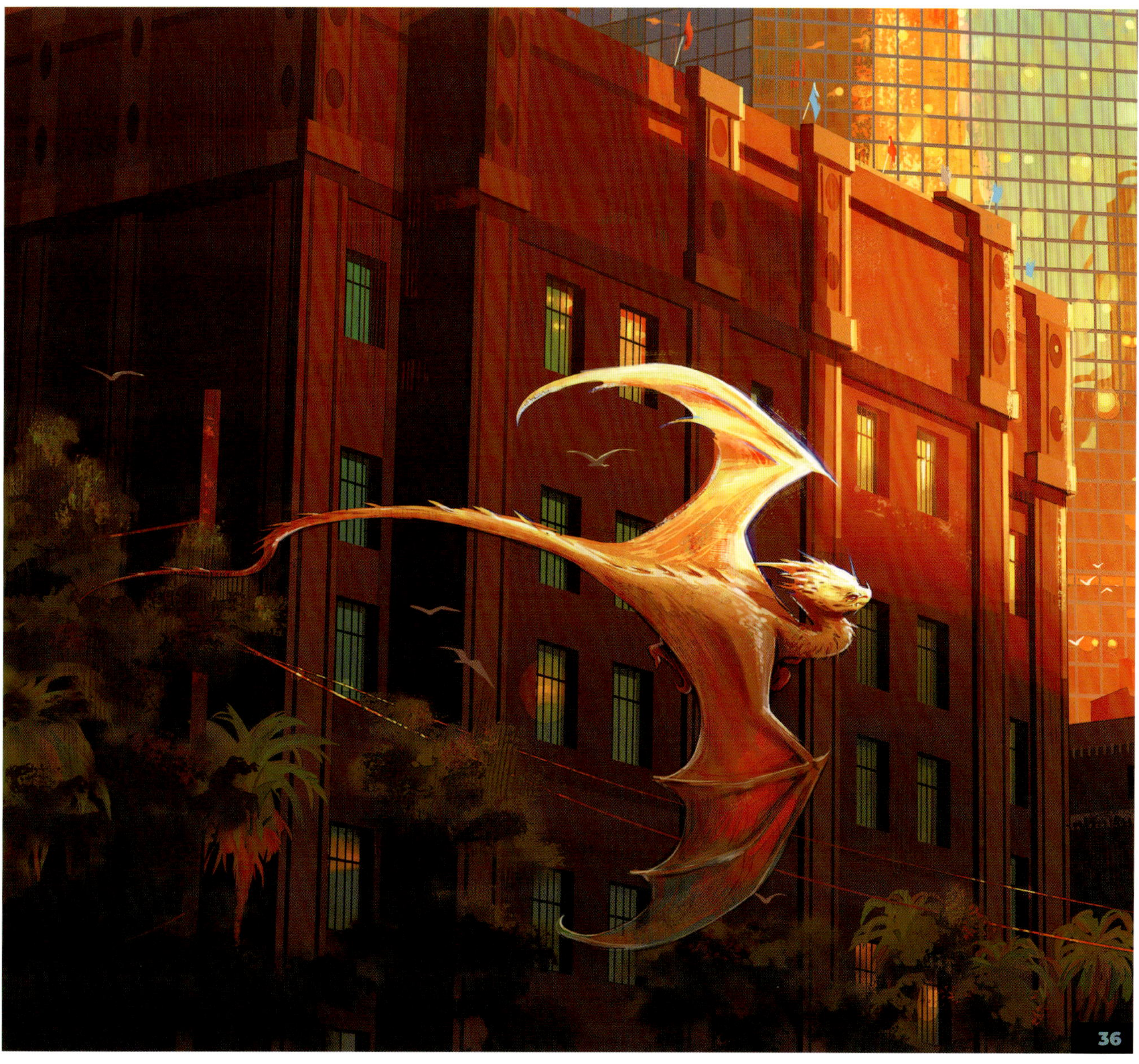

36 A close-up of the foreground, with an additional detail pass.

36 FINAL TOUCHES ON THE FOREGROUND

Now I begin a final detail pass across the foreground. I spend a lot of time sitting back and examining if the scaling and composition are reading in the desired way. I notice that the windows on my nearest foreground building appear too large, wide, and out of scale. I can slyly change this impression by adding additional vertical window leading. This is enough of a shift that the windows no longer distract me.

Next, I notice that the baby dragon doesn't 'pop' forward adequately, so I add some small details to encourage it to 'pop' towards the viewer. I add a subtle dark rim around the dragon's perimeter using a soft, painterly brush on a Multiply layer. This slight drop shadow effect increases the contrast around the dragon's silhouette and draws it forward in space. This is a technique I picked up from examining masterful oil paintings. I also add a few additional brushstrokes of grainy highlights along the exterior of the dragon's form. I use one more Multiply layer to deepen the darkest shadows, and an additional Screen layer to lighten the brightest highlights. This slight expansion of the value range helps to solidify the dragon in the foreground. I finish off my foreground detailing pass with a few additional scale cues: seagulls, along with some multicoloured flags on the building's roof.

37 FINAL TOUCHES ON THE BACKGROUND

Moving from the foreground to the background, I find that the mama dragon still 'pops' forward a bit too much for my liking. I use a Selective Colour adjustment layer to push the neutrals ever so slightly further from black, in just the shadow mass of the mama dragon's body. With that final push, I feel that she sits solidly behind the middle-ground window tower. I also use a grainy scattered dot brush to indicate some noisy atmospheric air debris in front of her shadowed lower wing and body. I sharpen the edges of her silhouette in the highlight areas, and soften the edges in the shadow areas. Finally, I paint a few more specular highlights on the window tower to add some interest to the open blue space it occupies. While doing this, I notice that the reflection on the right face of the tower feels nonsensical and distracting given the angle, so I mostly paint it out, leaving some vague indications of colour and shape.

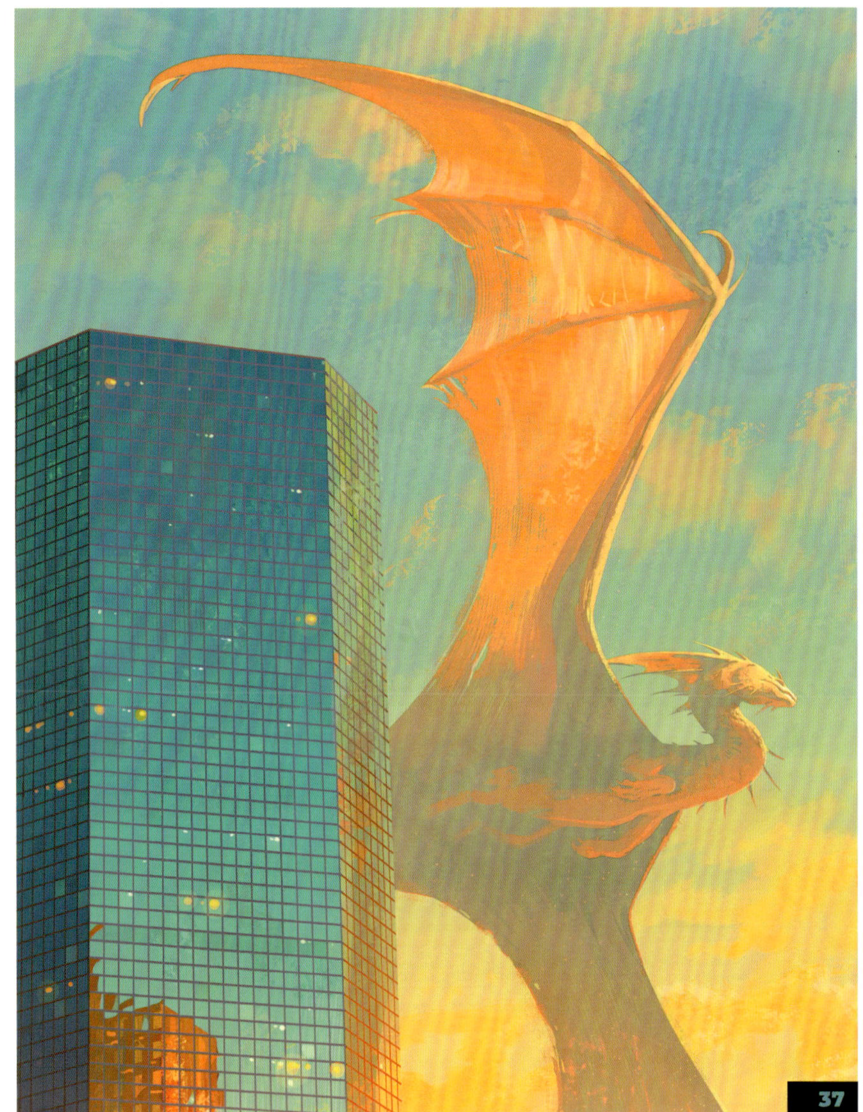

37 A close-up of the background, with an additional detail pass.

38 COMPOSITIONAL ELEMENTS

Let's take a moment to discuss the composition of this image. My intention is for the viewer's eye to be drawn to the baby dragon first. I've used both value contrast and detail contrast to accomplish this. The baby dragon contains the highest level of value contrast (visual contrast between light and dark tones), which automatically draws the eye. The noisy, detailed silhouette, full of little pockets of lighter and darker colour, works together with the value contrast to establish the baby dragon as a primary focal point.

In the same way that the eye is drawn towards contrast, it also instinctually follows gazes, both in life and in artwork. We are naturally curious about where somebody is looking and what they're looking at (even if that somebody is a painted dragon). We follow the little dragon's gaze to the right, but our eye path is interrupted by the dark face of the office building on the bottom right. This vertical form encourages the eye upward, and we follow the lower wing until we reach the mama dragon. The swoop of her upper wing then discourages the eye from straying off the canvas, and we instead follow the light column of sky on the left back towards the foreground, with the foreground building faintly pointing us along the way. This creates a closed feedback loop that encourages viewers to explore the composition without being drawn off the page.

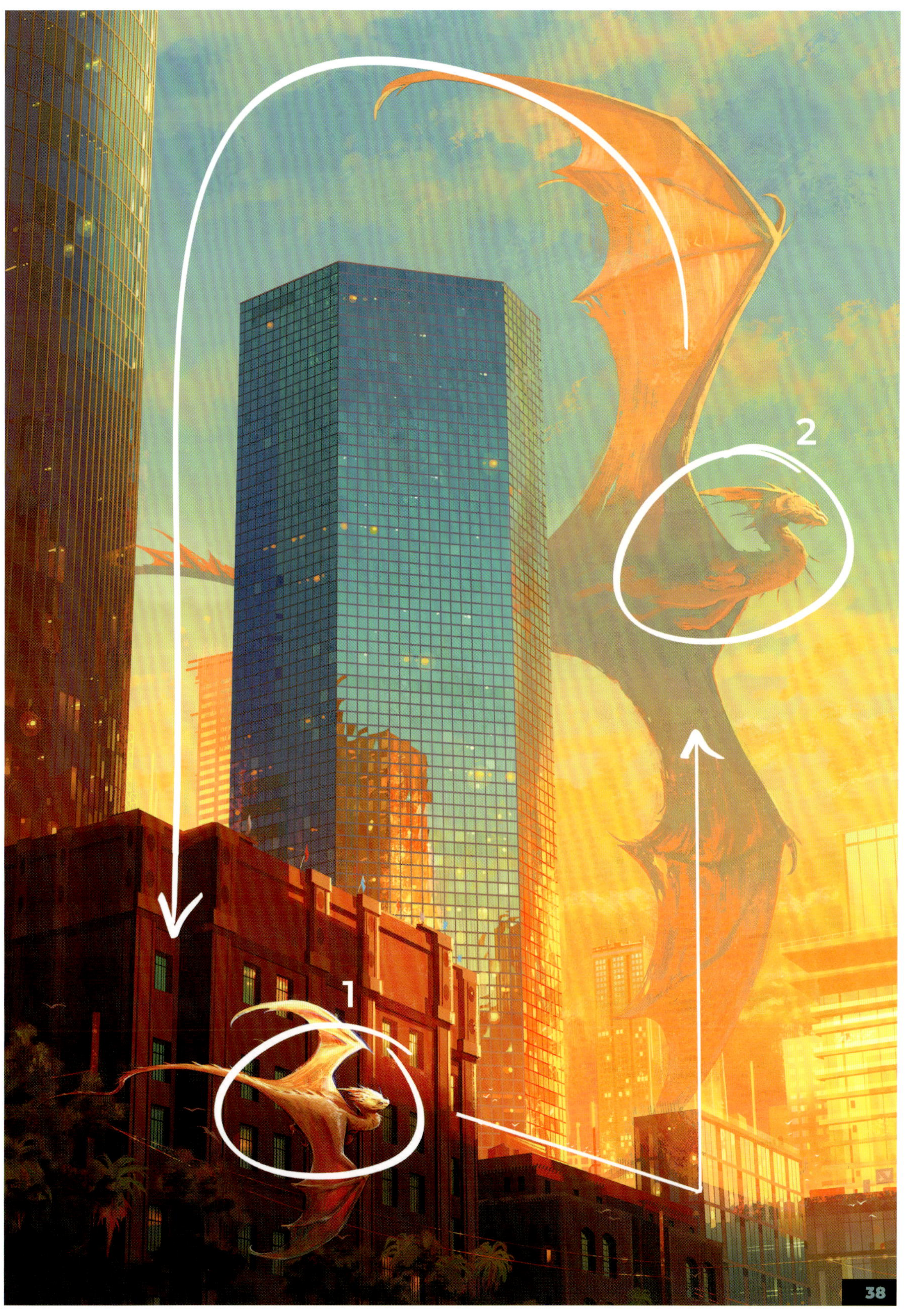

38 A diagram depicting the desired eye path through the image.

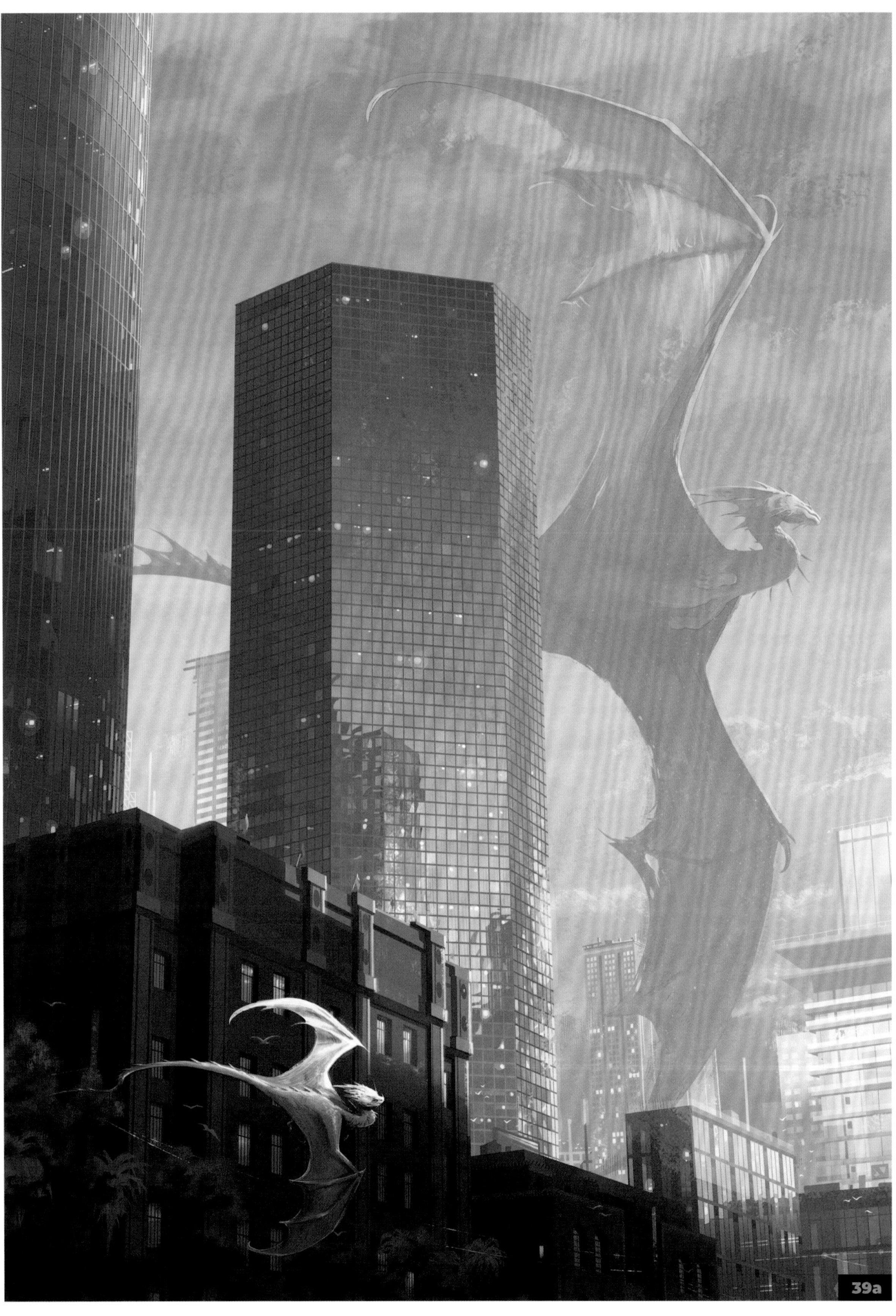
39a

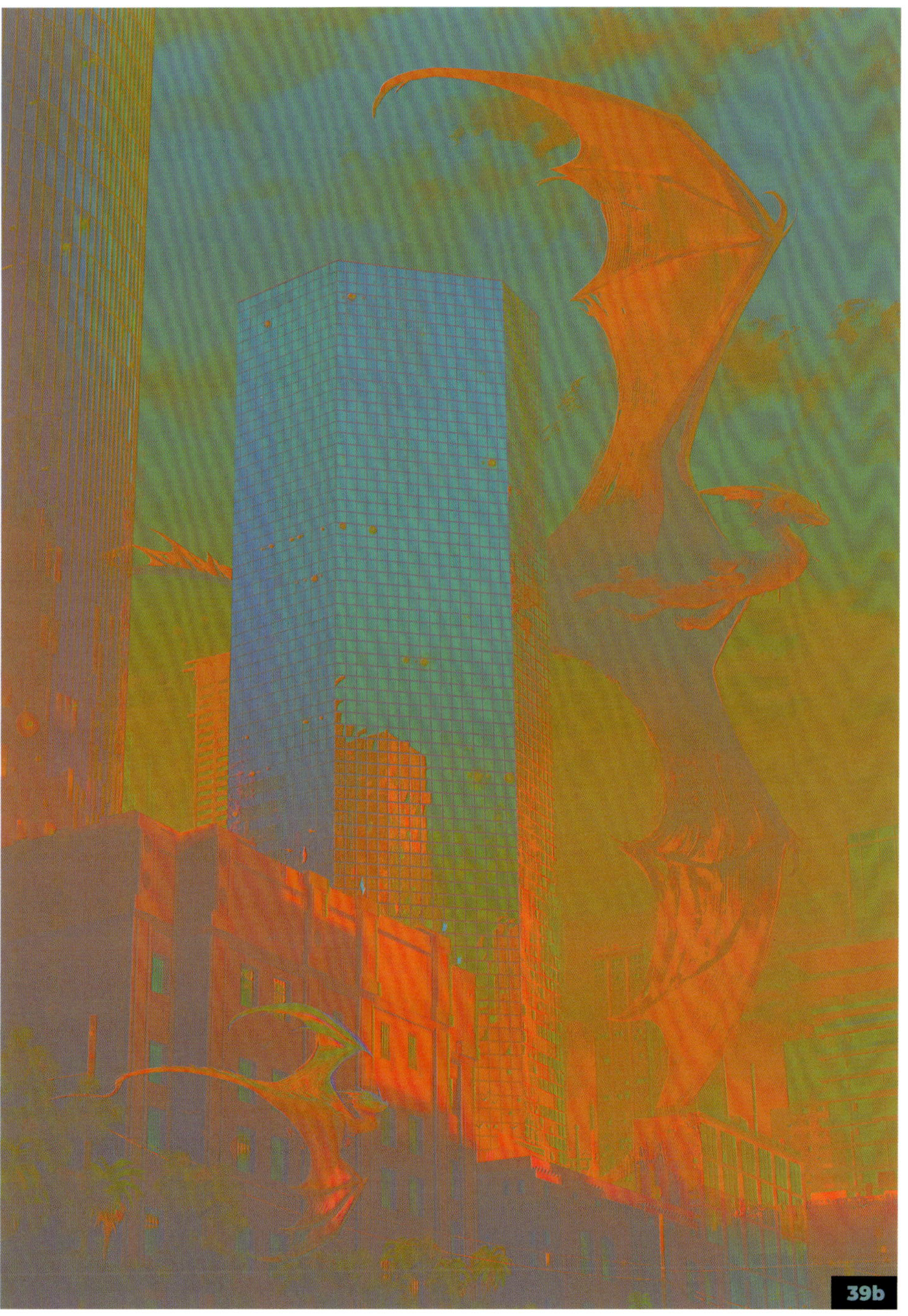

39a & 39b Examining the near-final image in pure value and hue.

39 EXAMINING THE PAINTING IN VALUE & HUE

Examining the final painting in pure value **(39a)**, take note of how the baby dragon clearly 'pops' forward in space, while the mama dragon almost blends into her surroundings in some areas. It's interesting to note how the hue contrast picks up slack in depicting form and detail in areas of low value contrast, especially on the mama dragon **(39b)**.

If you want to view your own paintings in pure value and hue, try leaving a layer filled with pure black set to Colour at the top of your Layer menu to check your values, and a layer filled with a midtone grey set to Luminosity at the top of your Layer menu to check your hues. These digital layer styles aren't perfect, but they can be very helpful in the process of simplifying and improving your compositions.

JUNGLE RUINS

NATHAN FOWKES

Creating the illusion of depth is one of my all-time favourite artistic techniques. As we compose pictures, we are not simply creating a place or depicting an event, we are carefully designing an emotional experience for our audience. When it comes to creating depth and perspective in a piece of artwork, we must build a powerful sense of presence to draw the viewer in.

For this project, I will be constructing a scene that takes us through many layers of foreground, foliage, and architecture, and into a deep background. I'll show you how to set up the perspective and how to implement techniques to create the illusion of depth where it is needed most.

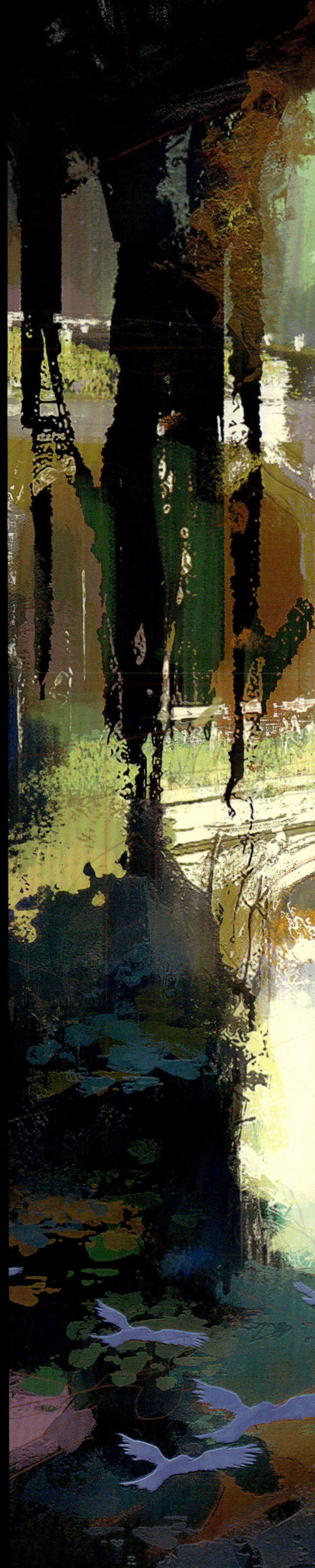

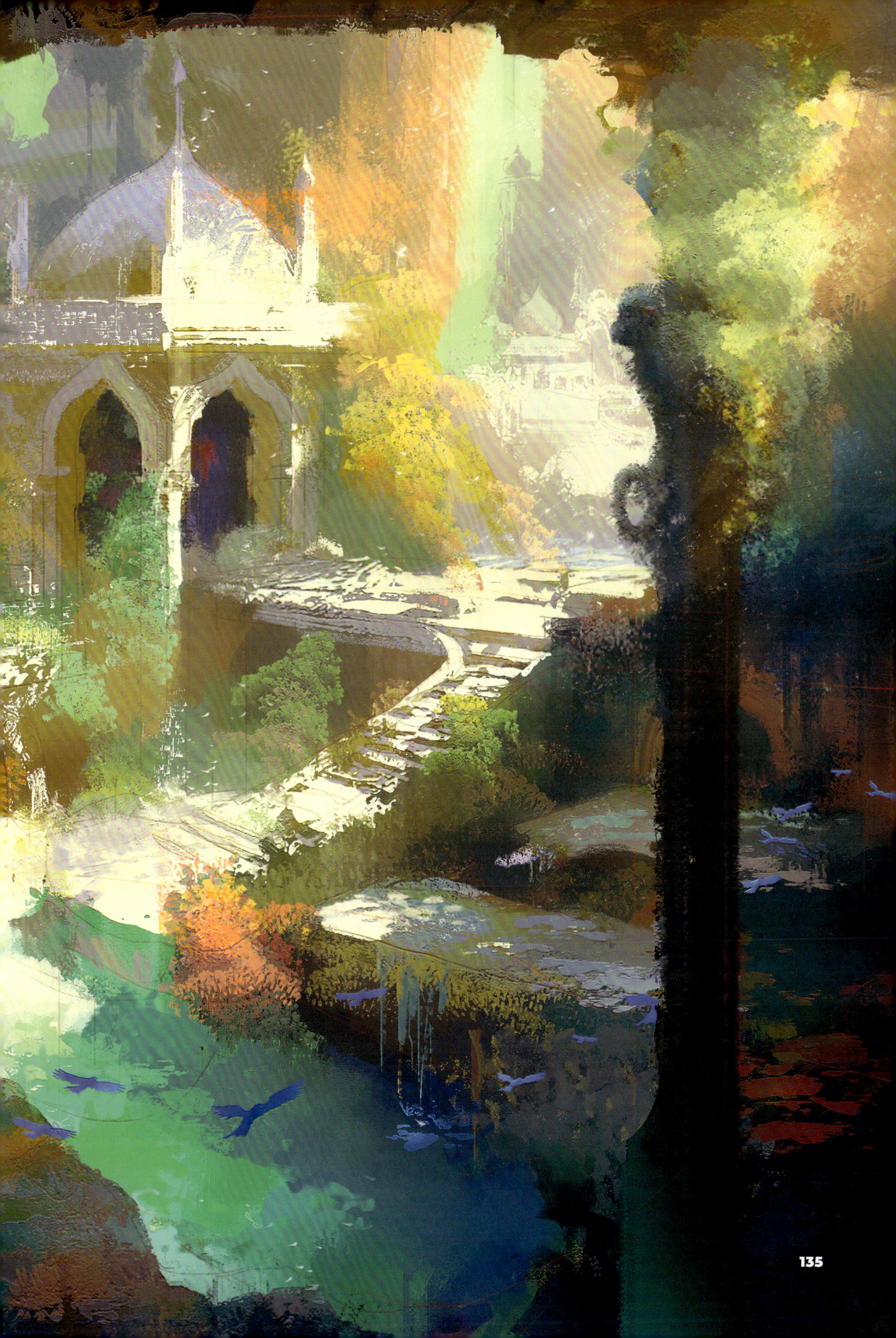

01 SETTING THE HORIZON

A grid that shows a perspective point of view (POV) is a good place to get started. This example is a standard two-point perspective set-up. I always begin with the eye-level line, which is also the horizon line, and decide where it will be placed for the scene. I place it lower on the page, as we will be looking up into tall architecture and trees, but I still want enough space below eye level to show a significant ground plane.

02 AN INITIAL IDEA

And here's my first idea – which, of course, means I'm likely going to reject it. I originally thought it would be fun (and a great display of perspective) to include a lot of vertical architecture and trees, with a lone figure in the foreground for scale. There might be a little footbridge for a stream and pond, so the perspective of reflections could also be shown, but in the end I abandon this idea. I feel it's a little too generic to suit the interest of you, the reader, and it would need a substantial downward perspective for variety.

03 LOOKING DOWN

A deep, downward view is not as common as some other perspectives used in art, but it's one that art students may want to add to their repertoire. It's rarer because we go through most of our lives viewing the world at eye level, where the horizon would be in view if there was nothing obstructing it. For most of us, a steep downward view is reserved for occasions when we're hiking in the mountains, looking down from a cliff, or in some other potentially dangerous situation. So this viewpoint can convey danger, but it can also give us a powerful bird's-eye view of the world, which conveys a sense of omniscience. With this in mind, for my next sketch I create a downward-looking three-point perspective, which will add drama and more interesting architectural shapes.

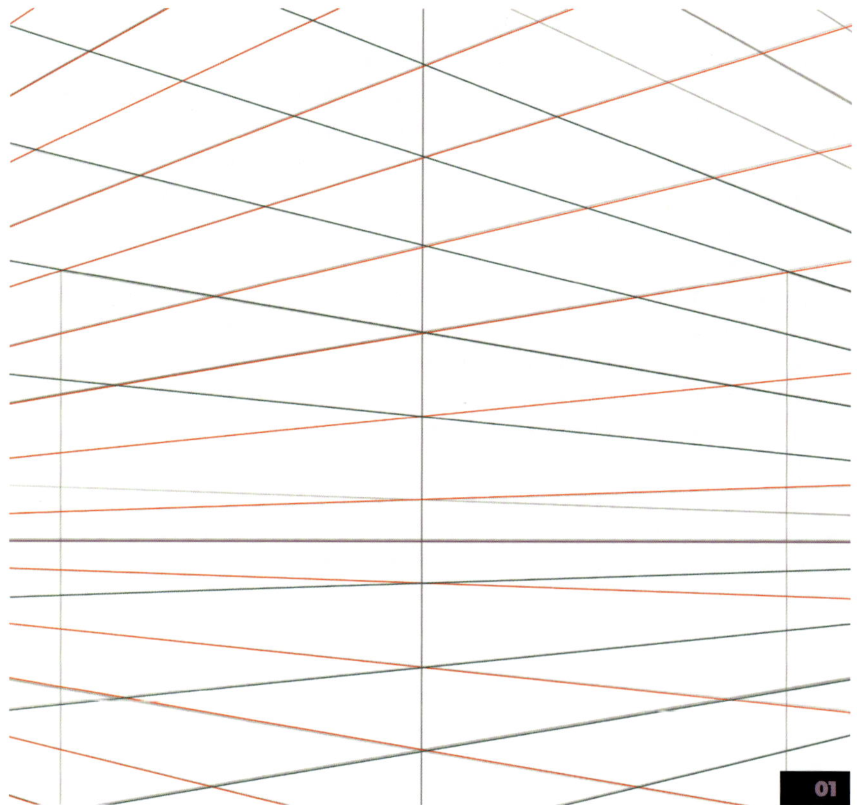

01 Two-point perspective layout that begins with the eye-level line placement.

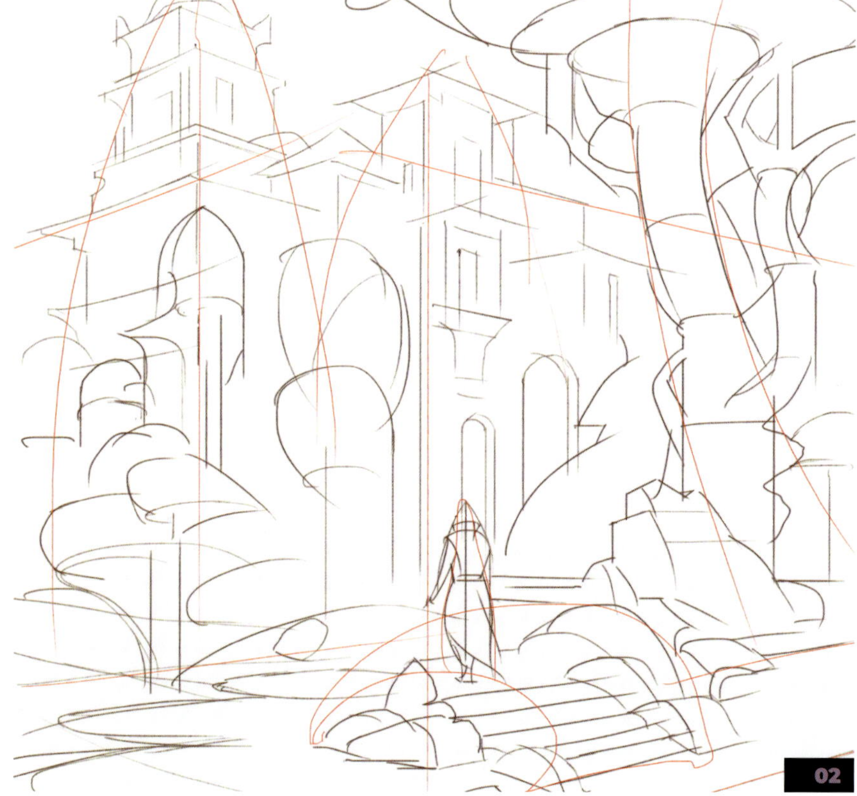

02 An initial idea using a low-eye-level POV, which I eventually discard.

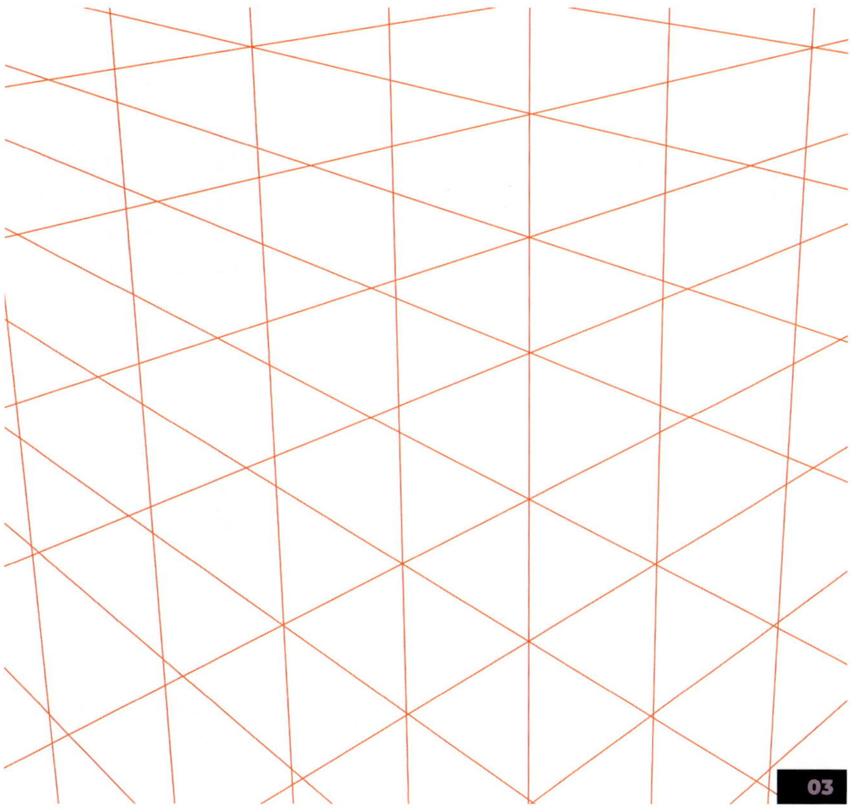

03 A three-point perspective POV layout, featuring a downward view.

VIEWPOINT

When creating an image, I almost always begin by establishing the viewpoint. Will I use a very low one, like a worm's-eye view looking up into a vast world? Or will it be a viewpoint that's very high in the picture plane – a bird's-eye view, peering down to create an omniscient feeling? Another option is a standard, middle-of-the-picture eye-level point of view, which is the way humans usually experience the world. For extreme points of view, very high or very low, you will probably want to use a three-point perspective, where your verticals converge towards a vanishing point. Making this decision up-front will help you get your painting heading in the right direction from the start.

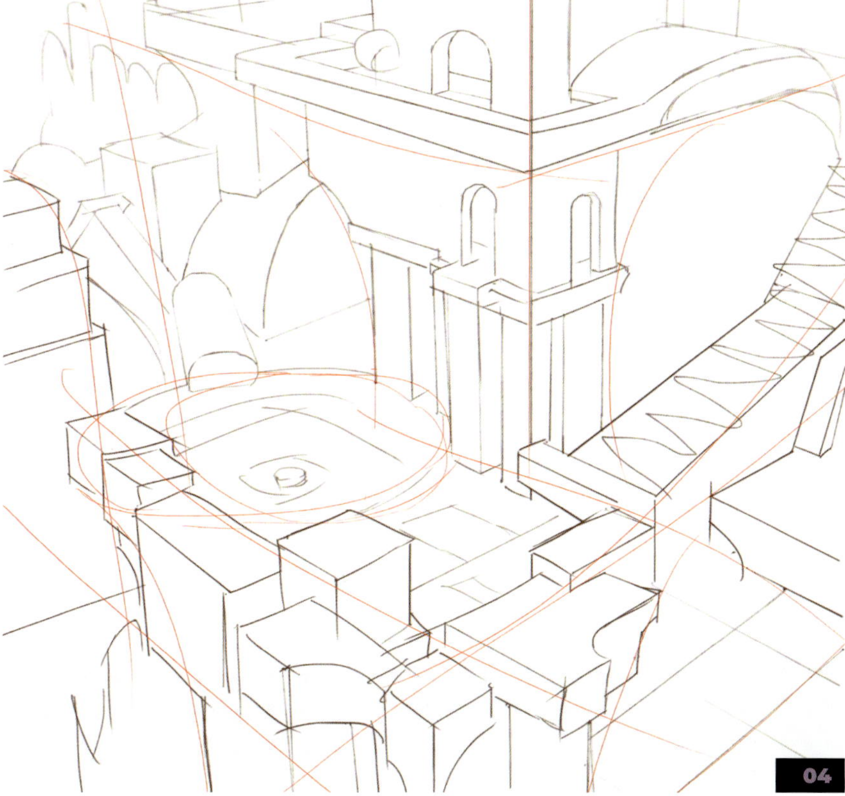

04 An initial idea using a high-eye-level POV.

04 LOOKING DOWN

Here's my perspective sketch based on this new point of view. It's a courtyard surrounded by quarried stone ruins, and the downward view creates an aura of mystery and helps the location feel like a discovery. Large stones flare into the foreground to create a feeling of depth in the rest of the image, while the stairs to the right and fallen blocks to the left follow perspective lines leading away from the viewer to create more depth, too. The columns and windows to the right of the centre are a potential focal area. I like this sketch, and maybe I will do more with it someday, but I ended up rejecting it for this project. For this tutorial, I want to create an image that uses a significant perspective looking both upwards and downwards.

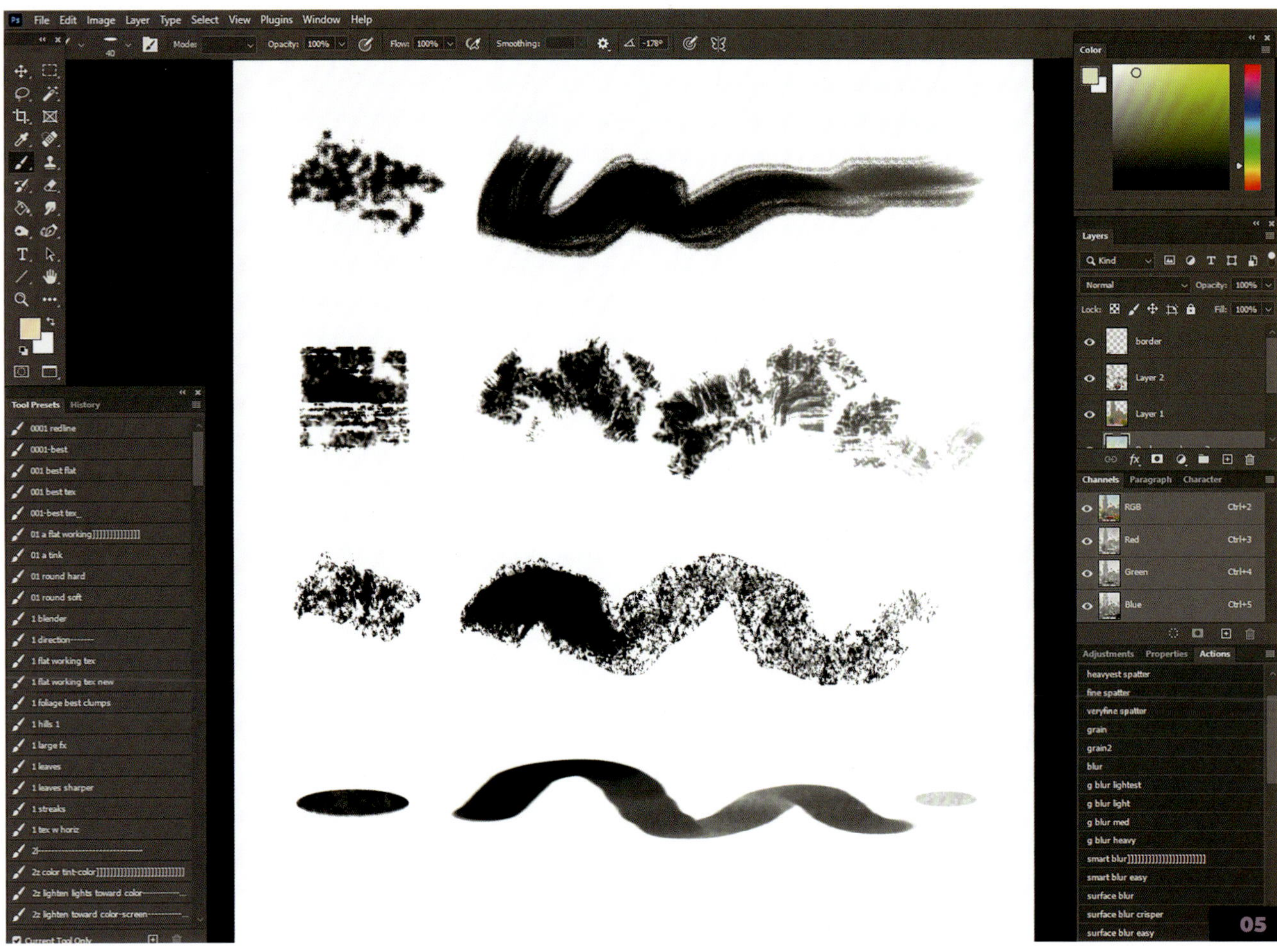

05 This is my Photoshop layout and the typical brushes I use for digital painting.

05 SOFTWARE SET-UP

I will be painting digitally in Photoshop from this point forward. Digital painting is the ideal medium for commercial illustration and production work, as it is efficient for making changes and adjustments when receiving notes and requests from clients. The digital brushes I use are fairly simple, and many of them come as standard with Photoshop. They mostly resemble chalk or a flat paintbrush and use pen pressure to determine the opacity and thickness of the stroke. I lean towards brushes that create organic strokes with texture. There are also a few speciality brushes that I'll show you later in the tutorial.

06 WARMING UP

Since I've not yet been satisfied with my perspective sketches, I decide to break away and have a little fun, playing a bit of hooky from this project, but at the same time doing something to help me get into it more. I love landscape sketching, especially places filled with mood, and I figure a moody, misty swampland will be a great study in depth. I take the opportunity to experiment with principles that we will go much deeper into later in this chapter: edges, temperature, and texture.

07 QUALITY OF DEPTH

Looking closer at the warm-up image, you can see how I use heavy textures and visual activity in the foreground, then the textures and colours become softer, cooler, and more grouped into the background. You will also notice some dark orange accents in the foreground – all of these elements combine to help push this area forward in contrast to the passive distance. This sketch is an absolute blast and helps me to get my head around creating a quality of depth. I'm ready to dive back into ideas for a final image.

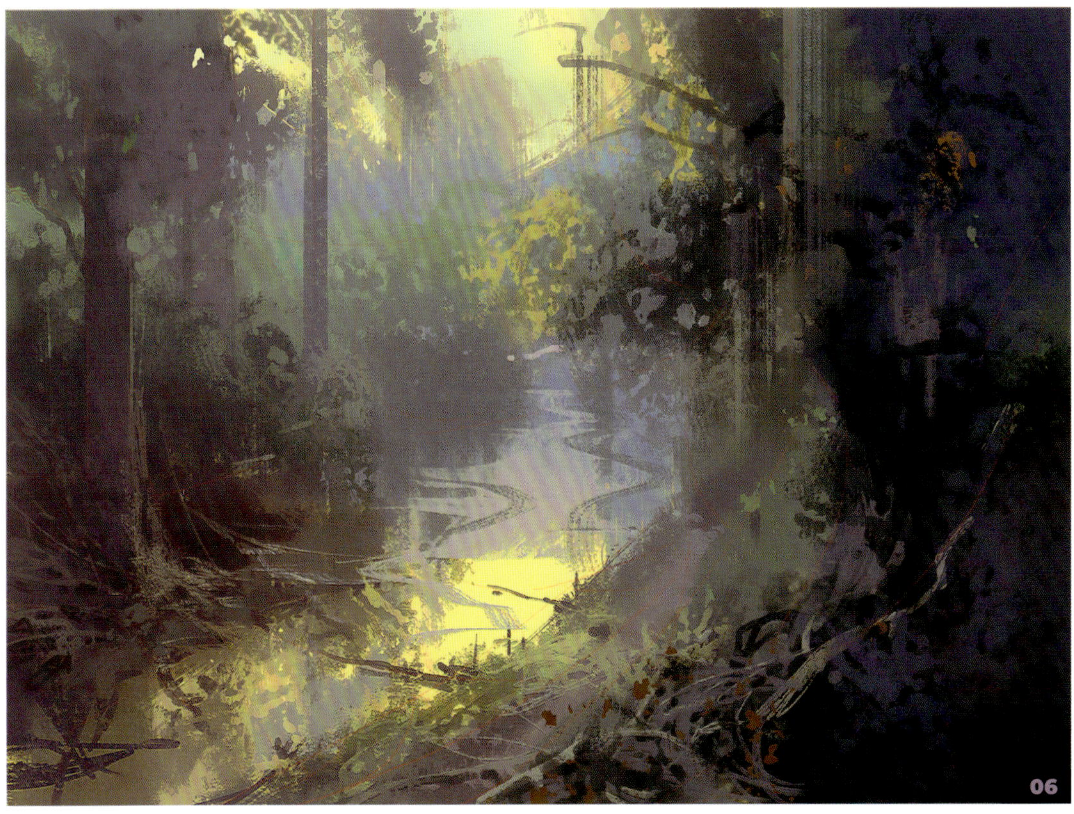

06 A warm-up study, practising techniques in preparation for the project.

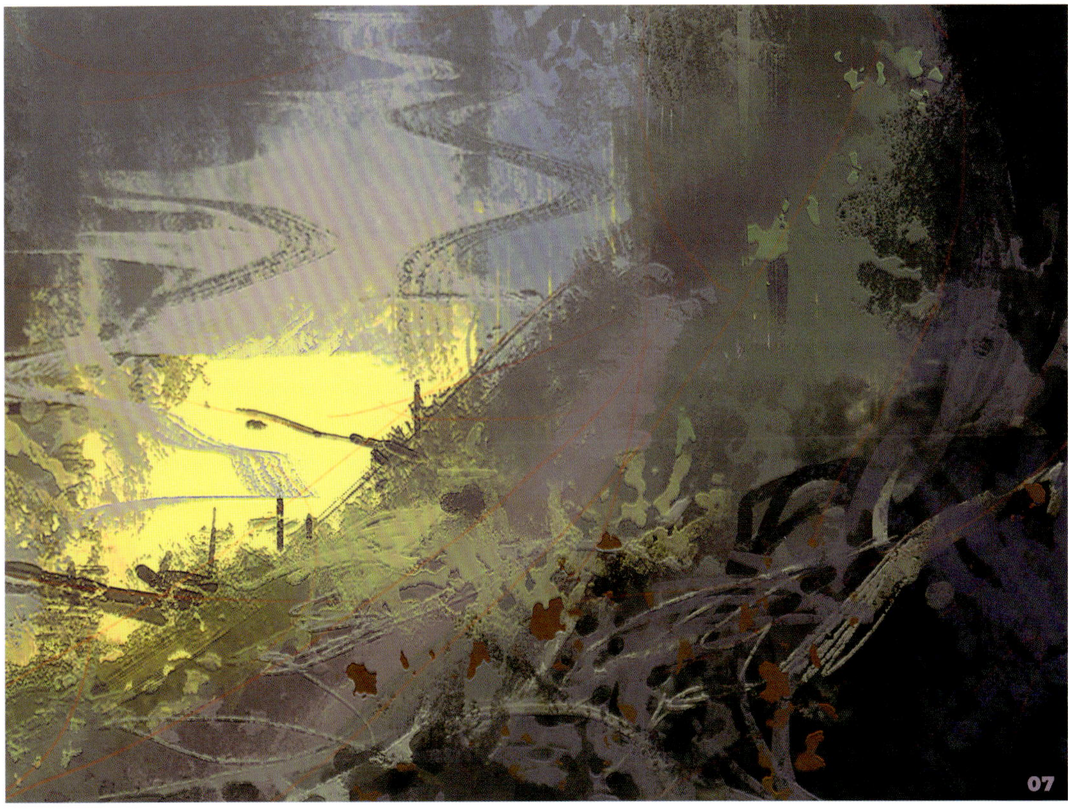

07 A crop of the warm-up image to show texture and detail.

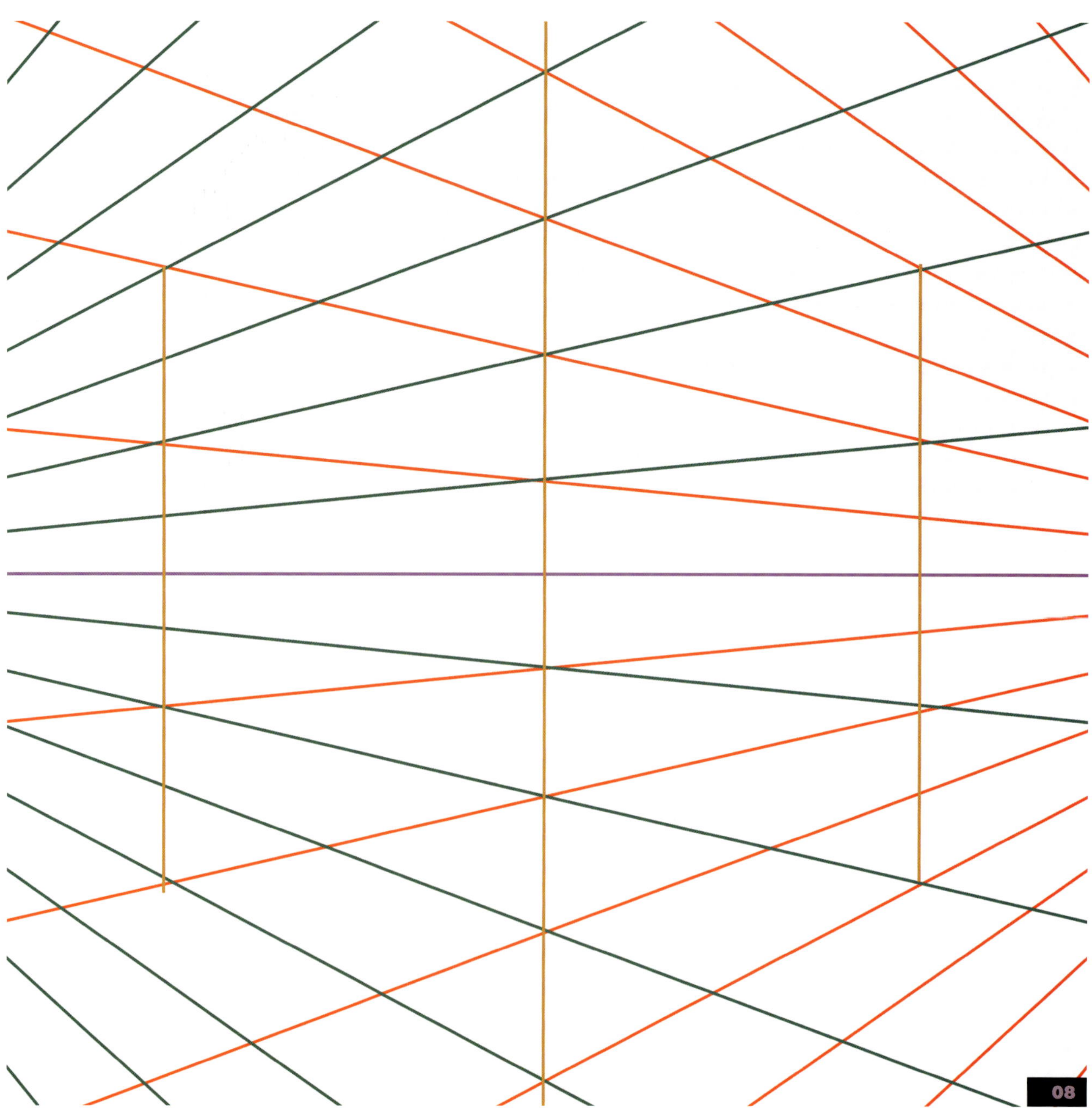

08 An expanded version of the mid-eye-level perspective grid.

08 EXPANDING THE VIEW

I decide to use the same perspective grid from step 01 for this project. It's a reliable point of view that keeps the eye-level line towards the middle. This way, we can direct the viewer's eye as far left, right, upwards, downwards, near, or far as desired. It potentially provides the full range of three-dimensional possibilities. I choose to expand the grid to allow for a high perspective, but also to enable me to push deeply into the ground plane. This will provide the opportunity to thoroughly explore a broad point of view for the scene, and a square frame will allow me an equal amount of horizontal and vertical space in which to build a composition.

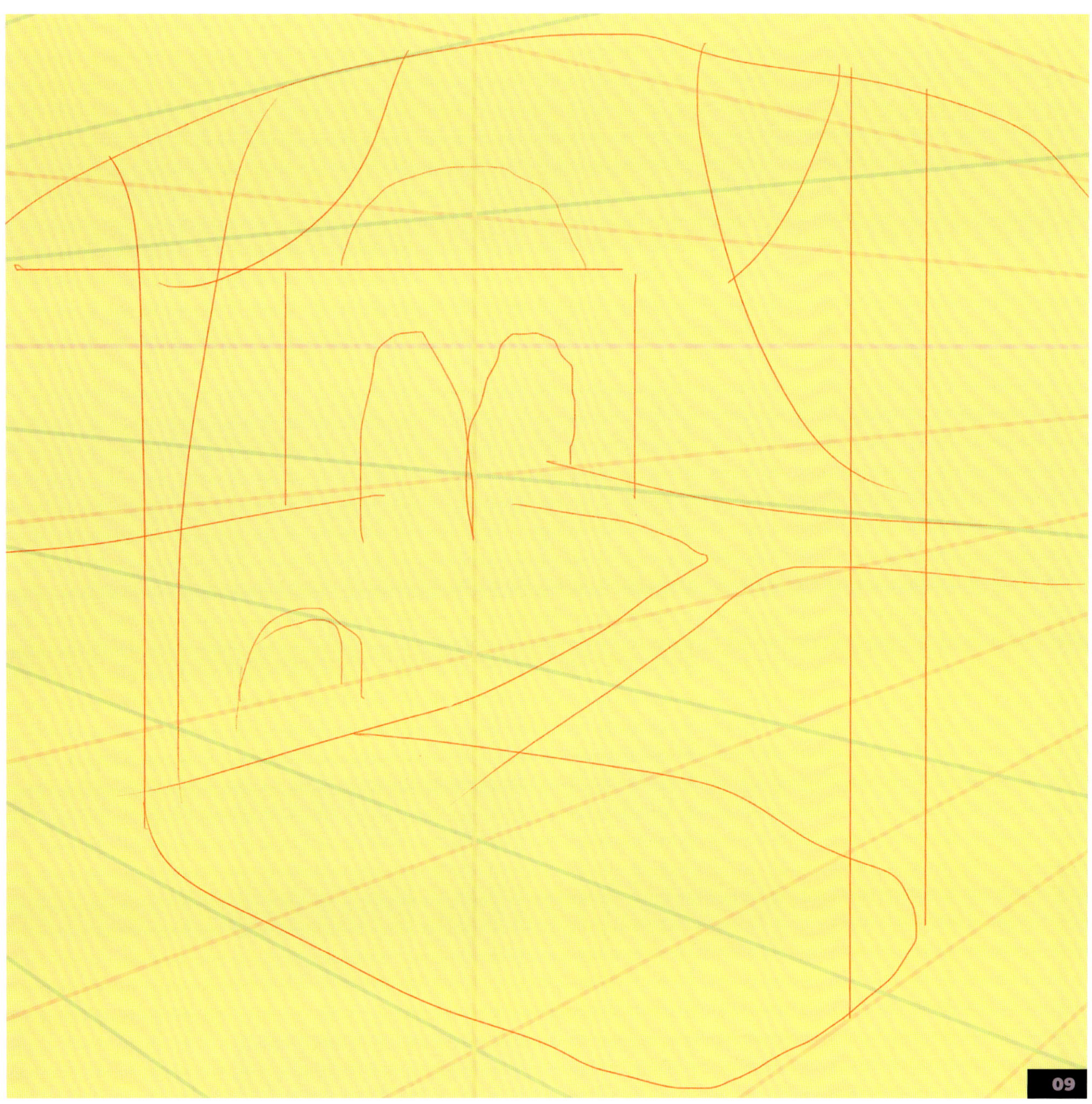

09 A very simple layout drawing to begin an exploratory colour comp.

09 A SIMPLE START

Now let's get going on the idea for the final image. I'm preparing for a scene that has a central domed pavilion, raised bridge-ways, and a staircase that takes us down to a lower pool. The painting will be filled with foliage and have a strong framing foreground. I want the scene to be full of history, as it will be in a state of ruin and decay. You may have noticed that my drawing for this step is childishly simple – that's all I want at this point. I'll be treating my first pass as a colour comp to see how things go, and then I hope to flesh out the image from there, beginning with the yellow base colour. Despite my simple drawing, I do have my perspective lines visible and will carefully follow them as I go. It's a good idea to keep your perspective lines slightly visible as you work because it's so easy to get caught up in individual areas of the painting and lose track of the direction in which the brushstrokes need to go. Many times I've seen students unintentionally let their brushwork deviate to a generic horizontal position because they're not used to thinking in terms of steep perspective.

EMPHASIZING DEPTH

A painting must translate the three-dimensional world into something that feels convincing on a two-dimensional surface. That means we can't simply draw and paint things the way they really are – it just doesn't work. My process is to use every trick and technique I can to make the closer areas advance in the scene and the further away areas recede.

Take a look at the rusty coin on the top left: would a coin really look like this? The truth is that I have heavily cheated it. I've used several types of contrast to differentiate between the advancing and receding edges: value contrast (relative lightness or darkness), temperature contrast (warm versus cool), texture contrast (rough versus smooth), and edge contrast (soft versus hard). Note that the receding edge is the exact opposite of the advancing edge – the value is darker, the temperature cooler, the texture removed, and the edges softer. Most notable is the way I've pushed warm colours to the front, while using cool colours towards the back. Heat tends to visually come forward and cool tends to visually recede. I have pulled out all the stops to make this coin feel three-dimensional. It was rendered two-dimensionally with painting tools in Photoshop, but is designed to feel completely 3D.

Take a careful look at each of the other images and you will see that I've utilized this effect of advancing and receding edges wherever possible throughout the tutorial painting. Without this technique, the scene would feel much flatter, and even confusing. Further edges might feel like they're coming forward and then the whole image falls apart, and nobody wants that.

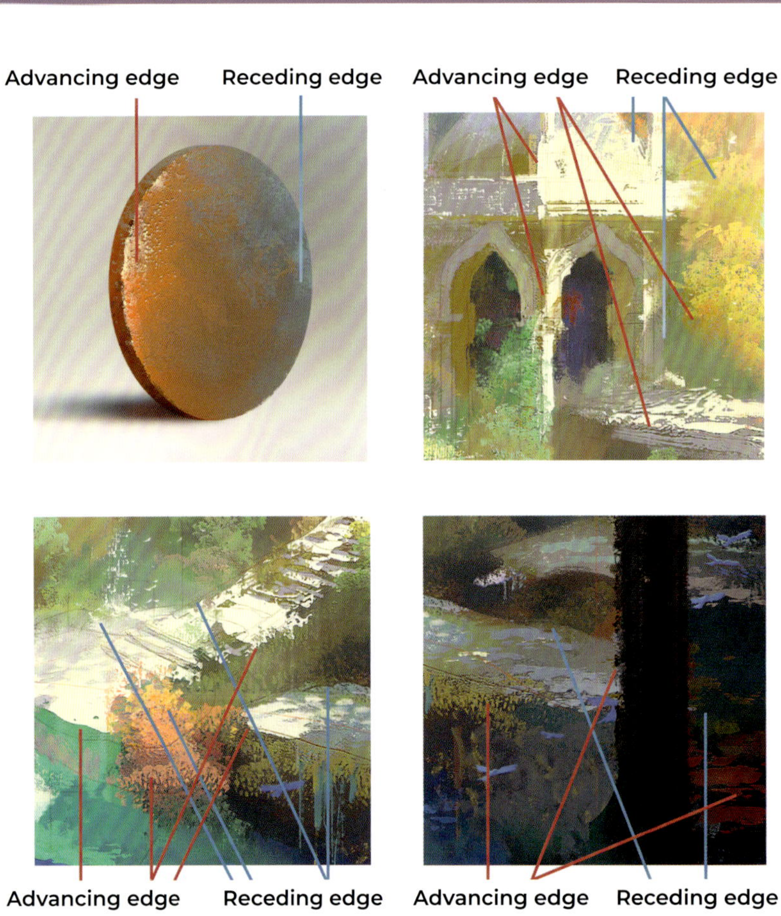

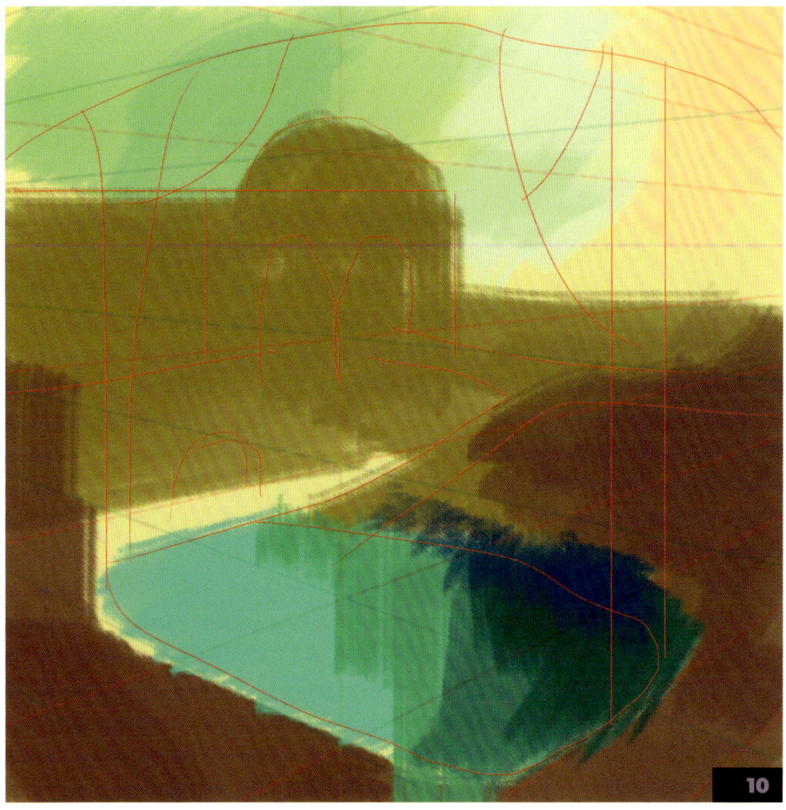

10 Initial simple block-in to begin the colour comp.

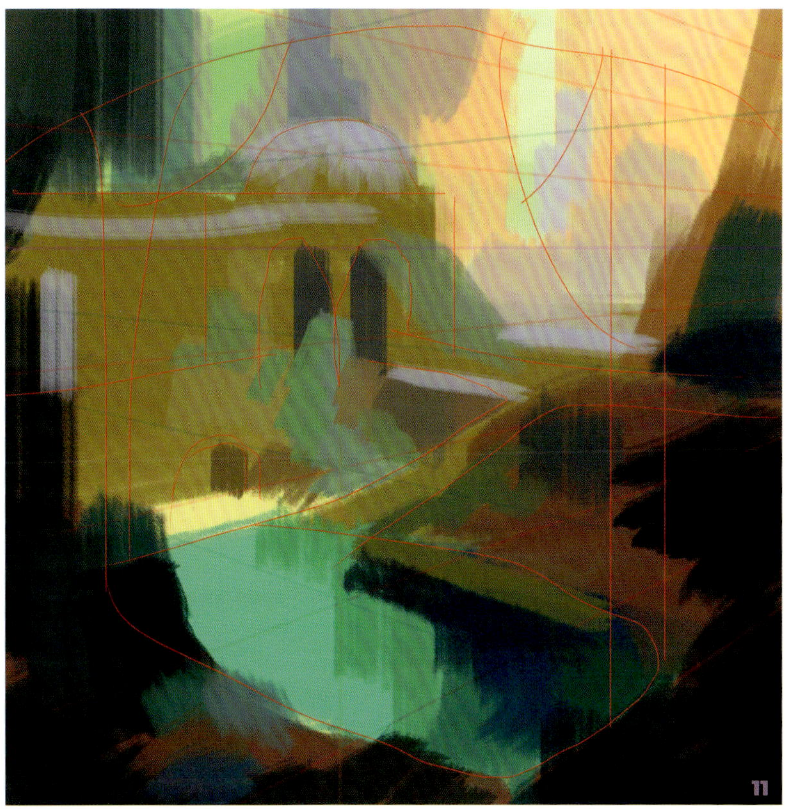

11 Overall block-in of the shadow colours.

10 BLOCKING IN

As we get started with the painting, I should define my terminology. I'm referring to this initial process as a 'comp'. This term started out as shorthand for 'comprehensive sketch' a century or more ago. It was the proof-of-concept sketch that would be sent to an art director or publisher for initial approval. When roughing out a comp, I find it useful to keep things very simple, so I'm blocking in the building silhouette as if it's made of warm stone. There's an emerald pool in the centre and a greenish sky for a surreal, alluring quality. This colour in the sky is also very practical, as it harmonizes with the pool of water and yet also feels quite distant to the warmer colours in the foreground. The area surrounding the pool is simply brown earth.

11 COLOURS IN SHADOW

It's now time to start building more variety, while also keeping the various elements grouped and organized by treating everything as if it's in shadow. There is no rule about painting light or shadow first; it just depends on the needs of an individual scene. For this image, it makes most sense to paint an overall shadow block-in and then work the light into it. When a scene has less light and more shadow, I will often choose to begin this way. I am addressing one light source here, however, which is light from the sky. The blue sky shines cool light down onto the top planes, and I've started to indicate this. The green foliage begins to appear now as well, bridging the gap between the emerald of the pool and the browns of the earth.

I have also roughed-in an initial background. My vivid background oranges might seem counter-intuitive to the idea that warm colours advance and cool colours recede, but I'm juggling competing needs for this painting. The depiction of depth is nearly at the top of the list of importance, but at the very top is visual interest – I want a luminous, engaging overall image and this orange will help me to create that. It will also help to show how to stack competing needs. There will be several areas in this painting that will transition from cool to warm, then back to cool again into the distance.

12 FOREGROUND & GEOMETRY

There are two major additions in this step. First, a simple foreground to provide the image with an additional layer of depth. A foreground like this can sometimes double the sense of space and depth in a scene. The overhang is an arch shape to unify with the shape of the dome and the windows in the middle ground. Second, I add a sense of geometry anywhere I can. Crafting a top plane, front plane, and side plane into objects and structures intensifies the quality of form and depth. At this point, front and side planes consist of the local colour of the objects (the colour of the object itself regardless of any light) and cooler light from the sky illuminating the top planes. Note that even though the painting is very loose so far, I ensure that all structures follow the perspective lines.

13 ADDING THE LIGHT

And now, the addition of light! It's time to add direct sunlight and the light that bounces into adjacent shadows. We have already discussed the usefulness of cool skylight from above, and bounce light is equally important because it illuminates plane changes in the shadows. It also creates a luxurious glow of warmth for the scene. The sunlight comes in from the right at about a 45-degree angle, and this does three things: it clearly defines the front and side planes, it illuminates the top planes, and it gives a nice diagonal to the cast shadows. Diagonal angles can add a bit of action to a scene and, as I'm hoping for a strong sense of engagement in this image, every little bit helps.

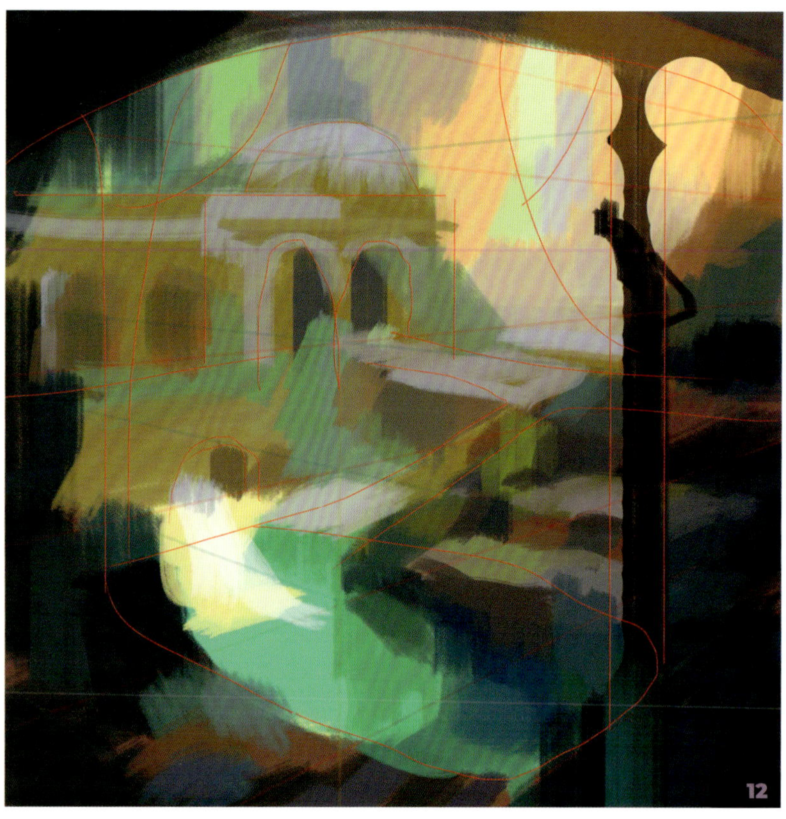

12 Adding a foreground and geometric planes into the structures.

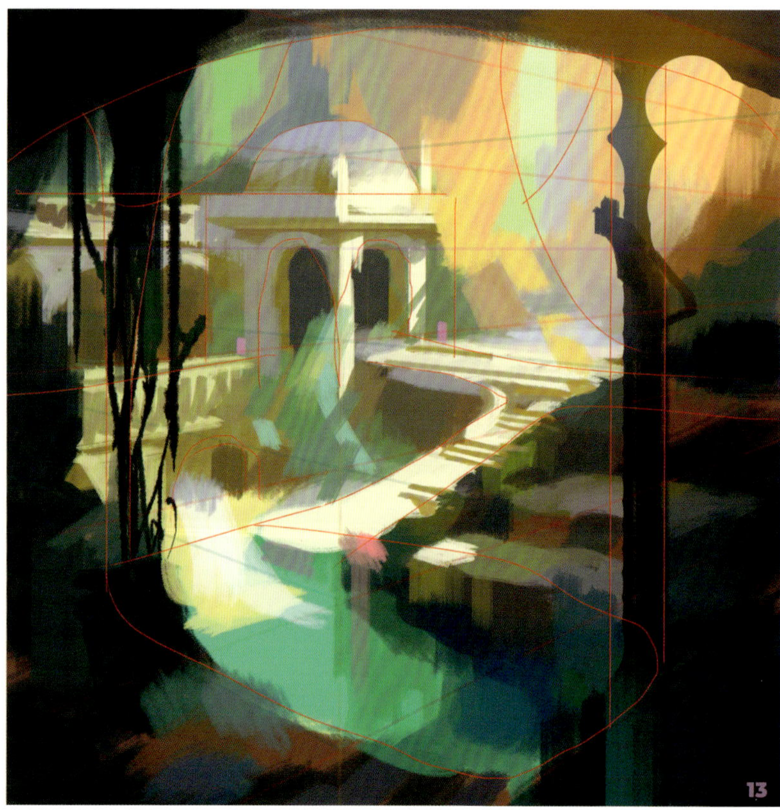

13 Direct sunlight enters the scene from the right at a 45-degree angle.

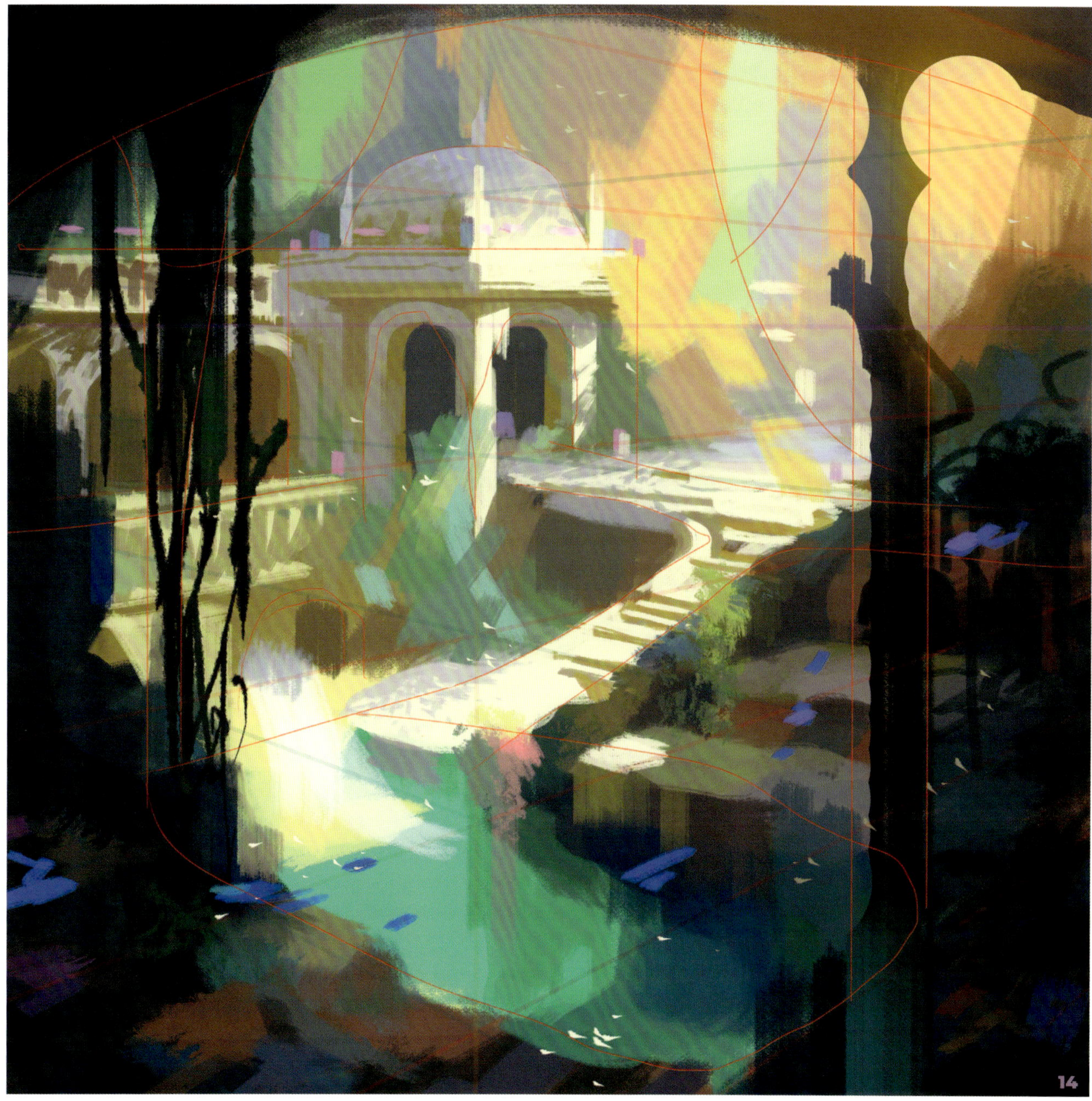

14 For the final comp step, I add multiple types of contrasting visual interest.

14 VISUAL INTEREST

This is the last step of the comp, so it's time for a sprinkle of visual interest. I plan to paint the architecture in a state of ruin, but still beautiful. This can be achieved by making it overgrown with grasses and vines, but also with colourful flowers. Where the foliage has no flowers, it will be lush with verdant leaves. Later I will show you how this foliage can be employed to convey a great deal of layering and depth. I have mentioned visual interest and engagement several times, but all the foliage, lighting, and water are not quite enough for me yet, so I decide to add bluebirds! These birds are not just about throwing another colour at the image; they are actually an important part of the creation of depth. There is the foreground column and the bluebirds, and then there is the foreground landmass, pool, stairs, platform, building, and so on, layering all the way into the far distance and sky. That's how to plan out as much depth as possible in a scene.

A QUALITY OF PURPOSE

Every painting has a purpose, whether it's to be hyperreal, completely abstract, or anywhere in between. Every line you draw and every stroke you make should be designed to serve that purpose, especially when creating perspective and depth. The moment you lose that sense of purpose and start mindlessly putting in details and contrasts, you create distractions that will work against the painting. The purpose of the painting we're working on here is to create an intriguing environment filled with depth cues. It's very easy to drift off course and let distractions creep into such a complicated environment.

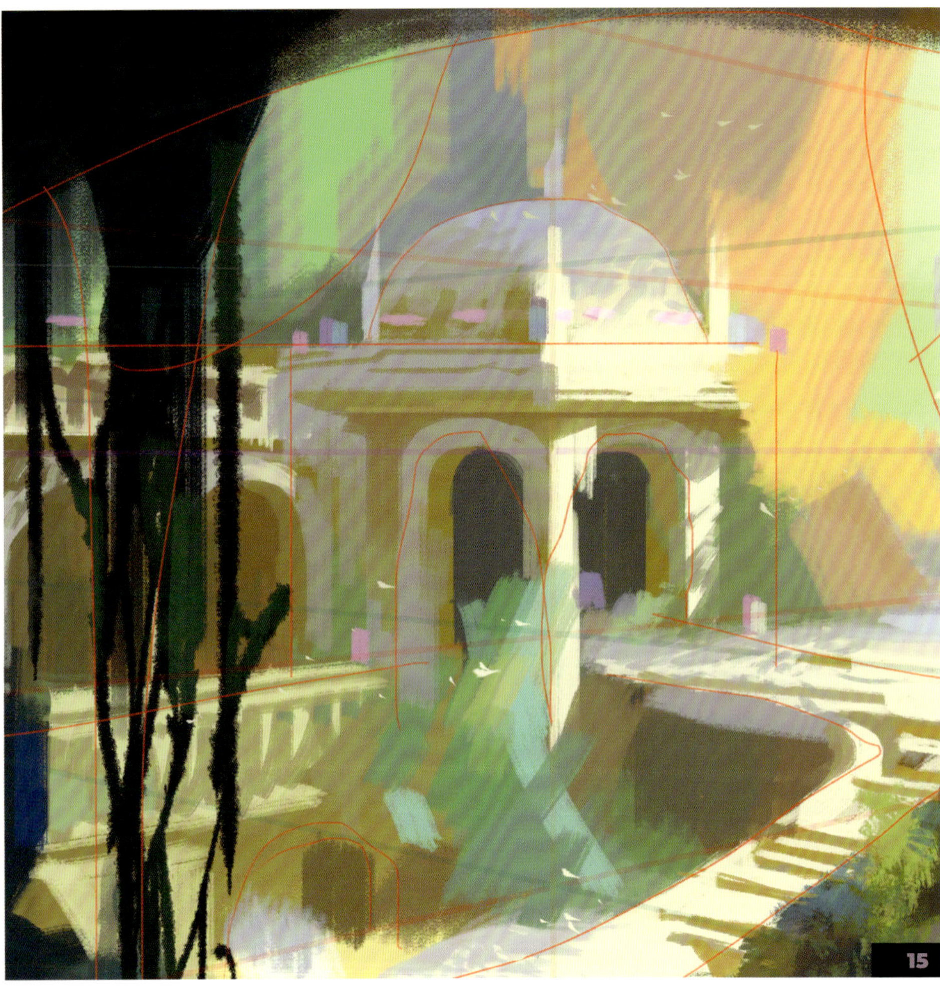

15 Close-up of the comp, showing how dappled light can be used.

15 DAPPLED LIGHT

This close-up demonstrates the value of dappled light and shadow, which creates action and visual interest while also adding depth and presence. Dappled light can be used to suggest there is something out of frame blocking the light, which reminds the viewer that the picture is one piece of a larger world. It also creates visual interest and can act as a transition from well-lit areas into places where the sunlight is blocked entirely. For instance, look at the top of the dome. It would normally be in full sunlight, but that would create more attention than I want in that area. This is not a painting about a dome – the dark entryways beneath are much more important. Dappled light suggests that trees and foliage are blocking the light from hitting the top of the dome, creating visual interest in that area, but not too much, with the light blocked in less important areas.

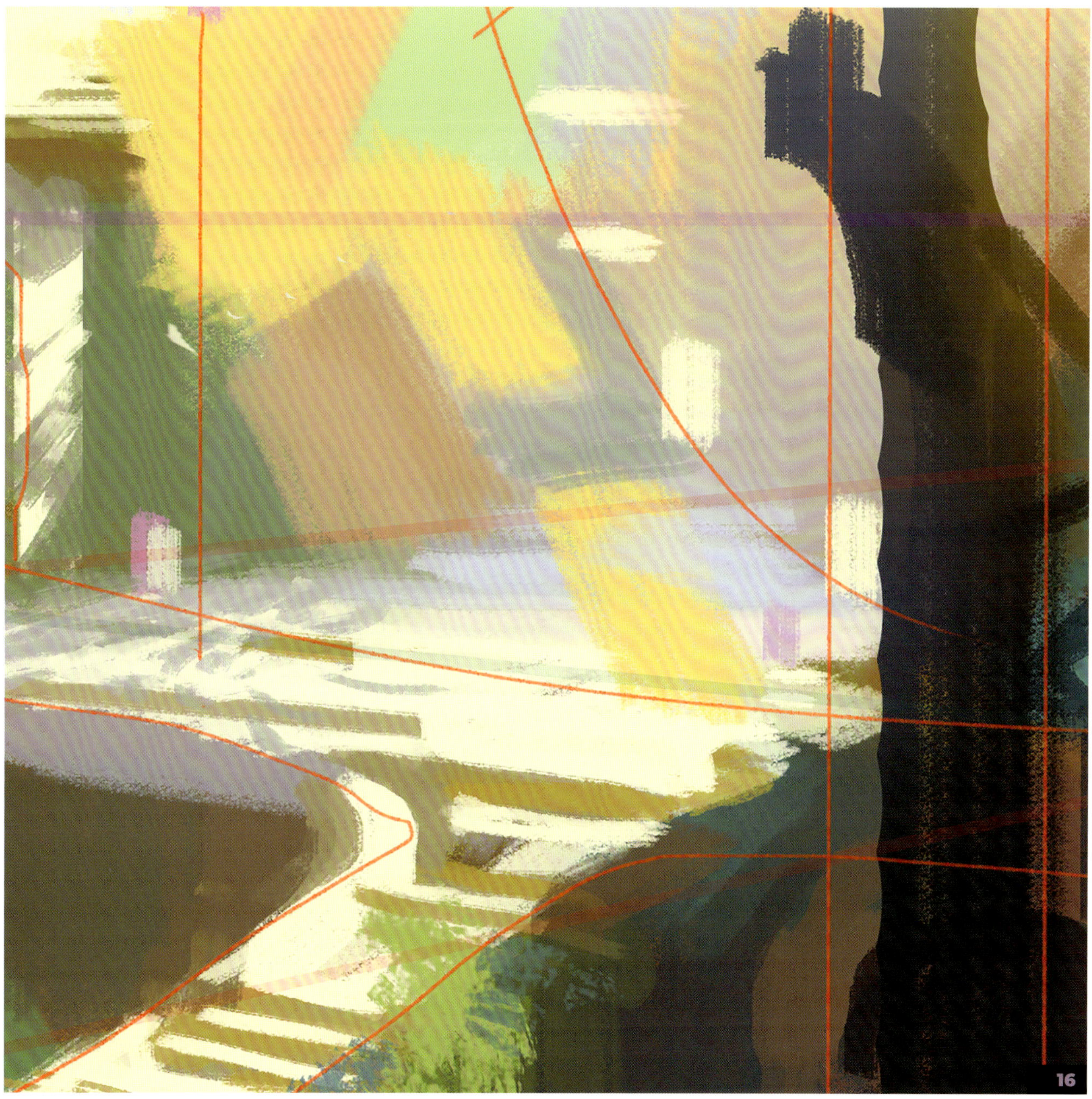

16 This simple and somewhat abstract close-up is an example of three important ideas at play: edge, temperature, and overlap.

16 EDGE, TEMPERATURE, & OVERLAP

This close-up highlights three ideas of great importance: edge, temperature, and overlap. They are so essential that this tutorial will discuss them at length later, but for now, this example establishes the important ideas. Take note of the sunshine and warmth where the staircase meets the platform, and how the platform transitions further and further back into cooler temperatures and lost edges. The hard edges at the top of the staircase help it to advance, while the complete disappearance of edges further back helps it to recede. As for temperature, the heat in front advances and the cooler distant temperatures on the platform strongly recede. Then there is a large, diagonal yellow stroke just past the top of the staircase touching the platform. It's only a single stroke, but it represents where warm, overgrown foliage will come down and meet the platform, so this one area offers a microcosm of great depth created by edge, temperature, and overlap.

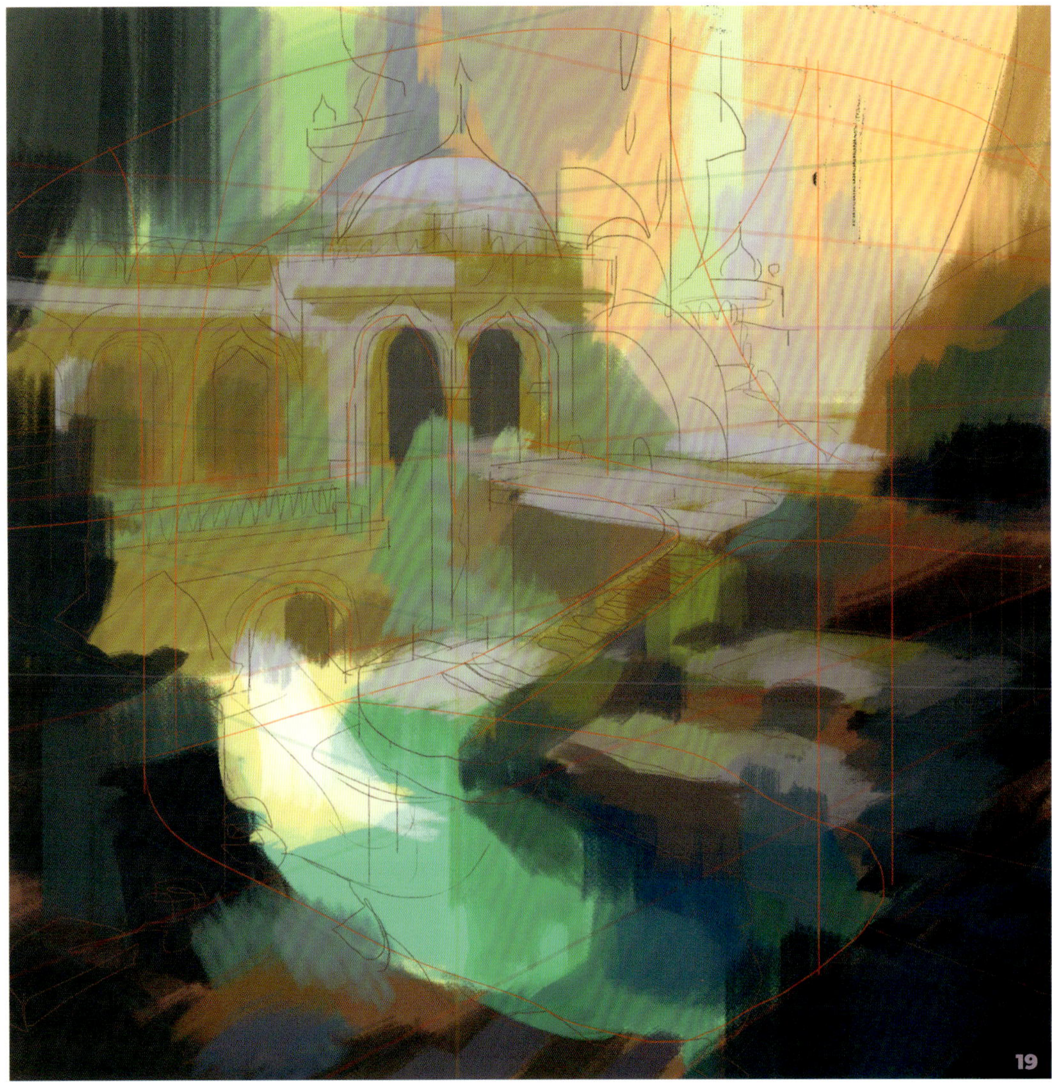

19 Initial block-in using an earlier stage from the comp.

19 PREPARING FOR COLOUR

There's really good news before we start to introduce colour: the early shadow block-in for the comp has all the information we need to get going. I take that same layer and overlay the line drawing on top. This will set us up beautifully to begin working in more information, especially for the direct light.

20 LIGHT SHOWS FORM

The approach we use for the lighting can be a huge advantage in conveying perspective and depth, but if we don't use some smarts and finesse, the lighting can turn into a lost opportunity. Let me use the idea of dappled lighting to illustrate. Light falls across form and form follows perspective, so light hitting a surface stretches across it in a way that shows that object's depth and form. We want to make sure that almost every mark we put down serves this purpose. Notice here how the dappled light carefully follows the shifting angles of the perspective and recedes into the distance. I'll be careful to get that effect into the painting where appropriate.

21 LIGHT IN PERSPECTIVE

Here's a second way light falls across surfaces. Instead of stretching with the perspective, as in the previous example, these spots of dappled light lie flat. They still convey depth as they recede and flatten into the distance. When would light be like this, versus the previous example? It depends on the position of the light source and where it's hitting surfaces. Light at the far right of this picture is much closer to the light source and would tend to lie flat like this. Light to the far left of our picture would angle away from the light source and would more likely resemble the previous illustration.

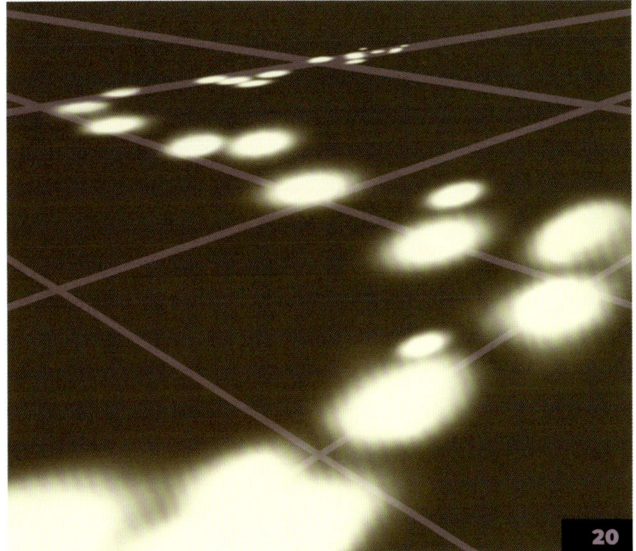

20 Light falling across surfaces will conform to perspective.

21 In this perspective grid, the dappled light lies flat.

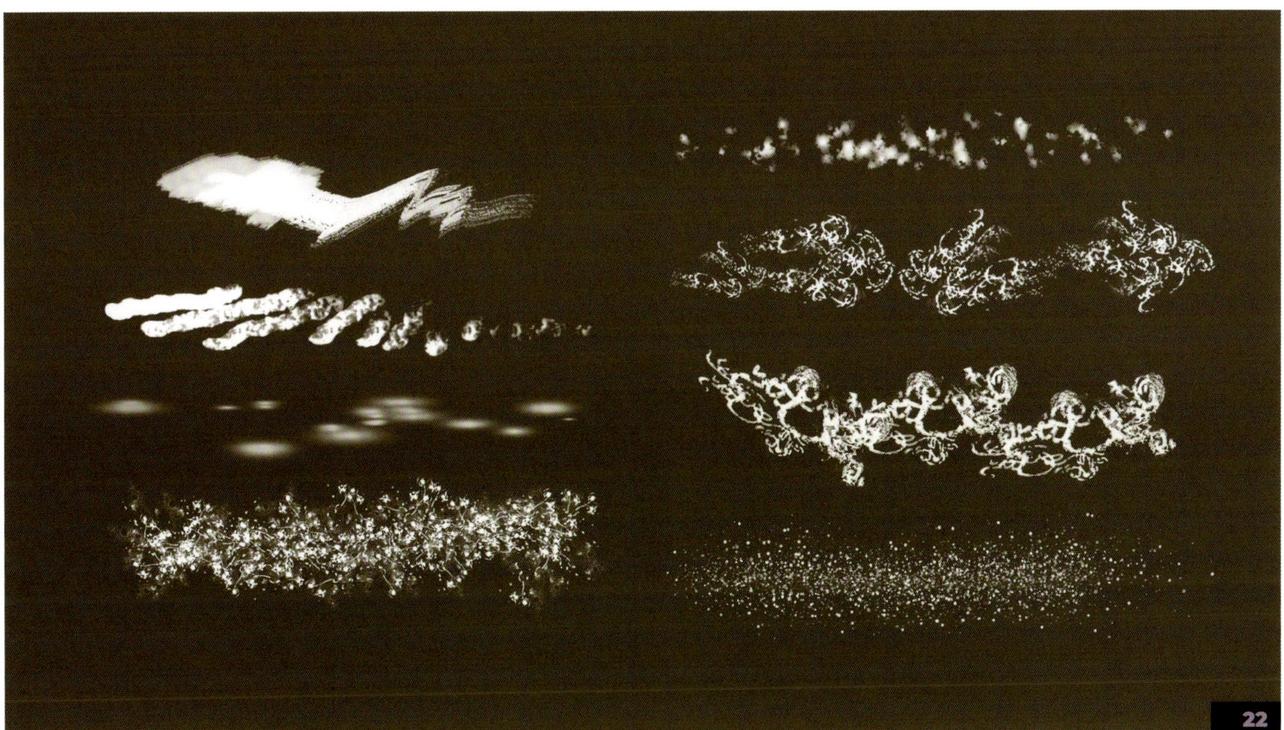

22 These are strokes and textures made by speciality Photoshop brushes that I'll be using to lay in the light.

22 CUSTOM BRUSHES

A tremendous amount of information can be conveyed with a single brushstroke. It can be thought of like this: *put the right colour in the right place, in the right shape, with the right edge, and the right texture.* With that in mind, I'll be using a few speciality brushes for this project. These are all strokes made by custom Photoshop brushes to create different effects, ranging from simple textures to dappled light to ornate foliage. Though I mostly use very basic and simple brushes, I've experimented a lot with this sort of thing over the years, including scanning watercolour strokes to produce an organic effect. Some of those brushes are used here. I don't at all mind if you scan and use these textures, but better than that would be to experiment and come up with something unique to you.

23 ADDING LIGHTING

Here is the image with the first lighting added. The light hits all of the planes that face to the right, as well as the top planes that are not otherwise obstructed. However, the obstructions are hugely important. This is a scene of beautiful ruin, lushly overgrown; the foliage and fallen blocks have a major impact on where the light is and where it isn't. This is of great value because it allows us to add light wherever we want and avoid it wherever it would create a distraction. Note that I am using scattered light and dappling, as shown in the previous steps.

24 LIGHTING QUALITY

This close-up shows the quality of light more clearly. I really enjoy approaching light like this because it's suggestive of form and detail without having to do an excessive amount of rendering. Note that the shadows have two aspects here: form shadows and shadows cast onto adjacent planes and objects. I really must emphasize the usefulness of this approach; you can be quick, loose, and expressive, and as long as your strokes of light follow form and perspective, they will feel right. This is how a painting can feel both loose and finished at the same time.

25 CREATING DEPTH IN FOLIAGE

Now that the image is ready for foliage, let me show you the primary technique I will use. This is simply a Photoshop brush with a little scattered placement so that it turns with the direction of the brushstroke. It has a thin textural shape that's hard and opaque on one side but soft and transparent on the other. It would take you about two minutes to make a brush similar to this. The significant aspect for this purpose is the overlap; as I stroke side to side from back to front, the brush creates an extraordinary feeling of depth, and I plan to capitalize on this effect. This isn't the only type of foliage I will use, as I don't want the image to look repetitive and artificial, but this technique will get the most usage and shows you my general approach.

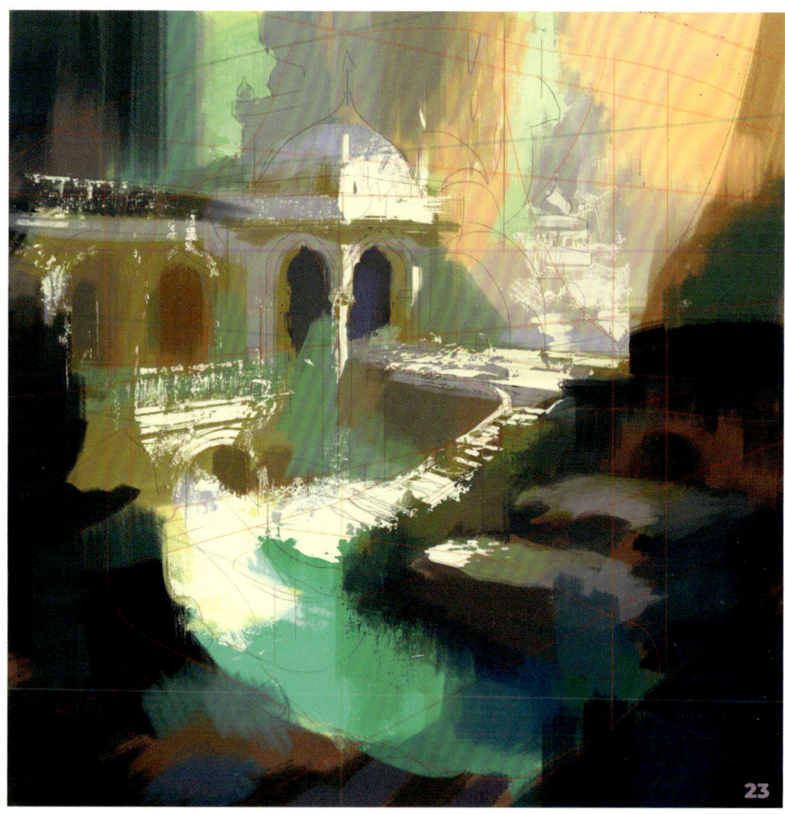

23 The light is laid in and carefully designed to follow depth and perspective, as well as to create visual interest.

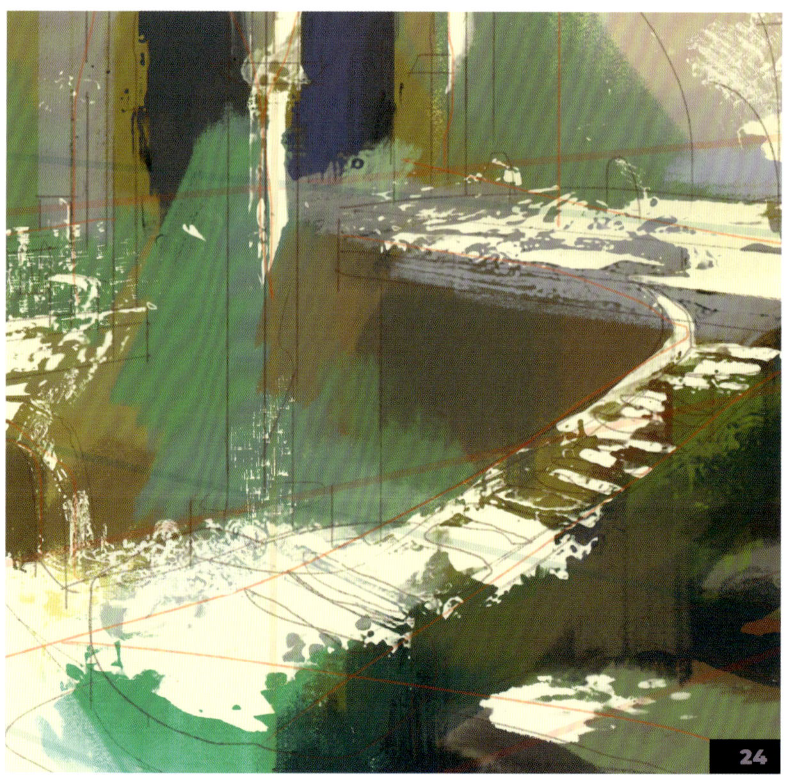

24 A close-up to show the light describing the objects it falls upon.

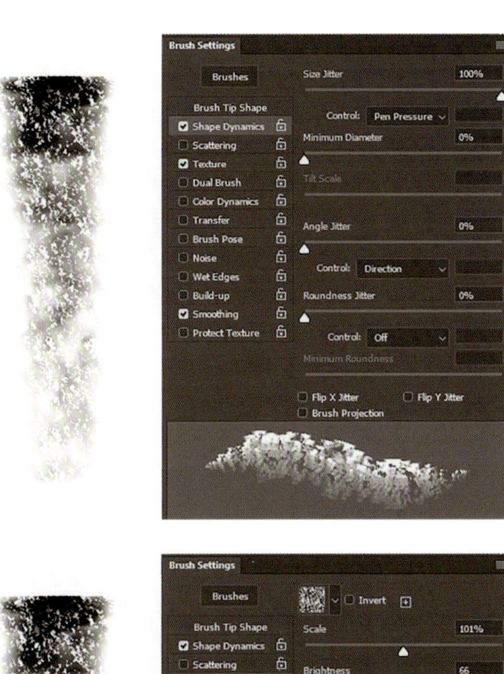

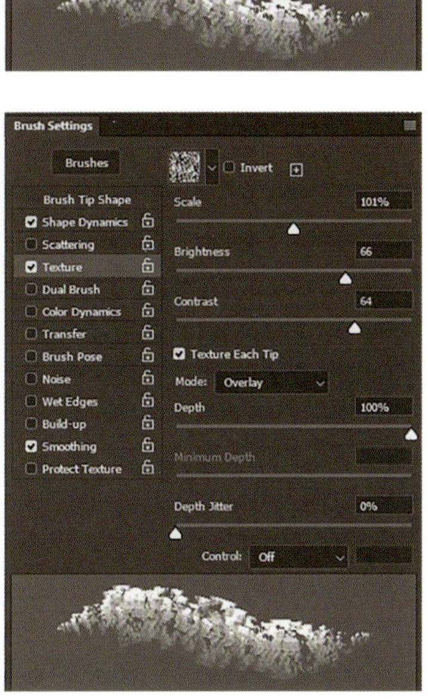

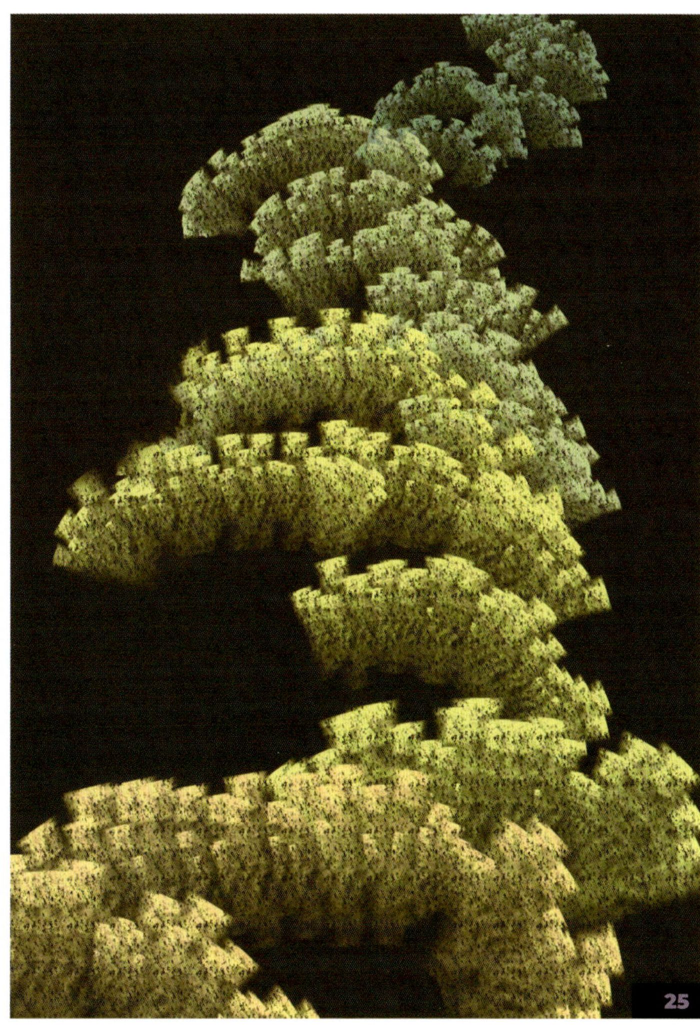

25 This will be my primary technique to create depth in the foliage through overlap.

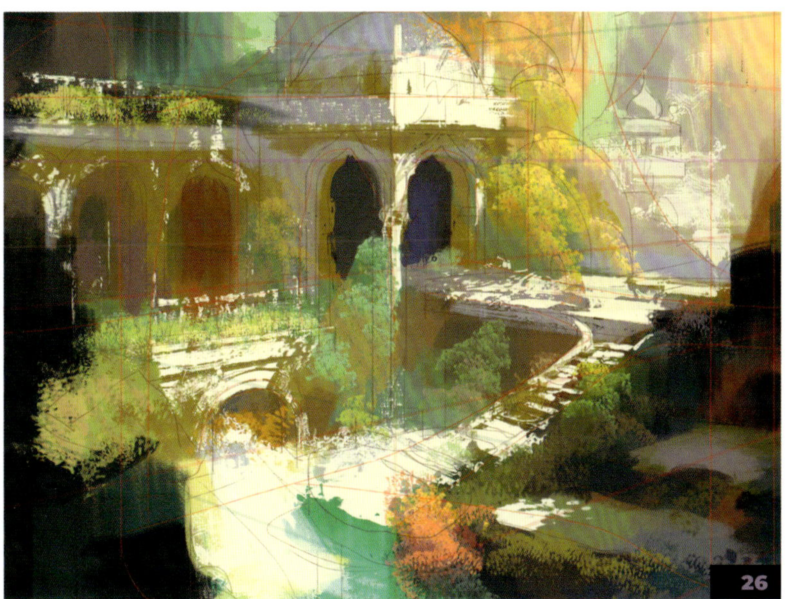

26 The addition of overall foliage in overlapping shapes.

26 ADDING THE FOLIAGE

The painting is now starting to take shape. Here you can see the foliage really overgrowing and wrapping around the building and structures. This wrap-around is important. If you can start the foliage behind something and have it grow around, towards the viewer, you can achieve plenty of depth. This is also a situation where the generally warm shadow colour is greatly beneficial; if you lay the foliage strokes over it and let them gradually blend, it will feel like there's lots of rendering when in actual fact there isn't.

CREATING DEPTH WITH OVERLAP

You might be surprised by how useful something as simple as overlap can be. Placing one thing in front of another automatically creates a quality of depth, so I constantly emphasize this idea in my work, layering as many elements in front of one another as is reasonable. In this demonstration, the final painting has some thirty levels of major overlap. The challenge laid out at the beginning of this chapter was: how do we create the illusion of a three-dimensional world on a two-dimensional page? Overlap is possibly the easiest of all the techniques listed in this chapter and yet it's equal in its three-dimensional authority.

Take a look at the graphic made of squares below **(A)**. They are simple and grey, with no significant qualities of contrast, and are all exactly the same size – yet they still feel like they are moving significantly away from us in space because of the quality of overlap. I am doing the same thing through the entirety of this demonstration, most notably with buildings and foliage.

Look at the top area of the painting section shown below **(B)**. I was careful to start the foliage behind the building, paint it wrapping around in front, then come down and partially cover the platform. The platform then transitions forward to the steps; you can see the indication of more overlapped foliage in front of the steps. From there, foliage comes from behind the middle-ground blocks and gradually makes its way to the front. That's about fourteen layers of overlap, which does worlds of good for the perception of depth in the image!

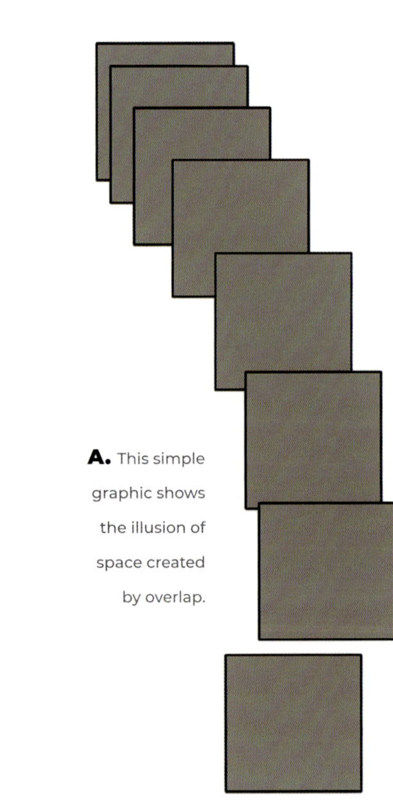

A. This simple graphic shows the illusion of space created by overlap.

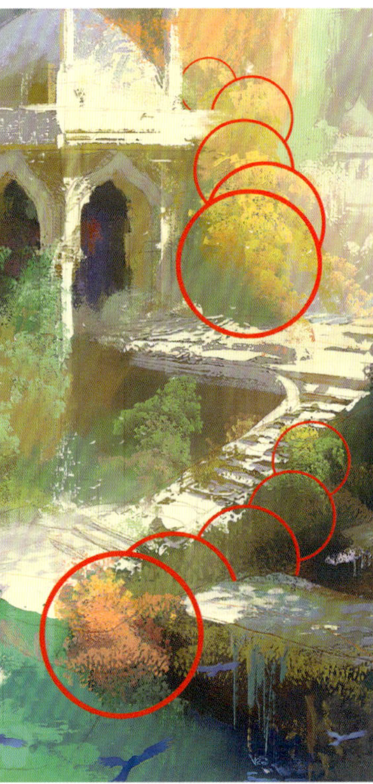

B. The red outlines highlight many layers of overlap as the foliage intertwines with the architecture.

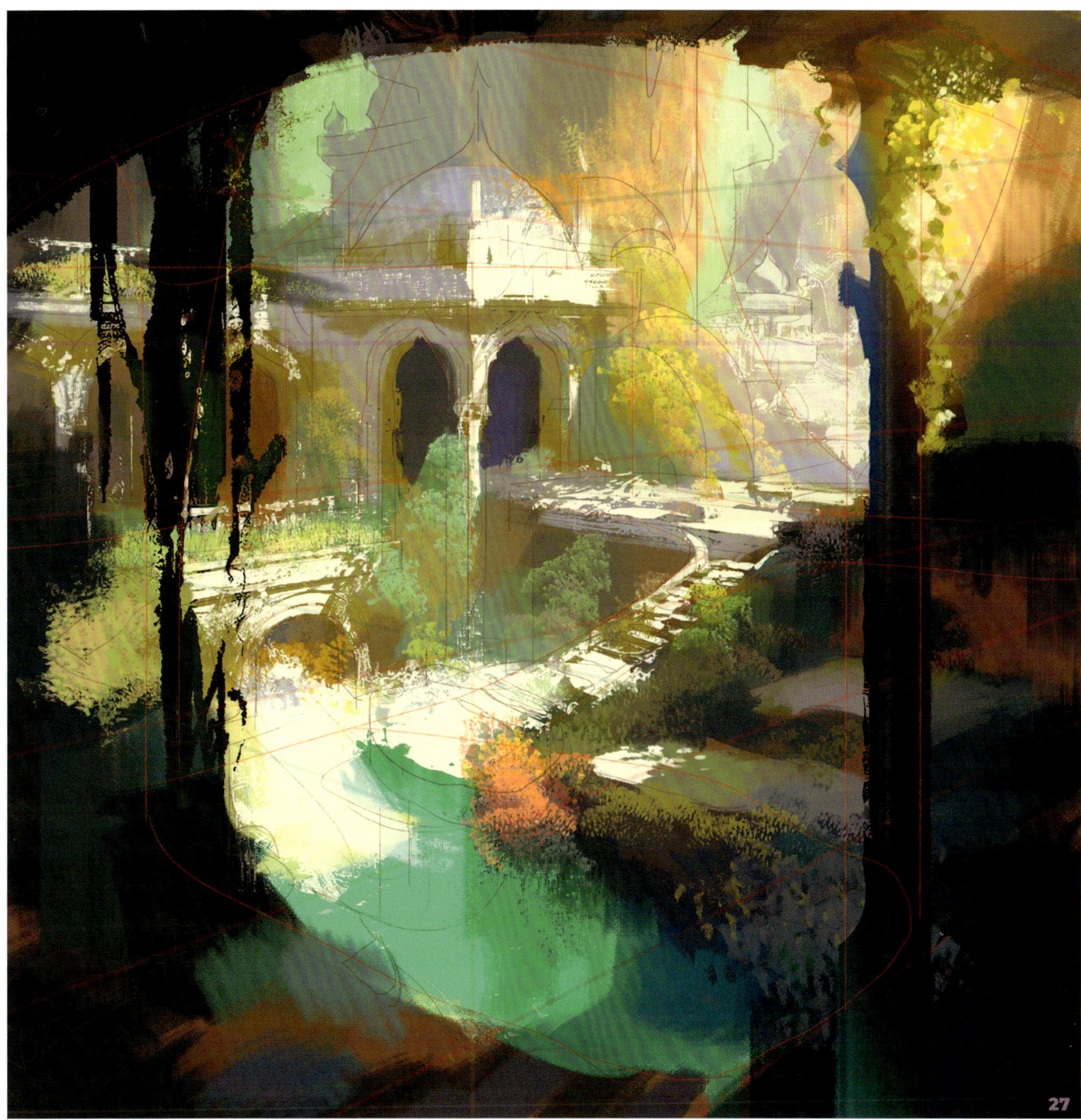

27 Introduction of the foreground as a framing element.

27 ADDING THE FOREGROUND

Here's the addition of the foreground, and just like in the comp, it adds lots of space to the environment. I keep it dark so it feels like the image is opening into a luminous world. Note that the foreground has perspective built into the top area. It's subtle but at the very top middle there are stonework shapes in a diminishing perspective that point towards the main pavilion. And don't forget the monkey – that little blue shape towards the top of the right column will eventually become a monkey, hanging out and looking into the scene!

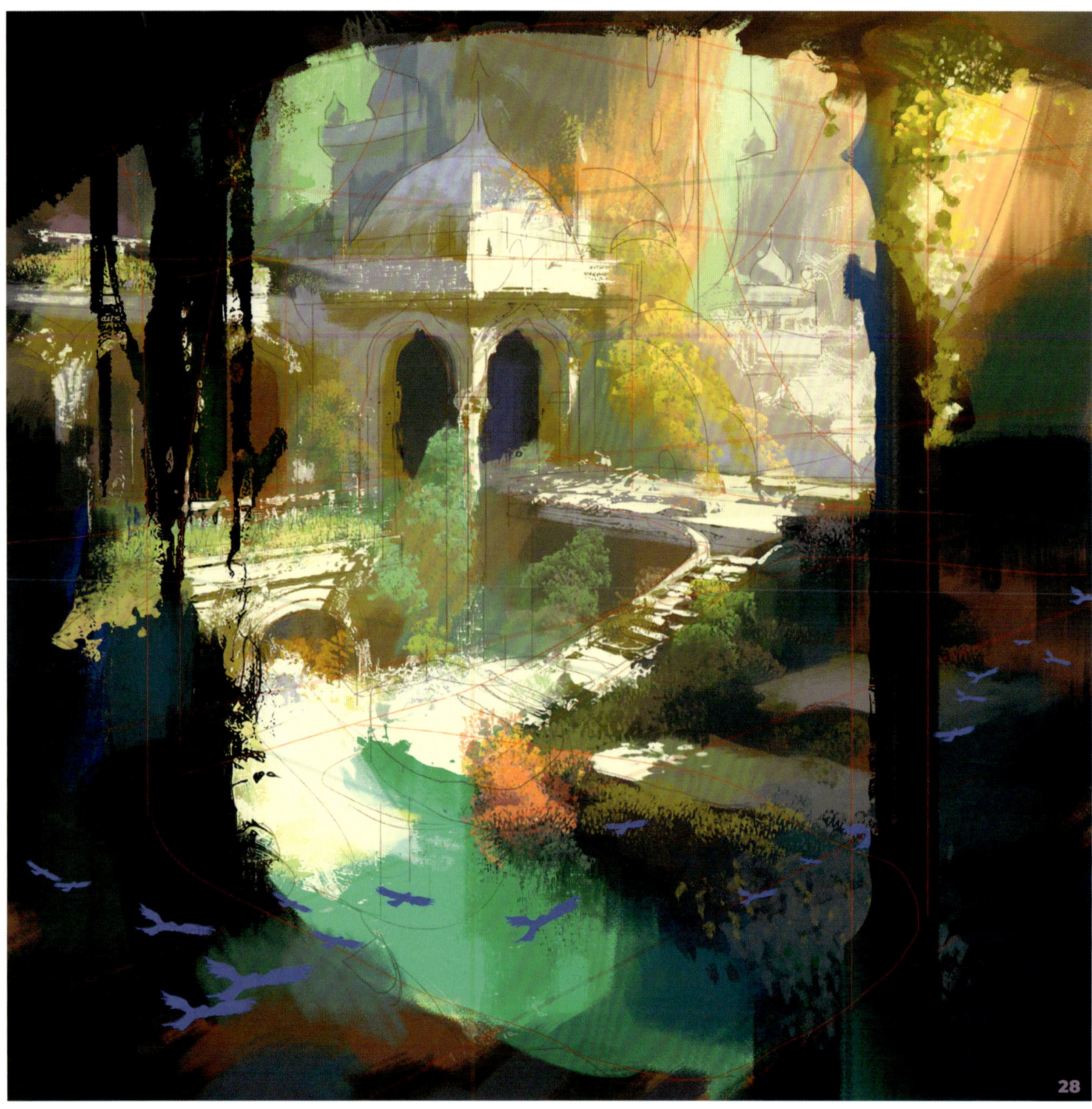

28 The addition of birds into the scene and enhanced layering throughout the image.

28 BUILDING MORE DEPTH

I touch up some of the foliage and architecture shapes, and add a flock of bluebirds in the foreground. My hope is that everyone who studies this image and the gallery section that follows will be in some way delighted. This requires careful design of visual interest, like the bluebirds in this setting. I can take advantage of them not just for visual interest, but to provide a major depth cue. Notice how I have them carefully following perspective lines and diminishing in size from left to right.

I also enhance the general overlapping in the scene – for example, adding darker tones behind the dome to create a layered effect moving further and further back into space. I introduce structures in the far background that follow the perspective of the scene and give the effect of an expansive complex of abandoned buildings.

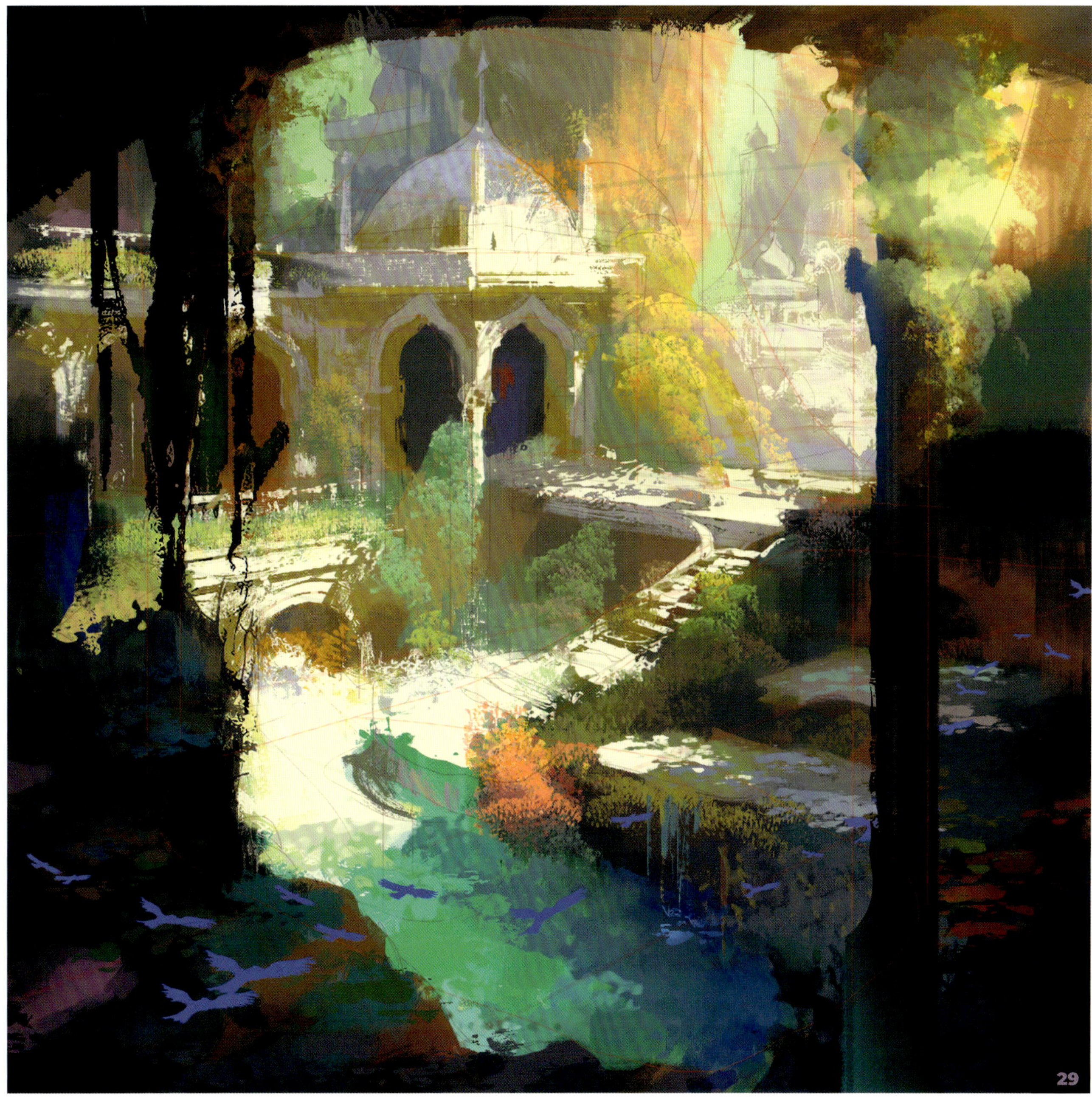

29 Plane changes in the foreground, middle ground, and centre pavilion are more clearly defined.

29 PAVILION PLANE CHANGES

To move the image towards a strong finish, the central pavilion needs some attention, as does the foreground. I add the suggestion of a little more detail in these areas, especially plane changes. The underside planes of the pavilion would receive some warm bounce light, which helps to define the geometry and perspective there. I add more emphasis to the top planes and side planes in the foreground and middle ground; the top planes and foliage are illuminated with sky light, and the side planes are kept darker and simpler. This effect wraps all the way around the foreground to where it meets the stairway. It provides just enough definition to these areas to consider them almost finished.

THE DESIGN OF CONTRAST FOR DEPTH

As artists, so much of what we do involves designing contrast, so I keep a little list in my head of what I consider to be foundational contrasts: value, shape, edge, colour hue, colour saturation, and texture. I am constantly considering where to put them, where not to put them, and how much to use them. You will see throughout this tutorial that these foundational contrasts are especially utilized to create depth.

30 THE PAVILION UP CLOSE

Here's a close-up to better show what was discussed in the previous step. I'm trying to find that balance between loose expressive painting and creating enough structure to feel complete. Notice the warm bounce light in the arched underside of the doorway and the underside planc of the overhanging structure. I combine that with the shadowed side planes on the left of the pavilion to create a clean definition of front, side, and underside planes – everything we need for a complete sense of form. Then there's the dome atop the structure; even though it falls into shadow, the cool sky light helps the form to appear rounded.

Take a good look at the stacked, illuminated effect of the foliage. Form, form, form, and depth, depth, depth – that's what it's all about here, even if my technique is a bit rough and scratchy!

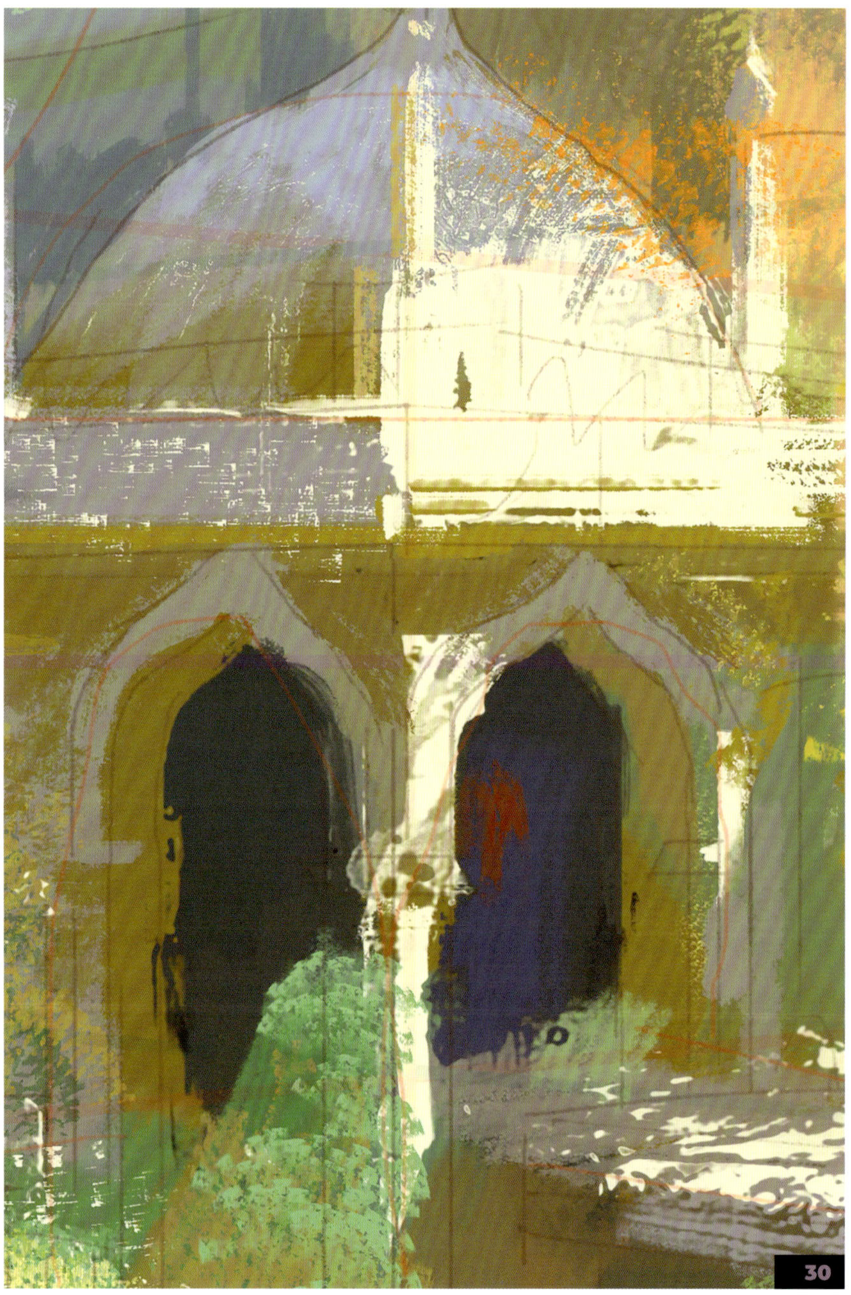

30 A close-up to show the three-plane structure of the pavilion, with front, side, and underside planes.

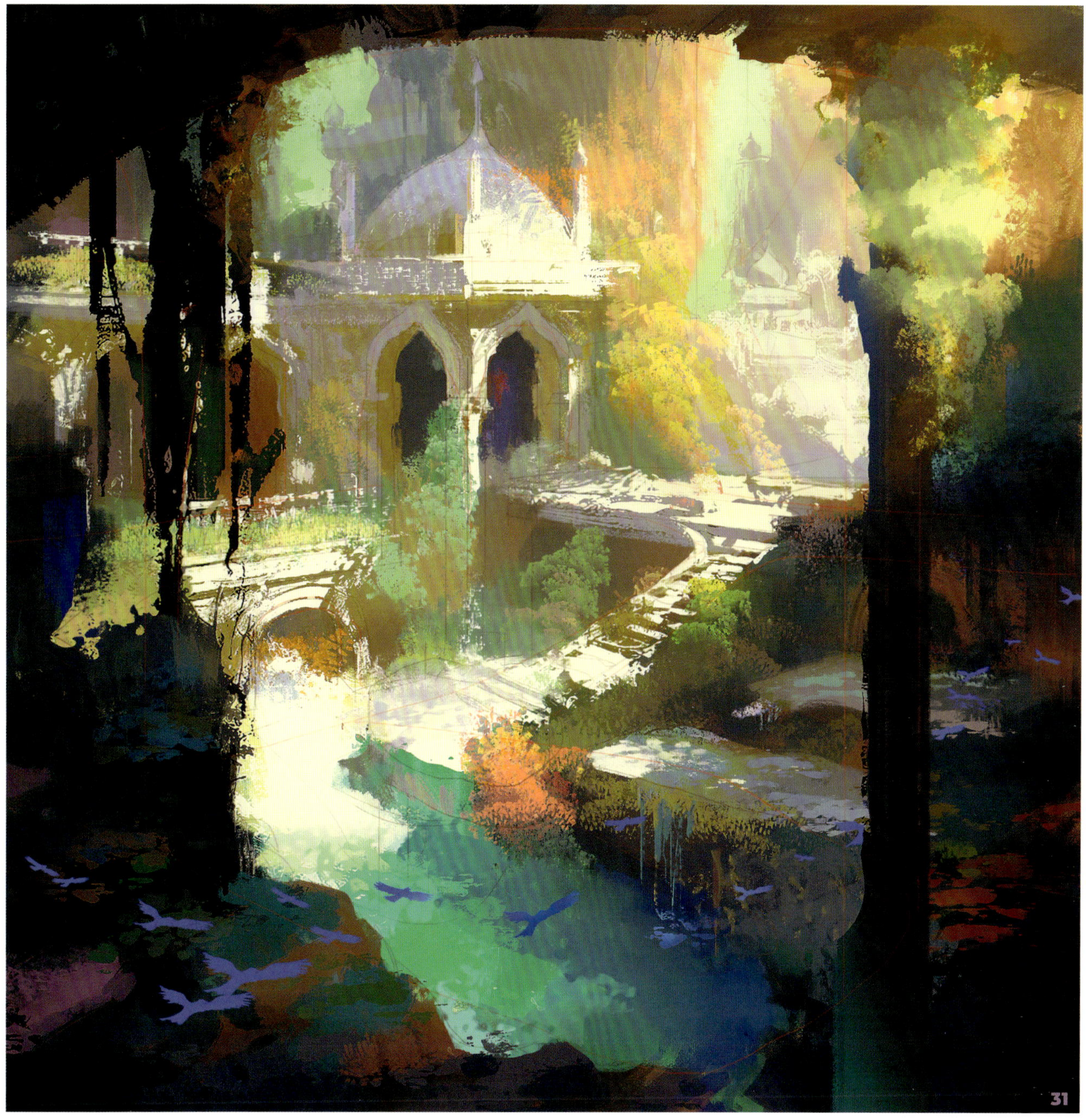

31 The finesse stage is where I remove small distractions and add small enhancements.

31 FINESSING CONTRAST DESIGN

The image is close to completion now! I call this my 'finesse' stage, where I carefully look over the image to check for strong design of contrast. Any little spot that calls too much attention to itself and advances too much in space must be excised from the painting. I conduct a 'search and destroy' to remove all such occurrences. Additionally, more important areas may need enhancement and more design of contrast. I carefully choose what kind of contrast is appropriate; the most likely choices are contrast of value, edge, colour, and texture. An idea I've been very struck by over the years is how a small five per cent improvement in the design of contrast can make the difference between a good painting and a great painting. This stage is critical.

32 EMBOSSING EFFECT

This is a crop-in on a Photoshop embossing layer. I don't often use this layer effect, because it can easily start to look too artificial, but since this image is all about depth, I decide to pull out all of the stops and demonstrate any techniques that can help. The emboss layer creates a quality of thickness, similar to the effect of using a thick impasto in an oil painting. The effect will be masked onto the final painting very selectively; carefully manipulated so it's strongest in the foreground and in the illuminated areas, but diminishes down to nothing in the distance. If a uniform emboss layer was dropped over the entire image without any design thought, it would give the painting a flattened look instead of adding depth.

33 ADDING THICKNESS

Here's an area of the painting with the emboss layer applied. You can see how it adds a bevel to the texture, with the illusion of light hitting the upper side of the textures and a small drop shadow on the lower side. This effect adds a thickness to the texture of the painting that helps it to advance in space. Notice that the effect is much diminished in the shadows and in the deeper darker areas I've taken it out completely.

34 TEMPERATURE & LAYERS

Before revealing the final image, these next few steps will take you through some close-ups of important techniques in action. In this section of the image, notice how there is much more heat and colour contrast in the foreground and middle ground, transitioning back to a much cooler colour palette behind. This technique provides an area of visual interest in the front that pops forward in contrast to the more passive background. Also note the layering; there are layers of foliage in front, then layers of architecture, then layers of foliage again, then more architecture, gradually taking us back to the green sky. These many layers of overlap create an intriguing quality of depth.

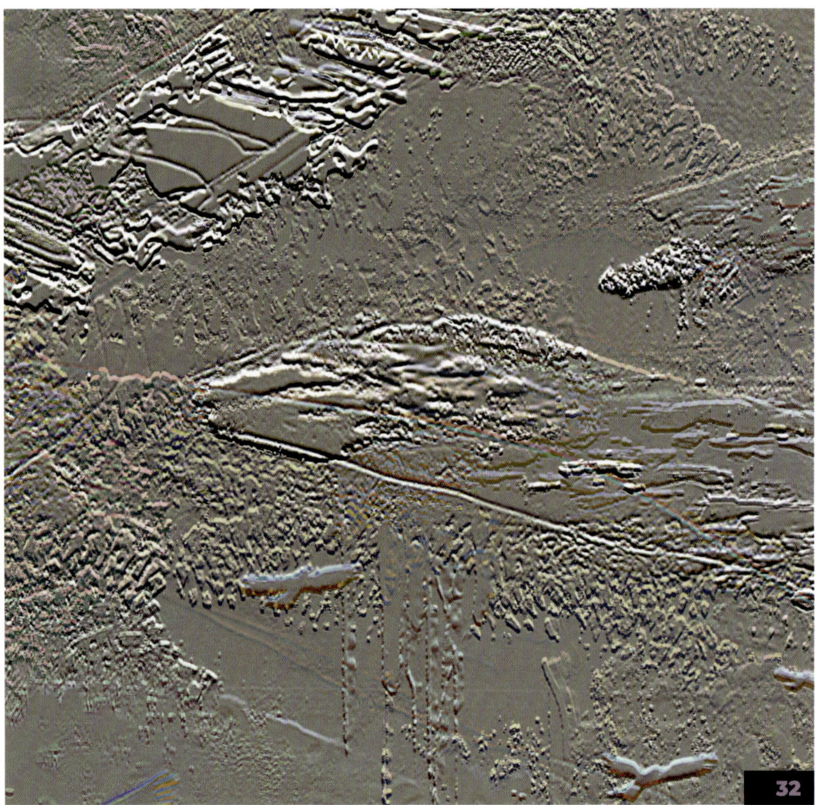

32 Close-up of a Photoshop emboss layer, to be applied very selectively to add texture to the painting.

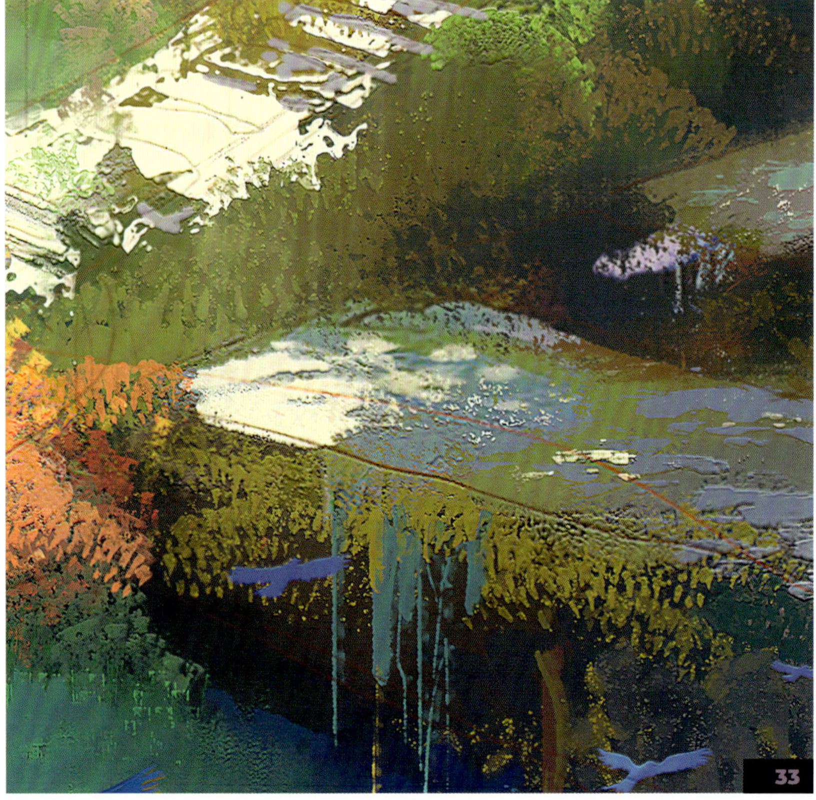

33 A crop-in showing the bevelled effect of the emboss layer on the painted textures.

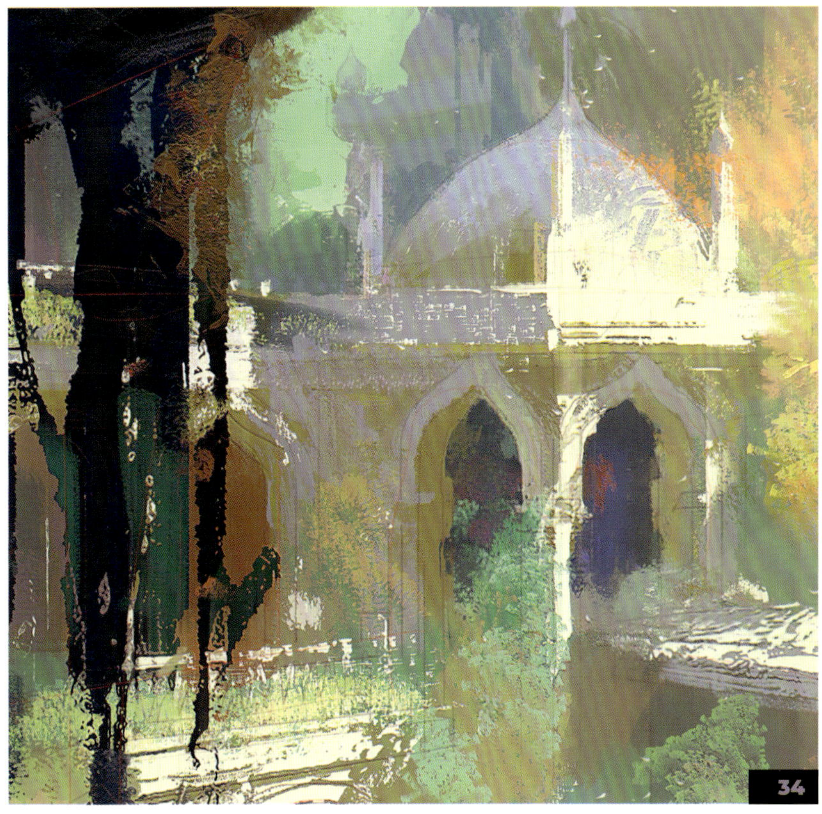

34 Detail view of the pavilion area.

THE POWER OF NOTHING

'Nothing' can be powerful, because anything that's placed next to areas of 'nothing' will feel important. We think so much about what we need to put into a painting that we sometimes forget the importance of leaving things out. My own work is becoming more and more about how much information I can leave out. Does this weaken a painting? I don't think so. In my experience it does exactly the opposite – it makes an image more potent, more purposeful. This is because a heavy edit leaves only the elements that are critical to the success of the painting. It's like a distillation process, taking away impurities until only the pure form is left.

35 Detail view of the foreground and the duct that runs underneath the building.

35 VARYING TEXTURE

This area of the painting shows the kinds of textures used in the foreground and middle ground. Observe these textures, as well as noticing where texture isn't used. Texture becomes meaningless if it's used everywhere, whereas it can be quite powerful when used selectively. Notice how attention is given to texture in the top planes in the foreground, but is absent in the side planes. This helps to maintain the simplicity of the foreground while still providing form through plane changes. Also, take a look at the illuminated passive area in the centre of this close-up: it's completely devoid of detail, which allows adjacent areas to have more emphasis. This is particularly important because the surrounding foliage needs a strong texture, and the jade pool needs to have visual activity also.

CREATING DEPTH WITH TEMPERATURE

Distant objects usually appear cooler in colour than those closer to the viewer; this is because light from the sky bounces around and infuses into the atmosphere. This effect is often referred to as 'atmospheric perspective'. Our eyes and brains are very used to this effect, so we inherently feel that objects with cooler colour temperatures and lower contrasts are far away, and therefore that objects with warmer colour temperatures are closer to us.

Take a look at this landscape study from a trip to the jungles of Central America **(C)**. It shows a misty, humid environment with a lot of atmospheric perspective in the distance. Note how the distant mountains become increasingly cooler the further they recede. The jungle environment also contains many warm local colours in the foliage, and I was able to emphasize that quality to produce the effect of the foreground advancing in the painting. I'm taking advantage of what appears naturally, but I'm designing it and giving it emphasis.

Now take a look at the two crop-ins of the pavilion painting. In the top-left image **(A)**. note how the most distant elements are lower in contrast and cooler in temperature. I have fun while painting, adding the green sky for example, but I don't let that disturb the quality of atmospheric distance. The crop-in example to the right **(B)** shows the platform area, and it covers a lot of distance (a good fifty metres or more) from foreground to distant background. It's important that this quality of distance is conveyed to the viewer, so I use warm colours and contrasts that pop in the foreground and infuse cool colours into the distant platform. Cool skylight naturally falls into the shadowy top planes and I can use that to my advantage.

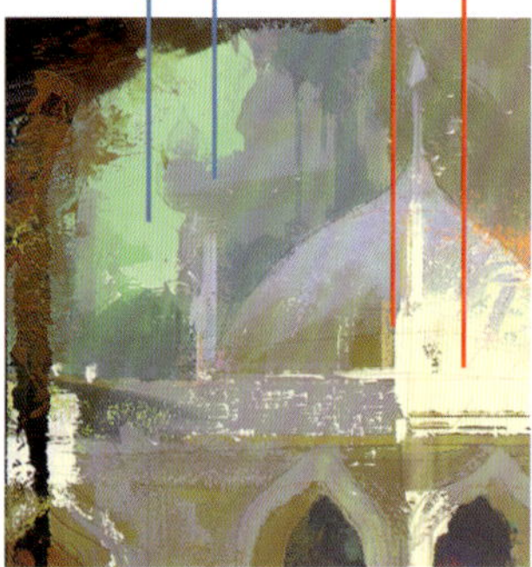

A. Crop-in showing atmospheric effects in the distance and advancing warm light on the structure.

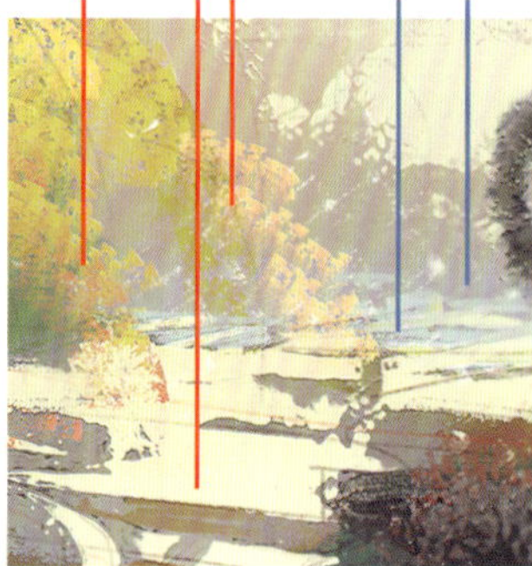

B. Crop-in showing cool light on the distant top planes and advancing warm light in the front.

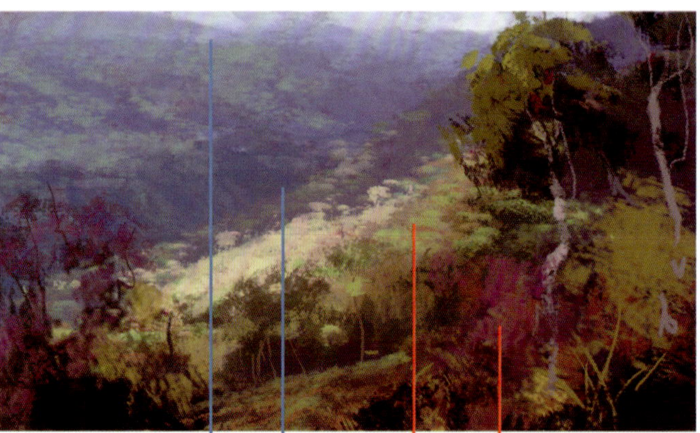

C. Landscape study showing receding atmospheric cool temperatures and advancing warm local colours.

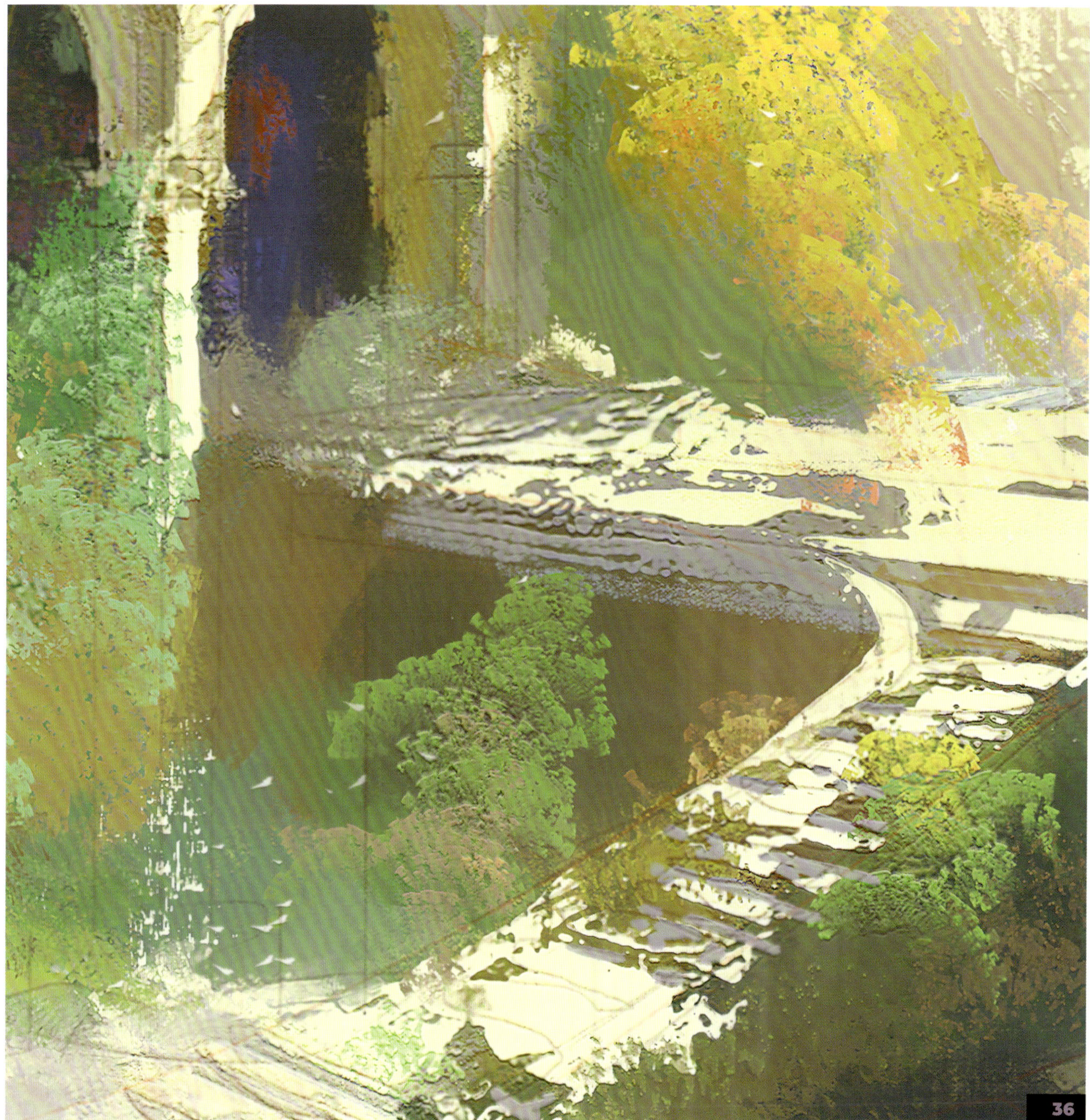

36 Cast shadows used to show the form of the stairs.

36 FORM THROUGH SHADOWS

Don't forget about cast shadows! They can be very subtle, but if your painting features direct sunlight, they must be present. Take a look at this close-up area of the stairs: they are rendered in an understated way, but the presence of cast shadows lets our eyes know there is form there. This is a useful way we can avoid distracting amounts of rendering while still letting the eye know there is form present.

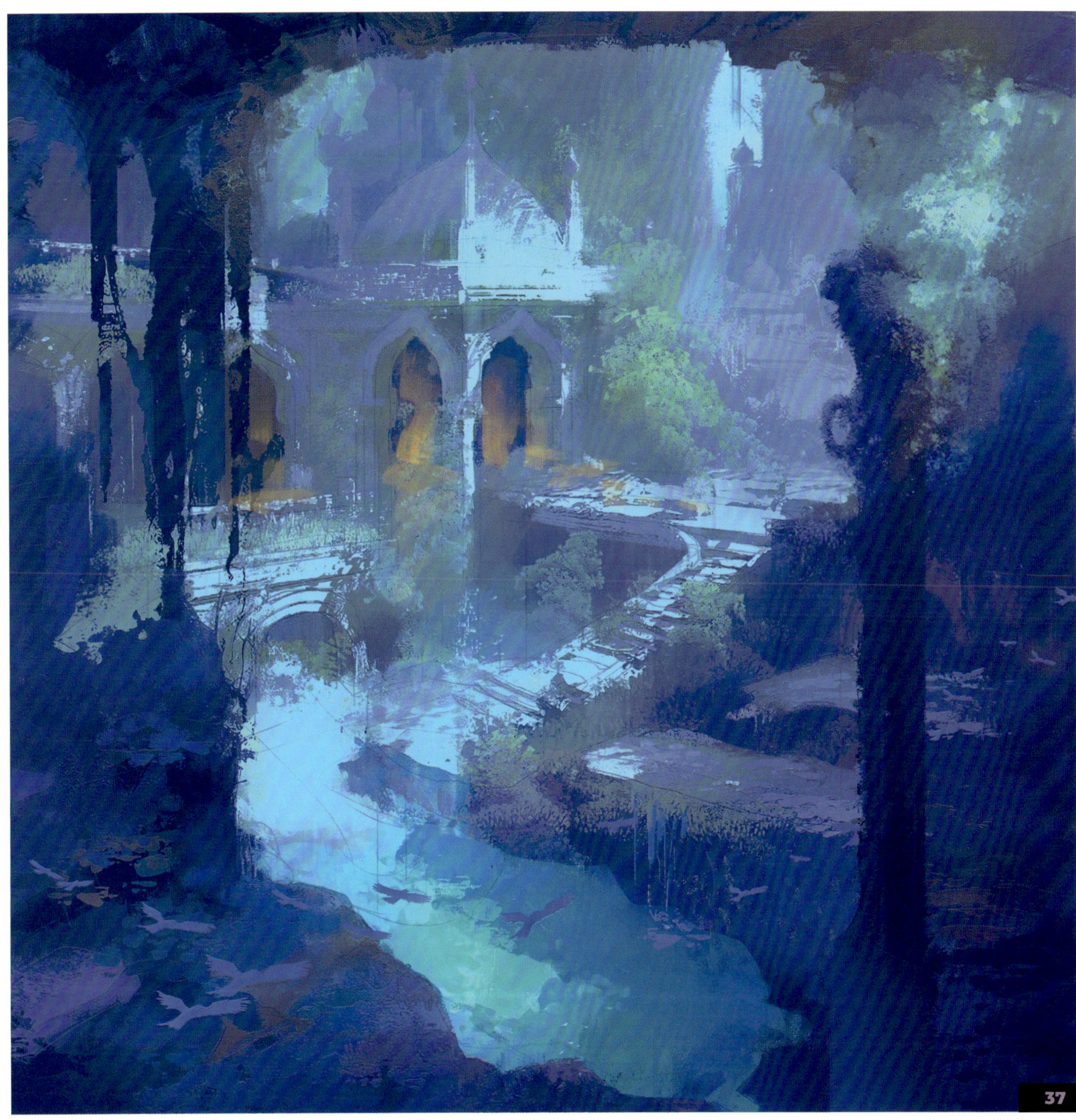

37 An alternative night-time version of the painting.

37 DEPTH IN THE DARK

I find it fun – and an excellent learning exercise – to try out alternative versions of a painting once it's relatively complete. This is a night-time version, which I feel holds on to the sense of depth pretty well. It can be difficult to create depth in dark scenes; the tactics are somewhat different as we don't have warm sunlight to rely on. Instead the warm local colours in the foreground are emphasized, and warm light is added in the central pavilion. This pulls our eye right past the foreground and firmly sets the middle ground apart from the distance.

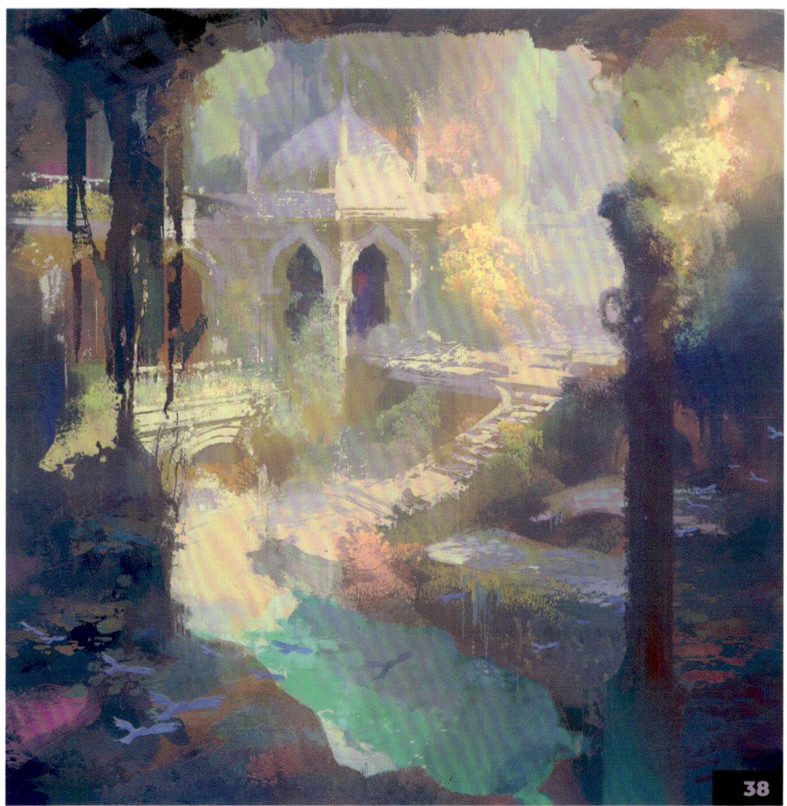

38 A version with more colour contrast and less value contrast.

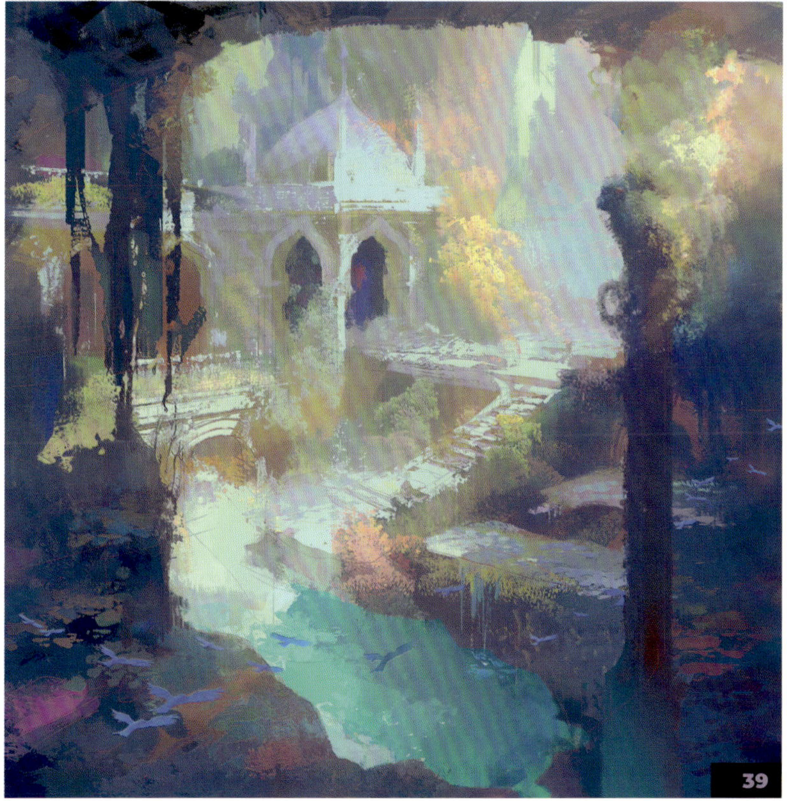

39 A fantasy version of the painting, with an unnatural cold light source in the daytime.

38 MORE COLOUR, LESS CONTRAST

This is a version with more colour contrast and less value contrast. I find it enjoyable to experiment with warmth and rich colour, and this version is a good example of how adjusting the value contrast can change the depth of the scene. The sense of depth is greatly reduced when the value contrast is reduced. This version has a much flatter and more decorative quality than the final painting will have. I wouldn't call it better or worse, just different, and it's good to be versatile in our abilities.

39 UNNATURAL COLD LIGHT

Occasionally I like to try out 'fantastical' environments. This example shows cold light in a warm environment during the daytime. It feels unreal because the local colours and the colour of the light source are at odds, and outside of what actually occurs in nature. It's not natural, so it's supernatural – a world of fantasy. This alternative shows that even when a fantastical effect is applied, the techniques used to create perspective and depth are still valid and still do their job successfully. None of these alternatives won out as the final piece, but creating experiments like these can help to expand an artist's skill set and assist in making the right design choices in the future.

THE FINAL PIECE

I now switch focus back to my main piece in its intended variation. It's almost there, but before calling a painting complete, I apply a few final techniques. First, I flip the image horizontally to see a mirror-image view. When you've been looking at a piece of work for a long time, it's worth doing this to get a fresh look – anything that isn't working will then become more obvious. Second, I always try to 'sleep on it' and take a fresh look the next day, if time allows. I almost always notice things that need improving. In this painting, there are some planes that don't quite read in perspective, so I give these clarity; this usually means a defined front plane, side plane, and under plane. There are also some harsh edges in the foreground with too much contrast, causing them to call too much attention to themselves. I always try to keep in mind the central purpose of an image, and for this piece, it's about an overall sense of depth and perspective, not a focus on foreground elements. I also sprinkle a few little white birds here and there for visual interest, and to give the painting further life and movement. Now I can call the painting complete.

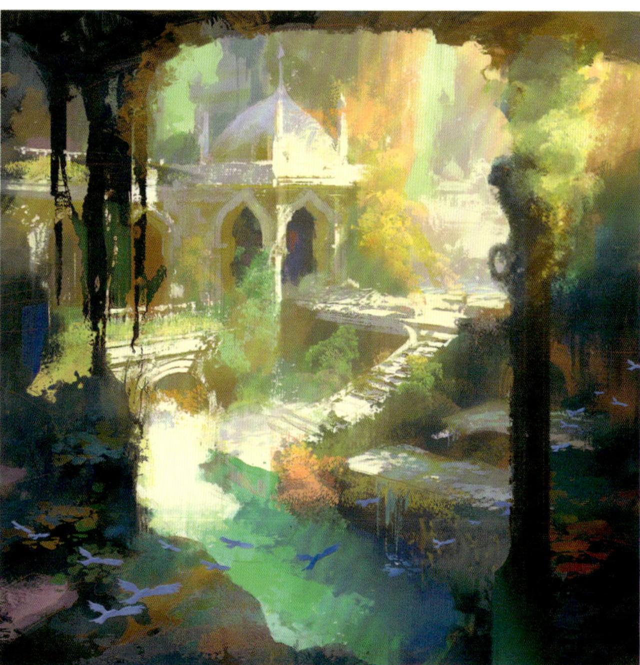

Jungle Ruins. The final painting.

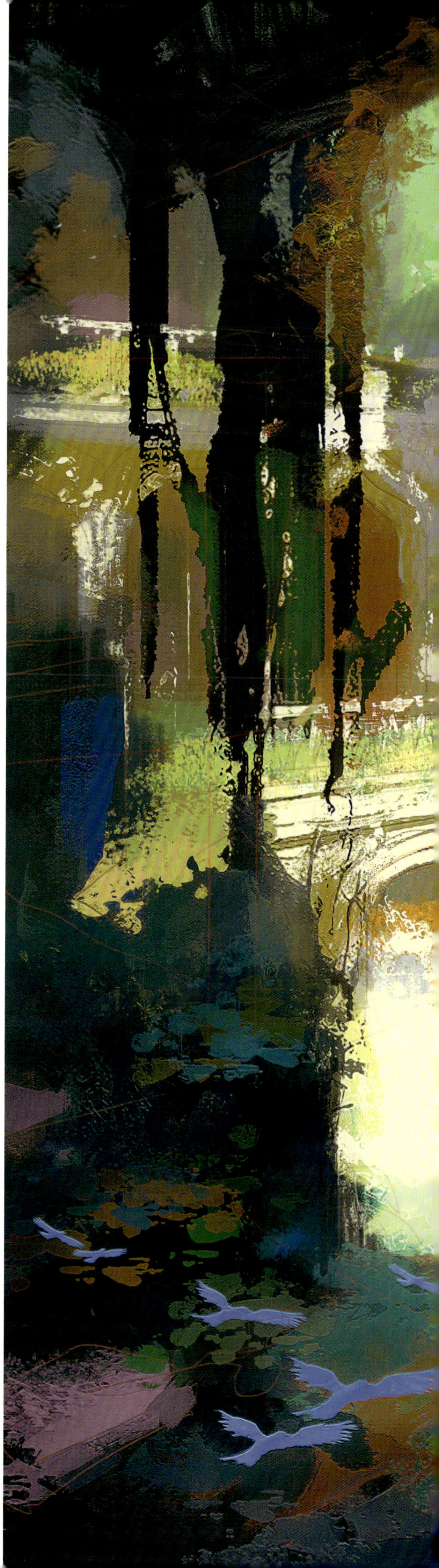

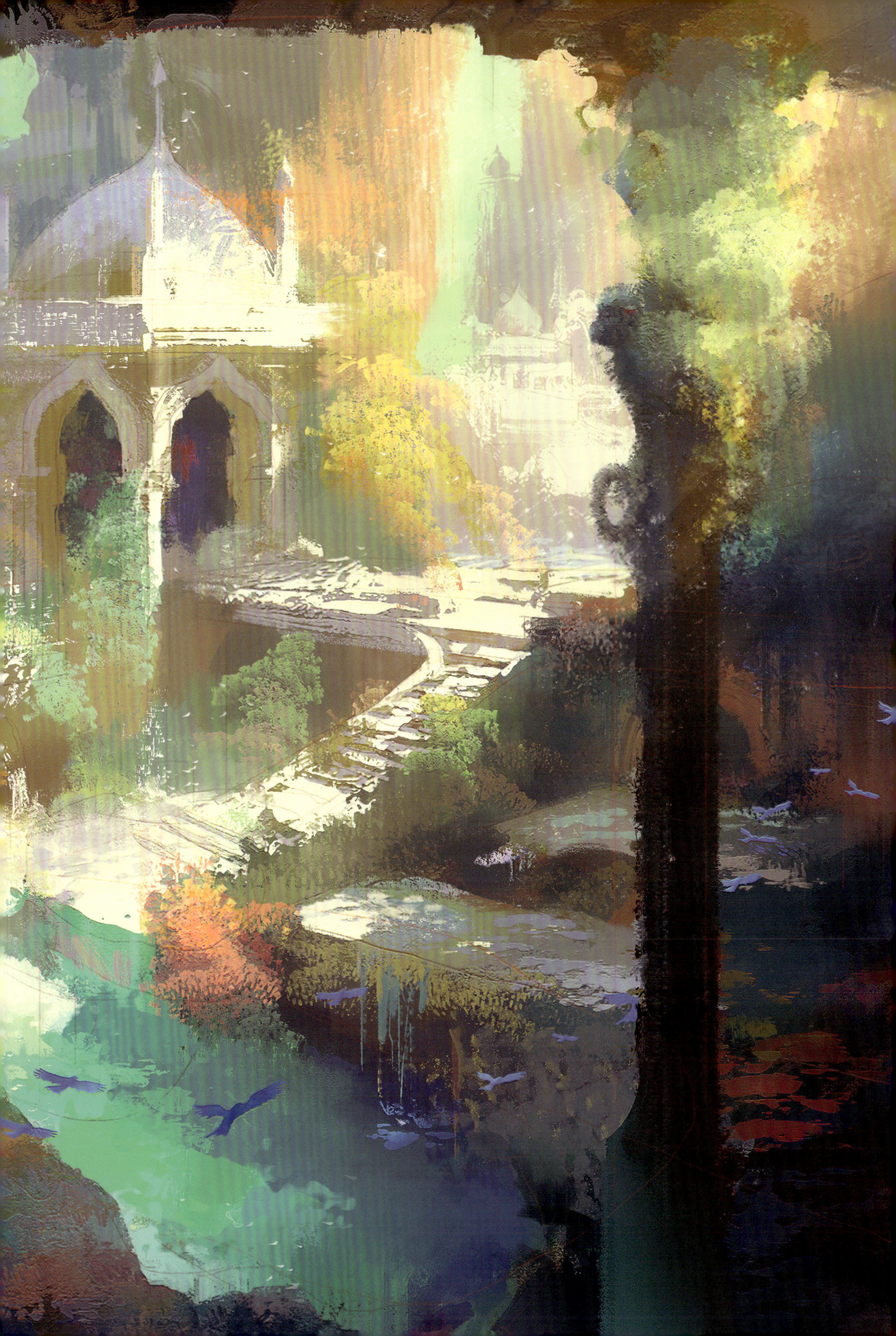

OLD MINING TOWN

ORENJIKUN

Perspective is an absolutely crucial fundamental in my drawing and painting. I love using wide-angle lenses to show more information on the canvas, and as a result, I delve into a lot of distorted perspective. Portraying depth and distance in my art helps me to develop a sense of space in the scene to tell stories and strengthen narratives. I'm particularly interested in studying how depth can help to create cinematic compositions.

In this piece I'll be emphasizing the use of one-point perspective and will aim to portray a sense of distance using this simple approach. I'll be using Photoshop to draw and paint digitally, exploiting the tools digital painting offers, such as duplicating flat assets and distorting them in perspective.

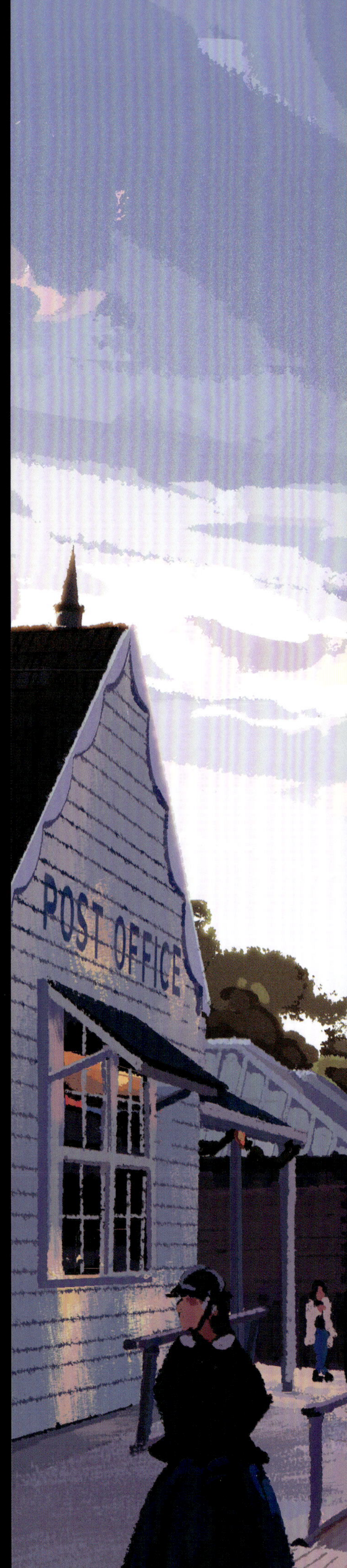

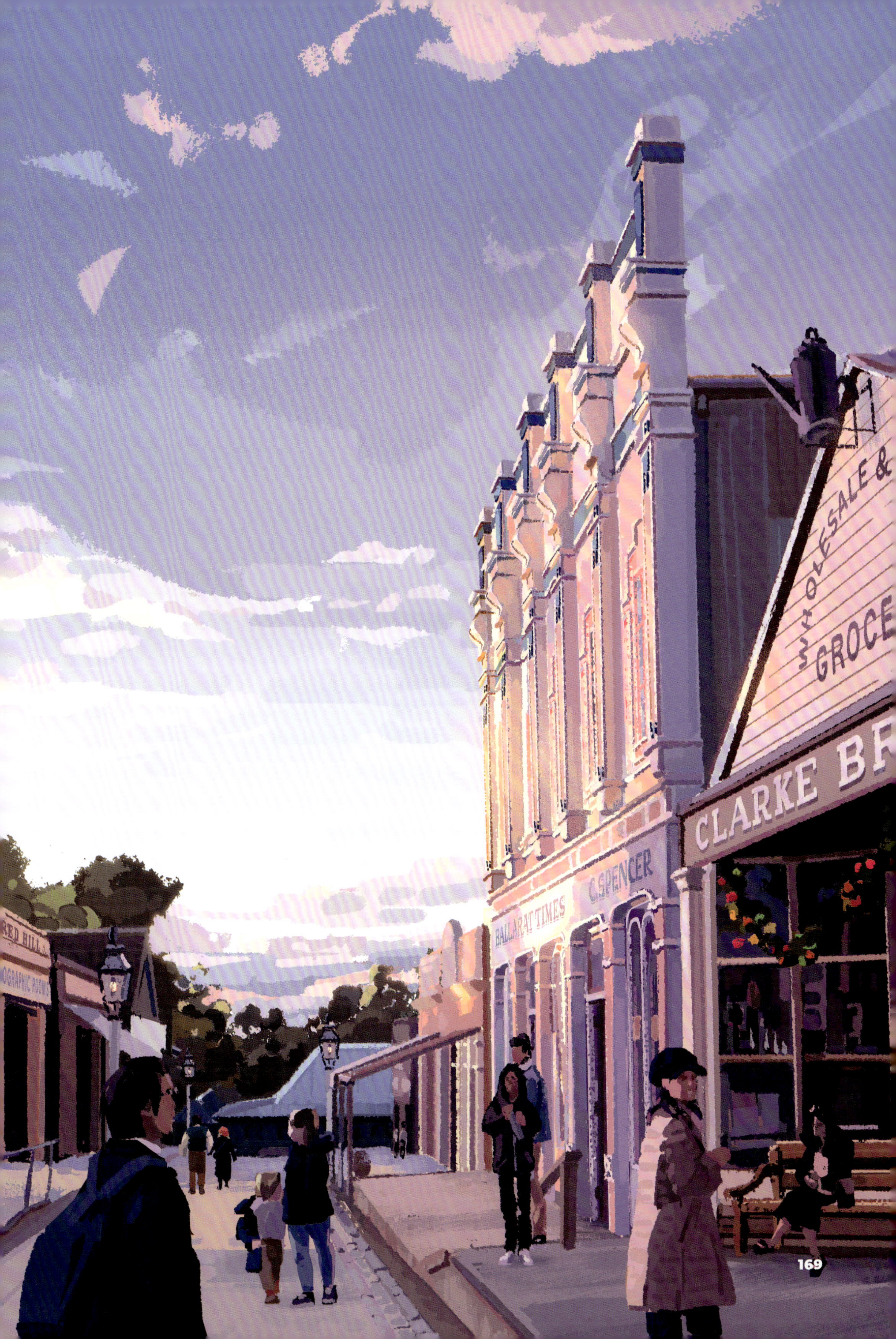
OLESALE &
GROCE
CLARKE BR
C.SPENCER
BALLARAT TIMES
RED HILL
OGRAPHIC ROOMS

01 GATHERING REFERENCES

The first step of creating a composition is to gather references and inspiration. I took this photo when visiting Sovereign Hill, a historic outdoor museum with preserved buildings and machinery from its time as a mining town during the gold rush in 1800s Australia. I love how the light hits the facade of the building, highlighting the intricate ornamentation and features. There is also an opportunity to exercise intermediate/advanced perspective techniques with the complexity of building facades.

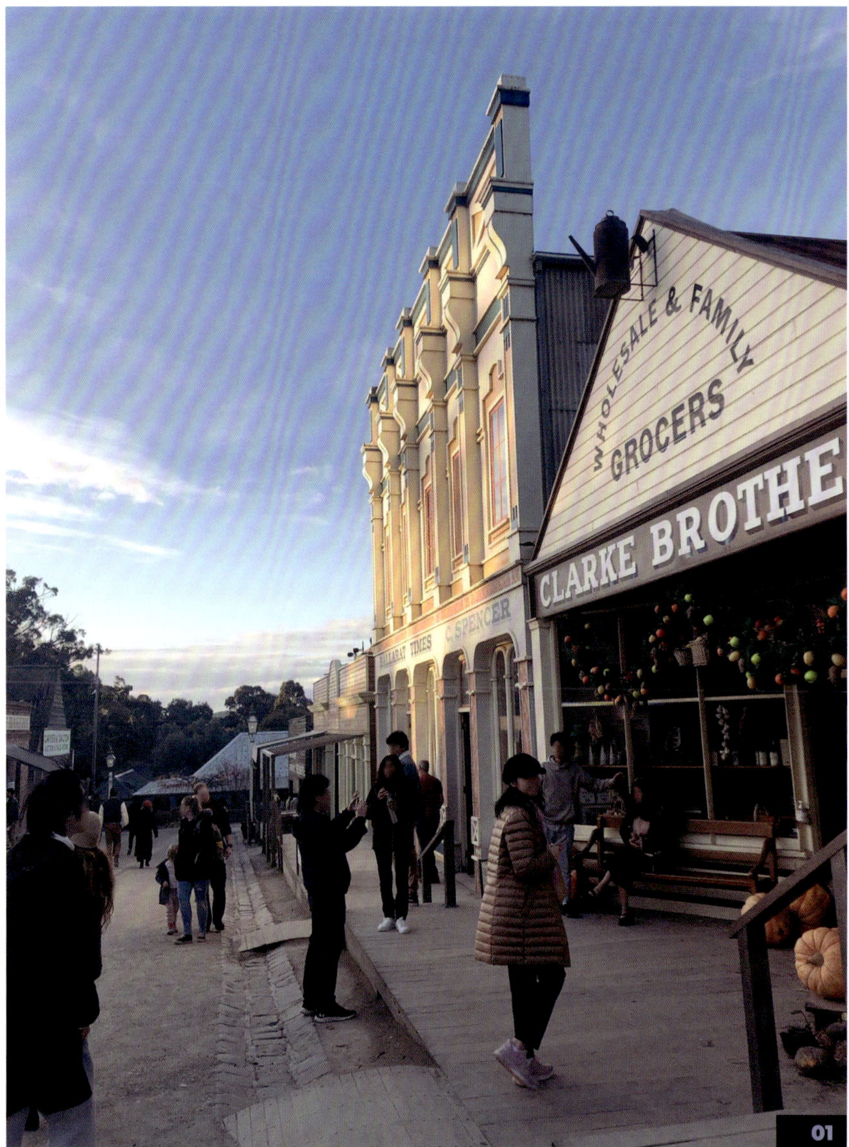

01 Photograph of Sovereign Hill from my phone, capturing a beautiful quality of light and crisp air.

02 INTENTIONS

To supplement my own photos, I research online to find more references **(02a)**, as I would like to extend the composition to a really wide pan **(02b)**. Before starting an artwork, I must carry out extensive research to clarify the intention of the piece, be it through colour, mood, subject matter, composition and layout, emotion, location, or whatever specifics I intend to portray. Although not a direct reference of the location and features, some other photos I took can be used to reference colours, lighting, textures, and materiality.

This piece is not intended to be an exercise in background/environment design, but rather an attempt to capture the essence of the light. As such, there won't be a lot of emphasis on design, but rather trying to use the existing built environment to compose the image in an appealing way, through shapes, textures, and light.

03 THUMBNAIL SKETCH

I begin with a rough thumbnail sketch to lay out the general outline of the composition. The composition features three-point perspective with one of the points on the canvas, developing a focal point and movement into the middle of the composition. I deliberately choose a simpler, wider-angle composition to provide more freedom with the expression of shapes and rhythms in the absence of a more obvious indication of perspective. Along the vertical axis, I intend to form a rhythm of shapes and lines, finding appealing proportions and contrasts between positive and negative space.

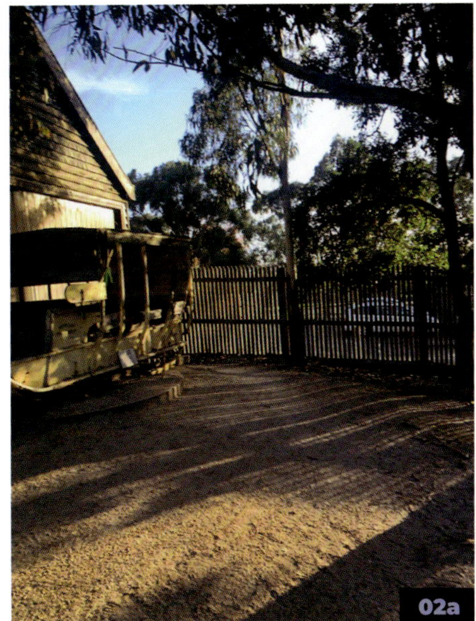

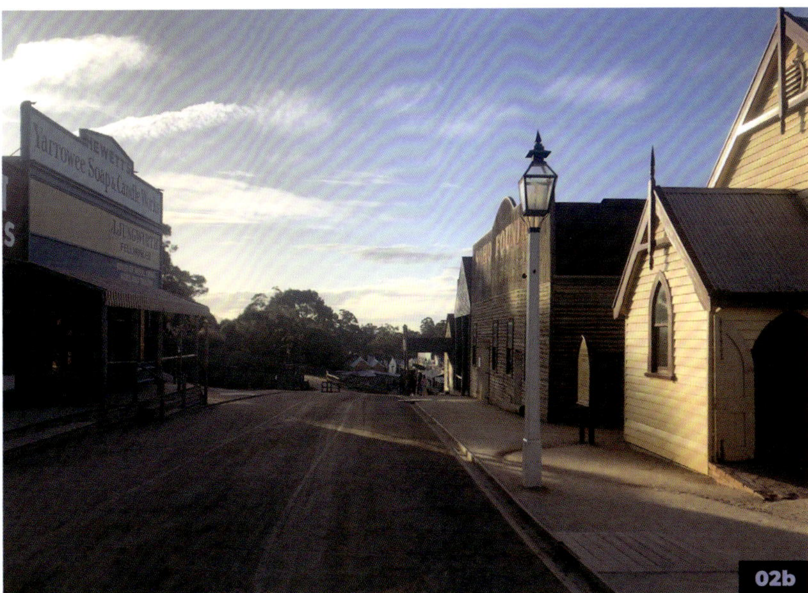

02a & 02b Additional photographs for lighting reference and inspiration.

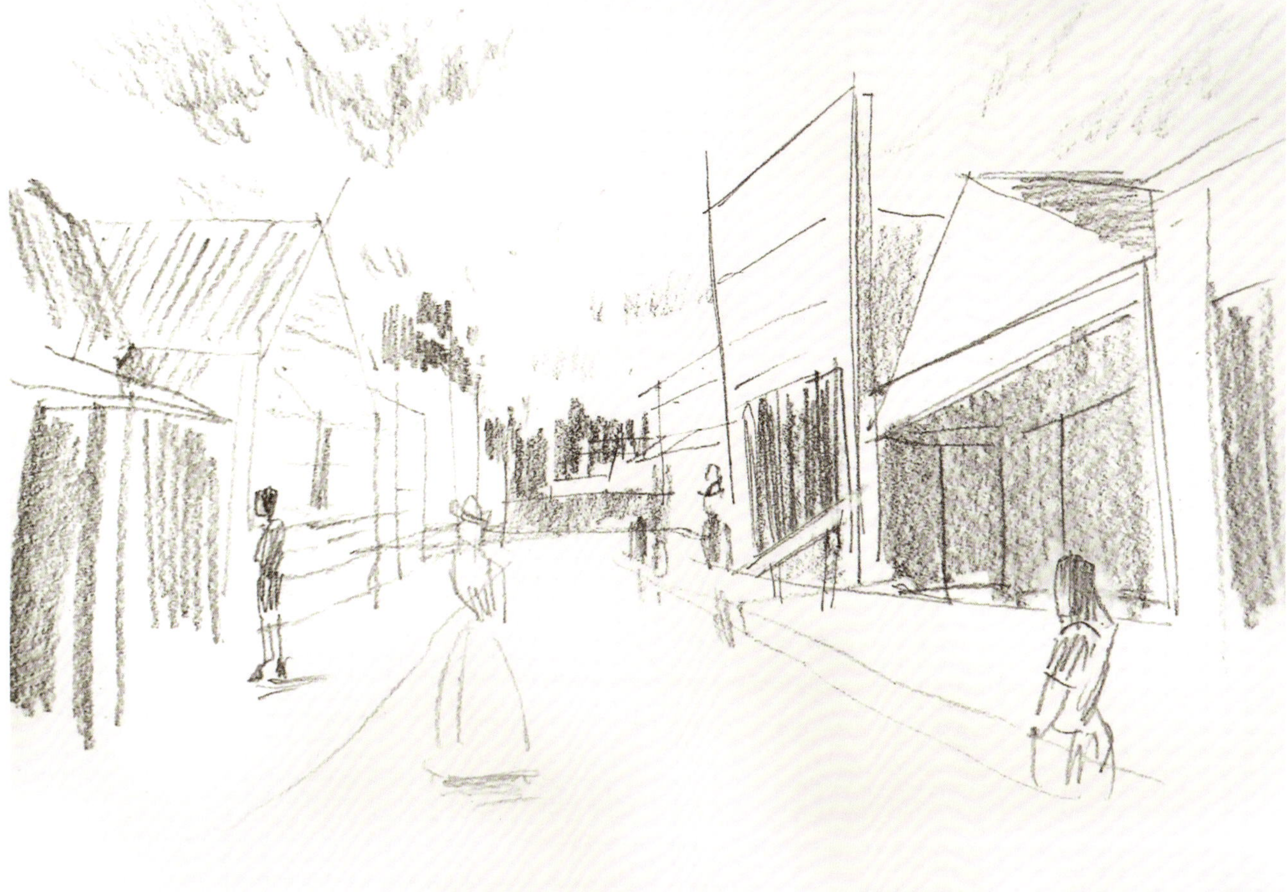

03 An A5-sized pencil sketch to find the composition.

04 COLOUR ROUGH

Next I paint out a rough colour sketch with large shapes and planes. I keep it simple and clear, with perspective in mind, thinking about the horizon line and vanishing point. I don't let the perspective overwhelm the process at this point, as I want to let my compositional instinct be the priority. Keep the textures and colour transitions basic to capture the simplest shapes and colours. At this stage, you should focus on how the thumbnail reads to see if the shapes and colours appear as intended, and on selling the dimensionality of the forms and masses.

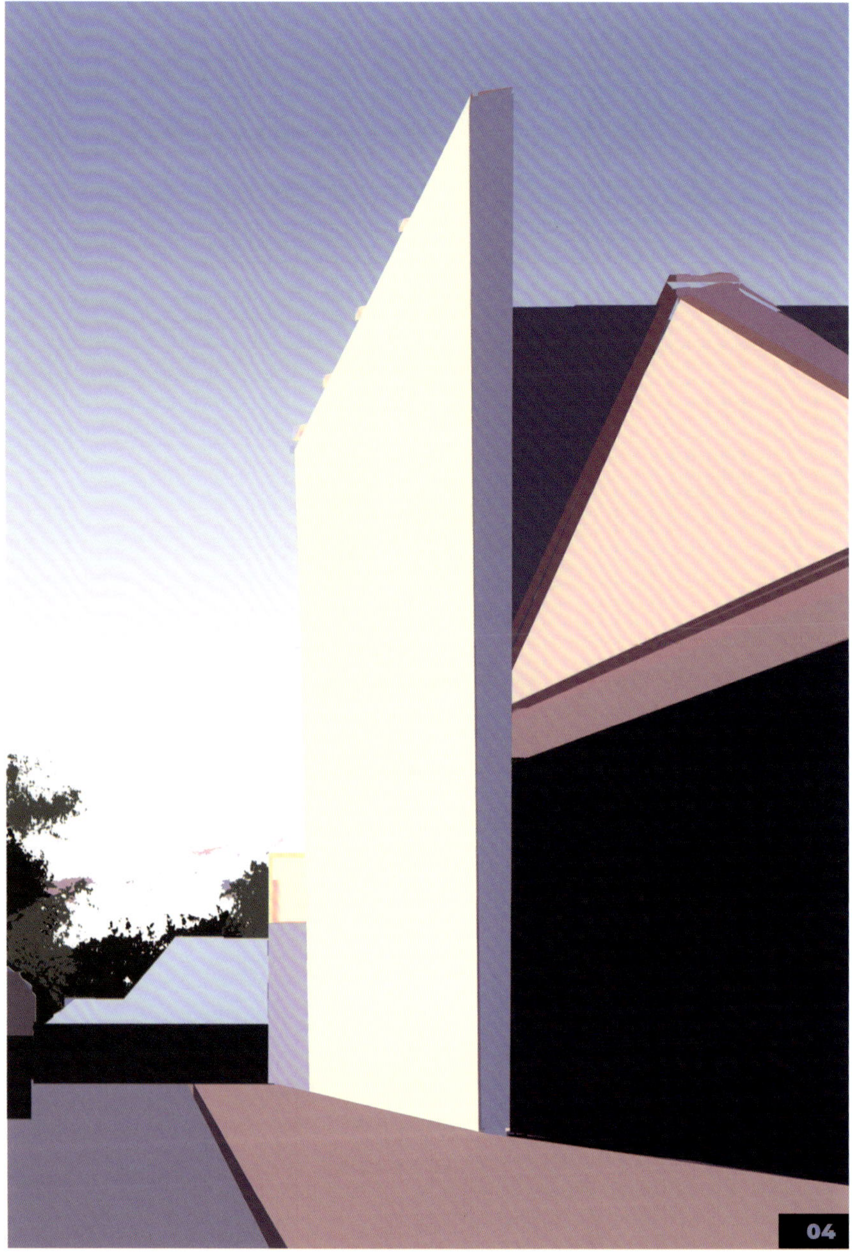

04 A basic blockout of the composition with reduced values and tones to focus on composition and clarity.

KEEP IT SIMPLE

Start out as simply as possible. Don't overwhelm yourself with fancy brushes, textures, or blending. Those are the kinds of things that are added as a finishing touch or polish to a piece, and are not necessary when developing the composition and blockout of objects and shapes. You don't want to add polish and detail only to have to change it completely when you realize there is a fundamental mistake with the composition or perspective.

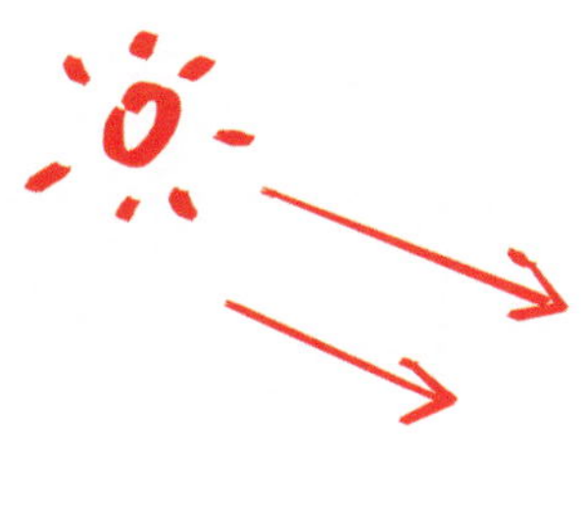

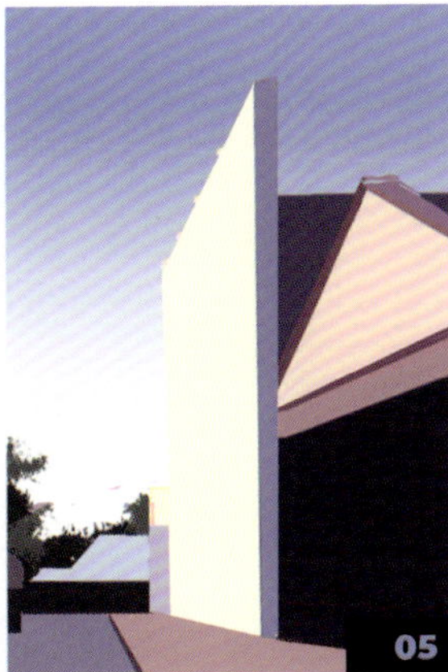

05 The light source is coming from the left of the composition.

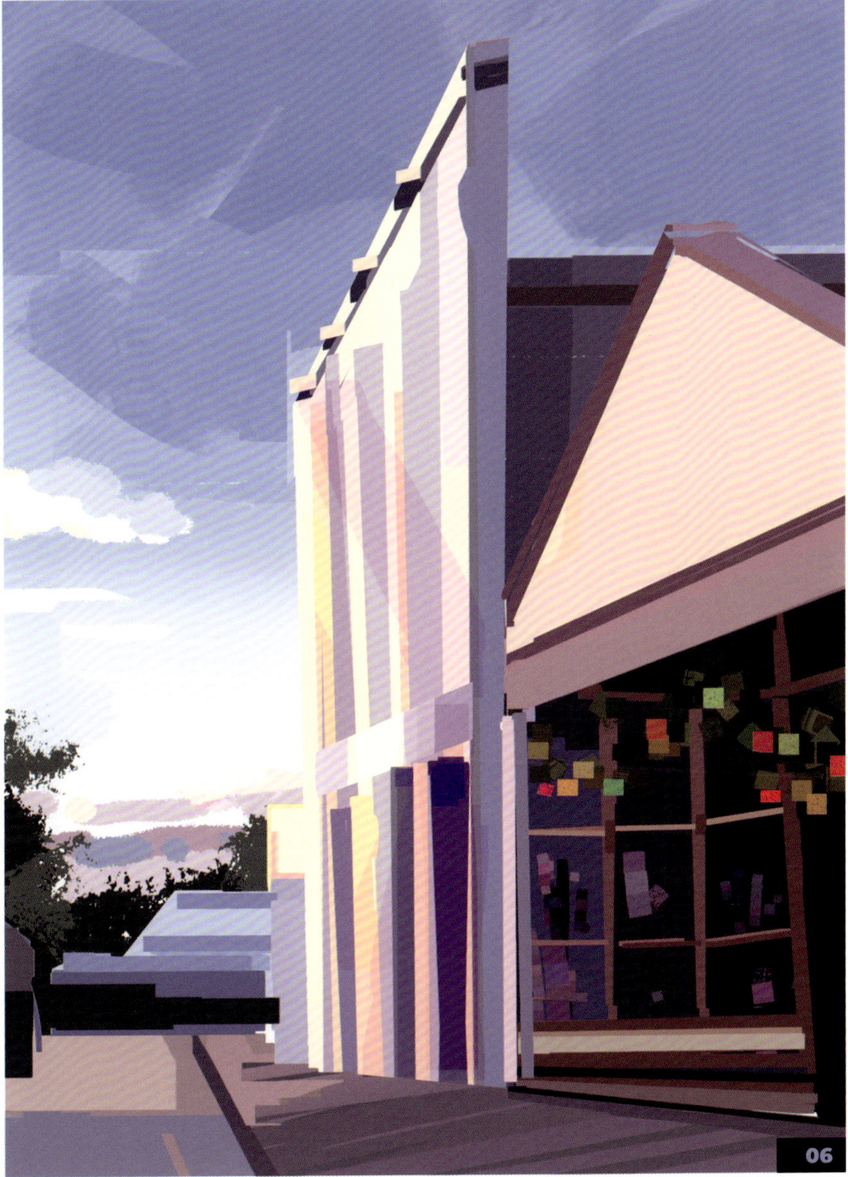

06 A rough colour study from reference to set the tone for the rest of the piece.

05 LIGHT SOURCE

The light source in this scene will be the sun, coming from the left of the composition and in front of the viewer, in accordance with the reference. Translated onto the canvas, this means the planes facing the viewer and facing to the right will be in shadow. As you paint, keep the established light source in mind and ensure it is consistent throughout the composition. Additionally, try to identify the colour and mood of the light source. For example, my reference features a beautiful golden glow with a crisp, cold atmosphere. It's important to identify the intention of the lighting and continue to bring it out through each step of the process.

06 BUILDING UP THE STUDY

Continuing with the quick colour study, I consolidate the shapes with lighting and shadow to indicate form and lay down a rough 'colour key' to inform the mood and lighting going forward. I need to solve the approach to the colours here, as it's important to emphasize the quality of light, while also keeping the lighting consistent.

I expand the range of shadow tones to define the recesses and protrusions of the buildings, using them to depict the turning planes and heighten the sense of three-dimensionality and space. A particular point of interest is the soft spot of light on the triangular facade: a small but precious detail. This quick 'colour study' stage of the process takes me about twenty-five minutes.

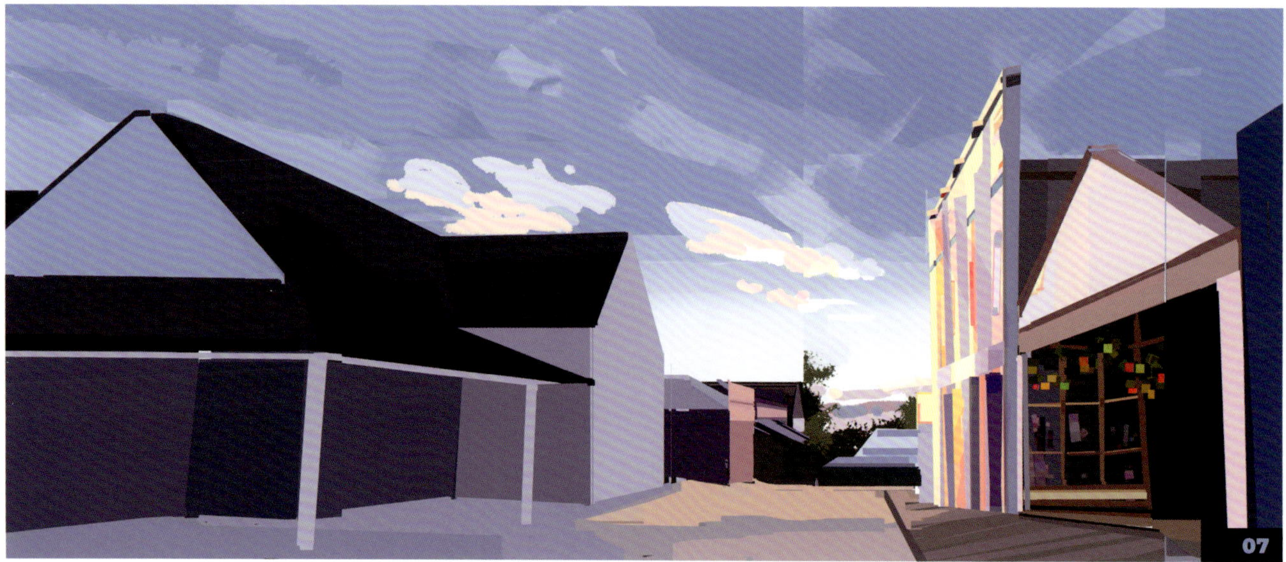

07 The basic compositional layout, extended from the initial study, keeping the colours and shapes simple to help find the composition.

07 EXTENDING THE SCENE

Once I'm happy with the colour study, I commit to the composition and extend the canvas. Quickly and loosely, like before, I paint out the large shapes and quickly describe the volumes of the buildings to grasp the larger picture. The main turning planes are depicted with flat shapes of colour. The aim is to lay out the volumetric space of the composition while keeping the graphic read in mind on the two-dimensional plane of the image.

Consistent shadows and lighting remain a priority as new elements are added without direct lighting reference. It's important to portray these new elements as believably as possible to marry the composition together. This step is the real first layout of the composition – feel free to chop and change at this stage to find an appealing breakup of shapes. You can freehand the perspective at this point, but keep in mind how objects would look as they recede into the distance.

FREEHAND PERSPECTIVE

Starting with a perspective grid early on in the process, especially when finding the composition, can be restrictive. Try expressing the narrative and mood of the composition freely first, adhering to perspective in a freehand manner, and then correct it at a later stage once the intention of the composition is established.

08 PERSPECTIVE GRID

Once I've roughly laid down the larger shapes and forms, I place a vanishing point on the horizon and lay out the perspective grid. In almost any composition set in three-dimensional space, perspective plays a large role in the composition. It's always necessary to define the perspective, even with the most simple perspective grid, as the smallest deviation away from it can be detected by the human eye and will look 'off'. Here the vertical perspective converges at a point above the horizon line, since the horizon line is low on the canvas, indicating that the camera is tilting upwards. I don't lay out guides for the horizontal perspective as I intend to depict it with a more naturalistic, pseudo-curvilinear style.

09 LEADING LINES

Following the perspective grid, I quickly tweak the main 'leading lines' of the buildings so that they recede correctly towards the vanishing point; for example, the angle of the large rooftop on the left, and the placement of the blue decoration on the right facade. These are some of the lines that naturally 'lead' the viewer's eye through the composition. To quickly note, since the scene is set on a hill, there will be another vanishing point for receding lines on the ground plane; however, this will require more care and attention, so will be solved at a later stage. For now, correcting the perspective of the greater leading lines is the priority.

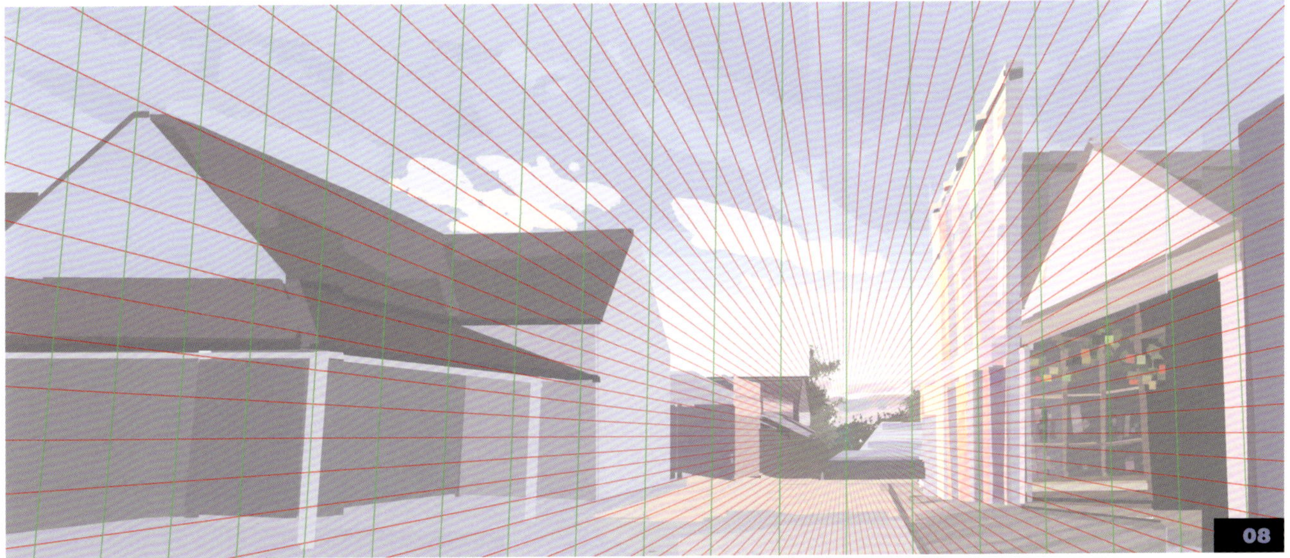

08 A grid overlay to correct the perspective going forward.

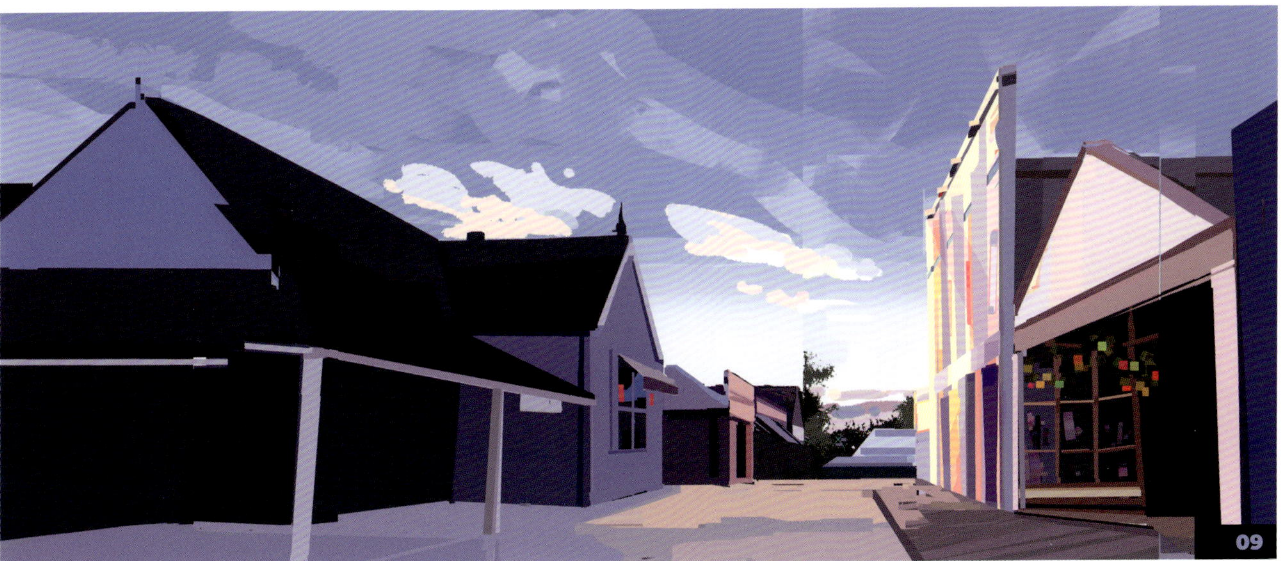

09 Correcting the study to fit the perspective grid.

YOU ARE PROBABLY NOT FORESHORTENING ENOUGH

Many artists have a tendency to draw foreshortened features on less of an angle than they really have. Take the orthogonal facade design **(A)**. If you were to depict it on an angle, you might depict it like diagram **D**. It looks right… or does it? The features are not foreshortened enough, indicating that the facade is wider than originally planned, more like diagram **B**. The correct amount of foreshortening **(C)** is actually more extreme than your instincts may tell you.

Developing a grasp of this concept can hugely improve your freehand perspective drawing. To correctly foreshorten these kinds of elements, you can find reference photos of similar perspectives. You can also quickly visualize the effect of foreshortening by putting the flat design up on a monitor and viewing your monitor at an angle, to get a feel for the effect.

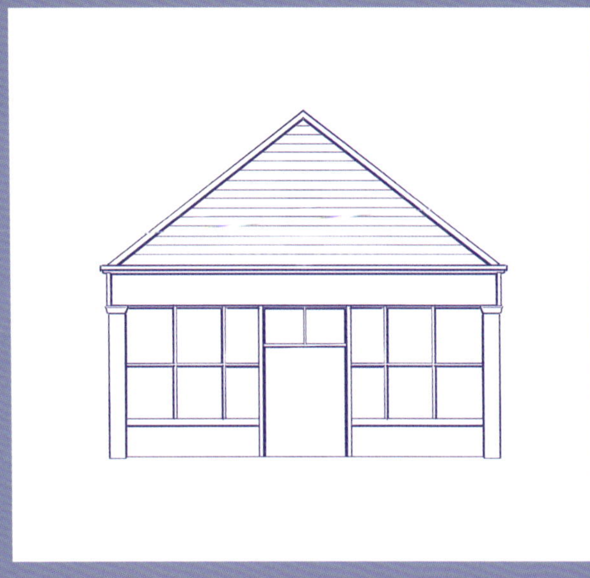

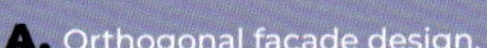

A. Orthogonal facade design.

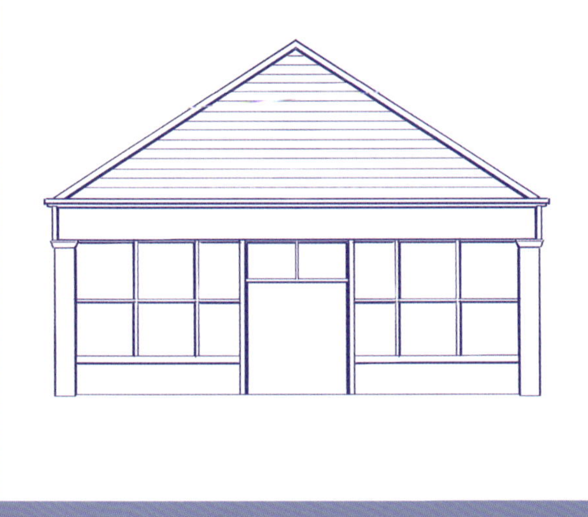

B. Incorrect facade width.

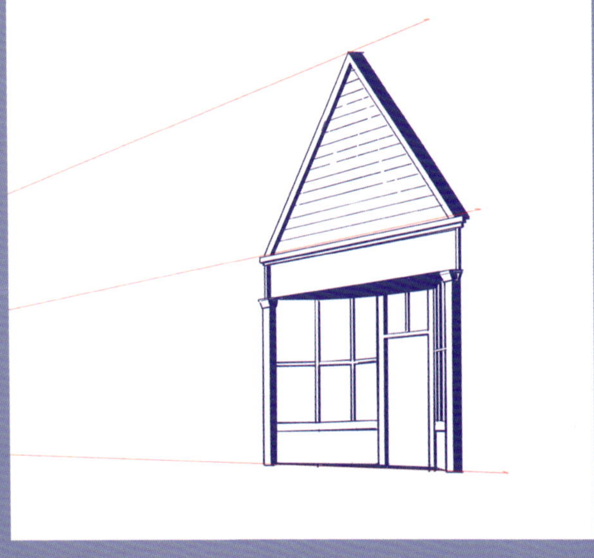

C. Correct foreshortening.

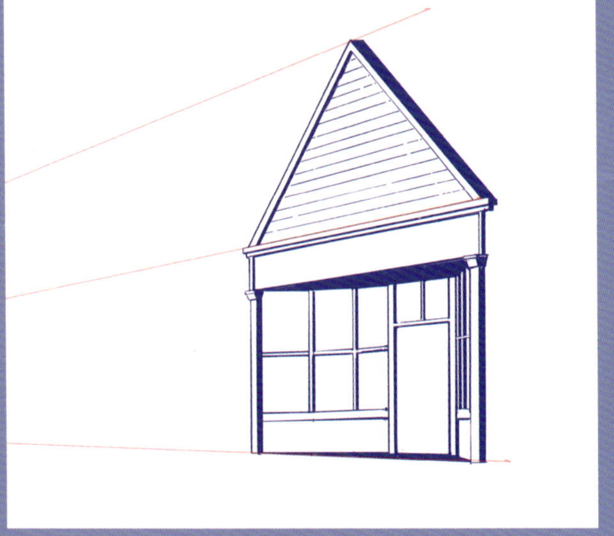

D. Incorrect foreshortening.

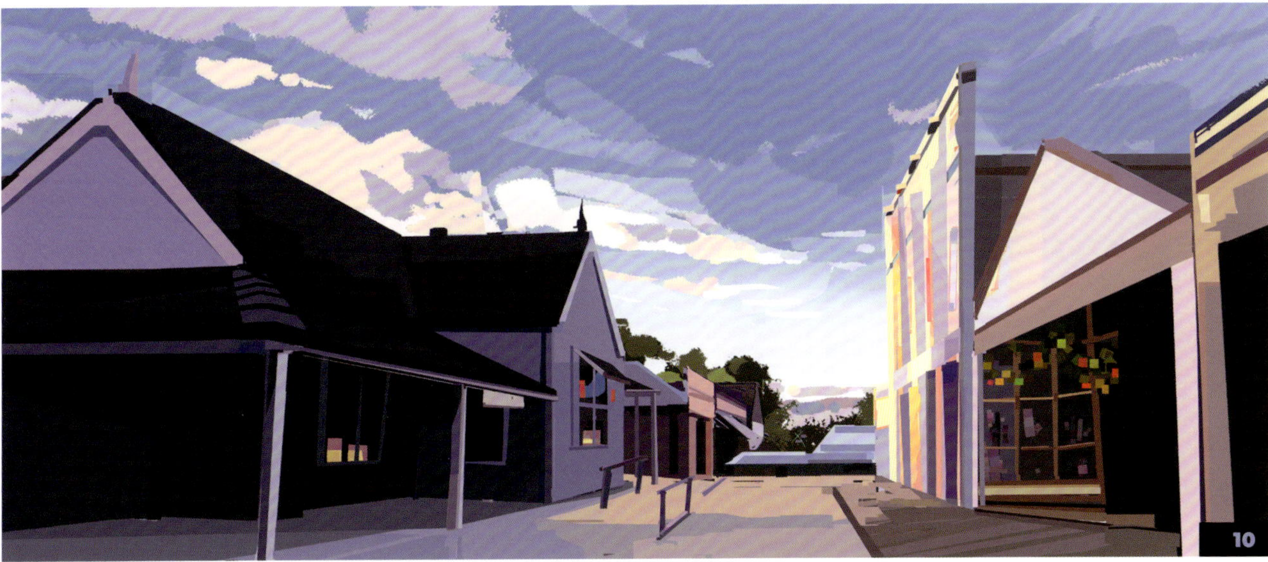

10 Adjusting the composition, shifting slightly to the left to help achieve balance.

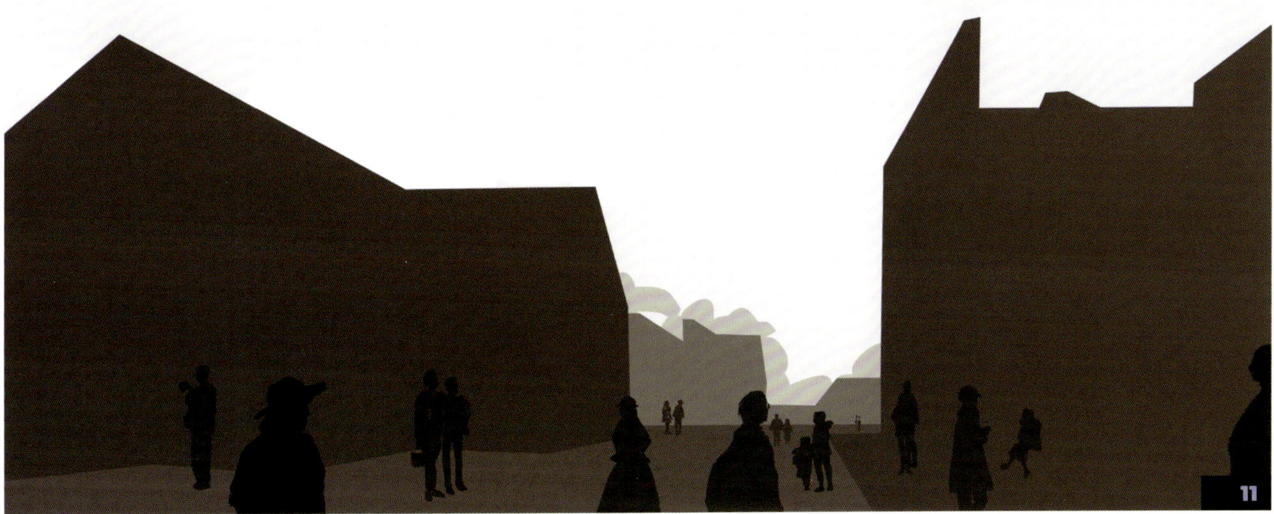

11 The greyscale breakdown of the foreground, middle ground, and background, showing balance and clarity.

10 COMPOSITION SHIFT

I decide to shift the composition slightly, to add more to the right side, as the left building is looking too large and monolithic. Incorporating more of the buildings that catch light on the right of the canvas brightens the image and brings the vanishing point towards the centre. When working on a piece, keep reviewing the composition by squinting, zooming out, and checking greyscale values. Don't get lost as you add finer details and don't let the intention of the image get away from you.

11 DEPTH & SEPARATION

Creating a clear separation of foreground, middle ground, and background is a simple but effective way to sell the depth of a composition. The overlapping of these elements helps to portray distance and scale, and the elements can be used compositionally to find appealing shapes and relationships. Don't neglect this simple but effective approach, and always refer to it throughout the process.

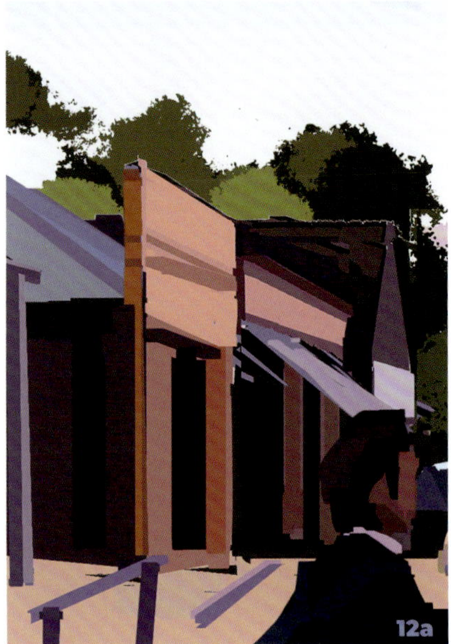

12a Facade with edge detail added to create thickness.

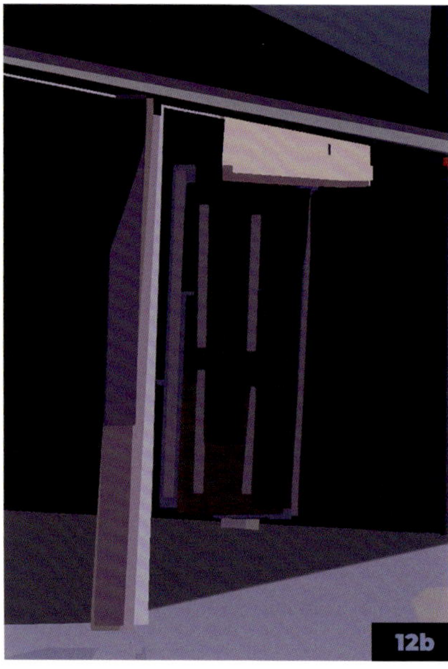

12b Detail of bevel added to the door to describe ornamentation.

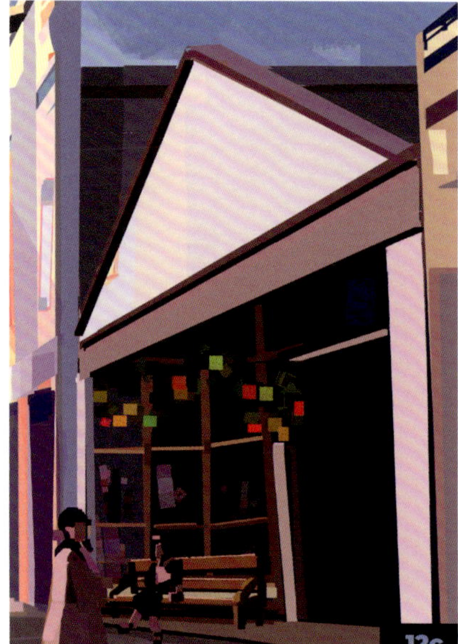

12c Pediment and signage with added volume.

12 BUILDING UP DETAIL

I continue to describe more shapes and forms while adhering to the perspective grid set in step 08. Adding details to the planes, just as simple faces, helps to solidify the perspective and add form and dimensionality to the buildings **(12a–c)**. The windows and awnings also adhere to perspective, strengthening the indication of depth and volume.

Scaling the amount of detail according to the distance from the camera is another way you can build a sense of depth in space. As objects recede into the distance, they lose focus. When painting digitally it can be tempting to zoom in really close and add detail to everything, but you should be selective with where you add detail, as it can not only affect the contrast and composition of the overall piece, but also how the depth of the piece is perceived.

13 ROOF CORNER

These receding roof tiles are tricky-looking elements to draw accurately, but the process is actually quite simple. The group of tiles recedes towards its own vanishing point **(13a)**, independent of the main vanishing point for the overall painting. You can 'eyeball' the tiles and play with spacing until the result feels right.

Smaller elements like these offer greater opportunity to play with shape language to find appealing breakups. For example, option **13b** shows a more 'correct' depiction of the tiles based on linear perspective rules. Although it looks very clean and correct, it lacks the personality of **13c**, which is drawn freehand, with slightly inconsistent spacing and angles. Distribute elements of 'wonkiness' throughout the piece to add a sense of character and shape appeal. This is not an exact science and very much depends on personal taste and experience. If you go too far, the result may look like a bad drawing, but getting it *just right* adds a new layer of expression and interpretation that will set your piece apart.

DETAIL IN PERSPECTIVE

A quick and easy way to add dimensionality to a flat facade is to add an indication of a thin extrusion or a bevel. By simply adding a thin shadow, a thin highlight, or a combination of both, you can enhance the illusion of complexity on a flat plane and add dimensionality.

13a Vanishing point, guidelines, and scaffolding for the tile detail.

13b Accurate representation of tiles in perspective.

13c Adding interest with a bit of 'wonk'!

14 CONSISTENT SCALE

As I continue to flesh out the space and composition, I pay close attention to scale, both with objects in relation to each other, such as building heights, windows, and doors, and with objects in perspective. The relation between these differently sized elements needs to be consistent. With the scale of the environment roughly in place, the stage is set to add characters that fit well into the scene.

With the help of my reference material, I carefully place some characters, blocking them in with simple shapes and a limited palette. As I'm not copying the figures exactly from reference, I adjust their placement and sizing to fit the context of the painting. This helps them to appear grounded and fit naturally in the space, scaled proportionately to the doorways and floor levels. Characters immediately add context to the scale of the environment, which is a crucial area to resolve, as well as adding liveliness and a sense of human touch and warmth to the space.

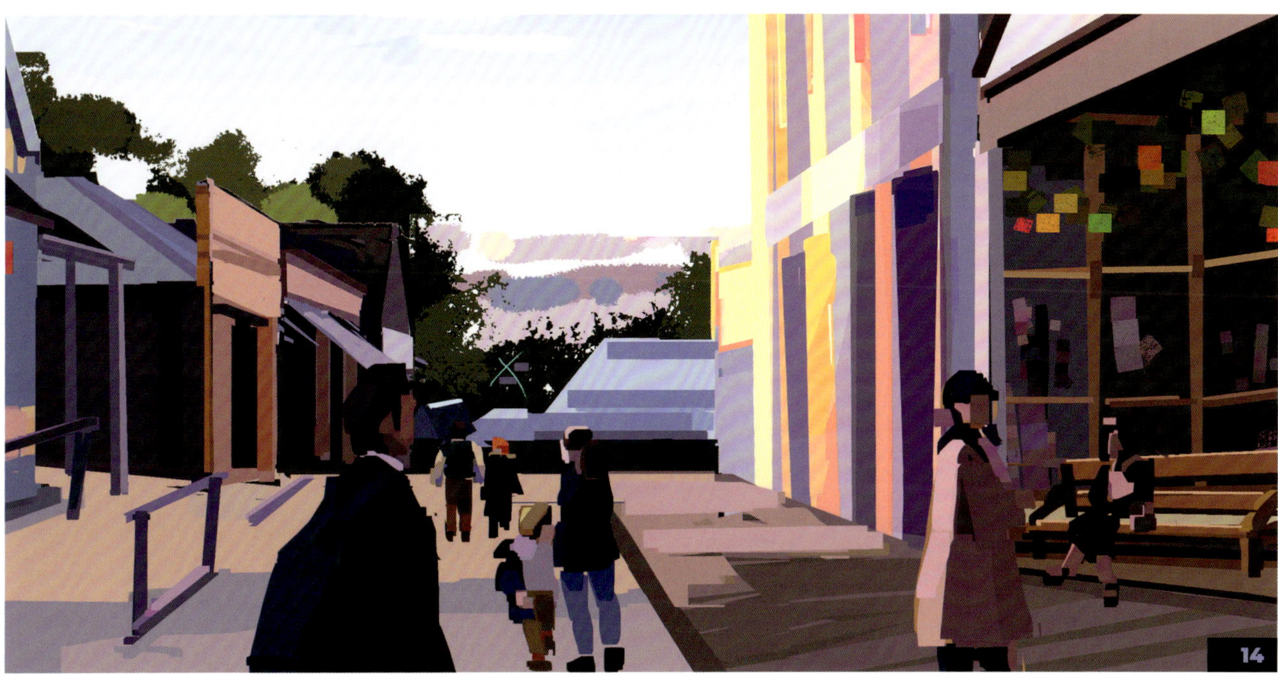

14 A close-up of the composition with added characters.

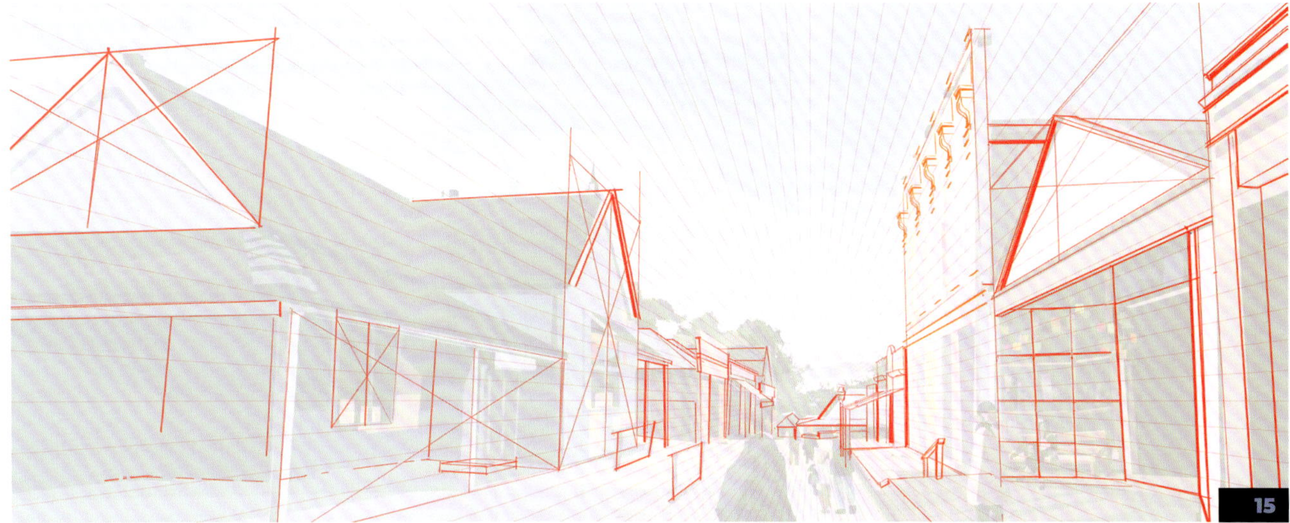

15 A revised drawing that makes corrections to the perspective and structure.

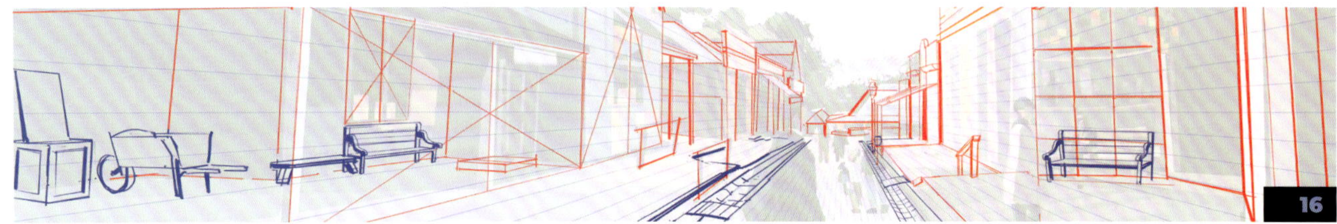

16 An additional drawover for the sloped ground and gutters, as well as some more set-dressing.

15 PERSPECTIVE CORRECTIONS

I want to create a new sketch that corrects the perspective and centre-lines of each major structure. Since this step is on a new layer that will be used as a guide, I adhere strongly to the grid to represent the perspective as correctly as possible. There will be an opportunity later to break away from it, but I want to lay out the most accurate pass first.

I check that orthogonals adhere to the perspective grid, that centre-lines are constructed correctly, that objects scale in line with the characters and other elements around them, and that the scale of receding objects makes sense. These guidelines will help to correct the painting in the next stage. This step is also necessary to clear up amorphous blobs of colour that don't describe much form yet. Small corrections like these may seem unnecessary, but they can be the difference between an amateur- and a professional-looking product.

16 THE GROUND PLANE

Next I wish to delineate the second vanishing point for the ground plane, which is actually sloping down since the site is situated on a hill. The slope is quite subtle and difficult to portray, so I need to be accurate to ensure that various cues are clear to communicate this visually. The second vanishing point is vertically in line with the first to communicate the slope. The sloped ground differentiates itself from the level deck in front of the shops on the right of the composition. The gutter on the left side is a little more naturalistic, depicting the unevenness of the imperfect slope, and a slight curve downwards shows the incline becoming steeper further down the slope. Once again, be accurate with this sketch, as it will help to correct the painting in the next stage.

FINDING CENTRE POINTS

To find the centre point of a rectilinear plane (one with straight lines), connect the opposite corners of the plane to form a cross. The point where those lines cross over is the centre of the plane and can be used to delineate forms within the plane, like window mullions, or to accurately plot shapes such as symmetrical triangles.

17 PERSPECTIVE DISTORTION

For an image to follow linear perspective, the horizontals must be perfectly horizontal, since the view is treated as if the viewer is looking straight on towards a vanishing point, eliminating the existence of the second point of perspective on the horizon line. However, due to the width of this canvas, and hence the wider 'camera' lens, a few optical corrections must be made towards the left and right edges of the canvas. As you extend the 'cone of vision' beyond 60 degrees, forms on the edge of the cone will begin to distort, similar to the principle of a fish-eye lens. (For more on the 'cone of vision', see page 190.)

We can execute this effect in a more freehand way to make the forms look more accurate and pleasing to the eye, simulating the real-life scenario of observing a scene **(17a)**. In real life, to observe a scene this wide, you would be required to look to the left and right, moving the approximation of vanishing points. So, in order to depict a panoramic view with a cone of vision beyond the regular human perception of 60 degrees, a bit of artistic liberty can be taken. Making a few small adjustments to subtly mimic curvilinear perspective produces a more naturalistic product, while keeping the principles of linear perspective in mind **(17b)**.

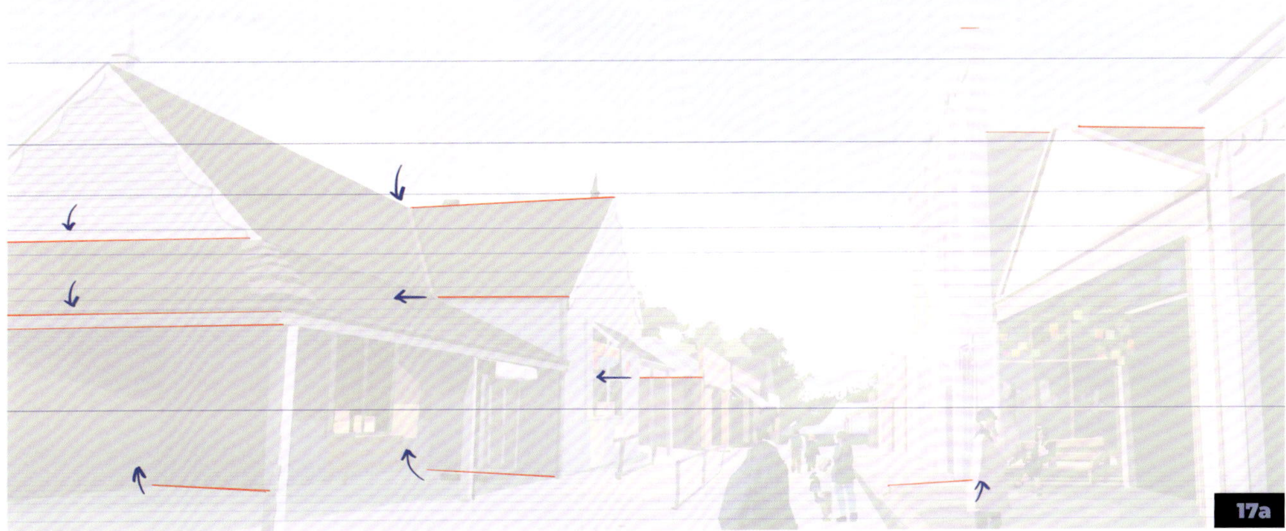

17a Slight adjustments to the horizontal perspective to mimic curvilinear perspective.

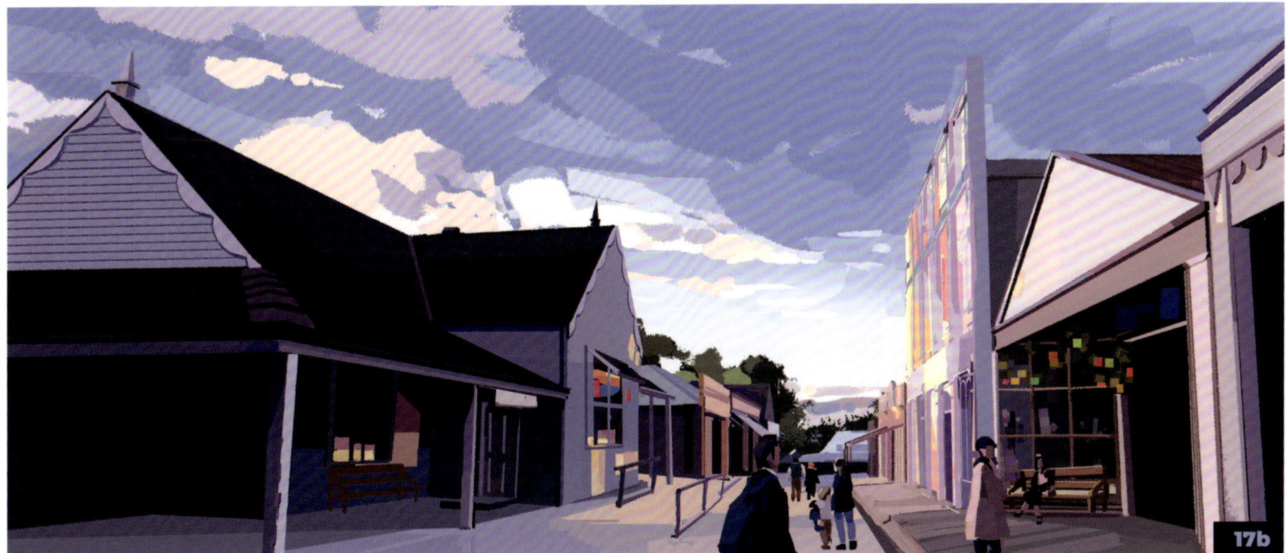

17b Slight curvilinear perspective introduced to bring in a more naturalistic feel.

18 FLAT FACADE ASSET

For drawing and painting highly detailed facades and building surfaces, you can leverage the editing capabilities of digital software. In this case, I design a flat asset for the tallest building **(18a)** and warp it onto the perspective grid, to accurately plot complicated details. I do this by transforming the corners of the asset plane to match the perspective grid **(18b)**. This flat design doesn't communicate a third level of depth, but plotting these details in two dimensions will help to accurately construct those extrusions and more complex three-dimensional forms later **(18c)**.

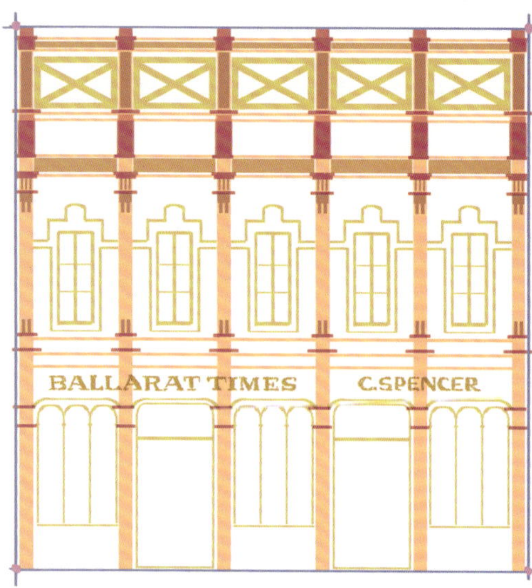

18a Flat facade design.

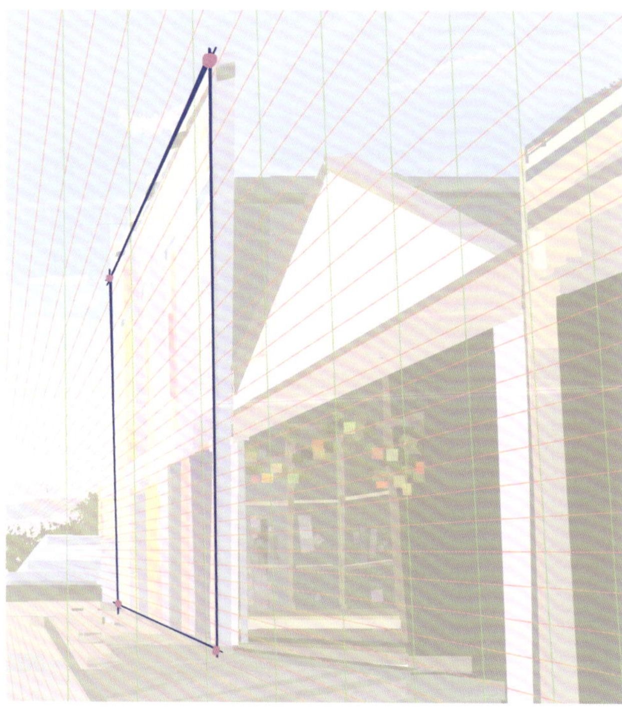

18b Planning the perspective and placement of the asset.

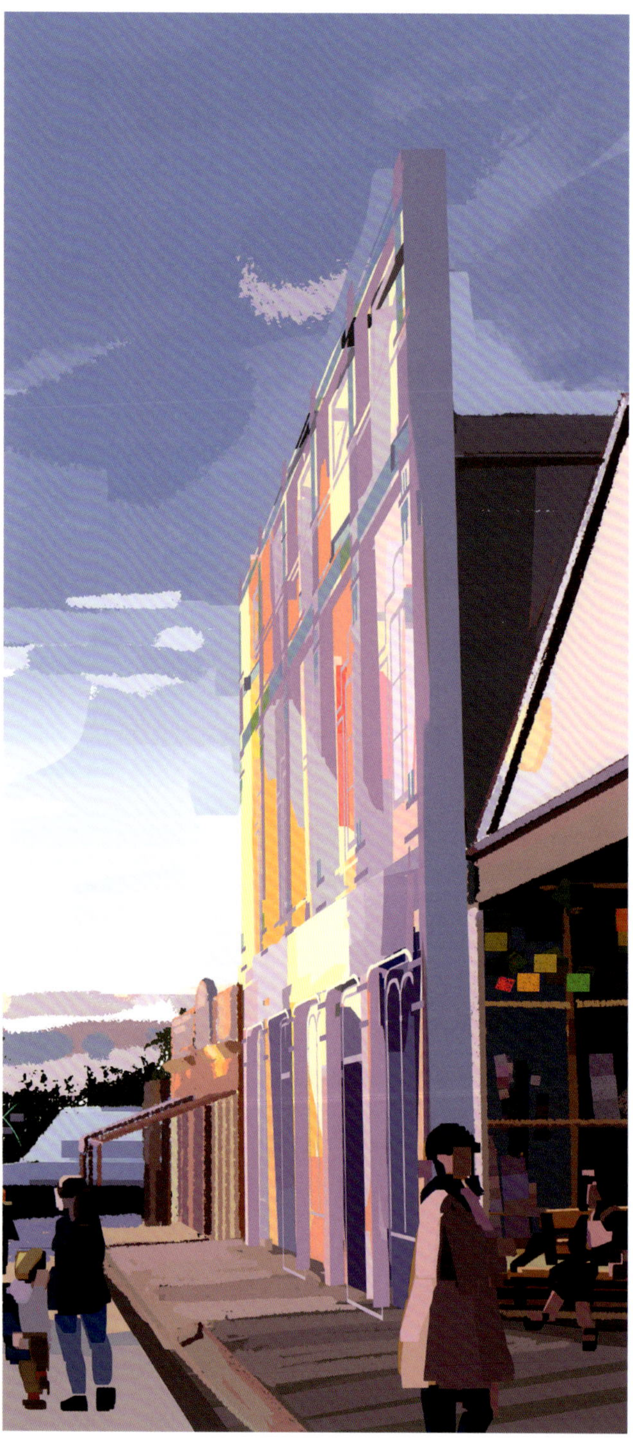

18c The flat design transformed into perspective.

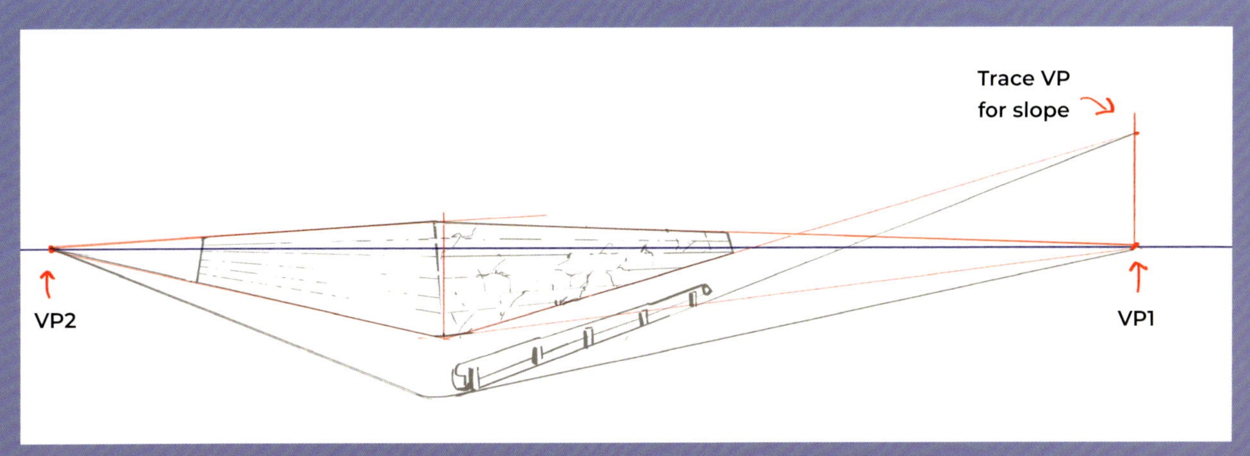

A. Constructing a slope in perspective.

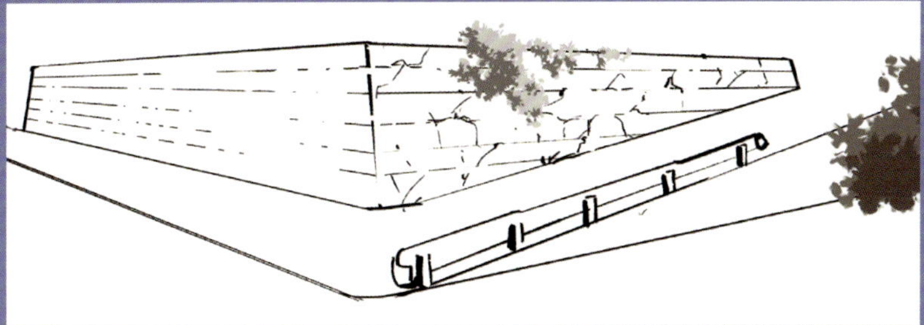

B. Slope in perspective.

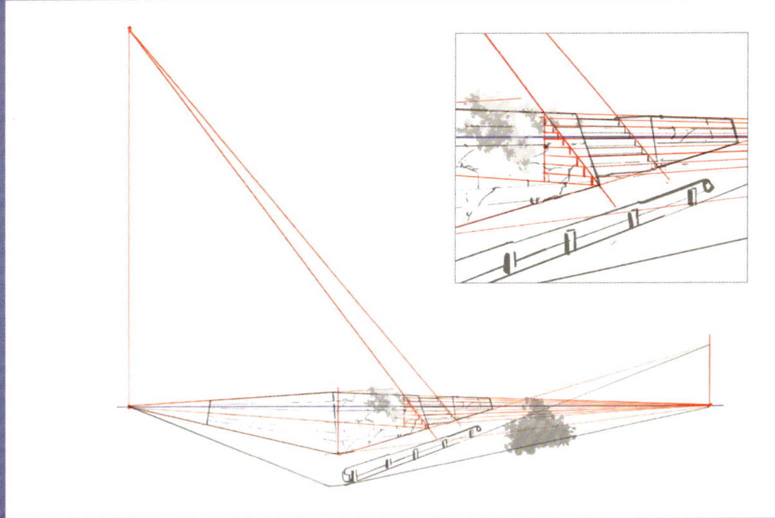

C. Constructing stairs in perspective.

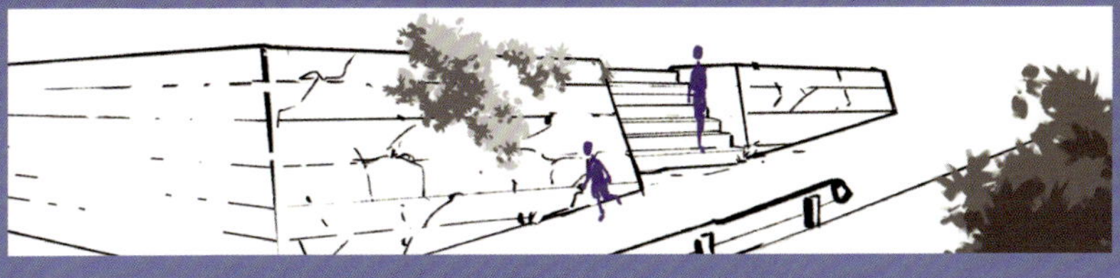

D. Stairs in perspective.

SLOPES & STAIRS IN PERSPECTIVE

Stairs and slopes can be tricky to construct in perspective. A solid structure can be achieved by adding another vanishing point directly in line with – above or below – the original vanishing point, depending on whether the incline is going up or down **(A)**.

To construct a slope, simply indicate it by adhering to the second vanishing point and have all other elements adhering to the first vanishing point **(B)**.

To construct stairs, draw the side plane of the staircase as a rectilinear (straight-edged) form, adhering to the regular vanishing point. Evenly divide this form with the number of risers desired. Next, find the slope of the stairs using the second vanishing point, vertically in line with the first. Using the spacing of the risers, the slope of the stairs, and the first vanishing point, construct the cross-section of the stairs, and then simply extrude this to a second vanishing point along the horizon line **(C)**.

Understanding how to construct stairs can open up a multitude of possibilities for drawing complex forms in perspective **(D)**.

19 BUILDING UP THE FACADE

I apply the flat design asset to the facade and replace the old sketch, but keep the colour information as a base for when I start to paint the details. Now I can address the three-dimensional facade elements mentioned in step 18. I isolate the facade and paint a single column in detail. This is my chance to get fancy with the rendering and implement finer details that will carry through to the final product. The image's colour palette is well-established at this point and can be used to inform the finer details and the subtler transition of colours required to achieve them. The use of shadow and light helps to delineate the different faces and curved transitions, building up the volume and structure of the column.

20 DUPLICATING COLUMNS

The facade features six identical repeating columns, so you can save some time by fleshing out a single column and duplicating it six times. It can be useful to duplicate assets you make during the

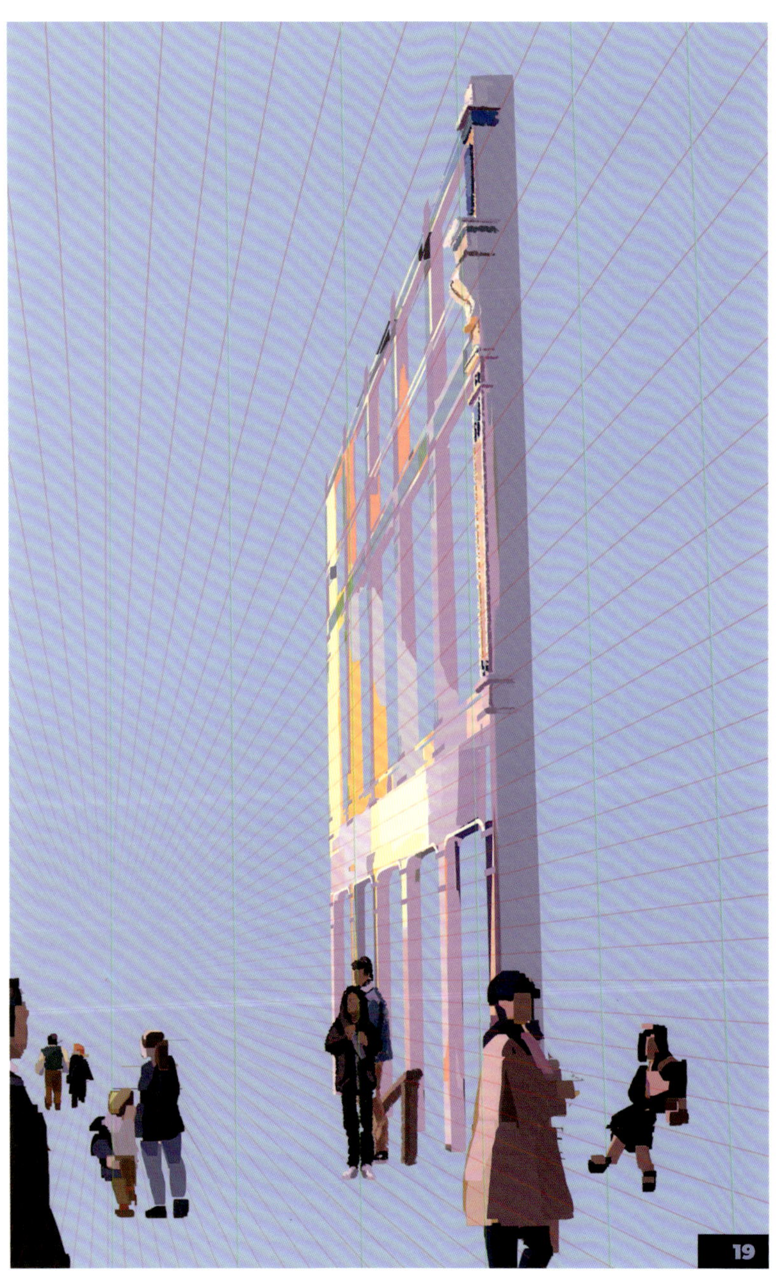

19 The isolated facade, with one detailed column with lighting and depth.

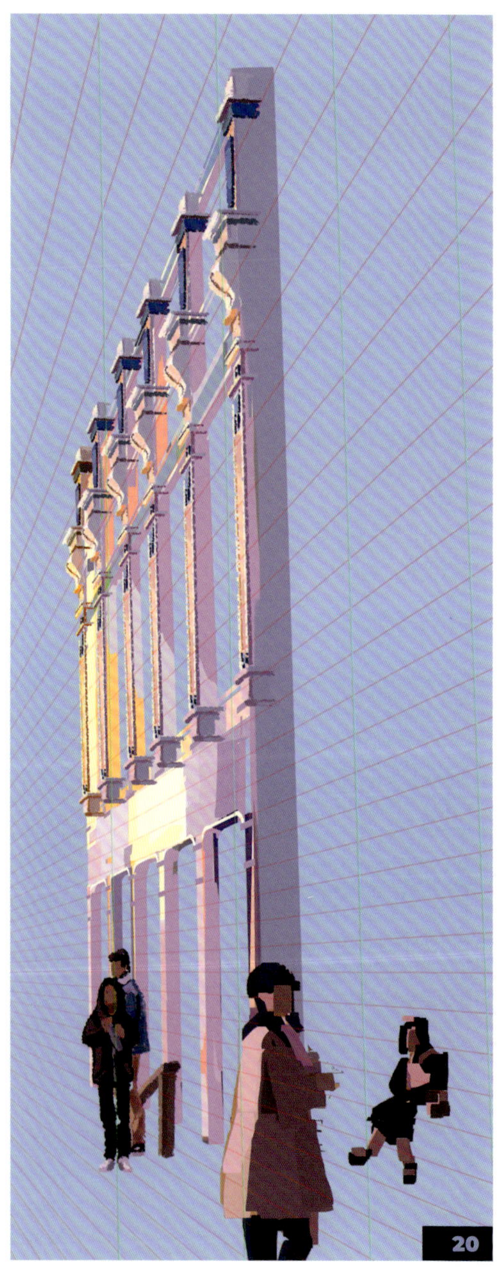

20 The isolated facade with a detailed column, duplicated and painted over.

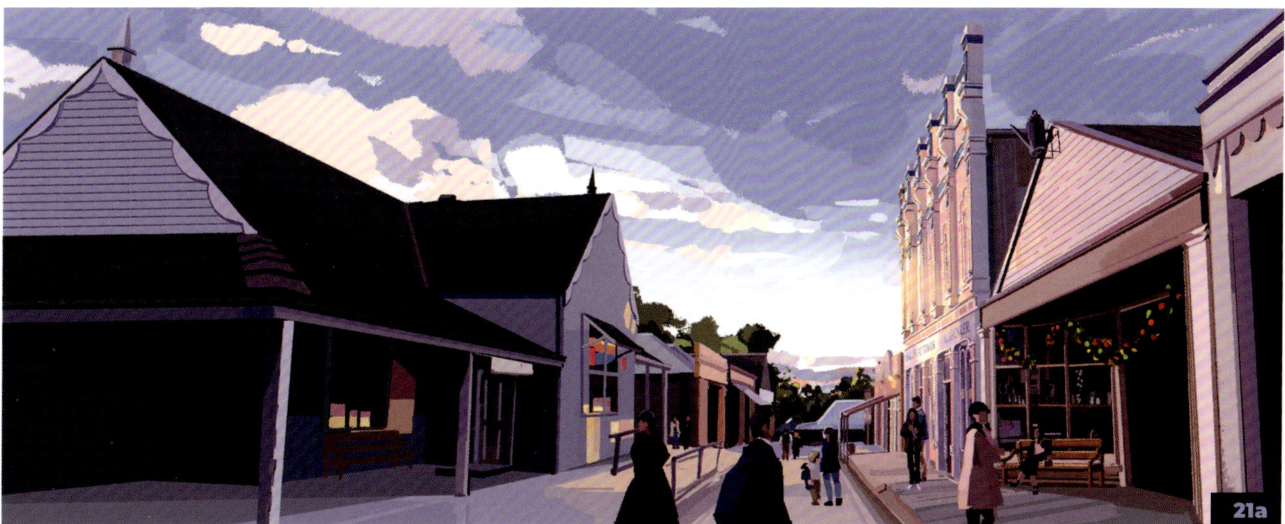

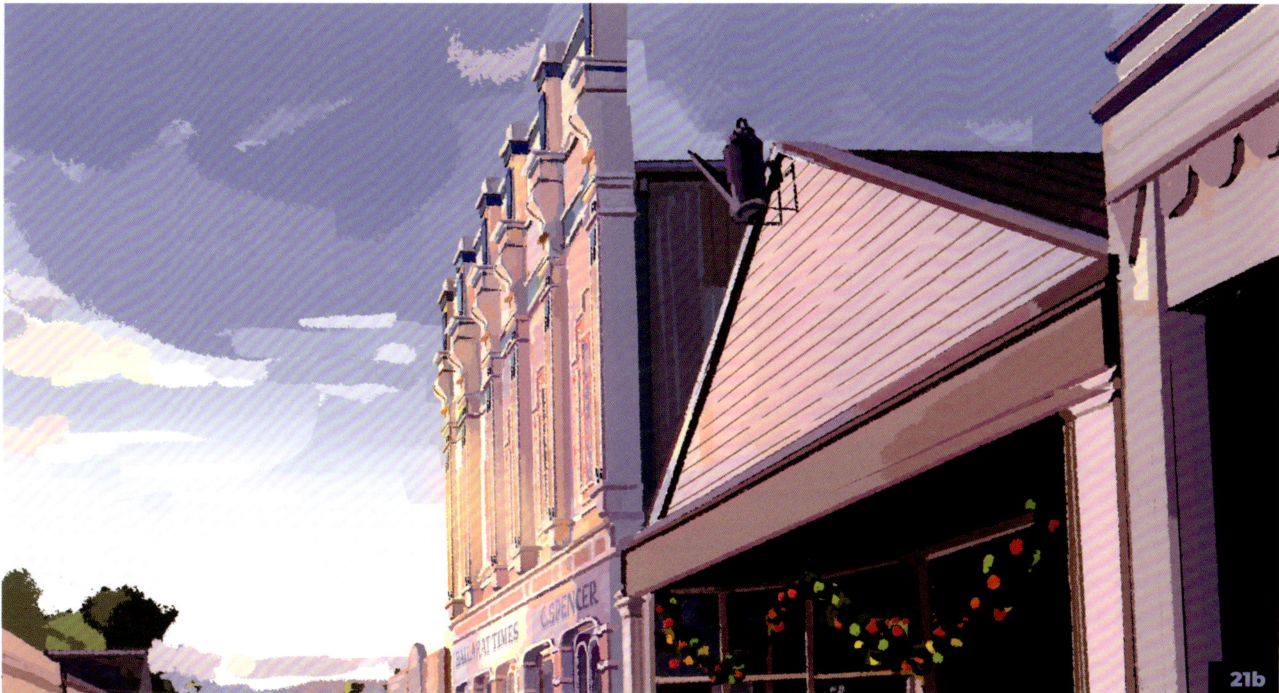

21a & 21b Completed facade detailing, with lighting and shadows painted over.

process, so look to utilize the assets you've made whenever you can, even from other paintings you've created in the past. This technique is extremely quick and efficient, as the result produced is a very faceted and dimensional facade. Make sure to paint over each column however, as the way lights and shadows fall on each column is different, and this will heighten the sense of depth.

21 TILES & BOARDS

At this point of the illustration, most of the composition and larger details are fleshed out. The next step is to add more texture and detail. However, it is important to note that the detail should support the perspective of the composition and adhere to the vanishing points. Adding tiles and the indication of wooden boards is a great way to reinforce the perspective and help the planes of the building read as they should **(21a, 21b)**.

25 SIGNAGE ASSETS

Building sign designs with text can be very difficult to draw in perspective. This is where the technique of warping a flat asset becomes especially useful. Like before, I transform the text by dragging the corners of the bounding box to match the perspective grid **(25a)**, and then scale the text into the right position on the building **(25b)**.

Aspects like arcs, curves, and spacing are all simplified when drawn orthogonally **(25c)**, and the time saved is especially important when doing client work. It also allows you to design more complexity and add more detail.

26 PEOPLE & DETAILS

Adding more people to the composition fills out the scene, distributing interest and various pops of contrast in areas that appeared flatter and uninteresting. Don't forget that you can 'design' the composition further than what you observe in reality. You can use different design elements and set-dressing to fill out a composition, such as trees and foliage, lamp posts and electrical wires, or whatever fits the setting.

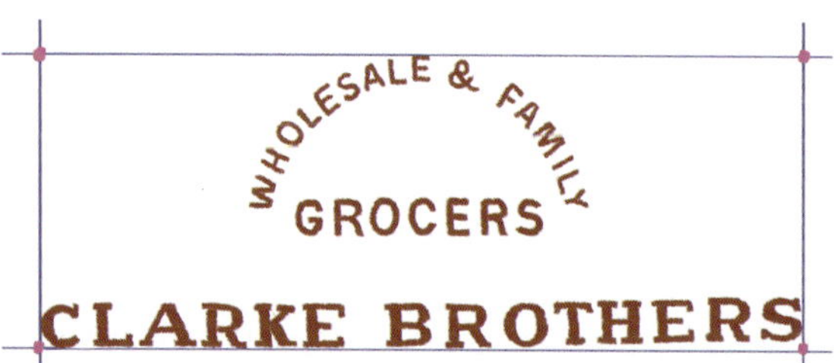

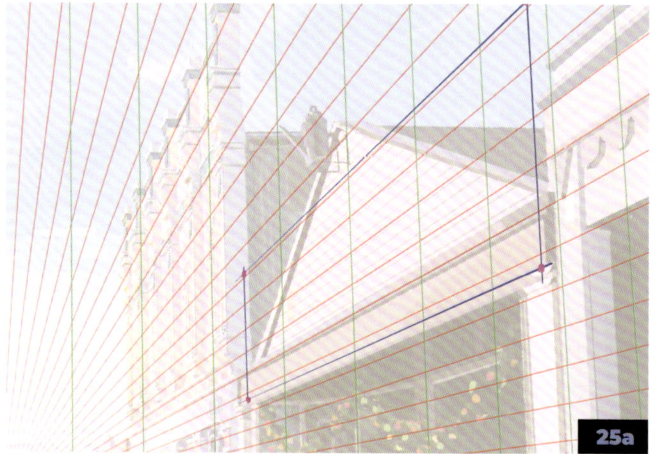

25a Transforming the bounding box to the perspective grid.

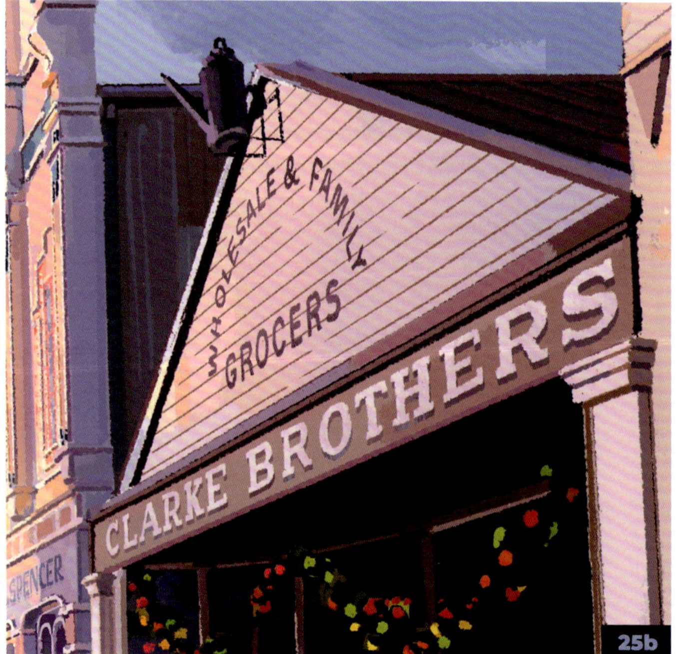

25b Painting over the transformed assets to blend them into the environment.

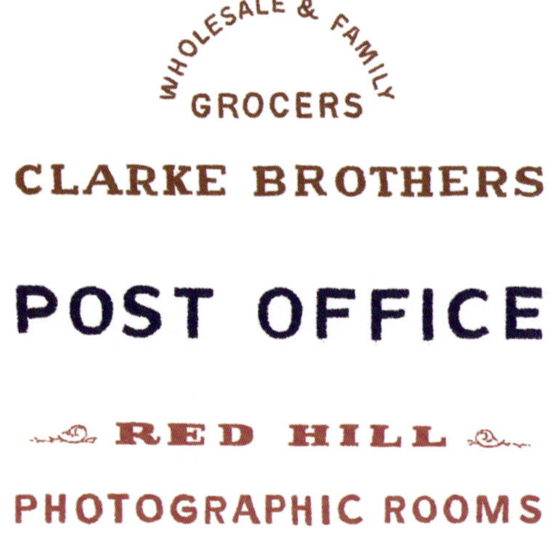

25c Text designs for the flat assets.

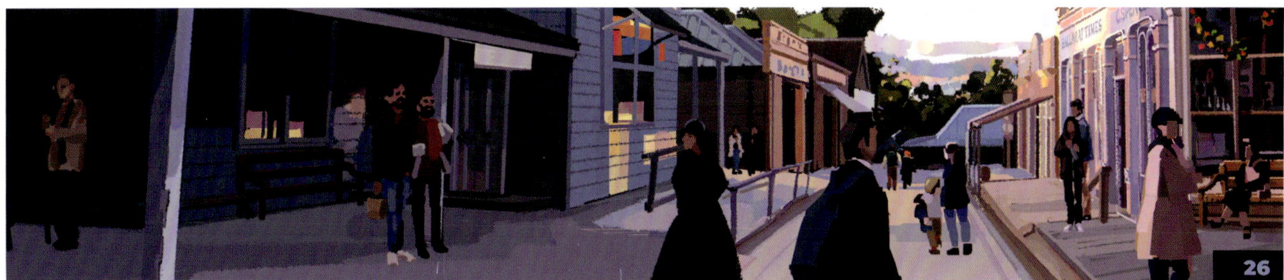

26 A close-up of the composition, further character additions using simple shapes and colours.

27a The initial colour-blocked ground plane lacks planar information.

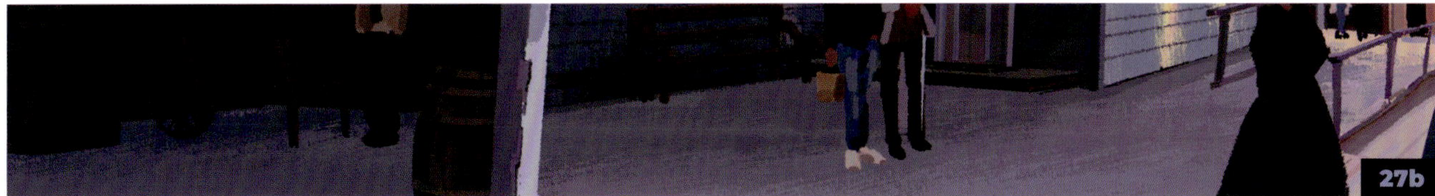

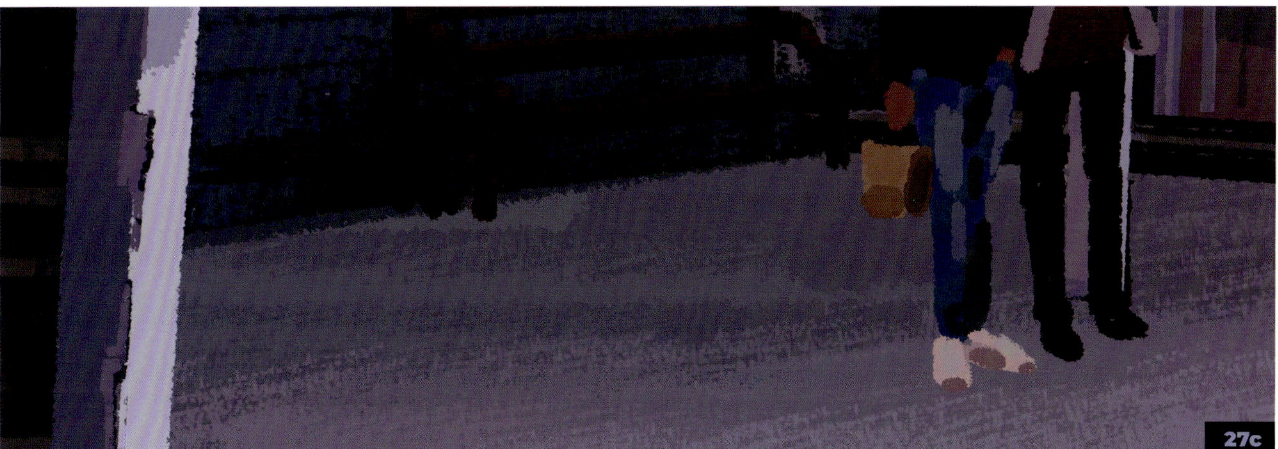

27b & 27c The textured ground plane, introducing complex colour transitions and directional planar information that indicates perspective.

27 TEXTURED BRUSHSTROKES

In order to avoid obfuscating the read of the ground plane, I use a directional texture to depict the subtle transition in the shadows. When I was using a larger flat brush earlier, I had trouble depicting the dimensionality of the ground plane – it made the perspective appear confusing **(27a)**. Even seemingly minor details, such as the direction of the brushstrokes, can have a profound effect on the composition **(27b, 27c)**. Be very aware of how every element and action can influence your results, and use these minute aspects intentionally to your advantage.

THE CONE OF VISION

The cone of vision is the extent of the vision of a viewer, out of a full 360-degree range. You can visualize this as a viewer stood in the centre of a circle, with each ordinal direction as a vanishing point. The typical person can experience clear vision within a 60-degree segment **(A)**. With a 60-degree cone of vision, you can only view one vanishing point at a time, with the others being outside of the cone of vision, or in a drawing sense, off the canvas.

By extending the cone of vision, the vanishing points in the drawing become closer together and distort the image. So, when three-dimensional forms extend outside of the cone of vision, they will begin to distort. When drawing in perspective, you don't always have to adhere to a 60-degree cone of vision, but it's important to be aware of image distortion and how it contributes to the narrative and storytelling **(B)**.

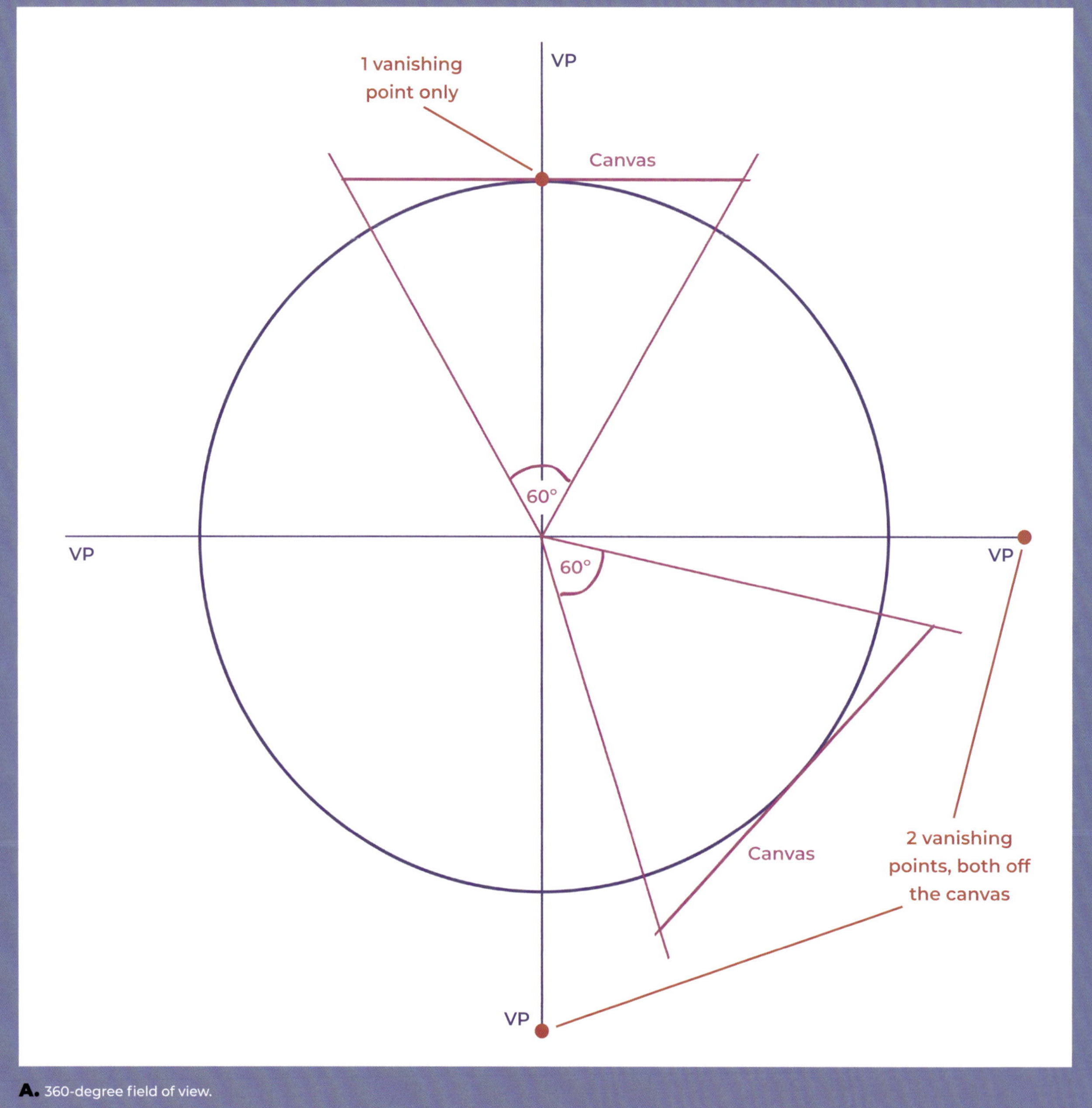

A. 360-degree field of view.

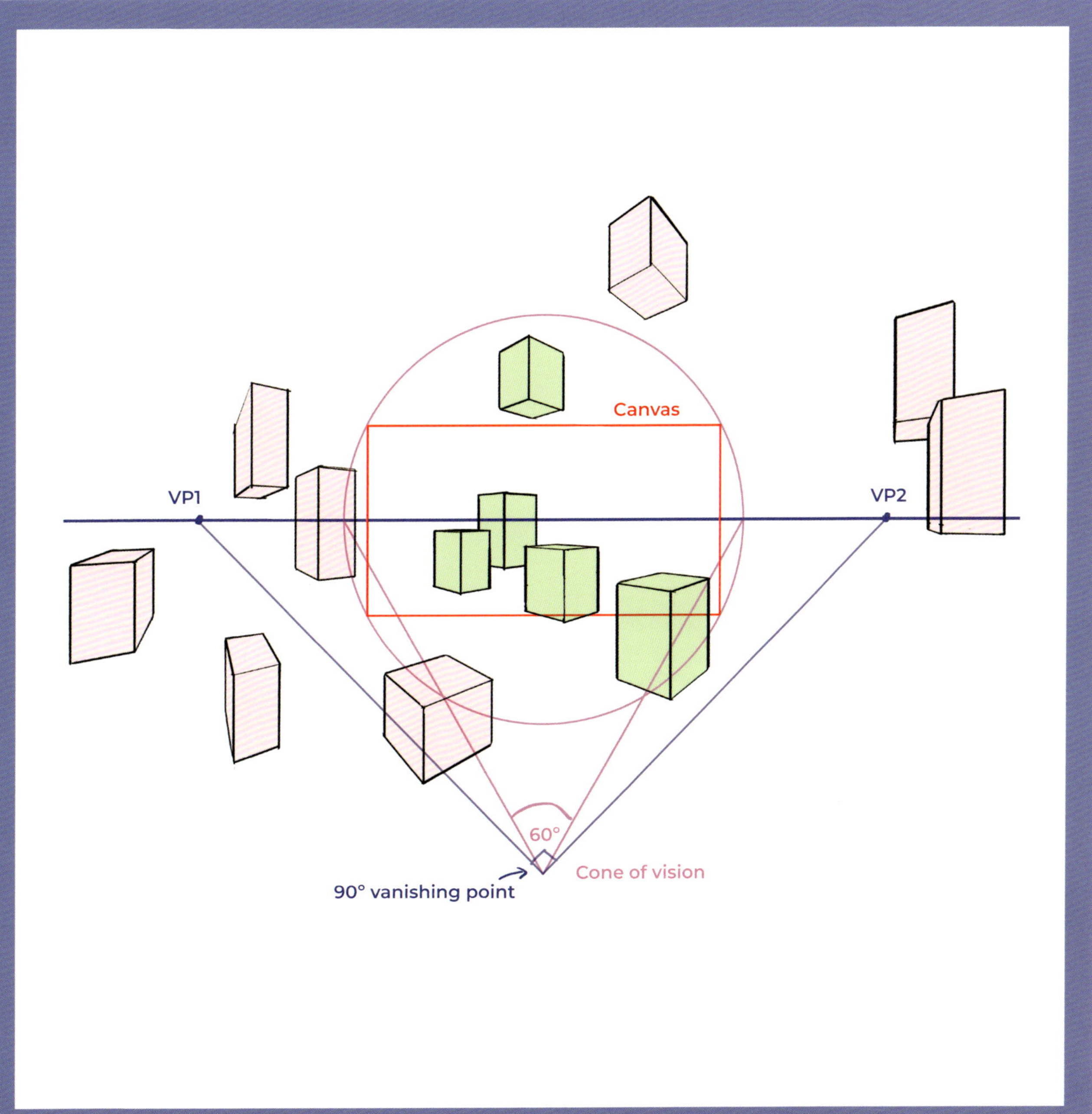

B. 60-degree cone of vision.

Widening and narrowing the cone of vision has the same effect as changing the lens length of a camera, so when thinking of composition cinematically, you can draw on knowledge of camera lens length and relate it to the cone of vision to help inform the perspective of your composition.

Greatly widening the cone of vision can cause distasteful distortion, at which point you can turn to fish-eye or curvilinear perspective to depict the distortions more naturalistically and develop more pleasing solutions to distortion.

Remember the cone of vision when placing vanishing points and setting up perspective grids.

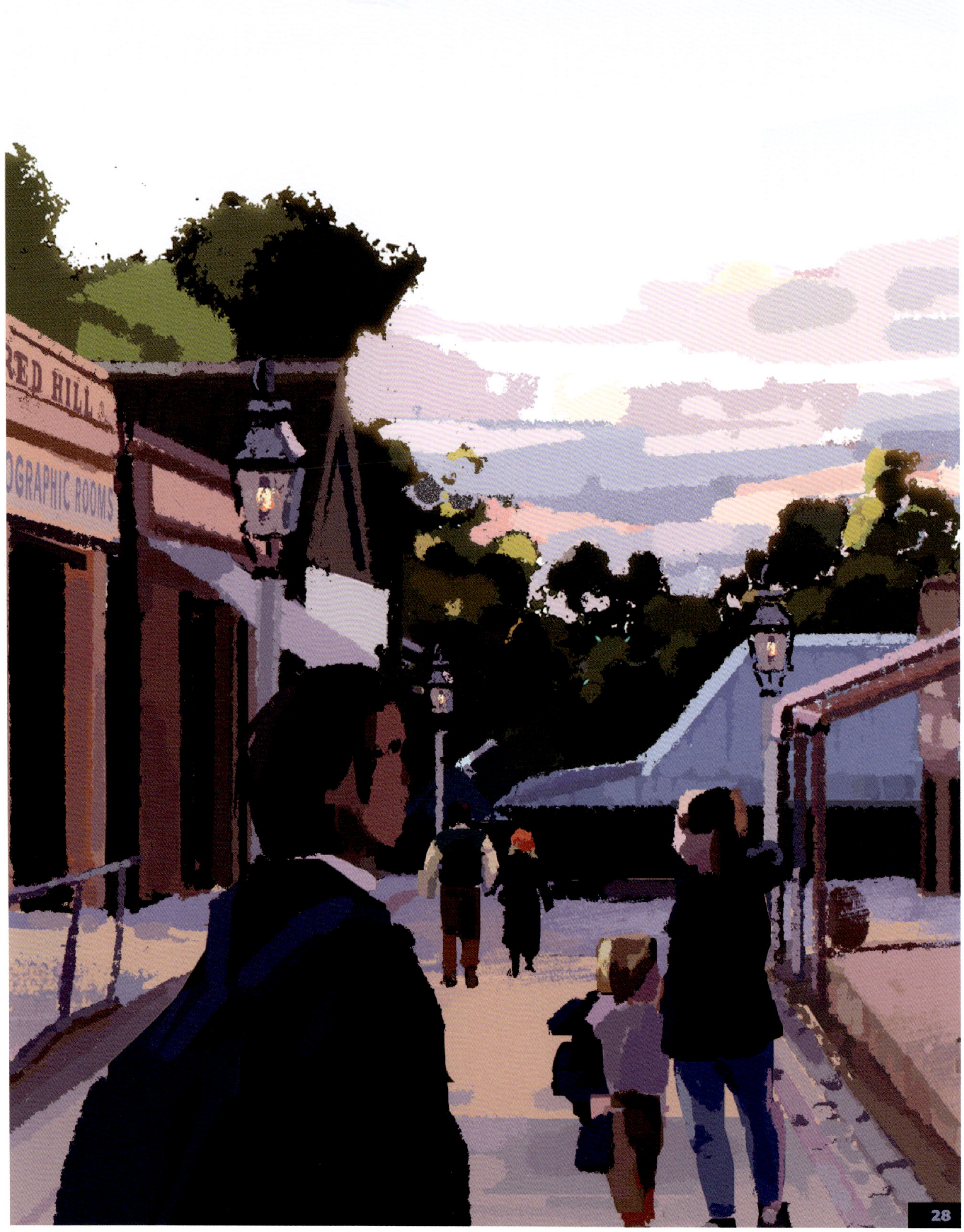

28 A close-up of the composition, featuring lamp posts as repeated elements receding in space.

28 SIZE & SCALE

To indicate the depth and scale of a composition, you can use repeated identical objects that recede into space. This image has lamp posts, for example, to which we can relate the scale of other objects in the scene. The wooden handrails are also used to this effect, solidifying the read of space and depth throughout the composition. The distribution of people throughout the space also contributes to this perception, and these important cues all work in tandem to relate the size, scale, and distance of all the elements in the painting. Added set-dressing also helps to fill out the composition.

29 SMOOTHING SHARP EDGES

Texture and edges can be jarring if they are too sharp **(29a)**. When edges are overly sharp, they can create undesired contrast and draw attention to areas that are unimportant, taking away from the intended focal points. Adjust the contrast of detail to direct and control the viewer's eyes, stating your intention through the composition. Texture can also help to exemplify the materiality of the object, with the direction of the brushstrokes here adhering to the direction of the wood grain, creating a softer transition and describing the materiality **(29b)**.

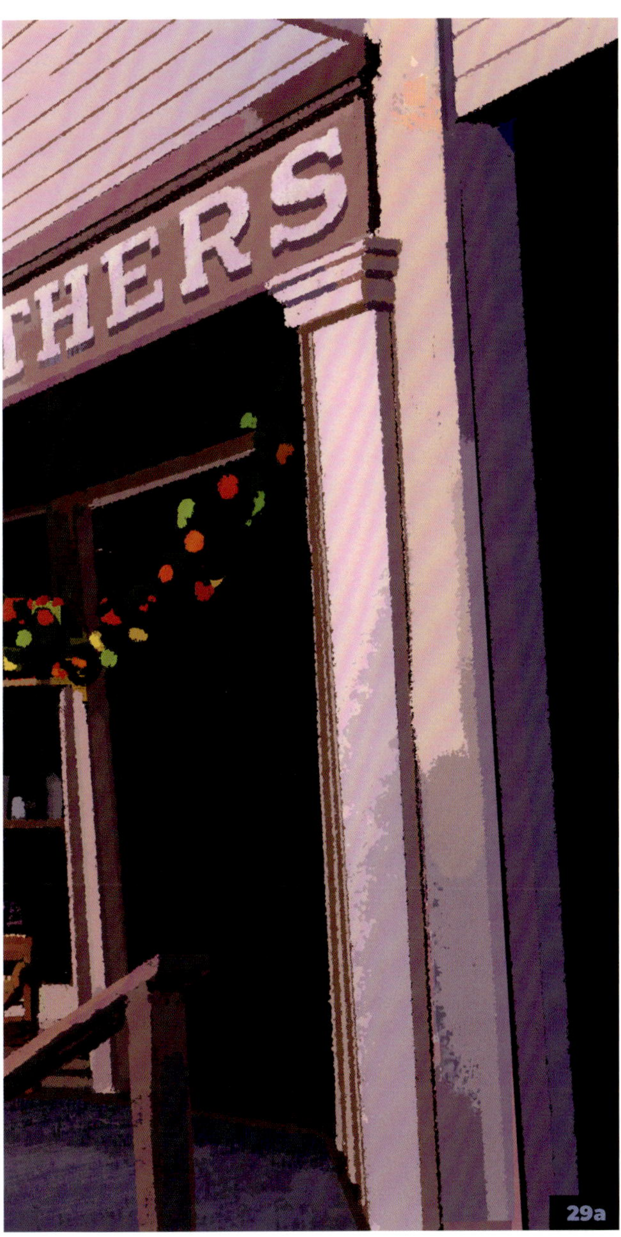

29a The initial colour-blocked columns lack textural information and are somewhat distracting.

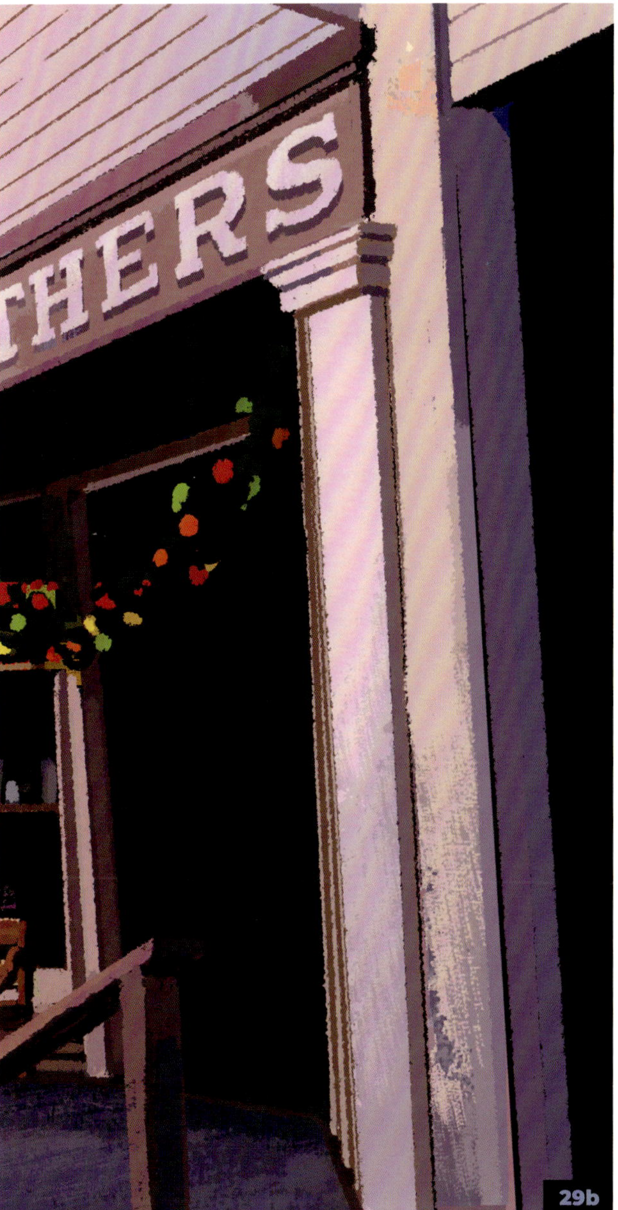

29b Softening sharp edges by introducing colour transitions and directional texture information.

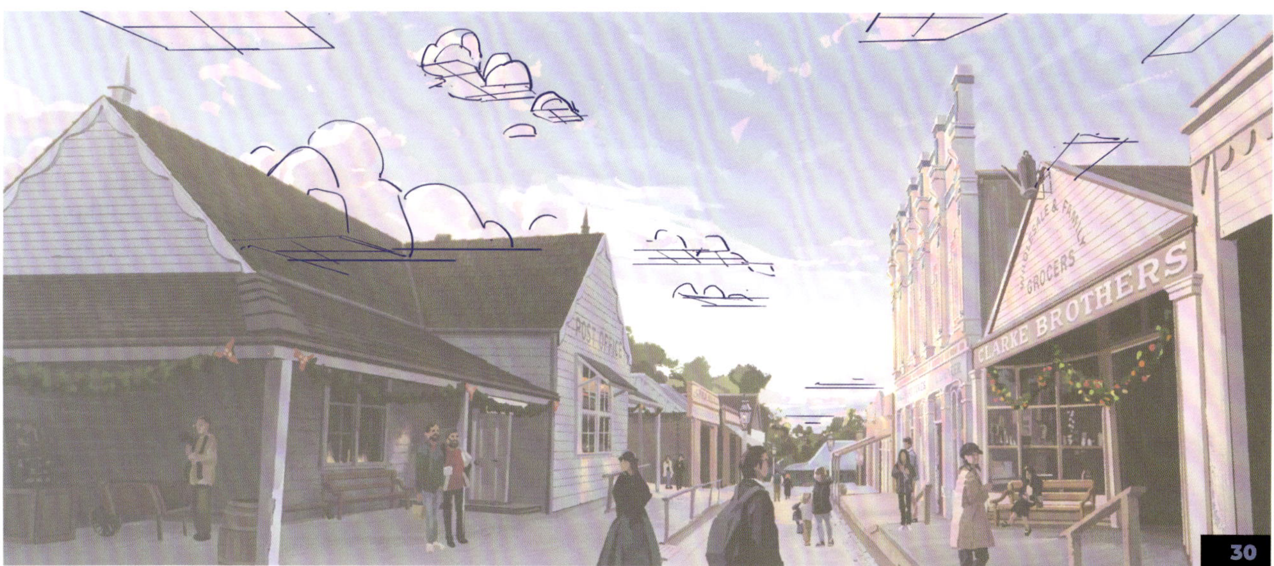

30 Drawing and painting volumetric clouds in perspective.

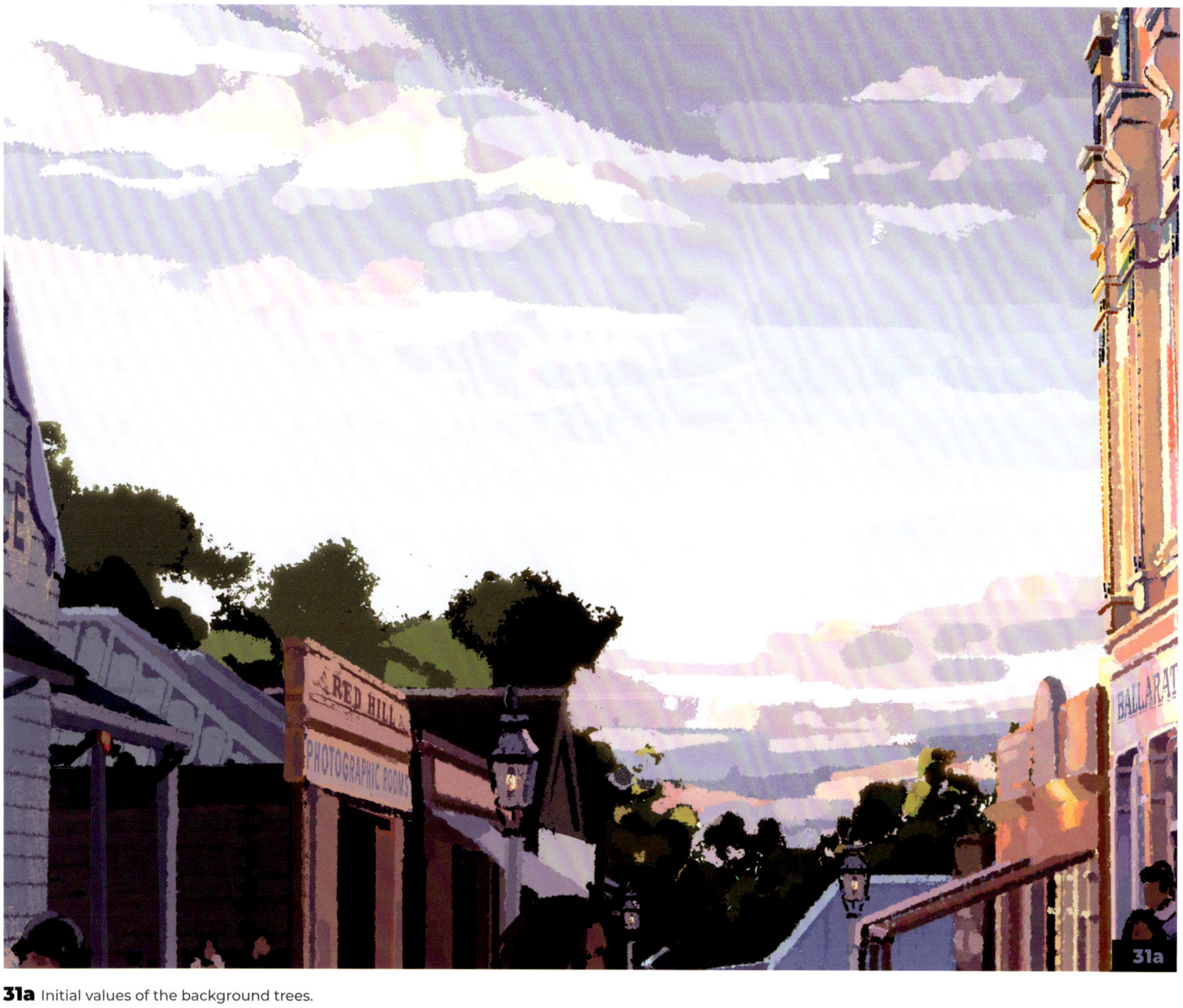

31a Initial values of the background trees.

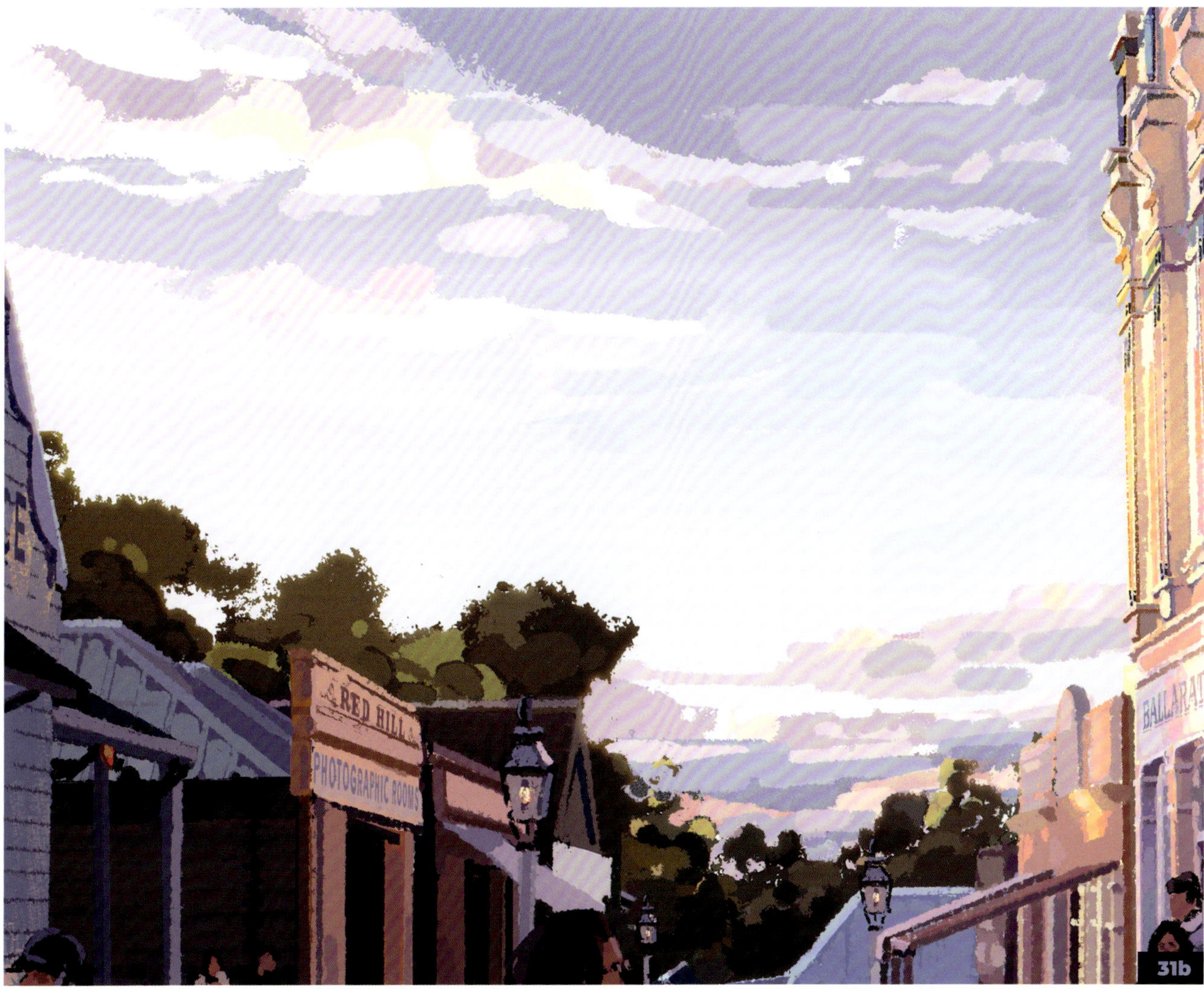

31b Adjusted value and tones to indicate 'atmospheric perspective'.

30 ADDING CLOUDS

The clouds must also be painted in a way that continues to accentuate the perspective of the piece. Remember to regard clouds as three-dimensional volumes, focusing in particular on the bottom plane of a cloud that we see from the ground. By simply depicting the bottom planes of clouds adhering to perspective and scaling them into the distance, the sense of volume and distance in the sky is immediately apparent. It can also be helpful to relate the scale of the clouds with other objects in the composition. Compositionally speaking, I add more clouds to the left of the canvas to contrast with the large area or darker value, and leave more of the blue sky visible on the right to allow the complexity of the facade to stand out. Controlling detail is an important element of creating an effective composition.

31 ATMOSPHERIC EFFECTS

Atmosphere can be used to add a sense of depth and distance without traditional perspective drawing. Since the trees and the sky in the background do not have any cues that indicate that they are in perspective, we can use the contrast or colour (or lack thereof) to help depict depth and distance **(31a)**. By washing out the trees with the same warm light that fills the sky from the left side, I can push the trees back into the distance, making their value closer to the sky. This appears to place them closer to the background sky and further away from the buildings **(31b)**. The colours in that area become more unified, decreasing their contrast and taking focus and attention away from the far background elements. This helps to keep the viewer's attention focused on the main middle-ground and foreground features.

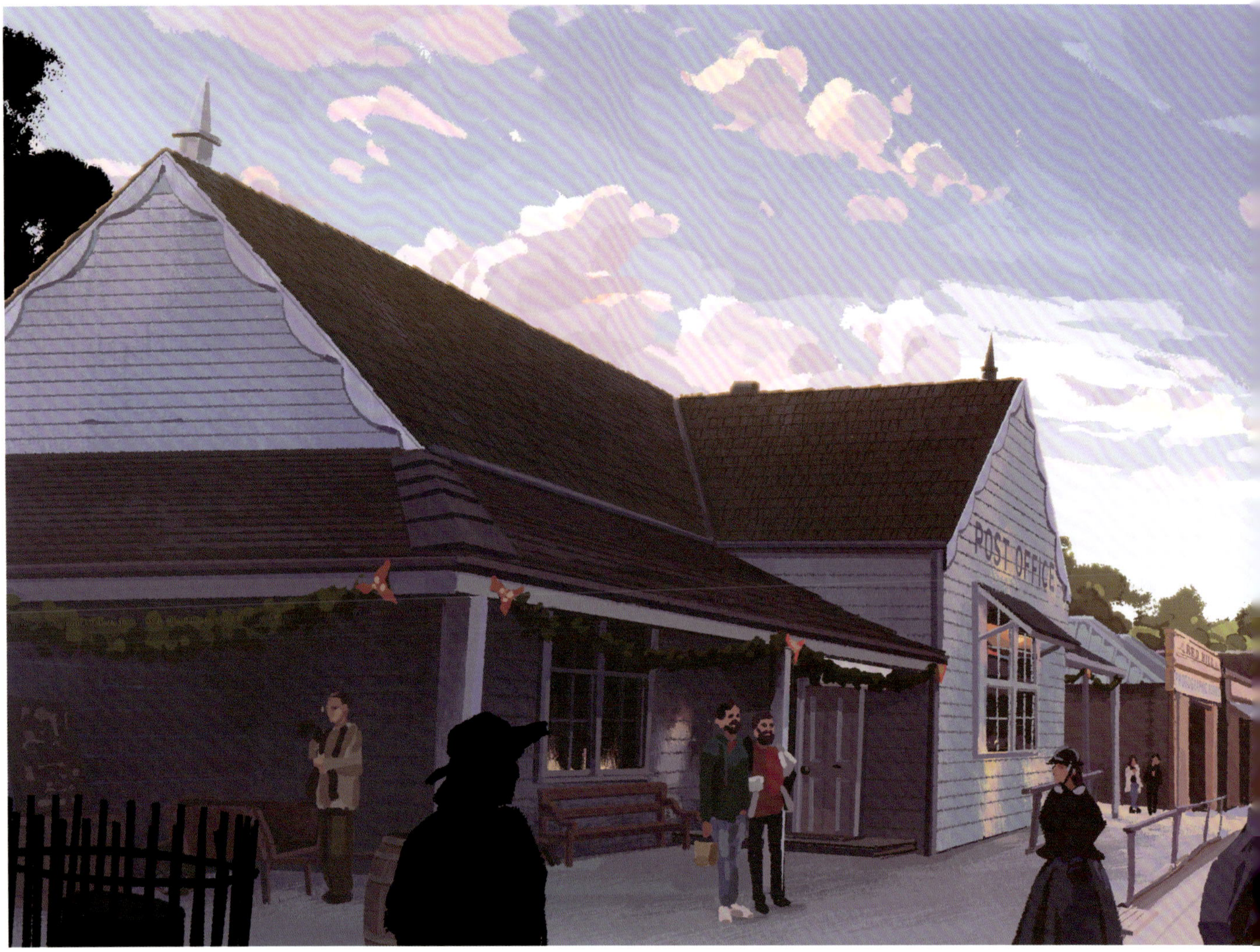

32 Adding more framing elements to the composition.

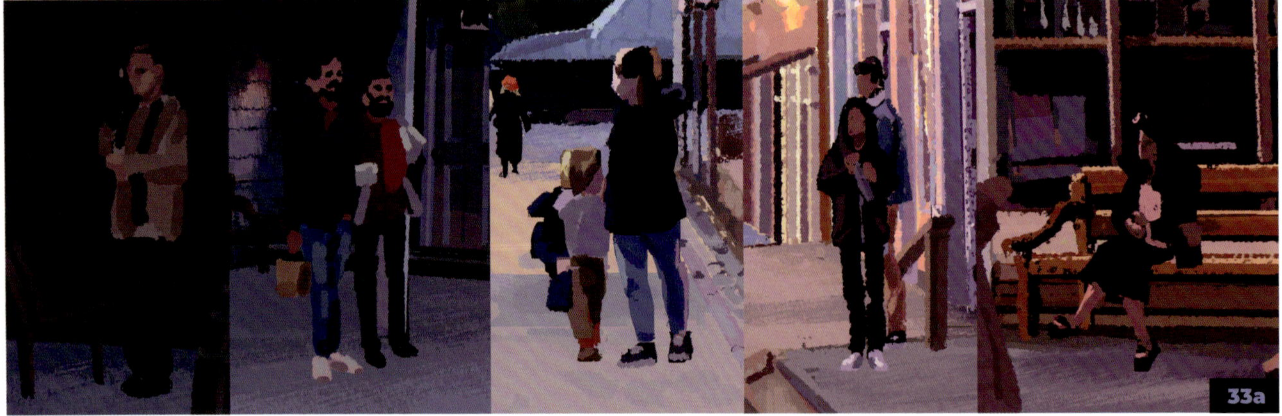

33a Close-ups showing characters and their points of contact with the ground.

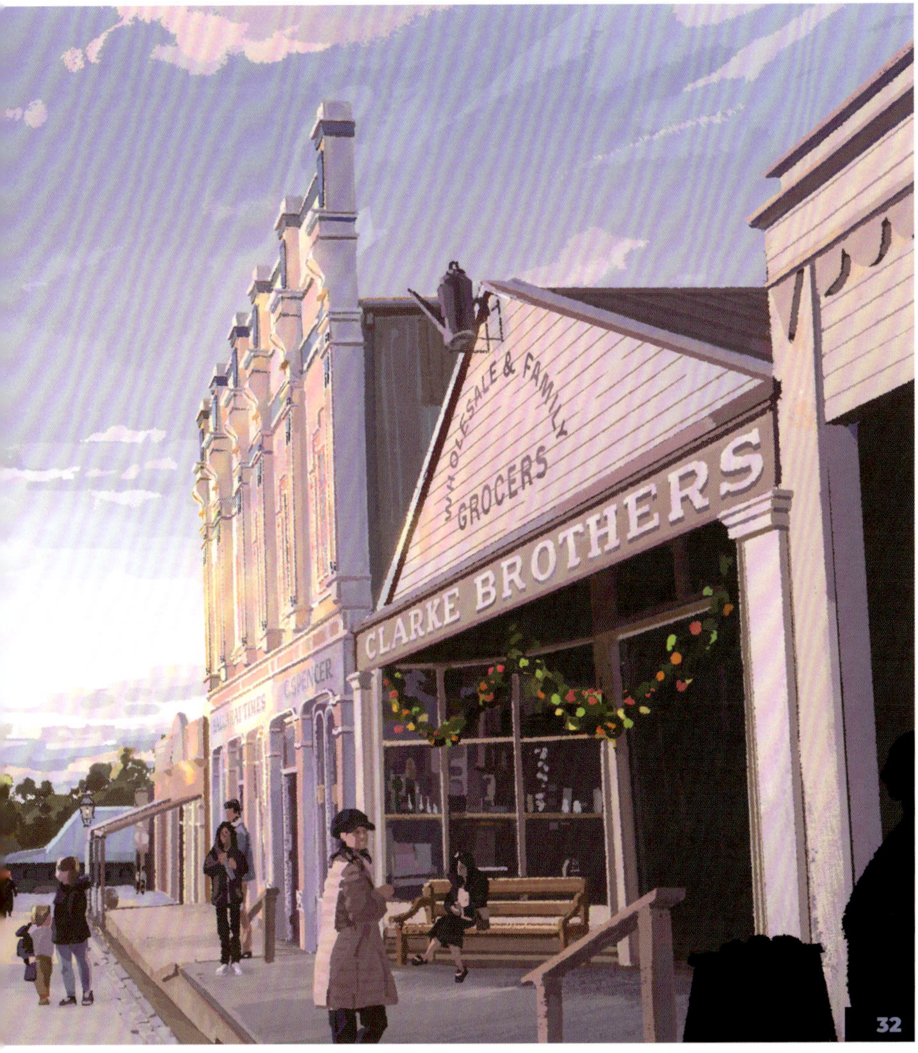

32 ADDITIONAL FIGURES

I introduce a few more people in the foreground to increase the range of distance portrayed in the composition. Adding more elements closer to the camera can heighten the viewer's sense of immersion into the scene, and is a good way to create a cinematic quality in your compositions. Much like how increasing dynamic range in exposure and values can increase depth and detail, increasing the dynamic range between the elements shown on the canvas can increase depth. To frame the composition a little more, I decide to add foliage to the top-left corner and some more set-dressing foreground elements.

33 AMBIENT OCCLUSION

Ambient occlusion refers to the shadows that form in an ambient-light setting, where the ambient light cannot reach, such as in deep crevices or where surfaces meet. Although most of the people and objects on the ground plane are enveloped in the shadow of the buildings **(33a)**, various sources of 'bounce light' enter the shadow region to form soft ambient-occlusion shadows where objects are touching the ground **(33b)**. Adding this soft shadow grounds the object, and forgetting to add it can often make the object feel like it's floating.

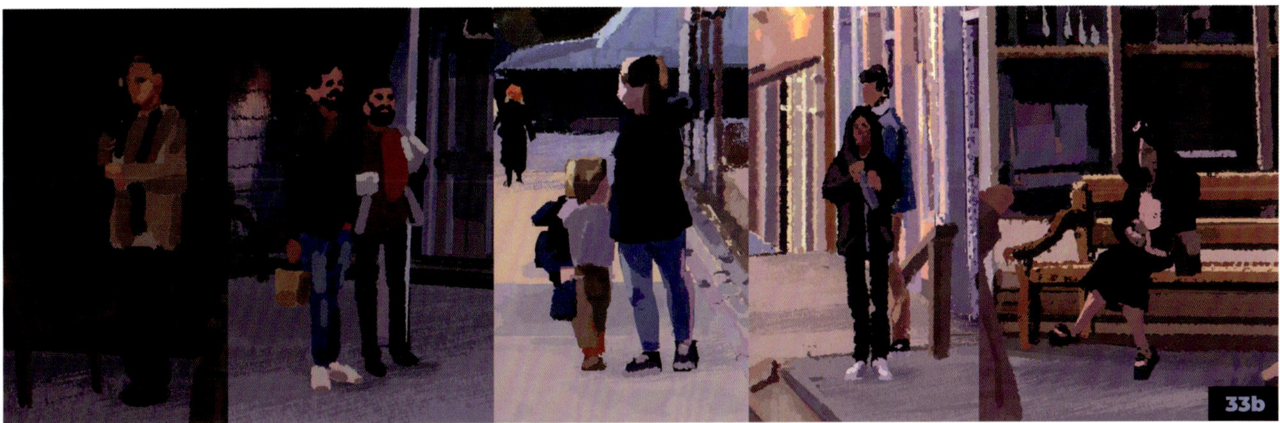

33b Close-ups after adding shadows to the characters for ambient occlusion.

34 LIGHTING EFFECTS

A subtle but effective finishing touch is the addition of light bleeds and glow. Depending on the strength of a light source, the light can often 'bleed' into its surroundings, appearing as a glow, and can have an ethereal quality. Look for areas in the composition where you have a strong light source, such as the brighter left side of the sky, or where the sun directly hits the building facades **(34a)**. Add an airbrushed glow to the area on a separate layer, and then set the layer to a blending mode such as Linear Dodge (Add) or Hard Light, depending on the quality of light you want to depict. These glows also serve to break up harder edges and reduce contrast in areas that are drawing too much attention **(34b)**.

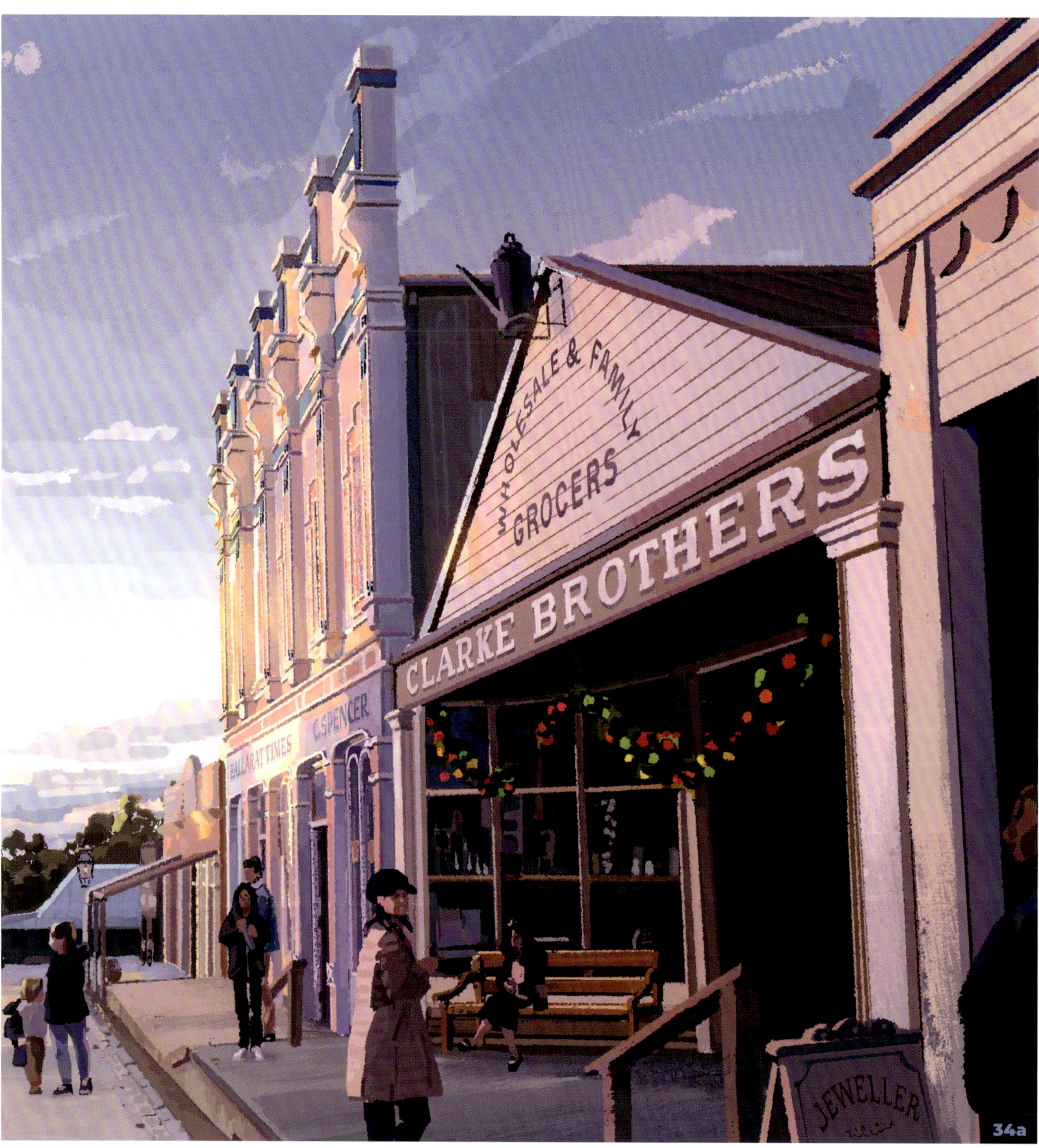

34a A facade with glow added to areas of direct lighting.

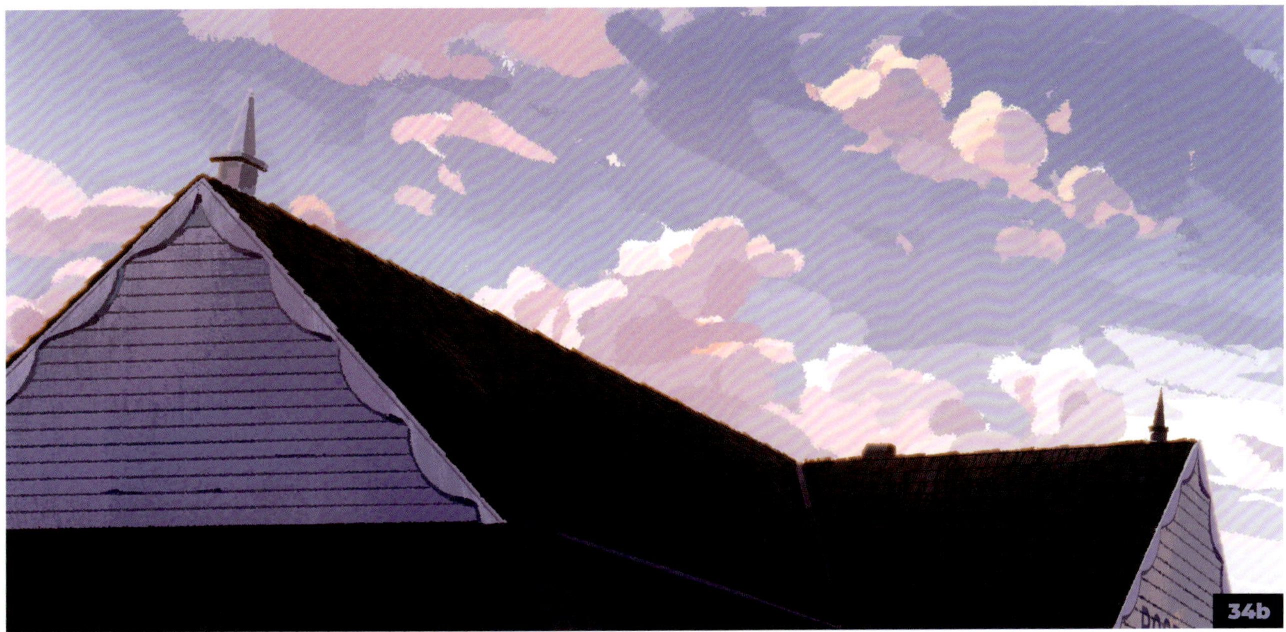

34b The roof in shadow, with light bleeding into it from the bright sky behind.

CHARACTERS IN PERSPECTIVE

When adding characters into the composition, it's important that their size and scale stays relative to each other, even at different distances from the viewer. This can be tricky to eyeball, but here is a mathematical tip to help keep your characters accurately placed in perspective.

Establish the relation of characters to the eye-level or horizon line. In this example, the horizon line cuts the silhouette of the characters at approximately chin level. Simply ensure that all of the characters adhere to that. If there are children or other smaller (or bigger) characters, keep their scale consistent relative to the character you are using for reference, which would in this case be the chin-level figure at the front.

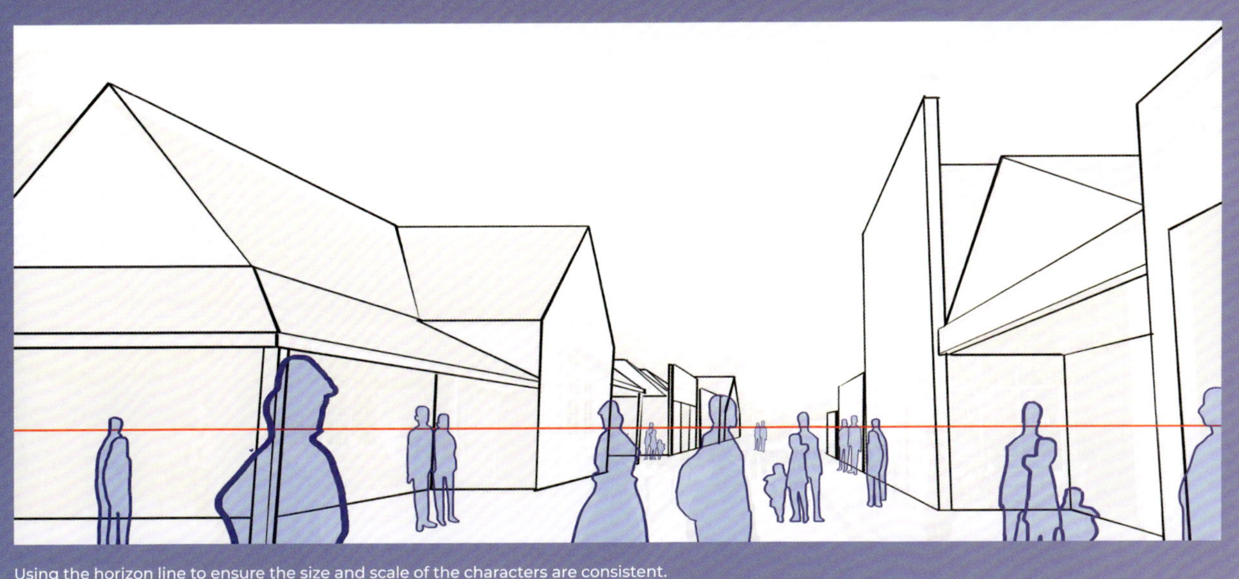

Using the horizon line to ensure the size and scale of the characters are consistent.

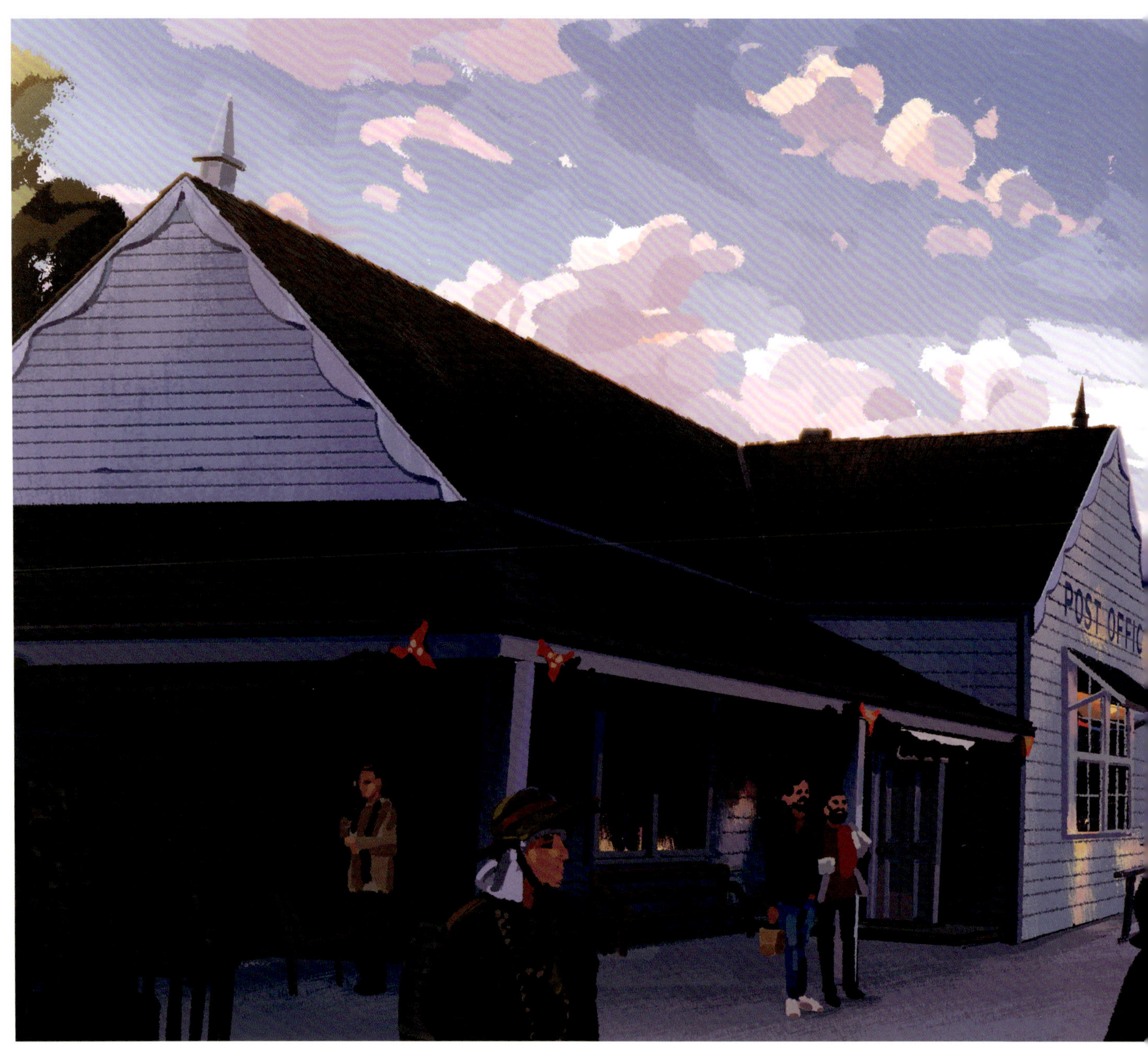

FINAL REFINEMENTS

At the final stage of a painting, it's good to re-evaluate the distribution of detail in the entire composition. When adding detail and polish to a piece, it can be easy to forget to account for the entire composition and the read you originally intended. Zooming out and looking at the entire composition as a thumbnail can help direct your efforts. Ensure that value, composition, and contrast are working together at the quick first read and are telling the story. Check for any unwanted areas of contrast and reduce detail there; find areas that look flat and increase their visual interest and detail.

Final image © Orenjikun

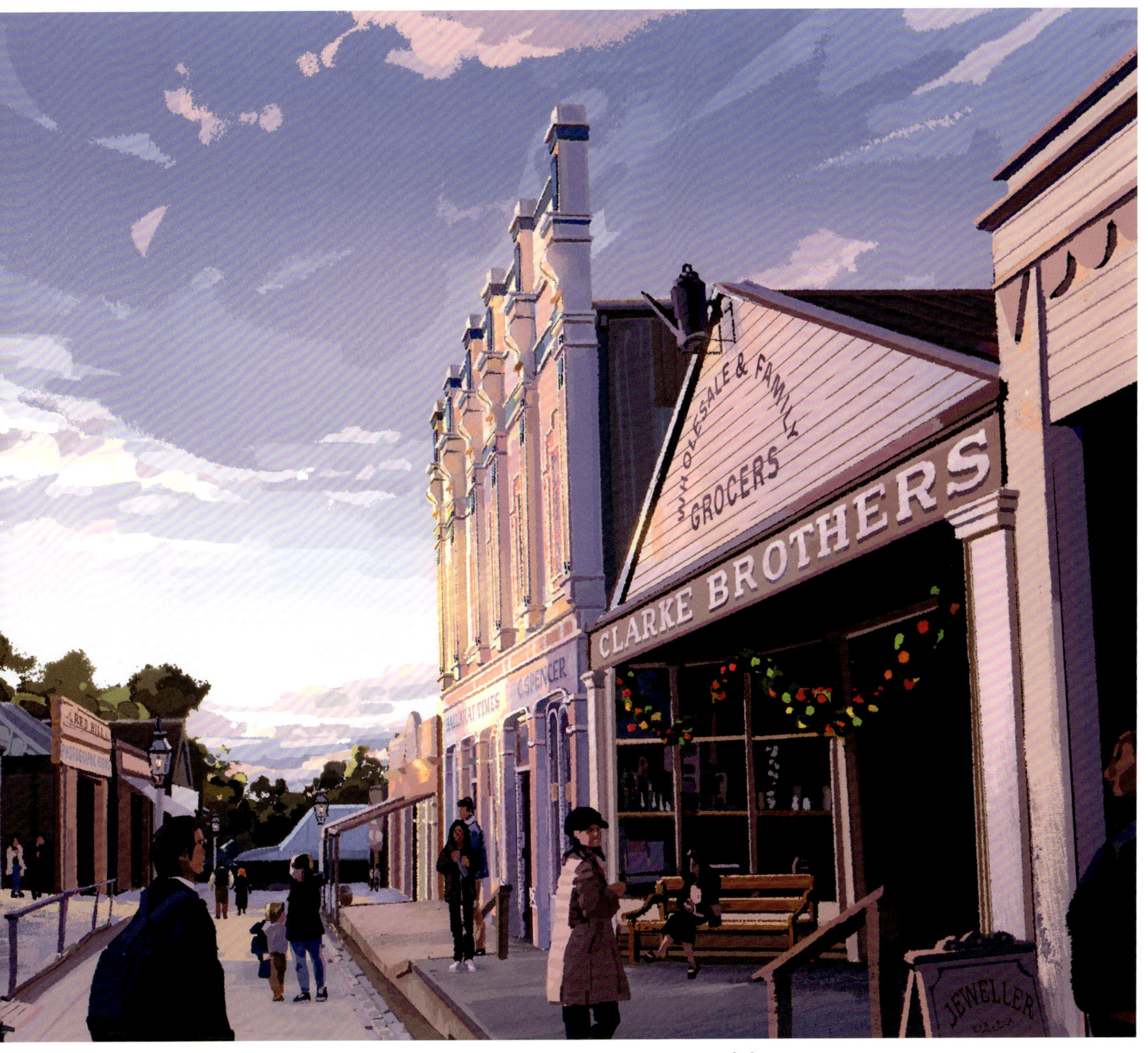

Old Mining Town. The final piece after a few more adjustments.

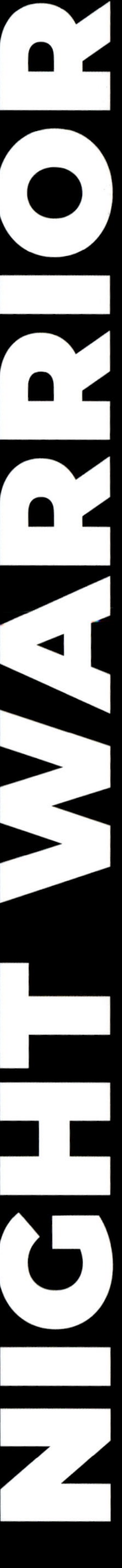

GUWEIZ

As someone who loves drawing in a more realistic and physical style, learning to manage perspective and depth has been really important. They are fundamental to conveying a precise, visually cogent composition to the viewer, making the piece that much more believable and convincing.

I love using perspective with dynamic camera angles, as they really bring out extraordinary ways to present my subjects and unlock numerous options when finding a good composition. Depth is a close companion, enabling the full three-dimensional space within the piece to be brought to life on top of a solid perspective framework.

For this tutorial, I will be drawing a full illustration consisting of both character and environmental elements, with a focus on showing how perspective and depth play their parts throughout the illustration process. We will also look at various techniques on how to approach building perspective for a complex scene or subject, as well as how to implement and apply the concept of depth at various stages. Beyond making use of perspective and depth as just guides or rules, we will also explore how deliberate choices in composition and subjects can make use of these core concepts to enhance the piece.

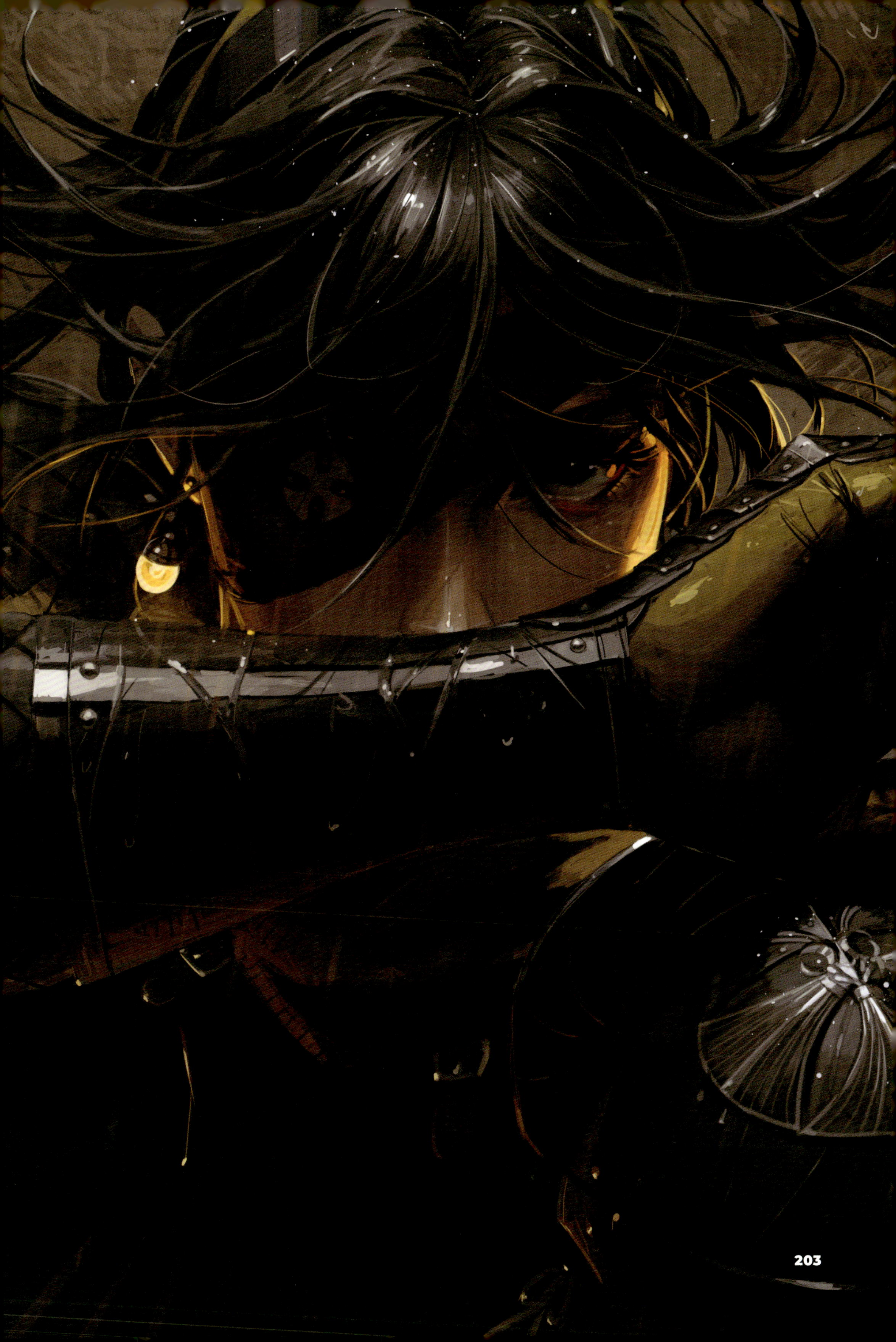

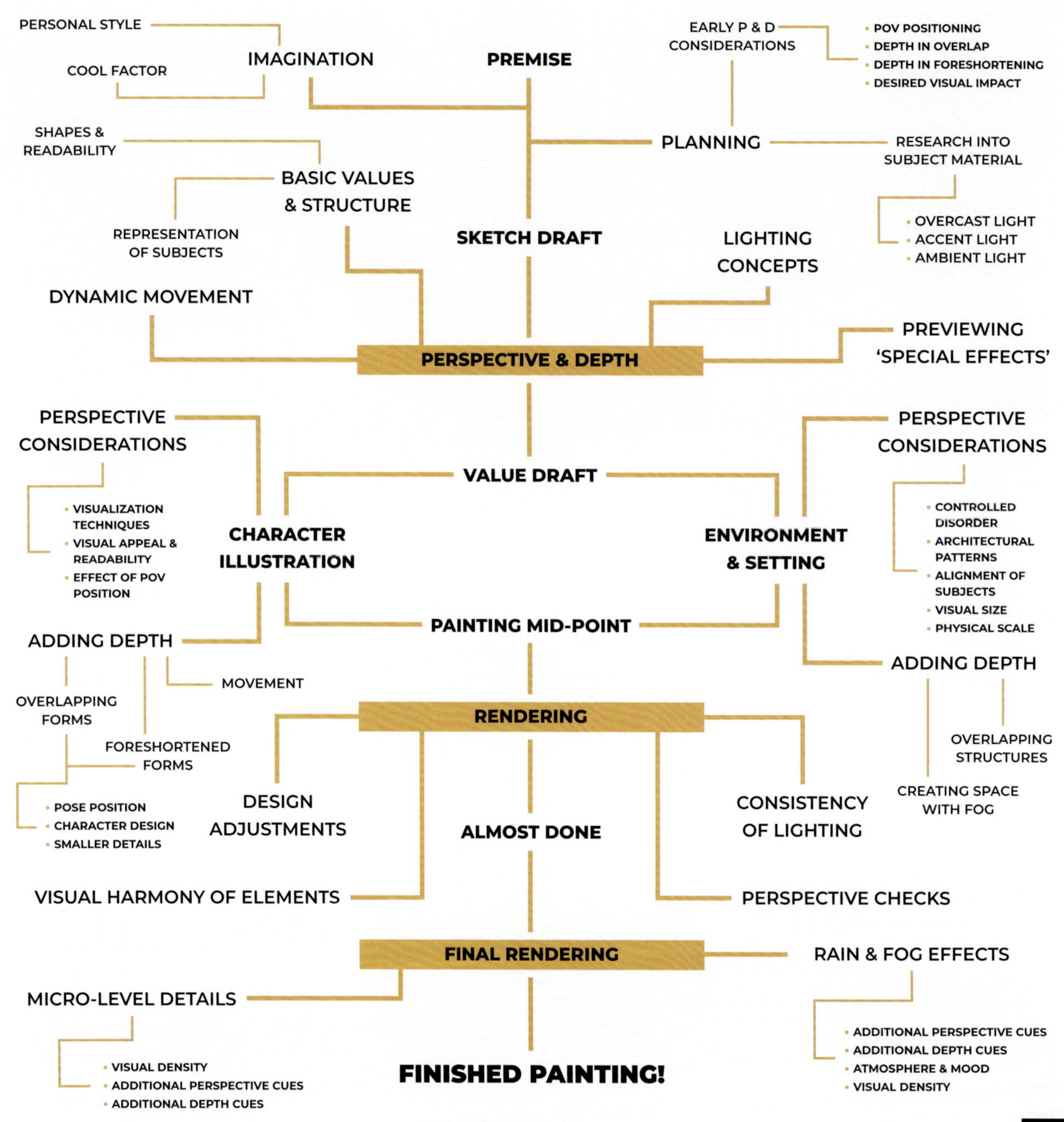

01 The planning process can differ very much from artist to artist; some may prefer jumping straight in, while others lean towards building up a solid reference board to start.

01 PRE-SKETCHING PLANNING

A little bit of pre-drawing preparation can go a long way in staying focused and on-target throughout the painting process. Coming up with an initial idea, justifications for why it works, and references to substantiate various parts of the planned composition are all parts of the prep that goes into generating a workable and interesting concept that's worth developing. During this initial stage, you should also start to consider how perspective and depth are going to be involved, not only as fundamentals but as possible force multipliers.

Is there a place in the composition where you can apply perspective deliberately as a way to add immersion? For example, using a close-up or angled view to create a more intimate feel with the subject, or using a wide view to capture the dramatic scope of the scene?

Is the composition idea sufficiently fleshed out with enough visual elements for there to be a sense of depth and space? For example, having multiple elements overlapping and layering over each other naturally in the scene can be great for implying realistic depth. Weather and lighting effects can also be tools to further reinforce this effect. You might also consider foreshortening as a way to imply depth, and by extension think about which elements of the piece are suited to this particular method, and which elements are not.

02 THE FIRST SKETCH

The purpose of the initial sketch is to capture, as quickly as possible, the major elements of the composition that you thought of in the previous step. For example, putting down the main subject, a rough representation of their surroundings, and balancing the canvas to the best of your ability will be the main goal here.

Beyond the basics, it's also a chance to start exploring and putting down placeholders for future elements of interest. For example, if an area could be used for showcasing ornate patterns later, you can mark it down. If lots of dynamic movement could be introduced to a specific part of the composition, you can sketch that out as well. If there's a chance to add authenticity with accurate and pretty architecture in the surroundings, you can rough that out now.

The rest of the painting process heavily rests on your ability to set up the overarching framework at this stage, so try your best to produce a rough but representative sketch with many interesting points. Fundamental aspects of perspective and depth remain very relevant, but right now you need to set up a composition that will be worth your time later on.

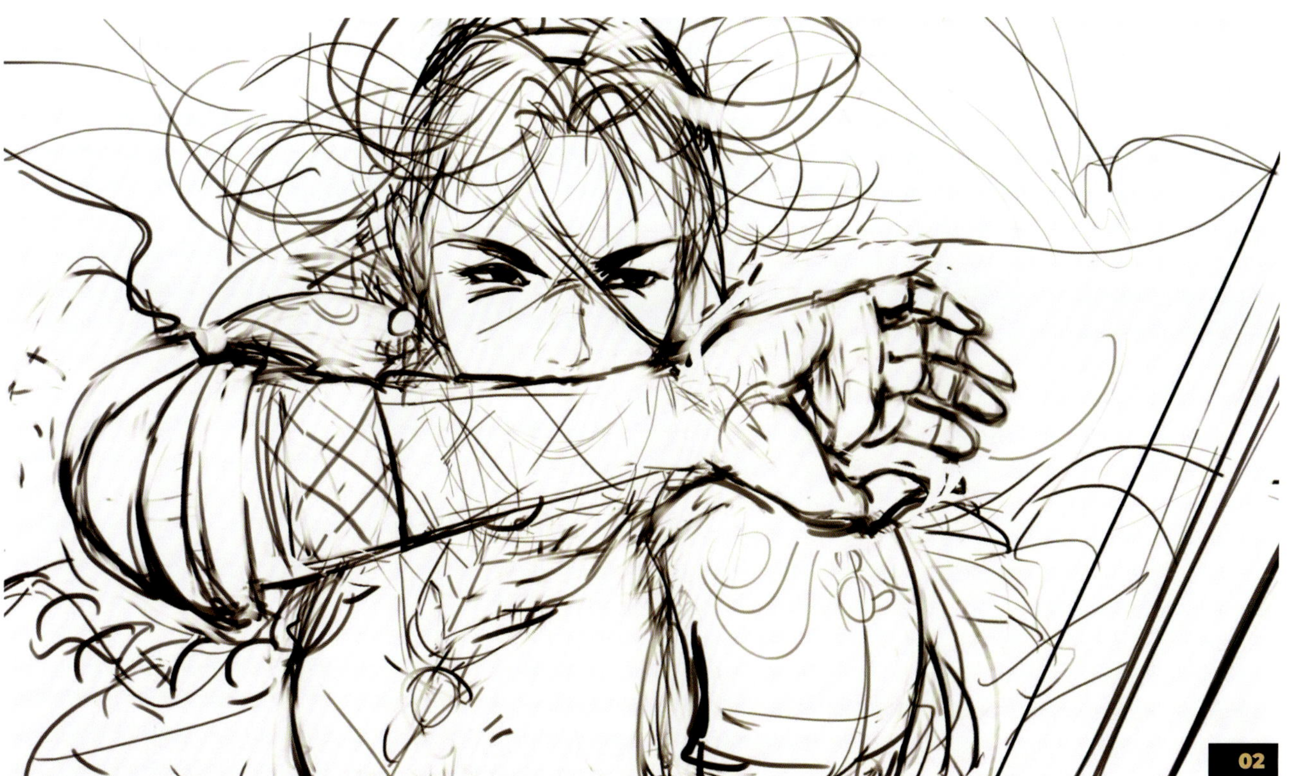

02 Speed and flexibility is the main priority for now, so roughness is acceptable as long as it remains readable; the drawing method should be whatever you are most comfortable with.

03 INTRODUCING VALUES

While line drafts are very time efficient, they lack the ability to fully depict comprehensive forms. A value draft can fill in that information gap and allow you to really get a clearer visual read on the composition. This is especially pertinent to situations where you don't yet have a complete idea of how you would like the end result to look. Being able to generate a quick preview can be incredibly helpful in clarifying your own expectations and direction for the piece.

A value draft also provides plenty of supplementary information about the structural forms of our subjects, and sets the groundwork for building good perspective and depth. It also provides a timely opportunity to make any major changes necessary before committing to a more precise and time-consuming portion of the workflow. For example, if the initial value draft exposes any problems, such as the composition lacking depth or being hard to read, you can immediately implement solutions to fix them. These solutions can include, but are not limited to: adjusting the local value of certain focal elements to elevate contrast in the region, fading out background objects with lighting to reduce their visual weight, or even moving major compositional elements around to improve the thumbnail's clarity.

You can approach this stage by thinking of values as two separate types that come together: local values and lighting values.

04 LOCAL VALUES

Think of local values as a sort of base brightness that belongs to each individual material. For example, the armour, cape, fabric, skin, hair, and elements in the background can each have their own local value.

Local value is not a fixed 'brightness number' per se, but rather it is determined by its relative brightness compared to every other material within the composition. As long as the comparative relationships between the materials are correct – for example light-coloured fabric receives a brighter local value than dark armour – you're ready to go.

With this knowledge, you can start putting together a combination of values that will work well for the illustration. Begin by laying down what you already have in mind, and continue from there. In this case, I start by giving the character black hair, lighter-coloured armour, and dark sections of fabric underneath **(04a)**. As this initial arrangement feels visually unbalanced, we can try out a different value scheme. By reversing the values of the fabric and armour, the overall value scheme feels a lot weightier than before, with smaller areas of brightness marking out the fabric highlights and face **(04b)**.

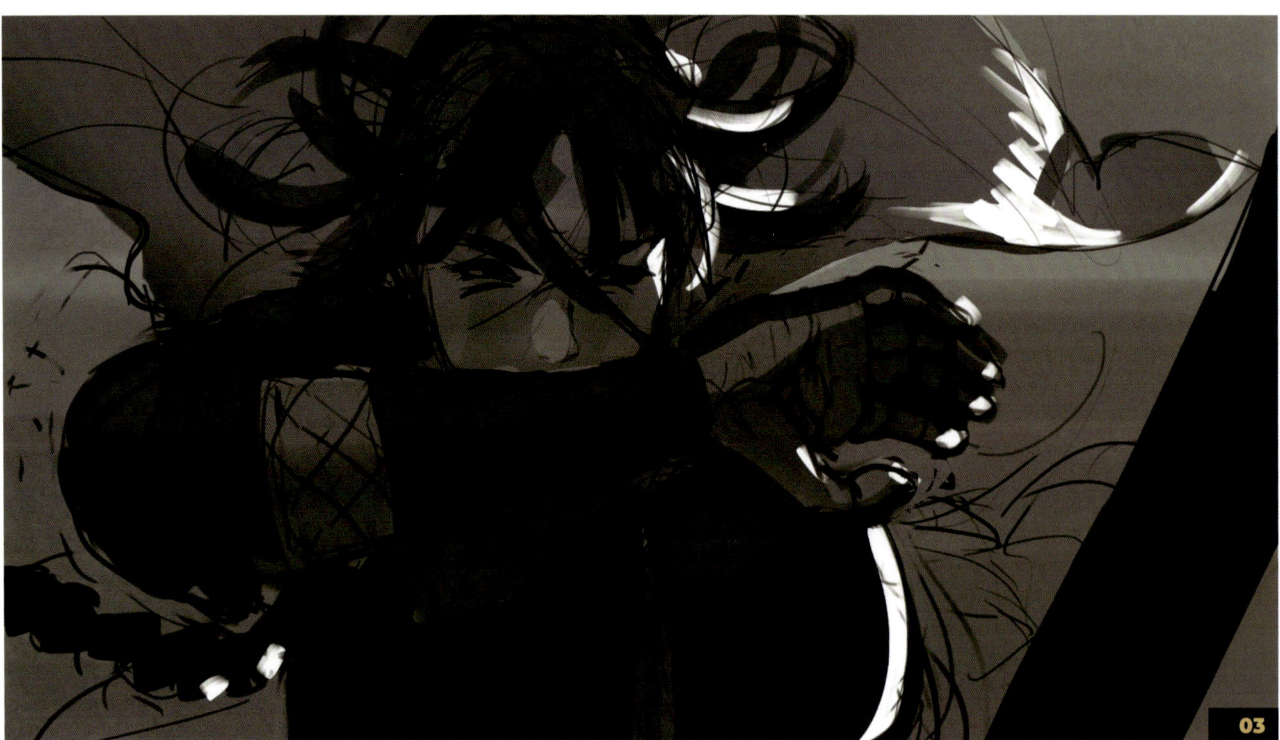

03 The desired result of this stage: to establish a simple but comprehensive value set-up accounting for both local and lighting values.

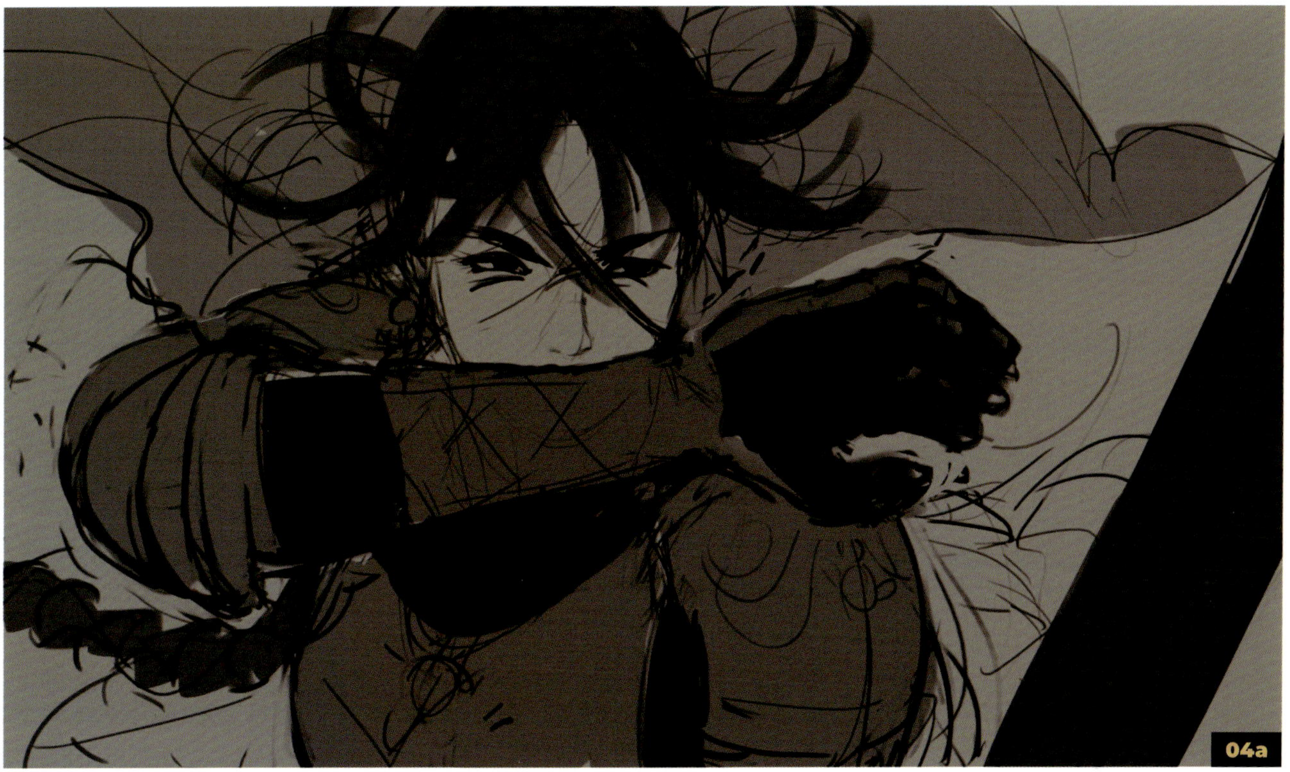

04a The initial trial of value combinations, which feels a little too bright across the character's silhouette.

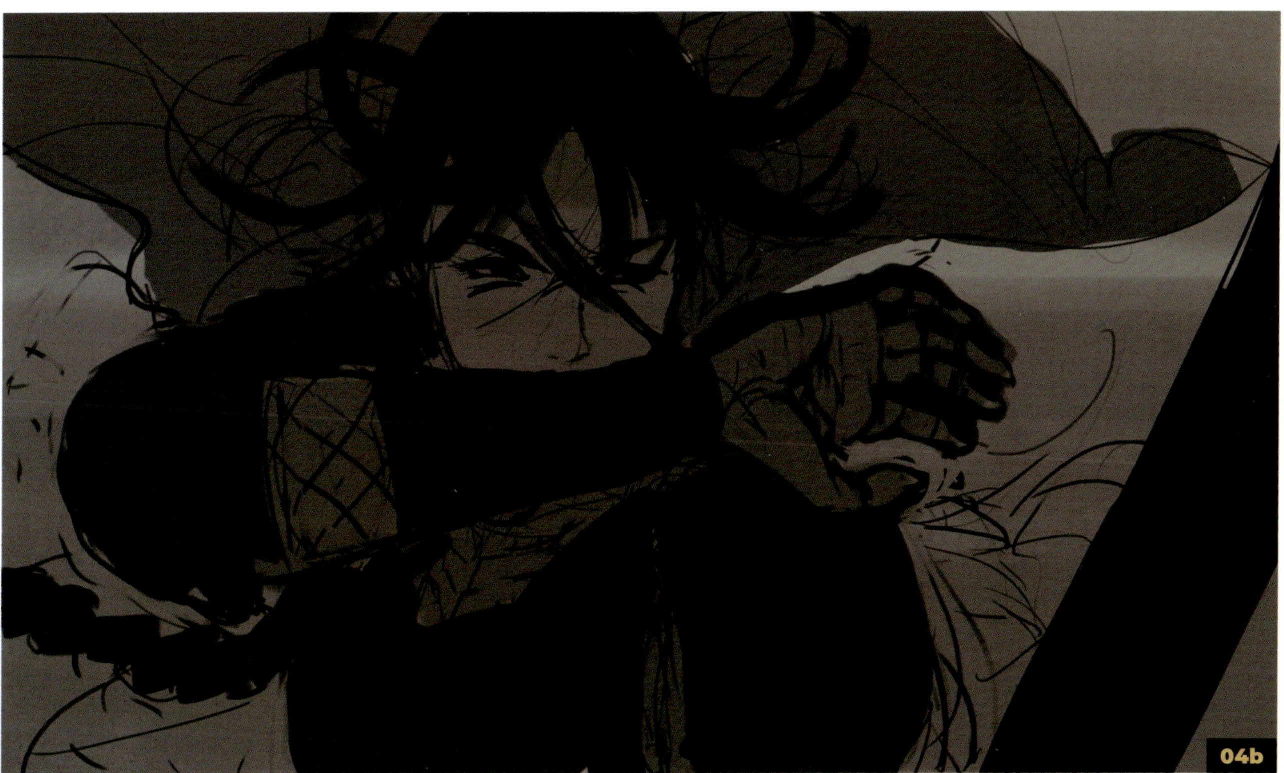

04b The revised combination has more cohesiveness around a generally darker presentation.

05 VALUES FROM LIGHTING

For now, tuck away your local values and turn your attention towards creating a simple but accurate overall lighting scheme. The two main goals here are simple: finding a lighting set-up that adds to the existing layout, and making that lighting set-up clearly readable.

To indicate the overcast, stormy scene that I have in mind, I start with a weak, diffuse light from above, with bright highlights on parts of the character that are wet with rain **(05a)**. In addition, I introduce some soft occlusion to the upper torso and neck areas where forms are close together and less exposed to light.

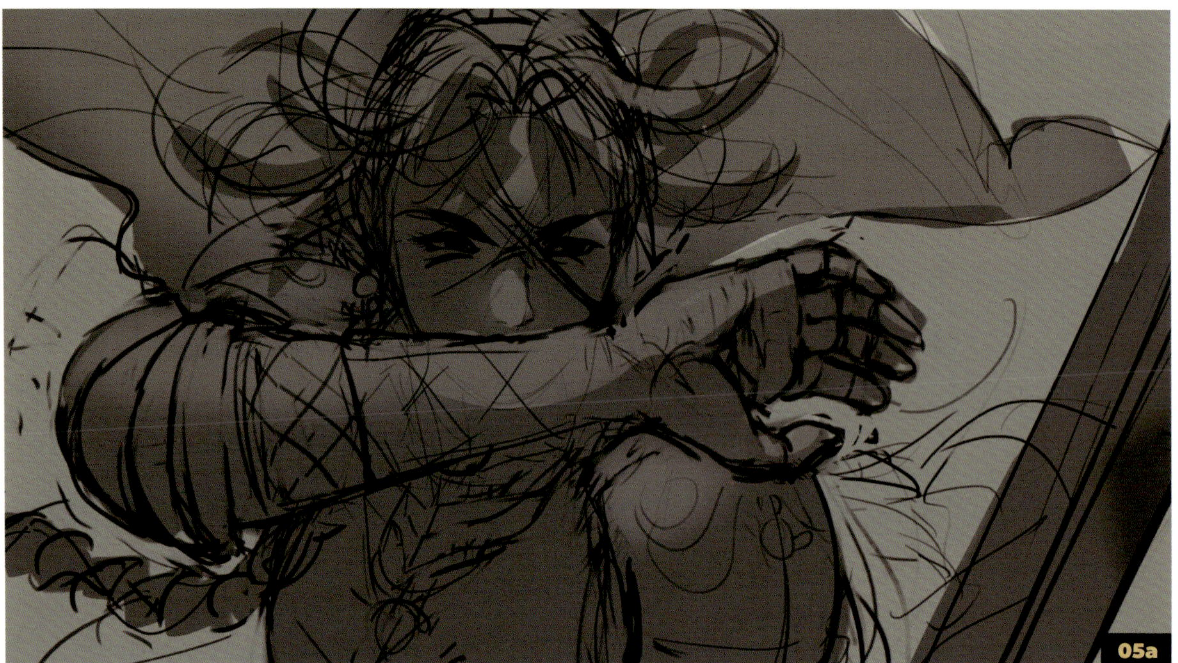

05a The isolated effect of the sky light.

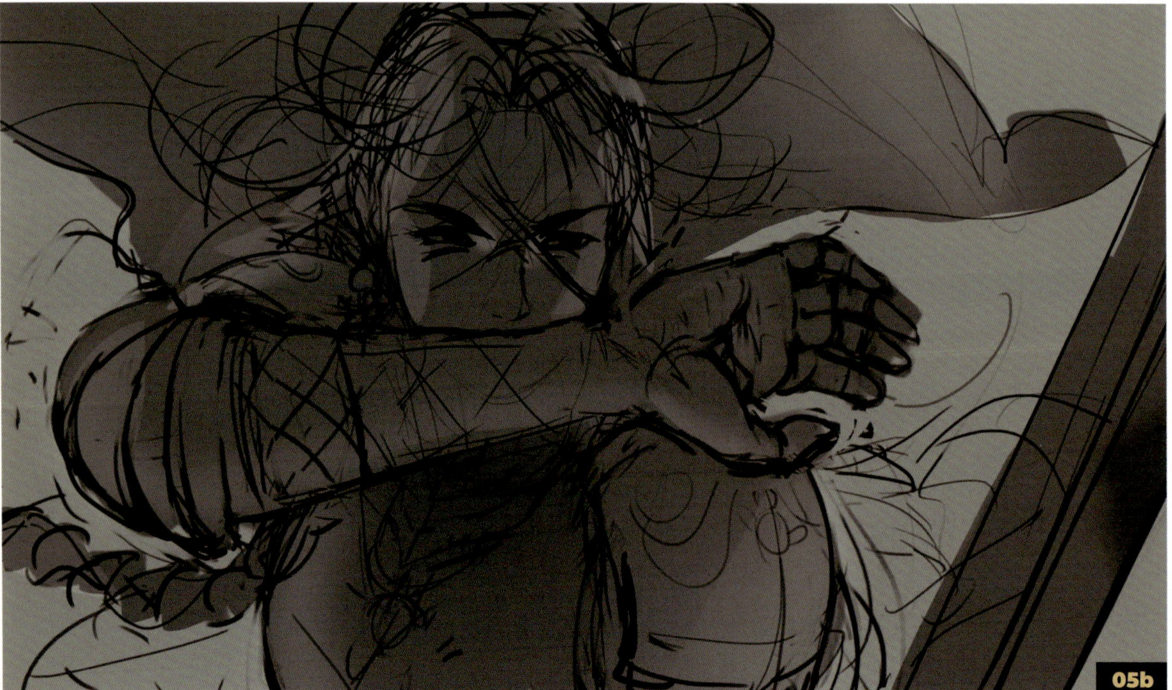

05b The effect of ambient light.

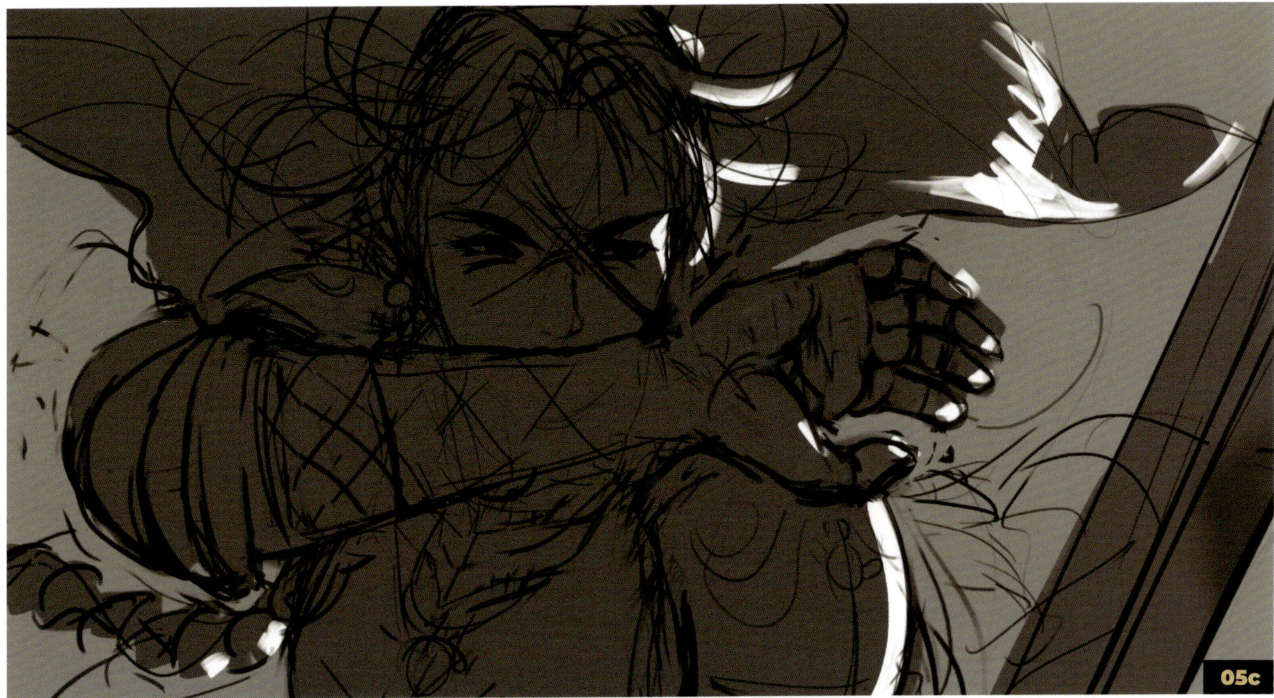

05c The effect of strong side lighting.

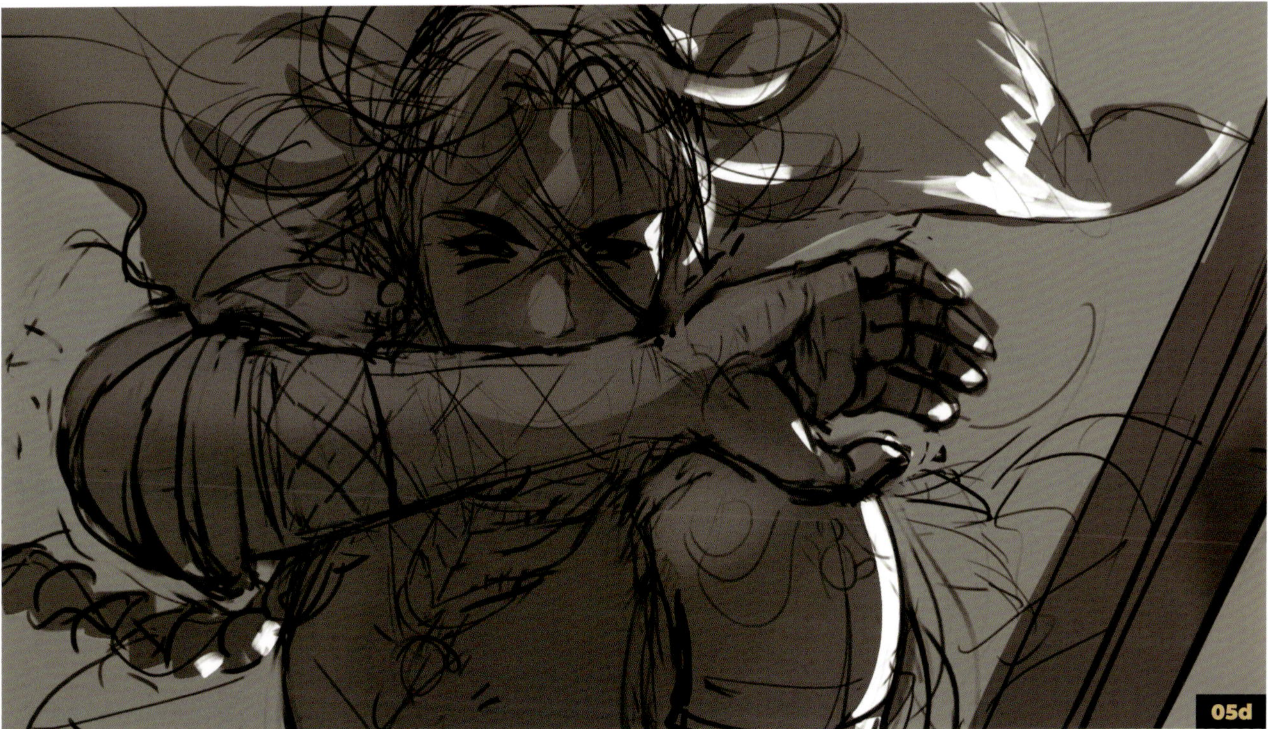

05d The combined effect of all light sources.

Next, introduce some ambient light coming from the surroundings **(05b)** – this is a key visual indicator for an outdoor lighting set-up. In addition, a strong direct light with a different colour and direction can be used as a tool to highlight focal areas **(05c)**, such as the face, as well as to demarcate overlapping forms, which in turn emphasizes depth **(05d)**.

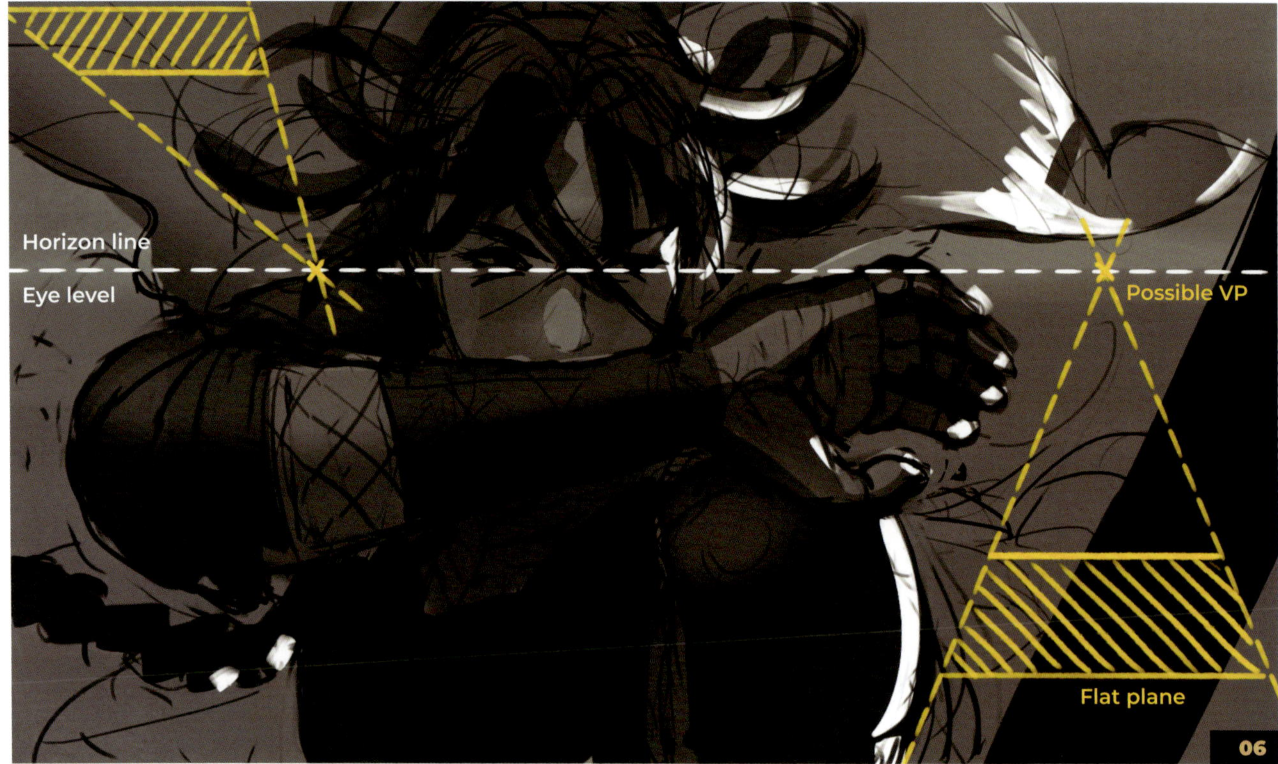

06 A few examples of planes that are parallel to the ground and therefore have vanishing points on the horizon line.

06 REFINING THE SKETCH: PERSPECTIVE

Now that you have a workable overall draft ready, you can begin to meaningfully tackle perspective. Begin with the helpful horizon line, defined simply as the perspective vanishing line for the ground. Every group of parallel edges that is also parallel to the ground will have vanishing points located on this same line.

As with any other set of perspective guidelines, the relevance and usefulness of this step derives from its association with key visual elements within the composition. In this case, the horizon line is immensely helpful as major elements in the scene will almost universally be aligned to the ground surface. The positioning of subjects – such as the character, the stairs they're standing on, the buildings and walls in the background, and even weather effects like rain or fog – all link to the orientation of the ground plane.

The directly forward-facing point of view (POV) also places the viewer's eye level on the horizon line. Alternatively, if the POV is angled down, or up at a significant angle, the horizon line may naturally leave our field of view.

With this simple guideline, you will be able to handle adjusting and adding elements to the scene in a much more controlled way, allowing you to proceed effectively with the next objective: creating a sense of space and depth.

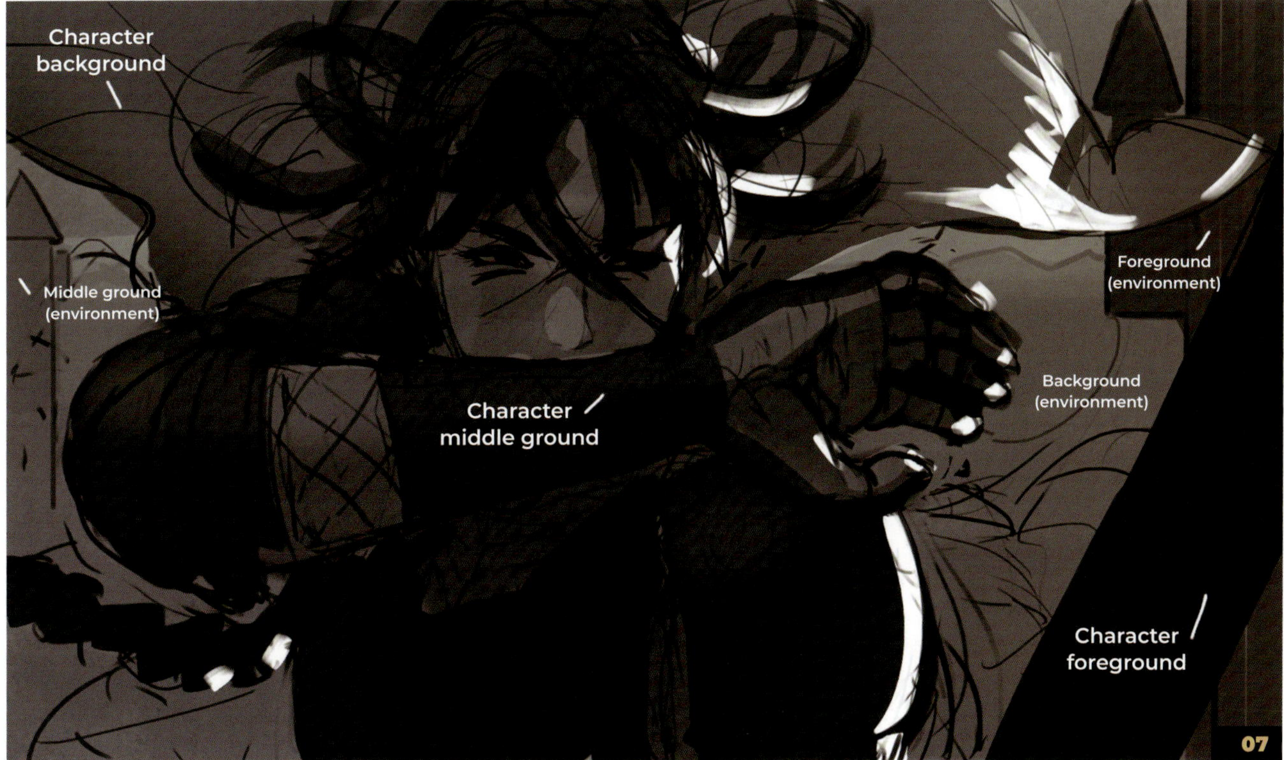

07 There is depth within the forms of the character (starting from the extreme foreground with the sword) and also within the background (using the buildings and far mountains as distance indicators).

07 REFINING THE SKETCH: ADDING DEPTH

A useful tip to remember is that you can only display as much spatial depth in your illustration as you are able to visibly landmark. You may have a grandiose, spatially vast composition you wish to convey, but to actually express it, you need concrete elements drawn to perspective, to scale, and placed strategically.

Take the example of a scene overlooking a huge metropolis. In order to convey the scale and depth of the city, you can't simply draw a few nearby buildings in detail and expect the audience to fill in the rest. It's easy to leave out things in the far distance as you focus on visually dominant elements you can see in the foreground or middle ground, so you have to be mindful of this full spectrum as you add various elements to the scene.

Similar to drawing a bounding box using two diagonal points, you need recognizable markers at each end of the space you wish to depict. For example, you can show one group of elements right in front of the viewer, and then another group farther away on the other end. Ideally, you would introduce additional visual landmarks across this space to further reinforce the perception of depth. These landmarks could be anything, from a hand in the foreground to a mountain range on the horizon.

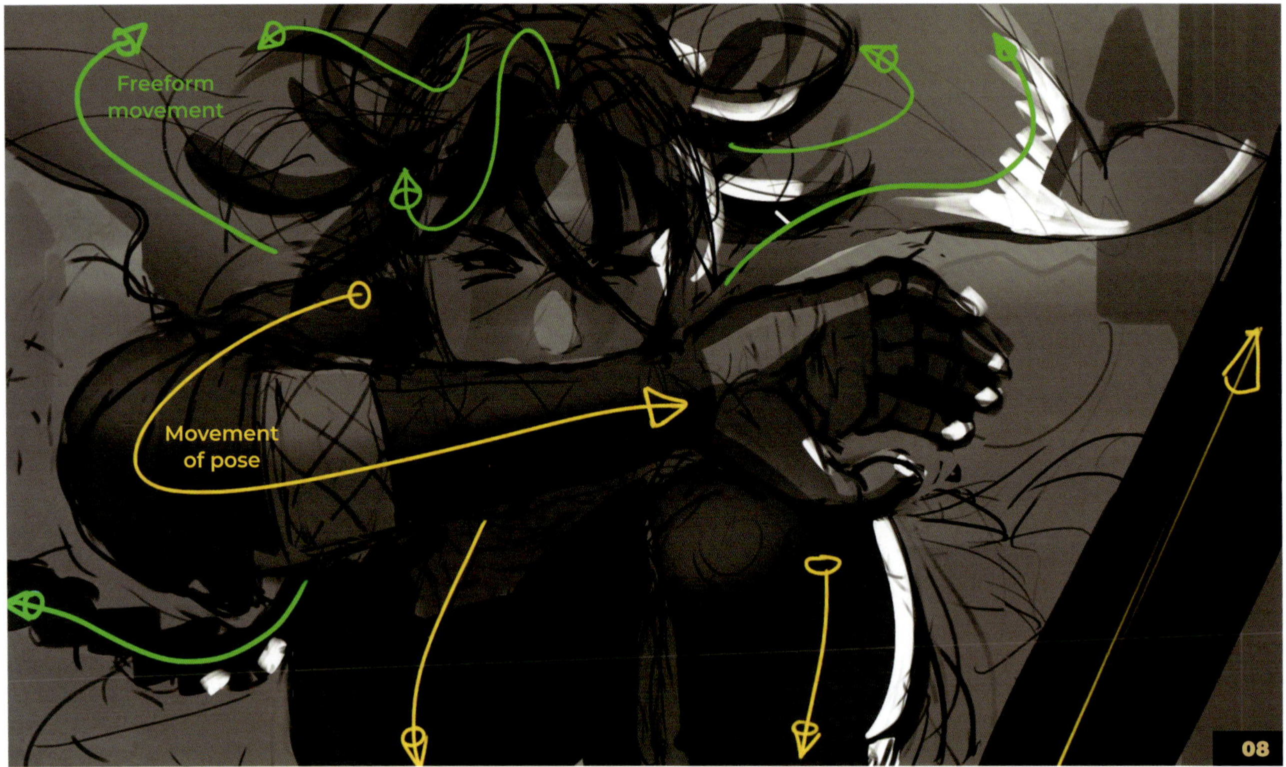

08 Movement lines can help to visualize or plan for dynamic motion in the composition. A good rule of thumb is to plan for movements that loop around to each other without pointing directly away from focal areas.

08 ADDING DYNAMIC MOVEMENT

Dynamic scenes can be crafted in many different ways. Besides applying the common technique of including various forms in motion, you can also incorporate perspective and depth cues into said motion to create an even more immersive composition.

By adopting a close-up POV to the character, you bring in perspective distortion that becomes an asset, as you can use it to visualize movement across depth. For example, imagine comparing a distant view of a runner with a close-up view. The former presents information matter-of-factly, whereas the latter is focused on speed and action by showing exactly how the body is moving across your view in three-dimensional space.

As in the example, you first need an innately dynamic subject to take advantage of these effects – such as a pose in which the character is exerting and moving, rather than being still. Physical aspects of the subject, such as their pose and the billowing wind, will make up the basis of this scene's dynamic effect.

Having the character's movement occur across a three-dimensional space, rather than just a single axis, is a great way to make things look even more dynamic. By having elements such as the hair and cape not only moving along the canvas in the composition but 'into' and 'out of' the canvas can add greatly to a scene's immersion – especially in conjunction with the close-up perspective, which clearly visualizes these elements moving across layers of depth.

'S' CURVES

The incorporation of 'S'-shaped curves into soft, moving elements is very effective. An 'S' curve is a curve that reverses direction once, compared to a simple 'C' curve, which maintains its direction throughout its length. When drawing flowing elements, such as the edges of fabric, or strands of material such as hair, using 'S' curves can impart a much more believable and detailed look. These curves can also take on variation and asymmetry, such as having some flatter curves, or a soft start followed by a strong recurve.

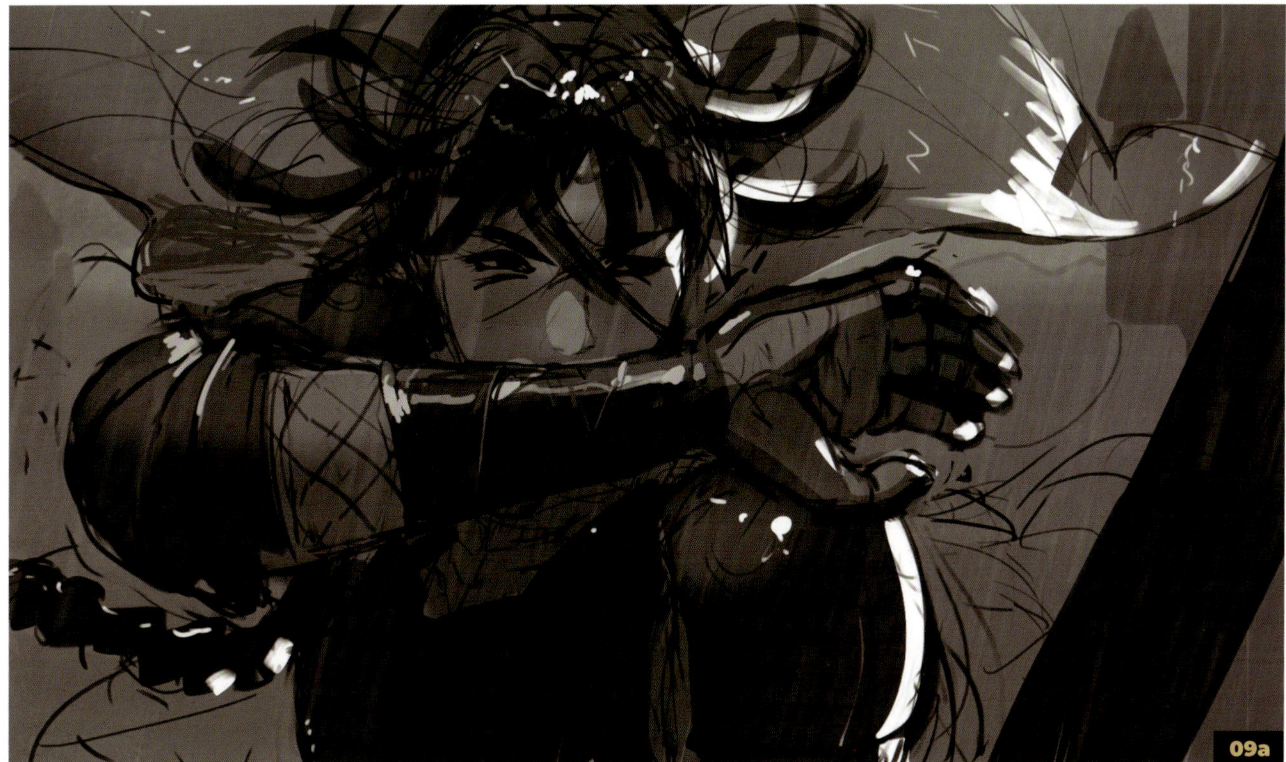

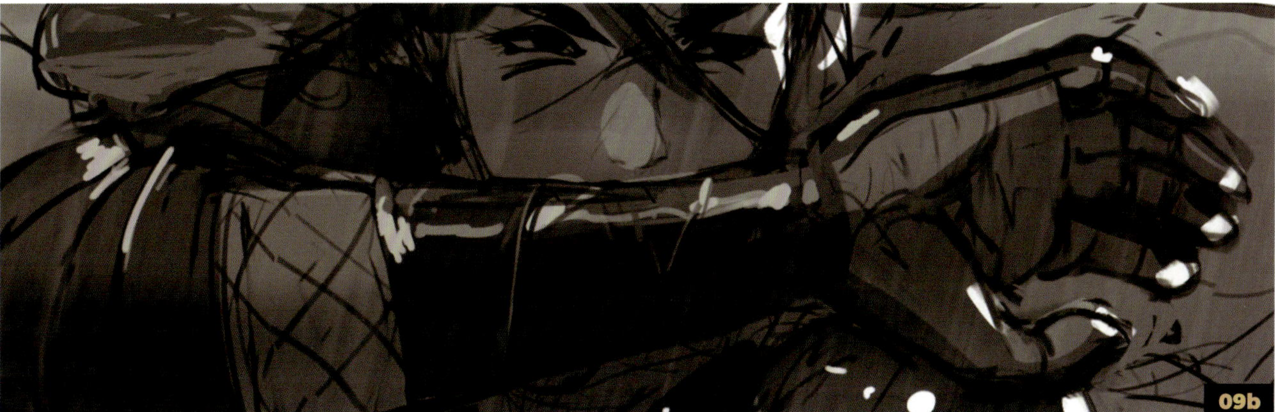

09a & 09b To strike a balance with your ease of painting, you can make use of layers to temporarily hide 'noisy' effects such as rain.

09 PREVIEWING EFFECTS

We're often tempted to think of environmental effects like rain and fog as finishing touches that come right at the end, rather than an aspect to tackle early on. Adding too many visual elements too early in the process can make it difficult to paint in an organized way.

However, these effects are no less important a part of the composition than anything else, as they have the potential to alter and affect many aspects of the piece. For example, wet surfaces become more reflective to lighting sources, while heavy rain and fog affect the perception and depth of elements in the distance.

Therefore, it is beneficial to start accounting for them now as we build the core of the composition. We introduce wet surfaces on our character by using sharp highlights at points where the sky reflects off these areas into our POV. To account for the rain and fog, we can use a soft brush to lighten and blend distant areas. To emulate the density of raindrops, a dense particle brush followed by motion blur works well **(09a, 09b)**.

The combined effect of these changes impacts the composition significantly, and gives us a peek into what the finished piece might look like.

AN ALTERNATIVE PERSPECTIVE ON PERSPECTIVE

One-, two-, and three-point perspective layouts are terms most beginner artists have heard. Naturally, you might tend to see them as predefined models with which to plan a composition. While these examples are helpful as templates, the use of perspective and vanishing points can extend well beyond the basics you commonly see used.

In order to go beyond the basics, though, you have to understand the significance of each vanishing point within the grand scheme of the composition. The core concept to start from is that *a vanishing point is as relevant as the compositional elements that make use of it*.

A simple example would be that of a box – its respective vanishing point is relevant because a large proportion of its defining edges recede towards that point. If you have many boxes that are all aligned with that point, the scene 'becomes' a one-point-perspective composition **(A)**. However, if the boxes are in disarray, then that specific vanishing point becomes arbitrary and a lot less intuitive as an anchor **(B)**.

If we introduce major visual elements that align with the vanishing point, that point now regains its significance, despite the exclusion of minor elements **(C)**.

When considering a realistic POV, you can think of vanishing points as simple guides to help visualize how things become smaller as they move further away relative to the viewer. These guides can be attached to any visually important element within the composition – for example, corridors and walls in an indoor setting, or trees and clouds in an outdoor setting.

The catch is that most elements within the frame are going to be at different distances away, meaning that a massive number of vanishing points would be needed to account for every axis of depth.

Imagine facing a wall directly head-on, with the wall's closest tile being in the middle **(D)**. The physical reality is that each edge, being further from your POV than the centre of the square, will have visually smaller tiles.

However, the further away the entire wall is from your POV, the weaker this effect. To give an extreme example, if the centre tile of the wall is one unit away from the POV, and the edge tiles are each two units away, the difference in visual size will be massive. If the centre is 999 units away from us and the edges are 1,000 units away, then this perspective distortion can effectively be ignored, as you can still see the entire wall at essentially the same distance.

The same principle applies in illustration, too, as artists tend to ignore very minor perspective distortion (for example, when drawing the aforementioned wall from the front at a moderate distance). However, if you want to draw a much closer POV with a wider lens, it might mean having

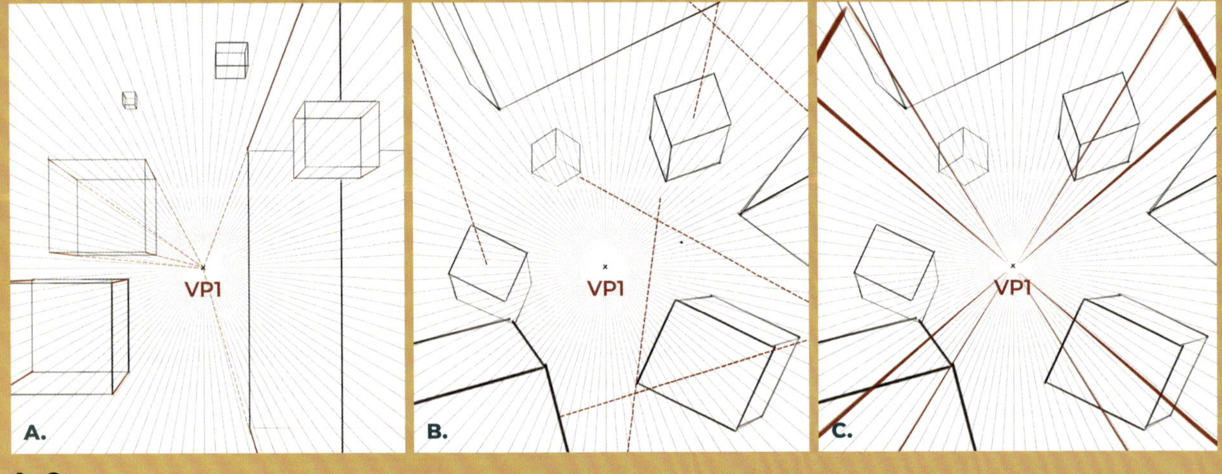

A.–C. Examples of how a one-point perspective set-up can be subverted or reinforced.

to account for the distance differences along the wall itself, therefore needing much more distortion. Extreme distortion across a flat plane can be difficult and unintuitive to calculate and depict.

To make things easier, you can introduce more 'obvious' directions of perspective (E). If you pick a clear angle of approach, the perspective distortions will occur along distinct axes, allowing you to 'override' the need for curved perspective lines. Rectilinear lenses in real life serve the same purpose of straightening out curved perspectives, and work best when shooting subjects at distinct angles.

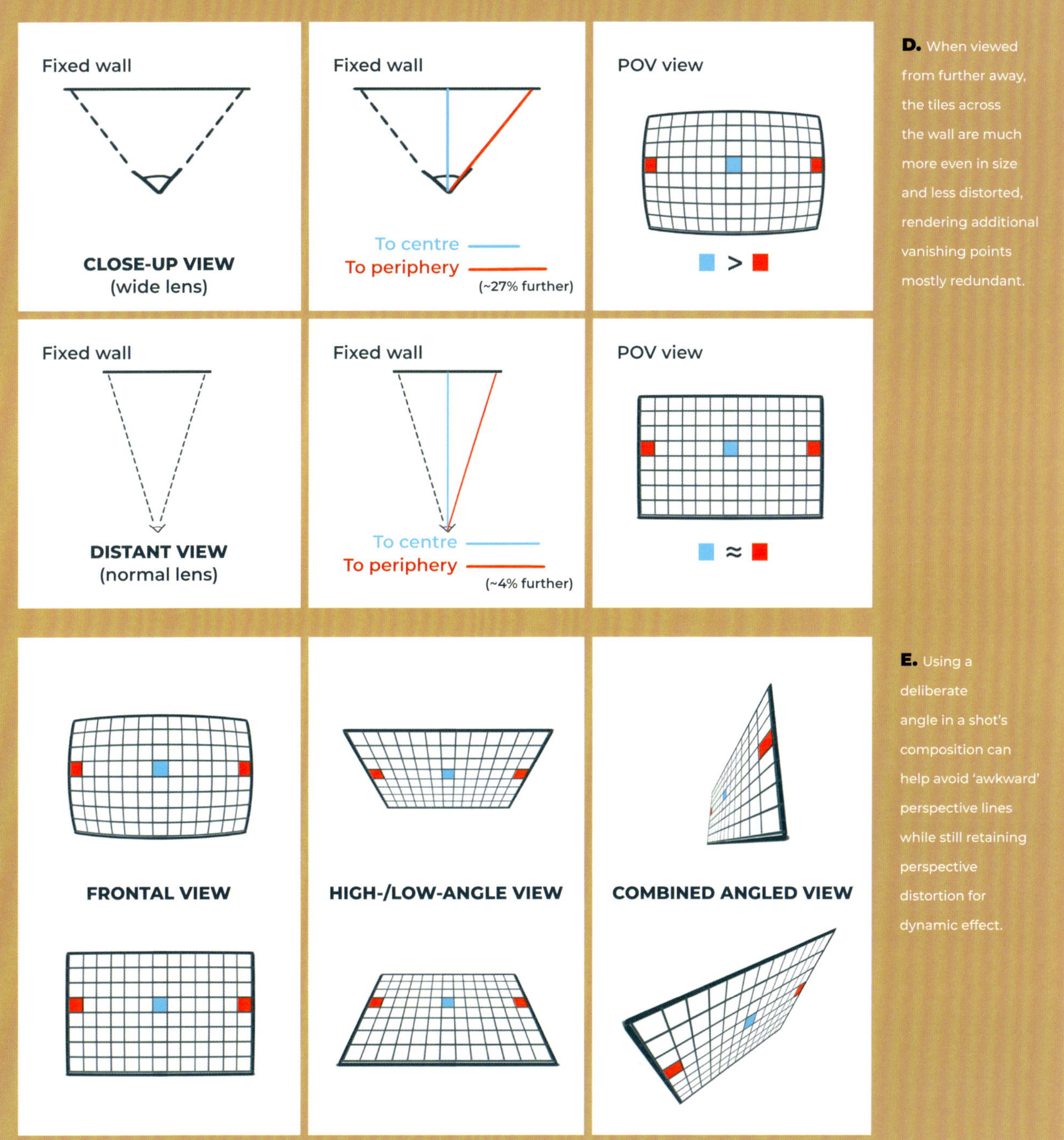

D. When viewed from further away, the tiles across the wall are much more even in size and less distorted, rendering additional vanishing points mostly redundant.

E. Using a deliberate angle in a shot's composition can help avoid 'awkward' perspective lines while still retaining perspective distortion for dynamic effect.

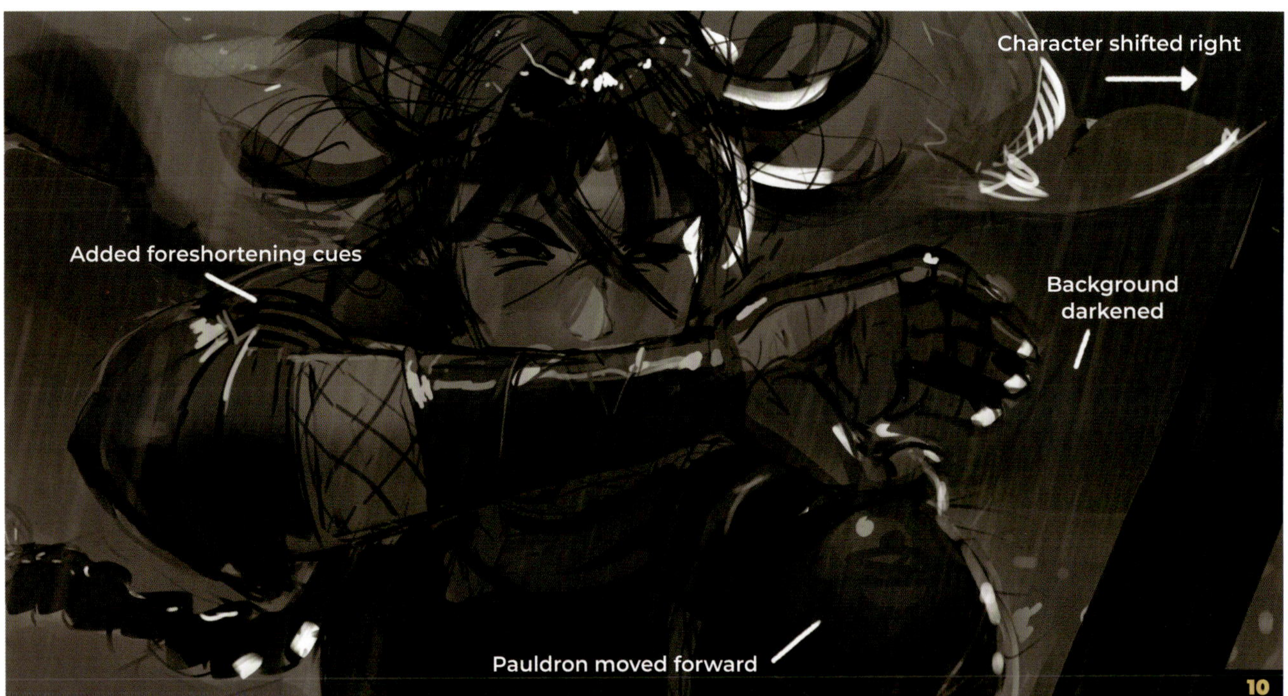

10 While individual fixes during this phase should be relatively minor, given the rigorous planning process, the sum of their parts can develop and improve the composition as a whole significantly.

10 REFRESHING THE COMPOSITION

Interspersing some free-painting into an organized process is an excellent way to make adjustments flexibly. During this process, it's equally important to review the changes occurring throughout the piece as it is to move forward with improving the composition. Look out for fundamental-level mistakes that need fixing, such as perspective-related errors. Check for misaligned edges, excessive or insufficient foreshortening, or depth lost during the drawing process.

In this case, you may need to tune the brightness of the highlights that you have just added to their respective materials, or to more accurately represent the underlying forms. The character's forward shoulder and pauldron could also be enlarged in line with the perspective view, given their proximity to the viewer's POV.

As you make these changes, it's helpful to constantly observe and compare 'before and after' stages to see how they impact the big picture. For example, an attention-grabbing element on one side of the canvas can make for a good focal point, but may also add excessive weight that needs to be balanced out.

Experiment and test out new ideas by marking potential areas of interest on the character, or adding architecture in the background. If the scene feels too bright or too dark so far, consider adjusting the overall values using a Curves adjustment layer.

11 CHARACTER: OVERVIEW

While we often strongly associate depth and perspective with environmental elements, they are also a key consideration when illustrating characters. It's a little less intuitive trying to reconcile grids and vanishing points with the more organic, dynamic forms present in a character, which can make perspective difficult here.

A helpful method for tackling perspective is to break down the character's form into manageable blocks **(11a)**. In this case, the head, upper torso, forearms, and upper arms are each represented by a 'box of best fit'. In turn, these simple guide boxes facilitate the process of drawing their represented forms in proper perspective, and in accurate relation to each other.

However, if you jump right into working in perspective with these individual boxes, things can get overwhelming really quickly. To start yourself off on the right foot, consider how you can represent the character as a whole with a single 'box of best fit' **(11b)**. A meaningful 'best fit' would be aligned with the character's axis of intent, which is the direction of their gaze or pose in this case.

With this central frame of reference, you can better understand the relative position of each individual form within the character, enabling you to draw them in perspective effectively.

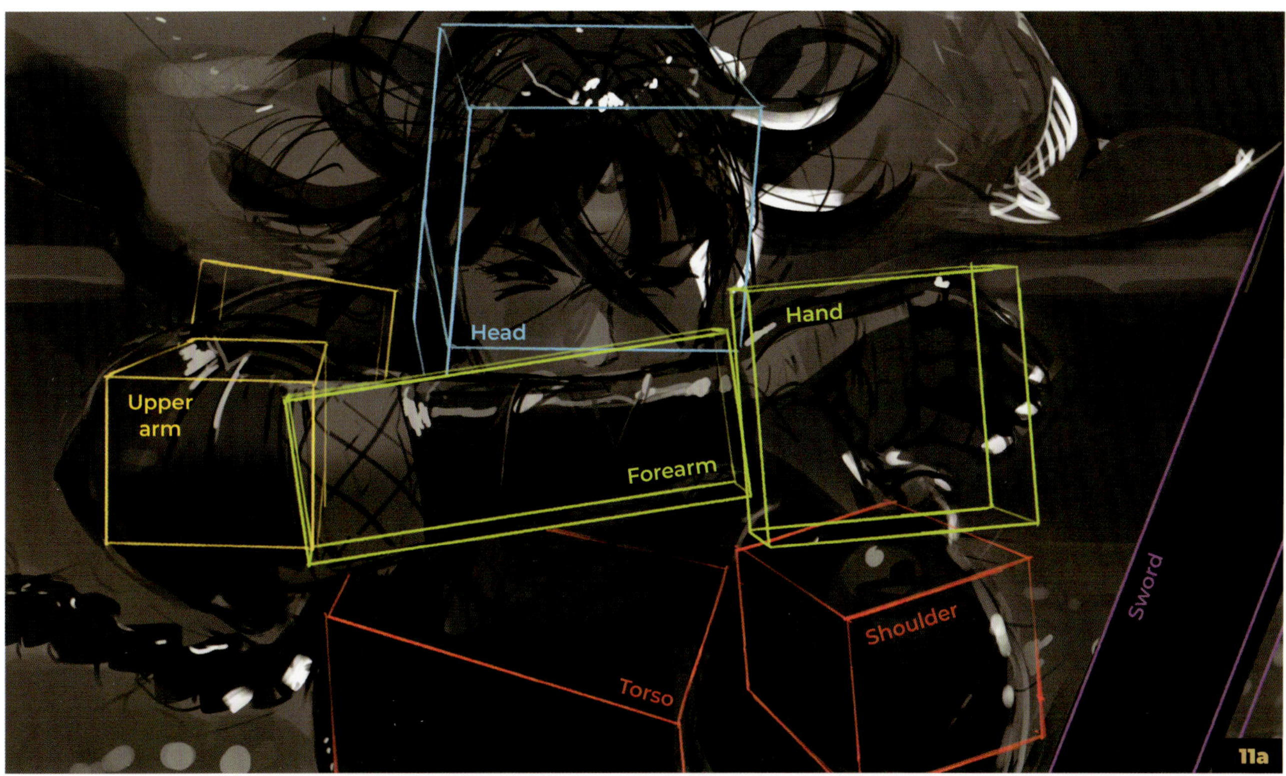

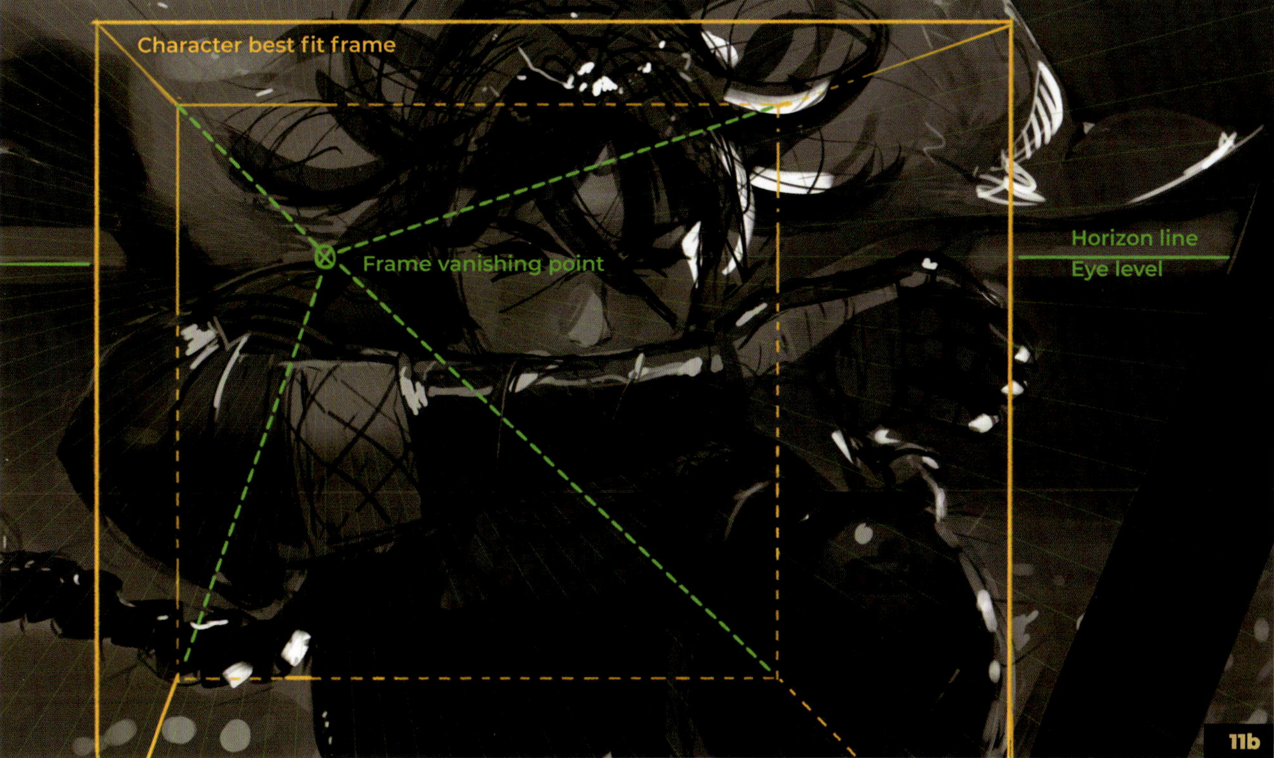

11a & 11b The top image shows a possible breakdown that can represent the individual forms.

The bottom image illustrates a possible 'best fit' frame that could be used for the character.

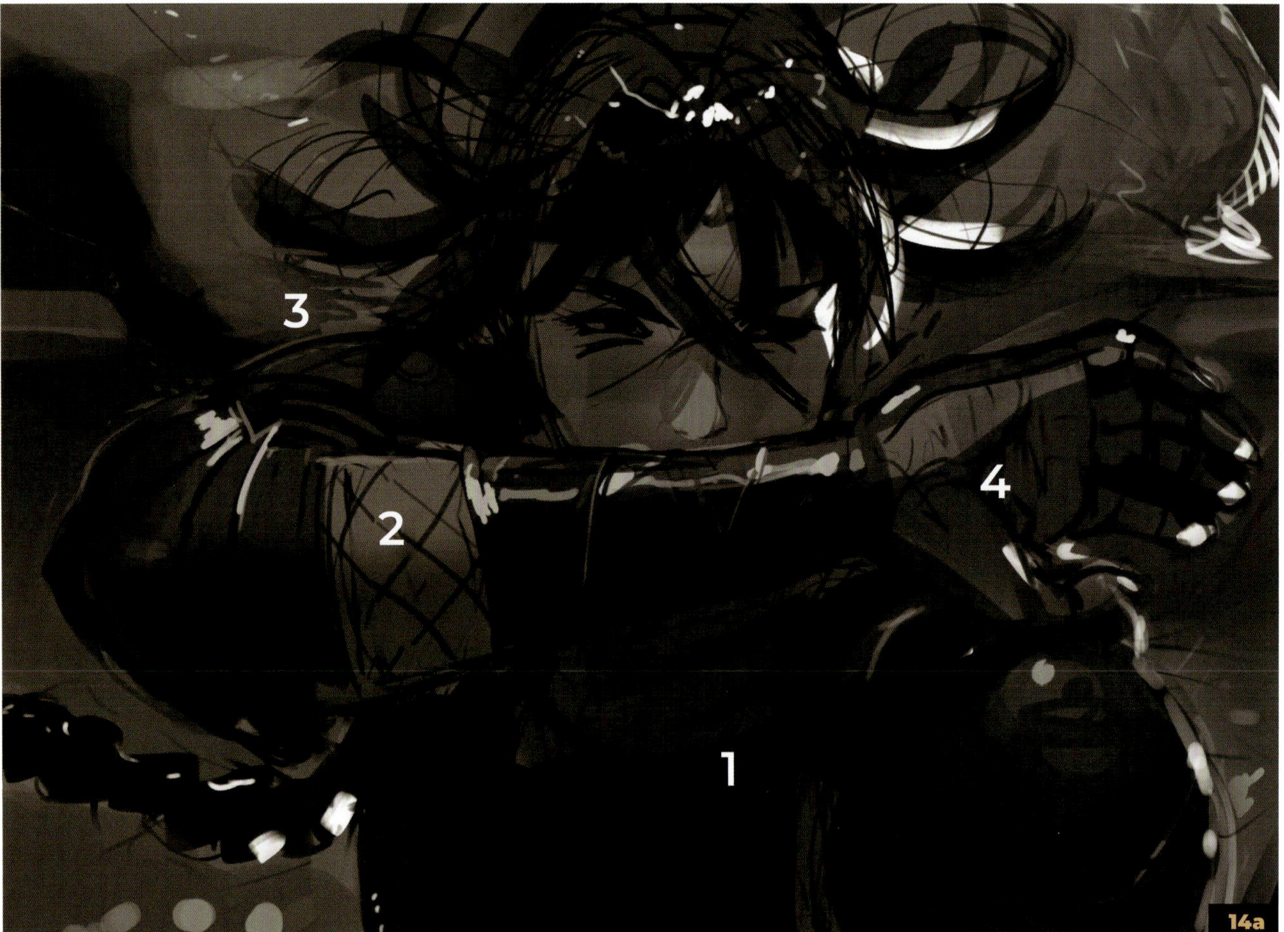

14a & 14b Before and after adjustments: **1)** stronger occlusion on cuirass, **2)** darkened fabric material, **3)** sharper reflection, taking into account contour of pauldron, and **4)** adjusted forearm and hand pose.

14 CHARACTER: LIGHTING

Now that you have a good understanding of how the character is drawn in proper perspective and depth, it's time to revisit your lighting set-up.

This scene will have three light sources to account for: the overcast lighting, which hits the character evenly from above; the ambient light, which comes from the overcast sky being reflected by the surroundings onto the character; and finally the accent or side light, which is from a separate source of illumination that highlights a part of the character's silhouette.

While you have already captured these basics in a very methodical manner, there is still a lot of room for improvement and adjustment.

The aim now is to assess the character's appearance as a whole, tweaking lighting strength and local values to better suit the composition **(14a, 14b)**. For example: increasing the ambient occlusion factor for the torso area to better distinguish the upward-facing portion; darkening the fabric portion of the forearm to create a more cohesive value block; and adjusting the overcast light to be less evenly reflected to account for the foreshortened forms.

As you paint, you may spot mistakes that you can fix as you go. For example, the leading forearm and hand have been adjusted to be more proportionate.

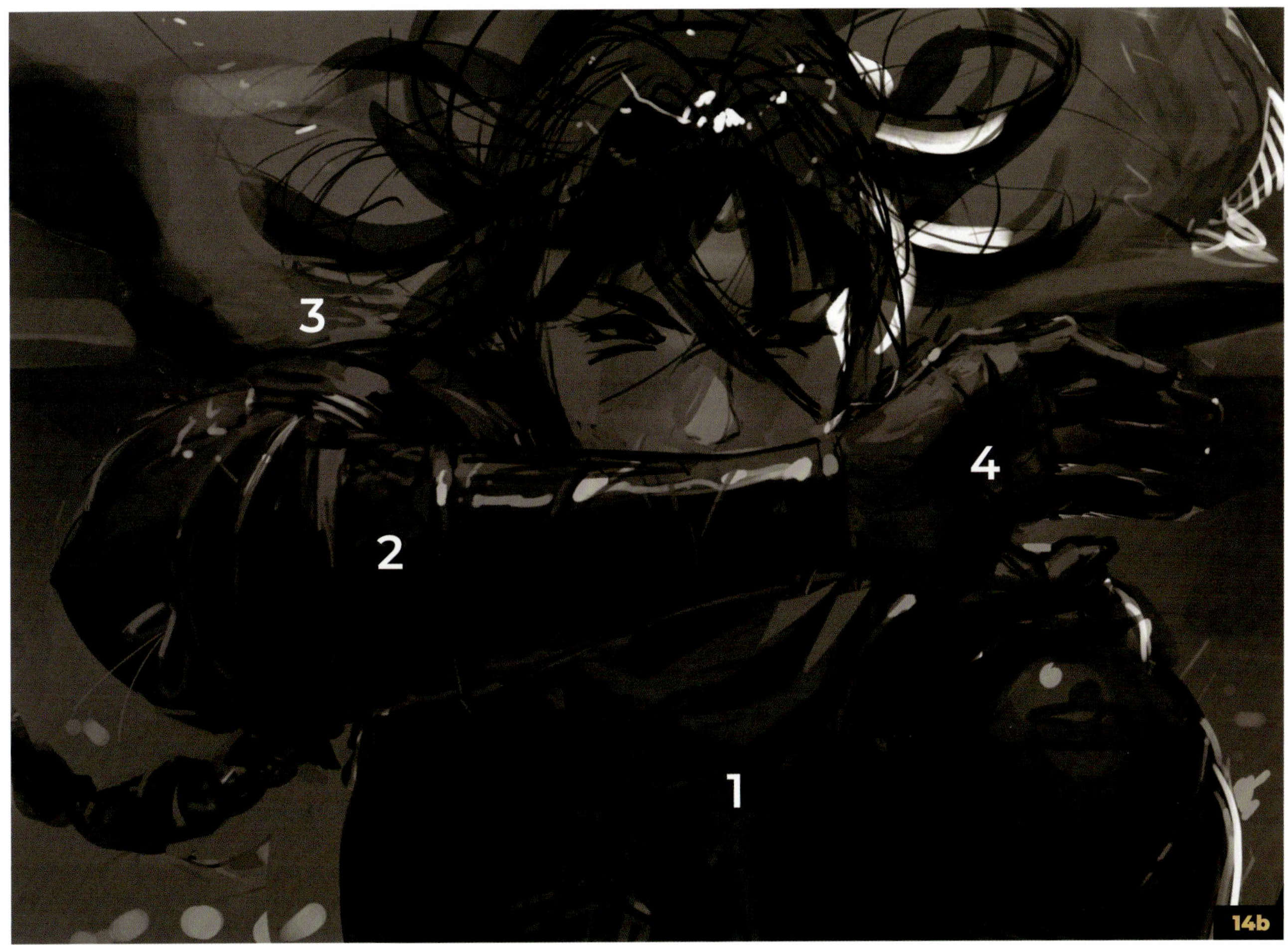

LIGHTING CONSIDERATIONS

Overcast lighting might be comparatively soft, but it is still bright enough for light to be bounced off the ground, nearby buildings, and even raindrops and fog onto the character. The best way to express this effect is usually by adding a soft, weak light cast upwards and from the side onto the character.

With a highly specular surface, these same areas might directly reflect the surroundings as an image, rather than just be softly lit by diffuse lighting.

To think about how lighting strikes a specific point, put yourself in that POV and imagine how the scene in front of you looks. Where is the brightest point? Is it generally brighter above or below? What about the light coming in from the side?

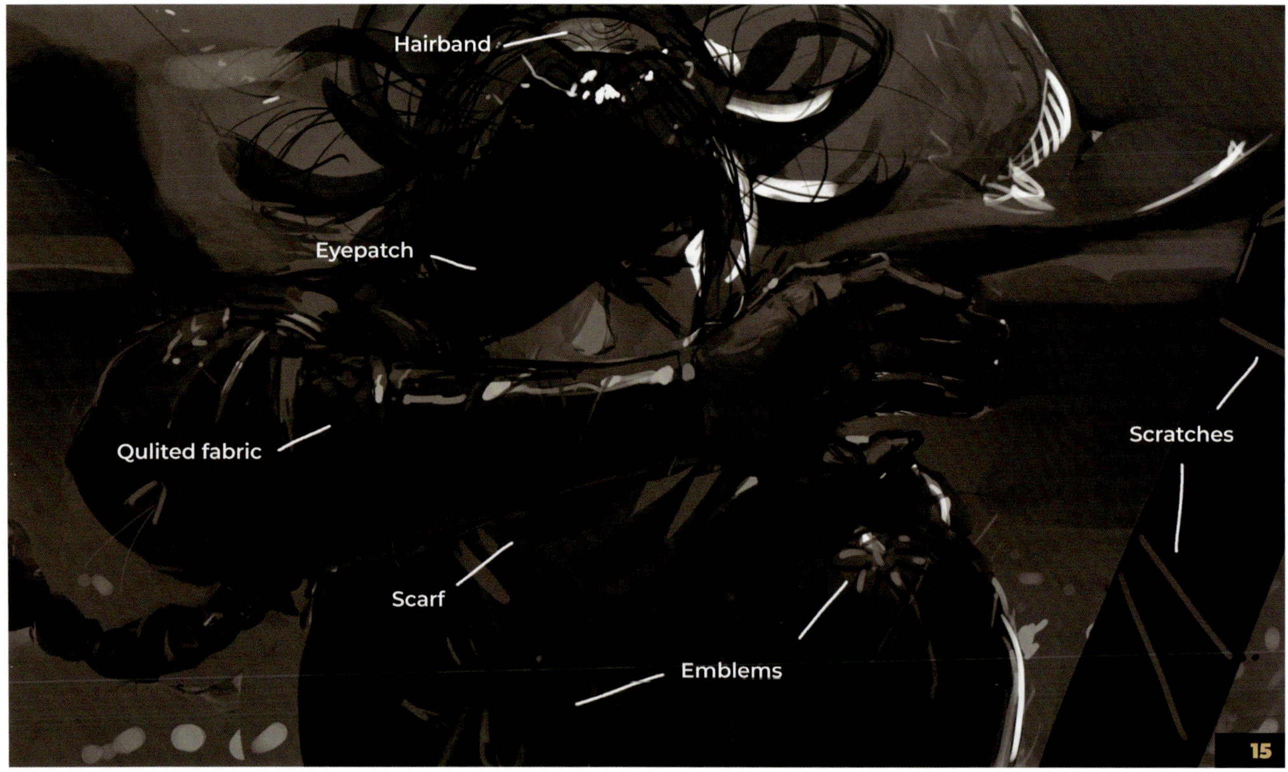

15 Introduction of multiple new textures, patterns, and objects on this first detail pass; more of the complex details are left as temporary placeholders.

15 CHARACTER: INTRODUCING DETAILS

Now that you have a solid foundation for the character, you can begin exploring options for developing the visuals further.

Detailing is necessary when you need to create something that is sufficiently information-dense and polished. This process can involve adding texture, patterns, or entire elements to make the subject more interesting. Beyond the basic 'filling in of empty space', there are plenty of opportunities within the detailing process that you can seize to reinforce perspective, or even to add another tier of depth to the composition.

First, consider introducing contour-following elements (such as the hairband, eyepatch, scarf, and arm wraps), which provide direct feedback on the perspective at various points in the composition. These can add clarity to the drawing process, giving you visible anchors with which to check that perspective is being correctly shown.

Second, on a smaller scale, textures and repeating patterns can be a more subtle but equally effective option (for example, scratches or seams aligned in perspective). You can even apply them to those above elements directly, such as the quilted layer on the arm wrap, which is a very succinct way to convey the contour of the forearm.

Single motifs like the one on the pauldron and chestplate can also be used to directly indicate the perspective of the surface they're attached to.

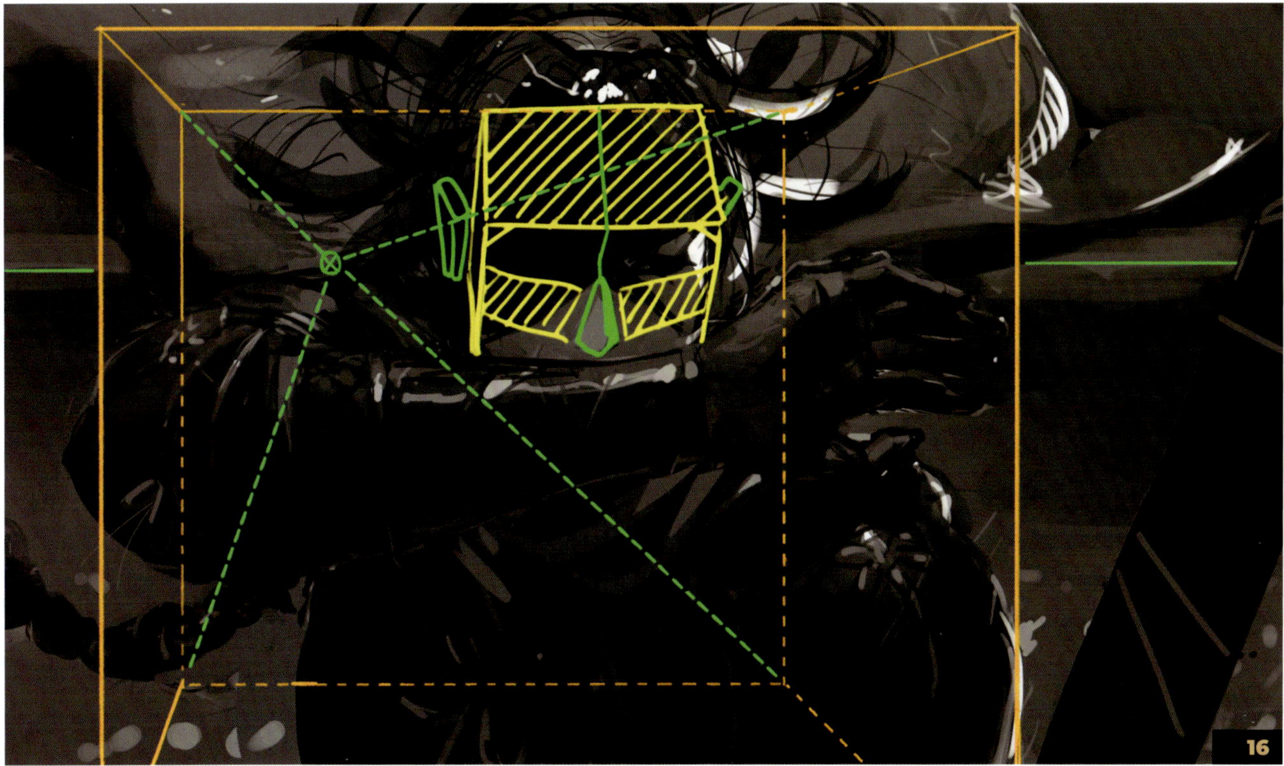

16 The basic structure of the face is broken down into perspective with upper- and lower-facing surfaces indicated to facilitate lighting the forms.

16 FACES & PERSPECTIVE

The face is often a natural point of focus for character illustrations, yet it can feel disproportionately difficult to approach given its apparent complexity. Rather than trying to figure it out in a single leap, look at the face as yet another group of forms that need to be understood and then drawn in perspective.

You can break down the face and subdivide it into relevant shapes, just as before. First, identify the forehead, nose, and ears as the most prominently protruding forms. Second, subdivide the remaining surfaces to account for the eyes, cheeks, and mouth area.

Recall the one-point grid from earlier. Using the perspective information it provides, you can figure how each part of the face should appear from your chosen POV. As we see the face very slightly from the left (our view), we should see a little more of the near cheek, and slightly less of the far cheek. As the side lighting is interacting from the less visible side, we should be careful not to over-expose it.

You can apply this similar deduction process to the rest of the face: the nose, eyes, cheeks, brow, and forehead are all drawn with a very slight asymmetry to account for perspective.

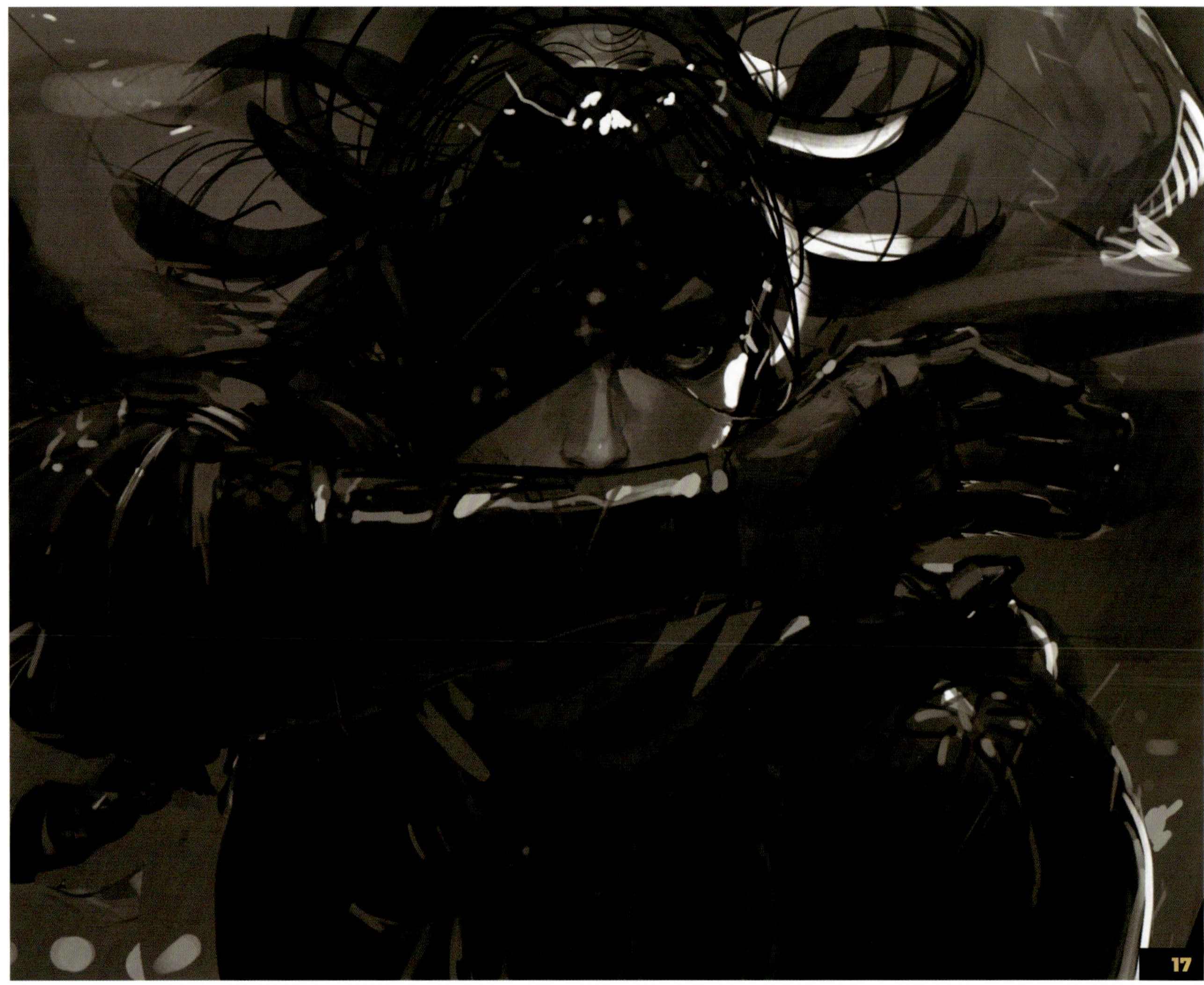

17 The first painting pass over the facial features can be a big jump from the previous stage; the change in how the face reads will naturally require further tuning and adjustment.

17 FACES & DEPTH

Recall how 'overlapping' and 'foreshortening' are two techniques used here to depict depth. Understanding of these concepts is equally relevant to the process of drawing a portrait. Overlapping forms may be less self-evident in this context, as facial features rarely obfuscate each other from the front view, but there are some subtle key areas of note.

As the character's head is slightly lowered, the tip of the nose will start to obscure the nostrils and the base of the philtrum from this POV. Due to the POV being close-up and slightly to the left, the character's far-side cheek also partially overlaps and obscures the ear. This depth cue is critical in providing visual information regarding the structure of the face – an unobscured ear from this perspective would imply that it's growing right out of the character's cheekbone!

Foreshortening is a lot more self-explanatory here, as you can see that the sides of the nose, edges of the brow, eye sockets, temple, cheekbones, and bottom of the cheek all show more foreshortening from this perspective. To reflect these foreshortened surfaces accurately, make sure to light these surfaces in a way that is consistent with the existing three-light set-up.

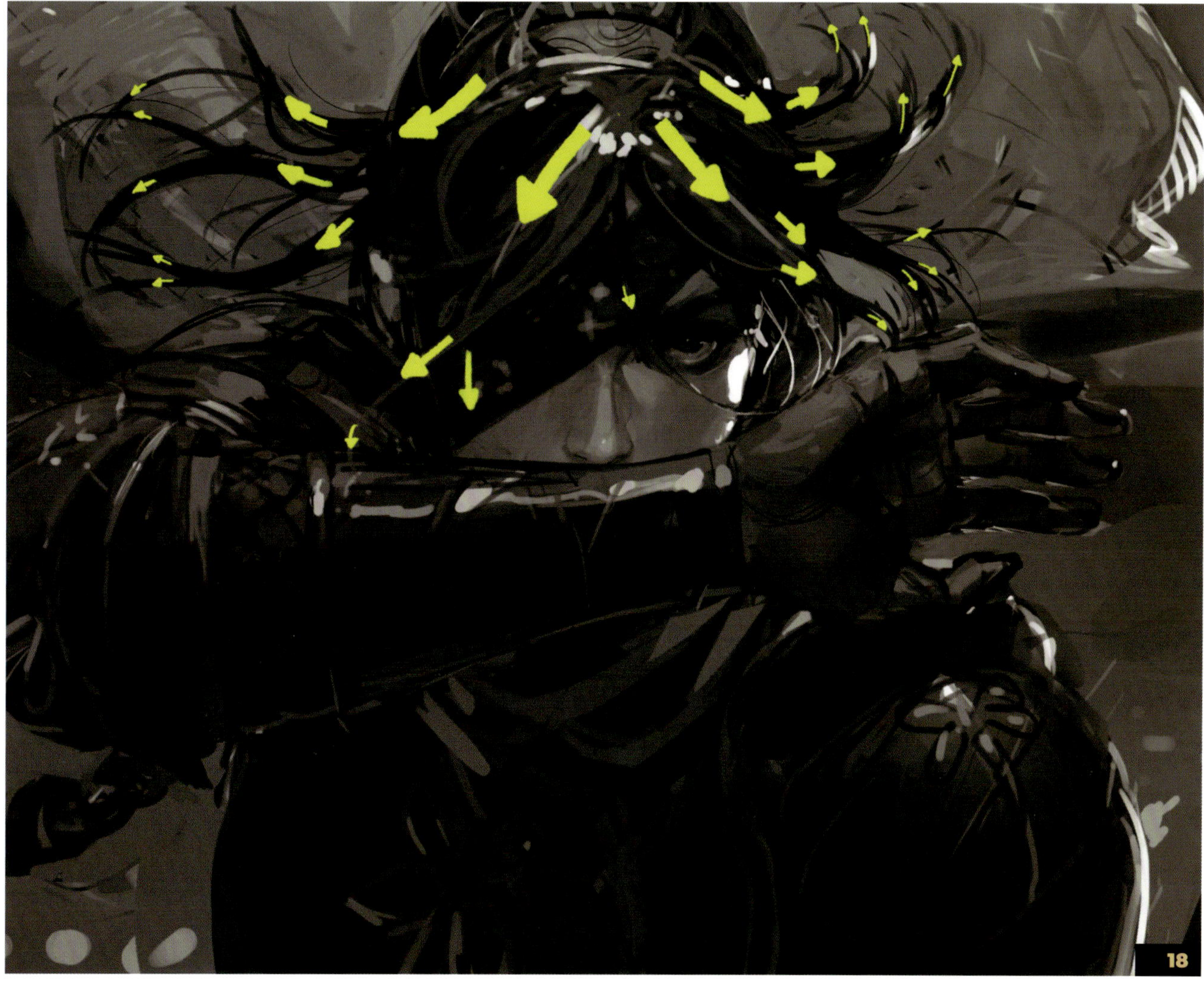

18 The movement of hair in the depth axis is difficult to clearly portray at this stage, but can be temporarily indicated with strong curves, especially towards the tips of strands.

18 HAIR

The next challenge is drawing hair in motion. To start, you can think of hair almost like a helmet sitting on top of the head and sharing much of the same perspective grid. In many cases, the apparent perspective of the hair actually conveys much of the information on how the character's head is positioned. As this character's head is slightly lowered from this POV, in a bracing pose, you should correspondingly see more of the top of her hair as well.

From here, we can start thinking about how the individual strands and 'bundles' of hair flow from the established base. This is also a great opportunity to add more dynamic movement to the composition. Rather than drawing evenly sized strands or blocks moving in an artificially uniform manner, you can add overlaps, desynchronizations, and size differences to the strands to make the movement look organic. The natural overlapping is also a great way to add further depth cues within the space the hair occupies.

To avoid excessive messiness that can unintentionally break up the visual flow, I find it helpful to first draw large 'blocks' of hair organized towards the axis of movement, with overlapping medium and small strands added in later. The visually dominant large blocks define and anchor the movement direction, while the medium and small shapes add a layer of controlled messiness and believability.

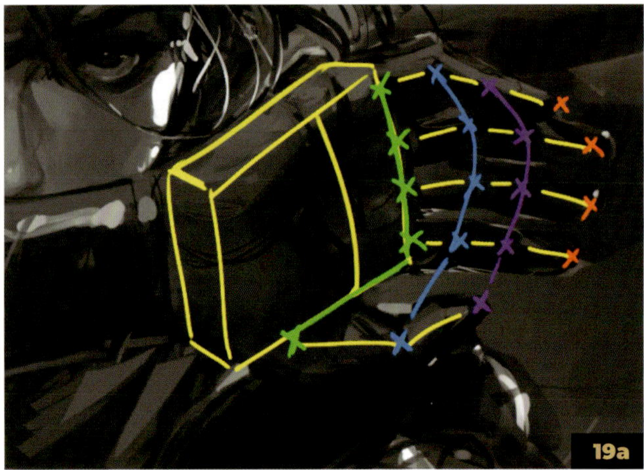

19a Knuckles and joints align along a smooth arc in this pose.

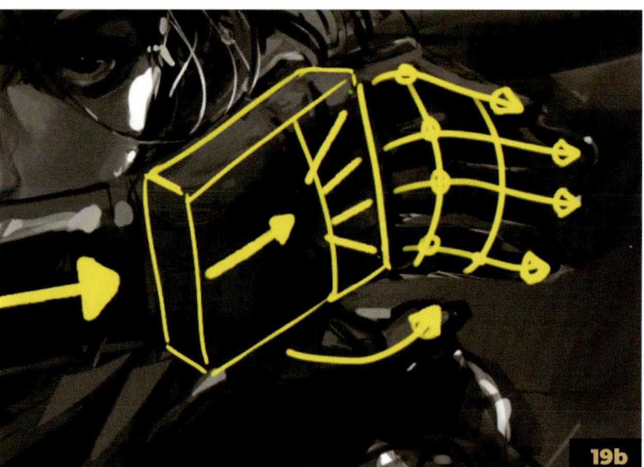

19b The flow of gesture from wrist to fingertip.

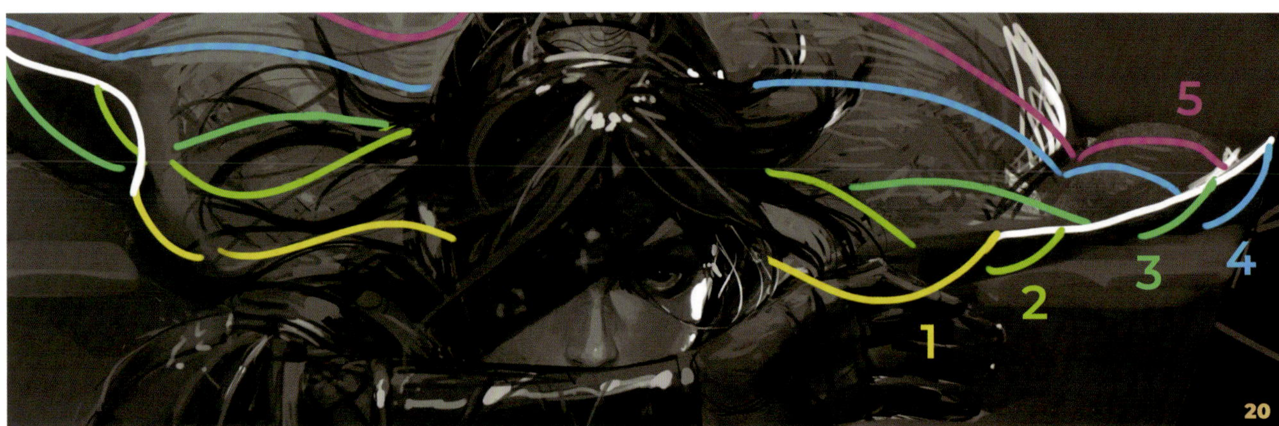

20 One possible way to break down the form of the cape in perspective: abstracting out individual edges within the 'cross-section' of the cape, using overlaps to add depth.

19 HANDS

Detailed hands are often a challenge to draw, not just because of how complex they are, but also because you can tell straight away when something about them isn't drawn right. Uncommon hand poses or difficult perspectives can add to this challenge. As before, you can break hands down into manageable portions.

First, identify the position and rotation of the palm. It's usually the least variable part of the hand, making it the best candidate to serve as a perspective anchor point for the rest of the hand. In this case, the palm is rotated outwards in a bracing position. Based on this, you can add the thumb and fingers accordingly. Taking a photo of your own hand can be an amazing visual aid.

Second, look at the relevant joints. Each finger has three, including the knuckle, while the thumb has two. After the initial sketch, you should locate these joints and 'link up' each finger **(19a)**. For example, the knuckles occupy one curve, the next joint the next curve, and so on. The lines essentially help you to check the length of each finger segment and keep the fingers within a realistic range of movement.

Conveniently, this technique also helps to smooth out the visual flow of the hand gesture/pose **(19b)**, and assists greatly in finding the right perspective for each finger segment.

20 ILLUSTRATING FABRICS

There are a few techniques that can help you to draw flowing fabrics in a foreshortened perspective. Fabrics are unique in that they are both soft and flexible, like hair, but also often exist as a singular large body. Because of this, they take on many properties of flowing hair, such as the abundance of S-curved sub-shapes that help to delineate motion. However, the main added challenge is that fabrics tend to terminate on single, continuous edges, whereas hair can get away with an element of messiness at the ends. As you draw the character's cape, your approach therefore has to take into account

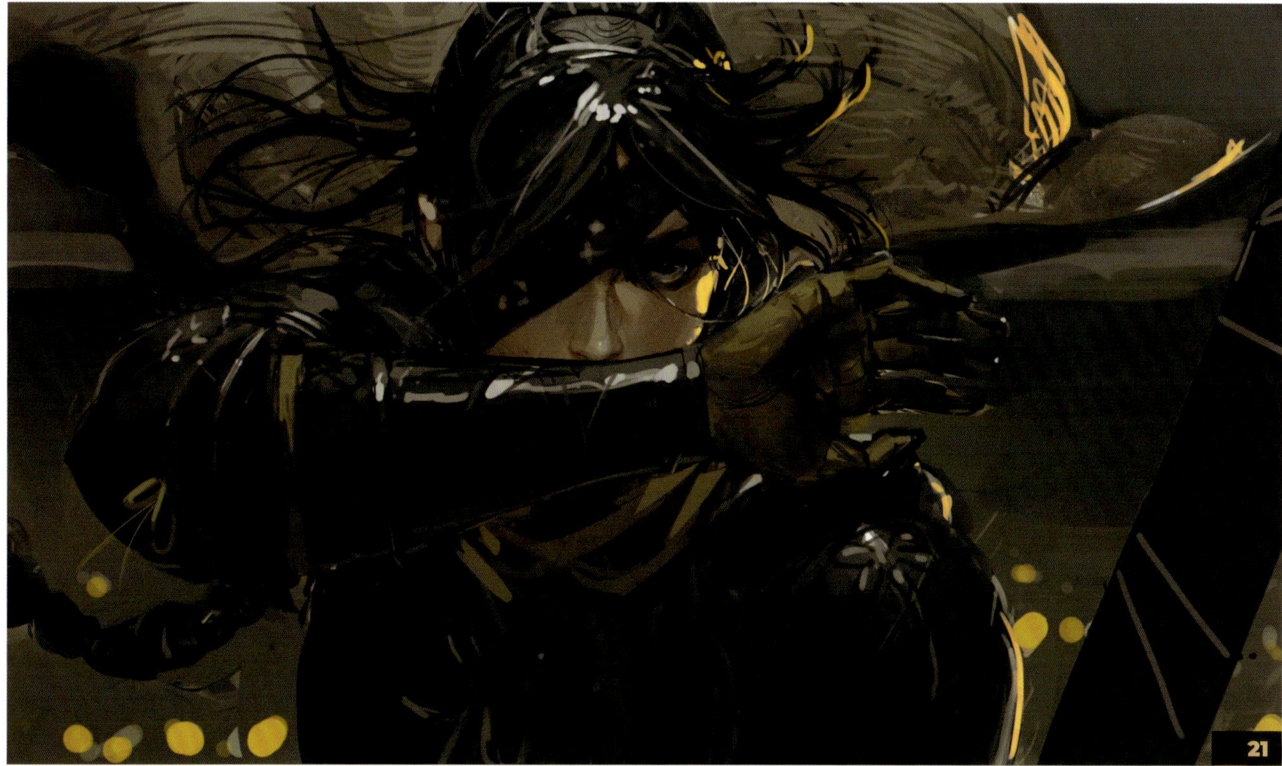

21 A preview of what the illustration should look like after your first colour pass, including both local and lighting colour.

the continuous nature of the fabric. Similar to many of the previous techniques, you can begin by mapping out a simplified form of the cape. Fortunately, you can regard the cape as a 2D object for most of this process.

Add a series of horizontal, continuous cross-section lines, one behind the other. These lines represent the contour of the cape at each point in depth. The curvature of these lines, their distance from each other, and their overlaps represent changing forms in the cape. To avoid drawing a cape that looks stiff and starched, it's best to constantly mix in variations in each of the above factors, avoiding extended sections where the lines run parallel to each other.

21 INTRODUCING COLOUR

While the greyscale sketch has been a very useful tool in setting up the foundations of the composition, colour will be your first look at the idea brought to life. It's helpful to keep things simple and organized in the beginning. Rather than figuring out the full spectrum of hues that you might want to use right at the start, begin with a straightforward colour scheme that directly accounts for the main colours involved.

Depending on your choice of composition, the colouring stage will vary in its complexity. For the purposes of this tutorial, you will adopt a relatively simple, practical colour scheme where a select few vibrant colours are supported by natural lighting and muted tones that populate most of the composition.

Similar to when you drafted the values early on, you can split the process into two distinct segments: local colour and lighting colour. Making this clear distinction at this early stage will help you to keep on top of what each colour is, as well as why it's there.

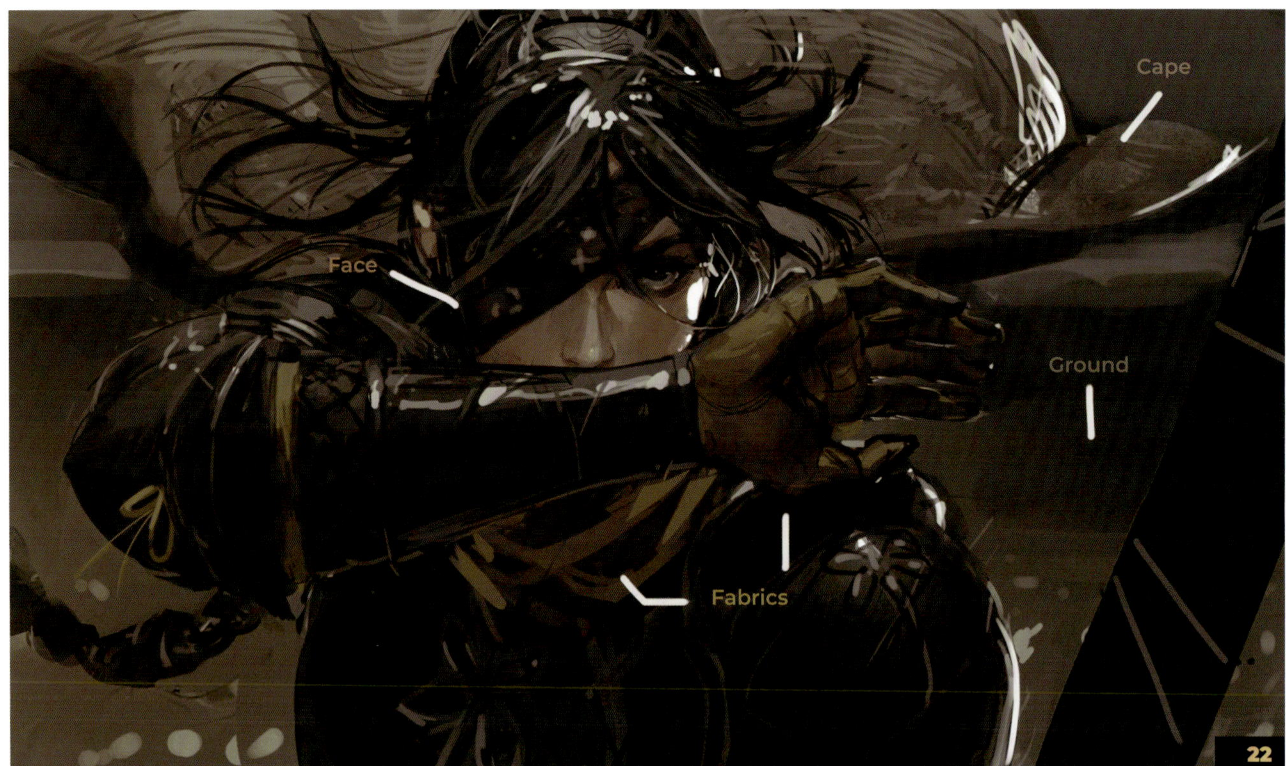

22 Assignment of local colours to each separate material; a simple but wide range of colours is a good place to start.

22 LOCAL COLOUR

You can think of the local colour as the base colour an object carries in colourless lighting. In this composition, most of the local colour will be located on the character. To apply the local colour, you can use a layer in Soft Light or Overlay mode to paint over the relevant areas. Here, I introduce the skin tone as well as a yellow tone for the fabric under armour. Aside from just adding the appropriate colour to our chosen subject, this also creates contrast between different elements of the character's design.

Recall how character design plays a part in reinforcing perspective and adding depth by introducing useful elements. Local colour further builds on this effect by giving those elements more contrast where necessary. For example, if you have a dark grey curtain beside a red and white one, you would essentially only see two major groupings in greyscale – dark and bright – as much of the contrast between red and black would be lost. Compare this to after the colour is restored, where you can see three very distinct blocks. This distinction contributes towards clarifying areas where contrast represents a change in depth, or where a form is foreshortened in perspective.

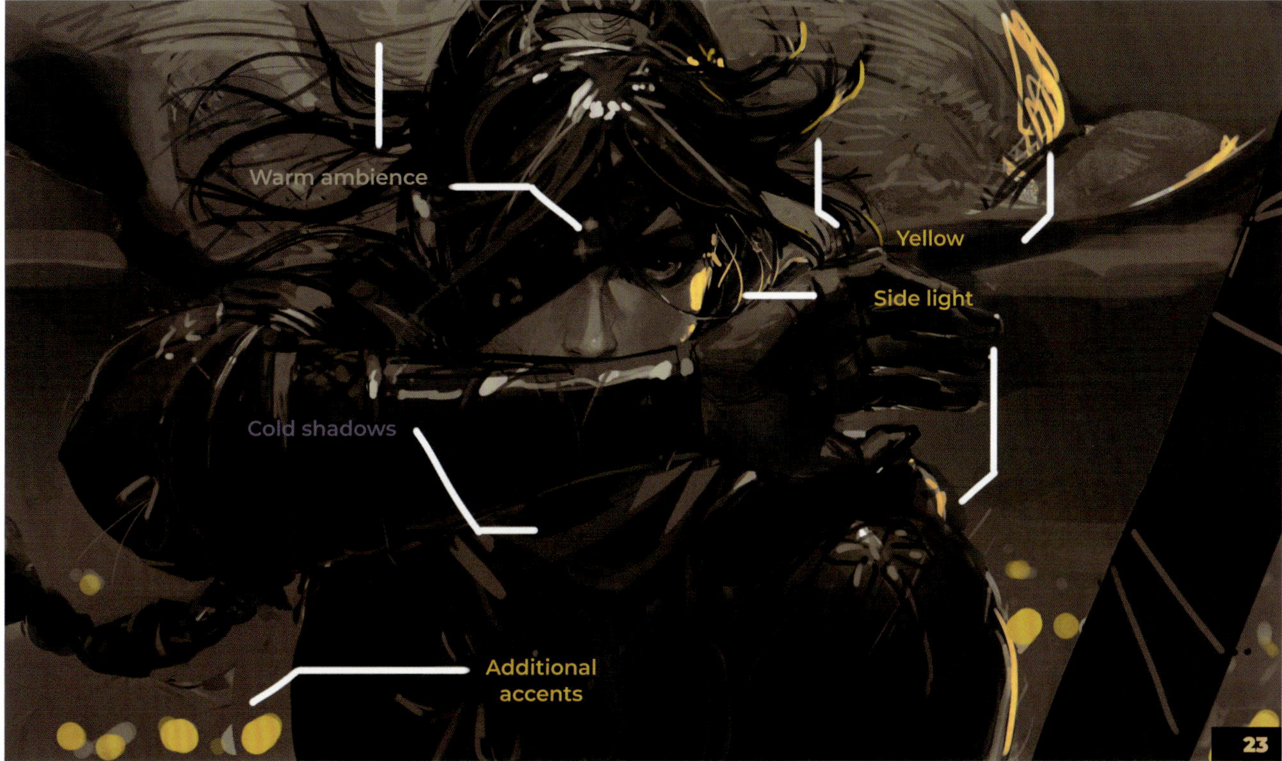

23 Isolated effects of lighting colour, without local colour; ideally, each light source should provide its own distinct colour to maximize clarity.

23 LIGHTING COLOUR

Next you can look at the colour imparted by that lighting, which you can subdivide into three parts.

First, there is a soft but substantial overhead light source coming from the overcast sky. For this light source, I choose a slightly warm, greenish tone to reflect the presence of storm clouds. To visualize this effect in the composition, I use a layer in Selective Colour mode to introduce a slight tint of yellow in the 'neutral' range and a little blue in the 'black' range.

Second, there is a strong, direct light source coming from the right side beyond our field of view. For this light source, I choose a very warm orange to keep it clearly distinct from the other sources of illumination. This is crucial, as without it, bright values indicating lighting can easily be conflated as coming from the same light source, even if multiple sources are present. For example, the highlights from the rain on the armour are bright, and in greyscale can be confused with the light coming from the right.

Third, there is a weak and soft ambient light coming primarily from the character's surroundings. It's the easiest to see coming from below, where it's the sole light source. For this, I choose a desaturated grey, similar to that of the sky. This colour matches the character's physical position (high up near a castle's citadel), as well as accounting for the predominantly grey stone architecture.

24 REBALANCING THE COMPOSITION

Now that you have introduced the first pass of colour to the composition, you'll be able to get a much better read on it as a whole. There may very likely be emergent issues that you need to resolve now that you can see them.

For example, the initial introduction of local colour may not have been precisely what you anticipated. If the yellow fabric is too oversaturated, it may 'pop' a little too much, disrupting the illusion of space by pushing itself very far forward in depth. Alternatively, the skin tone may be undersaturated, indicating that you may need to add a bit more vibrance or risk it blending in too much with the surrounding space.

A method I use to facilitate this checking process is to compare the image's current state with its pre-change state. By overlaying these two stages as layers and then going back and forth, I can easily spot mistakes that would otherwise have been difficult to detect. Being able to take a step back to reassess the piece after changes is critical in maintaining the integrity and perspective of the forms.

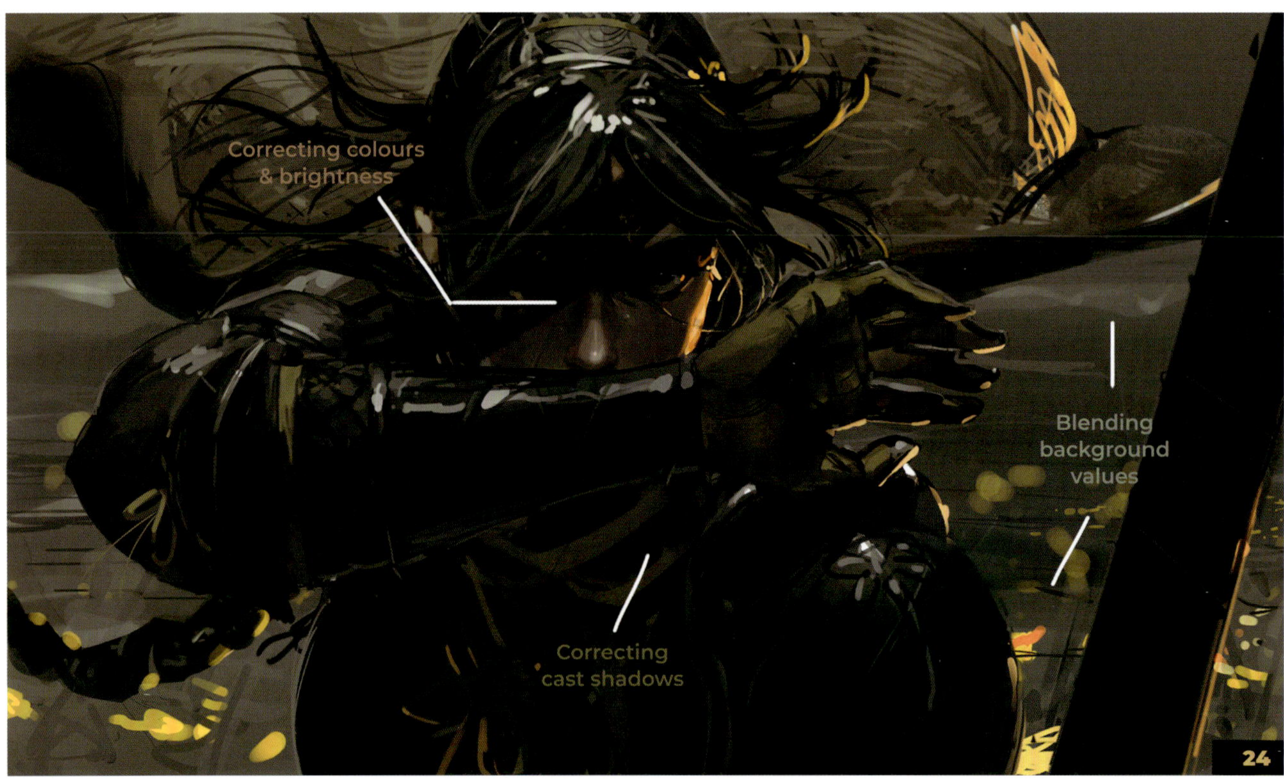

24 From the combined colour pass, further corrections and adjustments can be made. This is also an opportunity to trial different lighting ideas with full colour support.

25 STARTING ON THE ENVIRONMENT

With the main focus of the composition in place, you can divert your attention to further developing the setting and environment. As the goal is to create an illustration with a medieval theme, you need supporting elements in the surroundings to be authentic and readable to that end. Ideally, they should also be presented in a way that enhances the composition as a whole – for example, by introducing points of interest that flow naturally and draw the eye into the scene.

To give yourself a quantifiable goal, aim to have one architectural structure as the main background element, and then two or three additional structures off in the back that can further flesh out the scene. To round everything off, you could even draw smaller structures far off in the distance, to populate the image with a full range of depth.

The earlier groundwork during the value and colour drafting stage will come in very helpful here. Rather than having to figure out things from scratch, you can rely on the existing value/colour plan and build details over it.

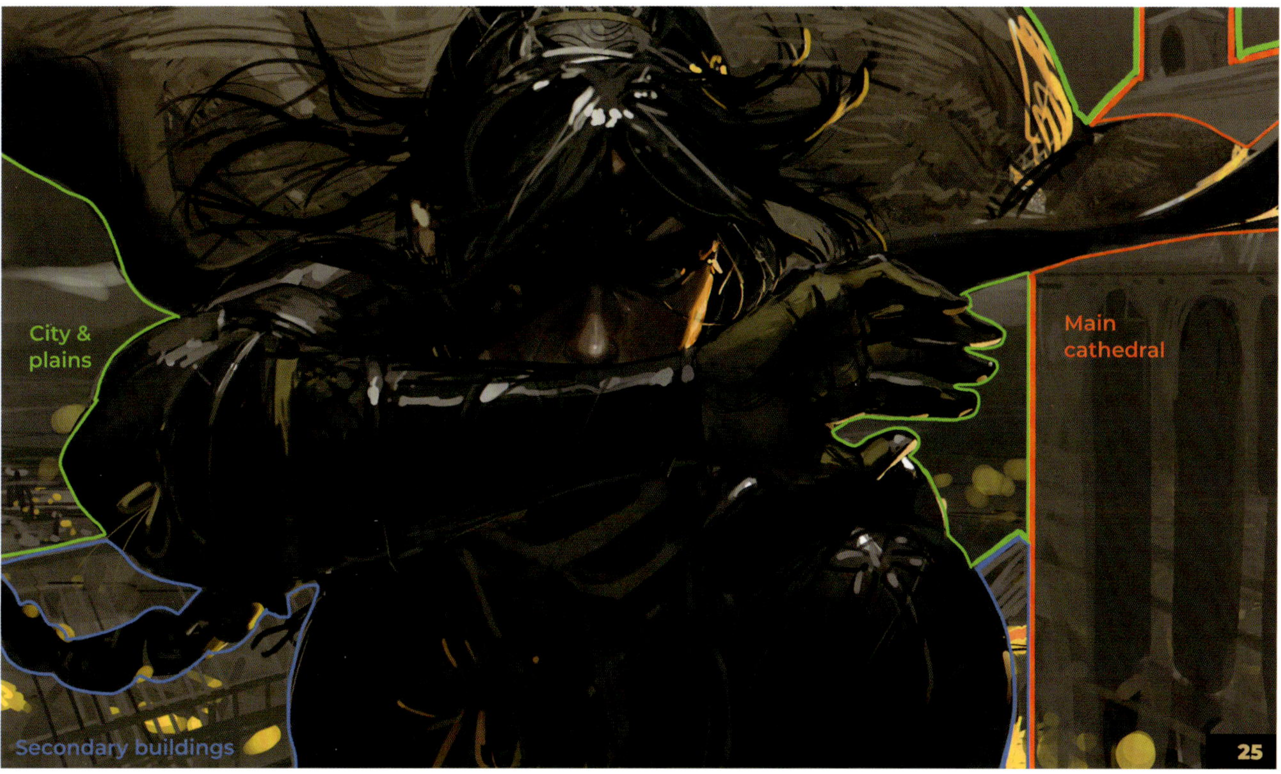

25 A simple breakdown of the background elements into manageable portions: the main cathedral and secondary buildings, followed by the distant city and plains.

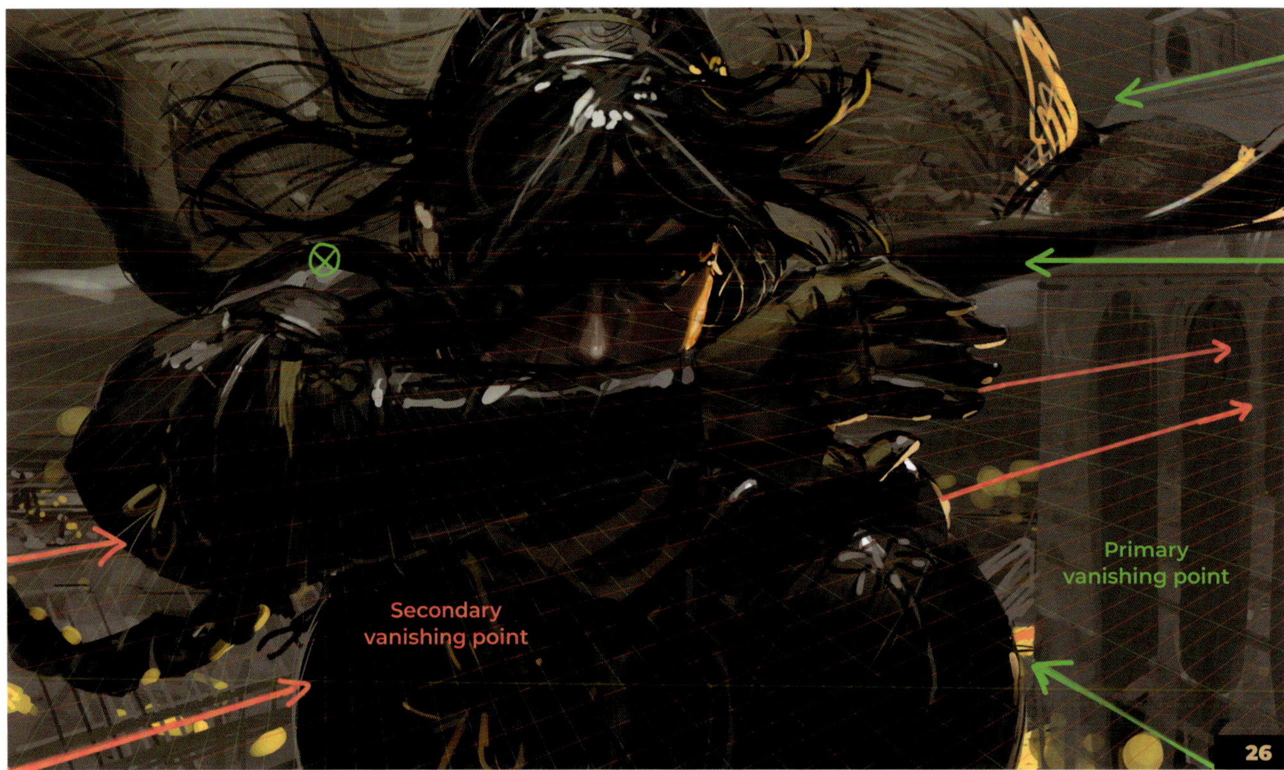

26 The use of two separate orientations for the background buildings, with the primary building being aligned with the character.

26 PERSPECTIVE IN THE ENVIRONMENT

Despite these structures playing a largely supporting role, a cohesive composition requires all of its parts to be drawn with proper accuracy. Any mistake at the fundamental level can become a weak link in the chain.

To make sure these structures are also drawn to proper perspective, you must first consider how they should be aligned. Taking the primary building as reference, consider drawing it parallel to the character's movement in perspective. To do so, simply borrow the previously used one-point perspective grid (indicated in green). Grouping the main elements in the same perspective will help to ground them as elements existing together in the same world.

For the supporting buildings, you can choose to yaw them a little to break off from the main axis of depth. This adds more of a natural touch to the city's layout and keeps things from feeling too much like an artificial corridor. As these buildings are yawed to a different rotation, the vanishing point of their major edges simply slides along the horizon line towards the right and out of frame (indicated in red).

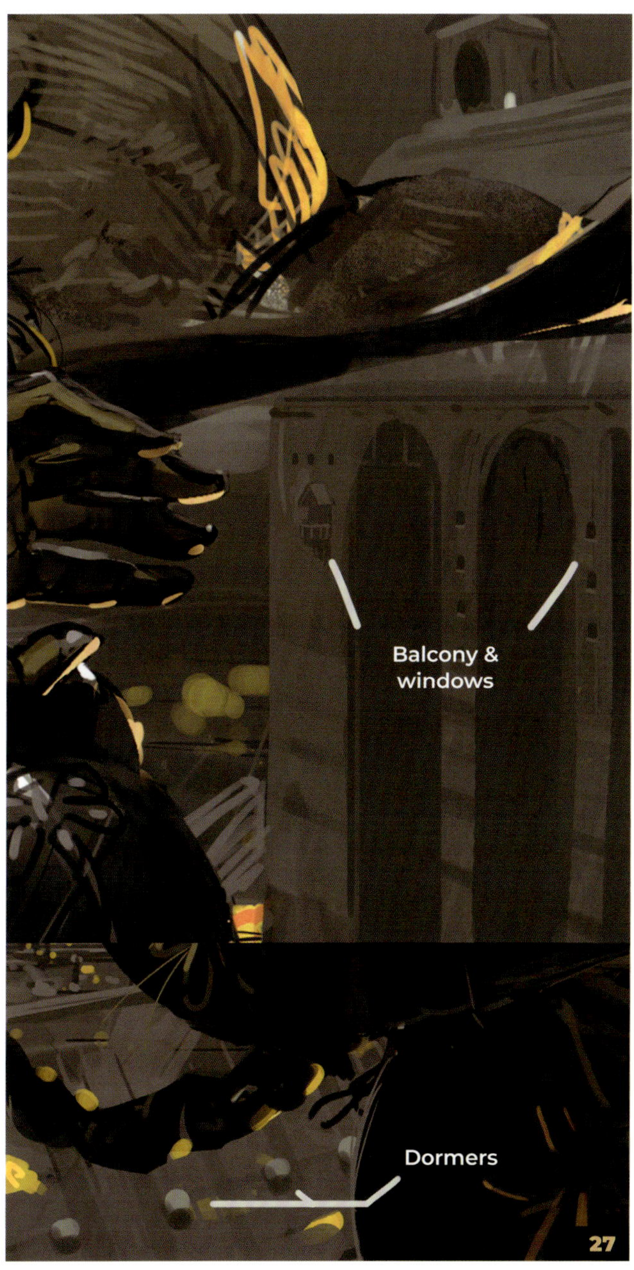

27 Simple windows, balconies, and dormers can provide a good read of scale and perspective, even as placeholder elements. As they are gradually replaced, their scale can carry over to the new structures being added.

27 PHYSICAL SCALE

The physical scale of objects is an incredibly important factor and determines how various elements in a scene are perceived. It is especially relevant when it comes to drawing convincing buildings and settings. As you begin to fill in more details on these buildings, scale becomes increasingly relevant.

Within the bounds of each individual structure, the size of sub-elements, such as doors and windows, gives crucial information about their scale relative to a person. Based on that information, the viewer can determine what kind of building it might be and what purpose it might serve.

Elements that you can intuitively use to gauge physical scale are 'relatable', human-interactable things, such as doors, windows, and walkways. These elements also provide scale context for other, less immediately recognizable elements. For example, it's really difficult to tell how big a castle wall is until you see some windows, crenellations, or arrow slits.

Getting the physical sizes of the key background structures right is critical, as you need an accurate read and assessment of the existing configuration before you can further work on these elements.

CAPTURING AUTHENTICITY

Details are a wonderful part of illustration. They provide so much space and potential for both stylization and immersiveness. However, it can be difficult to know where exactly to start with the detailing process.

Real-world references are always a great place to begin. They come fully detailed, functional, and often very visually appealing in myriad ways. The main challenge is almost always in efficiently adapting and conveying the appeal of real-world objects into stylized, contextual versions that work for each composition. This process forces you to observe closely and think hard about which pieces of visual information make up the core of each object you want to capture. Similar to how you approached many earlier phases, you'll want to start large and then cascade down towards the finer elements.

Here's one of my favourite examples of a scene breakdown **(A)**. Hong Kong has some of the most visually iconic urban residential architecture in the world, but it can seem incredibly daunting to approach given the sheer visual density.

To ease yourself into the process, take a look at related themes to this illustration. Based on your needs here, the two main things you can look into are period architecture and armour design. Specifically, you can zoom in on the very ornate and visually appealing design of Gothic cathedrals and period plate armour.

However, you can't quite use these designs exactly as they are. Each and every composition has its own unique needs, and being able to observe and extract what makes each element iconic and expressive is the real key.

Characters offer another dimension of challenge, as complex poses can hide or exaggerate parts of the design, often unintentionally. For example, while the design of a Gothic cuirass can be really interesting, this specific pose and lighting situation focuses on the pauldrons, bracers, and gauntlet instead. In turn, these designs may also be seen from uncommon angles or perspectives that foreshorten or obscure their iconic motifs.

To draw a Gothic-themed cathedral, begin by breaking down its silhouette and finding the most prominent repeating pattern. You can then expand from there into smaller elements, such as the gables, spires, and flying buttresses **(B)**.

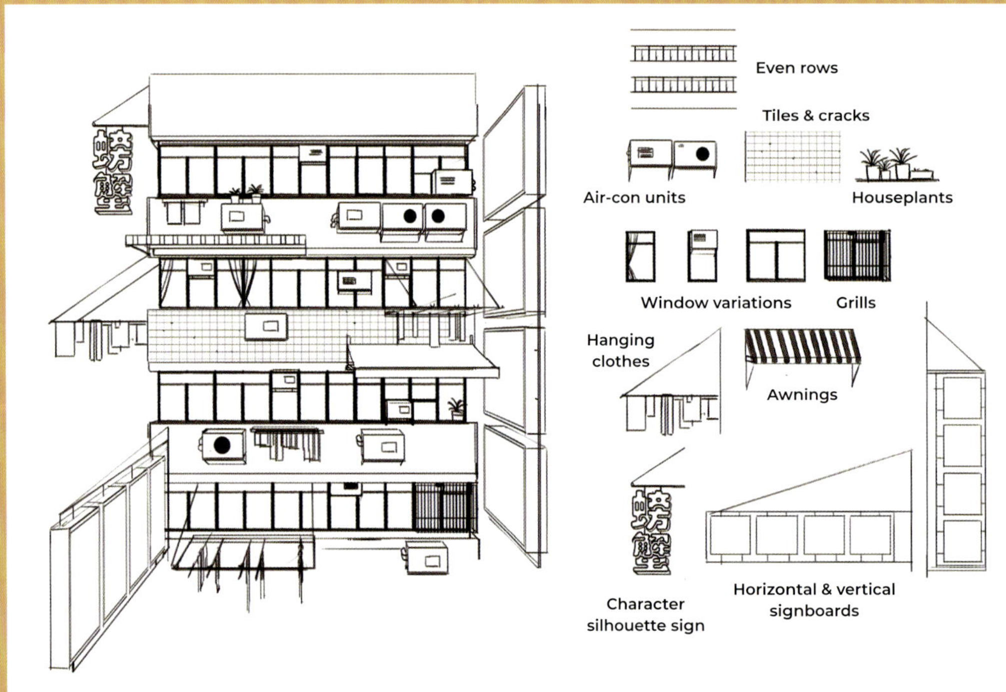

A. A simplified representation of a common apartment facade in Kowloon, Hong Kong, broken down into its iconic visual components.

Gothic armour design emphasizes a lot of parallel curves that form large, sweeping patterns across the otherwise smooth plate armour (C). More ornate variations tend to introduce similar patterns on a smaller scale as fine detailing, filling in previously empty space. With this knowledge, you can flexibly apply the design motif to your own illustration, applying it specifically to areas of visual focus. While it may not be fully authentic, doing so will add a significant degree of believability to your own variation!

Lastly, you can introduce minor details – scratches, dents, and even weather effects – as a final level of detail.

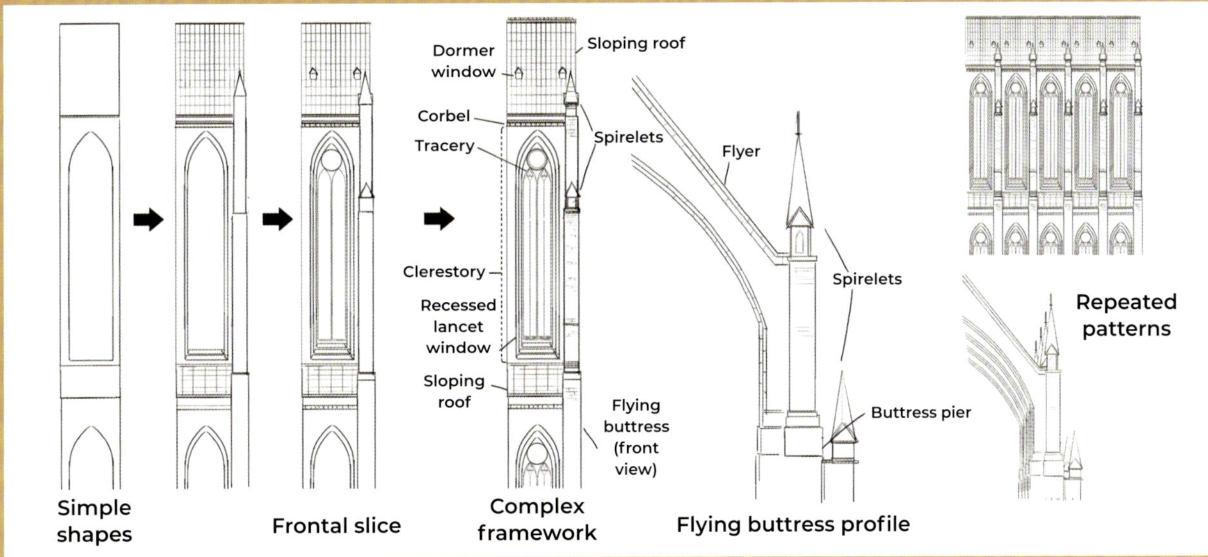

B. By capturing the likeness of the cathedral from the largest shapes, you can gradually progress up the level of detail, making use of its repeating visual properties.

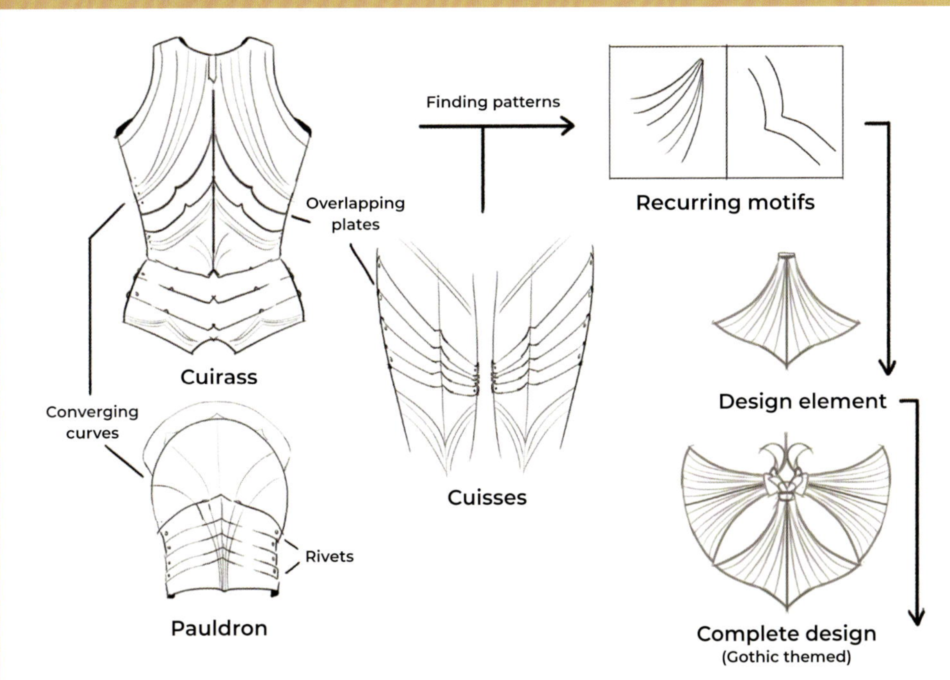

C. You can design and derive a stylized emblem by observing the main visual trends in Gothic armour design; this emblem will be used in the character's armour later on.

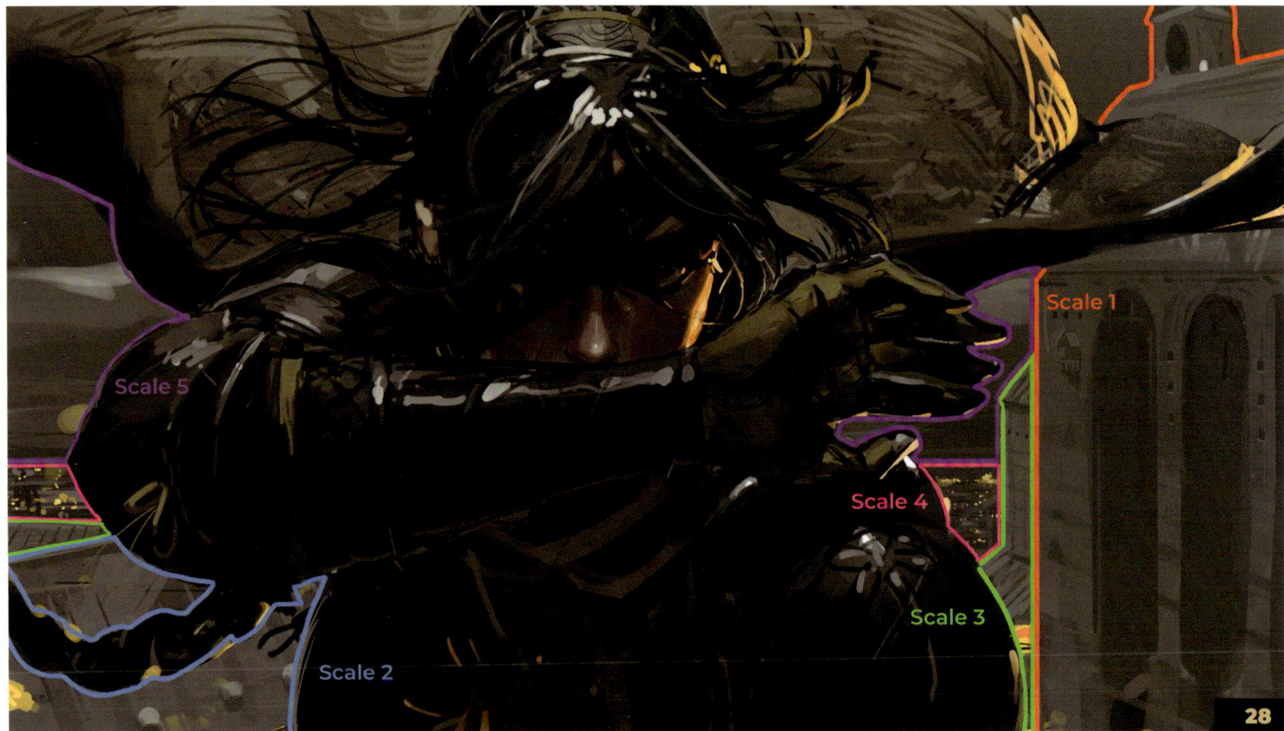

28 You can separate the receding visual scale into five segments. By ensuring that elements such as windows within each segment are distinct to their scale group, you can eliminate any potential discrepancies in physical scale.

28 VISUAL SCALE & DEPTH

The relative sizes at which elements appear on canvas are not only determined by their physical characteristics, as just discussed, but also by perspective. Visual size is the core principle behind perspective: as things recede into the distance, they get smaller visually, eventually 'vanishing' at the vanishing point.

The differences between the sizes of various elements provide critical information on their respective distances from the viewer's POV. But how can you tell whether a pixel's difference between two comparable elements on canvas is due to physical properties or perspective distortion?

In other words, you have to be clear whether building 2 is physically a lot smaller than building 1, or if it's just further away. To answer that question, your eye looks for common elements between different objects in the 3D space. You can avoid confusion by making sure there are comparable elements on both relevant buildings – for example, by ensuring windows of the same physical dimensions are visible on each structure.

To add another layer of perspective cues, an even-patterned spread of these common elements can be placed throughout each building, essentially tracing out a subtle perspective grid.

ELEMENTS OF UNUSUAL SCALE

If you want to introduce unusually large or small objects to draw attention within a piece, it's important to provide relevant context cues to make the distinction clear. A good way to do this effectively is to keep the 'wrongly scaled' objects in the minority, with the bigger part of the scene being to scale and in perspective.

For example, if you want to show that something Godzilla-sized is running amok in the city, it's important to make sure that it's the only entity with this extreme scale. Any mistakes relevant to scale can easily disrupt this illusion. For example, if a person in the foreground isn't drawn to perspective and is left unintentionally large, the viewer might assume they are Godzilla-sized too!

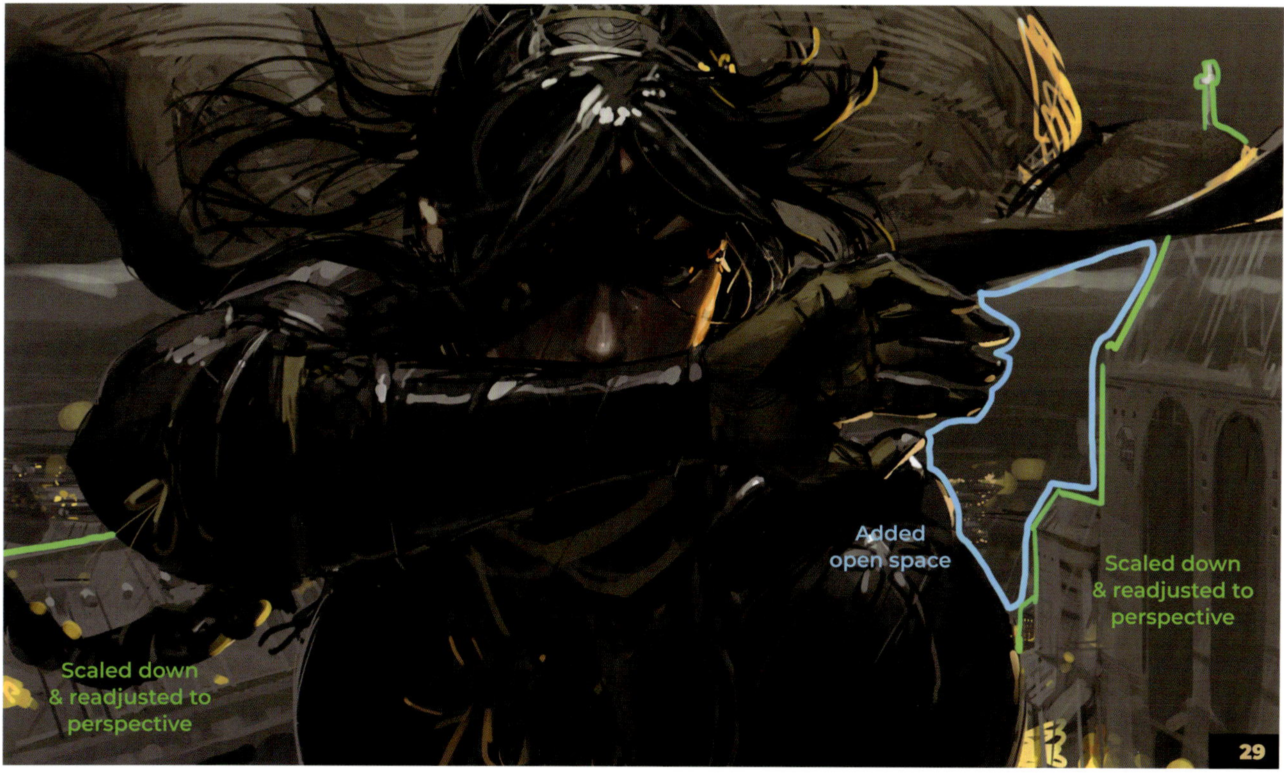

29 Using the Transform > Distort tool, I can 'pull' the existing structure into the new perspective. The increased negative space also allows the area more room to breathe.

29 FLEXIBLE PROCESS

Accurate perspective and depth management are foundational parts of the painting process that you cannot afford to skip over. However, this doesn't mean you need to be completely mono-directional when it comes to your workflow.

As you paint, you'll sometimes chance upon a new design or arrangement that you like and wish to develop further. For example, after some trial and error, I find a new arrangement of the existing buildings that results in a more visually appealing and balanced composition. Rather than erasing and starting from scratch, I first crudely move the existing elements into the desired position, and then iron out the change in perspective and scale after that. The handy one-point grid is an easy way to keep relevant edges in line and organized during this transition. Using this approach, I can make substantial, necessary alterations to the background composition without completely sacrificing my previous work.

Adaptability is increasingly relevant as you may find errors or necessary adjustments later in the painting process that can require significant changes. In an ideal world, you would get things right on the first try, but realistically, this is a handy solution when you inevitably find issues to fix!

30 REPEATING PATTERNS

As you saw during the drawing process of the character, repeating patterns are great for reinforcing perspective. They give viewers plenty of solid visual information to work out exactly what they are looking at, and from what angle and distance.

Authentic medieval architecture has plenty of iconic repeating motifs and patterns, which allow you to kill two birds with one stone by incorporating them here into the background structures.

Aside from ornate windows and carved reliefs, patterns aren't necessarily constrained to being textures wrapped around an existing form. The flying buttresses of the Gothic-style cathedral are also a way for repeating patterns to be applied. In this case, the added complexity in form also fits in well with the cathedral being a secondary focal point in the composition.

Simpler patterns also play a big part in filling in the gaps in detail. A row of parallel lines can be a great texture for visually lighter areas, such as rooftops, or act as a temporary 'in-perspective scaffold' for building more details upon later.

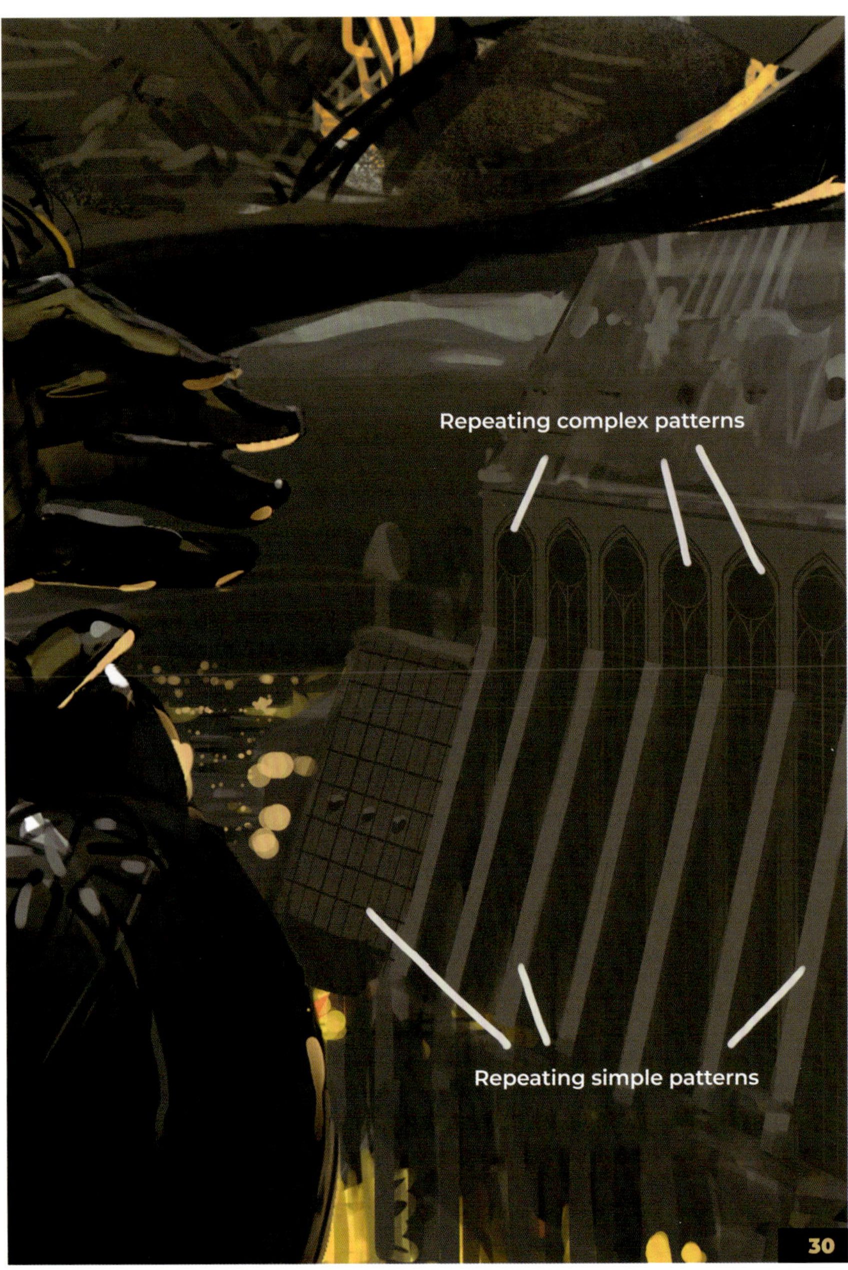

30 A mix of simple and complex patterns can help the building to be readable and interesting from both afar and up close.

INTENTIONAL IRREGULARITY

While aligning elements to a common grid is a great way to represent perspective, especially over a large space, allowing room for variation can add a more natural look. Here, different buildings across the city may take on different specific vanishing points along the horizon line, depending on their rotation and position. Vertically rotated surfaces may even have vanishing points on top or below the horizon line! The key is to keep enough elements to the main grid while allowing some minor elements to deviate.

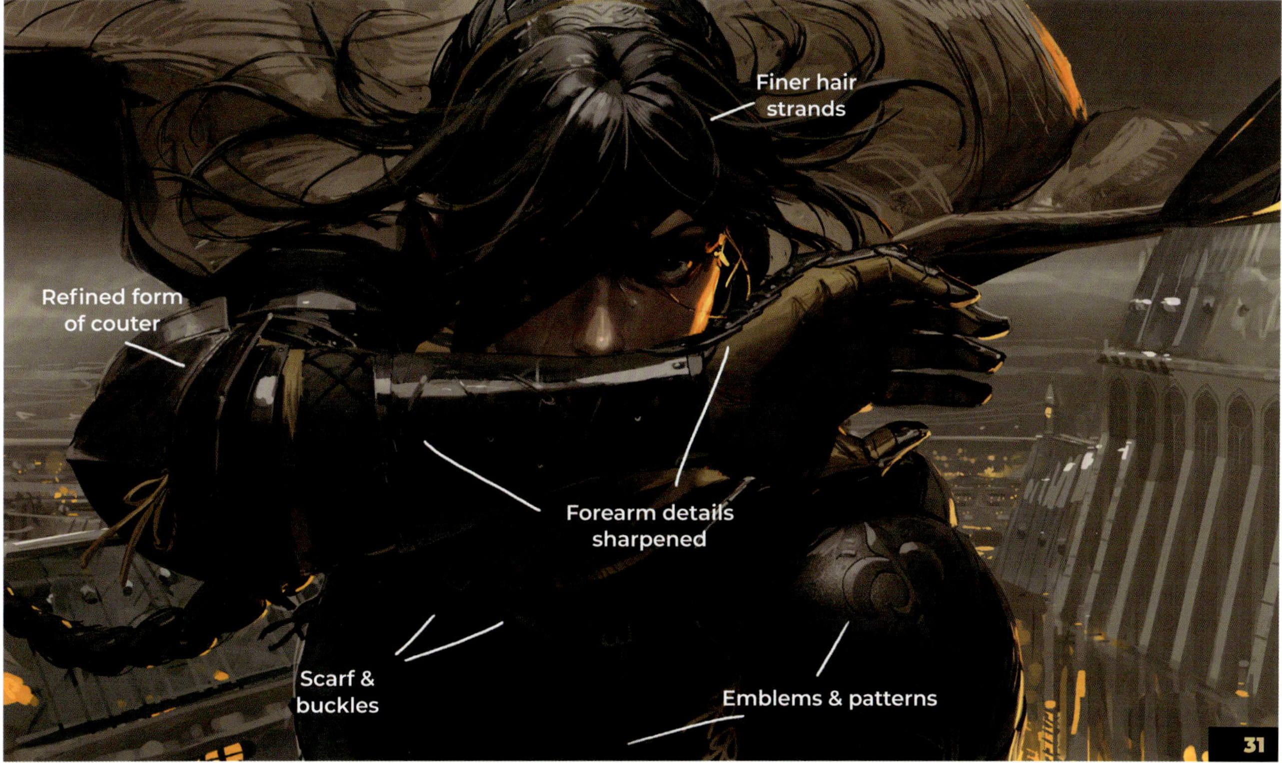

31 Many areas on the character are further developed, especially armour edges and details. This step can be referred to as 'cleaning up'.

31 DENSITY & BELIEVABILITY

As your composition takes form with details being filled in across the canvas, previously adequate areas can start to feel comparatively lacking or empty. This is because in terms of visual density and sharpness, those areas are starting to fall behind. This isn't an issue for distant regions of the setting, but may require remedying if it happens to key focal areas on the character.

As you are going for a more realistic visual style, you need to bring these areas of interest up to par. This process can be tedious and challenging in the sense that it requires you to fully re-examine much of your composition, going through it with a fine-toothed comb to redraw it precisely.

It's important to note that this refining process can draw on a variety of sources. Increased complexity of form, more texturing, and weather effects like rain or snow are all possible tools you can make use of to increase detail.

During this process, you can also experiment with different colour tones or brightnesses, to see which fits your vision the best.

Depending on the preferred visual style, some artists may opt to control and reduce excess details instead. The rule of thumb is that as long as the level of information density matches the importance of that region, the viewer generally won't find it jarring.

32 CONSISTENCY & HARMONY

As you continue to develop the composition organically, muscle memory can slightly push your illustration away from the original perspective plan. This is where the foundation drawing you set up thus far really shines, allowing new details you add to 'ride along' the existing forms with full confidence.

You need to make sure your original lighting plan stands the test of time and change too. While the existing value set-up may have been more than enough for an earlier stage of the process, you can improve it to more precisely reflect your intention. For example, toning down some excessively bright highlights to reflect the overcast sky more accurately, and adjusting the local values of certain materials to better match.

When these factors are adjusted, the sense of depth can be unintentionally impacted as well, blending unwanted elements together, while possibly excessively separating others. This is something important to pay attention to, especially if the changes are overarching and substantial.

For example, if you've replaced a previously simple element with a more complex one, such as adding protrusions to the armour, you'll need to account clearly for how this new form appears in the same lighting set-up.

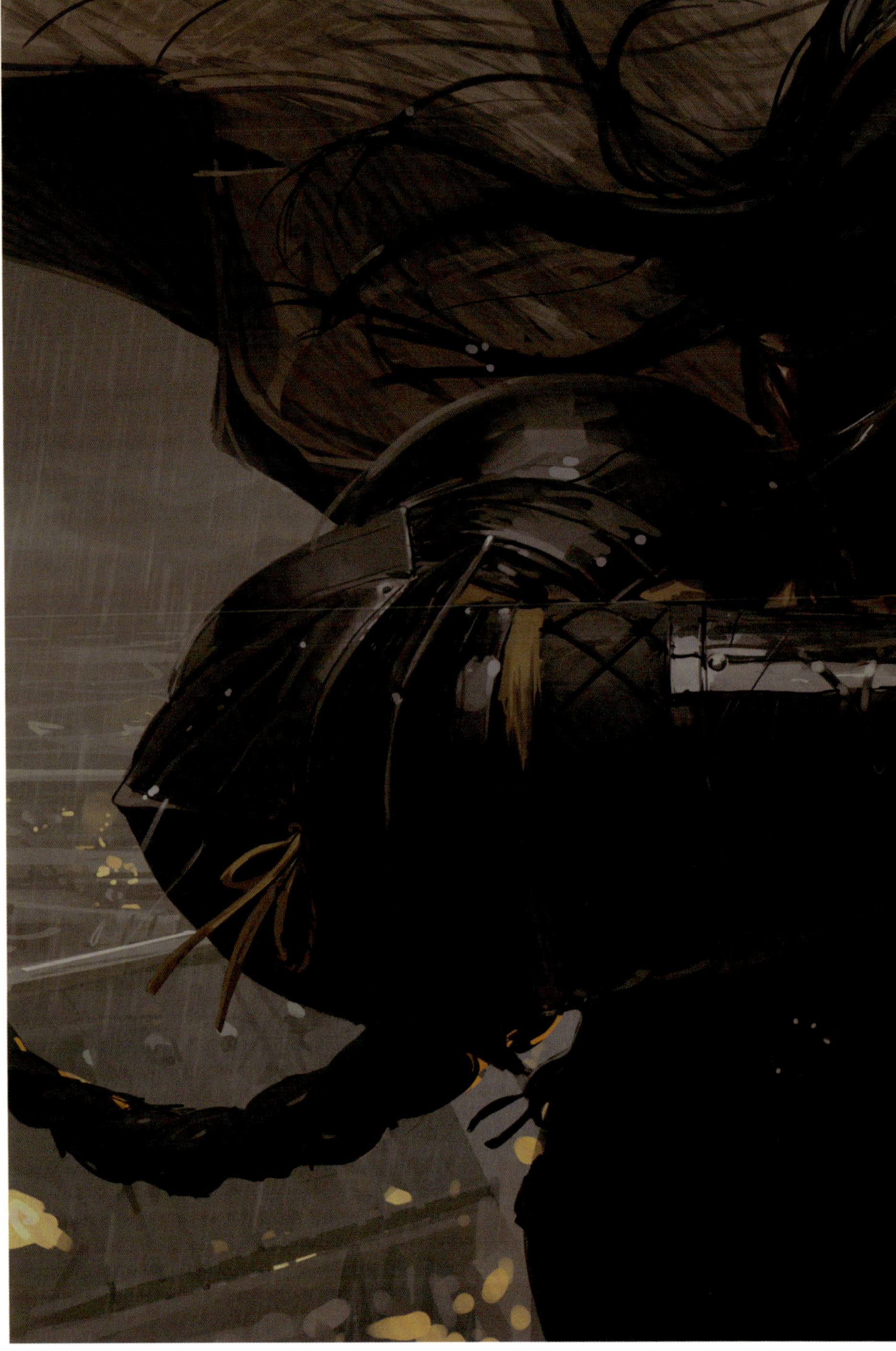

32 Continued revision to the composition including a modified, more angled pose, along with the softening of lighting and rain effects in the background.

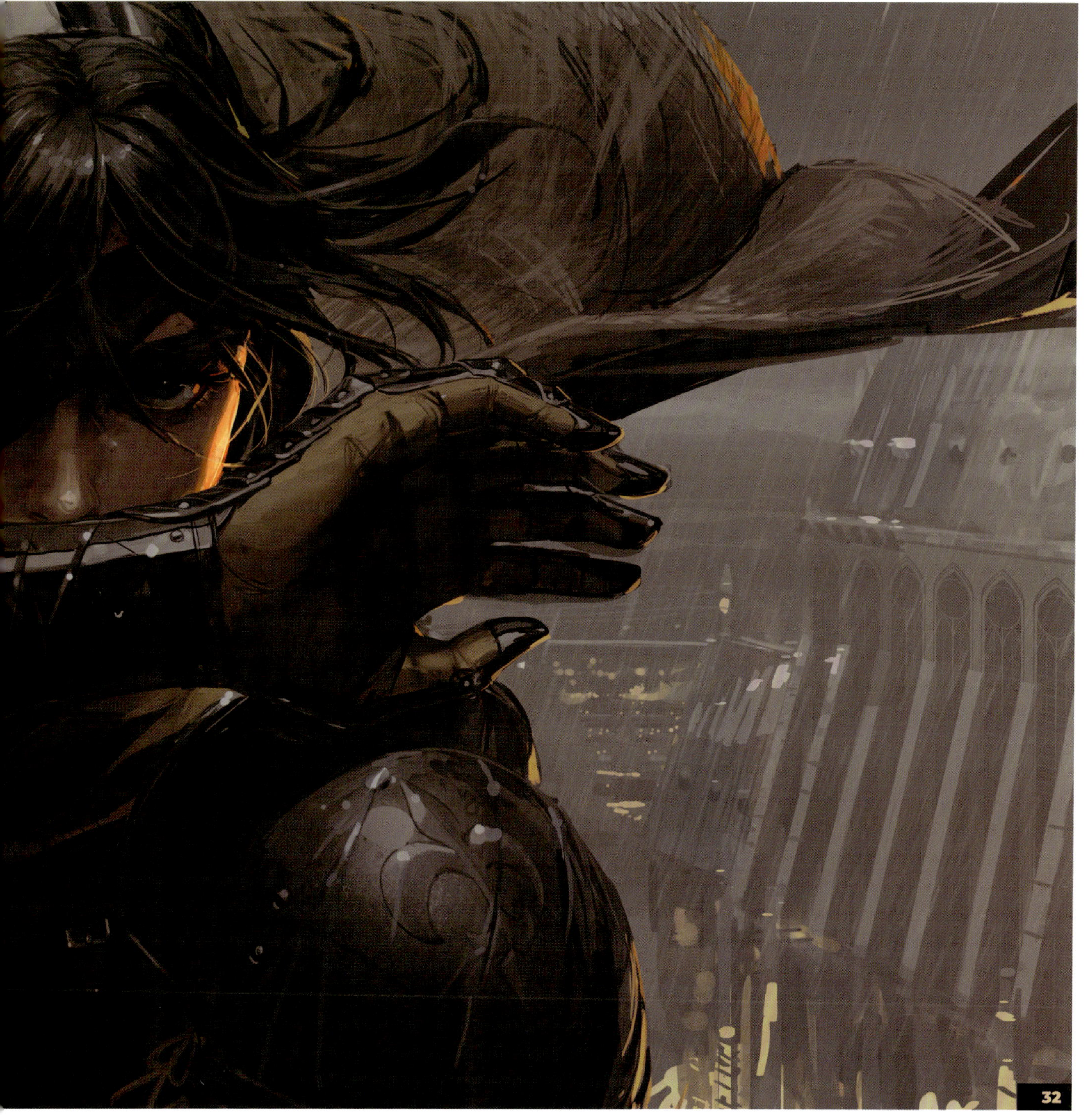

32

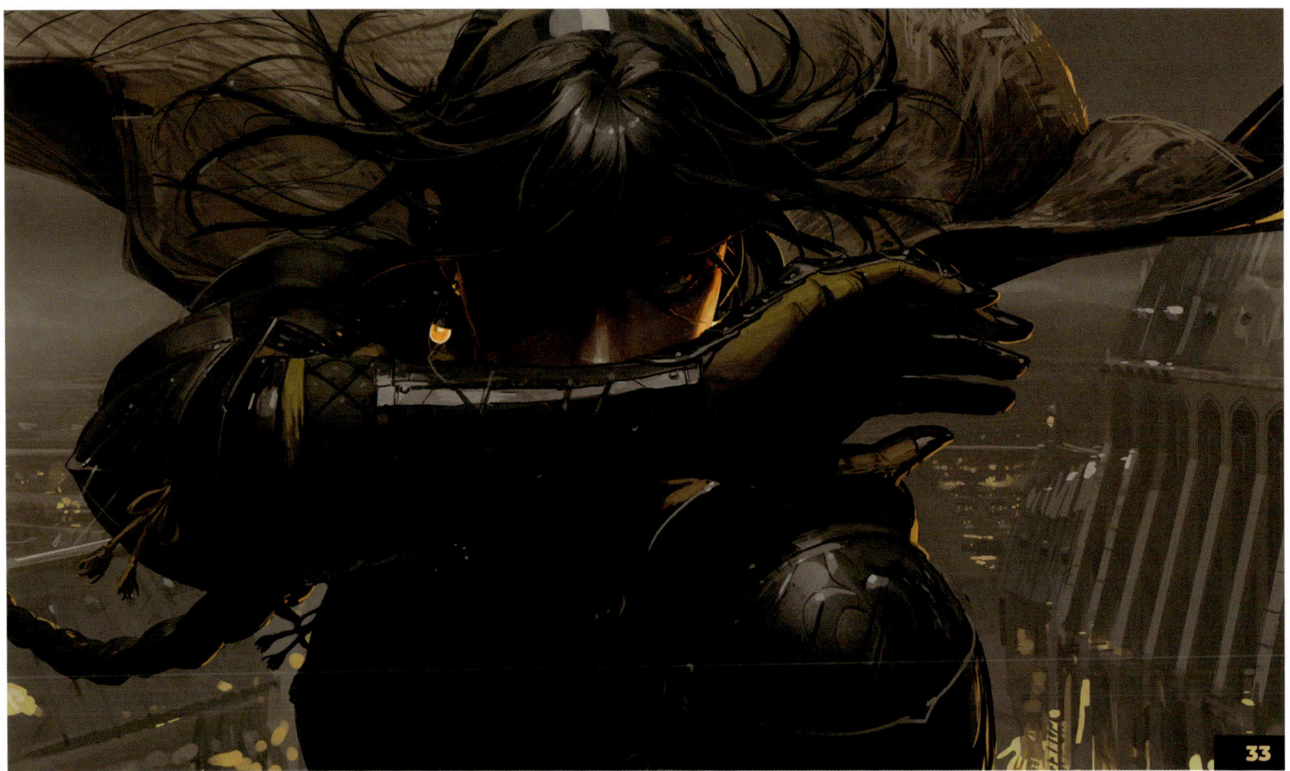

33 The head and hand of the character are adjusted for perspective, while the torso and forward shoulder are rotated to create a stronger forward/backward relationship and sense of depth.

33 CHARACTER REFINEMENT

Scale is a key indicator of perspective and depth in an environment, but the same very much applies to the character as well. As you smooth out rough areas of the character, 'uncertainty' in the form of vague lines is cleaned out, and hidden scale mistakes may be unveiled.

This is also a great time to refer to the diagrams on pages 226–227. This will help you to find certain discrepancies in your illustration. For example, the head and hand of my character are visually too small relative to the forward shoulder, leading to a visual read of the shoulder protruding too far forward in perspective, contradicting the pose diagram. This also meant the depth of the pose was thrown off and didn't make physical sense. By visually enlarging the head and hand, I can push these forms forward and closer to the correct POV, which is in line with the originally intended pose.

Furthermore, the diagrams also help me to adjust other parts of the character, including some proportion problems in the cuirass, as well as perspective and pose problems in the forward shoulder.

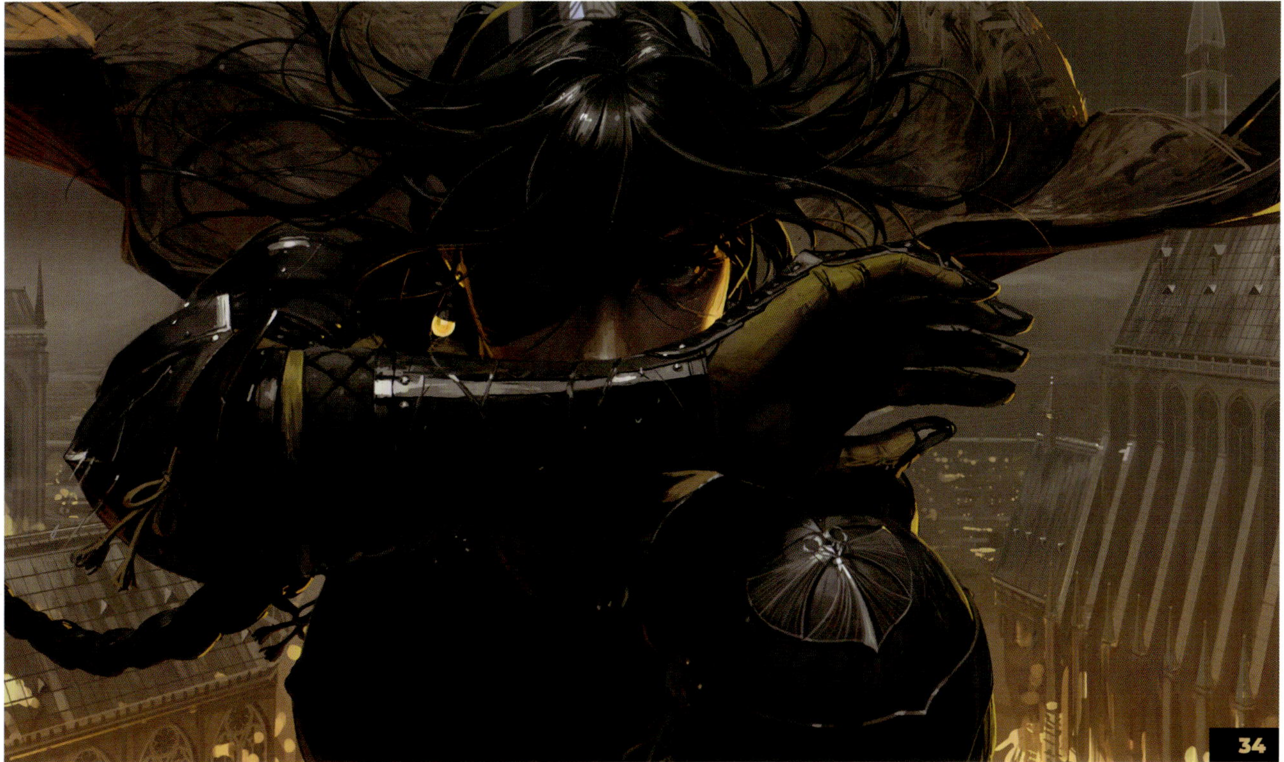

34 Addition of sharper highlights, along with the filling-in of ambient lighting and added character detail, brings the illustration to a higher resolution.

34 MORE CHARACTER REFINEMENT

After taking the drawing to the next stage of accuracy, you can confidently begin re-introducing areas of highlight, or strong reflection of light on the character. While these highlights can be deceptively small, they convey a lot of information on the underlying shape and form. Additionally, they are also a strong cue for perspective, based on how exactly the light is reflected off the wet surfaces in this POV. Looking at a mirror at different perspectives will produce very different reflected images.

Highlights also extend the full range of your value scheme, upping the contrast of the piece in a controlled, subtle manner.

You can also turn your attention to higher-resolution details, such as revisiting the motif planned for the forward pauldron. Instead of having a simpler bevelled insignia, you can 'upgrade' this to a motif that incorporates more physical volume and pattern. Recall the emblem designed on page 237.

The repeated pattern of the lines adds not only a stronger visual density, but also allows the emblem to be properly wrapped around the top of the pauldron in perspective. By leaving a gap between the emblem and the surface below, it can also add a physical sense of space and depth between the two elements.

The dark space on the character's right eye area unfortunately merges with the dark hair to create an unintended negative space. To resolve this, you can add a visually distinct element, such as a gold insignia, to fill in the blank space.

35 REFINING THE ENVIRONMENT

Turn your attention towards the background – similar to the polishing pass you did for the character, the same principles apply to the environmental elements as well.

While you clear out rough areas of the draft and paint in detail, it's key to maintain your attention on the perspective in which each detail is drawn. Fortunately, simple patterns such as the roof tiles are able to act as a subtle perspective grid, making it much easier to work on surrounding details and forms. They also provide an organized medium to introduce wear and tear in perspective. In addition, you can use them to introduce a degree of natural non-uniformity and realism by creating a slightly uneven reflection across the tiles.

Alongside smaller details and polish, you can also think about ways to improve the interaction between the background and character. To supplement and provide a source for the warm tones on the character, you can introduce a gentle overarching source of warm light from below. This addition not only introduces a wider range of hue shift from ground to sky, but also from near to far, which doubles up as a strong depth cue in both directions.

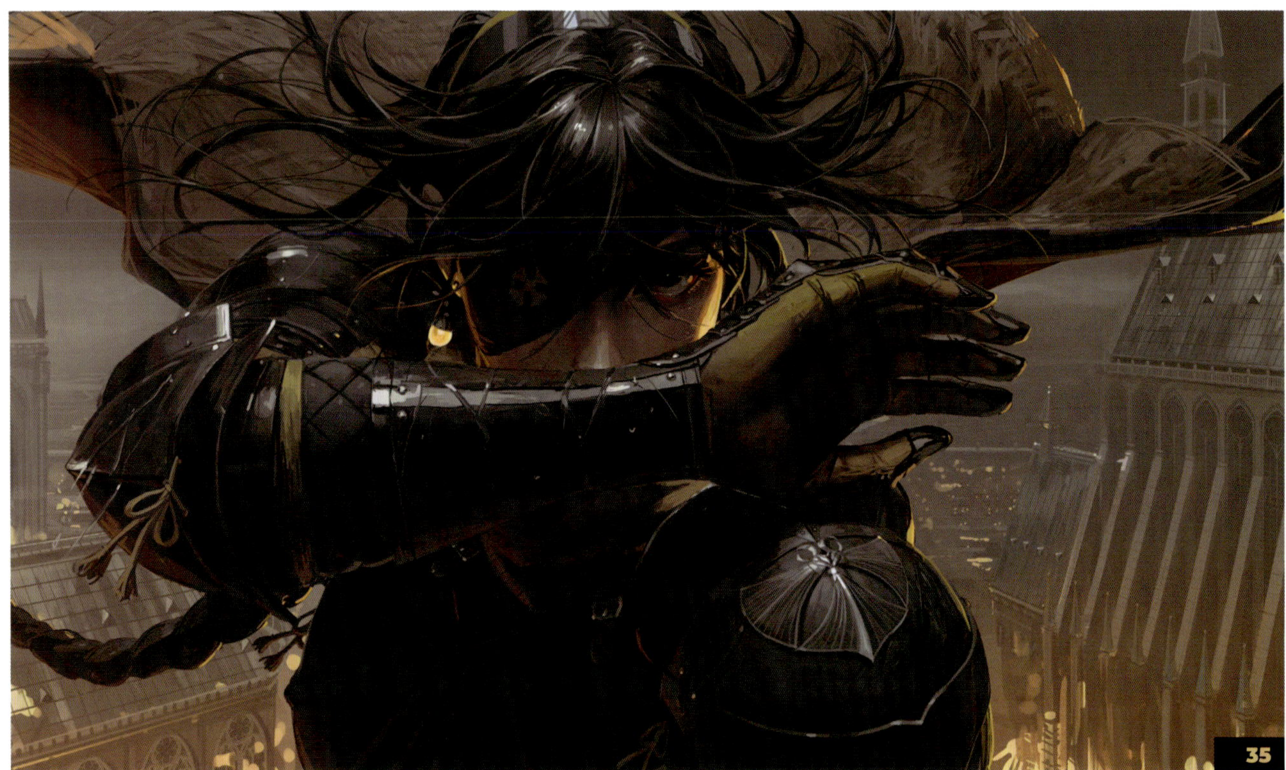

35 Completing the details of the main cathedral and secondary building with the addition of an extra architectural element in the distance. The introduction of a general warm ambience from below supports accent lighting on the character.

36 FOG & ATMOSPHERIC EFFECTS

Fog or other atmosphere-revealing effects are flexible sources of visual separation and depth indication that can be used to adjust the composition based on your needs. Finding ways to indicate space between overlapping elements can often be challenging, especially in relatively sparse scenes such as this one. Physically speaking, there just aren't enough additional structures or forms that you can slot in between them.

A combination of air and light in the form of fog can be a perfect stand-in for these situations. By using a soft brush, we can separate out distinct elements that require a bit more space between each other, introducing a highly customizable amount of depth. However, you should keep in mind that too strong an effect can be counterproductive as well.

Besides being helpful as a localized remedy for excessively blended forms, fog can also be a great tool to add depth on its own. The translucent nature of fog can be a subtle but precise indicator of distance and depth, with areas further from the viewer being more opaque, while leaving nearby elements relatively clear.

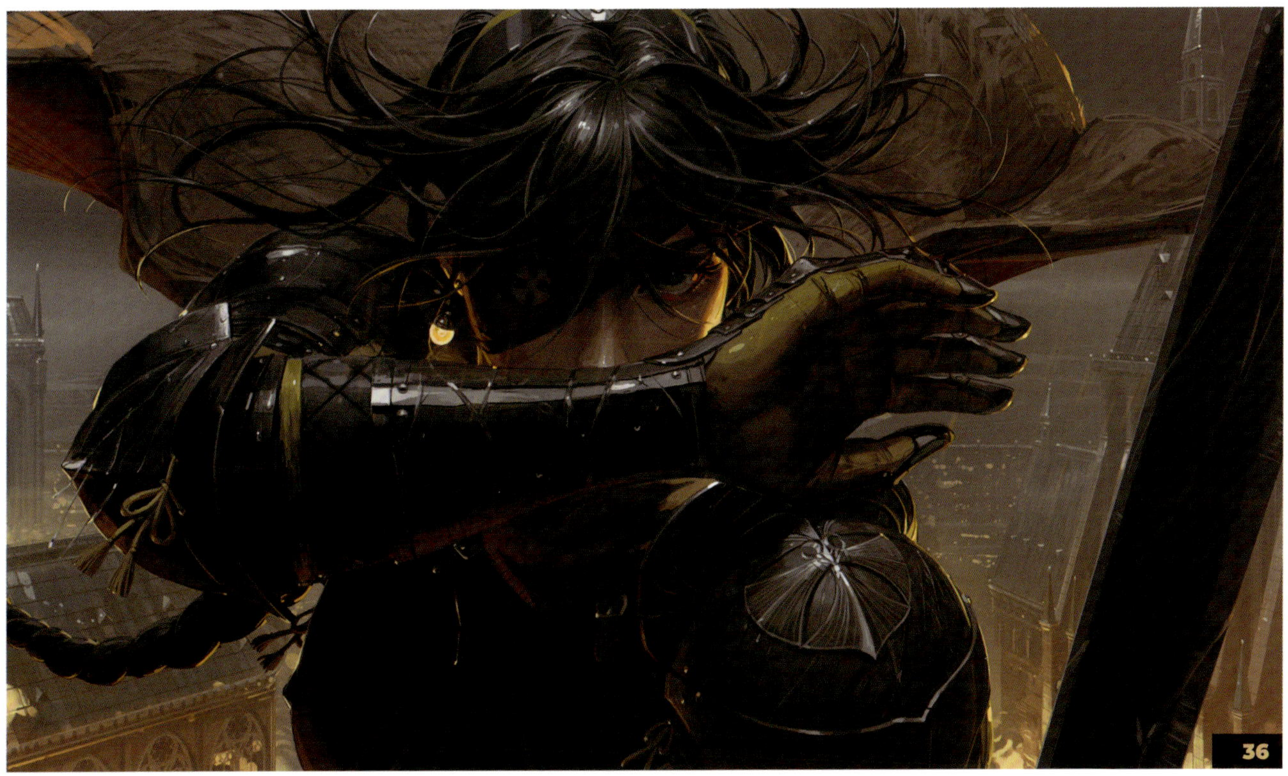

36 Lifting the values of the background beyond the main cathedral with a fog to add visual depth. Warmly lit fog on the left side adds more space between the secondary building and distant tower.

TEXTURE & MATERIAL

Texture and material often inadvertently fall into the 'afterthought' or even optional category of items to work on, especially due to their seemingly small visual presence on canvas. It can be tempting to think of them as decals that you stick on to an already finished product, rather than visually critical parts of the composition that reveal information about the forms beneath. This information can range from physical characteristics of the subject, such as lighting and contour, all the way to visual perspective and perceived depth. For this showcase, let's take a closer look at the current illustration.

The rain in the setting adds a wet sheen to many surfaces on the character, increasing how much light they directly reflect in this POV (A). This added material property is especially helpful when drawing foreshortened areas of the character, such as her right arm. With a more light-diffusing or 'clay-like' material, contoured forms such as her right pauldron may be more easily blended with the rest of the upper arm, as the material reflects light evenly around itself. While this type of material excellently facilitates the formation of visual shapes around lighting and shadow, it isn't ideal to use here, as the foreshortened arm requires more definition beyond what the downcast lighting can provide.

The 'shinier' material, however, allows you to indicate changes in contour and perspective much better. It's just like how the reflective surface in a mirror tends to be very sensitive to change as we move around it, while a piece of white paper looks very much the same from multiple angles.

The raindrops flowing off the armour are an additional aspect of 'texture' to consider. Their irregular nature can work to your benefit, breaking up the highly patterned and straight-edged armour visually. The shape and path of the drops also lends additional clues to the motion, perspective, and foreshortening of the subject.

Next, take a look at cracks and scratches on the armour (B). While you might tend to sketch these in as single lines, you can develop them further by giving these imperfections actual form. For smaller scratches, combine a dark and bright line to respectively indicate the indented and newly exposed

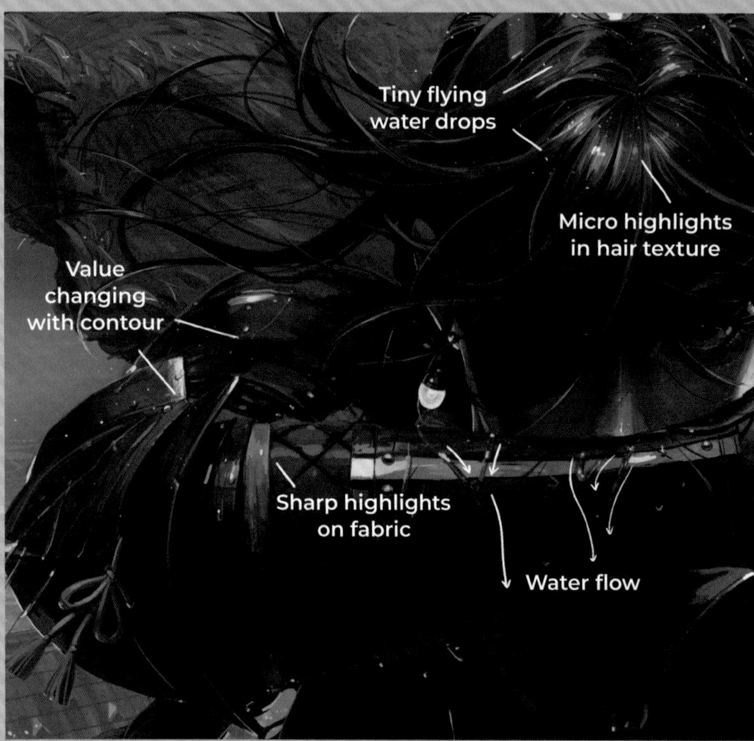

A. Like in real life, the path of water drops usually merge, but not diverge. This is a subtle characteristic that you can use to make your effect more convincing.

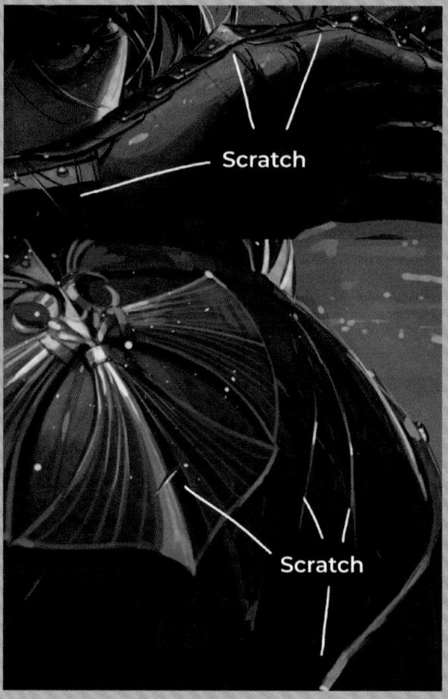

B. Cracks and scratches layered on top of existing detail can introduce a deeper complexity to the forms and also add a narrative aspect to the composition.

edges. For larger cuts, the same effect applies, except you can add further chips to these new edges to create a more natural, weathered look. It's also important to contour this texture around a curved form, or foreshorten them in perspective.

Lastly, for textures that are far away in the scene, such as the wet stone and roof tiles, you can afford to be slightly less precise and use fewer brushstrokes (C). However, you do need to make accurate use of the few brushstrokes you use. The size, value, and colour of each indicates substantial form and structure in these elements. For example, the strong reflection of light implies a reflective (and hence wet) surface, while a smattering of small pinpricks of highlights represent the complexity and details on them.

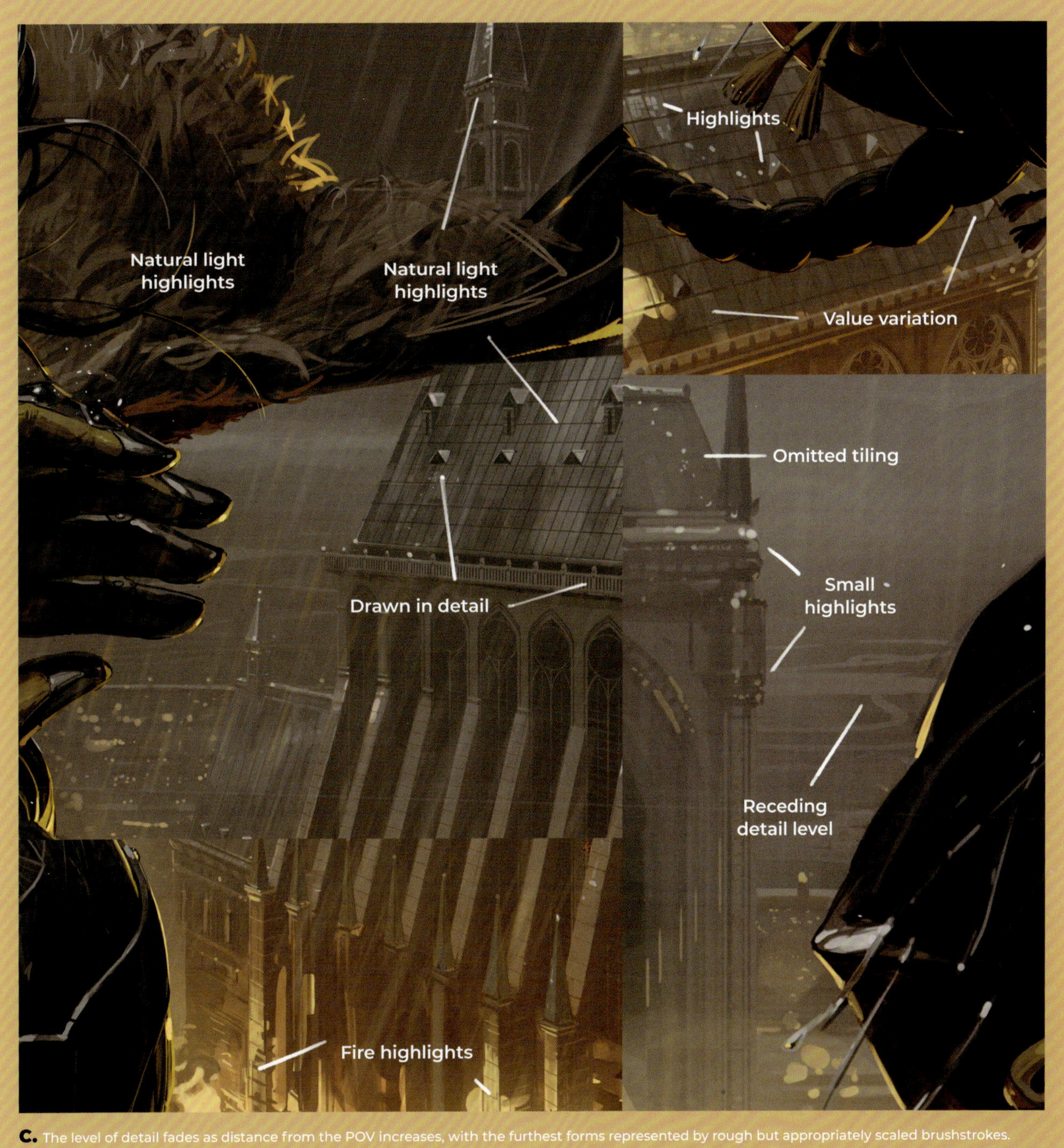

C. The level of detail fades as distance from the POV increases, with the furthest forms represented by rough but appropriately scaled brushstrokes.

37 RAIN EFFECTS

Rain effects also play a role similar to fog – they fill in empty space with a visible element, which can introduce depth into a sparse scene. Rain also adds a substantial amount of visual noise that can serve as extra detail, but can also disrupt the composition unintentionally. This can be managed by toning the effect carefully, or erasing areas of rain strategically to ensure focal areas do not get overridden.

The way rain falls in a largely parallel motion makes it a great source for perspective reinforcement. By aligning this directional movement to the appropriate perspective, you can visually make the rain fall towards the character along the direction of the wind.

Another important distinction is that rain isn't nearly as fuss-free as fog. By adding rain, you are committing also to visualizing its effects on various elements in the piece. For example, you have to add a wet effect to the armour, hair, and surroundings to make the rain effect convincing. However, this effort is not without reward, as it adds an additional layer of believability to your subject.

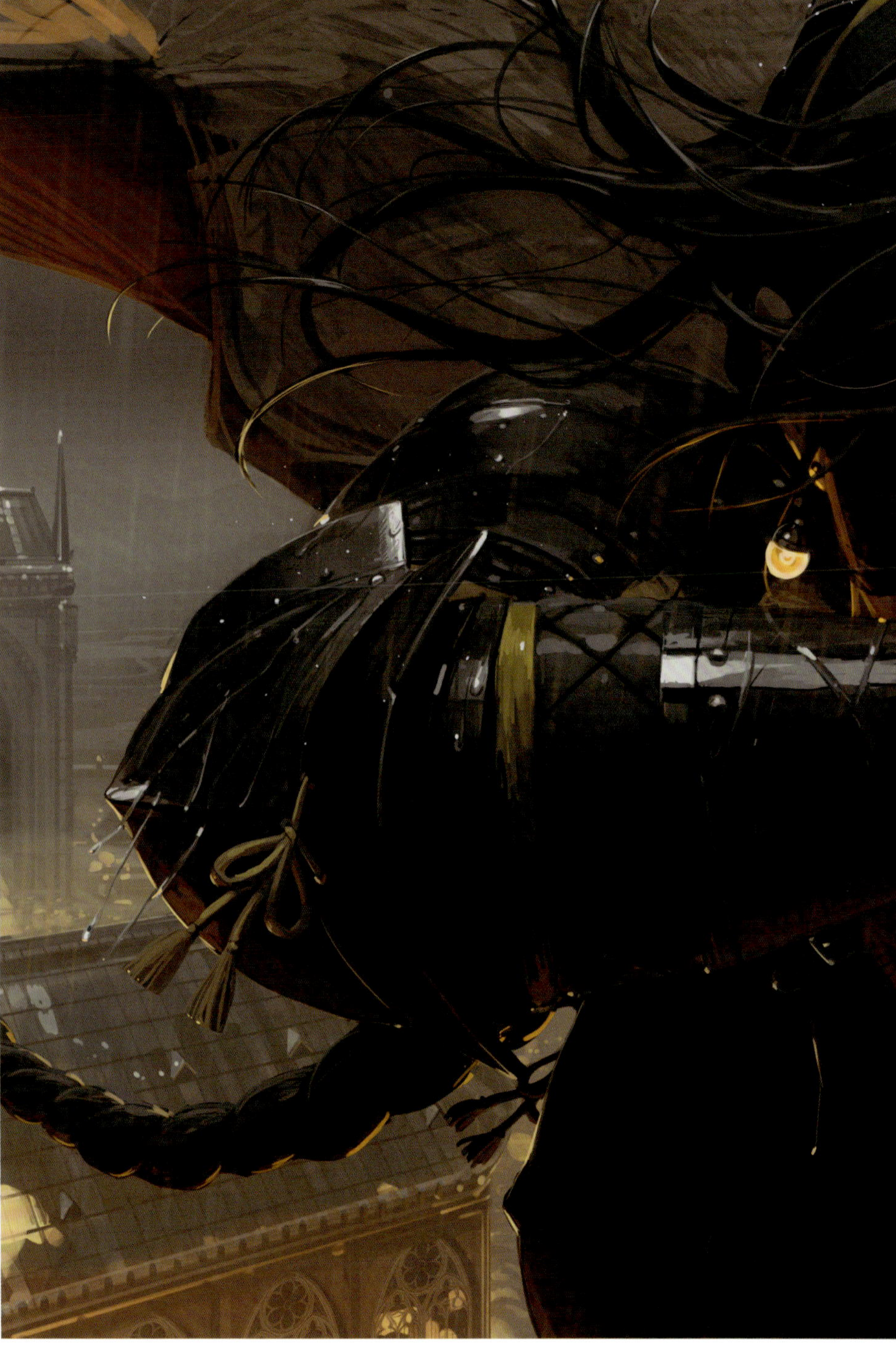

37 The rain effect is created by applying Motion Blur to a field of particles. Repeating this with smaller particles and less blur further from the POV creates a layered depth effect.

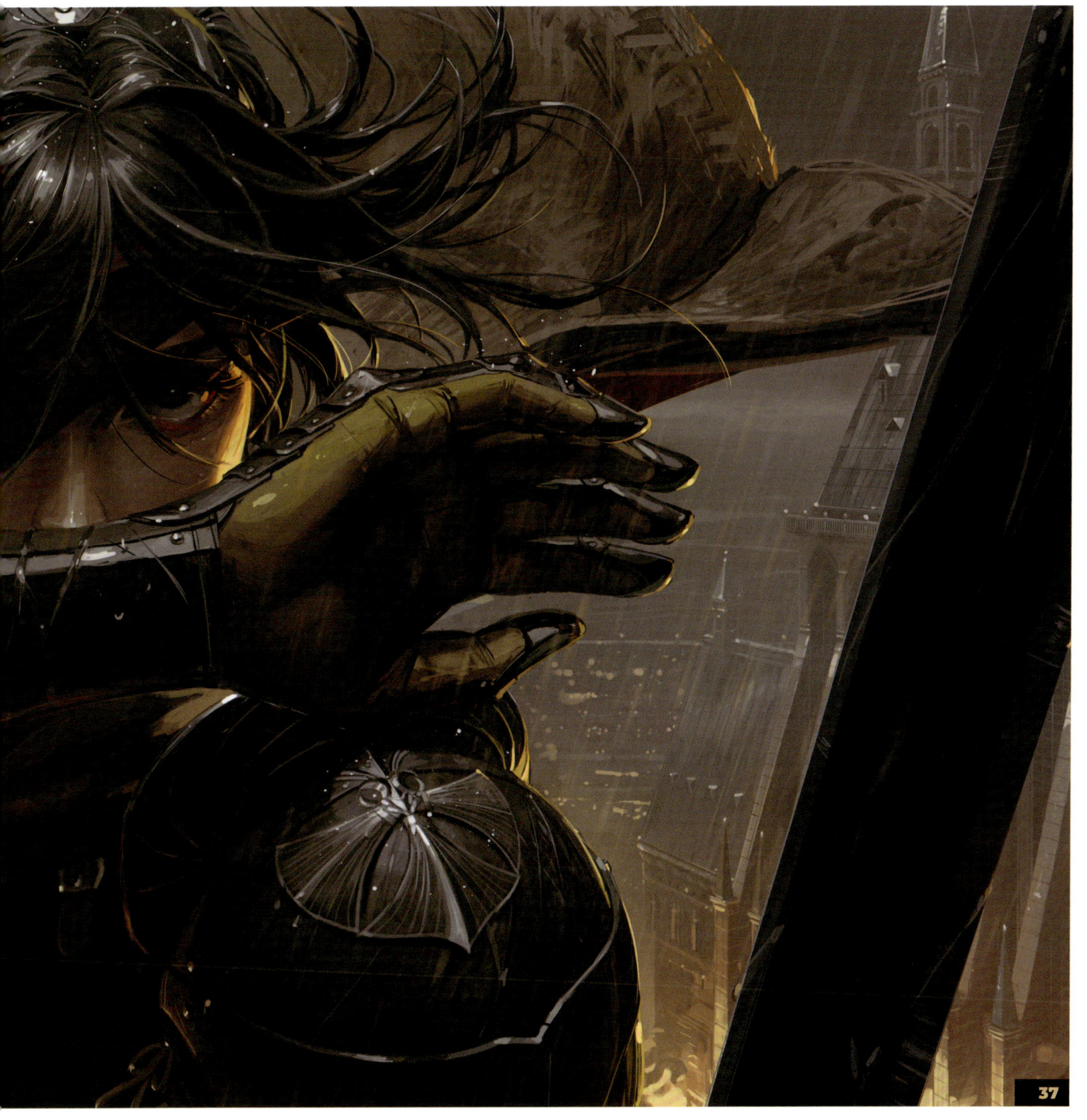
37

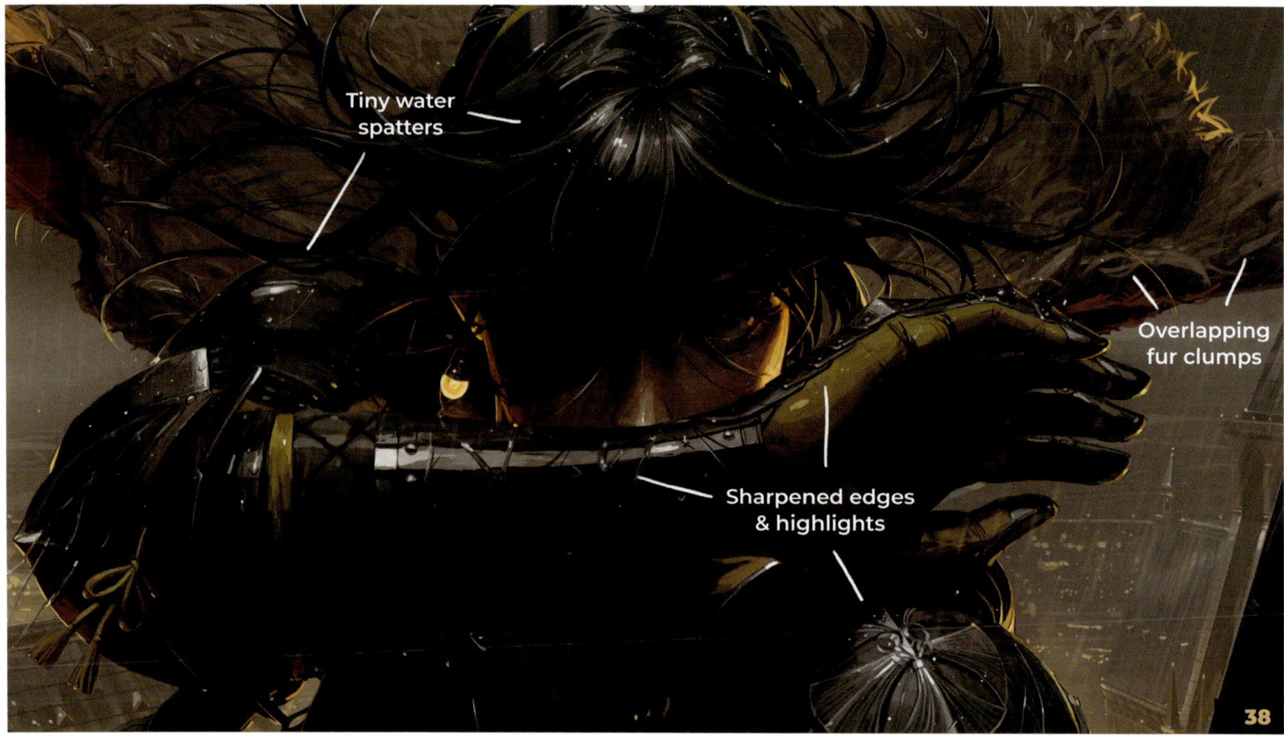

38 The core areas of visual focus near the face all receive another detail pass, adding tiny, pixel-sized highlights and shapes. The cape also receives an upgrade, both in material and depth presentation.

38 MICRO-LEVEL CHARACTER DETAILS

In this last stage, you can start introducing some micro-level textures and details to the piece to fully bring it to completion. These new additions may be small on canvas, but are unique in their ability to raise the overall range of detail. But how much of this detail do you need to add? Rather than going up and down the entire character adding detail in every nook and cranny, you can opt to be a little more strategic with your efforts.

For example, instead of spending hours adding scratch marks to areas of the armour in shadow, painting a couple of scratches across highlights is much more efficient in creating a stronger visual presence. Similarly, a few sharp but tiny highlights on armour edges and areas where the rain hits can indicate the wetness of the material very efficiently. Lastly, the fine nature of the fabric and hair can be demonstrated mainly at the focal areas with just a few strands and pixel-wide highlights and crease lines.

On pages 248–249, you saw how textures can also serve as perspective cues, with overlaps and contoured details reflecting the forms underneath. The fur cape is the biggest beneficiary of this concept, with small overlapping clumps much more clearly indicating depth compared to the smooth version from earlier.

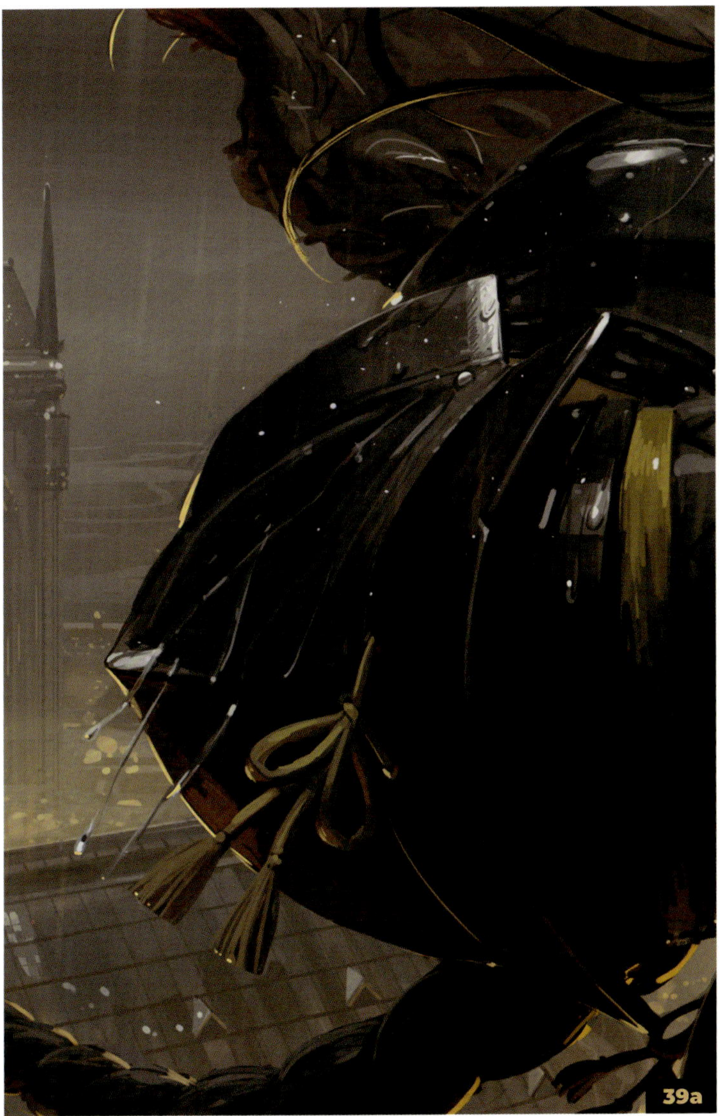

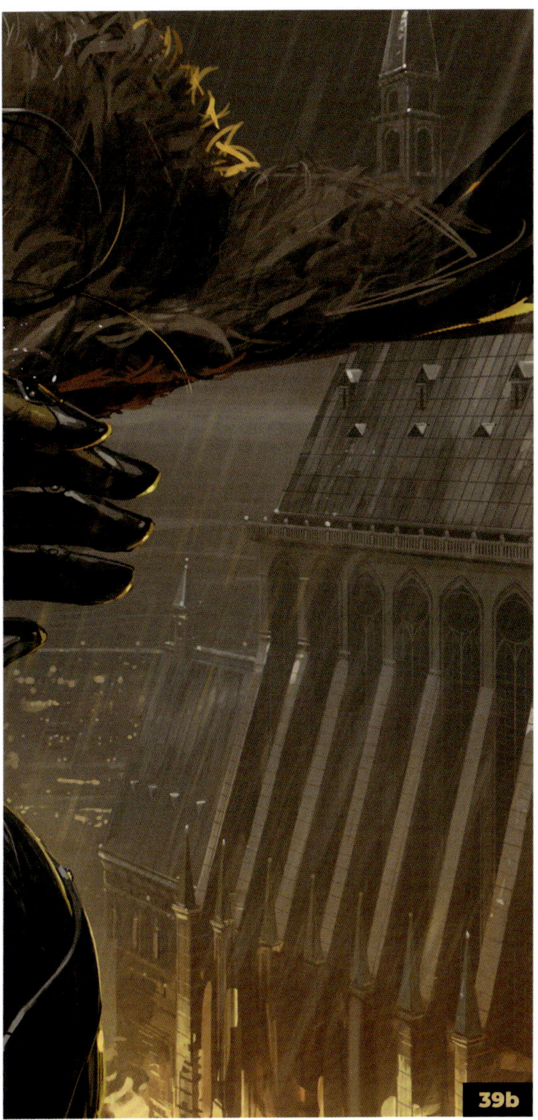

39a & 39b The bulk of the work here is to add small highlights from the wet surfaces to visibly indicate the architectural forms, and to balance their values in accordance with the depth of the scene.

39 MICRO-LEVEL ENVIRONMENT DETAILS

The environment and backdrop can also do with some micro-details. Much of this process is similar, adding small highlights and brushstrokes to indicate the complexity of form of the various buildings. As with before, there is no need to excessively draw in extreme detail, as long as the general visual impression of detail is achieved.

In fact, excess detailing left unbalanced can be counterproductive, creating a potentially incorrect visual read of certain elements being much closer and more visible than they need to be in the scene.

The balance between levels of detail throughout the composition is a subtle indicator of depth as well, with elements placed further from the viewer naturally being seen in less fidelity than closer subjects.

Last but not least, recall the importance of visual scale and how it impacts perspective and distance. Given the large expanse the background stretches over, scale needs to be managed especially carefully. For example, a building far away can have its drawn detail kept low, with individual roof tiles omitted and replaced with tiny highlights to indicate its distance.

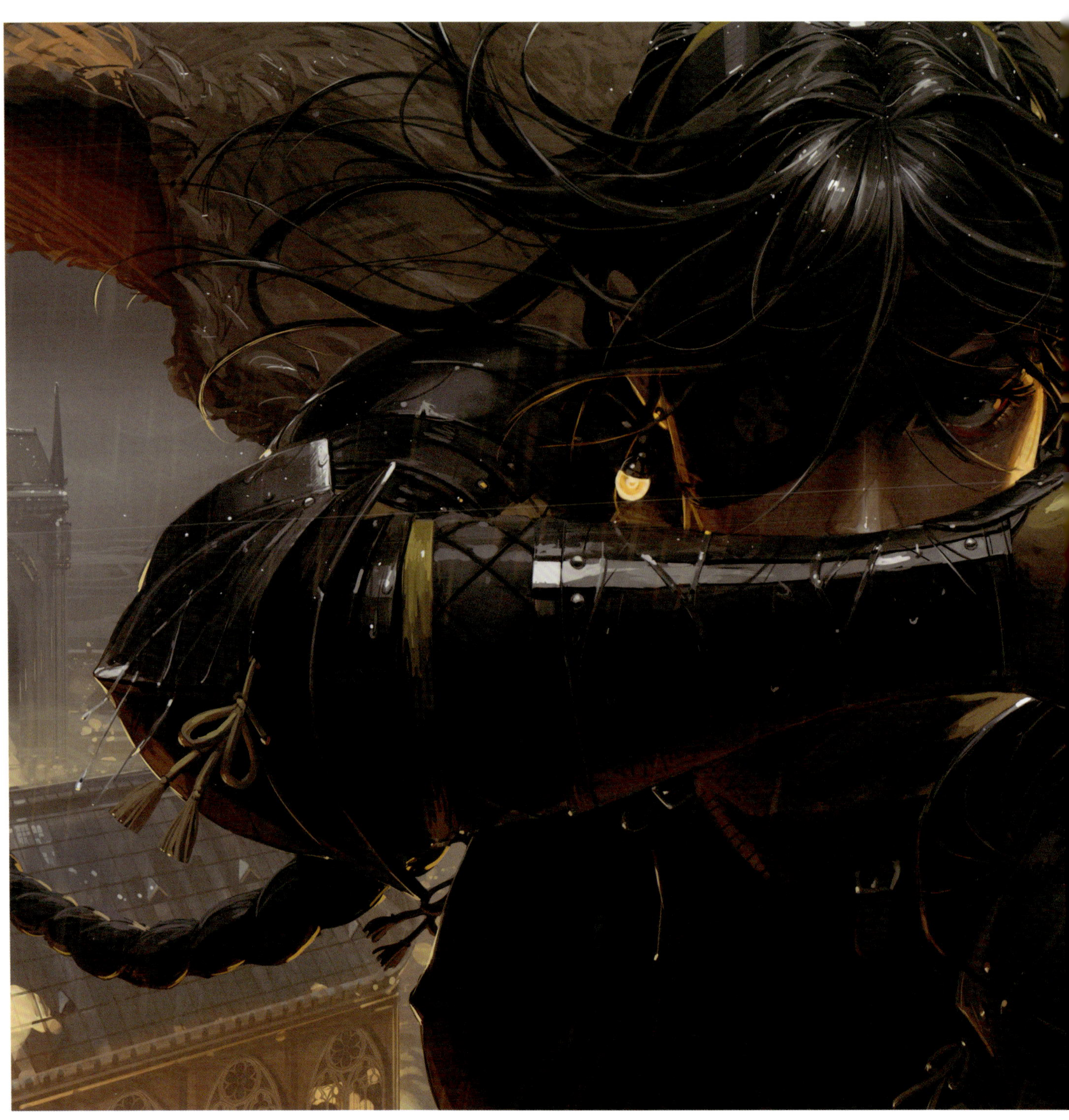

Night Warrior. The finished painting.

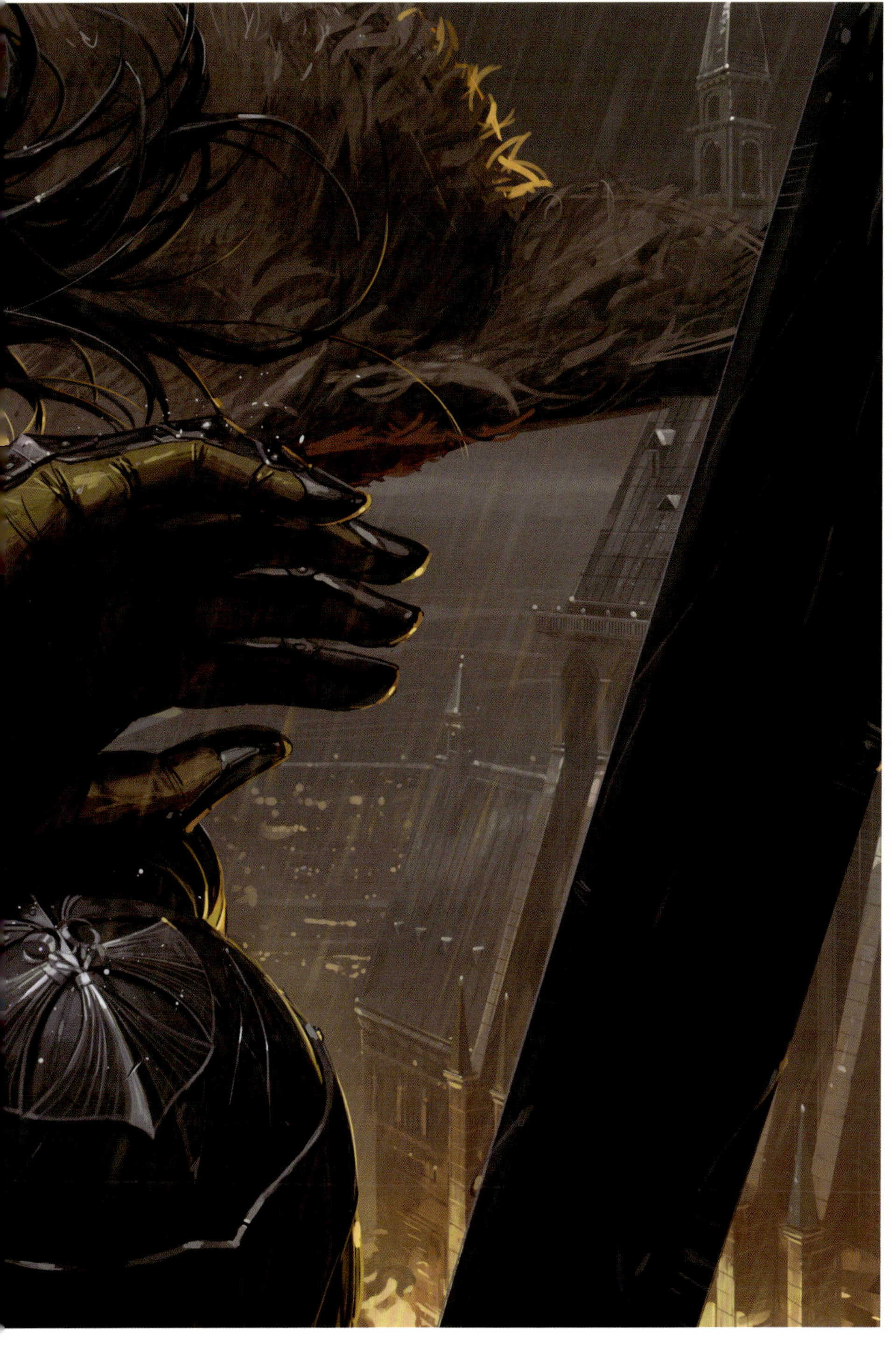

THE FINAL IMAGE

At the very end of the process, it's useful to take a few steps back in order to look at the big picture, and allow your own eyes to flow around the piece organically. This is a great method for spotting where your gaze naturally falls, and if the focal areas are sufficiently 'finished'.

Another method you can use to make the final pass is to split the image evenly, vertically and horizontally, into four parts. Sometimes more minor interactions between peripheral elements can be forgotten as you manage the big overall picture. Looking at each part alone can provide a new perspective on how the level of detail and depth works specifically within the isolated frames, and help you fix these minor mistakes.

Congratulations, you've come to the end of the tutorial! I hope this has been a helpful read and showed the importance of managing perspective as a fundamental pillar of the piece, alongside techniques of applying visual depth to create an immersive composition. These skills have been invaluable for me in designing compositions in my own work, and I hope they will be for you too.

Final image © Guweiz

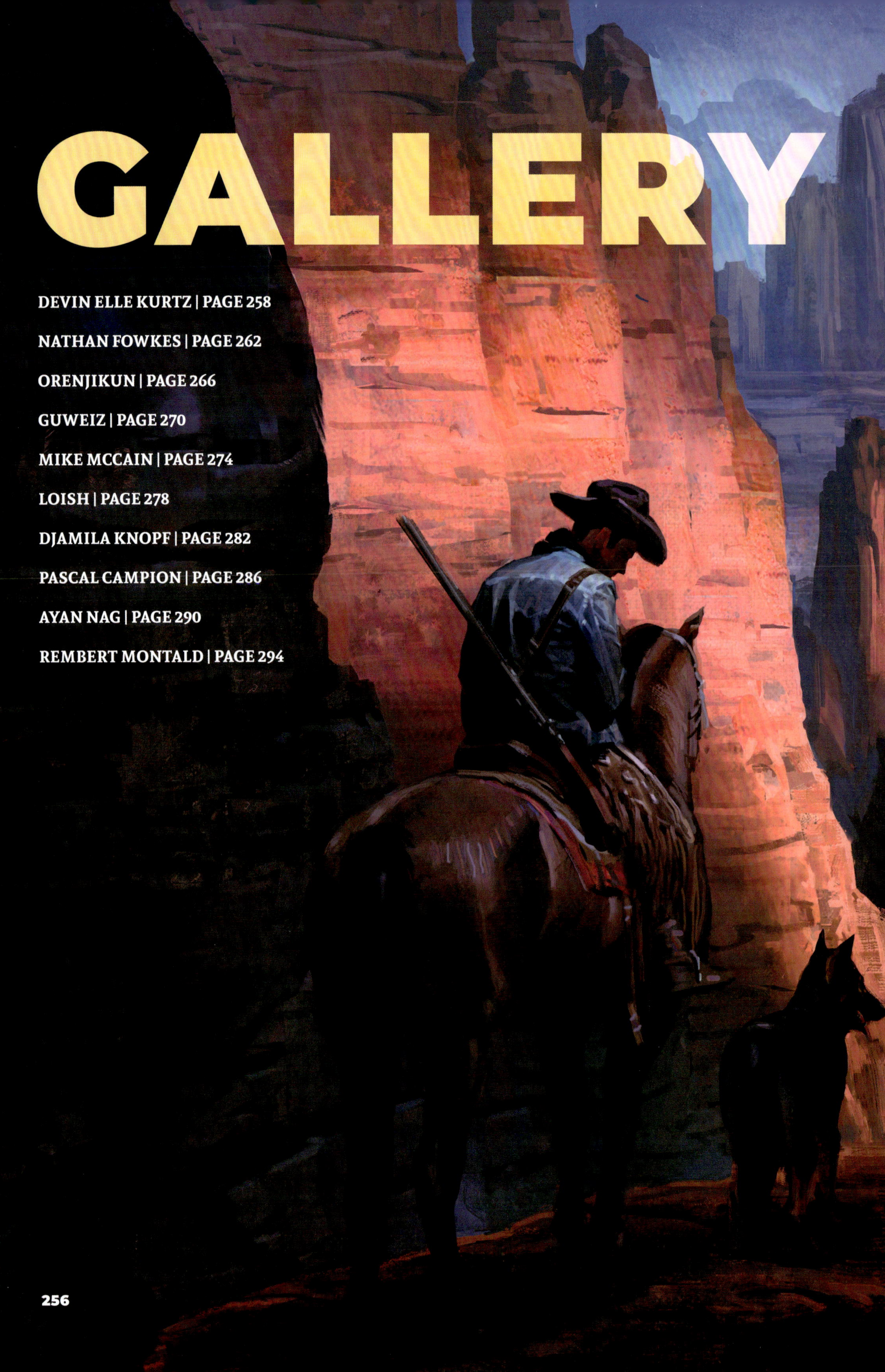

GALLERY

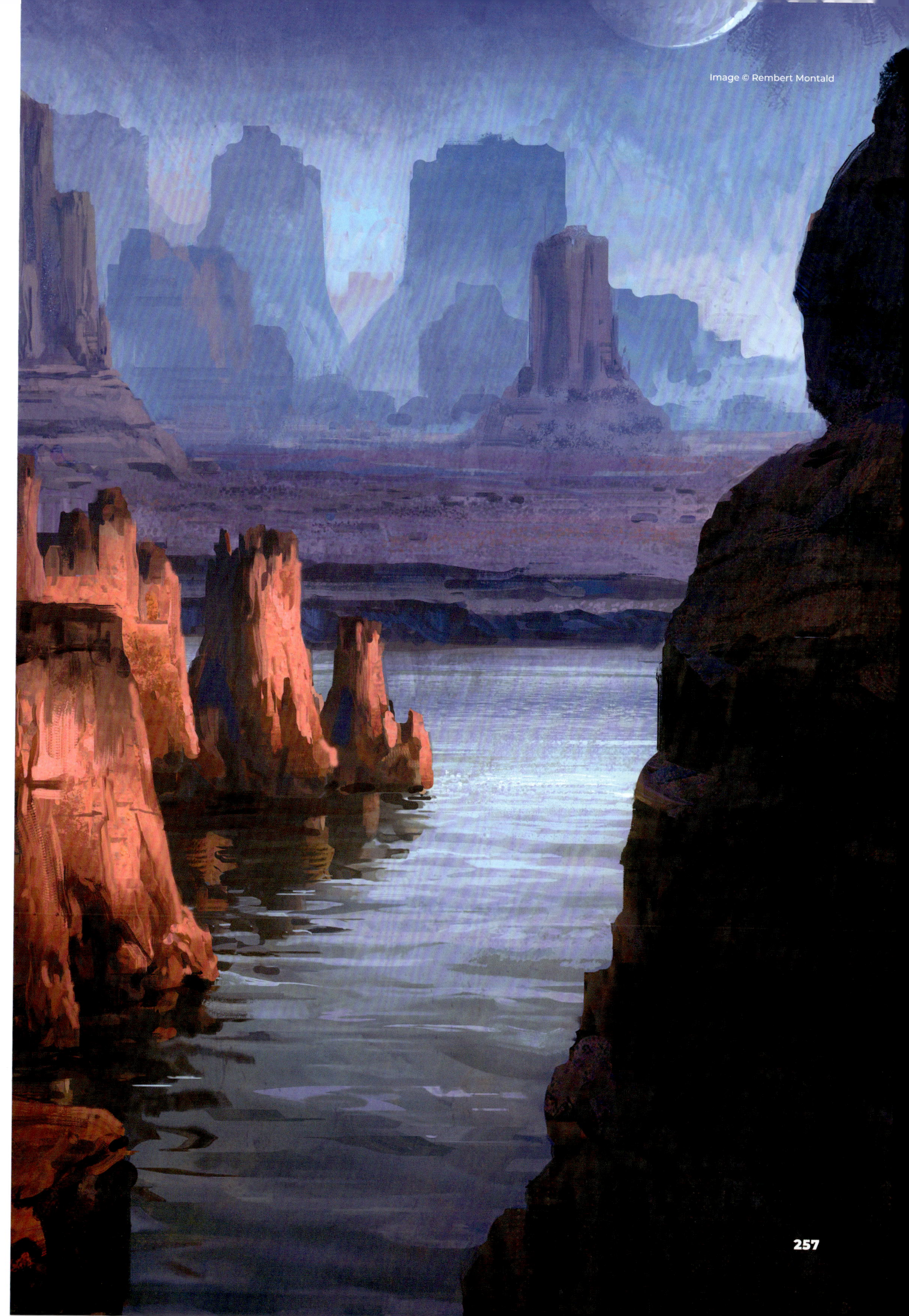

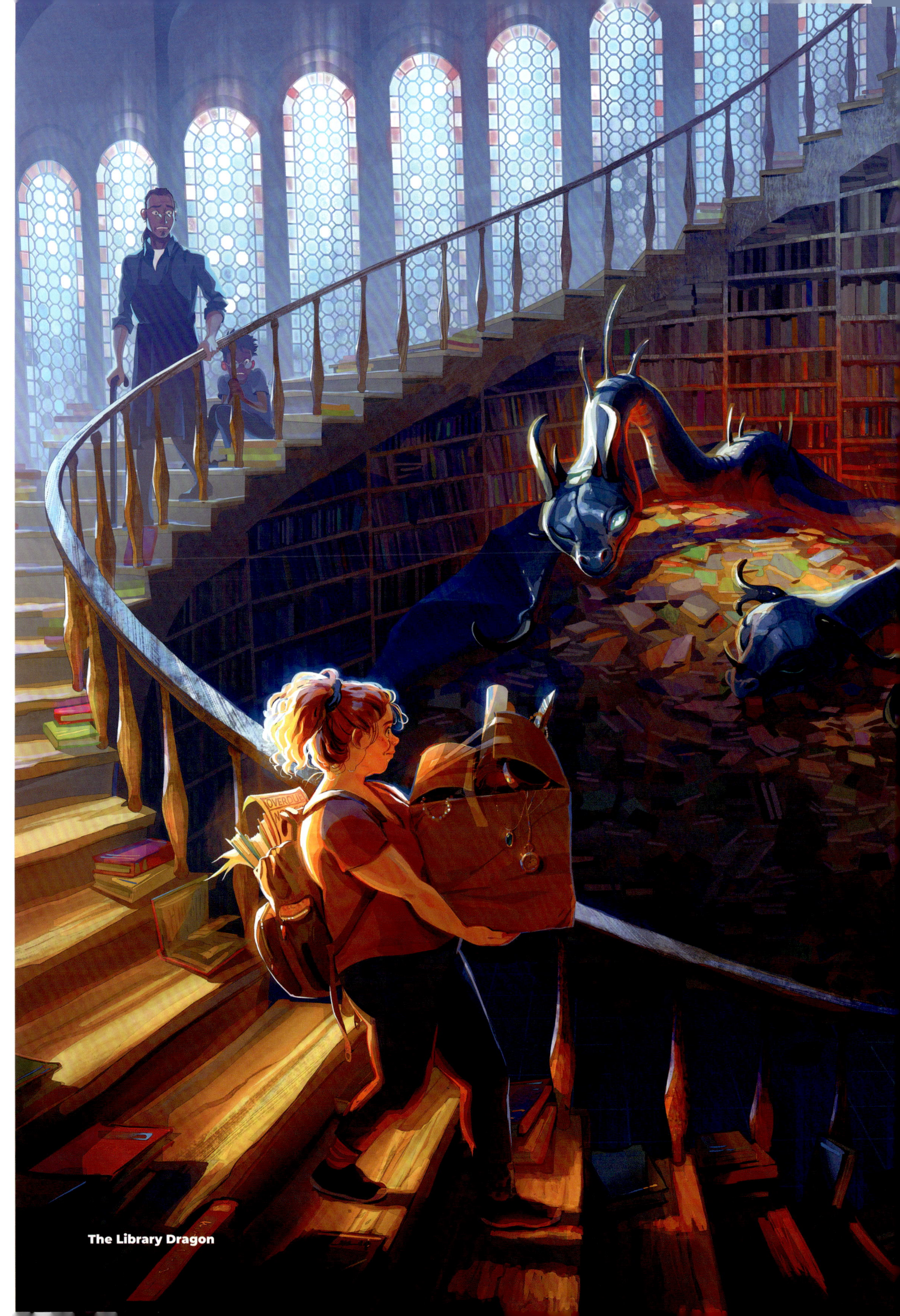

The Library Dragon

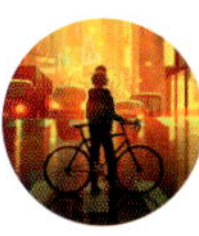

Dragon Migration

My goal with this image is to inspire awe and majesty. The boy walking the bike provides a conduit into the scene, but the viewer's willingness to step into his world hinges on a believable read of the scale, depth, and perspective. I painted this image from a very rough sketch, but took a lot of care when detailing the buildings to tighten the scaling, foreshortening, and one-point perspective.

I was careful to dramatically scale down the detail size and detail level of each layer of buildings to force a quick recession into the distance, with some of the most distant buildings nearly becoming pure silhouette. It can feel strange to forego so much detail in distant scenery, but it can sometimes prove the best solution to imply a great amount of distance and atmosphere, especially in a somewhat graphic style like this.

Repeating elements, such as the dragons here, are an excellent way to cue viewers into the depth of a scene. One of the most distant dragons interacts directly with a humongous skyscraper in the distance, and that connection with a known object immediately helps viewers to understand how large these imaginary creatures are. Their overlap, both in front of and behind buildings, also helps to clarify the scenery.

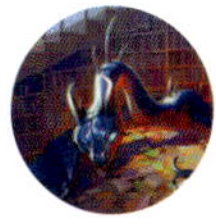

The Library Dragon

After sketching the thumbnail for this painting, I hopped over from Photoshop into SketchUp to model the spiral staircase. SketchUp is a 3D architectural design software with a free web version and is very easy to learn. There are multiple full intro courses that professionals have uploaded to YouTube for free, and I taught myself to use the software in a couple of weeks using only free resources. I find SketchUp very useful, as it allows me to create my own reference or base layer for tricky perspectives, like this spiral staircase, quite easily.

I used value to separate each layer of depth in the image. The girl and foreground staircase are given the widest range of values with the most contrast. The middle ground, with the two-headed book dragon, is given a constrained value range, with the darks lightening to a midtone. The background with the librarian and his assistant is considerably lightened to a narrow range of midtone values. Purple light from the stained glass windows catches stirred-up particles from the dusty old books and sets the upper third of the image back in space.

Colour temperature also helps to solidify the space and depth read, with the warmest reds, yellows, and oranges all situated in the foreground and middle ground. The background is neutral and cool, aside from magenta pops in the windows.

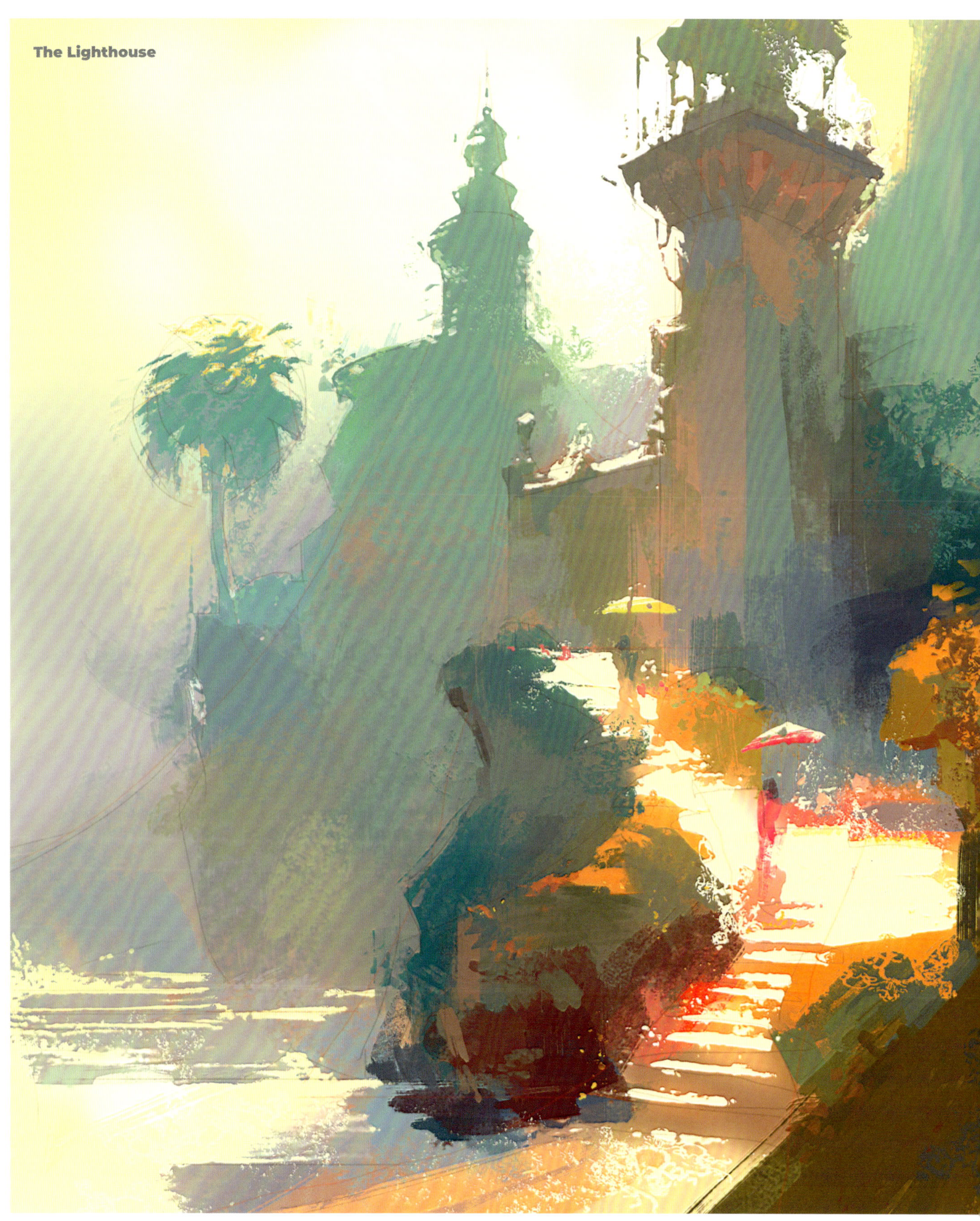
The Lighthouse

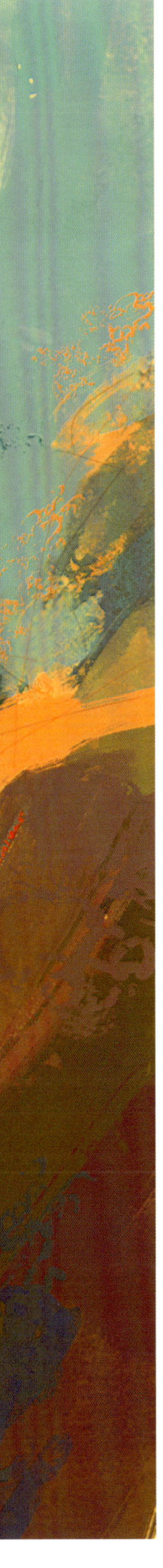

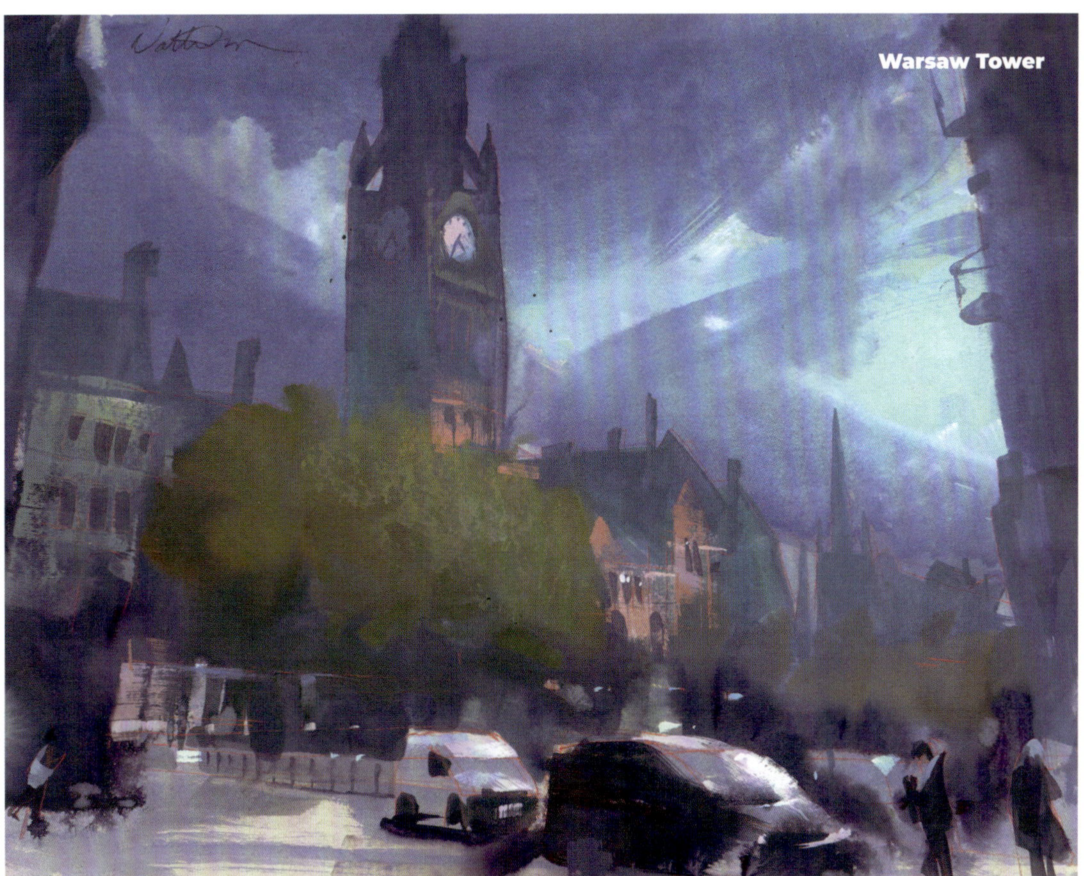
Warsaw Tower

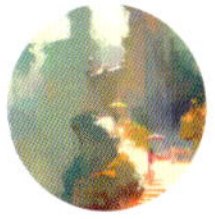

The Lighthouse

The depth cues in this painting include the high contrast in the foreground and lower contrast and lost edges to the far background, lots of heat at the front that moves to cooler greens and purples in the far background, plus lots of atmosphere and lack of detail in the background cliffs and structure. The stairs are also important. I love using pathways, roads, and stairs as they create depth and intrigue, leading the viewer through the image.

As I used fairly standard depth cues, I tried to be a little playful with the colour palette. In real life, it would be unlikely to see that much orange in the foreground and the atmosphere certainly wouldn't turn so green for the background building. But this isn't about depicting reality – it's meant to be an interesting, enjoyable, and engaging painting. My hope is that there's a surprise factor in the way colour has been used.

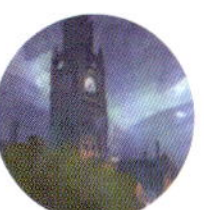

Warsaw Tower

I wanted to change the medium for this painting, as depth and perspective are critical considerations regardless of your medium or technique. The other images in this gallery are imaginary, but this one is a stylization of a real place. It captures an overcast, stormy day in Warsaw, Poland and is painted in watercolours, with a little opaque gouache in the highlights.

The major depth cue is the cars coming into the foreground. I intentionally painted the closest car black and the more distant car white. This is an invention on my part to force a quality of depth into the scene. The strong highlights on the cars capture the real-life lighting, but I emphasized this to get a real zing out of them for additional contrast. The buildings and trees recede into the distance, losing detail and gaining increasingly more sky colour until they virtually disappear.

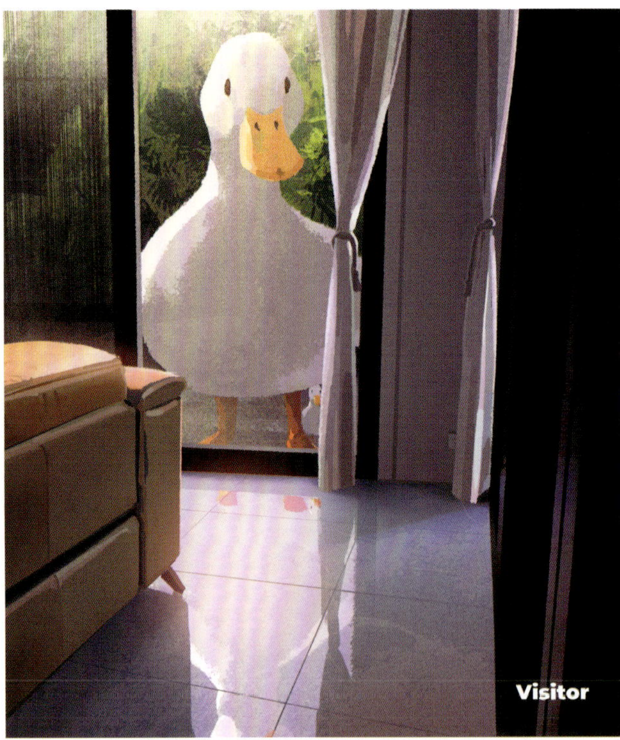
Visitor

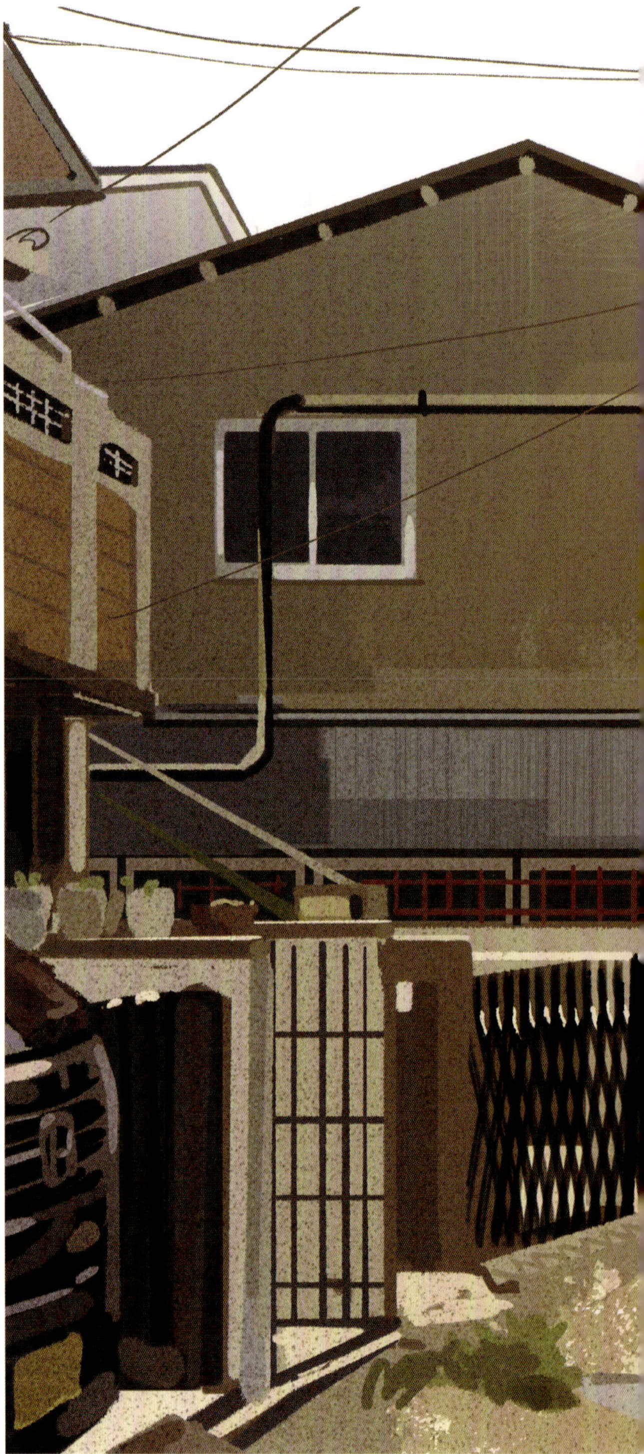

ORENJIKUN

What I love most about drawing in perspective is its ability to bring your imagination to life. Perspective and depth can have a large impact on the tone and mood of an artwork. Ask yourself, what statement are you trying to convey? What is the narrative? What is the intention? Decisions you make about eye level, lens length, and vanishing points affect every single choice you make down the line, so thinking about perspective from the start is crucial.

Although I believe a strong fundamental and practical knowledge of perspective drawing is important, I often like to begin a painting loosely, without hard guidelines, allowing my instinct and sensibility to inform the perspective of a composition. However, this is not a substitute for taking the time to learn and grind out your fundamentals!

Thinking about the narrative and considering the image as if I'm a director with a camera on a film set are what inform my choice of perspective. I ask myself, how should I stage the subject for the camera? From what viewpoint do I want to capture the scene? What lens length would best depict it? I'm still in the process of learning what makes a composition look cinematic, but I believe it's down to developing a strong narrative or feeling, and portraying that in a compelling way.

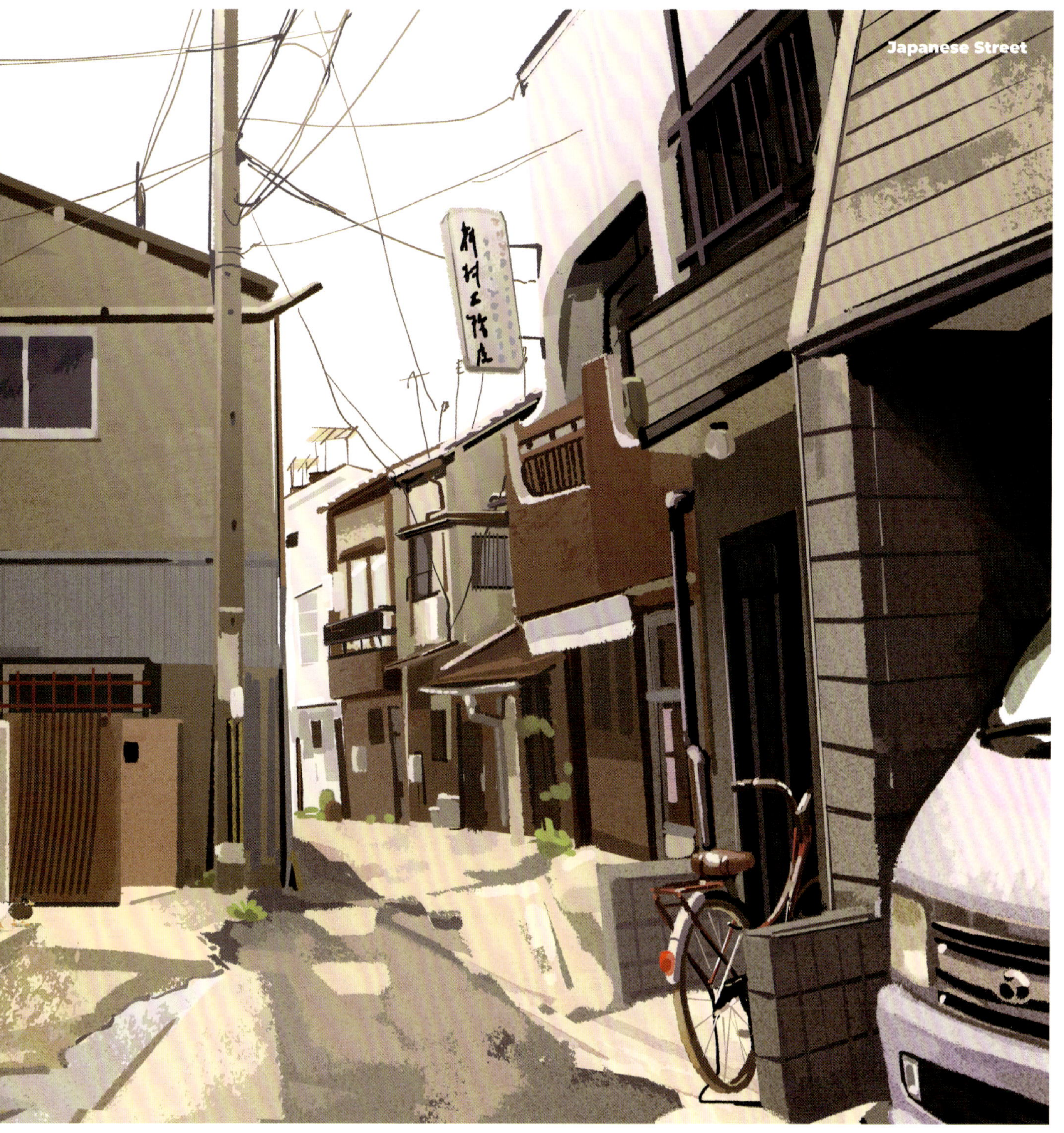

Japanese Street

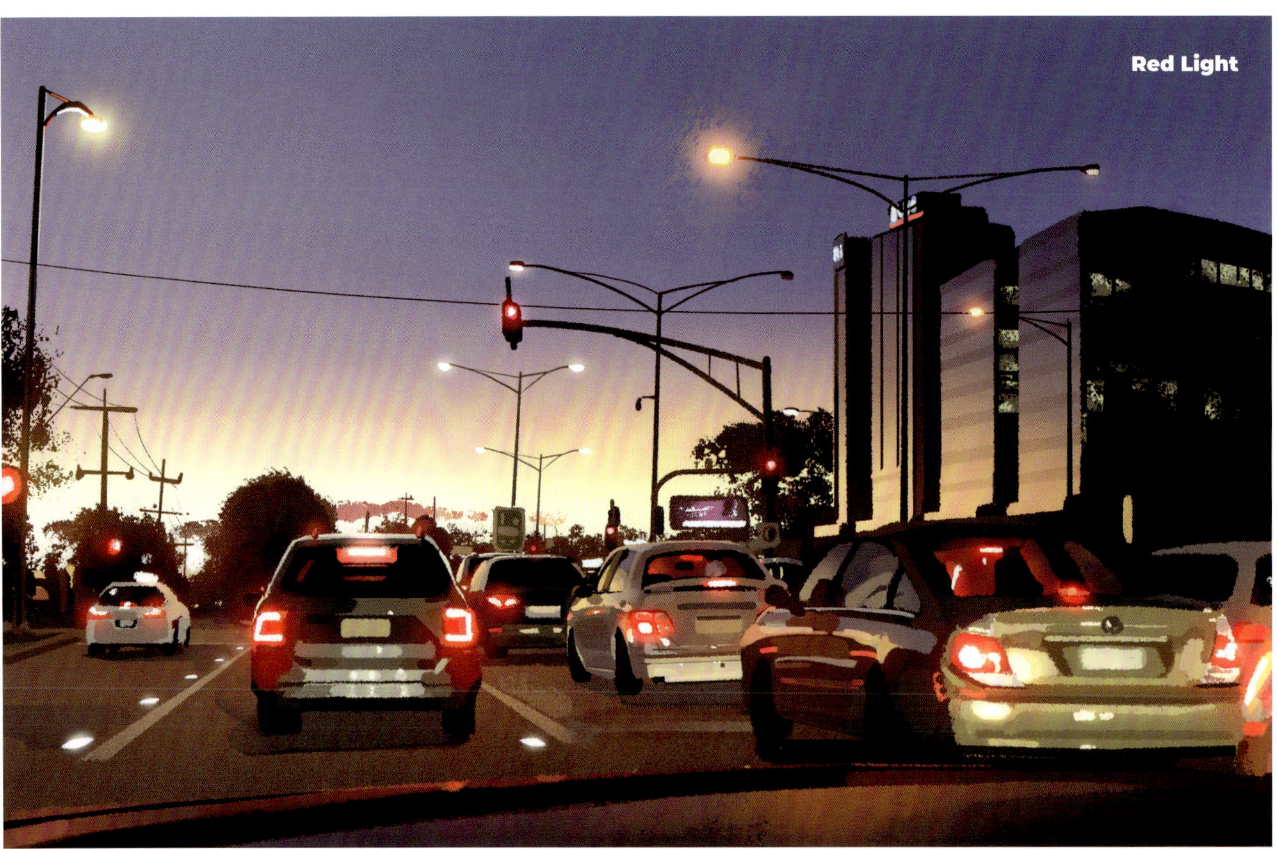

Red Light

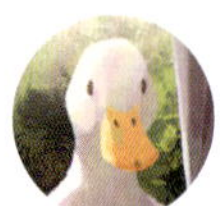

Visitor

Here I used perspective and scale to show the contrast in size between the regular-sized room and the outlandishly large duck. Notice that there is a slight indication of vertical perspective. Following the same perspective, the reflection in the tiles serves as another cue to ground the fantastically large duck in the scene. The lighting also helps to convey a sense of depth. A soft glow from the top of the image bleeds into the exterior, but is not present for interior parts of the composition. This division of lighting serves as an effective separation of the background and middle ground, enhancing the sense of depth and providing clarity where scale and perspective cues aren't present.

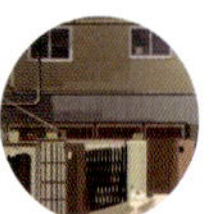

Japanese Street

Based on my travels to Japan, this painting depicts an unassuming, humble alleyway, full of character in its winding paths, myriad of textures and materials, and patchwork, undulating asphalt. To capture the charm of the reference, I freehanded the perspective, allowing a rhythm to dance through the image. The verticals feature a playful rhythm, finding appealing shapes in the positive and negative space.

Lighting can also provide important cues to the depth of the space. The large facade on the left of the composition occludes the sun, which provides a light source from behind and to the left. With the open path, light is able to shine through and catches on the left of the buildings on the right-hand side of the alleyway. Showing where light will and won't reach can help to convey the dimensionality of the forms.

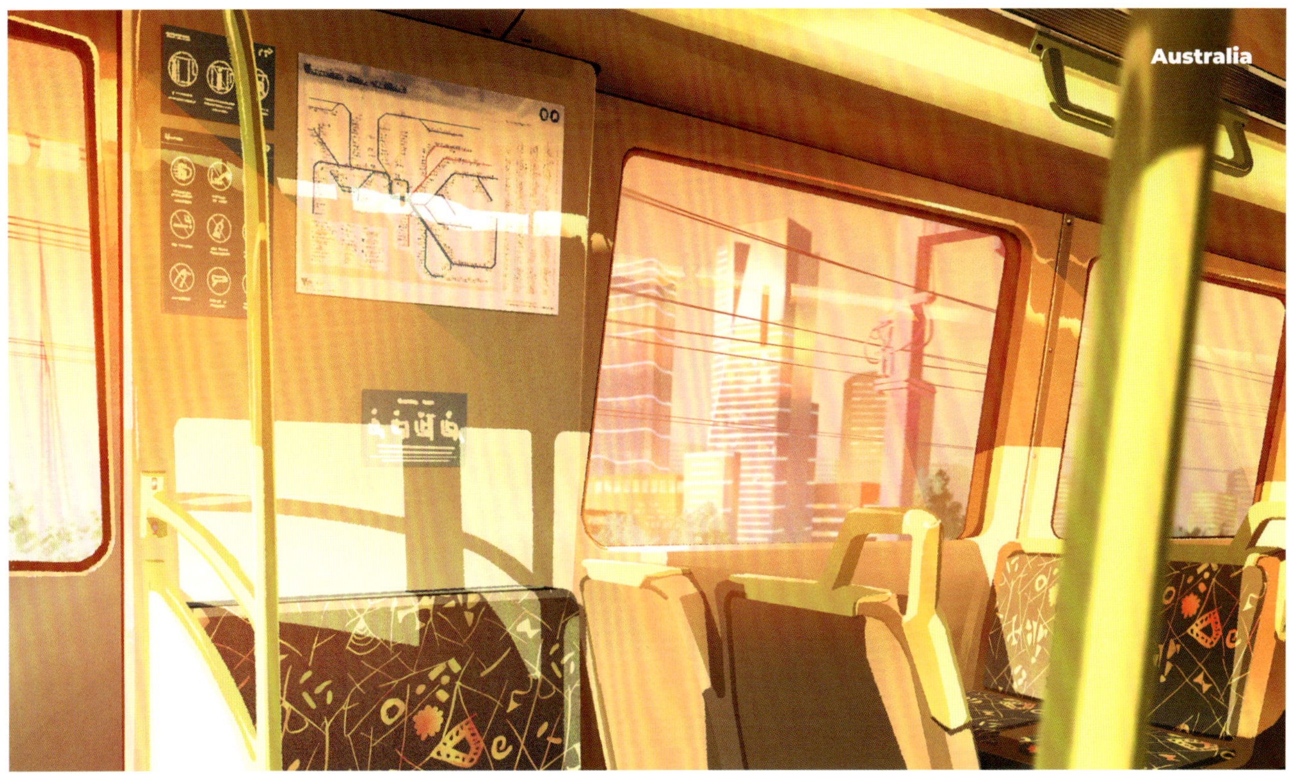
Australia

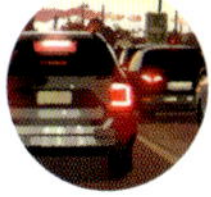

Red Light

This busy traffic scene is captured from the viewpoint of a passenger in a car. The overlapping of cars scaling into the distance serves as the primary cue for depth and perspective, filling the composition with a myriad of red lights scattered across the viewer's vision. This is supported by the lamp posts and electricity pylons, as well as some of the indications of receding distance in the office buildings, power lines, and road markings.

A sense of atmospheric perspective is illustrated through the sky, with the gradient softening towards the horizon line. Although the trees and foliage shapes are graphic and low detail, the atmospheric perspective serves as a simple but effective cue for depth, separating the distance between each group of foliage. The atmospheric perspective is further reinforced with a similar scaling reduction of detail, with objects receiving less detail and fidelity the further away they are from the camera.

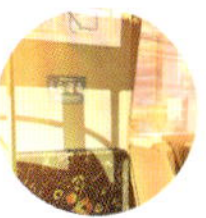

Australia

This is the Melbourne Metro train, with the iconic Eureka Tower in the background. I chose a view that is close and personal, hoping to evoke a sense of familiarity and nostalgia. The composition was created from scratch without a direct reference, and therefore the accurate placement of elements – such as the city background through the window and the foreground pole – was impossible. With the ability to construct the composition from my imagination, however, I was able to overlap the elements in a realistic and believable way to create a pleasing composition. The overlap of the background, middle ground, and foreground enhanced the sense of depth, while still featuring iconic features of the Melbourne Metro.

A further sense of depth is added through scale and various nods to camera specificities. The city skyline in the background is clearly far away in the distance, as you can see the top halves in their entirety. The foreground pole occupies a large amount of the frame and is blurred, indicating that it's outside of the depth of the focus range, being much closer to the camera. There is also a slight horizontal motion blur on the exterior to imitate the effect of blurred movement due to the camera shutter speed being too slow to capture the movement sharply.

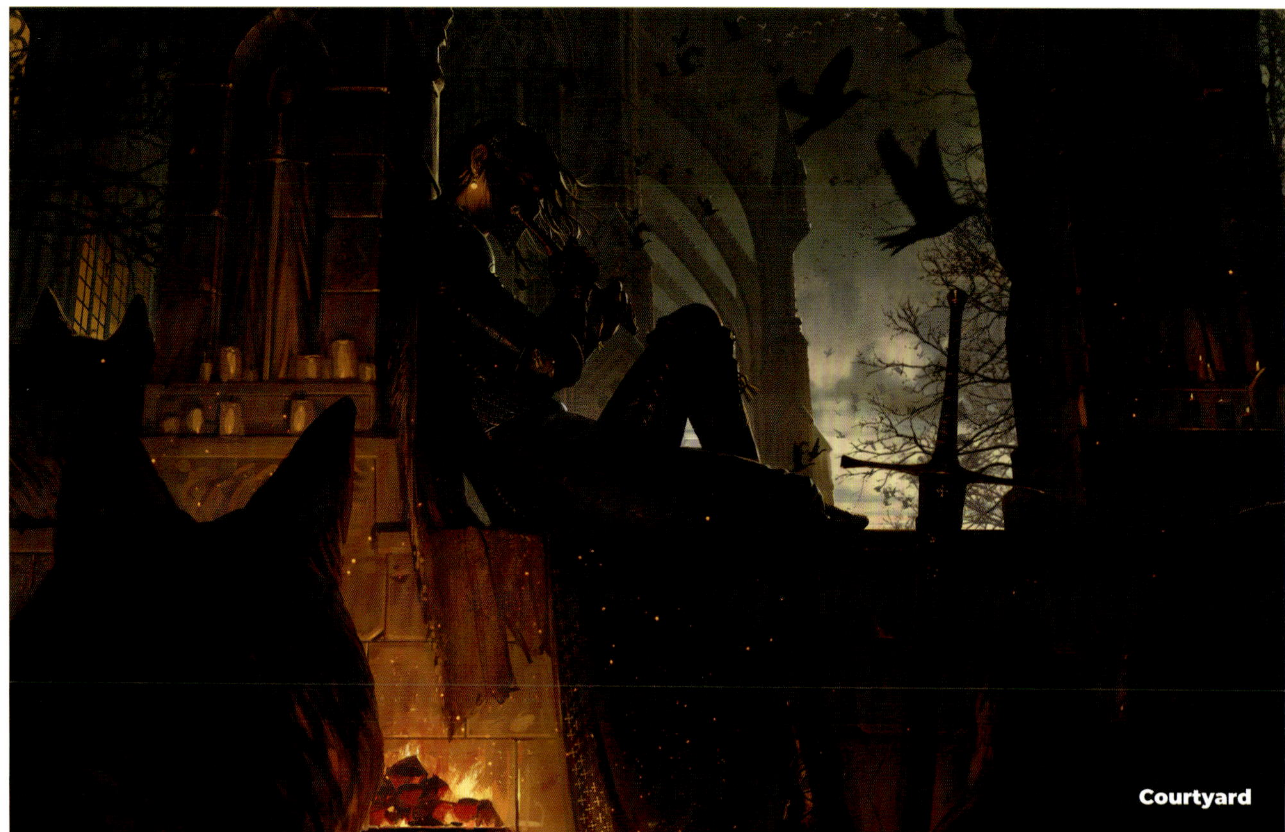

GUWEIZ

Perspective and depth are core concepts that I like exploring in my work. As an artist who prefers drawing in a realistic, immersive visual style, being able to harness them to design a variety of 'shot set-ups' has not only been enjoyable, but incredibly helpful in adding more variation and quality to my art.

Can we make this element more exciting by adding foreshortening? Or perhaps seeing it from a low angle will make it more dramatic? What about our proximity to the character? Are we too far away and detached, or too close and seeing distorted proportions? Does the scene feel fleshed out with a deep layering of relevant elements, or is it too sparse and flat in areas?

A well-executed, spatially deep composition drawn in accurate perspective offers the audience a unique first-person view into an imaginary world.

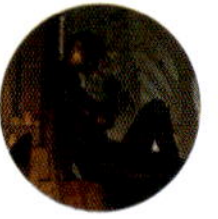

Courtyard

My goal was to juxtapose the character against a detailed and visually interesting gothic cathedral. A low angle works especially well to capture the full depth and iconic details of the scene in frame. This is an easy way to capture a close, low-angle scene to allow vertical edges to converge upwards slightly. This subtle but important perspective cue comes in very helpful here.

Separating each overlapping element can be more challenging due to the lighting set-up, with substantial light sources in both the foreground and background creating a weaker near-to-far brightness gradient. As such, the distinction between each layer of depth here is achieved mostly via rim light. Depth can also be added in various ways in the foreground, with the wolves in the extreme foreground being very obvious indicators, while the ridged forms on the columns serve as smaller, but equally useful cues.

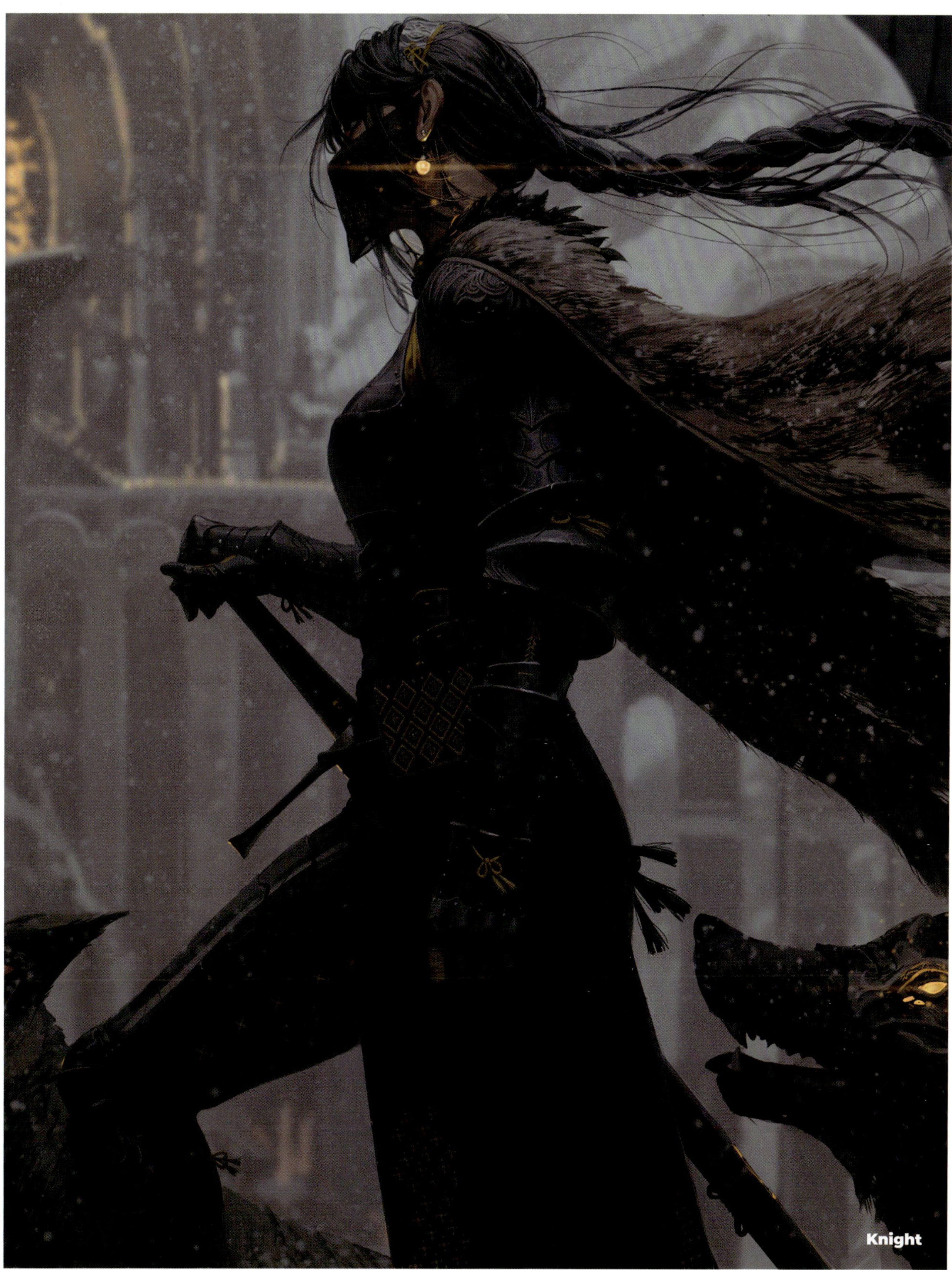

Knight

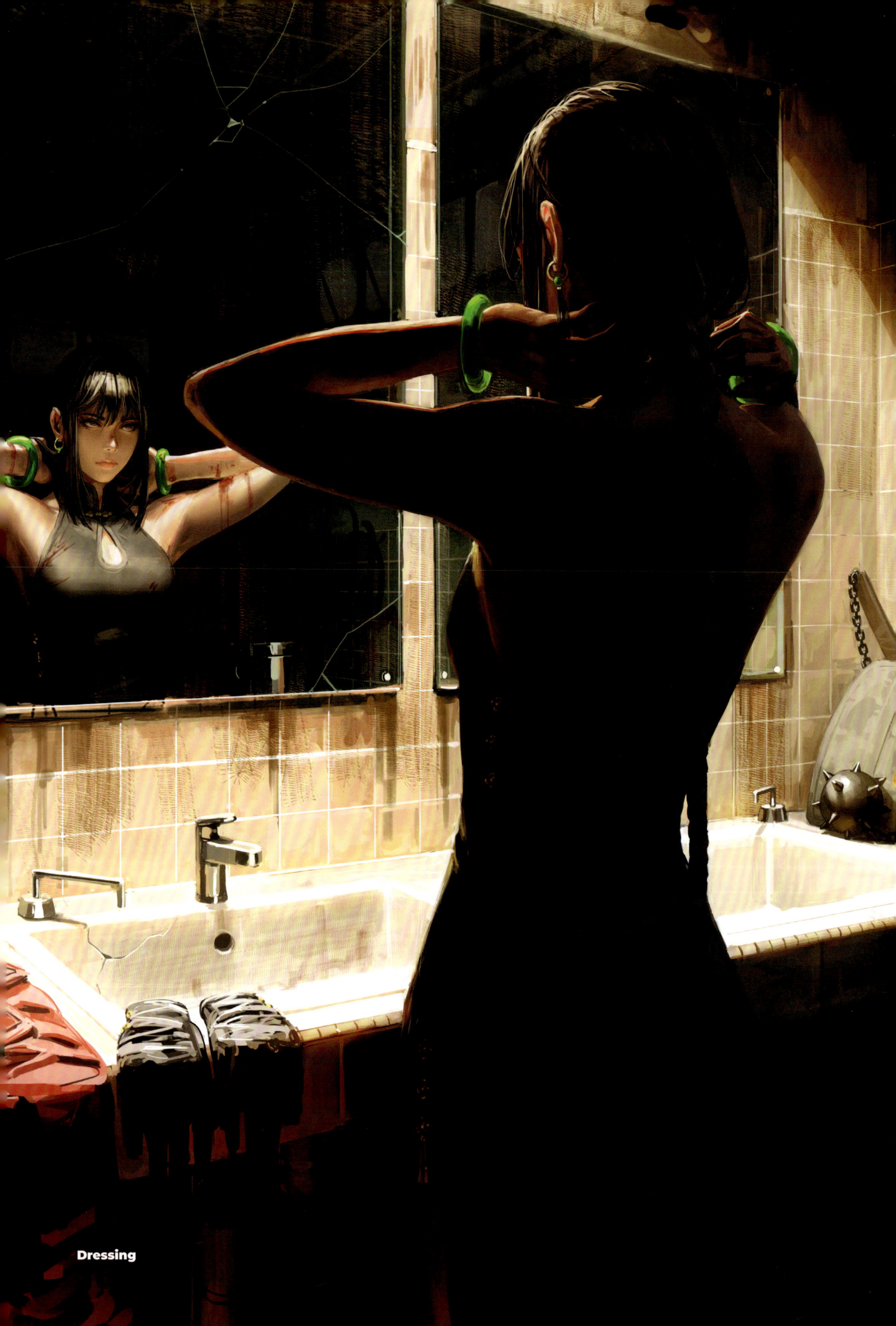

Dressing

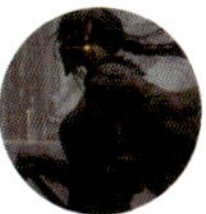

Knight

A simple, medium-distance shot allows you to see most of the character's body, which is important in indicating her pose and movement in this context. The shot is close enough to feel immersive, but not so much that the pose's readability is affected. I chose a low-angle view to complement the character's direction of movement up the stairs, as well as to accentuate the height and grandeur of the structures in the background. From this angle, you can see the structures from below, providing a unique perspective and opportunity to draw more expressive and visually clear forms; for example, the underside of arches.

A gentle blur is applied to the far background to create a stronger depth-of-field effect. The lighter, blue-greyish colour creates a value separation that also reinforces the distance of the structures from our POV. This effect is complemented by snow particles fading in size from the foreground to the background.

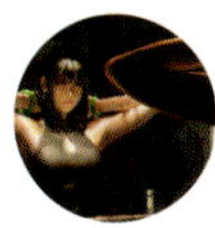

Dressing

A neutral angle can be a surprisingly effective way to make use of perspective. While less immediately dramatic than a high or low angle, the neutral position creates a much clearer perspective distinction between elements above and below the eye level. In turn, this distinction helps to clarify the POV height effectively to the viewer. I chose a height slightly lower than the character's head to create a slightly mysterious feel, an option that wasn't available to either a high (too exposing) or low (too concealing) angle view.

Mirrors and reflections are an excellent way to increase depth in a scene, especially if the physical setting is more constrained and limited. Here I was able to extend the depth of the scene from the character and wall all the way into the mirror image and onto the other side of the entire room. When drawing the reflection, think of it as simply seeing a duplicate of the room on the other side of a mirror-shaped hole.

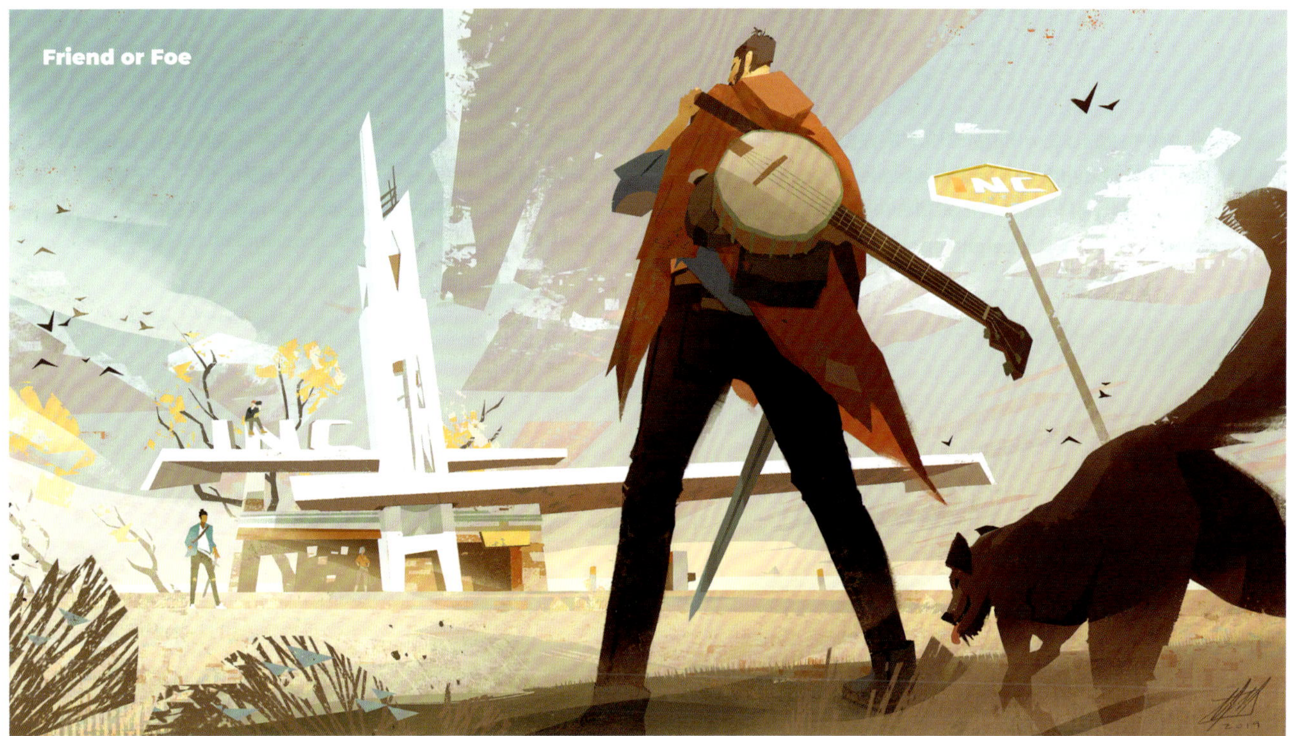

Friend or Foe

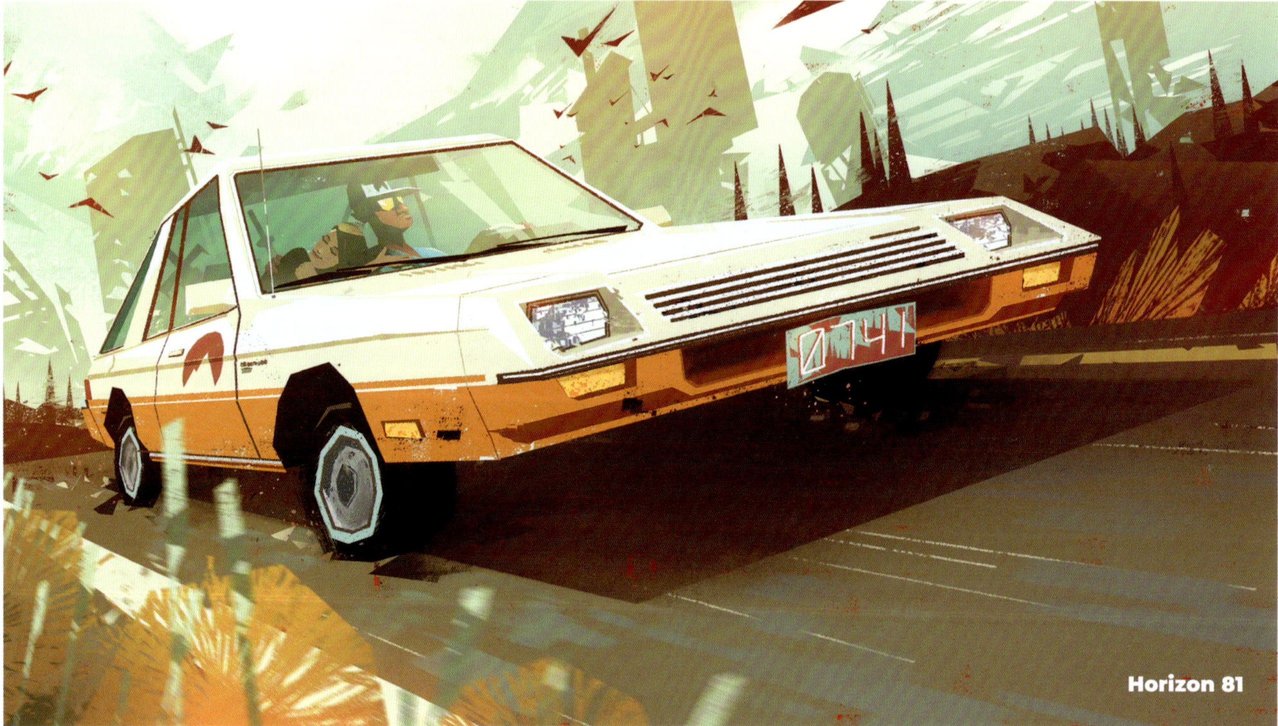

Horizon 81

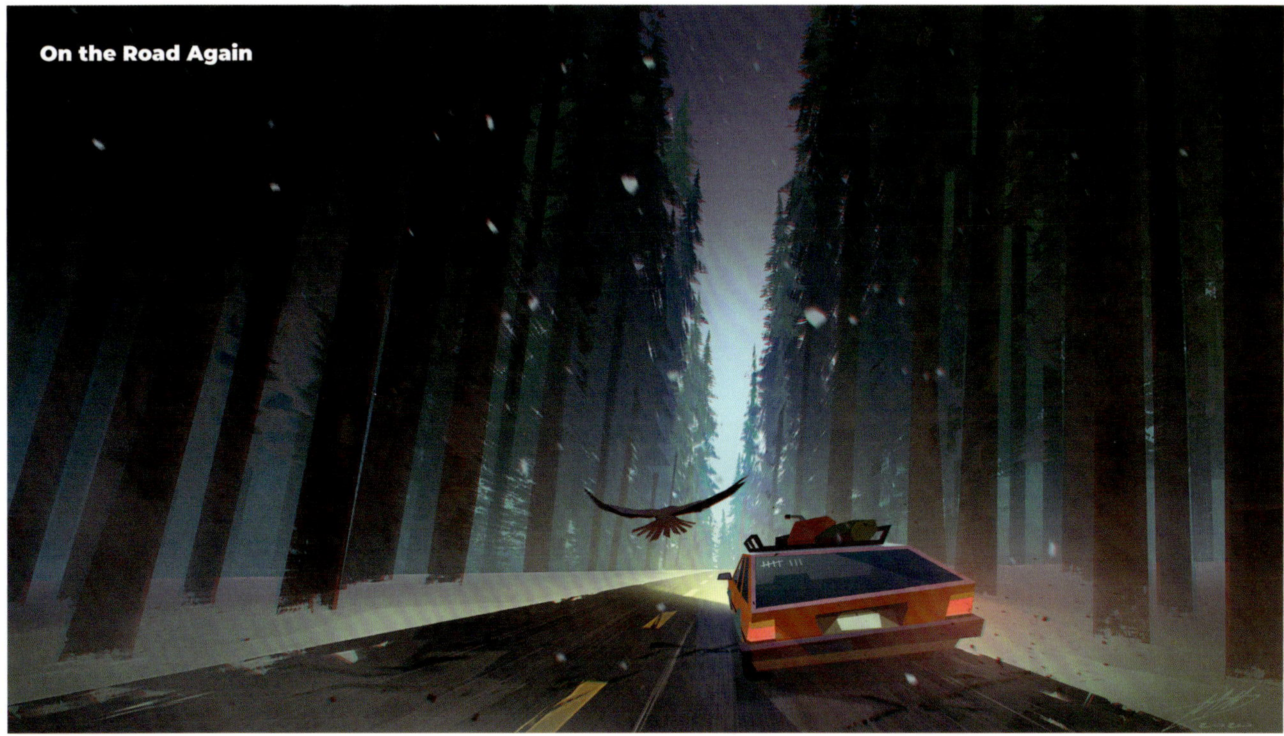
On the Road Again

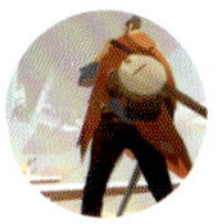

Friend or Foe

I tried to push perspective and depth in this scene. Though I struggled to figure out how to depict a believable character at such a low angle, it was a fun challenge to see how far I could push it. I like to place the camera low in a scene to exaggerate our feeling of scale and perspective. This can be an effective way to bring the viewer into a scene, as well as adding drama and impact.

Repeating elements can be a great way to convey depth. You can assume the foreground figure is roughly the same height as the figures in the distance, which suggests how far back in space those figures must be.

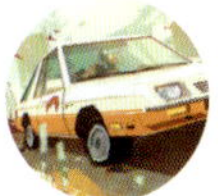

Horizon 81

This is one of the first imaginative paintings where I really tried to push and break free from a traditional perspective set-up. It felt very freeing to pursue energy and impact over technical accuracy. I based the car on reference photographs. Whenever I use a photo reference with perspective in it, it's helpful to consider how wide the camera field of view is. In this case, my reference photo was taken on a long lens from quite far away (with a narrow field of view). As I wanted the camera to feel closer in the painting, I drew the car with a much more obvious perspective to it.

All of these exaggerated images still require a good intuition for perspective and depth, allowing you to start to see where you can stretch and break the rules impactfully. It's like how a solid understanding of form and anatomy is still required to draw really stylized characters.

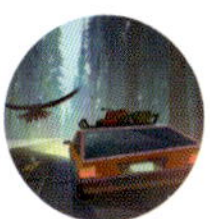

On the Road Again

This painting is based on my memory of driving through a forest in Oregon. I remember a feeling of symmetry from the flat forest extending straight up and out to the horizon line and wanted to capture a sense of that scale and speed. This painting is a good example of how creative decisions can create a believable feeling of perspective, beyond what 'correct' perspective techniques can offer. While it's based on a strong one-point perspective set-up, I suggested a second vanishing point above the image, putting the viewer low to the ground looking up. I also skewed the scene to heighten the sense of immediacy and energy.

Perspective and depth are part of my overall compositional choices. The clean graphic elements of this composition – the triangle of sky, the flat road, the repeating vertical trees – all work together to provide the feeling of speeding off towards the horizon.

LOISH

I started out as a character artist, so a lot of my ideas about capturing depth are based on the principles needed to convey a character. This means that I tend to use a lot of organic shapes when constructing a drawing, which makes perspective – especially technical approaches like two-point perspective – feel really difficult and counter-intuitive. It took me a while to figure out how to convey depth in my environment paintings, but over time I learned a few helpful tricks, such as using colour, lighting, and contrast to my advantage to establish a sense of three-dimensionality. I also started experimenting with perspective in my interior paintings by constructing a grid before starting the sketch. In this gallery I'll share some of my favourite tricks and techniques for capturing depth.

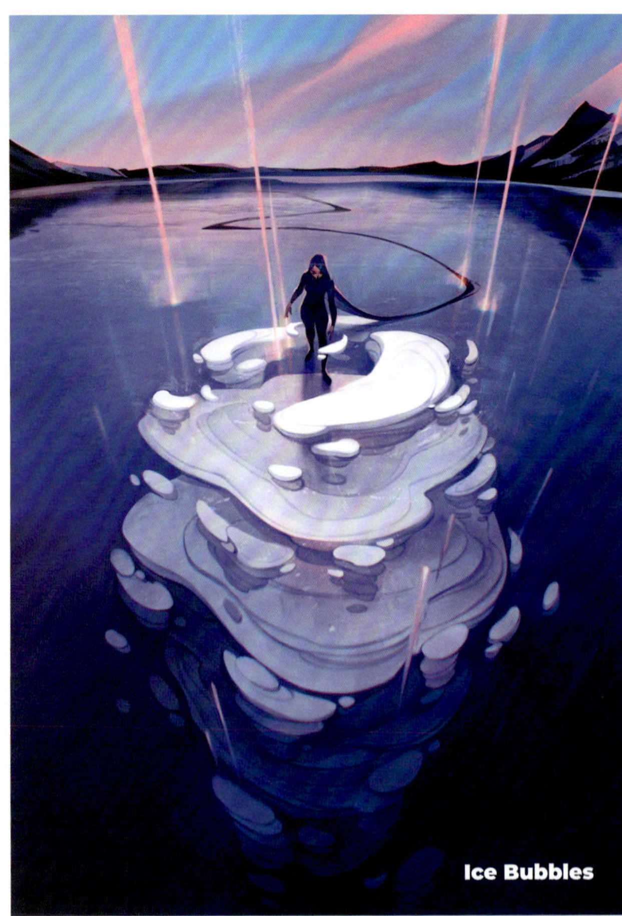
Ice Bubbles

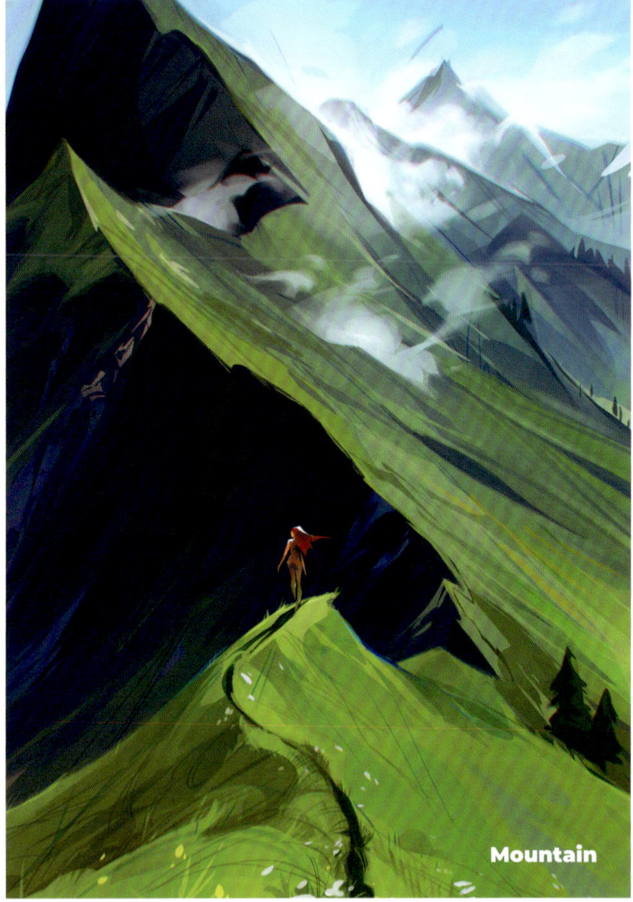
Mountain

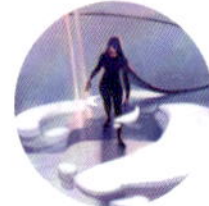

Ice Bubbles

I wanted to create the feeling of ice bubbles rising up from the depths of the icy ocean. The bubbles closest to the viewer are highest in contrast, while the bubbles further away are darker and fading from view. The sky transitions from a deep blue to a pale pink, and the ice fades from a lighter blue to a deep, dark blue towards the bottom. These gradients help to establish the composition, as well as depth and scale, in a landscape image.

To give this painting a somewhat curved perspective, I drew pink lines of light and energy rising up from the ice. These follow the movement of the perspective and are intended to be decorative, but also help the viewer to understand the perspective in the scene. I love using decorative elements to help convey the sense of space and scale. Here I used the character's hair to lead the eye towards the horizon, suggesting the long and winding path she has travelled.

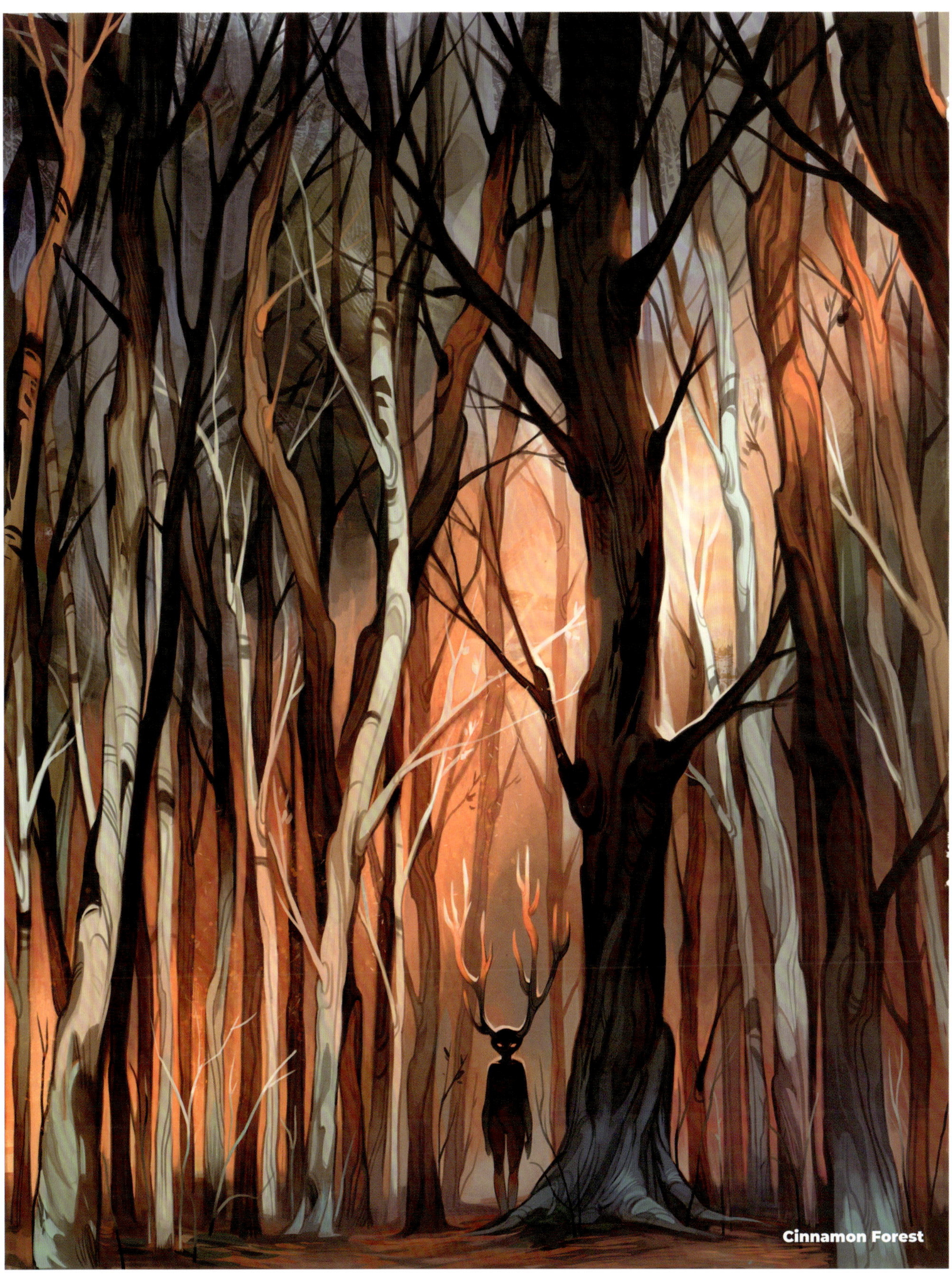

Cinnamon Forest

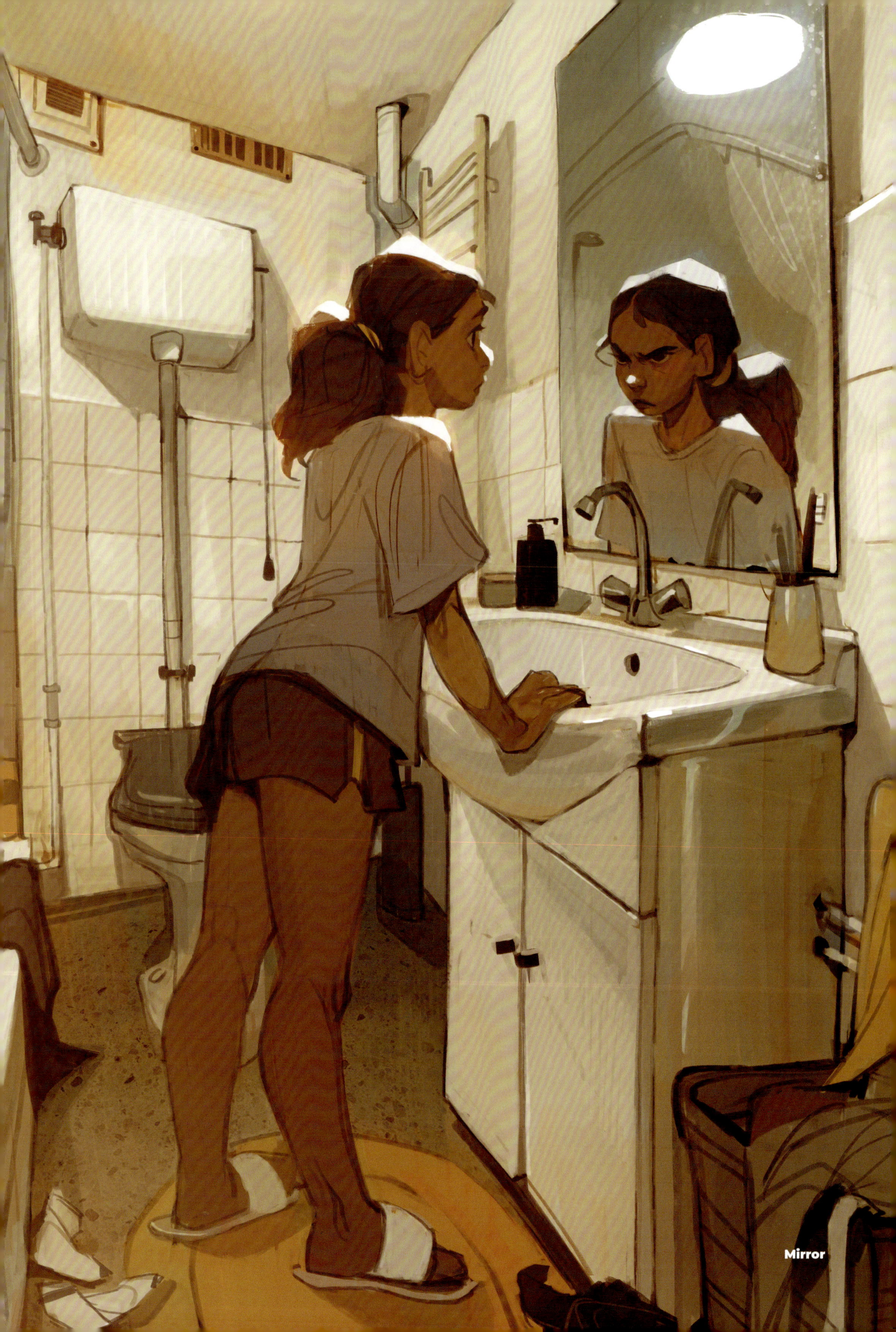

Mirror

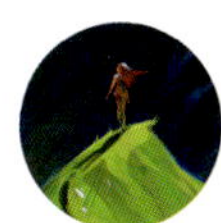

Mountain

When painting mountains, I've found that one of the most helpful ways to convey depth is by using atmospheric perspective. This involves making elements that are further away lower in contrast and more desaturated, as seen in the more distant peaks here. Adding the highest amount of contrast and vibrancy to the foreground elements helps the viewer know where to look, but it also creates a sense of how much distance there is between the foreground character and the landscape beyond.

Adding clouds and mist to mountain ranges can communicate which peaks are closest to the viewer, and which are further away. Here I used clouds and mist to separate the tallest peak from those behind it. When it comes to organic shapes like mountains, I really like adding colour in a way that follows the contours of the shapes. Here I tried to add lines and shapes along the edges of the mountain to help convey its basic form, boosting the three-dimensionality and sense of scale.

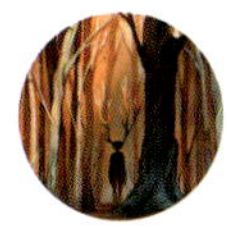

Cinnamon Forest

Lighting played a huge role in establishing the depth in this scene. By painting a beam of light passing over the trees, it becomes clearer to see which trees are in the foreground and which are in the background. The use of colour also helps to convey depth, as it is linked to the lighting. The areas that catch the light are warmer in tone, and areas in shadow are cooler in tone. These warmer areas feel closer to us than the cooler, more desaturated areas.

When conveying depth, it's helpful to play around with different shapes and levels of complexity. Positioning sharper, finer details in the foreground – like the smaller twigs near the ground – and softer, lower contrast elements in the background helps to establish which areas were intended to be closer to the viewer. Forests can feel endlessly deep and complex, which is something I wanted to capture. I found it useful to draw the trees on different layers, gradually stacking one layer over the next. This helped to give the forest a feeling of density and thickness.

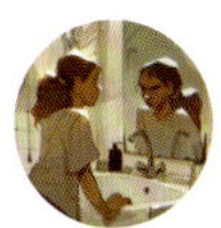

Mirror

I found it really helpful to create a grid beforehand to establish the perspective of the space. I did this by simply copying and pasting a premade grid onto the canvas, and transforming it digitally to construct the perspective. This was especially helpful for capturing the tiles. Once the grid is in place, it's fairly easy to make sure that all of the additional elements – including the pipes, mirror, sink, and other accessories – follow the basic perspective lines.

If you create the highest level of contrast in the focal point area, and lower the contrast in other areas, it will help to move some elements to the foreground and other elements to the background. In this case, the focal point is around the head and reflection of the character. Background elements are lower in contrast. Painting a sharp highlight on the character can help to separate them from the background. This is a way of using lighting to establish a sense of depth. Here I used a bright highlight on her head and shoulders to help position her in this space.

DJAMILA KNOPF

I find perspective and depth to be two of the most challenging aspects of painting environments. It took me a long time to wrap my head around these concepts and eventually use them to my advantage. Nothing makes a painting appear 'off' as quickly as flawed perspective, but if done right, it will lend solidity to any given scene.

It can also be an excellent storytelling device through how it places the viewer in relation to the subject matter. Is the viewer in the middle of the action, or far away? Are they on the same eye level as the person in the painting, or are they viewing the scene from high up in the sky or low to the ground? I love how perspective and depth can pull you into the artwork, creating the impression that there is a greater world beyond the picture frame.

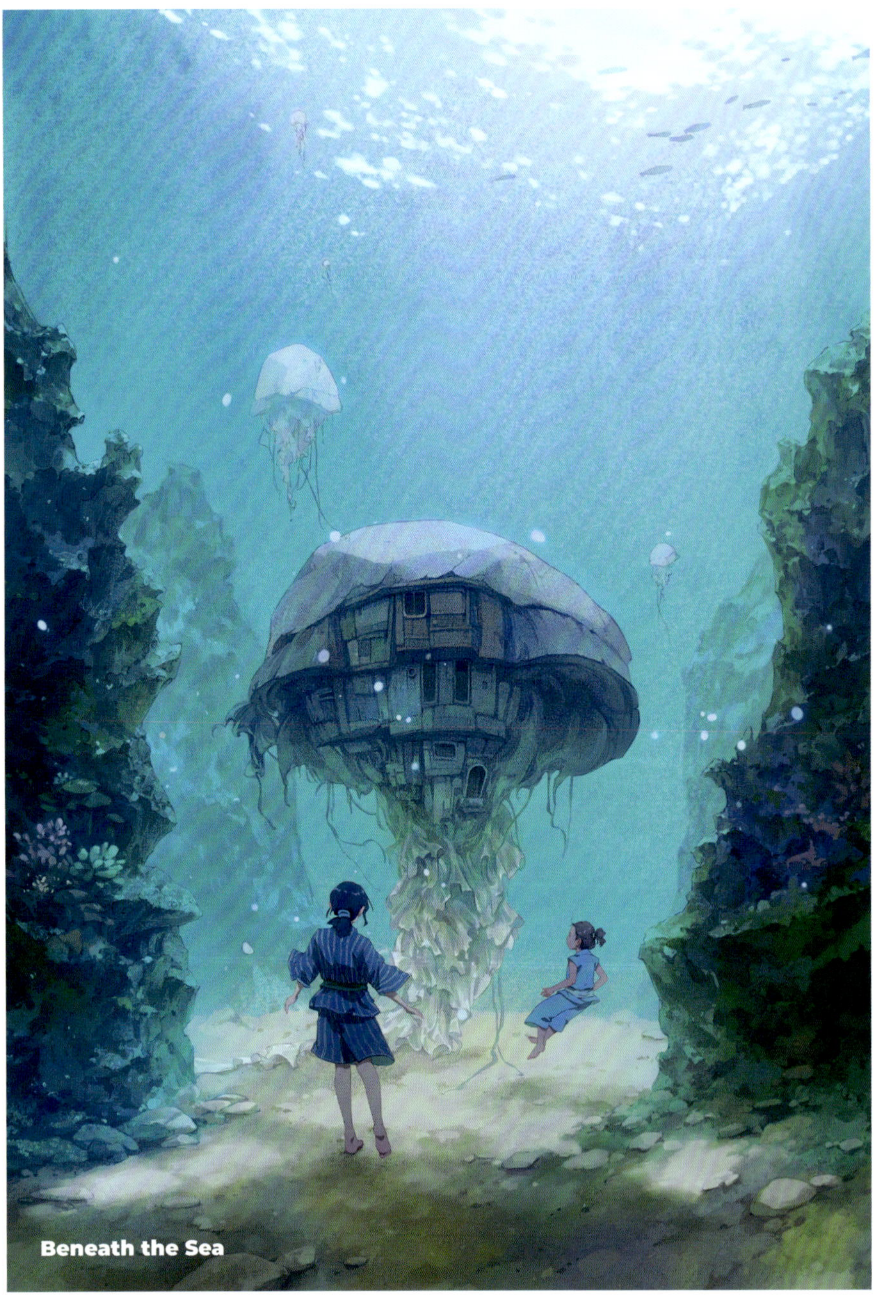

Beneath the Sea

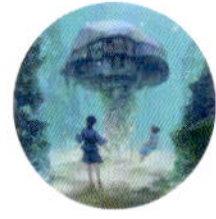

Beneath the Sea

This painting is a good example of how colour and value can be used to convey perspective and depth. The coral reefs in the foreground are repeated in a similar fashion throughout the scene, but those closest to the viewer have a broader value range (i.e. more contrast), greater colour variation, and more detail than those further back. The greater the distance between the viewer and the object, the hazier and more washed out it will appear, since there are more water molecules obstructing the view. As they are closer to the viewer, the coral formations in the foreground appear bigger than those further away.

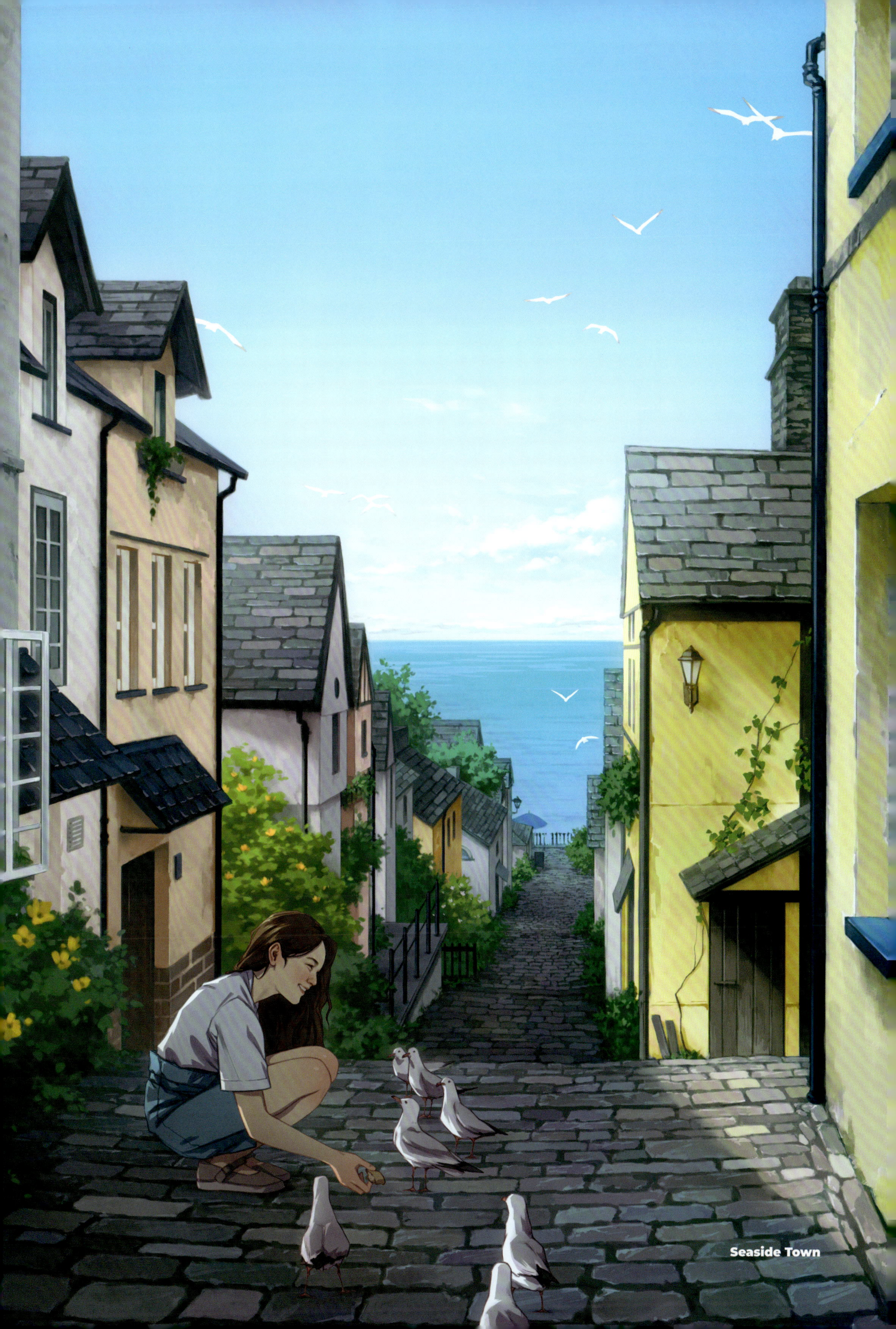

Seaside Town

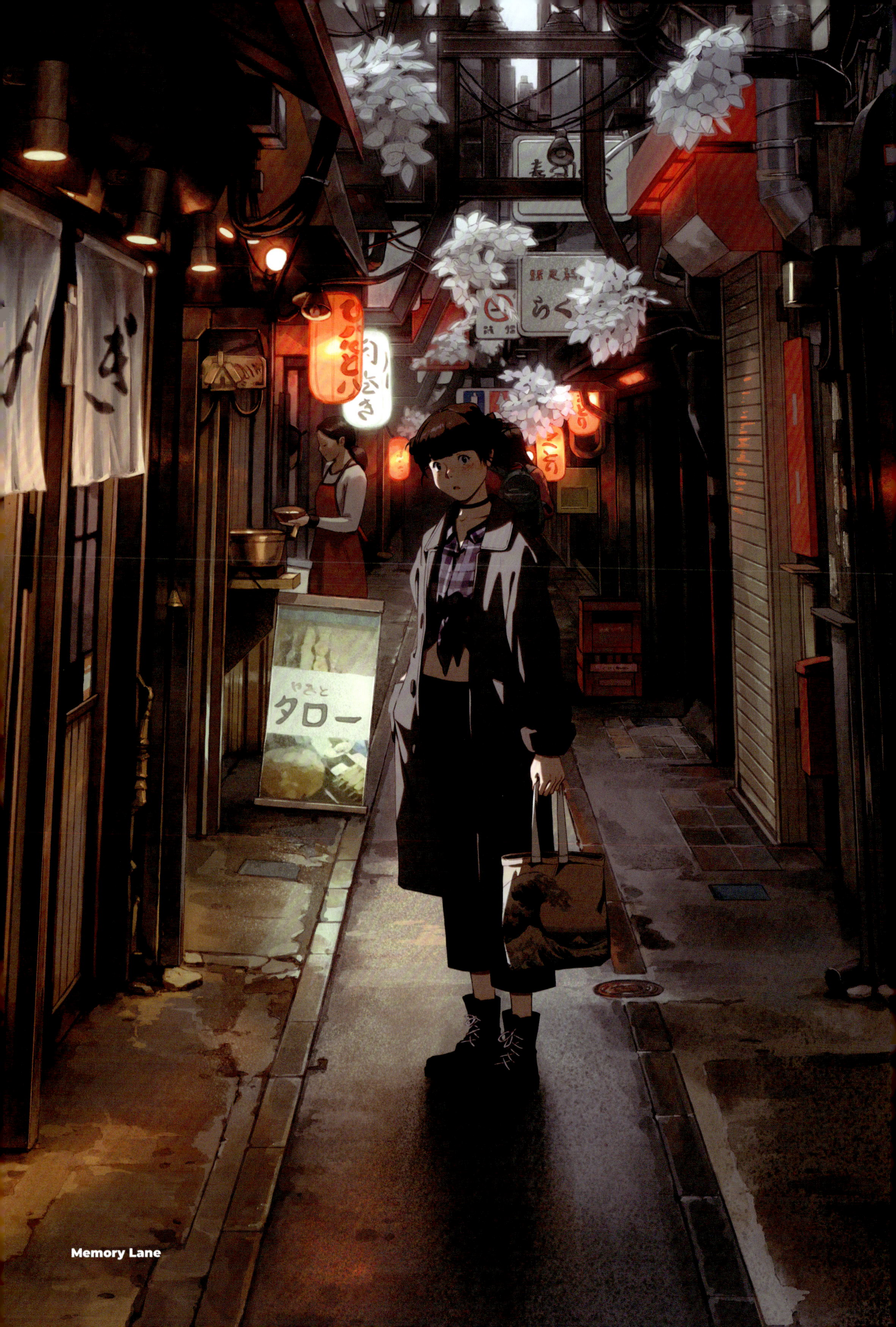

Memory Lane

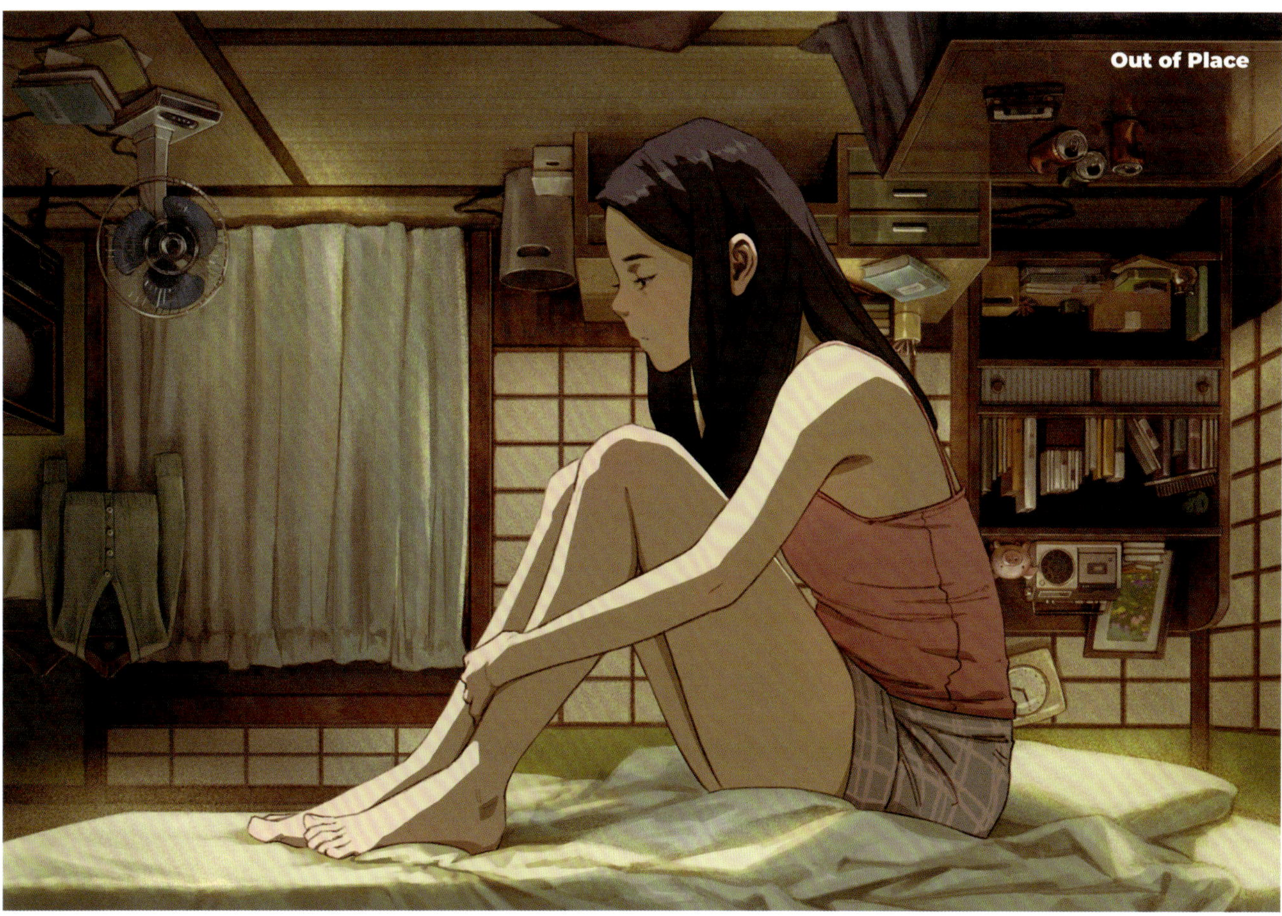
Out of Place

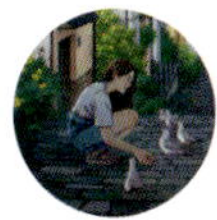

Seaside Town

I love little alleyways, in real life and in paintings, because they give me a cosy feeling combined with a sense of mystery, inviting me to step into them and explore. In this illustration, the converging lines draw the viewer's attention towards the centre of the image: the sea. By focusing on the water, rather than the character, I was able to create a feeling of vastness, like the image opened up right in front of me. By default, alleyways will create the illusion of depth, as the houses and street appear to decrease in size the further away they are. The cobblestones, clouds, and birds also help to create this effect.

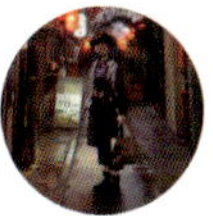

Memory Lane

This illustration depicts an alleyway with a very different mood to the seaside scene. The one-point-perspective and converging lines pull the viewer into the scene, but the further you look into the alley, the denser and more closed-off it appears, rather than giving an unobstructed view. The lines point towards the character's head, to guide the viewer's attention there and make it the focal point. I also wanted to create a sense of intimacy between the character and the viewer by placing the horizon line roughly at human eye level, as if the viewer is the one who stumbled upon the character on the street. The effect would have been very different if I'd placed the viewpoint much higher or lower.

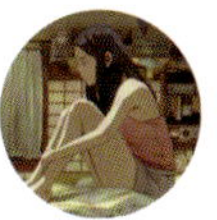

Out of Place

When it comes to perspective, this painting was a fun experiment and a bit of a mind-bender. It illustrates how you can have fun breaking expectations and flipping conventional viewing habits, quite literally, on their head.

The upside-down room might look odd at first glance, but it still follows a simple one-point perspective grid to ground the scene. The converging lines of the floor and tabletop create depth and point towards the character as the focal point. I brought the character and bedding forward by applying a higher contrast, compared to the other elements in the room.

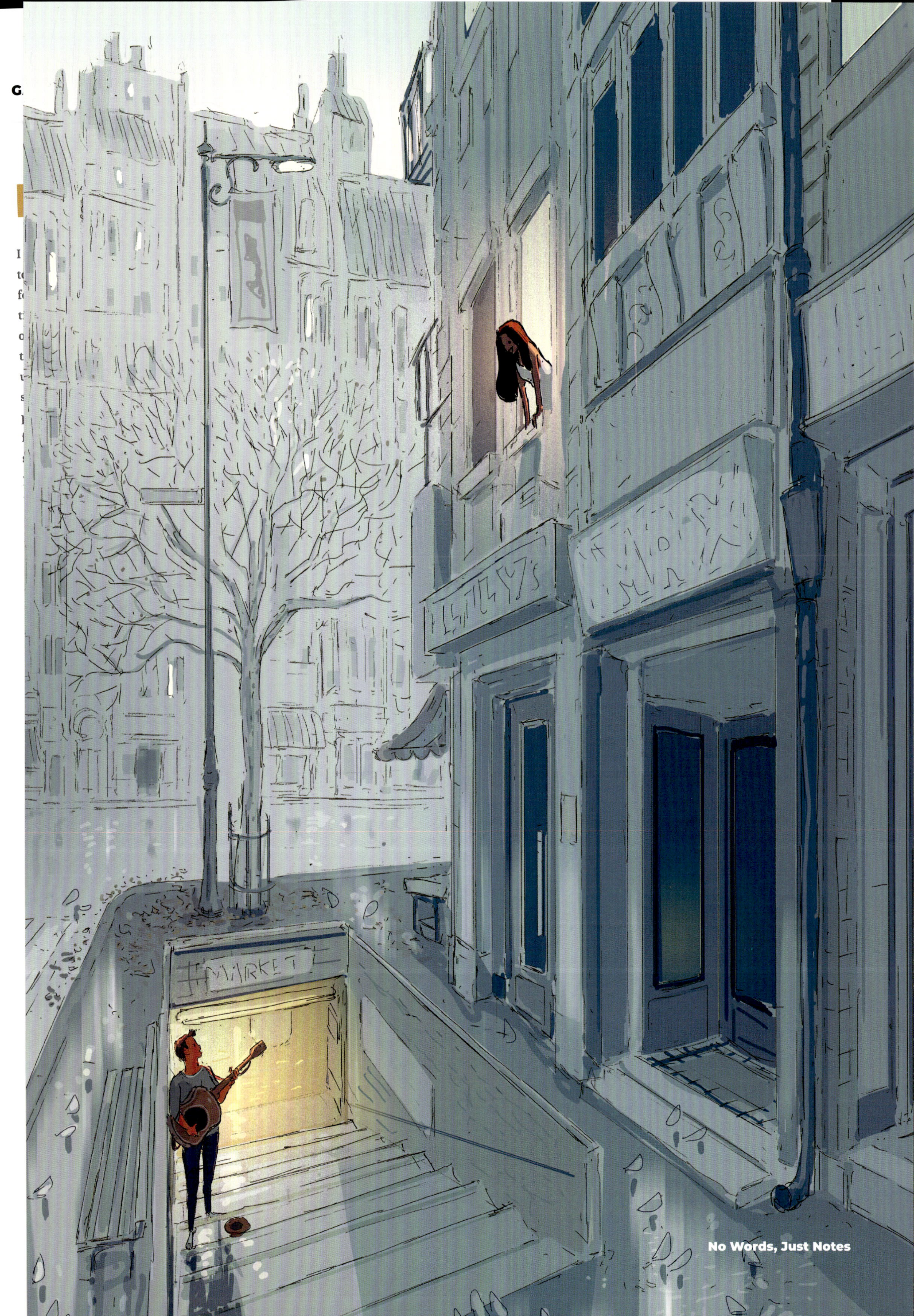

No Words, Just Notes

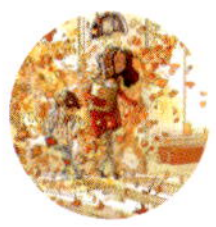

And Then Came Fall

This image has a fairly classic approach to depicting depth through a simple use of perspective and classic overlaying of planes. The table with the pumpkins is the foreground. It's bigger in proportion than the middle ground, which is where the woman and child enter through the door. The man watching the scene stands in the background.

It's classic because it's effective. The audience's eyes read the three main planes of the image and project it in space, just like we do for what we see in the real world. The light flooding through the door serves as a visual anchor, reinforcing the sense of space within space, which is a major element in much of my artwork. If I can convince the audience's eyes that they are looking at a space, and that within this space, there are other smaller spaces, it creates a sense of scope, which is the idea that there is more depth in the image that initially appears.

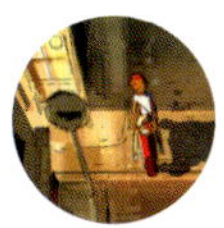

Saturday Evening

I grew up in the south of France where we had narrow streets, Vespas, and strong light creating shapes against the buildings. I pushed the depth in this image, using a birds-eye point of view. This is often used in film to signify that it's not a single person's point of view, but a general way of letting the audience know something that will be necessary to the unfolding story. This overhead camera angle shows the audience where the action takes place and the main elements that will come into play.

The painting was inspired by a song by Francis Cabrel called 'Samedi soir sur la terre', which translates to 'A Saturday evening on earth'. The song is about a boy and a girl who meet at a local dance and fall for one another. The song goes on to suggest that this story is happening over and over in the same village, in the same country, on the same planet. I've always loved the idea that we all live similar stories, but our own relationship to the world makes them unique. I used this birds-eye perspective to convey the familiar and universal nature of the story, then used light and spot colour to capture the uniqueness of the moment. By showcasing the characters in the light, I was saying: this is their world, their story, even if the tale is a classic one.

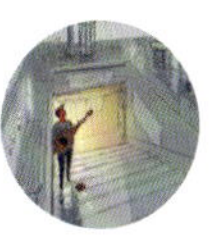

No Words, Just Notes

I used basic perspective notions to create a distance between the audience and the main anchor of the image (in this case, the characters). This distance varies from image to image, depending on the effect I'm trying to achieve. Here, I wanted the audience to feel as if they're witnessing the song. There is an almost voyeuristic implication to the composition, as if we shouldn't be watching this intimate moment. It creates a sense of participation from the audience and strengthens the emotional relation to the story. The strong directional lines lead the audience into the image, but because of the romantic nature of the story, I tried not to overpower the image with their presence, which is why they are sketchy and not too dark. The directional lines reinforce the story, rather than taking away from it. The drawing is there to support the story, not overpower or distract from it.

I always think in terms of stories. It's both a curse and a gift. It's a curse because there are different ways to approach visual storytelling, but it's a gift because it's inbuilt in my way of seeing the world. Everything I do tends to have space and time built into it. The basis for storytelling, especially in one image, is the idea that something has happened before what is depicted in the image and something will happen after. What the viewer sees is a moment in between moments. This helps the viewer's mind to imagine a world bigger, richer, and livelier than what is depicted on the canvas. The image itself offers enough indication of space, composition, and intent on the part of the characters to suggest possible stories.

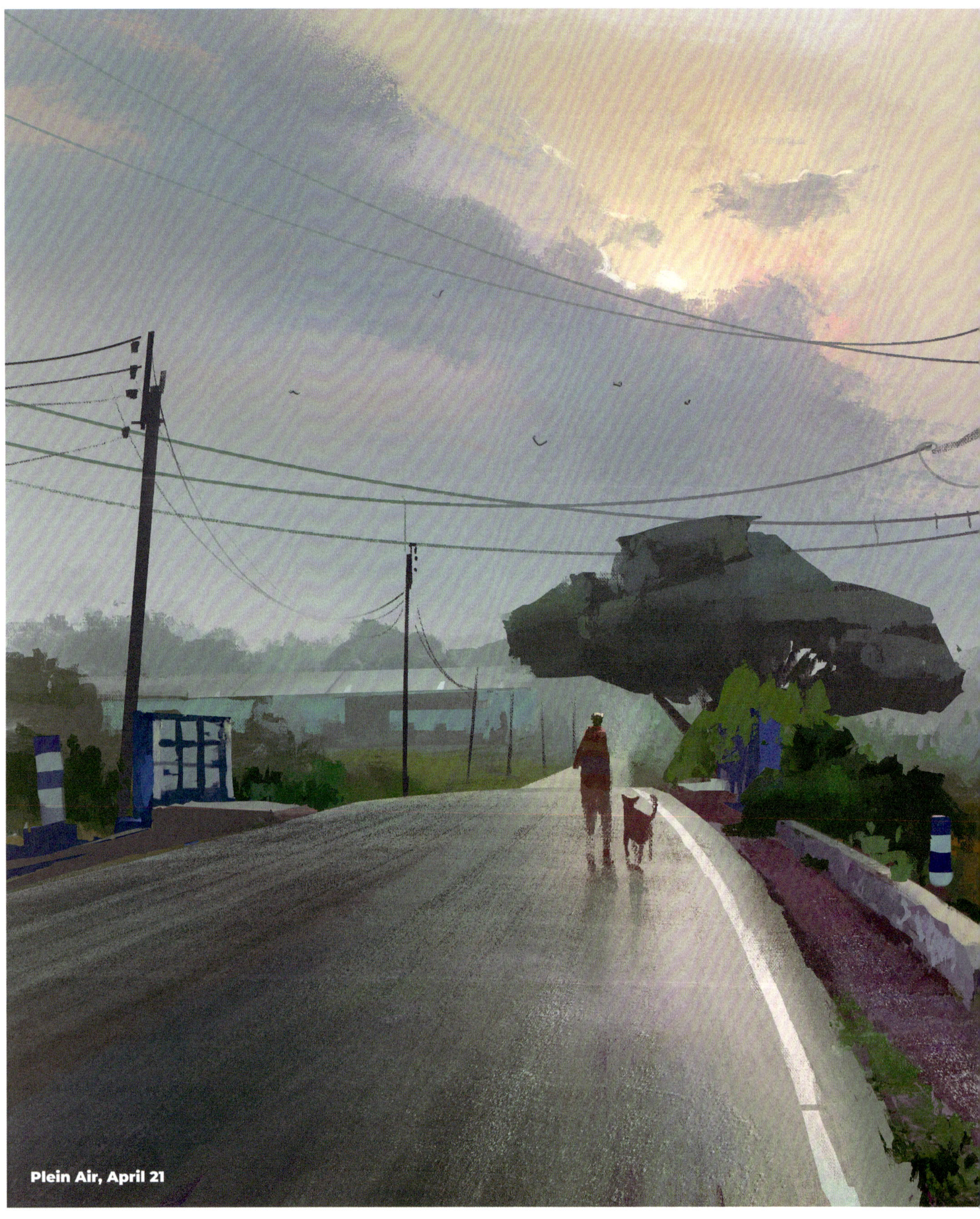
Plein Air, April 21

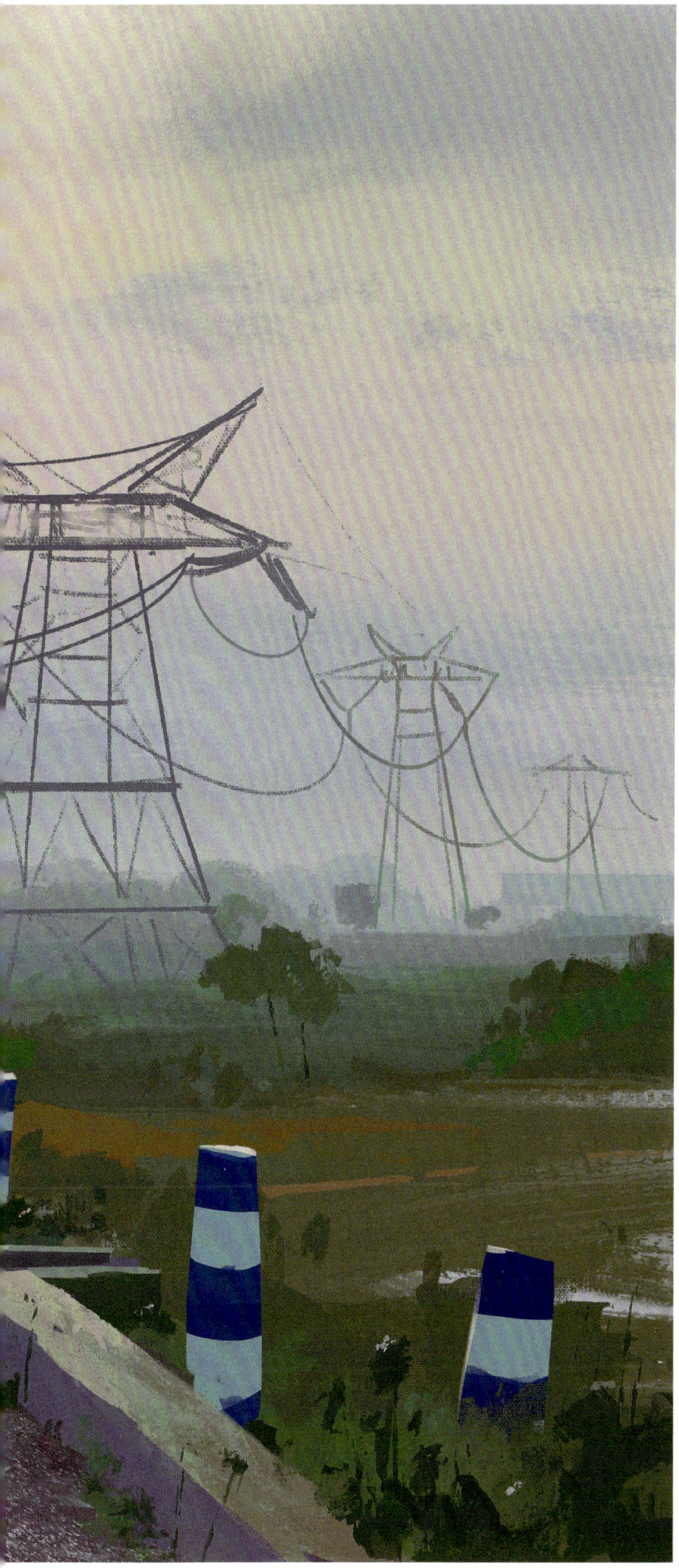

AYAN NAG

Perspective in visual mediums is inherently a technical and calculative aspect. While the basics of one- or two-point perspective are quite simple, it can rapidly increase in complexity when you add in additional vanishing points. The introduction of curved perspective lines, complicated shapes in perspective, and various other elements can prove a challenge even to the best of artists.

I typically approach perspective in a simpler way. Perspective is used to create an illusion of 3D space on a 2D surface, but you don't need super-complicated set-ups or pinpoint precision to accomplish this. A clear understanding of the core fundamentals is all you need. These pages will discuss a few key elements of perspective that I regularly make use of in whatever I'm painting.

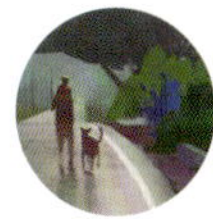

Plein Air, April 21

This painting can be considered one-point perspective. While there is a secondary vanishing point, the primary VP dominates the other by a large margin. We often observe repeating objects in the world around us. Understanding how they help us to navigate space, and how we can use that in our paintings, is one of the most important lessons in perspective. Put simply, objects get smaller the further they are away from us. Using this in your artwork will not only create depth, but it will help you to establish scale.

Notice how I used big, medium, and small repetitions across the canvas. The biggest repeating objects in the composition are the electricity pylons, followed by the telegraph poles. The smallest objects are the blue-white concrete posts near the bridge. If you connect each of them using imaginary lines, they frame the subjects nicely. They also create converging leading lines to create motion in the composition.

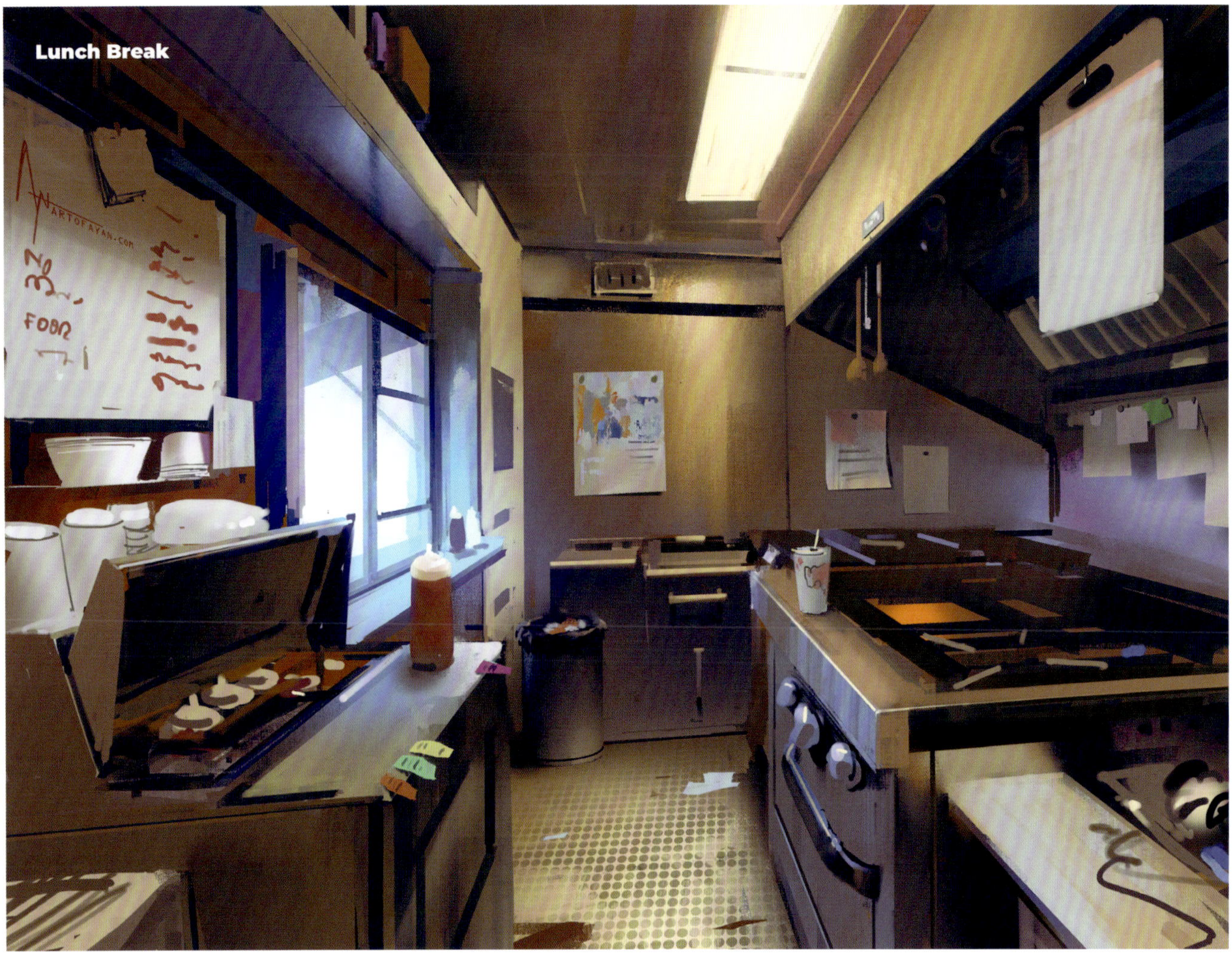

Lunch Break

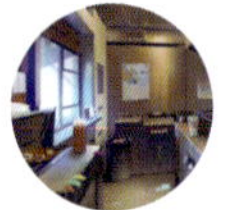

Lunch Break

This painting is a classic example of one-point perspective, with all of the lines converging into a single vanishing point. (Though if you look closely, there is a hint of a second vanishing point also.) Every object in the painting appears to be perfectly aligned to create the illusion of a 3D space. If you pay close attention to how the various elements are rendered, however, you will notice that the shapes are quite loose and gestural. As long as the big shapes are working well, you can get away with a lot of inaccuracies. Lines don't need to be completely straight and similar objects don't need to look the same. As long as these parameters are within a certain range, everything will make sense.

Notice how I used the floor texture to create an extra layer of depth and believability to the composition. While in real life everything in the image would have some kind of texture, as an artist you have the option to be selective about what to show and how to show it. The perspective-morphed texture acts as a filler of negative space and helps to unify the perspective and depth I'm trying to sell to the viewer.

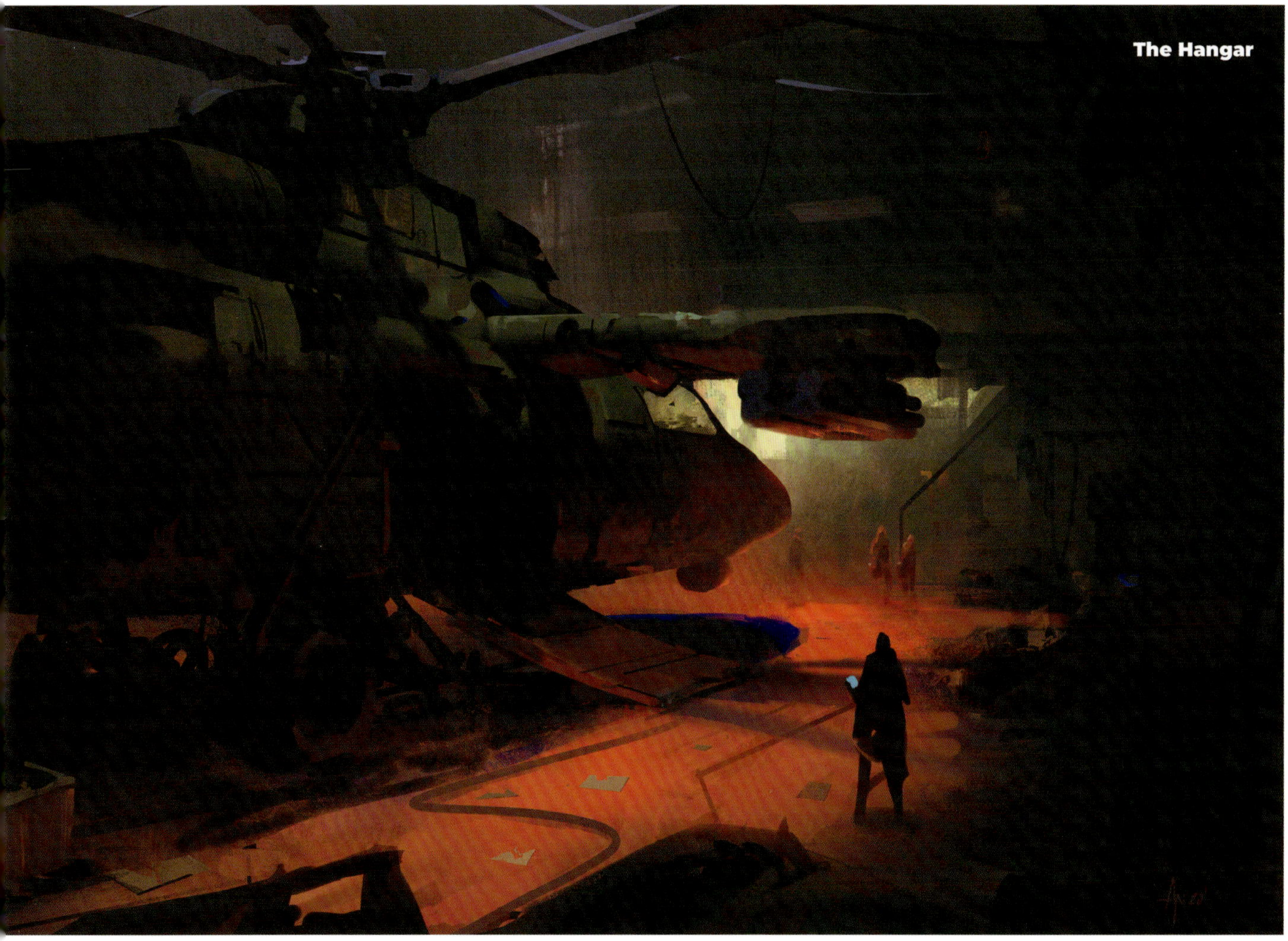

The Hangar

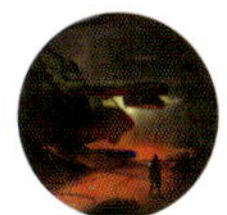

The Hangar

This painting has two dominant vanishing points. While the helicopter appears to be the main subject, it's not. If you squint your eyes, the first thing that you will notice is the silhouette of the character in the foreground. Secondary focus goes to the front of the helicopter, which leads the eye towards the secondary character in the background. Using this kind of careful overlapping and shape language can enable you to tell your story in a more effective way.

Another method to achieve perspective is to regulate the amount of detail. Objects in the distance will appear less detailed than those in the foreground. While the state of the object remains the same, our vision loses its sharpness after a certain distance. Selectively detailing the part that's closer to the viewer (such as the helicopter), while simplifying the objects further away (such as the characters in the background), will automatically improve your paintings.

Using leading lines for storytelling is another great way to compose your frames. Perspective lines found in architecture, and most manmade objects, offer numerous opportunities for this. I often use existing perspective lines and shapes found in an object to frame my subjects and further the storytelling.

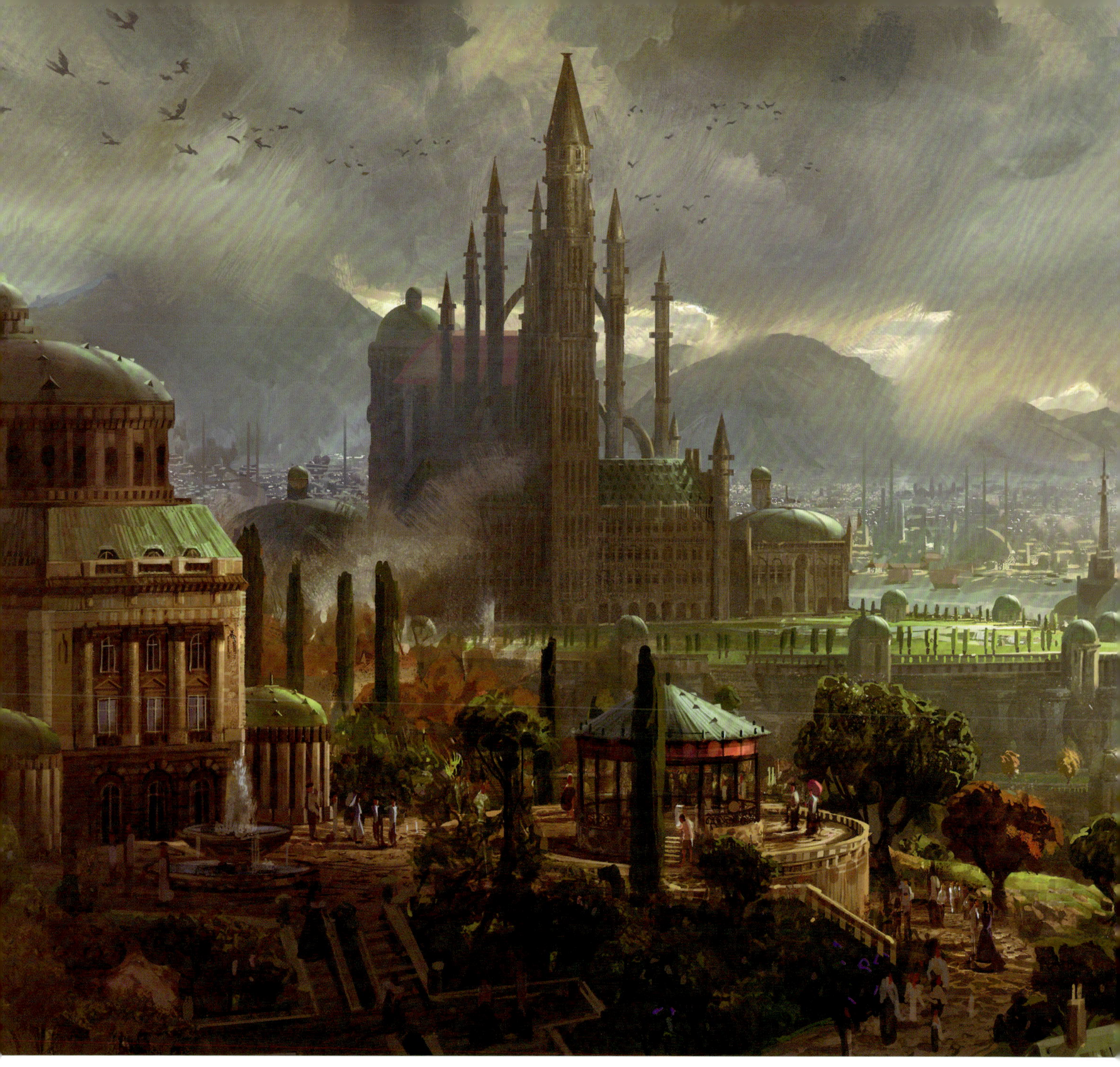

REMBERT MONTALD

Depth, for me, is a feeling, not a grid or mathematical calculation. When I draw or paint, I close my eyes and envision what it feels like to be in the place I'm trying to illustrate. What can I feel, smell, or hear? I try to remember a point in my life when I experienced something similar. All these memories combined create a mood, which is what interests me most.

Perspective and depth create a powerful visual trick, fooling the eye into thinking that a flat surface has depth. The Greeks and Romans used a method called *Trompe l'oeil*, which means 'deceives the eye'. They used this to enhance architecture and create dramatic perspective in murals. Italian sculptor and architect Gian Lorenzo Bernini used this trick in architecture to make a hallway appear narrower at the end than it actually was.

Familiarizing yourself with perspective and vanishing points will greatly benefit your artwork. You can exaggerate depth and fool the audience, but as the creator of the trick, you must avoid being fooled by the illusion yourself. Remember that it's a trick and work to master it. Like many concept artists, I used to rely on atmospheric perspective. Now I try to create perspective using local colours and overlap instead. Solid drawing skills always win over easy tricks.

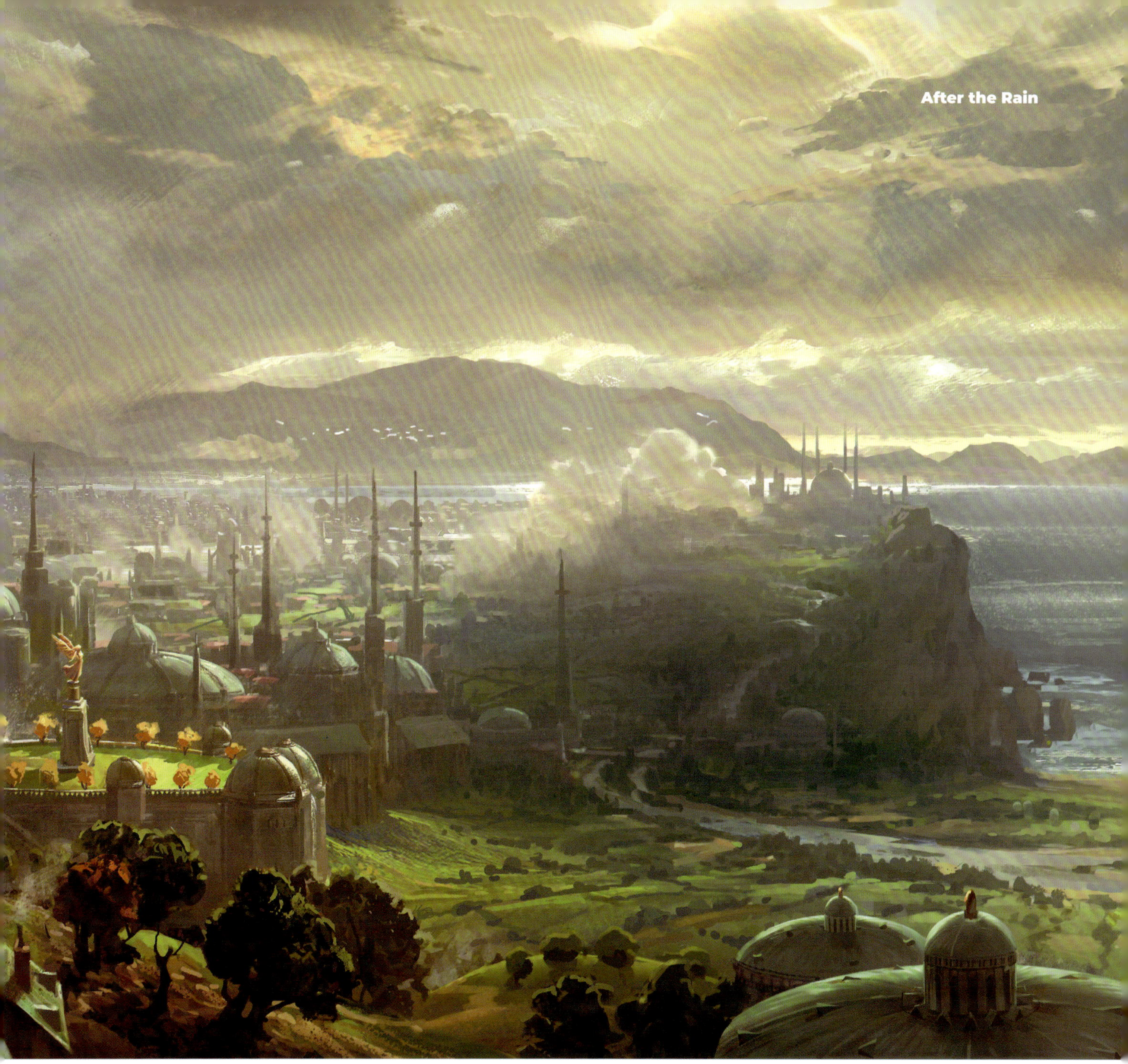

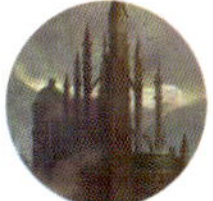

After the Rain

Here I tried to depict a vast scene with atmosphere. As it was all drawn by hand, the first step was to create a grid. I established the hues and values – cooler and lighter in the background, and darker and warmer in the front – before I began defining any architecture. After the values and hues were established, I started to think more carefully about the scale. How large is the city? How big is a street, or a house compared to a bigger building, such as a church? I started in the background and worked towards the front. For the final touch, I painted in all of the smaller details and the tiny people, trying to keep the scale in mind.

It's a common mistake to forget about perspective in the sky. Here I played with the clouds to establish greater depth. The further back you go, the smaller and closer the shapes are. I wanted to depict European weather near the coast, where it's usually very cloudy with pockets of sunlight moving over the landscape and peeking through the clouds.

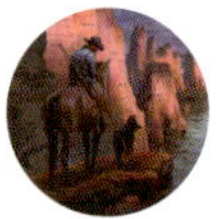

End of the trail

This painting was inspired by a road trip to Monument Valley in Utah. I fell asleep in the car and woke up with the sun rising to reveal these big rock silhouettes. It's also homage to the masters of Western painting.

The scale was relatively easy to capture. There is a cowboy with his horse and dog in the foreground, and I had the freedom to make the rock formations any size. This meant I had to rely on atmospheric perspective to create a sense of depth. I wanted the hues of the setting sun to strike through the scene. Notice how the reds become purpler when the atmosphere fades into the blues in the background. You can also observe how the ripples in the water vary in shape and size as they recede into the distance. The rocks create overlap, which is very important in creating the illusion of depth.

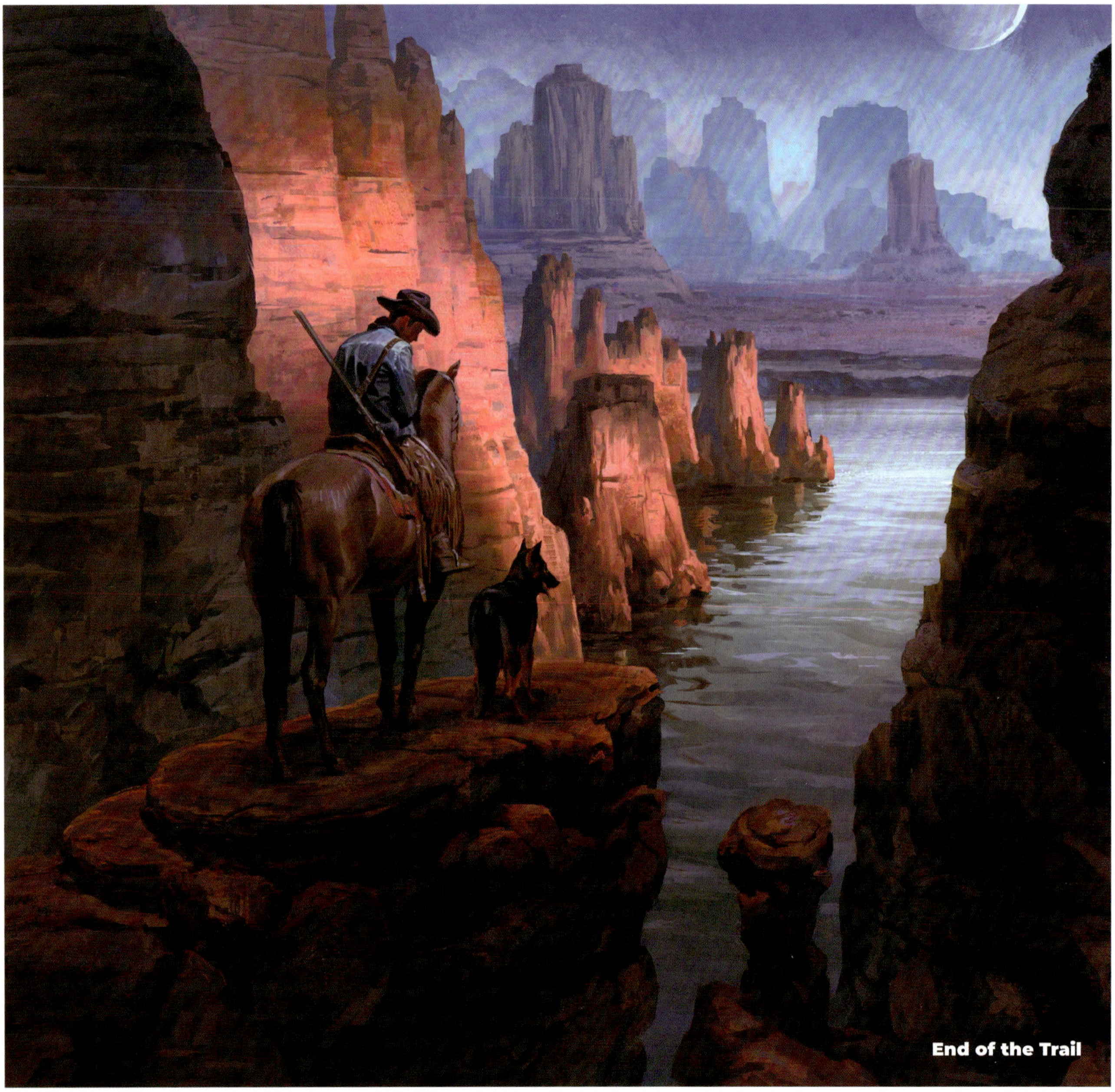

End of the Trail

Subway Sketch

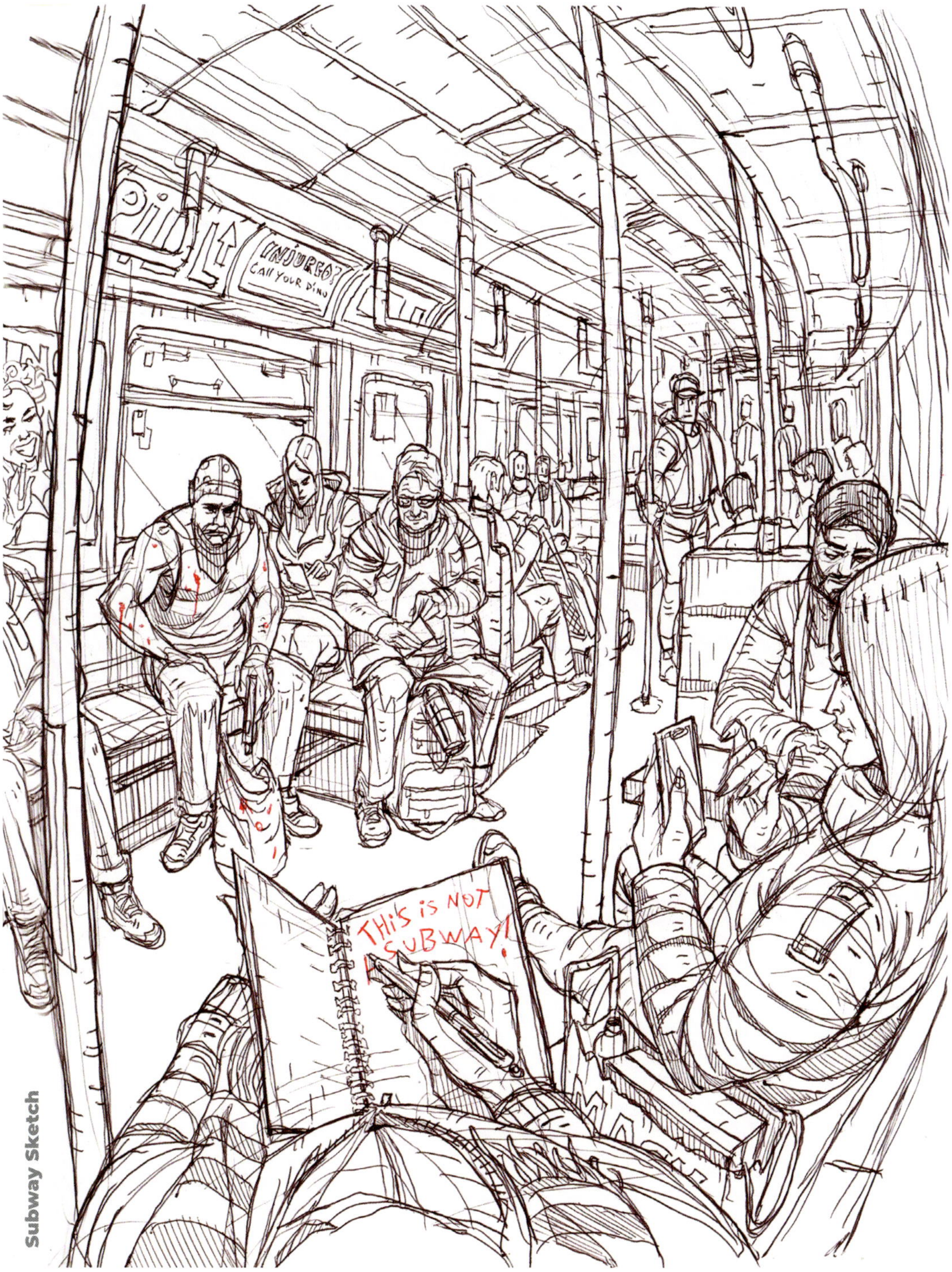

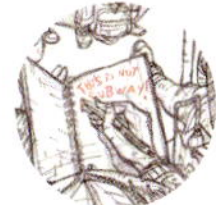

Subway Sketch

I create this kind of sketch in my sketchbook when I'm out and about, hence why all the lines are a little wonky. With line drawings and sketches, it's more difficult to rely on values to create depth. You can use hatching instead, though it can become a laborious task. Instead I like to rely on scale, bringing a few objects very close to the camera and exaggerating the vanishing points. This is also known as fish-eye perspective. Notice how the poles in the middle communicate the depth. Try finding a strong repetitive motif that you can scale back into the distance.

CONTRIBUTORS

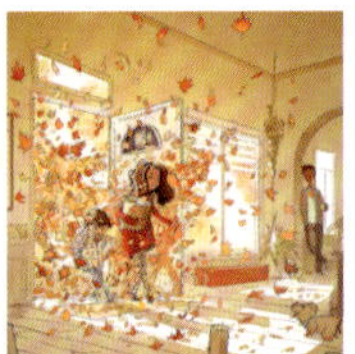
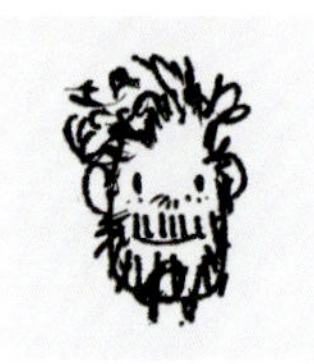

PASCAL CAMPION

Director, production designer, & story development | campionpascal.com

Pascal has worked as a director, storyboard artist, production designer, book illustrator, creative director, mentor, and teacher in the animation industry for the past twenty years, with companies including Disney and The New Yorker. His art book *The Art of Pascal Campion* was published with 3dtotal in 2022.

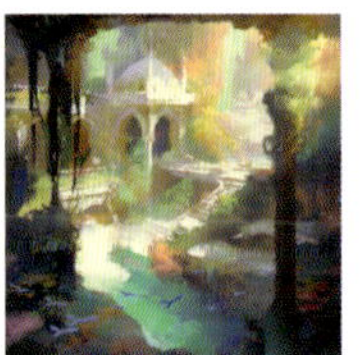
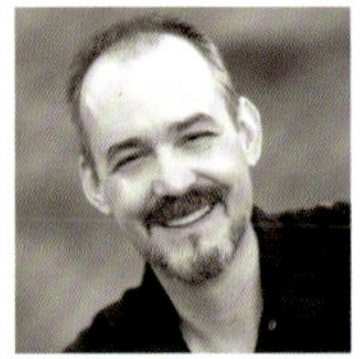

NATHAN FOWKES

Animation artist & fine artist | nathanfowkes.com

Nathan is a Los-Angeles-based feature animation artist who has worked on films for DreamWorks, Disney, Blue Sky Studios, and Paramount. He is a guest lecturer at ArtCenter College of Design and has taught at Los Angeles Academy of Figurative Art, Laguna College of Art and Design, and online at Schoolism.com.

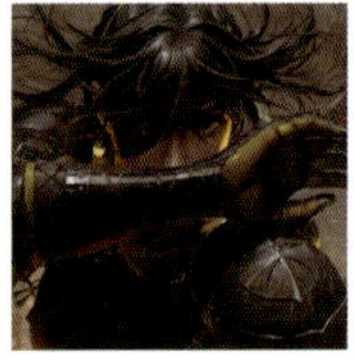
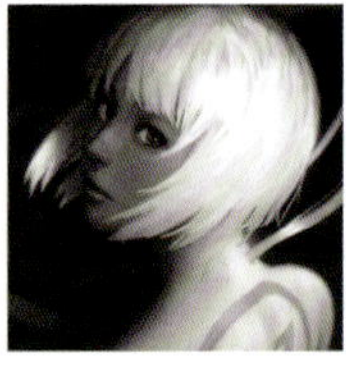

GUWEIZ

Freelance artist | instagram.com/guweiz

Based in Singapore, Guweiz works on a freelance basis in illustration, concept design, and art education. He enjoys creating personal artwork and has published two 3dtotal art books: *Guweiz: The Art of Gu Zheng Wei* and *The World of Guweiz: The Art of Gu Zheng Wei.*

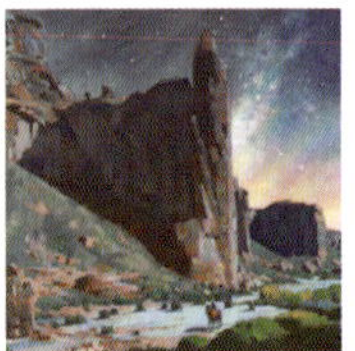
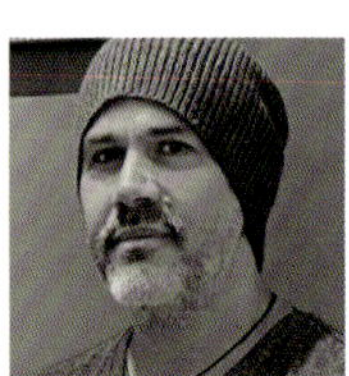

MIKE HERNANDEZ

Artist | mikehernandezart.com

A native Angeleno, Mike is a plein-air painter skilled in gouache, oil, and acrylic, whose works have featured in galleries and online publications. He has worked as a production designer, art director, and concept artist at DreamWorks Animation, and is a nationwide sought-after workshop instructor.

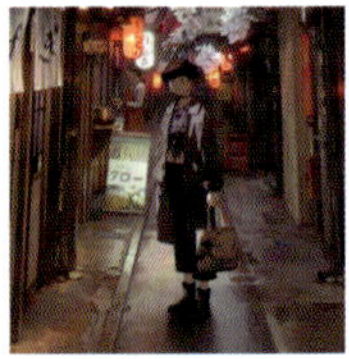
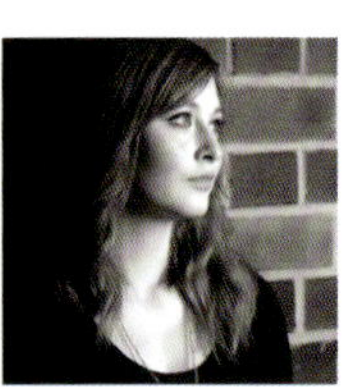

DJAMILA KNOPF

Illustrator | djamilaknopf.com

Djamila is an independent artist and Schoolism instructor based in Leipzig, Germany. Primarily focusing on personal projects, she creates illustrations that evoke a sense of wonder and nostalgia. Her 3dtotal art book *Komorebi: The Art of Djamila Knopf* was published in 2020.

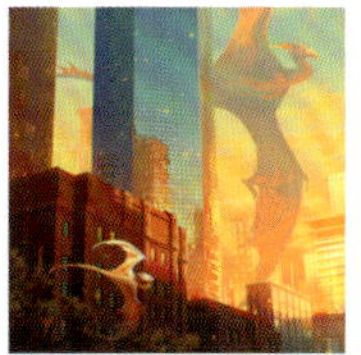
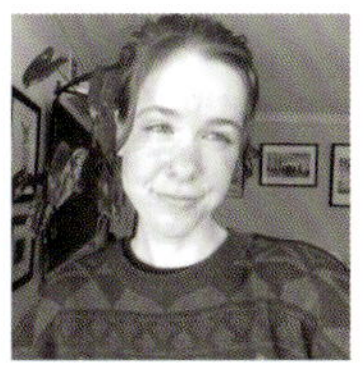

DEVIN ELLE KURTZ

Illustrator & environment artist | devinellekurtz.com

Based in San Diego, Devin has worked in the animation industry as a supervising background painter on Netflix's *Disenchantment*. Other clients include Mondo, Dark Horse, HarperCollins, and Disney. Her 3dtotal art book *Windows to Worlds: The Art of Devin Elle Kurtz* was published in 2021.

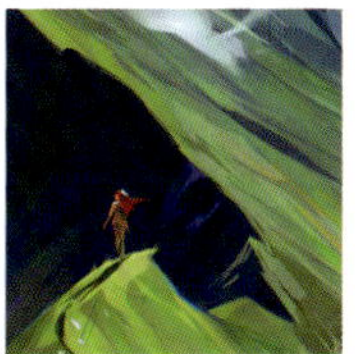
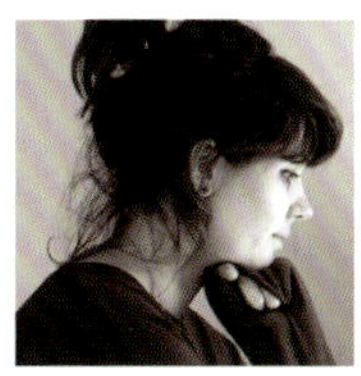

LOISH

Digital artist | loish.net

Loish (aka Lois van Baarle) is a digital artist who divides her time between creating personal art and making tutorials and other learning content for artists. She has three art books with 3dtotal: *The Art of Loish: A Look Behind the Scenes*, *The Sketchbook of Loish: Art in Progress*, and *The Style of Loish : Finding an Artistic Value.*

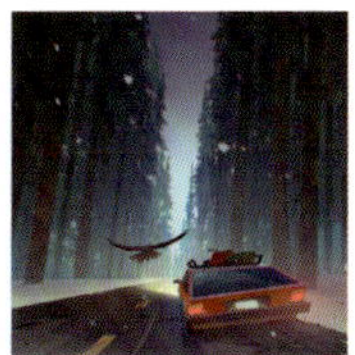
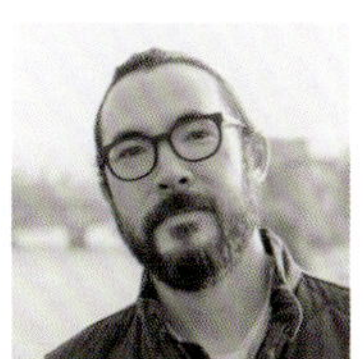

MIKE MCCAIN

Art director & illustrator | mikemccain.art

Mike is an LA-based artist fuelled by exploring and painting out in nature. Credits include *The Boy, the Mole, the Fox and the Horse* (art director) and *Spider-Man: Across the Spider-Verse* (visual development).

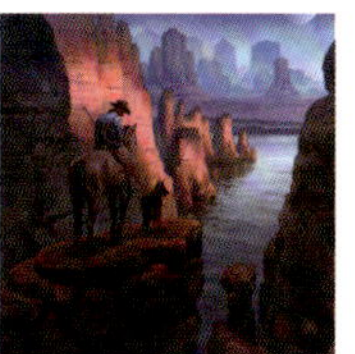
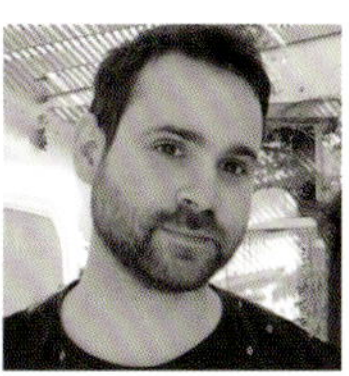

REMBERT MONTALD

Storyboard & concept artist | artstation.com/sharkyspoon

Intrigued by the intricacies of visual storytelling, Rembert pursued an education in animation and art in RITCS Brussels, Belgium, and Gobelins, Paris. He has lived and worked globally and believes the best way to tell a story is to show it.

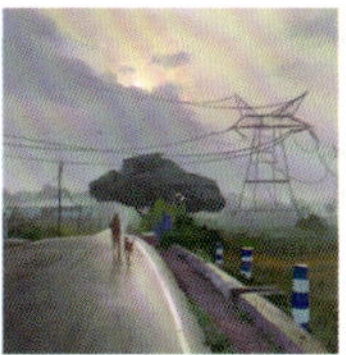
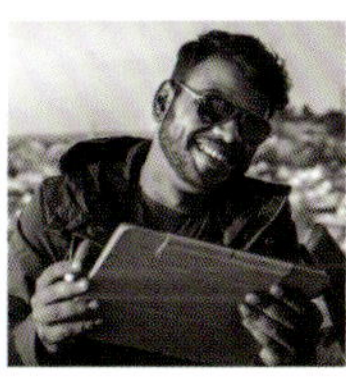

AYAN NAG

Illustrator | artofayan.com

Ayan is an Indian artist who's passionate about exploring and bringing his perspective to life through art. He loves creating new worlds and discovering beauty in the everyday. He has worked with studios including Axis Studios, Psyop, Passion Pictures, Procreate (Savage Interactive), and Ubisoft.

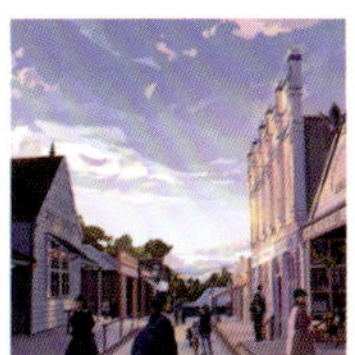
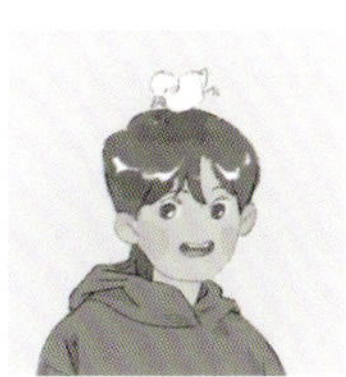

ORENJIKUN

Background artist for animation & games | instagram.com/orenjikun

Orenjikun is a self-taught artist who primarily lends his skills to the animation industry for background layout and paint. In his spare time he enjoys creating educational art content and attending conventions, where he sells his art.

INDEX

P

R

S

T

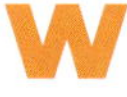

3dtotalPublishing

3dtotal Publishing is a trailblazing, creative publisher specializing in inspirational and educational resources for artists.

Our titles feature top industry professionals from around the globe who share their experience in skilfully written step-by-step tutorials and fascinating, detailed guides. Illustrated throughout with stunning artwork, these best-selling publications offer creative insight, expert advice, and essential motivation. Fans of digital art will enjoy our comprehensive volumes covering Adobe Photoshop, Procreate, and Blender, as well as our superb titles based around character design, including *Fundamentals of Character Design* and *Creating Characters for the Entertainment Industry*. The dedicated, high-quality blend of instruction and inspiration also extends to traditional art. Titles covering a range of techniques, genres, and abilities allow your creativity to flourish while building essential skills.

Well-established within the industry, we now offer over 100 titles and counting, many of which have been translated into multiple languages around the world. With something for every artist, we are proud to say that our books offer the 3dtotal package:

LEARN • CREATE • SHARE

Visit us at store.3dtotal.com

3dtotal Publishing is part of 3dtotal.com, a leading website for CG artists founded by Tom Greenway in 1999.

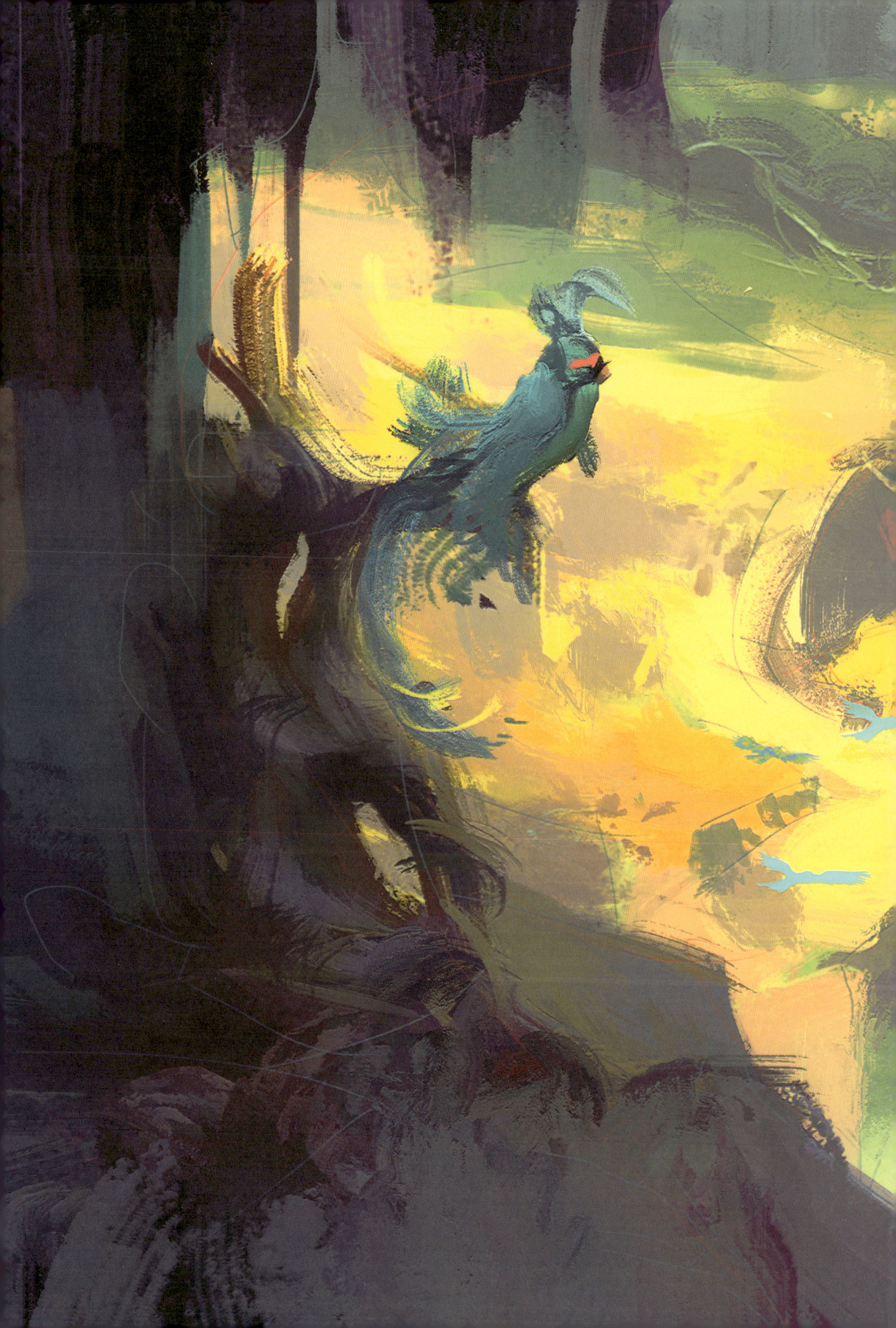